Proceedings of the

Fourth ACM SIGPLAN Symposium on Principles & Practice of Parallel Programming PPOPP

San Diego, California
May 19-22, 1993

Sponsored by the
Special Interest Group on Programming Languages,
Association for Computing Machinery

The Association for Computing Machinery
1515 Broadway
New York, New York 10036

Soft Cover ISBN: 0-89791-589-5

Additional copies may be ordered prepaid from:

ACM Order Department
P.O. Box 64145
Baltimore, MD 21264

1-800 342-6626
1-410 528-4261 (Outside US, MD and AK)

ACM Order Number: 551930

Fourth ACM SIGPLAN Symposium on Principles and Practice of Parallel Programming (PPoPP)

CONFERENCE COMMITTEE

General Chair

Marina Chen, *Yale University*

Program Chair

Robert Halstead, *DEC Cambridge Research Lab*

Program Committee

David Callahan, *Tera Computer Company*
David Culler, *University of California, Berkeley*
Carla Ellis, *Duke University*
Robert Halstead, *DEC Cambridge Research Lab*
Monica Lam, *Stanford University*
Olaf Lubeck, *Los Alamos National Laboratory*
Bart Miller, *University of Wisconsin, Madison*
Dan Reed, *University of Illinois*
Guy Steele, *Thinking Machines Corporation*
Michael Wolfe, *Oregon Graduate Institute*
Aki Yonezawa, *University of Tokyo*
Hans Zima, *University of Vienna*

Local Arrangements Chair

Young-il Choo, *Yale University*

Conference Treasurer

Katherine Yelick, *University of California at Berkeley*

Publicity Chair

Anne Rogers, *Princeton University*

External Referees

Sarita Adve
Siegfried Benkner
Roman Blasko
Peter Brezany
Jeff Brown
Barbara Chapman
Charles Consel
Andrea Dusseau
Joe Fasel
Seth Copen Goldstein
Jeffrey Hammes
Jan Hulman
R. Bruce Irvin
Wayne Joubert
Jim Larus
Maria Lucka
Takashi Matsumoto
Satoshi Matsuoka
James Moore
Hans Moritsch
Rob Netzer
Adam Sah
Klaus Erik Schauser
Andreas Schwald
Margaret Simmons
Jaswinder Singh
Toru Sugimoto
Marian Vajtersic
Jens Volkert
Thorsten von Eicken
Harvey Wasserman
Katherine Yelick

Foreword

It gives us great pleasure to introduce this collection of papers presented at the Fourth ACM SIGPLAN Symposium on Principles and Practice of Parallel Programming, held on May 19–22, 1993, as part of the 1993 ACM Federated Computing Research Conference in San Diego, California. Parallel computation is an increasingly vital part of computer science, and we are happy that the seed planted at the first meeting of this series, in New Haven, Connecticut, in July 1988, has grown and flourished.

As the field of parallel computing develops, it is important that researchers and practitioners working in different subfields not lose touch with each other. Accordingly, the goal of this series of meetings has been to provide a forum where the best current research in operating systems, languages, compilers, and tools for parallel programming can be presented to a broad parallel programming audience. As with the previous meetings of this series, we sought submissions that (1) center on experiments and comparative evaluation of parallel software, (2) report on new ideas in languages, compilers, and environments for parallel programming, or (3) summarize experience with parallel programming in a way that illustrates general principles. Reflecting the growing maturity of the field, we especially sought papers containing results derived from actual implementation on parallel machines and papers containing results applicable to highly parallel machines.

We received 96 submissions, each of which was read by three or more referees, usually Program Committee members. The Program Committee met on December 4–5, 1992, and selected 26 of these papers for presentation at the Symposium and publication in these Proceedings. This is the largest number of papers yet presented at a PPoPP conference and we are pleased with their high quality and their great range. These papers cover the spectrum from models of parallel computing to implementation techniques, from Fortran to actors, and from compilation algorithms to application development tools and case studies, thus satisfying the goal of broadly covering the active areas of parallel programming research.

Many people have contributed to making this conference happen. We thank the Program Committee and the external referees for their responsiveness and their exemplary devotion to duty, which was evident in the thoroughness and thoughtfulness of their reviews as well as in many other ways. We are grateful to David Wise, the FCRC Conference Chair, for his support and overall help in organizing this fourth PPoPP Symposium. We thank Donna Baglio at ACM Headquarters, who patiently coached us in our dealings with the ACM. We thank Chris Hatchell for his staff support in Marina Chen's office. Finally, we are indebted to Michelle Gillespie for her invaluable administrative support in collecting the submissions, arranging the Program Committee meeting, handling correspondence, and assembling these Proceedings.

Marina Chen
General Chair

Bert Halstead
Program Chair

Author Index

Table of Contents

Thursday, May 20, 1993

Friday, May 21, 1993

LogP: Towards a Realistic Model of Parallel Computation

David Culler, Richard Karp,* David Patterson,
Abhijit Sahay, Klaus Erik Schauser, Eunice Santos,
Ramesh Subramonian, and Thorsten von Eicken

Computer Science Division,
University of California, Berkeley

Abstract

A vast body of theoretical research has focused either on overly simplistic models of parallel computation, notably the PRAM, or overly specific models that have few representatives in the real world. Both kinds of models encourage exploitation of formal loopholes, rather than rewarding development of techniques that yield performance across a range of current and future parallel machines. This paper offers a new parallel machine model, called LogP, that reflects the critical technology trends underlying parallel computers. It is intended to serve as a basis for developing fast, portable parallel algorithms and to offer guidelines to machine designers. Such a model must strike a balance between detail and simplicity in order to reveal important bottlenecks without making analysis of interesting problems intractable. The model is based on four parameters that specify abstractly the computing bandwidth, the communication bandwidth, the communication delay, and the efficiency of coupling communication and computation. Portable parallel algorithms typically adapt to the machine configuration, in terms of these parameters. The utility of the model is demonstrated through examples that are implemented on the CM-5.

Keywords: massively parallel processors, parallel models, complexity analysis, parallel algorithms, PRAM

1 Introduction

Our goal is to develop a model of parallel computation that will serve as a basis for the design and analysis of fast, portable parallel algorithms, *i.e.*, algorithms that can be implemented effectively on a wide variety of current and future parallel machines. If we look at the body of parallel algorithms developed under current parallel models, many can be classified as impractical in that they exploit artificial factors not present in any reasonable machine, such as zero communication delay or infinite bandwidth. Others can be classified as overly specialized, in that they are tailored to the idiosyncrasies of a single machine, such as a particular interconnect topology. The most widely used parallel model, the PRAM[13], is unrealistic because it assumes that all processors work synchronously and that interprocessor communication is free.

*Also affiliated with International Computer Science Institute, Berkeley.

4th ACM PPOPP,5/93/CA,USA

Surprisingly fast algorithms can be developed by exploiting these loopholes, but in many cases the algorithms perform poorly under more realistic assumptions[28]. Several variations on the PRAM have attempted to identify restrictions that would make it more practical while preserving much of its simplicity [1, 2, 14, 19, 23, 24]. The bulk-synchronous parallel model (BSP) developed by Valiant[30] attempts to bridge theory and practice with a more radical departure from the PRAM. It allows processors to work asynchronously and models latency and limited bandwidth, yet requires few machine parameters as long as a certain programming methodology is followed. We used the BSP as a starting point in our search for a parallel model that would be realistic, yet simple enough to be used to design algorithms that work predictably well over a wide range of machines. The model should allow the algorithm designer to address key performance issues without specifying unnecessary detail. It should allow machine designers to give a concise performance summary of their machine against which algorithms can be evaluated.

Historically, it has been difficult to develop a reasonable abstraction of parallel machines because the machines exhibited such a diversity of structure. However, technological factors are now forcing a convergence towards systems formed by a collection of essentially complete computers connected by a communication network (Figure 1). This convergence is reflected in our LogP model which addresses significant common issues while suppressing machine specific ones such as network topology and routing algorithm. The LogP model characterizes a parallel machine by the number of processors(P), the communication bandwidth(g), the communication delay(L), and the communication overhead(o). In our approach, a good algorithm embodies a strategy for adapting to different machines, in terms of these parameters.

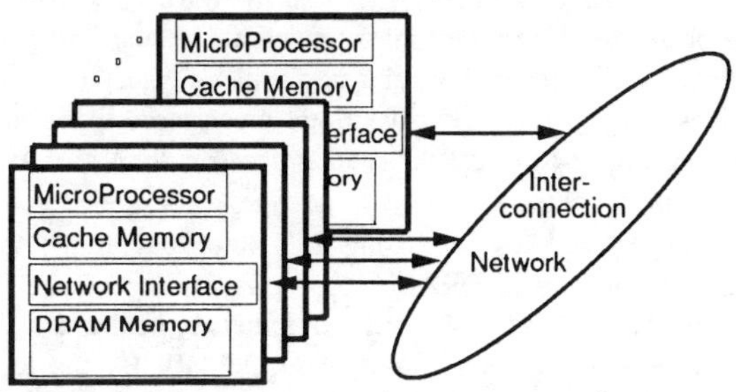

Figure 1: *This organization characterizes most massively parallel processors (MPPs). Current commercial examples include the Intel iPSC, Delta and Paragon, Thinking Machines CM-5, Ncube, Cray T3D, and Transputer-based MPPs such as the Meiko Computing Surface or the Parsytec GC. This structure describes essentially all of the current "research machines" as well.*

We believe that the common hardware organization described in Figure 1 will dominate commercial MPPs at least for the rest of this decade, for reasons discussed in Section 2 of this paper. In Section 3 we develop the LogP model, which captures the important characteristics of this organization. Section 4 puts the model to work, discussing the process of algorithm design in the context of the model and presenting examples that show the importance of the various communication aspects. Implementation of these algorithms on the CM-5 provides preliminary data towards validating the model. Section 5 presents communication networks in more detail and examines how closely our model corresponds to reality on current machines. Section 6 compares our model to various existing parallel models. Finally, Section 7 addresses several concerns that might arise regarding the utility of this model as a basis for further study.

2 Technological Motivations

The possibility of achieving revolutionary levels of performance has led parallel machine designers to explore a variety of exotic machine structures and implementation technologies over the past thirty years. Generally, these machines have performed certain operations very well and others very poorly, frustrating attempts to formulate a simple abstract model of their performance characteristics. However, technological factors are forcing a convergence towards systems with a familiar appearance; a collection of essentially complete computers, each consisting of a microprocessor, cache memory, and sizable DRAM memory, connected by a robust communication network. This convergence is likely to accelerate in the future as physically small computers dominate more of the computing market.

Microprocessor performance is advancing at a rate of 50 to 100% per year[17], as indicated by Figure 2. This tremendous evolution comes at an equally astounding cost: estimates of the cost of developing the recent MIPS R4000 are 30 engineers for three years, requiring about $30 million to develop the chip, another $10 million to fabricate it, and one million hours of computer time for simulations[15]. This cost is borne by the extremely large market for commodity uniprocessors. To remain viable, parallel machines must be on the same technology growth curve, with the added degree of freedom being the number of processors in the system. The effort needed to reach such high levels of performance combined with the relatively low cost of purchasing such microprocessors led Intel, Thinking Machines, Meiko, Convex, IBM and even Cray Research to use off-the-shelf microprocessors in their new parallel machines[5]. The technological opportunities suggest that parallel machines in the 1990s and beyond are much more likely to aim at thousands of 64-bit, off-the-shelf processors than at a million custom 1-bit processors.

Memory capacity is increasing at a rate comparable to the increase in capacity of DRAM chips: quadrupling in size every three years[16]. Today's personal computers typically use 8 MB of memory and workstations use about 32 MB. By the turn of the century the same number of DRAM chips will offer 64 times the capacity of current machines. The access time falls very slowly with each generation of DRAMs, so sophisticated cache structures will be required in commodity uniprocessors to bridge the difference between processor cycle times and memory access times. Cache-like structures may be incorporated into the memory chips themselves, as in emerging RAM-bus and synchronous DRAM technology[17]. Multiprocessors will need to incorporate state-of-the-art memory systems to remain competitive.

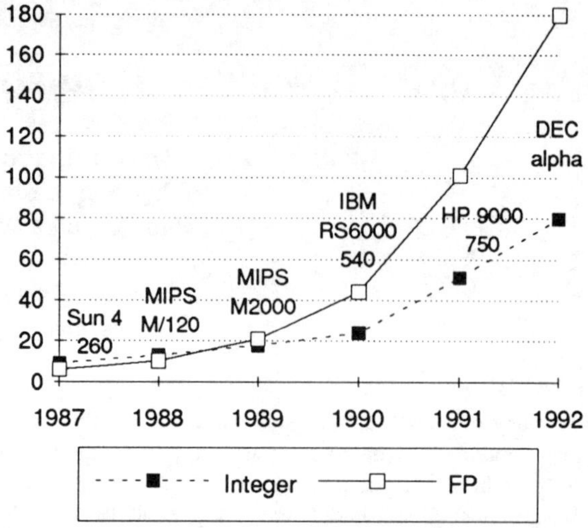

Figure 2: *Performance of state-of-the-art microprocessors over time. Performance is approximately number of times faster than the VAX-11/780. The floating point SPEC benchmarks improved at about 97% per year since 1987, and integer SPEC benchmarks improved at about 54% per year.*

Since the parallel machine nodes are very similar to the core of a workstation, the cost of a node is comparable to the cost of a workstation. As the most expensive supercomputer costs less than 25 M$ for the processors and memory, and since the price of workstations have remained at about 5-10 K$, the largest parallel machines will have a few thousand nodes. This economic observation is valid today, with no vendor producing a system with more than two thousand nodes.

Summarizing, we can expect that the nodes of parallel machines of the 1990s will be capable of computing hundreds of Mflops and capable of storing hundreds of megabytes. The number of such nodes will not scale into the millions, *so parallel algorithms will need to be developed under the assumption of a large number of data elements per processor*. This has significant impact on the kinds of algorithms that are effective in practice.

Network technology is advancing as well, but it is not driven by the same volume market forces as microprocessors and memory. While new media offer much higher network bandwidth, their realizable performance is limited by the interface between the network and the node. Currently, communication bandwidth through that interface lags far behind internal processor memory bandwidth. The lack of attention paid to the network interface in current microprocessors also means that substantial time is lost on each communication operation, regardless of programming style. Although the interface is improving, processors are improving in performance even faster, so we must assume that *high latency and overhead of communication, as well as limited bandwidth* will continue to be problems.

There appears to be no consensus emerging on interconnection topology: the networks of new commercial machines are typically different from their predecessors and different from each other. Operating in the presence of network faults is becoming extremely important as parallel machines go into production use, which suggests that the physical interconnect on a single system will vary over time to avoid broken components. Finally, adaptive routing techniques are becoming increasingly practical. Thus, attempting to exploit a specific network topology is likely to yield algorithms that are not very robust in practice. An abstract view of the latency and bandwidth properties of the network provides a framework for adapting algorithms to the target machine configuration.

No single programming methodology is becoming clearly dominant: shared-memory, message-passing, and data parallel styles all have significant popularity. Thus, the computational model should apply regardless of programming style. The technological factors discussed above make this goal tractable as most recent parallel machines support a range of programming styles using roughly similar hardware mechanisms[31].

The essential message is clear: technological forces are leading to massively parallel machines constructed from at most a few thousand nodes, each containing a powerful processor and substantial memory, interconnected by networks with limited bandwidth and significant latency. This renders both PRAM and network models inappropriate as a foundation for algorithm development since they do not accurately predict performance of programs on real computers. Our conclusion is that a new model which captures the technological reality more faithfully is needed.

3 LogP Model

Starting from the technological motivations discussed in the previous section, programming experience, and examination of popular theoretical models, we have developed a model of a distributed-memory multiprocessor in which processors communicate by point-to-point messages. The model specifies the performance characteristics of the interconnection network, but does not describe the structure of the network.

The main parameters of the model are:

L: an upper bound on the *latency*, or delay, incurred in communicating a message containing a word (or small number of words) from its source module to its target module.

o: the *overhead*, defined as the length of time that a processor is engaged in the transmission or reception of each message; during this time, the processor cannot perform other operations.

g: the *gap*, defined as the minimum time interval between consecutive message transmissions or consecutive message receptions at a processor. The reciprocal of g corresponds to the available per-processor communication bandwidth.

P: the number of processor/memory modules. We assume unit time for local operations and call it a cycle.

Furthermore, it is assumed that the network has a *finite capacity*, such that at most $\lceil L/g \rceil$ messages can be in transit from any processor or to any processor at any time. If a processor attempts to transmit a message that would exceed this limit, it stalls until the message can be sent without exceeding the capacity limit.

The parameters L, o and g are measured as multiples of the processor cycle. The model is *asynchronous*, *i.e.*, processors work asynchronously and the latency experienced by any message is unpredictable, but is bounded above by L in the absence of stalls. Because of variations in latency, the messages directed to a given target module may not arrive in the same order as they are sent. The basic model assumes that all messages are of a *small size* (a simple extension deals with longer messages).

In analyzing an algorithm, the key metrics are the maximum time and the maximum space used by any processor. In order to be considered correct, an algorithm must produce correct results under all interleavings of messages consistent with the upper bound of L on latency. However, in estimating the running time of an algorithm, we assume that each message incurs a latency of L.[1]

3.1 Discussion of parameters

This particular choice of parameters represents a compromise between faithfully capturing the execution characteristics of real machines and providing a reasonable framework for algorithm design and analysis. No small set of parameters can describe all machines completely. On the other hand, analysis of interesting algorithms is difficult with a large set of parameters. We believe that LogP represents "the knee of the curve" in that additional detail would seek to capture phenomena of modest impact while dropping parameters would encourage algorithmic techniques that are not well supported in practice.

We have resisted the temptation to provide a more detailed model of the individual processors, such as cache size, and rely on the existing body of knowledge in implementing fast sequential algorithms on modern uniprocessor systems to fill the gap. An implementation of a good parallel algorithm on a specific machine will surely require a degree of tuning, but if the issues raised by the level of detail embodied in LogP are not addressed, it would seem that the algorithm design is incomplete.

Fortunately, the parameters are not equally important in all situations; often it is possible to ignore one or more parameters and work with a simpler model. For example, in algorithms that communicate data infrequently, it is reasonable to ignore the bandwidth and capacity limits. In some algorithms messages are sent in long streams which are pipelined through the network, so that message transmission time is dominated by the inter-message gaps, and the latency may be disregarded. In some machines the overhead dominates the gap, so g can be eliminated. One convenient approximation technique is to increase o to be as large as g, so g can be ignored. This is conservative by at most a factor of two. We hope that parallel architectures improve to a point where o can be eliminated, but today this seems premature. More specific rationale for the particular parameters and their role is provided in the remainder of the paper.

3.2 Discouraged loopholes and rewarded techniques

The LogP model eliminates a variety of loopholes that other models permit. For example, many PRAM algorithms are excessively fine-grained, since there is no penalty for interprocessor communication. Although the EREW PRAM penalizes data access contention at the word level, it does not penalize contention at the module level.

The technique of multithreading is often suggested as a way of masking latency. This technique assigns to each physical processor the task of simulating several virtual processors; thus, computation does not have to be suspended during the processing of a remote request by one of the virtual processors. In practice, this technique is limited by the available communication bandwidth and by the overhead involved in context switching. We do not model context switching overhead, but capture the other constraints

[1] There are certain anomalous situations in which reducing the latency of certain messages actually increases the running time of an algorithm. These arise primarily when the computational schedule is based on the order of message arrival, rather than the information contained in the message.

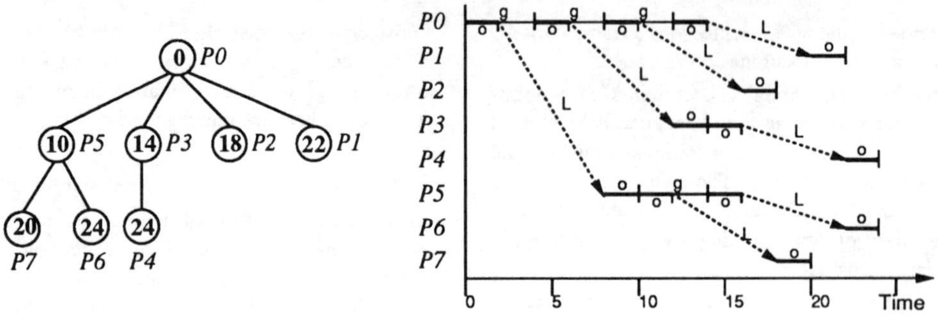

Figure 3: *Optimal broadcast tree for $P = 8, L = 6, g = 4, o = 2$ (left) and the activity of each processor over time (right). The number shown for each node is the time at which it has received the datum and can begin sending it on. The last value is received at time 24.*

realistically through the parameters o and g. Moreover the capacity constraint allows multithreading to be employed only up to a limit of L/g virtual processors. Under LogP, multithreading represents a convenient technique which simplifies analysis, as long as these constraints are met, rather than a fundamental requirement[26, 30].

On the other hand, LogP encourages techniques that work well in practice, such as coordinating the assignment of work with data placement, so as to reduce the communication bandwidth requirement and the frequency of remote references. The model also encourages the careful scheduling of computation and overlapping of computation with communication, within the limits imposed by network capacity. The limitation on network capacity also encourages balanced communication patterns in which no processor is flooded with incoming messages.

Although the model is stated in terms of primitive message events, we do not assume that algorithms must be described in terms of explicit message passing operations, such as send and receive. Shared memory models are implemented on distributed memory machines through an implicit exchange of messages[12]. Under LogP, reading a remote location requires time $2L + 4o$. Prefetch operations, which initiate a read and continue, can be issued every g cycles and cost $2o$ units of processing time. Some recent machines migrate locations to local caches when they are referenced; this would be addressed in algorithm analysis by adjusting which references are remote.

3.3 Broadcast and Summation

As a concrete illustration of the role of various parameters of the model, we sketch optimal algorithms for two simple problems: broadcast and summation. The solutions are quite different from those on the PRAM.

First, we consider the problem of broadcasting a single datum from one processor to $P - 1$ others. The main idea is simple: all processors that have received the datum transmit it as quickly as possible, while ensuring that no processor receives more than one message. The source of the broadcast begins transmitting the datum at time 0. The first datum enters the network at time o, takes L cycles to arrive at the destination, and is received by the node at time $L+2o$. Meanwhile, the source will have initiated transmission to other processors at time $g, 2g, \ldots$, assuming $g \geq o$, each of which acts as the root of a smaller broadcast tree. As indicated in Figure 3, the optimal broadcast tree for p processors is unbalanced[2] with the fan-out at each node determined by the relative values of L, o, and g. Observe that the processor overhead of successive transmissions overlaps the delivery of previous messages. Nodes may experience idle cycles at the end of the algorithm while the last few messages are in transit.

To obtain an optimal algorithm for the summation of n input values we first consider how to sum as many values as possible within a fixed amount of time T. This produces the communication and computation schedule for the summation problem. The pattern of communication among the processors again forms a tree; in fact, the tree has the same shape as an optimal broadcast tree[20]. Each processor has the task of summing a set of the elements and then (except for the root processor) transmitting the result to its parent. The elements to be summed by a processor consist of original inputs stored in its memory, together with partial results received from its children in the communication tree. To specify the algorithm, we first determine the optimal schedule of communication events and then determine the distribution of the initial inputs.

If $T \leq L + 2o$, the optimal solution is to sum $T + 1$ values on a single processor, since there is not sufficient time to receive data from another processor. Otherwise, the last step performed by the root processor (at time $T - 1$) is to add a value it has computed locally to a value it just received from another processor. The remote processor must have sent the value at time $T - 1 - L - 2o$, and we assume recursively that it forms the root of an optimal summation tree with this time bound. The local value must have been produced at time $T - 1 - o$. Since the root can receive a message every g cycles, its children in the communication tree should complete their summations at times $T-(2o+L+1), T-(2o+L+1+g), T-(2o+L+1+2g), \ldots$. The root performs $g - o$ additions of local input values between messages, as well as the local additions before it receives its first message. This communication schedule must be modified by the following consideration: since a processor invests o cycles in receiving a partial sum from a child, all transmitted partial sums must represent at least o additions. Based on this schedule, it is straight-forward to determine the set of input values initially assigned to each processor and the computation schedule. Notice that the inputs are not equally distributed over processors. (The algorithm is easily extended to handle the limitation of p processors by pruning the communication tree.)

The computation schedule for our summation algorithm can also be represented as a tree with a node for each computation step. Figure 4 shows the communication schedule for the processors and the computational schedule for a processor and two of its children. Each node is labeled with the time at which the step completes, the wavy edges represent partial results transmitted between processors, and the square boxes represent original inputs. The initial work for each processor is represented by a linear chain of input-summing

[2]A special case of this algorithm with $o = 0$ and $g = 1$ appears in [4].

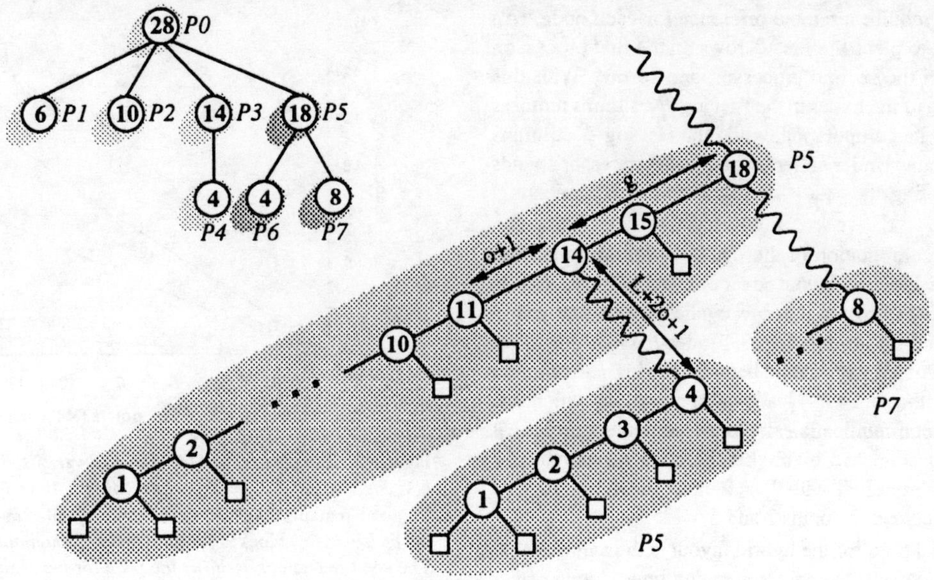

Figure 4: *Communication tree for optimal summing (left) and computation schedule for a subset of processors (right) for* $T = 28, P = 8, L = 5, g = 4, o = 2$.

nodes. Unless the processor is a leaf of the communication tree, it then repeatedly receives a value, adds it to its partial sum and performs a chain of $g - o - 1$ input-summing nodes. Observe that local computations overlap the delivery of incoming messages and the processor reception overhead begins as soon as the message arrives.

4 Algorithm Design

In the previous section, we stepped through the design of optimal algorithms for extremely simple problems and explained the parameters of our model. We now consider more typical parallel processing applications and show how the use of the LogP model leads to efficient parallel algorithms in practice. In particular, we observe that efficient parallel algorithms must pay attention to both computational aspects (such as the total amount of work done and load balance across processors) and communication aspects (such as remote reference frequency and the communication schedule). Thus, a good algorithm should co-ordinate work assignment with data placement, provide a balanced communication schedule, and overlap communication with processing.

4.1 Fast Fourier Transform

Our first example, the fast Fourier transform, illustrates these ideas in a concrete setting. We discuss the key aspects of the algorithm and then an implementation that achieves near peak performance on the Thinking Machines CM-5. We focus on the "butterfly" algorithm [8] for the discrete FFT problem, most easily described in terms of its computation graph. The n-input (n a power of 2) butterfly is a directed acyclic graph with $n(\log n + 1)$ nodes viewed as n rows of $(\log n + 1)$ columns each. For $0 \leq r < n$ and $0 \leq c < \log n$, the node (r, c) has directed edges to nodes $(r, c+1)$ and $(\bar{r}_c, c+1)$ where $\bar{r}_c$ is obtained by complementing the $(c+1)$-th most significant bit in the binary representation of r. Figure 5 shows an 8-input butterfly.

The nodes in column 0 are the problem inputs and those in column $\log n$ represent the outputs of the computation. (The outputs are in bit-reverse order, so for some applications an additional rearrangement step is required.) Each non-input node represents a complex operation, which we assume takes one unit of time. Implementing the algorithm on a parallel computer corresponds to laying out the nodes of the butterfly on its processors; the layout determines the computational and communication schedules, much as in the simple examples above.

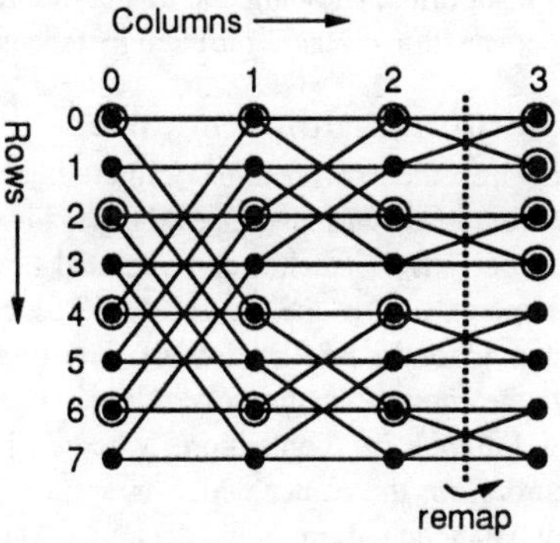

Figure 5: *An 8-input butterfly with* $P = 2$. *Nodes assigned to processor 0 under the hybrid layout are circled.*

4.1.1 Data placement and work assignment

There is a vast body of work on this structure as an interconnection topology, as well as on efficient embeddings of the butterfly on hypercubes, shuffle-exchange networks, etc. This has led many researchers to feel that algorithms must be designed to match the interconnection topology of the target machine. In real machines, however, the n data inputs and the $n \log n$ computation nodes must be laid out across P processors and typically $P << n$. The nature of this layout, and the fact that each processor holds many data elements has a profound effect on the communication structure, as shown below.

A natural layout is to assign the first row of the butterfly to the first processor, the second row to the second processor and so on. We refer to this as the *cyclic* layout. Under this layout, the first $\log \frac{n}{P}$ columns of computation require only local data, whereas the last $\log P$ columns require a remote reference for each node. An alternative layout is to place the first $\frac{n}{P}$ rows on the first processor, the next $\frac{n}{P}$ rows on the second processor, and so on. With this *blocked* layout, each of the nodes in the first $\log P$ columns requires a remote datum for its computation, while the last $\log \frac{n}{P}$ columns require only local data. Under either layout, each processor spends $\frac{n}{P} \log n$ time computing and $(g\frac{n}{P} + L) \log P$ time communicating, assuming $g \geq 2o$.

Since the initial computation of the cyclic layout and the final computation of the blocked layout are completely local, one is led to consider ***hybrid*** layouts that are cyclic on the first $\log P$ columns and blocked on the last $\log P$. Indeed, switching from cyclic to blocked layout at any column between the $\log P$-th and the $\log \frac{n}{P}$-th (assuming that $n > P^2$) leads to an algorithm which has a single "all-to-all" communication step between two entirely local computation phases. Figure 5 highlights the node assignment for processor 0 for an 8-input FFT with $P = 2$ under the hybrid layout; remapping occurs between columns 2 and 3.

The computational time for the hybrid layout is the same as that for the simpler layouts, but the communication time is lower by a factor of $\log P$: each processor sends $\frac{n}{P^2}$ messages to every other, requiring only $g(\frac{n}{P} - \frac{n}{P^2}) + L$ time. The total time is within a factor of $(1 + \frac{g}{\log n})$ of optimal, showing that this layout has the potential for near-perfect speedup on large problem instances.

4.1.2 Communication schedule

The algorithm presented so far is incomplete because it does not specify the *communication schedule* (the order in which messages are sent and received) that achieves the stated time bound. Our algorithm is a special case of the "layered" FFT algorithm proposed in [24] and adapted for the BSP model[30]. These earlier models do not emphasize the communication schedule: [24] has no bandwidth limitations and hence no contention, whereas [30] places the scheduling burden on the router which is assumed to be capable of routing any balanced pattern in the desired amount of time.

A naive schedule would have each processor send data starting with its first row and ending with its last row. Notice, that all processors first send data to processor 0, then all to processor 1, and so on. All but L/g processors will stall on the first send and then one will send to processor 0 every g cycles. A better schedule is obtained by staggering the starting rows such that no contention occurs: processor i starts with its $\frac{in}{P^2}$-th row, proceeds to the last row, and wraps around.

4.1.3 Implementation of the FFT algorithm

To verify the prediction of the analysis, we implemented the hybrid algorithm on a CM-5 multiprocessor[3] and measured the performance of the three phases of the algorithm: (I) computation with cyclic layout, (II) data remapping, and (III) computation with blocked layout. Figure 6 demonstrates the importance of the communication schedule: the three curves show the computation time and the communication times for the two communication schedules. With the naive schedule, the remap takes more than 1.5 times as long as the computation, whereas with staggering it

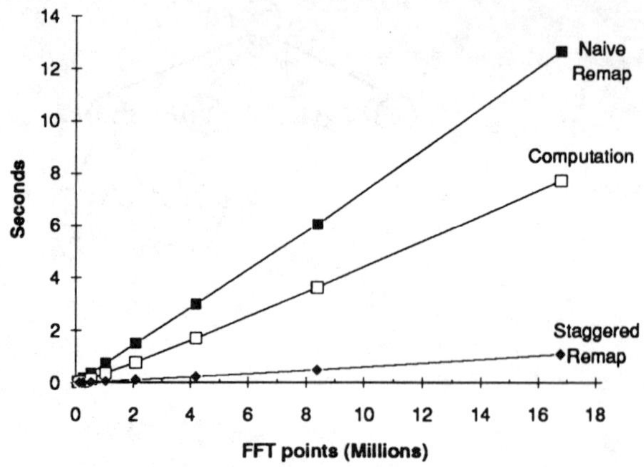

Figure 6: *Execution times for FFTs of various sizes on a 128 processor CM-5. The compute curve represents the time spent computing locally. The bad remap curve shows the time spent remapping the data from a cyclic layout to a blocked layout if a naive communication schedule is used. The good remap curve shows the time for the same remapping, but with a contention-free communication schedule, which is an order of magnitude faster. The X axis scale refers to the entire FFT size.*

takes only $\frac{1}{7}$th as long.

The two computation phases involve purely local operations and are standard FFTs. Figure 7 shows the computation rate over a range of FFT sizes expressed in Mflops/processor. For comparison, a CM-5's Sparc node achieves roughly 3.2 MFLOPS on the Linpack benchmark. This example provides a convenient comparison of the relative importance of cache effects, which we have chosen to ignore, and communication balance, which other models ignore. The drop in performance for the local FFT from 2.8 Mflops to 2.2 Mflops occurs when the size of the local FFTs exceeds cache capacity. (For large FFTs, the cyclic phase involving one large FFT suffers more cache interference than the blocked phase which solves many small FFTs.) The implementation could be refined to reduce the cache effects, but the improvement would be small compared to the speedup associated with improving the communication schedule.

4.1.4 Quantitative analysis

The discussion so far suggests how the model may be used in a qualitative sense to guide parallel algorithm design. The following shows how the model can be used in a more quantitative manner to

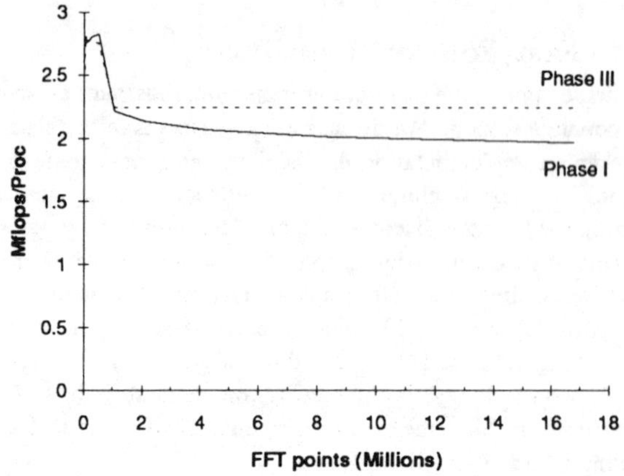

Figure 7: *Per processor computation rates for the two computation phases of the FFT in Mflops (millions of floating-point operations per second).*

[3]The CM-5 is a massively parallel MIMD computer based on the Sparc processor. Each node consists of a 33 Mhz Sparc RISC processor chip-set (including FPU, MMU and 64 KByte direct-mapped write-through cache), 8 MBytes of local DRAM memory and a network interface. The nodes are interconnected in two identical disjoint incomplete fat trees, and a broadcast/scan/prefix control network. The implementation does not use the vector accelerators which are not available at the time of writing.

predict the execution time of an implementation of the algorithm. From the computational performance in Figure 7 we can calibrate the "cycle time" for the FFT as the time for the set of complex multiply-adds of the butterfly primitive. At an average of 2.2 Mflops and 10 floating-point operations per butterfly, a cycle corresponds to $4.5\mu s$, or 150 clock ticks (we use *cycles* to refer to the time unit in the model and *ticks* to refer to the 33 Mhz hardware clock). In previous experiments on the CM-5[31] we have determined that $o \approx 2\mu s$ (0.44 cycles, 56 ticks) and, on an unloaded network, $L \approx 6\mu s$ (1.3 cycles, 200 ticks). Furthermore, the bisection bandwidth[4] is 5MB/s per processor for messages of 16 bytes of data and 4 bytes of address, so we take g to be $4\mu s$(0.44 cycles, 56 ticks). In addition there is roughly $1\mu s(0.22\ cycles, 28\ ticks)$ of local computation per data point to load/store values to/from memory. Analysis of the staggered remap phase predicts the communication time is $\frac{n}{P}\max(1\mu s + 2o, g) + L$. For these parameter values, the transmission rate is limited by processing time and communication overhead, rather than bandwidth. The remap phase is predicted to increase rapidly to an asymptotic rate of 3.2MB/s. The observed performance is roughly 2MB/s for this phase, nearly half of the available network bandwidth.

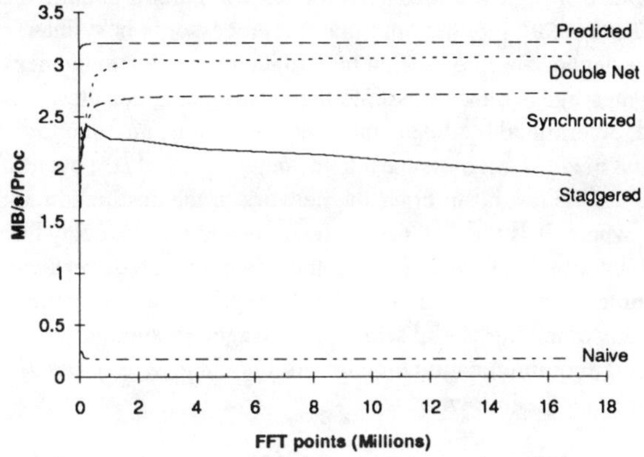

Figure 8: *Predicted and measured communication rates expressed in Mbytes/second per processor for the staggered communication schedule. The staggered schedule is theoretically contention-free, but the asynchronous execution of the processors causes some contention in practice. The* synchronized *schedule performs a barrier synchronization periodically (using a special hardware barrier). The* double net *schedule uses both data networks, doubling the available network bandwidth.*

The analysis does not predict the gradual performance drop for large FFTs. In reality, processors execute asynchronously due to cache effects, network collisions, etc. It appears that they gradually drift out of sync during the remap phase, disturbing the communication schedule. To reduce this effect we added a barrier synchronizing all processors after every $\frac{n}{P^2}$ messages.[5] Figure 8 shows that this eliminates the performance drop.

We can test the effect of reducing g by improving the implementation to use both fat-tree networks present in the machine, thereby doubling the available network bandwidth. The result shown in Figure 8 is that the performance increases by only 15% because the network interface overhead (o) and the loop processing dominate.

[4]The bisection bandwidth is the minimum bandwidth through any cut of the network that separates the set of processors into halves.

[5]For simplicity, the implementation uses the hardware barrier available on the CM-5. The same effect could have been achieved using explicit acknowledgement messages.

This detailed quantitative analysis of the implementation shows that the hybrid-layout FFT algorithm is nearly optimal on the CM-5. The computation phases are purely local and the communication phase is overhead-limited, thus the processors are 100% busy all the time (ignoring the insignificant L at the end of the communication phase). Performance improvements in the implementation are certainly possible, but without affecting the algorithm itself.

4.1.5 Overlapping communication with computation

In future machines we expect architectural innovations in the processor-network interface to significantly reduce the value of o with respect to g. Algorithms for such machines could try to overlap communication with computation in order to mask communication time, as in the optimal summation example. If o is small compared to g, each processor idles for $g - 2o$ cycles between successive transmissions during the remap phase. The remap can be merged into the computation phases, as in the optimal algorithms[27]. The initial portion of the remap is interleaved with the pre-remap computation, while the final portions can be interleaved with the post-remap computation. Unless g is extremely large, this eliminates idling of processors during remap.

4.2 LU Decomposition

We now discuss one other problem that has been carefully studied on parallel machines and show how the LogP model motivates the development of efficient algorithms for it. Here we provide only a qualitative assessment of the key design issues. The long version of this paper also contains a discussion of sorting and connected components[9]. For details of the implementation of connected components and analysis under the LogP model see [29].

Linear algebra primitives offer a dramatic example of the importance of careful development of high performance parallel algorithms. The widely used Linpack benchmark achieves greater than 10 GFLOPS on recent parallel machines. In this section we examine LU decomposition, the core of the Linpack benchmark, to show that the key ideas employed in high performance linear algebra routines surface easily when the algorithm is examined in terms of our model.

In LU decomposition using Gaussian elimination, an $n \times n$ non-singular matrix A is reduced in $n - 1$ elimination steps to a unit-diagonal lower triangular matrix L and an upper triangular matrix U such that $PA = LU$ for some permutation matrix P. Since L and U are constructed by overwriting A, we will refer only to the matrix A, with $A^{(k)}$ denoting the matrix A at the start of step k. In the k-th elimination step, the k-th row and column of $A^{(k)}$ are replaced by the k-th column of L and the k-th row of U. This involves *partial pivoting* to determine the pivot, *i.e.*, the element in column k (below the diagonal) of largest absolute value, *swapping* the k-th and pivot rows of $A^{(k)}$, and *scaling* of the k-th column by dividing it by the pivot. Thereafter, the $(n-k) \times (n-k)$ lower right square submatrix of $A^{(k)}$ is *updated* to $A^{(k+1)}$:

$$A_{ij}^{(k+1)} = A_{ij}^{(k)} - L_{ik}U_{kj},\ i,j = k+1,\ldots,n$$

The row permutations that result from pivoting are carried along as part of the final result. The parallelism in this algorithm is trivial: at step k all $(n-k)^2$ scalar updates are independent. The pivoting, swapping and scaling steps could be parallelized with appropriate data layout.

To obtain a fast algorithm, we first focus on the ratio of

communication to computation. Observe that regardless of the data layout, the processor responsible for updating $A_{ij}^{(k)}$ must obtain L_{ik} and U_{kj}. A bad data layout might require each processor to obtain the entire pivot row and the entire multiplier column. Thus, step k would require $2(n-k)g + L$ time for communication [6] and $2(n-k)^2/P$ time for computation.

The communication can be reduced by a factor of 2 by choosing a *column* layout in which n/P columns of A are allocated to each processor. For this layout, only the multipliers need be broadcast since pivot row elements are used only for updates of elements in the same column. A more dramatic reduction in communication cost can be had by a *grid* layout in which each processor is responsible for updating a $(n-k)/\sqrt{P} \times (n-k)/\sqrt{P}$ submatrix of $A^{(k)}$. This requires each processor to receive only $2(n-k)/\sqrt{P}$ values, a gain of $\sqrt{P}$ in the communication ratio. Some of this advantage will be foregone due to the communication requirements of pivoting and scaling down a column that is shared by many processors. However, this cost is asymptotically negligible in comparison to the communication cost for update.

Our specification of the grid layout is incomplete since there are many ways to distribute A among P processors so that each receives a submatrix of A determined by a set of $n/\sqrt{P}$ rows and columns. The two extreme cases are *blocked* and *cyclic* allocation in each dimension. In the former case, the rows and columns assigned to a processor are contiguous in A while in the latter they are maximally scattered ($\sqrt{P}$ apart). It should be clear that blocked grid layout leads to severe load imbalance: by the time the algorithm completes $n/\sqrt{P}$ elimination steps, $2\sqrt{P}$ processors would be idle and only one processor is active for the last $n/\sqrt{P}$ elimination steps. In contrast, the scattered layout allows all P processors to stay active for all but the last $\sqrt{P}$ steps. It is heartening to note that the fastest Linpack benchmark programs actually employ a scattered grid layout, a scheme whose benefits are obvious from our model.

5 Matching the Model to Machines

The LogP model abstracts the communication network into three parameters. When the interconnection network is operating within its capacity, the time to transmit a small message will be $2o + L$: an overhead of o at the sender and the receiver, and a latency of L within the network. The available bandwidth per processor is determined by g and the network capacity by L/g. In essence, the network is treated as a pipeline of depth L with initiation rate g and a processor overhead of o on each end. From a purely theoretical viewpoint, it might seem better to define L to be a simple function of P. However, from a hardware design viewpoint, it might seem important to specify the topology, routing algorithm, and other properties. In this section, we consider how well our "middle ground" model reflects the characteristics of real machines.

5.1 Average distance

A significant segment of the parallel computing literature assumes that the number of network links traversed by a message, or *distance*, is the primary component of the communication time. This suggests that the topological structure of the network is critical and that an important indicator of the quality of the network is the average distance between nodes. The following table shows the asymptotic average distance and the evaluation of the formula for the practical case, $P = 1,024$.

Network	Ave. Distance	$P = 1,024$
Hypercube	$\frac{\log p}{2}$	5
Butterfly	$\log p$	10
4^{deg} Fat Tree	$4 \log_4 p - 2/3$	9.33
3D Torus	$\frac{3}{4} p^{1/3}$	7.5
3D Mesh	$p^{1/3}$	10
2D Torus	$\frac{1}{2} p^{1/2}$	16
2D Mesh	$\frac{2}{3} p^{1/2}$	21

For configurations of practical interest the difference between topologies is a factor of two, except for very primitive networks, such as a 2D mesh or torus. Even there, the difference is only a factor of four. Moreover, this difference makes only a small contribution to total message transmission time, as discussed below.

5.2 Unloaded communication time

In a real machine, transmission of an M-bit long message in an unloaded or lightly loaded network has four parts. First, there is the *send overhead*; *i.e.*, the time that the processor is busy interfacing to the network before the first bit of data is placed onto the network. The message is transmitted into the network channel a few bits at a time, determined by the channel width w. Thus, the time to get the last bit of an M-bit message into the network is $\lceil M/w \rceil$ cycles. The time for the last bit to cross the network to the destination node is Hr, where H is the distance of the route and r is the delay through each intermediate node. Finally, there is the *receive overhead*, *i.e.*, the time from the arrival of the last bit until the receiving processor can do something useful with the message. In summary, the total message communication time for an M bit message across H hops is given by the following.

$$T(M,H) \quad = T_{snd} + \lceil \tfrac{M}{w} \rceil + Hr + T_{rcv}$$

Table 1 indicates that, for current machines, message communication time through a lightly loaded network is dominated by the send and receive overheads, and thus is relatively insensitive to network structure. Furthermore, networks with a larger diameter typically have wider links (larger w), smaller routing delays (r), and a faster cycle time because all the physical wires are short. All these factors reduce the transmission time. Thus, modeling the communication latency as an arbitrary constant, in the absence of contention, is far more accurate than simple rules, such as $L = \log P$. In determining LogP parameters for a given machine, it appears reasonable to choose $o = \frac{T_{snd}+T_{rcv}}{2}$, $L = Hr + \lceil \frac{M}{w} \rceil$, where H is the maximum distance of a route and M is the fixed message size being used, and g to be M divided by the per processor bisection bandwidth.

The send and receive overheads in Table 1 warrant some explanation. The very large overheads for the commercial message passing machines (nCUBE/2 and CM-5) reflect the standard communication layer from the vendor. Large overheads such as these have led many to conclude that large messages are essential. For the nCUBE/2, the bulk of this cost is due to buffer management and copying associated with the asynchronous send/receive communication model[31]. This is more properly viewed as part of the computational work of an algorithm using that style of communication. For the CM-5, the bulk of the cost is due to the protocol associated with the synchronous send/receive, which involves a pair of messages before transmitting

[6] We are assuming here that the $2(n-k)$ elements of the pivot row and multiplier column are distributed equally among processors and are communicated by an efficient all-to-all broadcast.

Machine	Network	Cycle ns	w bits	$T_{snd} + T_{rcv}$ cycles	r cycles	avg. H (1024 Proc.)	T(M=160) (1024 Proc.)
nCUBE/2	Hypercube	25	1	6400	40	5	6760
CM-5	Fattree	25	4	3600	8	9.3	3714
Dash[12]	Torus	30	16	30	2	6.8	53
J-Machine[10]	3d Mesh	31	8	16	2	12.1	60
Monsoon[25]	Butterfly	20	16	10	2	5	30
nCUBE/2 (AM)	Hypercube	25	1	1000	40	5	1360
CM-5 (AM)	Fattree	25	4	132	8	9.3	246

Table 1: *Network timing parameters for a one-way message without contention on several current commercial and research multiprocessors. The final two rows refer to the active message layer, which uses the commercial hardware, but reduces the interface overhead.*

the first data element. This protocol is easily modeled in terms of our parameters as $3(L+2o)+ng$, where n is the number of words sent. The final two rows show the inherent hardware overheads of these machines, as revealed by the Active Message layer[31].

The table also includes three research machines that have focused on optimizing the processor network interface: Dash[12] for a shared memory model, J-machine[10] for a message driven model, and Monsoon[25] for a dataflow model. Although a significant improvement over the commercial machines, the overhead is still a significant fraction of the communication time.

5.3 Saturation

In a real machine the latency experienced by a message tends to increase as a function of the load, i.e., the rate of message initiation, because more messages are in the network competing for resources. Studies such as [11] show that there is typically a saturation point at which the latency increases sharply; below the saturation point the latency is fairly insensitive to the load. This characteristic is captured by the capacity constraint in LogP.

5.4 Long messages

The LogP model does not give special treatment to long messages, yet some machines have special hardware (*e.g.*, a DMA device connected to the network interface) to support sending long messages. The processor overhead for setting up that device is paid once and a part of sending and receiving long messages can be overlapped with computation. This is tantamount to providing two processors on each node, one to handle messages and one to do the computation. Our basic model assumes that each node consists only of one processor that is also responsible for sending and receiving messages. Therefore the overhead o is paid for each word (or small number of words). Providing a separate network processor to deliver or receive long messages can at best double the performance of each node. This can simply be modeled as two processors at each node.

5.5 Specialized hardware support

Some machines provide special hardware to perform a broadcast, scan, or global synchronization. In LogP, processors must explicitly send messages to perform these operations.[7] However, the hardware versions of these operations are typically limited in functionality; for example, they may only work with integers, not floating-point numbers. They may not work for only a subset of the machine.

The most common global operation observed in developing algorithms for the LogP model is a barrier, as in the FFT example above. As discussed below, some parallel models assume this to be a primitive operation. It is simpler to support in hardware than global data operations. However, there is not yet sufficient evidence that it will be widely available. One virtue of having barriers available as a primitive is that analysis is simplified by assuming the processors exit the barrier in synchrony.

5.6 Contention free communication patterns

By abstracting the internal structure of the network into a few performance parameters, the model cannot distinguish between "good" permutations and "bad" permutations. Various network interconnection topologies are known to have specific contention-free routing patterns. Repeated transmissions within this pattern can utilize essentially the full bandwidth, whereas other communication patterns will saturate intermediate routers in the network. These patterns are highly specific, often depending on the routing algorithm, and amount of buffering in each router, as well as the interconnection topology. We feel this is an important message to architects of parallel computers. If the interconnection topology of a machine or the routing algorithm performs well on only a very restricted class of communication patterns, it will only be usable to a very specific set of algorithms. Even so, for every network there are certain communication patterns where performance will be degraded due to internal contention among routing paths. The goal of the hardware designer should be to make these the exceptional case rather than the frequently occurring case. A possible extension of the LogP model to reflect network performance on various communication patterns would be to provide multiple g's, where the one appropriate to the particular communication pattern is used in the analysis.

6 Other Models

Our model was motivated by the observation of a convergence in the hardware organization of general purpose massively parallel computers. Parallel systems of the next decade will consist of up to a few thousand powerful processor/memory nodes connected by a fast communication network. In this section we briefly review some of the existing computational models and explain why they fail to fully capture the essential features of the coming generation of machines.

[7] It is an unintended use of the model to synchronize implicitly without sending messages, *e.g.* by relying on an upper bound on the communication latency L.

6.1 PRAM models

The PRAM[13] is the most popular model for representing and analyzing the complexity of parallel algorithms. The PRAM model is simple and very useful for a gross classification of algorithms, but it does not reveal important performance bottlenecks in distributed memory machines because it assumes a single shared memory in which each processor can access any cell in unit time. In effect, the PRAM assumes that interprocessor communication has infinite bandwidth, zero latency, and zero overhead ($g = 0, L = 0, o = 0$). Thus, the PRAM model does not discourage the design of algorithms with an excessive amount of interprocessor communication. Since the PRAM model assumes that each memory cell is independently accessible, it also neglects the issue of contention caused by concurrent access to different cells within the same memory module. The EREW PRAM deals only with contention for a single memory location. The PRAM model also assumes unrealistically that the processors operate completely synchronously.

Although any specific parallel computer will, of course, have a fixed number of processors, PRAM algorithms often allow the number of concurrently executing tasks to grow as a function of the size of the input. The rationale offered for this is that these tasks can be assigned to the physical processors, with each processor apportioning its time among the tasks assigned to it. However, the PRAM model does not charge for the high level of message traffic and context switching overhead that such simulations require, nor does it encourage the algorithm designer to exploit the assignment. Similar criticisms apply to the extensions of the PRAM model considered below.

It has been suggested that the PRAM can serve as a good model for expressing the logical structure of parallel algorithms, and that implementation of these algorithms can be achieved by general-purpose simulations of the PRAM on distributed-memory machines[26]. However, these simulations require powerful interconnection networks, and, even then, may be unacceptably slow, especially when network bandwidth and processor overhead for sending and receiving messages are properly accounted.

6.2 Extensions of the PRAM model

There are many variations on the basic PRAM model which address one or more of the problems discussed above, namely memory contention, asynchrony, latency and bandwidth.

Memory Contention: The *Module Parallel Computer* [19, 23] differs from the PRAM by assuming that the memory is divided into modules, each of which can process one access request at a time. This model is suitable for handling memory contention at the module level, but does not address issues of bandwidth and network capacity.

Asynchrony: Gibbons[14] proposed the *Phase PRAM*, an extension of the PRAM in which computation is divided into "phases." All processors run asynchronously within a phase, and synchronize explicitly at the end of each phase. This model discourages excessive interprocessor synchronization. To balance the cost of synchronization with the time spent computing, Gibbons proposes to have a single processor of a phase PRAM simulate several PRAM processors. Other proposals for asynchrony include[7, 18, 21].

Latency: The *delay model* of Papadimitriou and Yannakakis[24] accounts for communication latency, *i.e.* it realizes there is a delay between the time some information is produced at a processor and the time it can be used by another. A different model that also addresses communication latency is the *Block Parallel Random Access Machine* (BPRAM) in which block transfers are allowed[1].

Bandwidth: A model that deals with communication bandwidth is the *Local-Memory Parallel Random Access Machine* (LPRAM)[2]. This is a CREW PRAM in which each processor is provided with an unlimited amount of local memory and where accesses to global memory are more expensive. An asynchronous variant which differs in that it allows more than one outstanding memory request has been studied in [22].

Memory Hierarchy: Whereas PRAM extends the RAM model by allowing unit time access to any location from any processor and LogP essentially views each node as in the RAM, the *Parallel Memory Hierarchy model* (PMH)[3] rejects the RAM as a basis and views the memory as a hierarchy of storage modules. Each module is characterized by its size and the time to transfer a block to the adjoining modules. A multiprocessor is represented by a tree of modules with processors at the leaves. This model is based on the observation that the techniques used for tuning code for the memory hierarchy are similar to those for developing parallel algorithms.

Other primitive parallel operations: The scan-model[6] is an EREW PRAM model extended with unit-time scan operations (data independent prefix operations), *i.e.*, it assumes that certain scan operations can be executed as fast as parallel memory references. For integer scan operations this is approximately the case on the CM-2 and CM-5.

The observation of the deficiences of the PRAM led Snyder to conclude it was unrealizable and to develop the *Candidate Type Architecture* (CTA) as an alternative[28]. The CTA is a finite set of sequential computers connected in a fixed, bounded degree graph. The CTA is essentially a formal description of a parallel machine; it requires the communication cost of an algorithm to be analyzed for each interconnection network used. The BSP model presented below abstracts the structure of the machine, so the analysis of algorithms is based on a few performance parameters. This facilitates the development of portable algorithms.

6.3 Bulk Synchronous Parallel Model

Valiant's Bulk Synchronous Parallel (BSP) model is closely aligned with our goals, as it seeks to bridge the gap between theoretical work and practical machines[30]. In the BSP model a distributed-memory multiprocessor is described in terms of three elements: (i) *processor/memory modules*, (ii) an *interconnection network*, and (iii) a *synchronizer* which performs barrier synchronization.

A computation consists of a sequence of *supersteps*. During a superstep each processor performs local computation, and receives and sends messages, subject to the following constraints: the local computation may depend only on data present in the local memory of the processor at the beginning of the superstep, and a processor may send at most h messages and receive at most h messages in a superstep. Such a communication pattern is called a h-relation.

Although the BSP model was one of the inspirations for our work, we have several concerns about it at a detailed level.

The length of a superstep must be sufficient to accommodate an arbitrary h-relation (and hence the most unfavorable one possible). Our model enables communication to be scheduled more precisely, permitting the exploitation of more favorable communication patterns, such as those in which not all processors send or receive as many as h messages. Valiant briefly mentions such refinements as varying h dynamically or synchronizing different subsets of processors independently, but does not describe how such refinements might be implemented.

Messages sent at the beginning of a superstep can only be used in the next superstep, even if the length of the superstep is longer than the latency. In our model processors work asynchronously, and a processor can use a message as soon as it arrives.

The BSP model assumes special hardware support to synchronize all processors at the end of a superstep. The synchronization hardware needed by the BSP may not be available on many parallel machines, especially in the generality where multiple arbitrary subsets of the machine can synchronize. In our model all synchronization is done by messages, admittedly at higher cost than if synchronization hardware were available.

Valiant proposes a programming environment in which algorithms are designed for the PRAM model assuming an unlimited number of processors, and then implemented by simulating a number of PRAM processors on each BSP processor. He gives a theoretical analysis showing that the simulation will be optimal, up to constant factors, provided that the *parallel slackness*, *i.e.* the number of PRAM processors per BSP processor, is sufficiently large. However, the constant factors in this simulation may be large, and would be even larger if the cost of context switching were fully counted. For example, in a real processor, switching from one process to another would require resetting not only the registers, but also parts of the cache.

6.4 Network models

In a network model, communication is only allowed between directly connected processors; other communication is explicitly forwarded through intermediate nodes. In each step the nodes can communicate with their nearest neighbors and operate on local data. Many algorithms have been created which are perfectly matched to the structure of a particular network. Examples are parallel prefix and non-commutative summing (tree), physical simulations and numerical solvers for partial differential equations (mesh), FFT and bitonic sorting (butterfly). However, these elegant algorithms lack robustness, as they usually do not map with equal efficiency onto interconnection structures different from those for which they were designed. Most current networks allow messages to "cut through" intermediate nodes without disturbing the processor; this is much faster than explicit forwarding.

The perfect correspondence between algorithm and network usually requires a number of processors equal to the number of data items in the input. In the more typical case where there are many data items per processor, the pattern of communication is less dependent on the network. Wherever problems have a local, regular communication pattern, such as stencil calculation on a grid, it is easy to lay the data out so that only a diminishing fraction of the communication is external to the processor. Basically, the interprocessor communication diminishes like the surface to volume ratio and with large enough problem sizes, the cost of communication becomes trivial. This is also the case for some complex communication patterns, such as the butterfly, as illustrated by the FFT example in Section 4.

We conclude that the design of portable algorithms can best be carried out in a model such as LogP, in which detailed assumptions about the interconnection network are avoided.

7 Summary

Our search for a machine-independent model for parallel computation is motivated by technological trends which are driving the high-end computer industry toward massively parallel machines constructed from nodes containing powerful processors and substantial memory, interconnected by networks with limited bandwidth and significant latency. The models in current use do not accurately reflect the performance characteristics of such machines and, thus are an incomplete framework for development of practical algorithms.

The LogP model attempts to capture the important bottlenecks of such parallel computers with a small number of parameters: the latency (L), overhead (o), bandwidth (g) of communication, and the number of processors (P). We believe the model is sufficiently detailed to reflect the major practical issues in parallel algorithm design, yet simple enough to support detailed algorithmic analysis. At the same time, the model avoids specifying the programming style or the communication protocol, being equally applicable to shared-memory, message passing, and data parallel paradigms.

As with any new proposal, there will naturally be concerns regarding its utility as a basis for further study. The model exhibits interesting theoretical structure; our optimal algorithms for broadcast and summation result in a formulation that is distinct from that obtained on the PRAM or various network models. These examples also demonstrate how an algorithm may adapt its computation and communication structure in response to each of the parameters of the model. We have observed that in specific situations some parameters become insignificant and one can work with a simplified model. The FFT example demonstrates that the elegant communication pattern that some algorithms exhibit on an element-by-element basis disappears when a large number of elements is allocated to each processor. This suggests that adjusting the data placement is an important technique for improving algorithms, much like changes in the representation of data structures. Furthermore, this example illustrates the importance of balanced communication, which is scarcely addressed in other models. These observations are borne out by implementations on the CM-5 multiprocessor. Very similar observations apply to parallel sorting, LU decomposition, and matrix multiplication.

We believe that the LogP model opens several avenues of research. It potentially provides a concise summary of the performance characteristics of current and future machines. This will require refining the process of parameter determination and evaluating a large number of machines. Such a summary can focus the efforts of machine designers toward architectural improvements that can be measured in terms of these parameters. For example, a machine with large gap g is only effective for algorithms with a large ratio of computation to communication. In effect, the model defines a four dimensional parameter space of potential machines. The product line offered by a particular vendor may be identified with a curve in this space, characterizing the system scalability. It will be important to evaluate the complexity of a wide variety of algorithms in terms of the model and to evaluate the predictive capabilities of the model. The model provides a new framework for classifying algorithms and identifying which are most attractive in various regions of the machine parameter space. We hope this will stimulate the development of new parallel algorithms and the examination of the fundamental requirements of various problems within the LogP framework.

Acknowledgements

Several people provided helpful comments on earlier drafts of this paper, including Larry Carter, Dave Douglas, Jeanne Ferrante, Seth Copen Goldstein, Anoop Gupta, John Hennessy, Tom Leighton, Charles Leiserson, Lesley Matheson, Rishiyur Nikhil, Abhiram Ranade, Luigi Semenzato, Larry Snyder, Burton Smith, Guy Steele, Robert Tarjan, Leslie Valiant, and the anonymous reviewers.

Computational support was provided by the NSF Infrastructure Grant number CDA-8722788. David Culler is supported by an NSF Presidential Faculty Fellowship CCR-9253705 and LLNL Grant UCB-ERL-92/172. Klaus Erik Schauser is supported by an IBM Graduate Fellowship. Richard Karp and Abhijit Sahay are supported by NSF/DARPA Grant CCR-9005448. Eunice Santos is supported by a DOD-NDSEG Graduate Fellowship. Ramesh Subramonian is supported by Lockheed Palo Alto Research Laboratories under RDD 506. Thorsten von Eicken is supported by the Semiconductor Research Corporation.

References

[1] A. Aggarwal, A. K. Chandra, and M. Snir. On Communication Latency in PRAM Computation. In *Proceedings of the ACM Symposium on Parallel Algorithms and Architectures*, pages 11–21. ACM, June 1989.

[2] A. Aggarwal, A. K. Chandra, and M. Snir. Communication Complexity of PRAMs. In *Theoretical Computer Science*, pages 3–28, March 1990.

[3] B. Alpern, L. Carter, E. Feig, and T. Selker. The Uniform Memory Hierarchy Model of Computation. *Algorithmica*, 1993. (to appear).

[4] A. Bar-Noy and S. Kipnis. Designing broadcasting algorithms in the postal model for message-passing systems. In *Proceedings of the ACM Symposium on Parallel Algorithms and Architectures*, pages 11–22, June 1992.

[5] G. Bell. Ultracomputers: A Teraflop Before Its Time. *Communications of the Association for Computing Machinery*, 35(8):26–47, August 1992.

[6] G. E. Blelloch. Scans as Primitive Parallel Operations. In *Proceedings of International Conference on Parallel Processing*, pages 355–362, 1987.

[7] R. Cole and O. Zajicek. The APRAM: Incorporating asynchrony into the PRAM model. In *Proceedings of the Symposium on Parallel Architectures and Algorithms*, pages 169–178, 1989.

[8] J. M. Cooley and J. W. Tukey. An algorithm for the machine calculation of complex Fourier series. *Math. Comp*, 19:297–301, 1965.

[9] D. E. Culler, R. M. Karp, D. A. Patterson, A. Sahay, K. E. Schauser, E. Santos, R. Subramonian, and T. von Eicken. LogP: Towards a Realistic Model of Parallel Computation. Technical Report UCB/CSD 92/713, UC Berkeley, 1992.

[10] W. et al Dally. The J-Machine: A Fine-Grain Concurrent Computer. In *IFIP Congress*, 1989.

[11] W. J. Dally. Performance Analysis of k-ary n-cube Interconnection Networks. *IEEE Transaction on Computers*, 39(6):775–785, June 1990.

[12] Lenoski D. et al. The Stanford Dash Multiprocessor. *IEEE Computer*, 25(3):63–79, March 1992.

[13] S. Fortune and J. Wyllie. Parallelism in Random Access Machines. In *Proceedings of the 10th Annual Symposium on Theory of Computing*, pages 114–118, 1978.

[14] P. B. Gibbons. A More Practical PRAM Model. In *Proceedings of the ACM Symposium on Parallel Algorithms and Architectures*, pages 158–168. ACM, 1989.

[15] J. L. Hennessy. MIPS R4000 Overview. In *Proc. of the 19th Int'l Symposium on Computer Architecture*, Gold Coast, Australia, May 1992.

[16] J. L. Hennessy and D. A. Patterson. *Computer Architecture—A Quantitative Approach.* Morgan Kaufmann, 1990.

[17] IEEE. *Symposium Record—Hot Chips IV*, August 1992.

[18] P. Kanellakis and A. Shvartsman. Efficient parallel algorithms can be made robust. In *Proceedings of the 8th Symposium on Principles of Distributed Computing*, pages 211–221, 1989.

[19] R. M. Karp, M. Luby, and F. Meyer auf der Heide. Efficient PRAM Simulation on a Distributed Memory Machine. In *Proceedings of the Twenty-Fourth Annual ACM Symposium of the Theory of Computing*, pages 318–326, May 1992.

[20] R. M. Karp, A. Sahay, E. Santos, and K. E. Schauser. Optimal Broadcast and Summation in the LogP Model. Technical Report UCB/CSD 92/721, UC Berkeley, 1992.

[21] Z. M. Kedem, K. V. Palem, and P. G. Spirakis. Efficient robust parallel computations. In *Proceedings of the 22nd Annual Symposium on Theory of Computing*, pages 138–148, 1990.

[22] C. U. Martel and A. Raghunathan. Asynchronous PRAMs with memory latency. Technical report, University of California, Davis, Division of Computer Science, 1991.

[23] K. Mehlhorn and U. Vishkin. Randomized and deterministic simulations of PRAMs by parallel machines with restricted granularity of parallel memories. *Acta Informatica*, 21:339–374, 1984.

[24] C. H. Papadimitriou and M. Yannakakis. Towards an Architecture-Independent Analysis of Parallel Algorithms. In *Proceedings of the Twentieth Annual ACM Symposium of the Theory of Computing*, pages 510–513. ACM, 1988.

[25] G. M. Papadopoulos and D. E. Culler. Monsoon: an Explicit Token-Store Architecture. In *Proc. of the 17th Annual Int. Symp. on Comp. Arch.*, Seattle, Washington, May 1990.

[26] A. G. Ranade. How to emulate shared memory. In *Proceedings of the 28th IEEE Annual Symposium on Foundations of Computer Science*, pages 185–194, 1987.

[27] A. Sahay. Hiding Communication Costs in Bandwidth-Limited Parallel FFT Computation. Technical Report UCB/CSD 92/722, UC Berkeley, 1992.

[28] L. Snyder. Type Architectures, Shared Memory, and the Corollary of Modest Potential. In *Ann. Rev. Comput. Sci.*, pages 289–317. Annual Reviews Inc., 1986.

[29] R. Subramonian. The influence of limited bandwidth on algorithm design and implementation. In *Dartmouth Institute for Advanced Graduate Studies in Parallel Computation (DAGS/PC)*, June 1992.

[30] L. G. Valiant. A Bridging Model for Parallel Computation. *Communications of the Association for Computing Machinery*, 33(8):103–11, August 1990.

[31] T. von Eicken, D. E. Culler, S. C. Goldstein, and K. E. Schauser. Active Messages: a Mechanism for Integrated Communication and Computation. In *Proc. of the 19th Int'l Symposium on Computer Architecture*, Gold Coast, Australia, May 1992.

Exploiting Task and Data Parallelism on a Multicomputer

Jaspal Subhlok, James M. Stichnoth, David R. O'Hallaron, and Thomas Gross
School of Computer Science
Carnegie Mellon University
Pittsburgh, PA 15213

Abstract

For many applications, achieving good performance on a private memory parallel computer requires exploiting data parallelism as well as task parallelism. Depending on the size of the input data set and the number of nodes (i.e., processors), different tradeoffs between task and data parallelism are appropriate for a parallel system. Most existing compilers focus on only one of data parallelism and task parallelism. Therefore, to achieve the desired results, the programmer must separately program the data and task parallelism. We have taken a unified approach to exploiting both kinds of parallelism in a single framework with an existing language. This approach eases the task of programming and exposes the tradeoffs between data and task parallelism to the compiler. We have implemented a parallelizing Fortran compiler for the iWarp system based on this approach. We discuss the design of our compiler, and present performance results to validate our approach.

1 Introduction

Many applications can be naturally expressed as collections of parallel or pipelined tasks, with coarse grained parallelism among the tasks, and finer grained parallelism within each task [7]. For example, a sonar spectral detection system consists of a sequence of parallel pipelines, where each pipeline consists of a sequence of downsampling time domain filters, followed by an FFT, thresholding, and other postprocessing operators [16].

Two widely used styles of parallelism for private memory multicomputers are data parallelism [9, 11, 20, 19, 10] and task parallelism [6, 13, 12, 14]. Data parallelism is typically expressed as a single thread of control operating on data sets distributed over all nodes. It is especially useful when the size of the data sets can be scaled to fit the size of the parallel machine. Task parallelism is typically expressed as a collection of sequential processes with explicit communication between them.

For some applications it is essential to exploit both styles of parallelism within the same program. In particular, for signal processing applications, physical considerations often make it impossible to arbitrarily increase the size of the data sets. Thus, it may be impossible for a single data parallel thread of control to use all nodes effectively. For example, in a signal processing application the number of input sensors can be limited by size, weight, power, and cost considerations. Further, the number of frequencies of interest is constrained by the sampling rate and the physical characteristics of the signal being analyzed. The result is that, as the number of nodes in modern multicomputers increases, it becomes increasingly difficult to use all nodes effectively on a single task. This phenomenon was encountered in [15], where it was shown analytically that at most 8 nodes could be used effectively in a purely data parallel sonar spectral detection system, primarily because the data set sizes are fairly small and cannot be increased.

The point is that, depending on the sizes of the machine and the data sets, the same source program can benefit from different styles of parallelism: data parallelism, task parallelism, or some combination of the two. In this paper, we discuss a practical approach to accomplish this. We have implemented a parallelizing Fortran compiler for the iWarp multicomputer [2, 3]. The key idea is that a *single source program* can be translated to fit a particular machine or data set size. The style of the generated code is based on compiler

Supported in part by the Defense Advanced Research Projects Agency, Information Science and Technology Office, under the title "Research on Parallel Computing," ARPA Order No. 7330. Work furnished in connection with this research is provided under prime contract MDA972-90-C-0035 issued by DARPA/CMO to Carnegie Mellon University, and in part by the Air Force Office of Scientific Research under Contract F49620-92-J-0131. This material is based upon work supported under a National Foundation Graduate Research Fellowship.

4th ACM PPOPP,5/93/CA,USA
© 1993 ACM 0-89791-589-5/93/0005/0013...$1.50

analysis and user hints.

We have used the compiler to explore the tradeoffs between task and data parallelism for some model programs operating on different size data sets. In particular, we compared a purely data parallel implementation and a pipelined data parallel implementation for two example programs, and observed that the best performance was obtained with different implementations for different data sizes.

Section 2 describes the programming model. Section 3 describes the compilation approach. Section 4 discusses the communication models used for generating data parallel and task parallel programs. Section 5 presents experimental results that compares the performance of programs compiled with different styles of parallelism. Section 6 discusses related work.

2 Programming model

The language we chose is Fortran 77 augmented with Fortran 90 array syntax and data layout statements based on Fortran D [1] and the emerging High Performance Fortran (HPF) standard [8]. The choice of Fortran was based on convenience and user acceptance. We have taken a source-to-source compilation approach; the output of the compiler is a Fortran 77 program (with calls to a communication library) for all the nodes in the system.

2.1 Data parallel constructs

Data parallelism is expressed using data layout statements, array syntax, and a simple parallel loop. For example:

```
C$      template t(n)
C$      align A(i,j) with t(i)
C$      align B(i,j) with t(j)
C$      distribute t(cyclic)

        do i=1,n
           A(i,:) = A(i,:) + B(:,i)
        enddo
```

This example uses `template`, `align`, and `distribute` directives to distribute the rows of array `A` and the columns of array `B` cyclically across the node array. In the example above, the *ith* loop iteration uses an array statement to add the *jth* column of `B` to the *ith* row of `A`. Moreover, each loop iteration is independent and can run in parallel with the other loop iterations.

2.2 Task parallel constructs

Task parallelism is expressed as special code regions called *parallel sections*. The body of a parallel section is limited to subroutines and loops. For ease of implementation, we require that these loops have constant bounds. The subroutines may contain data parallel operations. Each of these subroutine calls is followed by `input` and `output` directives, which identify the input and output parameters of the subroutine. The arguments in the `input` and `output` lists can be scalars, array slices with constant bounds, or whole arrays.

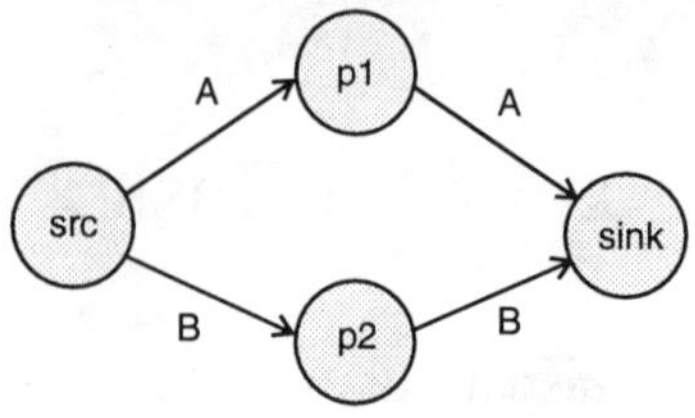

Figure 1: Data dependences for one loop iteration.

The body of a parallel section contains a task for each invocation of a subroutine call. We use subroutines to identify tasks because of programming and implementation convenience. A task is a single thread of control with well defined side effects. Tasks communicate with other tasks only through their input and output parameters. The communication is completely determined by the way the data would flow if the program was executed sequentially. A task waits for its inputs, executes, produces its outputs, and then terminates. Finally there is an implicit barrier synchronization at the end of a parallel section for data consistency. The following example illustrates task parallel programming:

```
C$      begin parallel
        do i = 1,10
           call src(A,B)
C$         output:  A,B
           call p1(A)
C$         input:  A
C$         output:  A
           call p2(B)
C$         input:  B
C$         output:  B
           call sink(A,B)
C$         input:  A,B
        enddo
C$      end parallel
```

This example consists of forty tasks, with ten tasks corresponding to each lexical subroutine call in the parallel section. During each iteration, a `src` task distributes array `A` to a task `p1` and array `B` to a task `p2`, which operate on their inputs and send their outputs to a `sink` task. The data dependences for one loop iteration are shown in Figure 1. Note that within each loop iteration, tasks `p1` and `p2` can execute in parallel, and that the loop iterations can be pipelined.

There are several important points to make about this task model. First, while the simple notion of a parallel section limits the class of parallel programs that can be expressed (e.g., communication between tasks is prohibited except on entry and exit), it allows for efficient implementation with relatively little analysis. Second, if the directives are correct and complete, then the parallel program has sequential semantics. Third, the compiler has the freedom to choose between several possible mappings of task parallelism onto a machine, and can even choose to ignore the directives and compile the program in a purely data parallel style.

3 Compilation approach

Figure 2 illustrates the main compilation steps. In this example, we start with a single source program consisting of two data parallel subroutines and a main program that calls them as tasks. The program is based on the 2D FFT model program discussed later. The compilation proceeds as independent data parallel and task parallel phases. The data parallel phase analyzes the array statements and parallel loops, and generates data parallel code for each subroutine called in the body of the parallel section.

The task parallel phase analyzes directives inside the parallel section and generates a layer of the hierarchical *uniform task graph (UTG)* that captures the dependence relationships between tasks. In this example, the top layer of the UTG consists of six tasks, two per loop iteration. The compiler then partitions the UTG into *modules*, forming a *module graph* where each node is a module, and each arc represents possible communication between nodes. A module is a unit for placement on the processor nodes and is compiled with the native Fortran 77 compiler. Finally, the modules are mapped to the physical machine, with each module assigned to a disjoint collection of nodes.

3.1 Compiling array statements

The core data parallel construct is the array assignment statement:

$$\mathtt{A}(f_1 : l_1 : s_1) = \mathcal{F}(\mathtt{B}(f_2 : l_2 : s_2))$$

where $\mathcal{F}$ is some element-wise intrinsic operator, and arrays `A` and `B` are assigned block-cyclic distributions using `template`, `align`, and `distribute` statements. Note that block distributions and cyclic distributions are both special cases of block-cyclic distributions.

The compiler determines the necessary communication for such a statement using the *owner-computes rule*, which states that the computation is distributed across the processing elements according to where the results are to be stored. In the best case, results and operands are stored on the same processor, and no communication is necessary. The worst case, however, is an all-to-all personalized communication, where every node must send data to every other node and

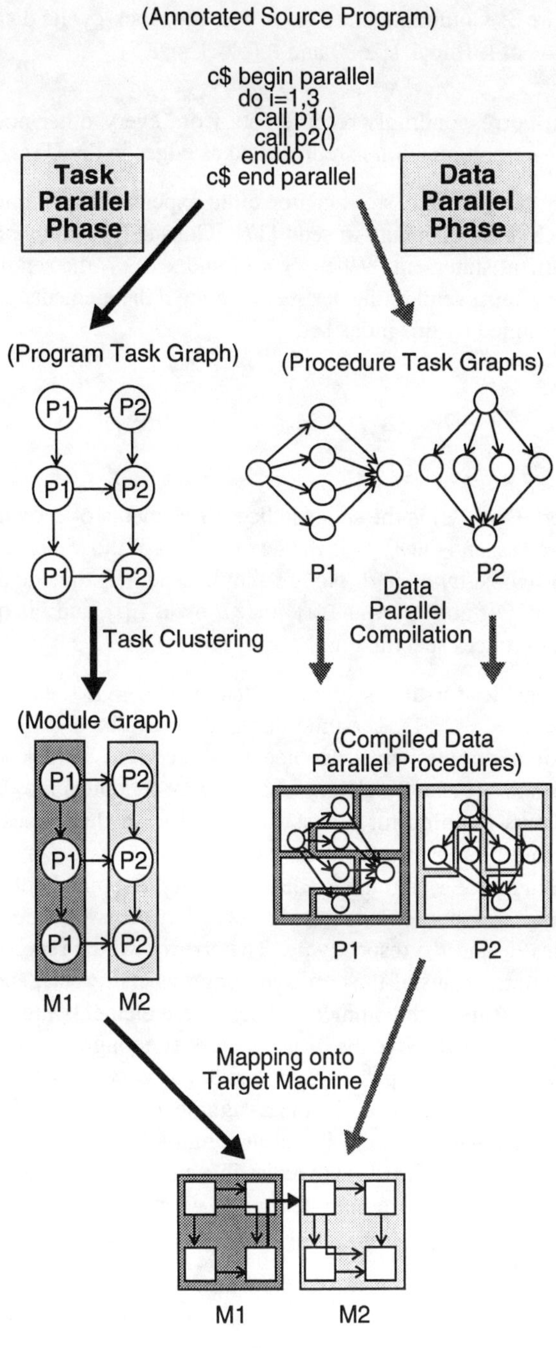

Figure 2: Compilation approach

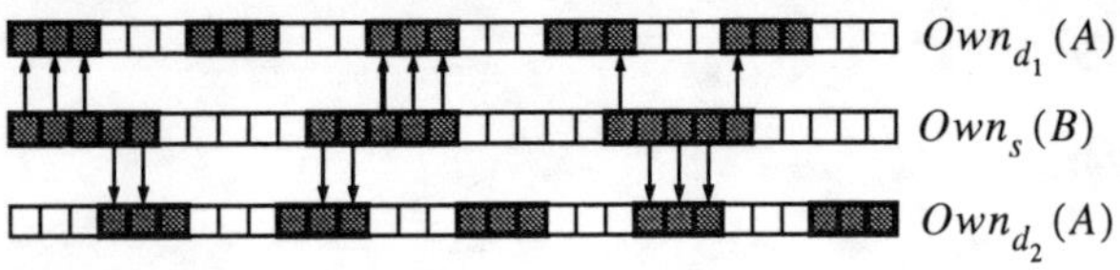

Figure 3: Communication for A = B, for block-cyclic distribution of A (block size 3) and B (block size 5)

must correspondingly receive data from every other node. Such communication is represented as edges in the UTG.

In the general case, it can be quite expensive to compute which array elements to send [17]: Consider the above assignment statement. When $f_2 = f_1$ and $s_2 = s_1$, the sending node s must send to the destination node d the elements of B determined by this index set:

$$Own_s(\mathtt{B}) \cap Own_d(\mathtt{A}) \cap (f_1 : l_1 : s_1)$$

where $Own_s(\mathtt{B})$ is the set of indices of elements of B owned by node s, and $Own_d(\mathtt{A})$ is the set of indices of those elements of A owned by node d. Node s should send B[i] to node d if and only if node s owns B[i], node d owns A[i], and i is one of the indices specified in the array slice $(f_1 : l_1 : s_1)$.

Consider for the assignment statement A = B (i.e., $f_1 = f_2 = s_1 = s_2 = 1$). Assume that both arrays have a block-cyclic distribution over two nodes, where A has a block size of 3 and B has a block size of 5. Figure 3 depicts the data transfers required for this statement. The shaded boxes in the middle row represent the elements of B owned by the sending node s, and the shaded boxes in the top and bottom rows represent the elements of A owned by the two receiving nodes d_1 and d_2, respectively. The arrows, which represent the intersections of the corresponding ownership sets, show the elements with common indices; these elements must be communicated. Note the irregularity, even though the block-cyclic distribution patterns are regular and easy to represent, as are the array slices in the assignment statement. This kind of communication is not uncommon, as such assignment statements are used to redistribute arrays. The situation becomes even more complex when we introduce non-unit strides s_1 and s_2 into the assignment statement.

Figure 3 illustrated the sender's task of determining which elements of an array to send. It is equally expensive for a node to compute the set of elements to receive. Although the algorithm to determine the elements to send is nearly identical to the algorithm to determine the elements to receive, in the general case, the respective algorithm must be executed on both the sending and receiving nodes. The similarity between the algorithms motivates the optimizations presented in Section 4.2.

3.2 Compiling parallel tasks

For task parallelism, the compiler has to address another set of issues. Most importantly, precise data dependence and communication relationships between tasks must be collected at compile time. Since the variables that a subroutine can access and modify are explicitly described in the `input` and `output` directives (including arrays and array sections), and since there are no conditional statements inside a parallel section, a data flow framework on array sections can statically determine the dependence and precise data movement between tasks.

The second major issue is clustering of tasks into modules. Task clustering determines the amount of computation in each module. In our current implementation, all tasks corresponding to a lexical procedure call constitute a module. This is a simple model that is based on the notion of treating a subroutine as a unit of parallel computation, and fits many applications.

Finally, the modules must be mapped onto the physical machine. This includes allocation of processor nodes and placement of modules on the node array. Allocation of nodes to modules determines the load balancing and is a critical factor for efficient execution. In the current implementation this is controlled explicitly by the programmer through directives. However, the compiler does provide a framework where a programmer can experiment with different processor allocations, simply by changing directives in the program.

4 Communication

An iWarp node is physically connected to 4 other nodes by 8 unidirectional *communication buses*. The iWarp communication system provides *logical channels* between adjacent nodes [3]. Data sent over different logical channels is kept separate. A *pathway* is a sequence of logical channels; pathways are also directly supported by the communication system and provide for "long-distance" connections between arbitrary pairs of nodes in the iWarp system. Like logical channels, pathways can be created and destroyed at runtime, with low overhead. Node programs can access pathways directly, one word at a time, without intervention from the runtime system.

Pathways are the fundamental building blocks for implementing a variety of communication styles on iWarp. An important style for the compiler is the *permanent network*, which is a collection of pathways created at the beginning of program execution and left in place for the duration of the program.

Pathways can also be used to implement a variety of message passing styles. The basic idea is to create a *transient pathway* that exists only for some duration during the execution of a program. One usage model is to transfer only a single message over a transient pathway . Each time there is a message to send from node n_i to node n_j, the program creates a pathway between the two nodes, transfers the data over the pathway, and then destroys the pathway. Different message passing styles can be constructed in this way by varying the behavior at the endpoints of the individual pathways.

In our compiler, permanent networks are used to transfer data between parallel tasks and to perform special-purpose communication primitives such as barrier synchronization and broadcasting. Message passing based on transient pathways is used for all other communications. The compiler partitions the communication resources on each node into two sets; one set is used exclusively for permanent networks, and the other set is used exclusively for message passing. The important points here are that the same pathway mechanism is used for all communication styles, and that the pathways can be manipulated directly by the user–level program, without intervention from the runtime system.

4.1 Data parallel communication

As discussed in Section 3.1, the compiler manages the movement of data from one node to another. Consider an element `B[i]` of an array `B` that is required for a computation on some node *N*. If `B[i]` is not stored on *N*, it must be moved to `B'[j]` for some array `B'` such that `B'[j]` is local to *N*. In general, the exact communication patterns for a data parallel program are not known at compile time, and therefore, some form of general-purpose message passing is required.

Several different message passing styles have been identified: The message passing system can buffer `B[i]` in temporary storage on the destination node, and then `B[i]` is moved from that buffer to the location `B'[j]`, where the application program expects it. This is an example of the station-to-station communication style [2]. However, such copying is wasteful; another style is to allow the communication system to place `B[i]` directly into `B'[j]` (door-to-door delivery [2]).

The sender computes the addresses of the elements `B[i]` to be transmitted, but note that in general `i` $\neq$ `j`. So for both communication styles, it is necessary to compute the index `j` for `B'[j]` This computation of `j` shares common subexpressions with the computation of `i`. To exploit these common computations, we developed a new communication style called *deposit model message passing*. The central idea behind deposit model message passing is that the sending node computes the destination addresses of the data on the receiving node, and passes these addresses along with the data. Rather than computing the destination addresses explicitly, the receiving node merely reads the addresses and deposits the received data into the appropriate memory locations. The key point is that the sending node computes the destination addresses, which eliminates the address computation on the receiver while imposing only a small additional burden on the sender.

Deposit model message passing incurs an additional cost. Since addresses must be passed along with the data, some part of the communication bandwidth is wasted. This overhead can range from small, when regular sections of the array can be sent in large blocks, to large, in the case of address-data pairs, when an explicit destination address is sent for each data item. This reduces the effective bandwidth of the communication system by at most a factor of two. However, in our experience, this is more than compensated for by the reduced workload on the receiving nodes.

Deposit model message passing is a general-purpose communication style that is not specific to iWarp. It can be used effectively by any parallelizing compiler for any private memory computer system. However, on iWarp, the direct word-level access to the pathways allows for another important optimization. The receiving node scatters the data to memory *directly*, as each data item arrives over the communication bus. The scattering occurs at the full 40 Mbytes/second bandwidth of the communication buses.

4.2 Task parallel communication

A program consists of a set of modules, each executing on a subset of available nodes. Each module consists of a set of tasks that potentially communicate, but only on entry and exit. In our model, a module is independent of other modules, and in the current implementation, modules are placed on disjoint sets of nodes on an iWarp machine. The interface between two modules is the message format used to transfer the input and output parameters.

Communication between modules conceptually consists of collecting the data in the sending module, sending the data to the receiving module, and distributing the data in the receiving module. A direct implementation would require the existence of nodes that have enough memory to hold all the data to be transferred. Also, at least 6 memory operations (a read and a write each for gathering, transferring, and distributing) would be required to transfer each word of data.

In the actual implementation, we create a permanent *snake* network in each module, as shown in Figure 4. We forward data on the snake network in a synchronized manner, such that the data reaches a designated *master* node in a canonical order. The master node, which is connected to the master node of the receiving module by a permanent inter-module pathway (shown as a thick arrow in Figure 4), simply forwards the data directly from the snake network to the intermodule pathway, and ultimately to the master node of the receiving module, *without ever placing the data in memory*. The data is distributed in a synchronous fashion similar to the way it is collected. This implementation requires only one memory read and write for every data element, and the data transfer is pipelined. Data can be transferred at the peak bandwidth of a single logical channel.

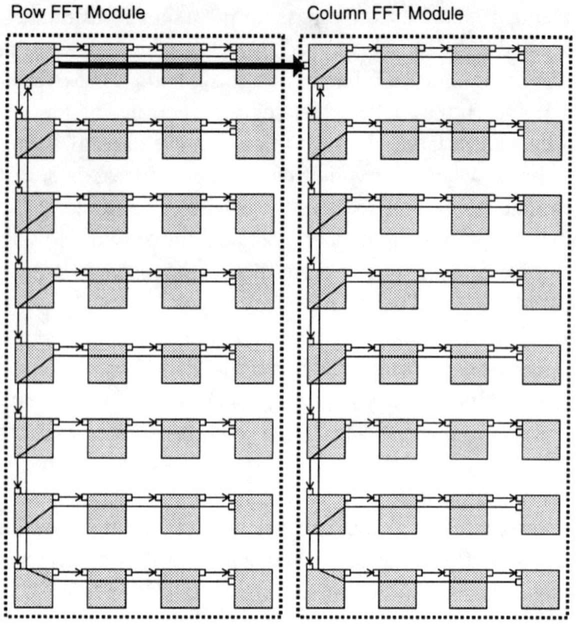

Figure 4: Networks for task parallel communication.

The bandwidth of one communication bus is an important limiting factor for this approach, and can limit the overall performance of an application. This phenomena was observed in the experiments that we discuss in the next section. Clearly, the performance can be further improved by transferring data in parallel between individual nodes in the modules, using, for instance, message passing to send individual data objects.

However, in our implementation model, a module is an independent process with a standard communication interface. The processing elements inside a module do not have any knowledge of the physical location or data distribution of other modules. This property is extremely important in situations where an application consists of several modules executing on different machines on a network, or when dynamic load balancing can change the computation and data distribution associated with a module. Thus, we have chosen a model that is applicable to a wide variety of computation environments, and is not tailored for our current implementation.

5 Experimental results

Depending on the size of the input sets and the machine, compiling with one style of parallelism may allow the source program to run faster than with another style. To illustrate the benefits that can be obtained from choosing between different styles of parallelism at compile time, we investigated a small but important example: the 2-dimensional Fast Fourier Transform (2D FFT). We first examine the implementation of a 2D FFT program, and then a program in which a 2D FFT is followed by a stage that analyzes the results and generates histograms.

5.1 Example: 2D FFT

The 2D FFT example inputs a sequence of m $n \times n$ complex arrays, and performs a 2D FFT on each array in sequence. This models the situation in real-time signal or image processing applications in which a stream of input comes from a collection of sensors. Each 2D FFT computation consists of two passes over the array. The first pass performs an independent 1D FFT on each of the n rows of the array. The second pass performs an independent 1D FFT on each of the n columns of the array. The output is an $n \times n$ array.

We chose the 2D FFT because of its intrinsic importance, because it is similar in its structure to many larger signal processing applications such as synthetic aperture radar imaging and sonar adaptive beam interpolation, and because it is a satisfying combination of the easy and the challenging: easy because the 1D FFT's on the rows (columns) are independent; challenging because it must scan both the rows *and* the columns of the input array, and therefore requires an efficient redistribution of data to achieve good performance. The Fortran program is of the form:

```
C$      begin parallel
        do i = 1,m
           call rffts(A)
C$         output:  A
           call cffts(A)
C$         input:  A
        enddo
C$      end parallel
```

The program, 2DFFT, consists of a parallel section, with calls to two subroutines inside a loop that iterates m times. Subroutine *rffts* is a data parallel procedure that produces a complex $n \times n$ array A, and then applies a 1D FFT to each row of the matrix. Subroutine *cffts* is a data parallel task that applies a 1D FFT to each column of array A, and then verifies the correctness of each element of the result matrix. The source of parallelism inside each task is a parallel loop statement.

To evaluate the impact of the input data size on the relative performance of data parallelism and task parallelism, we used the compiler to automatically map the same 2DFFT program onto a 64-node iWarp system in two different ways:

DP–2DFFT: *Purely data parallel.* The directives for task parallelism are ignored and the program is compiled as a single thread of control running on all 64 nodes. During each iteration of the outer loop, all nodes compute the row FFT's, transpose the data, and then compute the column FFT's. The parallelism is in the form of independent parallel loop iterations within each subroutine.

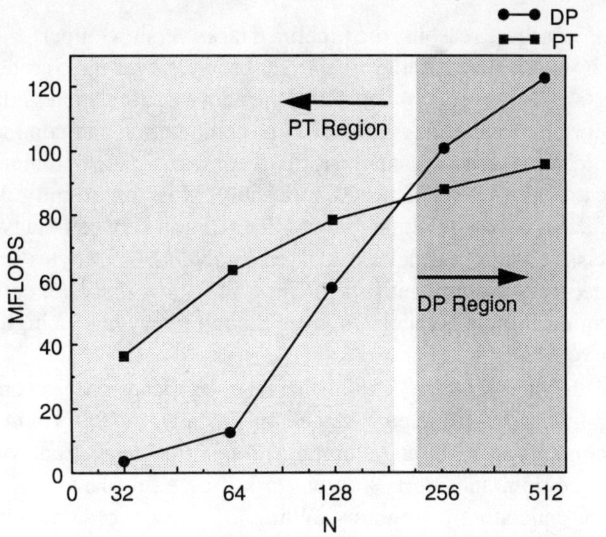

Figure 5: Performance of $N \times N$ 2DFFT on 64 nodes.

PT–2DFFT: *Pipelined tasks.* The same source program is compiled as a collection of pipelined data parallel tasks. Each task is compiled in exactly the same style as DP–2DFFT, but for 32 nodes rather than 64 nodes. The tasks that update the rows are clustered into one module and placed on 32 nodes. Similarly, the tasks that update the columns are clustered into another module and placed on the remaining 32 nodes. The parallelism is in the form of data parallel loops within each module, and pipelining between the two modules.

We do not consider a purely task parallel style, because for this example there are not enough tasks to keep the nodes busy.

We measured the performance of these two styles for different input sizes. Figure 5 compares the performance of the data parallel implementation with the performance of the pipelined tasks implementation. We observe that the pipelined tasks (PT–2DFFT) execute faster for the smaller data sizes, in this case $n < 256$. For $n \geq 256$, the purely data parallel style (DP–2DFFT) outperforms the pipelined data parallel version. The figure shows a crossover point near 200.

Figure 6 shows the measured performance as more processors are added to a fixed size 2D FFT problem (n = 128). We observe that the performance of both data parallel (DP–2DFFT) and pipelined tasks (PT–2DFFT) implementations is similar and improves approximately linearly as the number of processors is increased, up to 32 processors. However, when the number of processors is doubled to 64, the pipelined tasks version again shows the expected improvement, but the purely data parallel version shows a small improvement. This illustrates that, for some problem sizes, a fixed size 2D FFT problem can use a larger number of processors effectively when executing as pipelined tasks.

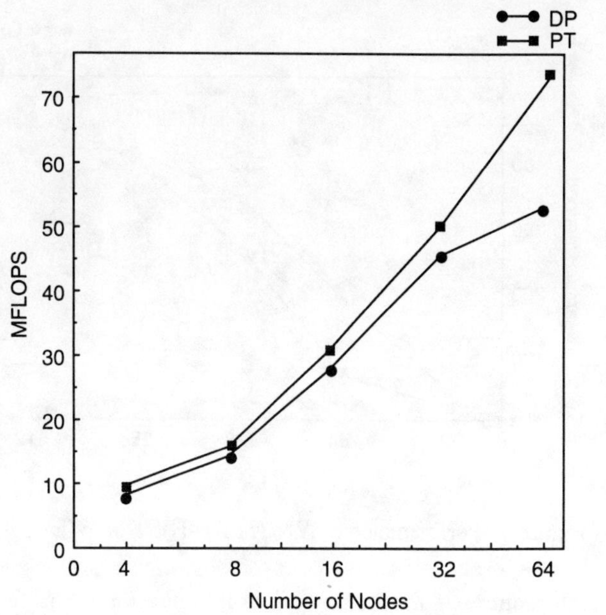

Figure 6: Performance of 2DFFT as a function of number of nodes.

5.2 Example: FFT–HIST

Our second example consists of a program containing a 2D FFT computation, followed by a result analysis stage which generates histograms and performs some other local computations. The Fortran program is of the form:

```
C$      begin parallel
        do i = 1,m
           call fft(A)
C$         output:  A
           call hist(A)
C$         input:  A
        enddo
C$      end parallel
```

We again build two versions of the same program for a 64-node iWarp system using the compiler. In the purely data parallel version (DP–FFT-HIST), a single thread of control executes on all 64 nodes. During each iteration of the outer loop, all nodes first compute the row FFT's, transpose the data, and compute the column FFT's. Next all nodes perform local analysis and collect local data for histograms. Finally histograms are generated using reductions over all processors. In the pipelined tasks version(PT–FFT-HIST), the program is compiled as two sets of tasks, each running on 32 nodes. Each task in the first set performs a 2D FFT computation, and each task in the second set generates histograms. Computation inside the tasks is data parallel.

It is important to note that there is a significant qualitative difference between this example and the previous one. The two stages in this example (i.e., a 2D FFT and a Histogram)

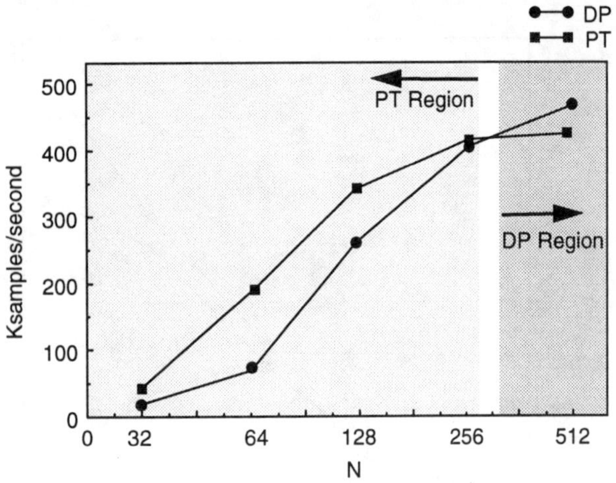

Figure 7: Performance of $N \times N$ FFT–HIST on 64 nodes.

each require significant amount of internal communication, while the stages in the previous example (i.e., 1D FFT's) required no internal communication.

The performance results obtained by executing the two versions of the program are shown in Figure 7. Note that since this computation is not dominated by floating point operations, our metric is the number of samples processed per second. We again observe that the results are qualitatively similar to those obtained for the previous example, The pipelined tasks version has better performance for data sizes up to around 300, and the data parallel version has better performance for larger data sizes.

5.3 Discussion of performance results

It is informative to analyze the results for the two examples. The first example consists of two separate 1D FFT stages. In the purely data parallel mode, each 1D FFT stage executes on all nodes in parallel, with no communication within each stage, but on transition between the two stages, a matrix transpose operation must be performed. Using pipelined tasks, the two stages are also data parallel, but in addition, the stages are pipelined. The transpose operation is merged with the transfer of data from one set of nodes to the other set of nodes, so there is no need for an explicit matrix transpose operation.

The main advantages of a task parallel approach in this example are:

- On each node, twice as many operations are performed between communication operations, since the same computation is mapped onto half as many nodes.

- For relatively small data sizes, transfer of data between disjoint sets of nodes can be implemented more efficiently than a matrix transpose.

For these reasons, the pipelined tasks version outperforms the purely data parallel version for problem sizes up to around 200. For larger problem sizes, the above factors are less important because the granularity of computation and communication increases, and the ratio of computation to communication ($O(\log n)$) increases noticeably. Most importantly, the fact that there is sequential communication between the two tasks along a channel with a fixed bandwidth (40Mbytes/sec) becomes a dominant factor, since all the data parallel communication is parallelized, even though it may have a higher overhead.

In the second example, there is significant global communication within each stage. Specifically, the 2DFFT task contains an all-to-all communication in the matrix transpose operation, and the Histogram task uses a set of reductions for generating histograms. While the number of communication steps is exactly the same in both implementations, all global communication in the pipelined tasks implementation is performed over half the number of cells. This reduces the communication overhead, particularly for small problem sizes where communication overhead tends to dominate. For this reason, pipelined tasks outperform purely data parallel implementations in this example for a larger range of data sizes.

We would like to point out that the smaller input sizes, for which the pipelined tasks version outperforms the purely data parallel version, are certainly of practical interest. For example, a sonar adaptive beam interpolation (ABI) application manipulates a sequence of $r \times c$ complex arrays. Like 2D FFT, ABI first manipulates the rows of the matrix, and then manipulates the columns. The parameter r is proportional to the number of sensors attached to a cable that is towed behind a ship, and c is the number of frequencies of interest. While c is typically large, on the order of 1000, r is typically small, on the order of 50. It is limited by cost and length of the cable, and simply cannot be increased to fit the number of nodes.

Often the only way to determine whether a purely data parallel implementation or a pipelined tasks implementation is more suitable for a particular computing situation is by experimentation. Therefore, we argue that it is extremely useful to have a system to experiment with the tradeoffs involved. This is especially important for problems that are dominated by global communication because communication characteristics during execution can change significantly when task parallelism is introduced in addition to data parallelism.

6 Related work

Compiling for private memory parallel computers has been an active area of research in the recent past and several different approaches have been discussed in the literature. We compare our approach to specific research projects using other approaches, and discuss their influence on this project.

Several research and production compilers have been built for compiling a program in data parallel fashion to a SPMD parallel program. These include the Fortran D compiler [10], SuperB [20], the Vienna Fortran compiler [5], and the Thinking Machines Fortran compiler [1]. The general approach is to take a sequential program in a conventional language (Fortran for the above three), possibly with directives to guide data layout and parallelism. The compiler parallelizes the program, typically using the owner computes rule to distribute the computation among nodes. We have also taken this approach for exploiting data parallelism. The data layout statements are similar to those used in Fortran D, Vienna Fortran, and HPF. However, we also exploit task parallelism, which is not addressed in these projects.

Assign [14] is a programming tool that is used to develop task parallel programs. The user specifies the parallel tasks and the communication between them, and the tool maps the tasks to physical nodes. Jade [12] extends this approach by allowing the programmer to augment the code with abstract data usage information instead of specifying communication explicitly. Our research has been motivated by the Assign project, and some aspects of our design are similar to Jade, but there are several important differences. We use an existing language and do not introduce any new language constructs. All auxiliary information is in the form of compiler directives, and therefore the base program is an ordinary sequential program. Furthermore, we also address data parallelism within the same language and compiler model.

One approach to exploiting data and task parallelism is to use a coordination language for expressing task parallelism. SCHEDULE [6] allows the user to express a set of tasks and their dependence relationships, and the system implements the task parallelism. PVM [18] provides user primitives that can be used to build heterogeneous parallel applications from components, which can potentially be data parallel tasks. Linda [4] provides a programming paradigm which can be used for expressing task parallelism, while the data parallelism may be expressed in a different data parallel language. Our approach differs from others discussed above in that we use the same framework for both task and data parallelism, and build on existing technology for parallelization of data parallel programs. We provide support for both kinds of parallelism inside Fortran programs, and a single compiler manages all parallelism. This is important for two reasons. First, it simplifies the task of writing a parallel program, since the user must deal with only one programming paradigm. Second, the compiler has the opportunity to manage the tradeoffs between task and data parallelism, as illustrated by our example programs.

7 Concluding remarks

Many real-world applications must exploit both task and data parallelism to achieve good performance. The size of the input data set is an important parameter that influences which style of parallelism is more appropriate for mapping a given computation onto a parallel system. We have developed a single framework that makes programming with task and data parallelism convenient: the user can develop programs in a single environment, and the compiler can make tradeoffs between task and data parallelism. Our measured results are preliminary, but it is becoming clear that it is important to exploit both task and data parallelism.

8 Acknowledgements

We would like to thank Susan Hinrichs for developing the iWarp's PCS communication tool chain, Thomas Stricker, Thomas Warfel, and Michael Hemy for their advice on message passing, Bwolen Yang for assistance with the FFT programs and iWarp measurements, Jim Wheeler at GE and Tom Stover at NAWC for teaching us about sonar signal processing, Jon Webb for advice on parallel loops, and Keith Bromley at NOSC for encouraging us to pursue a unified framework for task and data parallelism.

References

[1] ALBERT, E., KNOBE, K., LUKAS, J., AND STEELE, G. Compiling Fortran 8x array features for the Connection Machine computer system. In *Proceedings of the ACM SIGPLAN Symposium on Parallel Programming: Experience with Applications, Languages and Systems* (New Haven, CT, July 1988), pp. 42–56.

[2] BORKAR, S., COHN, R., COX, G., GLEASON, S., GROSS, T., KUNG, H. T., LAM, M., MOORE, B., PETERSON, C., PIEPER, J., RANKIN, L., TSENG, P. S., SUTTON, J., URBANSKI, J., AND WEBB, J. iWarp: An integrated solution to high-speed parallel computing. In *Supercomputing '88* (Nov. 1988), pp. 330–339.

[3] BORKAR, S., COHN, R., COX, G., GROSS, T., KUNG, H. T., LAM, M., MOORE, M. L. B., MOORE, W., PETERSON, C., SUSMAN, J., SUTTON, J., URBANSKI, J., AND WEBB, J. Supporting systolic and memory communication in iWarp. In *Proceedings of the 17th Annual International Symposium on Computer Architecture* (Seattle, WA, May 1990), pp. 70–81.

[4] CARRIERO, N., AND GELERNTER, D. Applications experience with Linda. In *Proceedings of the ACM SIGPLAN Symposium on Parallel Programming: Experi-*

ence with Applications, Languages and Systems (New Haven, CT, July 1988), pp. 173–187.

[5] CHAPMAN, B., MEHROTRA, P., AND ZIMA, H. Programming in Vienna Fortran. *Scientific Programming 1*, 1 (Aug. 1992), 31–50.

[6] DONGARRA, J., AND SORENSEN, D. A portable environment for developing parallel Fortran programs. *Parallel Computing 5* (1987), 175–186.

[7] FOX, G. The architecture of problems and portable parallel software systems. Tech. Rep. CRPC-TR91172, Northeast Parallel Architectures Center, 1991.

[8] HIGH PERFORMANCE FORTRAN FORUM. *High Performance Fortran Language Specification*, Jan. 1993. Version 1.0 DRAFT.

[9] HILLIS, D. W., AND STEELE, JR., G. L. Data parallel algorithms. *Communications of the ACM 29*, 12 (Dec. 1986), 1170–1183.

[10] HIRANANDANI, S., KENNEDY, K., AND TSENG, C. Compiler optimizations for Fortran D on MIMD distributed-memory machines. In *Proceedings of Supercomputing '91* (Albuquerque, NM, November 1991), pp. 86–100.

[11] KOELBEL, C., MEHROTRA, P., AND ROSENDALE, J. V. Semi-automatic domain decomposition in BLAZE. In *Proceedings of the 1987 International Conference on Parallel Processing* (August 1987), S. K. Sahni, Ed., pp. 521–524.

[12] LAM, M., AND RINARD, M. Coarse-grain parallel programming in Jade. In *Proceedings of the Third ACM SIGPLAN Symposium on Principles and Practice of Parallel Programming* (Williamsburg, VA, April 1991), pp. 94–105.

[13] LEE, E. A., AND MESSERSCHMITT, D. G. Static scheduling of synchronous data flow programs for digital signal processing. *IEEE Transactions on Computers C-36*, 1 (Jan. 1987), 24–35.

[14] O'HALLARON, D. The Assign parallel program generator. In *Proceedings of the 6th Distributed Memory Computing Conference* (Portland, OR, Apr. 1991), pp. 178–185.

[15] PRINTZ, H. *Automatic Mapping of Large Signal Processing Systems to a Parallel Machine*. PhD thesis, Department of Computer Science, Carnegie-Mellon University, 1991. Also available as report CMU-CS-91-101.

[16] PRINTZ, H., KUNG, H. T., MUMMERT, T., AND SCHERER, P. Automatic mapping of large signal processing systems to a parallel machine. In *Proceedings of SPIE Symposium, Real-Time Signal Processing XI* (San Diego, CA, Aug. 1989), Society of Photo-Optical Instrumentation Engineers, pp. 2–16.

[17] STICHNOTH, J. Efficient compilation of array statements for private memory multicomputers. Tech. Rep. CMU-CS-93-109, School of Computer Science, Carnegie Mellon University, Feb. 1993.

[18] SUNDERAM, V. S. PVM : A framework for parallel distributed computing. *Concurrency: Practice and Experience 2*, 4 (December 1990), 315–339.

[19] TSENG, P. S. *A Parallelizing Compiler For Distributed Memory Parallel Computers*. PhD thesis, Department of Computer Science, Carnegie-Mellon University, 1989. Also available as CMU Tech Report CMU-CS-89-148.

[20] ZIMA, H., BAST, H.-J., AND GERNDT, M. SUPERB: A tool for semi-automatic MIMD/SIMD parallelization. *Parallel Computing 6* (1988), 1–18.

ActorSpace: An Open Distributed Programming Paradigm

Gul Agha
Department of Computer Science
1304 W. Springfield Avenue
University of Illinois at Urbana-Champaign
Urbana, IL 61801, USA
Email: agha@cs.uiuc.edu

Christian J. Callsen
Department of Math. and Comp. Science
Frederik Bajers Vej 7E
Aalborg University
9220 Aalborg Øst, DENMARK
Email: chris@iesd.auc.dk

Abstract

We present a new programming paradigm called ActorSpace. ActorSpace provides a new communication model based on *destination patterns*. An *actorSpace* is a computationally passive container of actors which acts as a context for matching patterns. Patterns are matched against listed attributes of actors and actorSpaces that are *visible* in the actorSpace. Both visibility and attributes are dynamic. Messages may be sent to one or all members of a group defined by a pattern. The paradigm provides powerful support for component-based construction of massively parallel and distributed applications. In particular, it supports open interfaces to servers and pattern-directed access to software repositories.

1 Introduction

Our goal is to develop a programming paradigm to support scalable component-based software construction. We believe that large software systems can be modelled as massively parallel, distributed, and open systems. The task of mega-programming [32] requires support for coordinating autonomous software systems which may, for example, consist of active processes, distributed databases, and intelligent problem-solving experts. Some of the key issues concerning composition in such systems are related to reference and access scope rules. We have developed the ActorSpace model to provide a potential method for addressing these problem and for experimenting with different alternatives.

4th ACM PPOPP,5/93/CA,USA

ActorSpace extends actor-style point-to-point asynchronous communication with ***pattern-directed*** invocation and broadcasting. Point-to-point communication provides efficiency in a distributed system by allowing locality to be directly expressed and optimized. On the other hand, pattern-directed communication allows abstract specification of a group of recipients. Actor groups are defined using attribute patterns, scoped within a specified actorSpace: i.e., the potential targets of a message may be defined within a specific actorSpace using destination patterns. Note that actorSpaces may overlap, and in particular, may be nested. The intuition behind ActorSpace can be roughly given in terms of two metaphors as follows.

In mathematics, a set may be described in one of two ways: by enumerating its elements, or by specifying a characteristic function which defines a subset of a domain. Explicitly identifying objects corresponds to enumerating the elements whereas providing patterns of object attributes corresponds to specifying a characteristic function. Of course, in conventional mathematics the two characterizations are equivalent as mathematical objects are static. The mathematical metaphor breaks down since computational objects, like real-world objects, may dynamically change their behavior while retaining their identity.

A second analogy is with mailing lists and telephone directories in the real world. Individuals may appear in many lists. Each list may contain a set of attributes associated with the individual – as viewed by that list. More complex databases may allow retrieval of individuals using search based on patterns of attributes.

Broadcasting can be (and typically is) implemented in terms of message passing and does not extend the expressibility of the paradigm, but using the notion of a group of receivers provides greater abstraction – a system can hide the actual number of members and their location from an application process. The application may then leave it to the system to deliver a message to all appropriate receivers. This provides an abstraction that may be easily applied to replicating services, for instance to enhance reliability or increase performance. Moreover, in ActorSpace, services may be structured using nested actorSpaces; computations may then be successively localized. Alternately, diffusion scheduling may be obtained by successively transferring work using actorSpaces representing local neighborhoods of processors.

The ActorSpace model allows open flexible interfaces for pattern-directed retrieval from software repositories. For example, pattern-directed communication provides an appropriate model for supporting access to class libraries in a concurrent object-oriented programming environment. Consider each class as a 'factory' actor which may return its instances. The interface specifications of classes may be represented as attributes which are then used to dynamically access classes from the library.

Outline of the Paper

Section 2 describes our view of open systems and why we feel that openness in systems is useful. Section 3 briefly mentions related work with respect to open systems, process groups and broadcasting. Section 4 briefly describes the primitives of the Actor model. The following section informally defines ActorSpace. By adding a few primitives to the Actor model we obtain ActorSpace, while still retaining Actors as a special case of ActorSpace. Section 6 gives an example of an application, which demonstrates how the programming paradigm elegantly solves a specific problem. Section 7 briefly describes ongoing work on a prototype implementation of ActorSpace. The final section concludes the paper and discusses directions for future research.

2 Open Systems

We want to develop systems which offer resources to applications and reclaim resources after some application has finished using them. A particular class of such a system is distributed operating systems. Distributed operating systems provide resources to support the arrival, creation and later termination of distributed applications. We think of distributed systems or applications as being a set of active objects that compute and coordinate. Moreover, we would like the system to allow objects to exchange information even when the objects do not know each other in advance. In our terminology, each object plays the following roles during computation of a given problem:

Client: A client requests service from a server in order to perform a computation.

Server: A server provides a service to a (set of) client(s).

Manager: A manager surveys the system and adjusts it to suit needs as they arise.

Clients and servers are the "usual" clients and servers in the client–server model which can be implemented directly in language models such as Actors or Linda. Managers are not necessary for computation per se: they are needed in an administrative role to keep resources available in an open system and to maintain security and safety. Note that the above are roles rather than sorts or types; an active object may be a client requesting service from servers, while at the same time offering service to other clients, or a manager controlling other active objects.

The role of managers is what is new in open systems; in an open system clients cannot be trusted (for example, there is no way to know if they are buggy), so security must be enforced in order to prevent clients from contaminating a shared resource. Managers have authorization to perform powerful operations such as manipulating actorSpaces.

3 Related Work

Naming is a key issue in achieving openness in object-based systems that use sending of messages for coordination. In order to coordinate with an object, the "initiator" of the coordination must be able to name or identify the objects with which the coordination should take place.

Concurrent programming systems such as Actors [1], Emerald [21], Orca [6] and Concurrent Aggregates [11] support an object-based programming model, where objects may invoke methods in other objects by giving a reference to the object and parameters for the invocation. Open systems which use explicit references to objects and message passing as coordination primitives, usually offer a global naming service to which all objects have a reference. This naming service can then be queried for other references by accessing the accumulated data. Objects may register themselves if they want other objects to send messages to them.

On the other hand, ActorSpace supports *open interfaces* that allow pattern-based communication between processes which have no explicit reference to each other. Client applications may use the interface to access the services provided and perform communication with other applications, and terminate when their work has finished by exiting the system in a coherent state.

In newer operating systems, object groups or process groups are offered to support group-oriented applications, which are an important aspect of distributed systems. Generally, object groups can be viewed as an association of one name with a set of names (corresponding to members of the group), which when bundled with primitives for manipulation of groups and extension of communication primitives to groups of receivers support group oriented communication. Amoeba [22], the V Distributed System [10], and the ISIS toolkit [7] offer process or object groups, which for instance may be used for replication (to increase reliability or availability), or for faster access to services through selection of a local server instead of a non-local server.

Our work builds on the Actor model [1]. The *locality* property of Actors states that an actor may only send a message to an actor whose mail address has been explicitly given [18]. Furthermore, because mail addresses of new actors are unique, it is possible to reason it terms of subcomponents without interference caused by potential name collisions in an open system.

In other words, locality simplifies the task of reasoning about components in terms of their interfaces [4]. On the other hand, the locality property implies that two actors may communicate only if they have a common ancestor in the partial order defined by the causal chain of events. This has some drawbacks: for example, because the recipients must be explicitly known in the Actor model, changes in a group of potential receivers must be explicitly communicated. We address these difficulties with the ActorSpace model.

Linda [8, 16] provides process interaction through a globally shared memory with associative operations on the contents. Thus information is available so that anyone can potentially access it. Our goal is to provide an open access similar to Linda. At the same time, we offer locality for more efficient, secure communication.

Variations of the Linda model include first-class tuple spaces embedded in Scheme [20]. In this model, tuple spaces may be created dynamically, passed as arguments or returned as results of functions, and used in tuples or data structures. The behavior of tuple spaces may be customized, as tuple spaces define policies which allow customization of matching rules, conditions for automatic forwarding to other tuple spaces, blocking of other processes and exception handling for failures in tuple operations. Our notion of customizable actorSpace managers incorporates the power of the first-class tuple space model.

Note that in Linda and its variants (for example, [8, 20, 27]), processes must actively poll a tuple space and specify the type of tuple they want to retrieve. This model results in a number of significant differences with the ActorSpace paradigm. First, race conditions may occur as a result of concurrent access by different processes to a tuple space. Second, communication cannot be made secure against arbitrary readers – for example, there is no way of abstractly specifying that a process with certain attributes may not consume a tuple. In ActorSpace, by contrast, the visible attributes of a message's recipient are specified by the sender. Finally, in Linda, one cannot give an abstract specification which guarantees that communication is localized once initiated using patterns.

An earlier proposal using pattern-based data storage and retrieval was the *Scientific Community Metaphor* [25]. The Scientific Community Metaphor proposed problem-solving by pattern based access to a shared knowledge base by a community of computational agents, called *Sprites*. In fact, the Sprites model and Linda are remarkably close: the main difference between them is that Linda allows communication objects (tuples) to be removed from the tuple space whereas Sprites support only a monotonically increasing knowledge base [24].

Concurrent Aggregates [11] offers a communication style similar to Linda; clients name a group of actors when sending a message, and one of these actors will actually receive the message. Furthermore, Concurrent Aggregates supports nesting of aggregates, so that an entire group of aggregates may be targeted for a message. Note that membership and containment relationships in this model correspond to a strict hierarchy. On the other hand, actorSpaces may overlap arbitrarily.

The ActorSpace coordination primitives we develop include broadcasting messages to groups of receivers, also known as multicasting. Initial work was done on extending RPC to support replication [12], on broadcasting as a programming paradigm [15], and on protocols for reliable broadcasting [9]. Later work has focused on protocol design [23, 28] and on improving and supporting reliability of broadcasting protocols [7, 14, 22].

4 Actors

Actors are self-contained, interactive components of a computing system that communicate by asynchronous message passing. The basic actor primitives are:

create: creating an actor from a behavior description and a set of parameters, possibly including existing actors;

send to: sending a message to an actor; and,

become: an actor replacing its own behavior by a new behavior.

These primitives form a simple but powerful set upon which to build a wide range of higher-level abstractions and concurrent programming paradigms. The *create* primitive is to concurrent programming what definition of a lambda abstraction is to sequential programming: it extends the dynamic resource creation capability provided by function abstractions to concurrent computation. Each actor has a unique mail address determined at the time of its creation.

The *become* primitive gives actors a history-sensitive behavior necessary for shared mutable data objects. This is in contrast to a purely functional programming model and generalizes the Lisp/Scheme/ML sequential style sharing to concurrent computation.

The *send to* primitive is the asynchronous analog of function application. It is the basic communication primitive, causing a message to be put in an actor's mailbox (message queue). To send a message, the target of a communication needs to be specified. Finally, note that the arrival order of messages is nondeterministic but every message sent to an actor is guaranteed to be eventually delivered.

Practical actor languages incorporate a number of high-level abstractions such as higher order functions, inheritance, local synchronization constraints, RPC-style message-passing, and implicit functional parallelism (see, for example, [3, 19]).

5 ActorSpace

ActorSpace provides a set of coordination primitives that are independent of any specific architecture. Moreover, in the tradition of Linda and Actors, our intention is not to provide a programming language; rather we want to provide a set of coordination primitives that can be used for communication between concurrent computations. The computations themselves may be expressed in different programming notations. The run-time system for ActorSpace will support heterogeneity by selecting transport protocols and data representation formats at run-time, a task we feel is possible to perform automatically with good efficiency. By letting the communication primitives be identical on all architectures, ActorSpace provides powerful abstraction over the communication architecture.

ActorSpace adds several new concepts to Actors:

- *Attributes* are patterns which provide an abstract external description or view of an actor. Attributes may be generalized and specialized through conjunction and disjunction, respectively. Thus attributes may be embedded in a description lattice (e.g., see [5]). We do not further specify the representation of attributes, but as a simple realization, they may be based on the familiar property lists in Lisp. Pattern matching may be used to pick actors whose attributes satisfy a given pattern.
- *actorSpaces* are a scoping mechanism for pattern matching. Actors and actorSpaces may be made visible or invisible in an actorSpace. Visibility allows association of the mail addresses of actors with their attributes (as viewed by some registrar).
- *Capabilities* provide keys for secure access control, for example, in validating requests for visibility or attribute change requests.

Note that corresponding to each actorSpace is a *manager* who validates capabilities and enforces visibility changes. Although we describe default policies for actorSpaces, further customization may be obtained by manipulating managers (as we discuss later). We give an overview of the ActorSpace constructs and discuss some of the issues involved below.

5.1 Attributes and Pattern-Matching

ActorSpace provides two kinds of handles to access an actor: the usual actor mail address, which corresponds to the identity of an actor, and the attributes for an actor that are visible in some actorSpace. Patterns may be used to define groups of actors using their visible attributes. Abstractly, each actorSpace maps a pattern to a set of actor mail addresses by matching on its list of registered attributes of visible actors.

5.2 ActorSpaces

An *actorSpace* is a computationally passive container of actors and acts as a context for matching patterns. Patterns will only be matched against listed attributes of actors and actorSpaces that are *visible* in a specified actorSpace. An actorSpace is created by the expression create-actorSpace(capability) which returns a unique actorSpace mail address. The specified capability may be used to authenticate visibility operations in the actorSpace created. As with actors, actorSpaces may be visible in other actorSpaces. Thus, actorSpaces can be referred to by their actorSpace mail address or by a pattern.

5.3 Communication

ActorSpace communication is done using one of two primitives: send or broadcast. Both the primitives send a message asynchronously to the specified receiver(s). The sender specifies a set of receivers by giving a pattern and an actorSpace. The pattern is matched against all listed attributes of actors visible in the specified actorSpace.

When send(pattern@actorSpace,message) is used to send a message, a *single* target actor is non-deterministically chosen out of the group of potential receivers. This is useful when several actors are replicating a service offered to clients. For example, as the messages to the servers are distributed non-deterministically, the load *may* be balanced automatically by an implementation, and none of the clients need to know the exact number of potential receivers. Note that the actorSpace specification, here and below, may itself be pattern based.

When broadcast(pattern@actorSpace,message) is used to send a message, *all* of the actors whose attributes match the pattern receive the message. A reason for introducing broadcasts is that we want to allow the sender to specify the kind of potential receivers which should receive a message, without having to also worry about the number of receivers. Broadcasting could be simulated by explicitly sending a message to all actors in the group, but this requires that the sender know each of these actors. By simply specifying a pattern, the sender leaves it to the system to determine exactly *which* actors should receive the message. The broadcast primitive greatly simplifies expressing many applications. For instance, in search problems such as the Traveling Salesman, a new lower bound can be broadcast to all nodes participating in the search for the shortest route.

In ActorSpace, broadcasting is done by specifying a group of receivers that should receive a message. The run-time system then carries out the message delivery. We assume that message delivery is only finitely delayed, but that the message order is not necessarily preserved; thus, unlike other broadcast implementations [7, 22], we do not guarantee a global or partial order on broadcast messages. Broadcasts may be received by two actors in a different order and point to point messages may be interleaved between two broadcasts. If a global order on broadcasts to a specific group is desired, it can be obtained by sending all messages that are to be broadcast to a special actor whose sole purpose is to receive messages from group members, and then broadcast these serially to the group using some agreed upon protocol (cf. sequenced send in the actor language HAL [19]). However, better performance may be obtained by not guaranteeing any order on broadcast messages, when such an ordering is not necessary or desirable [7, 29], which is why we do not enforce any ordering of broadcasts.

5.4 Visibility in ActorSpace

When an actor or an actorSpace is created, it is *not* automatically placed in an actorSpace; thus it may not be subject to pattern matching on its attributes. Actors and actorSpaces must be made *explicitly* visible to be subject to pattern matching; thus the default preserves the locality properties of the Actor model. Actors are autonomous entities, so they are able to make themselves visible or invisible given an actorSpace. Since actorSpaces are computationally passive, however, they cannot make themselves visible or invisible in a given actorSpace. Visibility leads to the issue of security and the role of managers in the system. Managers are supposed to control the system and we clearly do not want every actor to have the ability to change the visibility of another actor or actorSpace.

We provide security by the standard technique of introducing *capabilities*: only the holder of *the capability* for an actor or an actorSpace can change its visibility. Capabilities are unforgeable unique keys that can only be created by calling the underlying system with the primitive new-capability(). Capabilities can be stored, compared, copied and, in some systems, communicated in messages. When creating an actor or an actorSpace, a capability may be bound to it, and only if this capability is presented, may an actor's visibility be changed. A capability may also be bound to more than one actor or actorSpace.

We introduce two new primitives for controlling visibility: make-visible(α,attributes@space,capability), which explicitly subjects the actor or actorSpace α to pattern matching inside a specified space, and make-invisible(actor,space,capability), which removes actors from the specified actorSpaces – and thus any other enclosing actorSpace. Finally, note that attributes of visible actors or actorSpaces may change. Such changes may be made with the change-attributes operation, using the same parameters as make-visible.

5.5 Garbage Collection

The presence of actorSpaces affects the garbage collection of both actors and actorSpaces. As long as an actor (or actorSpace) is visible in an actorSpace, it may be potentially reachable and thus cannot be garbage collected until the container actorSpace has been garbage collected. An actorSpace may be deleted if no actor has a way of accessing it (and, as with actors, no messages containing its mail address are pending).

However, when an actorSpace is garbage collected, the actors contained in that actorSpace themselves are *not* deleted, rather, they are no longer visible using the actorSpaces (which is moot since the actorSpace itself is no longer accessible). Conversely, when an actor is no longer reachable, and furthermore cannot potentially reach a reachable actor, a garbage collection algorithm may be able to delete it. Note that since actorSpaces are viewed as passive containers, garbage collecting them is simpler than actors: inverse reachability need not be considered. We will not discuss garbage collection further, but we expect that a garbage collection algorithm for the Actor model [30] may be adapted in designing a garbage collector for ActorSpace.

5.6 Fairness and Asynchrony

Generally, ActorSpace messages have the same properties as Actor messages: delivery is asynchronous, but is guaranteed to eventually happen. However, there are, a few exceptions which we describe briefly. Consider a message sent using a pattern which is not satisfied by any visible actor's attributes. In this case, the pattern matching may be suspended until at least one actor appears whose attribute is matched by the pattern. This allows asynchrony in attribute updates and pattern-based message passing. On the other hand, such a message could be considered an error – forcing additional synchronization.

Again, if a message was sent using the broadcast primitive and there is no actor whose name is matched by the pattern, there are several possibilities, including: the broadcast is discarded, the broadcast is suspended until there is at least one actor whose attributes match the pattern, or broadcasting could be persistent, so that any actor (existing or created in the future) whose attributes match the pattern, will receive the broadcast message *exactly once*. The last case may be useful in enforcing a protocol or assuming some other common knowledge in a group.

In our current implementation, send and broadcast messages are suspended until at least one actor arrives whose attribute matches the pattern for the broadcast. This is the cheapest option that avoids repeated synchronization that would otherwise be needed to address the asynchrony in the system. However, a particular choice of semantics cannot satisfy all requirements. By allowing actorSpace managers to be customized, we can vary the temporal constraints on the matching rules.

5.7 The Problem of Cycles

The consequence of an actorSpace being visible in itself can be quite catastrophic: if its attributes are matched by some broadcast message, an infinite number of messages may be generated by the message. In case of a pattern directed send, the damage is less significant: the message could be simply lost in an infinite forwarding loop. As part of the semantics of make-visible we do not allow an actorSpace to be made visible in itself, or recursively in any contained actorSpace. This avoids cycles in the directed acyclic graph defined by the visibility relation between actorSpaces.

In implementation terms, avoiding such cycles means that a visibility relation graph must be constructed before an actorSpace is allowed to be visible. Furthermore, since actors are encapsulated and should not be sent arbitrary bookkeeping messages, type information must be maintained to determine whether a mail address refers to an actor or an actorSpace.

An alternate strategy is to tag message and compare tags with those of previously sent messages. This may offer a way of trapping cycles of messages simply forwarded by actors as well. Again, we believe no single strategy will provide a universally desirable solution. The problem is probably best addressed by customizing actorSpace managers.

6 Example: A Dynamic Process Pool

This section presents an example of an application that can be efficiently expressed in the ActorSpace paradigm. We have chosen a dynamic process pool to demonstrate how ActorSpace elegantly solves some particular problems and how ActorSpace provides an open system for computing.

Consider a parallel system with a number of processors in a pool that can be allocated to solve problems. We consider algorithms for parallel problem-solving based on divide-and-conquer. Specifically, we envision a number of actors (which for efficiency reasons could be located on different nodes), which participate in solving the problem. All these actors reside in an actorSpace, and new actors may come along while the system is running to help to solve the problem. This is shown in figure 1.

The figure shows a processor pool located in a local actorSpace, which is not visible except to the client. Assume that an actorSpace called `ProcPool` contains a pool of available processors. The client could contain code as follows:

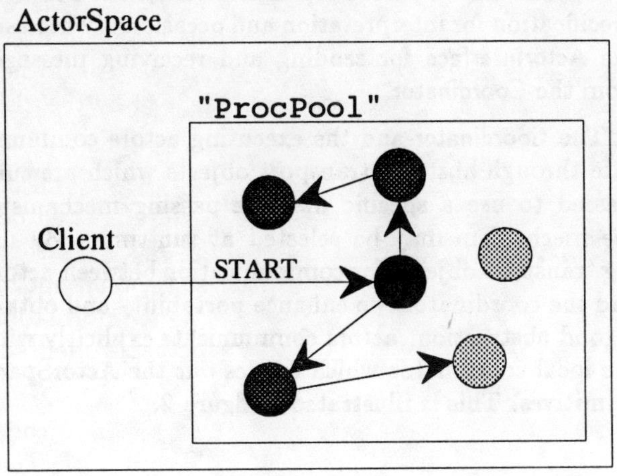

Figure 1: A processor pool where the actors participate in solving a problem. The Client starts by sending a problem into the pool, which is divided among the processors. The lighter circles denote newly arrived processes.

```
// Create a processor pool
..
// Create the job to be done
..
send(*@ProcPool,job,self);
// Wait for the answer to return
..
```

The client starts the data-processing by sending a message to an arbitrary processor inside the ActorSpace **ProcPool** and a return address for answers. Note that * in this example is a pattern that matches any attribute. Now, each of the processing actors might contain code as follows:

```
// Receive a new job
..
if job-too-big(job) then
  subjobs = divide-into-subjobs(job);
  // distribute the jobs among neighbors
  for i in "all subjobs" do
    send(*@MyNghbrProcs,subjobs[i],self);
  // Collect answers and merge
  ..
else
  result = process(job);
endif
// Return the answer
send(answer-destination,result);
```

The first processor which receives the job may decide that the job is too large to handle; it then divides the job into smaller subjobs, sends them to one of the other actors in its neighborhood processor pool and waits for the partial answers. Note that **MyNghbrProcs** is an identifier bound to some actorSpace. The binding will depend on the code for the particular processor – different processors may refer to different actorSpaces.

In particular, depending on the organization of the actorSpaces, the above divide and conquer can be done within a nested subspace. Thus, the broadcast can happen to representatives of a WAN whereas the subsequent distribution can be localized to be within a LAN.

Note that the processors in the pool do not have to know how many processors participate in solving the problem, and indeed, the number may vary during the computation. By only specifying that a message should be sent to one of the actors in the "current" actorSpace, one of the visible processors will receive the message, thereby receiving part of the problem. By letting the processors divide the job as the problem is analyzed, we remove a bottleneck around a master process in the more traditional "one master, multiple slaves" approach to parallelize problems. And by using patterns, the number of processors allocated to the task can be adjusted during execution – without having to stop the system.

7 A Prototype Implementation

The implementation of the first prototype for ActorSpace focuses on making a small system for initial experimentation with the ActorSpace coordination paradigm. We want to keep the prototype implementation small, thus we have limited its extent and kept the system simple. Instead of building a compiler which will compile the programming language, we have chosen to build a small sequential interpreter for interpreting the code associated with each method definition. An interpreter gives us the additional flexibility of easily loading behaviors at run-time. A future extension will include a byte-compiler which will compile the code into an intermediary form, similar to early implementations of other object–oriented programming languages (such as SmallTalk).

The system is designed in an object-oriented manner to allow maximal flexibility. To provide for an easy extension to accommodate heterogeneous computing, certain system-classes may be subclassed to provide transportation and data representation suitable for other architectures. The overall design of the prototype can be separated into two parts: the design of a single node, and the design of inter-node coordination.

7.1 Representation of Attributes

In our current prototype, attributes are concatenations of atoms, and patterns are regular expressions over atoms – rather analogous to the structure of files and directories in UNIX. Actors are actually created inside an actorSpace (their host space), although they are not visible in this actorSpace unless explicitly made so. Furthermore, they may be made visible in other actorSpaces, regardless of whether or not they are visible in their "host" actorSpace.

Patterns are resolved inside the sender's host actorSpace, unless the pattern explicitly refers to another actorSpace. This provides a structural communication hierarchy. The attributes of actorSpaces and actors may be combined to form a structured attribute (with a special combination operator '/'), much as is the case with file names in a conventional file-system such as in the UNIX file-system. In the same manner, a globally visible actorSpace which is the "root" of the tree of actorSpaces, is created automatically by the run-time system. This ensures that the first actorSpaces created by the users may be made visible to other users. On the other hand, such global visibility makes automatic garbage collection of actorSpaces generally infeasible, and therefore the current prototype provides explicit means of destroying actorSpaces.

7.2 Single-node Design

The single-node design associates all the executing actors on a node with a single local coordinator. Each node in our prototype implementation contains the following:

- A small sequential interpreter for the computations.
- An ActorInterface which allows methods defined in the actor behaviors to be invoked.
- A Coordinator which provides the main run-time support and carries out the ActorSpace coordination primitives.

A major goal of the implementation was to make the design of the interpreter, the ActorInterface and the Coordinator as modular as possible. We have achieved this by defining a communications format between the interpreter, the ActorInterface and the Coordinator. As far as the ActorInterface is concerned, behaviors allow the initialization of variables and parameterized invocation of methods. The Coordinator is only concerned with receiving requests, carrying them out, and possibly returning messages to the ActorInterface or the interpreter. The interpreter uses a parsed representation of the behavior specification for interpretation and occasionally accesses the ActorInterface for sending and receiving messages from the Coordinator.

The Coordinator and the executing actors communicate through abstract transport objects which are subclassed to use a specific message passing mechanism; the mechanism may be selected at run-time. By using transport objects for communication between actors and the coordinator, we enhance portability and obtain a good abstraction: actors communicate explicitly with the local coordinator which carries out the ActorSpace primitives. This is illustrated in figure 2.

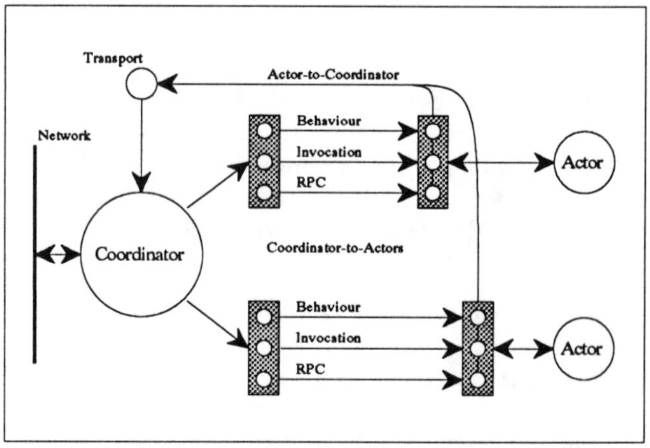

Figure 2: An overview of the design of a single node in ActorSpace.

The executing actors are supplied with three different message ports, each of which has a different purpose. The Behavior-port is used for sending the actor its next behavior. The Invocation-port is used for sending the actor any messages sent to it using send or broadcast. The RPC-port is used when an actor performs a system call that expects a return value, such as the creation of a new actor. In this case, the name of the new actor must be returned. All messages from an actor are sent to the coordinator's single port where the message, in turn, will be processed by the local coordinator.

7.3 Inter-node Design

The local coordinator connects to coordinators on other nodes using a (virtual) coordinator bus. This provides a transparent interface to actors that are located on other nodes in a network. The network is illustrated in figure 3.

A coordinator process uses the network connection to broadcast information to other coordinators in order

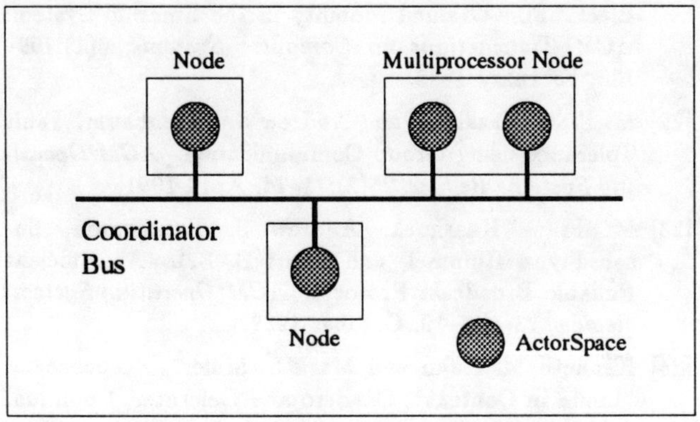

Figure 3: The connection of several coordinators on a (virtual) coordinator bus.

to maintain coherence of the state of ActorSpace. This state includes "live" actors and actorSpaces as well as visibility of actors. The coordinators automatically determine the location of an actor given its name and forwards any outgoing messages to the appropriate node using the network connection. The broadcast network does not rely on having a network with a hardware broadcast facility at its disposal. However, the current design needs a global ordering on individual broadcasts between coordinators to order visibility changes globally, so that all nodes have the same view of visibility in ActorSpace (although *not* necessarily the same order on broadcasts to actors). The broadcasting between the coordinators could, for instance, be done using either the Amoeba broadcast protocol [23] or a centralized broadcaster and sequencer [9]; both have orderings of some sort on broadcast messages.

8 Conclusions and Research Directions

Our ongoing work and further research includes a formal definition of ActorSpace based on a semantic definition of Actors and their MetaArchitectures [4, 31]. We intend to develop customizable managers to allow experimentation with different coordination and scheduling mechanisms. For example, this would allow experimentation with arbitration mechanisms which may be used instead of the current indeterminate choice that happens when a single actor is selected out of a group of actors. More powerful managers could use dæmons to monitor actors in an actorSpace and update attributes in order to maintain specified coordination constraints [2, 13]. Finally, it may be useful to allow persistent messages that would be automatically received by a new participant whenever it enters an existing group.

Acknowledgments

This research has been supported in part by the Office of Naval Research (ONR contract number N00014-90-J-1899), by the Digital Equipment Corporation, and by joint support from the Defense Advanced Research Projects Agency and the National Science Foundation (NSF CCR 90-07195). Christian J. Callsen is sponsored in part by a research fellowship from Århus University and Aalborg University, and a generous grant from the Danish Research Academy (V910219). The work was done in part while the second author was a visiting scholar at the Unviersity of Illinois.

The authors would like to thank Svend Frølund, Wooyoung Kim, Rajendra Panwar, Anna Patterson, Daniel Sturman, and Carolyn Talcott for helpful comments and stimulating discussions on the structure and problems of ActorSpaces, as well as critical reading of the manuscript. The first author would especially like to acknowledge a number of fruitful interactions with, as well as inspiration from the work of David Gelernter, Carl Hewitt, John Holland, Suresh Jagannathan, Ken Kahn, Henry Lieberman, Nicholas Carriero, Carolyn Talcott, Peter Wegner, and the late Alan Perlis.

References

[1] G. Agha. *Actors: A Model of Concurrent Computation in Distributed Systems.* The MIT Press, 1986.

[2] G. Agha, S. Frølund, R. Panwar, and D. Sturman. A Linguistic Framework for Dynamic Composition of Dependability Protocols. In *Proceedings of the Third IFIP Working Conference on Dependable Computing for Critical Applications*, pages 197–207, Palermo (Sicily), Italy, September 1992. IFIP.

[3] K. Wooyoung and G. Agha. Compilation of a Highly Parallel Actor-Based Language. In U. Banerjee, D. Gelernter, A. Nicolau, and D. Padua, editors, *Proceedings of the Workshop on Languages and Compilers for Parallel Computing.* Yale University TR DCS RR-915, 1992. to appear in LNCS, Springer-Verlag.

[4] Gul Agha, Ian Mason, Scott Smith, and Carolyn Talcott. Towards a Theory of Actor Computation. In *Third International Conference on Concurrency Theory (Concur '92)*, pages 565–579. Springer–Verlag, August 1992. LNCS 630.

[5] G. Attardi and M. Simi. Semantics of Inheritance and Attributions in the Description System Omega. In *Proceedings of IJCAI 81*, Vancouver, B. C., Canada, August 1981. IJCAI.

[6] Henri E. Bal, M. Frans Kaashoek, and Andrew S. Tanenbaum. Orca: A Language For Parallel Programming of Distributed Systems. *IEEE Transactions on Software Engineering*, 18(3):190–205, March 1992.

[7] Kenneth Birman, André Schiper, and Pat Stephenson. Lightweight Causal and Atomic Group Multicast. *ACM Transactions on Computer Systems*, 9(3):272–314, August 1991.

[8] Nicholas J. Carriero and David Gelernter. How to Write Parallel Programs: A Guide to the Perplexed. *ACM Computing Surveys*, 21(3):323–357, September 1989.

[9] Jo-Mei Chang and N. F. Maxemchuk. Reliable Broadcast Protocols. *ACM Transactions on Computer Systems*, 2(3):251–273, August 1984.

[10] David R. Cheriton and Willy Zwaenepoel. Distributed Process Groups in the V Kernel. *ACM Transactions on Computer Systems*, 3(2):77–107, May 1985.

[11] Andrew A. Chien and William J. Dally. Concurrent Aggregates. *Second ACM Symposium on Principles and Practice of Parallel Programming, SIGPLAN Notices*, 25(3):187–196, March 1990.

[12] Eric C. Cooper. Replicated Procedure Call. In *Proceedings of the 3rd Annual ACM Symposium on Principles of Distributed Computing Conference*, pages 220–232. ACM, August 1984.

[13] S. Frølund and G. Agha. A Language Framework for Muti-Object Coordination. In *Proceedings of European Conference on Object Oriented Programming*, 1993. To appear in LNCS, Springer-Verlag.

[14] Hector Garcia-Molina and Annemarie Spauster. Ordered and Reliable Multicast Communication. *ACM Transactions on Computer Systems*, 9(3):242–271, August 1991.

[15] Narain H. Gehani. Broadcasting Sequential Processes (BSP). *IEEE Transactions on Software Engineering*, SE-10(4):343–351, July 1984.

[16] David Gelernter. Generative Communication in Linda. *ACM Transactions on Programming Languages and Systems*, 7(1):80–112, January 1985.

[17] David Gelernter. Multiple tuple spaces in Linda. In E. Odjik, M. Rem, and J.-C. Syre, editors, *PARLE '89, volume 2, LNCS 366*, pages 20–27. Springer–Verlag, June 1989.

[18] C. Hewitt and H. Baker. Laws for Communicating Parallel Processes. In *1977 IFIP Congress Proceedings*, pages 987–992. IFIP, August 1977.

[19] C. Houck and G. Agha. HAL: A High-level Actor Language and Its Distributed Implementation. In *Proceedings of th 21st International Conference on Parallel Processing (ICPP '92)*, volume II, pages 158–165, St. Charles, IL, August 1992.

[20] Suresh Jagannathan. Customization of First-Class Tuple-Spaces in a Higher-Order Language. In E. H. L. Arts, J. van Leeuwen, and M. Rem, editors, *PARLE '91, volume 2*, pages 254–276. Springer–Verlag, June 1991. LNCS 506.

[21] Eric Jul, Henry Levy, Norman Hutchinson, and Andrew Black. Fine-Grained Mobility in the Emerald System. *ACM Transactions on Computer Systems*, 6(1):109–133, February 1988.

[22] M. Frans Kaashoek and Andrew S. Tanenbaum. Fault Tolerance using Group Communication. *ACM Operating Systems Review*, 25(2):71–74, April 1991.

[23] M. Frans Kaashoek, Andrew S. Tanenbaum, Susan Flynn Hummel, and Henri E. Bal. An Efficient Reliable Broadcast Protocol. *ACM Operating Systems Review*, 23(4):5–19, October 1989.

[24] Kenneth M. Kahn and Mark S. Miller. Response to: "Linda in Context", Carriero and Gelernter, Commun. ACM 32 (4):444–458, Apr. 1989. *Communications of the ACM*, 32(10):1253–1255, October 1989.

[25] William A. Kornfeld and Carl Hewitt. The Scientific Community Metaphor. *IEEE Transactions on Systems, Man, and Cybernetics*, 11(1):24–33, January 1981.

[26] Edward D. Lazowska. System Support for High Performance Multiprocessing. In USENIX *Workshop on Experiences with Distributed & Multiprocessor Systems (SEDMS III)*, pages 1–11. USENIX Association, 1992.

[27] Satoshi Matsuoka and Satoru Kawai. Using Tuple Space Communication in Distributed Object-Oriented Langu ages. In *OOPSLA '88 Conference Proceedings*, pages 276–284, November 1988. Published as ACM SIGPLAN Notices, volume 23, number 11.

[28] P. M. Melliar-Smith, Louise E. Moser, and Vivek Agrawala. Broadcast Protocols for Distributed Systems. *IEEE Transactions on Parallel and Distributed Systems*, 1(1):17–25, January 1990.

[29] Pat Stephenson and Kenneth Birman. Fast Causal Multicast. *ACM Operating Systems Review*, 25(2):75–79, April 1991.

[30] N. Venkatasubramaniam, G. Agha, and C. Talcott. Scalable Distributed Garbage Collection for Systems of Active Objects. In *Proceedings International Workshop on Memory Management*, pages 441–451, St. Malo, France, September 1992. ACM SIGPLAN and INRIA, Springer-Verlag. LNCS.

[31] Nalini Venkatasubramanian and Carolyn Talcott. A MetaArchitecture for Distributed Resource Management. In *Proceedings of the Hawaii International Conference on System Sciences*. IEEE Computer Society Press, January 1993.

[32] G. Wiederhold, P. Wegner, and S. Ceri. Towards Megaprogramming. *Communications of the ACM*, 35(11), November 1992.

[33] Akinori Yonezawa, editor. *ABCL: An Object-Oriented Concurrent System*. Computer Systems Series. The MIT Press, 1990.

Experiences Using the ParaScope Editor: an Interactive Parallel Programming Tool*

Mary W. Hall† Timothy J. Harvey‡ Ken Kennedy‡ Nathaniel McIntosh‡
Kathryn S. McKinley§ Jeffrey D. Oldham† Michael H. Paleczny‡ Gerald Roth‡

Abstract

The ParaScope Editor is an interactive parallel programming tool that assists knowledgeable users in developing scientific Fortran programs. It displays the results of sophisticated program analyses, provides a set of powerful interactive transformations, and supports program editing. This paper summarizes experiences of scientific programmers and tool designers using the ParaScope Editor. We evaluate existing features and describe enhancements in three key areas: user interface, analysis, and transformation. Many existing features prove crucial to successful program parallelization. They include interprocedural array side-effect analysis and program and dependence view filtering. Desirable functionality includes improved program navigation based on performance estimation, incorporating user assertions in analysis and more guidance in selecting transformations. These results offer insights for the authors of a variety of programming tools and parallelizing compilers.

1 Introduction

The complexity of constructing parallel programs is a significant obstacle to widespread use of parallel computers. In the process of writing a parallel program, programmers must consider the implications of concurrency on the correctness of their algorithms. Ideally, an advanced compiler could free the programmer from this concern by automatically converting a sequential program into an equivalent shared-memory parallel program. Although a substantial amount of research has been devoted to automatic parallelization, such systems are not consistently successful [1, 9, 6, 30, 33]. When automatic systems fail, the ParaScope Editor (PED) assists in parallelizing Fortran applications by combining programmer expertise with extensive analysis and program transformations [3, 27, 28].

This paper reports on the utility of PED as an interactive parallel programming tool in the ParaScope parallel programming environment [10]. Through user evaluation of PED, we assess existing functionality and suggest enhancements. The critiques confirm the usefulness of tools like PED and offer new insights for compiler writers and parallel programming tool designers in three key areas.

User Interface. We describe a new user interface that was designed and implemented based on previous evaluations [17, 25]. This interface enhances the original [28], unifying improved navigation and viewing of the program, its dependences, and information about its variables. User evaluation confirms the appropriateness of the interface but exposes the need for new features such as navigation assistance based on performance estimation and a facility enabling users to assert information about variable values.

Program Analysis. Dependence analysis specifies a partial order of a program's statements that preserves its meaning [5, 15]. For safety, the compiler must assume a dependence exists if it cannot prove otherwise. In ParaScope, analysis of interprocedural and intraprocedural constants, symbolics and array sections improve the precision of its dependence analysis [19, 27]. (We assume the reader is familiar with these analyses.) User evaluation confirms they are indispensable for discovering parallelism. In addition, more advanced symbolic analysis and exploiting user assertions in all analyses are essential when parallelizing many programs.

Transformations. Program transformations introduce, discover, and exploit parallelism without changing the meaning of the program. PED provides users with the same source-to-source transformations and accompanying analysis employed by ParaScope's compilers [8, 22], allowing users to apply transformations di-

*This research was supported by The Center for Research and Parallel Computation (CRPC) at Rice University, under NFS Cooperative Agreement Number CCR-9120008.

†Center for Integrated Systems, Stanford University, Palo Alto, CA 94305. ‡Department of Computer Science, Rice University, Houston, TX 77251-1892. §ENSMP (CRI), 35, rue Saint Honoré, F-77305 Fontainebleau Cedex, France.

4th ACM PPOPP,5/93/CA,USA

name	description & contributor	lines	procedures
spec77	weather simulation code Steve Poole, IBM Kingston & Lo Hsieh, IBM Palo Alto	5600	67
neoss	thermodynamics code Mary Zosel, Lawrence Livermore National Laboratory	350	5
nxsns	quantum mechanics code John Engle, Lawrence Livermore National Laboratory	1400	11
dpmin	molecular mechanics and dynamics program Marcia Pottle, Cornell Theory Center	5000	52
slab2d	2-D severe storm fluid flow prototype Roy Heimbach, National Center for Supercomputing Applications	550	9
slalom	benchmark program Roy Heimbach, National Center for Supercomputing Applications	1200	13
pueblo3d	hydrodynamics benchmark program Ralph Brickner, Los Alamos National Laboratory	4000	50
arc3d	3-D hydrodynamics code Doreen Cheng, NASA Ames Research Center	3600	25

Table 1: Analyzed and Parallelized Programs.

rectly. User evaluation reveals that access to transformations is not sufficient. Users found it difficult to determine which transformations to attempt and request that the system suggest a transformation or compound transformations.

This paper is organized into 4 more sections, related work and conclusions. In the next section, we present our evaluation methodology. Sections 3 through 5 discuss the three key areas in detail, briefly describing existing functionality, evaluating it and outlining obstacles to parallelization and proposed solutions.

2 Methodology

The experiences presented in this paper result primarily from a workshop held in July, 1991 at Rice University. Eight researchers from industrial sites and government laboratories attended. Each contributed a Fortran code to be parallelized with PED. Table 1 lists the workshop attendees with their programs. Additional evaluations result from two studies of parallel programming tools: one by Joseph Stein, a visiting scientist at Syracuse University [35], and another by Katherine Fletcher of Rice University and Doreen Cheng at NASA Ames Research Center [16].

At the workshop, we divided the attendees into groups of one or two people and assigned a researcher familiar with PED to assist each group. After a morning of introductory talks and a PED demonstration, the user groups parallelized their application with PED for the next two half days. They followed the work model described in Section 3.1.

We collected feedback from the workshop through two sources. First, the assistants recorded observations from the hands-on sessions with their user groups: which features were used, any difficulties encountered, and participants' comments. Each group also presented their experiences. We concluded with a lengthy discussion involving all attendees.

The contents of this paper are derived from the assistants' accounts and the discussions as well as talks by Stein and Fletcher on their experiences.

3 User Interface

3.1 Background

The user interface communicates PED's capabilities to programmers. Repeated evaluation of PED [17] and its predecessor PTOOL [2, 25] by compiler writers, application programmers and human interface experts has led to its current design. Although many of the features in the new PED interface are found in the original [28], it improves upon the original by providing more consistent and powerful features.

PED employs three user interface techniques to manage and present the detailed information computed by the system: (1) a book metaphor with *progressive disclosure*, (2) user-controlled *view filtering*, and (3) *power steering* for complex actions. The book metaphor portrays a Fortran program as an *electronic book* with analysis results annotating the source, analogous to a book's marginal notes, footnotes, appendices, and indices [37]. Progressive disclosure presents details incrementally as they become relevant [34]. View filtering emphasizes or conceals parts of the book as specified by a user [14]. Power steering automates repetitive or error-prone tasks, providing unobtrusive assistance while leaving the user in control.

The layout of a PED window is shown in Figure 1. The large area at the top is the *source pane* displaying the Fortran text. Two footnotes beneath it, the *dependence pane* and the *variable pane*, display dependence and variable information. All three panes operate similarly. Scroll bars can be used to bring other portions of the display into view, predefined or user-defined view filters may be applied to customize the display, the mouse may be used to make a selection, and menu choices or keyboard input may be used to edit the displayed infor-

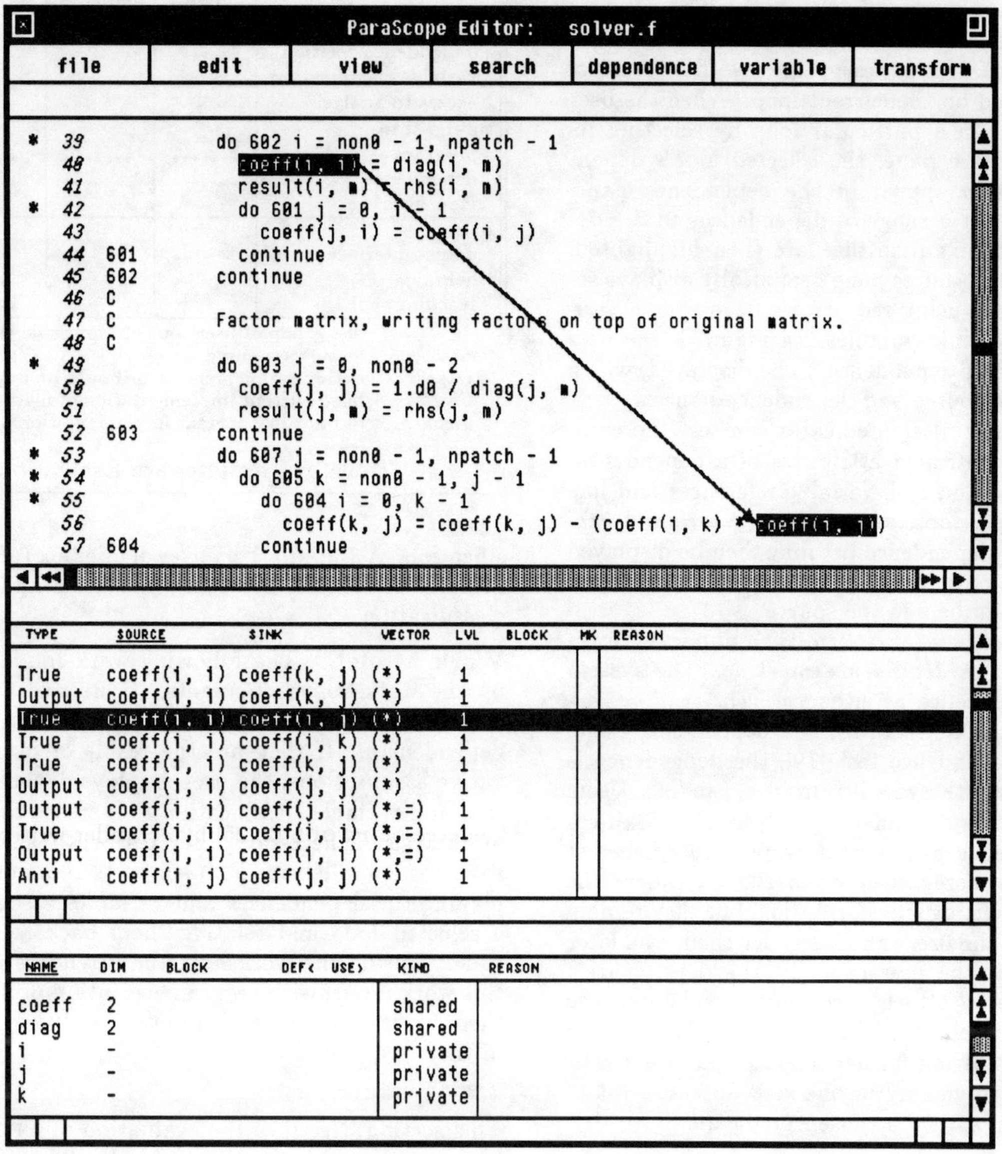

Figure 1: The ParaScope Editor.

mation. The Fortran text, the dependence information, and the variable information are each described below in terms of the information displayed, view filtering, and editing. We also discuss the work model best supported by PED and used during the workshop.

Fortran Source Code. Fortran source code is displayed in pretty-printed form in the source pane. At the left are marginal annotations showing the ordinal number of each source line and asterisks (*) which indicate the start of each loop. The ordinal line numbers for the statements in the *current loop* are highlighted with color (not visible in Figure 1). Source view filtering can be used to highlight or conceal source lines, based on either the text or the underlying semantics of each line. For example, source view filter predicates can test attributes of a line such as if it contains certain text, if it is a loop header, or if it is erroneous.

The source pane allows arbitrary editing of the program using mixed text and structure editing techniques [36]. The user has the full freedom to edit character by character or to use the power steering afforded by template-based structure editing. Incremental parsing occurs in response to edits, and the user is immediately informed of any syntactic or semantic errors.

Dependence Information. The editor reveals program dependences in a tabular list in the dependence pane. The display shows each dependence's source and sink variable references and characteristics such as dependence distance. PED uses progressive disclosure of dependences based on the current loop. When the user expresses interest in a particular loop by selecting its marker in the source pane, the selected loop's dependences immediately appear in the dependence pane. The user may select a range of dependences in the dependence pane to examine that are then highlighted. Simultaneously, the source pane graphically displays selected dependences using red arrows from source variable references to sink variables. In Figure 1, the user has selected a single dependence to be displayed, which is reflected in the source and dependence panes.

Dependence view filter predicates can test the computed and user-controlled attributes of a dependence, such as its source and sink variable references and line numbers, its type, loop nesting level, *mark* and *reason*. The filtered dependence list may then be displayed graphically all at once, one dependence at a time, or according to line numbers in the source.

The dependence pane also permits an important form of editing known as *dependence marking*. The system marks each dependence as either *proven*, *pending*, *accepted* or *rejected*. If PED proves a dependence exists with an exact dependence test [19], the dependence is marked as *proven*; otherwise it is marked *pending*. Users may sharpen PED's dependence analysis by marking a pending dependence as *accepted* or *rejected*. Rejected dependences are disregarded when PED considers the safety of a parallelizing transformation, but they remain in the system so the user can reconsider them at a later time. If desired, the user can edit the dependence's *reason* attribute to attach a comment explaining the classification decision. A *Mark Dependences* dialog box provides power steering for dependence marking by allowing the user to classify in one step an entire set of dependences that satisfy a chosen predicate.

Variable Information. The variable pane displays a list of variables with progressive disclosure similarly based on the current loop. The attributes of a variable include its name, definitions and uses outside the current loop, dimension, common block if any, and shared or private status. View filter predicates can test any of these attributes.

The variable pane also supports editing in the form of *variable classification*. Locating variables that may legally be made private to a loop body can greatly reduce the number of spurious dependences in a loop (see Section 4.1). Analysis automatically locates many such variables, but it is conservative and may classify variables as shared that may legally be made private. With variable classification, the user may edit a variable's *shared/private* attribute to correct overly conservative classifications for arrays and scalars. As with dependence editing the user may also edit a variable's *reason* field, attaching a comment regarding the variable's classification. A *Classify Variables* dialog box (analogous to *Mark Dependences*) provides power steering for variable classification.

	used	improve	like	dislike
user interaction				
dependence deletion	⋆⋆⋆⋆⋆⋆			⋆⋆⋆
variable classification	⋆⋆⋆⋆			
access to analysis		⋆⋆⋆		
navigation				
program	⋆⋆⋆⋆⋆⋆⋆	⋆⋆⋆⋆⋆⋆⋆	⋆⋆	
dependence	⋆⋆⋆⋆⋆⋆⋆	⋆⋆⋆⋆⋆	⋆⋆	⋆
view filtering	⋆		⋆	
other				
detect interface error	⋆⋆⋆			
help	⋆⋆	⋆	⋆⋆	
teaching tool			⋆⋆	

⋆: one group of users out of a possible seven
used: feature was used
improve: current implementation should be improved
like: liked current implementation of feature
dislike: did not like current implementation of feature

Table 2: User Interface Evaluation.

Work Model. The following work model was used by the workshop participants. Users select a loop for consideration and examine any parallelism inhibiting dependences. If they are the result of overly conservative assumptions, the user employs dependence deletion and variable classification to increase the precision of analysis. If necessary, they perform transformations to expose parallelism. PED supports this model by displaying the dependences and variables associated with a selected loop and relating them back to the source code. During the workshop, the attendees augmented this work model with program execution profiles to help them focus on the most computationally intensive loops in their program.

3.2 Evaluation

This section describes the evaluation of PED's user interface, as summarized in Table 2. The table lists a number of features in its rows and responses in the columns. Each of the five workshop groups, along with Fletcher and Stein, is represented by an asterisk, for a total of seven possible asterisks. Because the implementation of the interface described above was not robust at the time of the workshop, it was demonstrated but not used by the participants. Here, we address only issues that apply to both interfaces and are not addressed in the current implementation. This structure allows us to focus on user suggestions for improvement.

User Interaction. Users were comfortable with selecting a loop and then evaluating its dependences and variable annotations. Specifically, one user commented that having all information available in one window annotating the source code was preferable to the functional-based approach of Forge [31], which requires the programmer to bring up a series of windows to access the results of program analysis.

To correct overly conservative analysis, users performed both dependence deletion and variable reclassification to reflect their perception of the true program state. Variable reclassification proved to be the right level of abstraction. When users were able to determine a variable could be made private to a loop, changing the variable's classification and seeing the resulting decrease in dependences was effective. However, deleting individual dependences was too tedious for most users. One user disliked dependences as a paradigm and desired a higher level of abstraction based on variables. We discussed simplifying dependence deletion by introducing variable-based user assertions that the system would then use to automatically eliminate dependences (see Section 3.3).

Three users requested more access to all the analysis computed by the system in order to enhance their understanding of the program and provide insight into the reasons the system must assume dependences exist. For instance, one user felt that displaying array sections that summarize the portion of an array accessed by a loop, similar to those used in interprocedural analysis (see Section 4.1), would provide an intuitive representation of the accesses within the loop. Two other users requested that the system display constant values or ranges for loop bounds and subscript expressions. In general, they wanted access to any information the system uses to compute dependences in order to correct overly conservative analysis.

Program Navigation. Existing features in PED assist in navigating the source code. They include view filtering and annotations in the display. Source view filtering was not widely used during the workshop primarily because it was unfamiliar to the assistants. However, one group defined filters based on labels to help them understand a procedure's control flow (see Section 5.3). One user commented that they would have liked to apply view filtering to examine the procedure's loop structure; this feature is one of the predefined view filters. Another requested that the display annotations include a loop nesting depth indicator.

All users requested more assistance in locating the most computation-intensive procedures and loops in the program in order to better target their parallelization efforts. For this purpose, the users relied on external tools to profile their codes. They used the Unix utility *gprof* from Sun and Cray executions to derive procedure-level profiles. One user brought loop-level profiling available from Forge [31], which shows the loop structure of a procedure, with the number of iterations executed and its percentage of execution time. The users requested that similar profiling or static performance estimation be integrated into PED to help focus user attention on the loops where effective parallelization would have the highest payoff. ParaScope now includes a static performance estimator used to predict the relative execution time of loops and subroutines in parallel programs [26].

Several users wanted a graphical representation of the call graph, rather than the current textual presentation [21]. A visual program representation provides a much needed "big picture" when working with a large or unfamiliar program. Short cuts to accessing other procedures via this representation were also requested.

Dependence Navigation. In navigating dependences, the users requested a number of features subsumed by the current implementation. First, they needed to visit dependence endpoints quickly rather than having to scroll through the source. They wanted view filtering capabilities to examine in the source and dependence panes all dependences associated with a particular definition. They were comfortable with use-definition chains and requested a filter mechanism for viewing them.

The users also wanted additional navigational features to examine dependences with at least one endpoint outside the current loop, in another loop or even another procedure. Displaying dependences with endpoints outside the selected loop requires straightforward extensions to PED. For example, if a variable is used or defined outside the current loop, the variable display reveals that information. To find the reference(s) at the workshop, the users were forced to search the program. Now the user need only select the line number of interest in the USE or DEF field (see Figure 1), and the appropriate reference appears in the source pane.

Dependence endpoints spanning multiple procedures pose a more difficult problem. Because interprocedural side-effect information summarizes accesses, one endpoint may correspond to several reads or writes of an array in multiple procedure bodies. To fully support dependence navigation, PED must be able to display other procedures while iterating over all the endpoints corresponding to a dependence.

Other. Another ParaScope tool, the *Composition Editor*, compares a procedure definition to calls invoking it, ensuring the parameter lists agree in number and type [11, 21]. These types of errors exist in production codes because most compilers do not perform cross-procedure comparisons. Several mismatched parameters between a procedure call and its declaration as well as type errors were detected and subsequently corrected using this analysis. One user requested further analysis to ensure that common block declarations have the same shape in every procedure in which they appear and to perform static array bounds checking.

Two participants were eager to use PED as a teaching tool for parallel programmers at their institutions. They felt PED's tutorial nature could help explain parallel programming to novices. Two users found the interactive help facility useful, but one wanted it to provide more information. One user wanted the ability to print the program, dependences, and variable information.

3.3 Obstacles to Parallelization

User Assertions. Explicit deletion of dependences fails to capture the user's reason for eliminating a dependence. A user deletes a dependence or a group of dependences because of some additional knowledge about the program that the system is unable to detect statically. This information is usually at a higher level than a specific dependence. Users would prefer to specify a high-level assertion and then have the system respond by deleting associated dependences. They proposed adding a user assertion language.

To support user assertions, we first need to define an assertion language based on three important concepts. (1) Assertions should express program properties that are natural to a user. (2) Assertions should provide information to the system that is useful in eliminating dependences. (3) It should be possible for the system to verify the correctness of the assertions at run time.

For example, the assertion language could enable users to specify the value or range of values of a variable using familiar Fortran syntax. Two simple but very useful assertions encountered during evaluation were specifying relationships between two symbolic variables and the properties of *index arrays*, arrays used in subscript expressions of another array. Consider the following fragment from *pueblo3d*.

```
DO M = 1, 3
   MCN = ICN (M, IR)
   ...
   DO I = ISTRT(IR), IENDV(IR)
      ...
      ... = UF(I + MCN, 3)
      UF(I, M) = ...
ENDDO
```

This construction appears in 10 loop nests in *pueblo3d* and several of these consume the majority of the total execution time. MCN represents "my current neighbor" and is used to index linearized three-dimensional arrays. Relative to the above loop structure, this program ensures that MCN > IENDV(IR) - ISTRT(IR) and therefore, there are no loop-carried dependences on UF. As in this case, arriving at an appropriate and useful assertion may require some careful thought, but the system will be offering some assistance as well (see Section 4.3).

4 Program Analysis

4.1 Background

Discovering and evaluating potential parallelism in a program requires extensive program analysis. In particular, dependence analysis provides the fundamental paradigm for detecting parallelism. A loop that contains no *loop-carried* dependences may execute its iterations in parallel. Further, dependences are used to prove the safety of program transformations. This section briefly describes the dependence analysis and supporting analyses that are currently available in PED [27].

Dependence Analysis. PED detects data and control dependences. *Data dependences* are located by testing pairs of references in a loop. A hierarchical suite of tests is used, starting with inexpensive tests, to prove or disprove that a dependence exists [19]. *Control dependences* explicitly represent how control decisions affect statement execution [15].

Supporting Analysis. Scalar data-flow analysis, including def-use chains, constant propagation and symbolic analysis, provides additional information about the values and relationship of variables. They can vastly improve the precision of dependence analysis [19, 20]. Def-use chains expose dependences among scalar variables as well as linking all accesses to each array for dependence testing. A critical contribution of scalar data-flow analysis is recognizing scalars that are *killed*, or redefined, on every iteration of a loop and may be made private, thus eliminating dependences. Constant propagation can locate constant-valued loop bounds, step sizes and subscript expressions. Symbolic analysis locates auxiliary induction variables, loop-invariant expressions and equivalent expressions. It also performs expression simplification on demand.

Interprocedural Data-flow Analysis. One of the distinguishing features of PED's dependence information is the incorporation of an extensive suite of interprocedural analysis techniques that determine the effects of procedure calls on variables. Interprocedural constants are inherited from a procedure's callers and directly incorporated into the intraprocedural constants. *Flow-insensitive side-effect analysis*, including MOD and REF analysis, describes the variables that may be accessed on some control flow path through the procedure [4]. *Flow-sensitive side-effect* analysis, such as KILL analysis, describes accesses that occur on every possible control flow path [7]. *Regular section analysis* is also used to describe more precisely, when possible, the side-effects to portions of arrays [24].

4.2 Evaluation

Table 3 demonstrates the importance of existing analysis and the need for additional analysis for the programs described in Table 1.

Dependence Analysis. The *dependence* entry in Table 3 indicates whether dependence analysis locates parallel loops in each program. For all of the programs, the system is able to automatically detect many parallel loops. Small, inner parallel loops are almost always detected. However, outer loop parallelism is essential to achieving measurable performance improvements for applications programs on many parallel architectures, and it too often goes undetected. We discuss impediments and solutions for parallel loop detection in Section 4.3.

Scalar Kill Analysis. As illustrated by the *scalar kills* entry, almost all of the programs contain a loop

	spec77	neoss	nxsns	dpmin	slab2d	slalom	pueblo3d	arc3d
dependence	U	U	U	U	U	U	U	U
scalar kills		U	U	U	U	U	U	U
sections	U	U	U	U	U			U
array kills	N		N	N	N	N	N	N
reductions		N	N	N		N		N
index arrays				N		N	N	

U: existing analysis was used. *N:* additional analysis was needed.

Table 3: Analysis Used or Needed During Workshop.

that becomes parallelizable following scalar privatization. In the program nxsns, interprocedural scalar KILL analysis reveals a scalar variable is killed in a procedure invoked inside a loop. Experience using PTOOL, PED's predecessor, also suggests interprocedural scalar KILL analysis is useful in eliminating spurious dependences [25].

Interprocedural Side-effect Analysis. The *sections* entry indicates that scalar side-effect analysis or regular section analysis reduces the number of dependences on a loop containing a procedure call in six of the programs. Of the two remaining programs, one does not contain loops with procedure calls and analysis failed on the other. In spec77 and nxsns, interprocedural side-effect analysis reveals that loops containing procedure calls can safely execute in parallel.

4.3 Obstacles to Parallelization

There are several areas where existing analysis in PED is not sufficient to detect parallelism, but the users together with the workshop assistants were able to discover it. In many cases, more precise analysis can detect and eliminate overly conservative dependences. In others, static analysis will probably never be sufficient and user assertions are needed.

Array Kill Analysis. For loops in seven of the programs, array kill analysis would eliminate important dependences, revealing parallelism. In slab2d and arc3d, automatic privatization of one or more killed arrays is sufficient to prove that loops may be safely executed in parallel. Frequently, a temporary array is assigned and used in an inner loop and its value does not carry across iterations of the outer loop. In arc3d, an array is killed inside a procedure invoked in a loop, so interprocedural array kill analysis is required. To perform array privatization in slab2d, kill analysis must be combined with loop transformations. Because the need for array kill analysis has been discussed previously [6, 33], we do not elaborate further here.

Reductions. Five of the programs contain sum reductions which go unrecognized by PED. For example, computing the sum of all the elements of an array. Because addition is associative, the additions do not need to be performed in order and so the loop can be parallelized after restructuring the accumulation of the sum. The need and methods for recognizing reductions are well known and we do not elaborate here. However, transforming reductions in an interactive setting is complicated by the property that efficient execution requires an architecture-specific approach.

Symbolic Expressions. Static analysis cannot derive information about certain symbolic expressions, such as variables read from an input file or index arrays used in subscript expressions. Symbolic terms in subscript expressions are a key limiting factor in precise dependence analysis. One study found that over 50% of the array references in some numerical packages contained at least one unknown symbolic term [20]. The *index arrays* entry in Table 3 demonstrates that three programs contained index arrays in subscript expressions that prevented parallelization.

We are using a three-pronged approach to improving the precision of dependence information in the presence of symbolics: (1) sophisticated symbolic analysis; (2) *partial evaluation*, or compiling the program with all or part of an input data set [18]; and (3) incorporating user assertions to eliminate dependences (described from the user interface perspective in Section 3.3).

The following program fragment from the routine *filter3d* in *arc3d* demonstrates the type of advanced interprocedural symbolic analysis that would improve program parallelization.

```
      DO 15 N = 1, 5
        DO 16 J = 1, JM
          DO 16 K = 2, KM
            WR1(J,K) = Q(JPL,K,L,N)-Q(J,K,L,N)
16      CONTINUE

        DO 76 K = 2, KM
          WR1(JMAX,K) = WR1(JM,K)
76      CONTINUE
        ... = WR1(J,K)
        ...
15    CONTINUE
```

In the initialization routine, the assignment JM = JMAX $-$ 1 occurs, and this relation holds for the rest of the program. Given this symbolic relationship and array kill analysis, the DO 15 loop may be safely parallelized by privatizing WR1 and two other arrays. The ability to detect and propagate this type of relationship can greatly improve the precision of dependence analysis.

In other cases, symbolic values are read, making it virtually impossible for static analysis to determine actual dependences. Consider the following fragment from the program *dpmin*.

```
      DO 300 N = 1, NBA
         I3 = IT(N)
         J3 = JT(N)
         K3 = KT(N)
         ...
         F(I3 + 1) = F(I3 + 1) - DT1
         F(I3 + 2) = F(I3 + 2) - DT2
         F(I3 + 3) = F(I3 + 3) - DT3
         F(J3 + 1) = F(J3 + 1) - DT4
         F(J3 + 2) = F(J3 + 2) - DT5
         F(J3 + 3) = F(J3 + 3) - DT6
         F(K3 + 1) = F(K3 + 1) - DT7
         F(K3 + 2) = F(K3 + 2) - DT8
         F(K3 + 3) = F(K3 + 3) - DT9
  300 CONTINUE
```

The arrays IT(N), JT(N) and KT(N) are read from a file, so the system assumes dependences connect all references to F.

To assist the user in deriving assertions that eliminate spurious dependences, the system may be able to derive *breaking conditions* that eliminate a particular dependence or class of dependences. In the above, a breaking condition for loop-carried dependences between instances of F(I3+1) is that IT(N) is a permutation array (*i.e* all values for I3+1 are unique). While possible, it would take significantly more analysis for the system to derive breaking conditions to eliminate all dependences on F and parallelize the loop. The system must recognize that if IT(N) is a function satisfying the constraint $\text{IT(I)} + 3 \leq \text{IT(I+1)}$ (similarly for JT and KT), $\text{IT(NBA)} + 3 \leq \text{JT(1)}$ and $\text{JT(NBA)} + 3 \leq \text{KT(1)}$, all dependences may be eliminated.

A similar approach is being pursued by Pugh and Wonnacott [32]. They derive relational constraints on variables during dependence testing using a variant of integer programming, and these are presented to the user in their implementation.

5 Program Transformation

5.1 Background

PED supports a large set of transformations proven useful for introducing, discovering, and exploiting parallelism and for enhancing memory hierarchy use [27]. Figure 2 shows a taxonomy of the transformations available in PED. Transformations are applied according to a *power steering* paradigm: the user specifies the transformations to be made, and the system provides advice and carries out the mechanical details. The system advises whether the transformation is *applicable* (is syntactically correct), *safe* (preserves the semantics of the program) and *profitable* (contributes to parallelization). The complexity of many transformations makes correct application difficult and tedious by hand. Thus, power steering provides safe, profitable and correct application of transformations and incremental updates of dependence information to reflect the modified program.

Reordering transformations change the order in which statements are executed, either within or across loop iterations. They expose or enhance loop-level parallelism and improve data locality. *Dependence breaking* transformations eliminate storage-related dependences that inhibit parallelism. They often introduce new storage and convert loop-carried dependences to loop-independent dependences. *Memory optimizing* transformations expose reuse of memory locations in registers or cache.

5.2 Evaluation

Table 4 lists the transformations used for parallelizing each program. The rows describe the existing transformations used and the additional transformations needed.

It is notable that only a few of PED's transformations were used. The most commonly used transformation was scalar expansion, which transforms a scalar into an array to eliminate loop-carried dependences. Loop unrolling was the only other transformation used more than once. For the most part, the transformations in the table are commonly used in vectorization; however, in one example loop interchange of an imperfect loop nest was required.

As compared with the previous section, users were much better at reproducing analysis not provided by the system than at determining which transformations could improve parallelization. The users and their assistants mentioned that selecting among the large number of transformations is too overwhelming. It was not clear to them which transformations to attempt for a given loop nest.

5.3 Obstacles to Parallelization

To assist users in program parallelization, they requested more automated assistance for applying transformations and two additional transformations.

Transformation Guidance. While few transformations were performed on these programs, it was *not* be-

Figure 2: Transformation Taxonomy for PED.

Reordering		
Loop Distribution	Loop Interchange	Loop Fusion
Statement Interchange	Loop Skewing	Loop Reversal
Dependence Breaking		
Privatization	Array Renaming	Loop Peeling
Scalar Expansion	Loop Splitting	Loop Alignment
Memory Optimizing		
Strip Mining	Scalar Replacement	
Loop Unrolling	Unroll and Jam	
Miscellaneous		
Sequential ↔ Parallel	Loop Bounds Adjusting	
Statement Addition	Statement Deletion	

	spec77	neoss	nxsns	dpmin	slab2d	slalom	pueblo3d	arc3d
loop distribution		U						
loop interchange							U	
loop fusion		U						
scalar expansion		U	U	U				
loop unrolling			U			U		
control flow		N	N	N				
interprocedural	N							

U: existing transformation was used. *N:* new transformation was needed.

Table 4: Transformations Used and Needed During the Workshop.

cause opportunities for transformation did not exist. Indeed, a substantial amount of research has demonstrated the value of loop transformations in exposing parallelism. Cursory re-examination of the programs reveals opportunities for many transformations that enable parallelization of outer loops. These opportunities include fusion and interchange in pueblo3d and distribution in dpmin and neoss. However, when the users were confronted with the selection of transformations, they did not know which ones to explore.

Several users want the transformation selection to include only those which are safe and profitable for the currently selected loop. This structure would save them from sifting through the entire list of transformations for each loop. As a simple extension to the current system, it could evaluate the safety of all the transformations for a particular loop on demand and present only the safe ones. However, determining what transformations are profitable is much more difficult. Profitability not only depends on machine specifics, but on subsequent transformations.

According to the users, transformation advice should incorporate the compiler's parallel code generation algorithms for a particular architecture. Ideally, a user would select the architecture and request parallelization at the loop, subroutine or program level. The system would then automatically perform parallelization or describe the impediments to a desired parallelization. Impediments would be presented in a systematic fashion based on the relative importance of a loop or subroutine. The user could evaluate any impediments and correct overly conservative assumptions, thus enabling *semi-automatic* parallelization. Several users stressed the importance of providing consistent analysis and parallelization algorithms between the compiler and interactive tool.

Complex Control Flow. Three programs, neoss, nxsns and dpmin, were written in dialects of Fortran that do not support structured *if* statements and that require *do* loops to execute at least one iteration regardless of loop bounds. Possibly to compensate for constructs lacking in the language, programmers introduced complex control flow involving *goto* statements. Consider the following loop with GOTOs from neoss and the structured equivalent produced by hand during the workshop.

```
      DO 50 K= ...                          original
         <b1>
         IF (DENV(K) - RES(NR+1)) 100, 10, 10
10       CONTINUE
         <b2>
         GOTO 101
100      <b3>
101      <b4>
50    CONTINUE
                              ⇓ structured version
      DO 50 K=...
         <b1>
         IF (DENV(K) .GE. RES(NR+1)) THEN
            <b2>
         ELSE
            <b3>
         ENDIF
            <b4>
50    CONTINUE
```

The *gotos* make it difficult for the users to understand the original loop. Other variations of *if-then-else* constructs formed with *gotos* also appear in these programs. However, users were able to further transform and parallelize a loop of this sort after control flow was simplified by hand.

To assist users in this process, the simplification of complex control flow can be automated by recognizing and substituting structured idioms for unstructured control-flow when appropriate. The need for this transformation is unique to an interactive setting. It is not necessary in completely automatic systems or internally in interactive tools because control dependence suffices to understand control flow regardless of the language constructs.

Interprocedural Transformations. The program spec77 has a number of loops containing procedure calls in the key procedure *gloop*. Interprocedural analysis indicates that the loops may be safely parallelized, but the loops have at most twelve iterations, limiting the number of possible parallel threads. The procedures invoked in these loops however contain outer loops with many more iterations that may also safely execute in parallel. A solution that combines the granularity of the outer loop with the parallelism of the loop in the procedure is to perform loop interchange across the procedure boundary [23]. In some cases, loops in *gloop* contained multiple calls so the loops of the called procedures were first fused before applying interchange.

In order to enable transformations such as loop interchange and loop fusion across procedure boundaries, we must be able to move a loop into or out of a procedure invocation. We call these interprocedural transformations *loop embedding* and *loop extraction*, respectively [23]. Steve Poole brought spec77 to the workshop because he was familiar with this work and wanted to perform these transformations in PED. Embedding and extraction are not currently implemented in PED.

6 Related Work

A few other papers report on the effectiveness of existing automatic parallelizing compilers on large applications [9, 6, 12, 13, 33] and of interactive tools [9]. Two of these suggest compiler-programmer interaction to achieve parallelization [9, 33].

Blume and Eigenmann explore the effectiveness of KAP [29] applied to Perfect benchmark programs on an 8-processor Alliant [6]. Half of the programs demonstrate little or no improvement following parallelization. Using the transformation algorithms in KAP, scalar expansion is the only transformation that consistently improved performance on several codes. The compiler often fails to parallelize important loops, such as loops containing procedure calls, and sometimes parallelizes loops with insufficient granularity. These failures are in part because the compiler does not perform interprocedural analysis.

Eigenmann et al. present novel approaches for improving parallelization in four Perfect programs [12, 13]. These techniques include run-time dependence testing and aggressive use of synchronization to guard critical sections.

Singh and Hennessy examine parallelization of three programs on an 8-processor Alliant [33]. They observe that certain programming styles interfere with compiler analysis. These include linearized arrays and specialized use of the boundary elements in an array. To aid the compiler in selecting appropriate loops to parallelize, they suggest user access to profiling information and assertion facilities that allow specifying ranges of symbolic variables.

Cheng and Pase consider 25 programs running on an 8 processor Cray Y-MP, using Cray fpp, KAP/Cray and Forge to introduce parallelism [9]. Most of the parallel versions demonstrate a speedup of less than 2 over their vector counterparts. When using Forge, the only interactive tool, they offer two suggestions. First, the user should be given insight about what loops to parallelize, either through profiling or performance estimation. Second, they want the system to query for unknown scalar variable values and use these assertions in analysis to eliminate dependences.

Because PED contains some of the features recommended by these studies, our evaluation reveals how they work in practice. For example, most of these studies find interprocedural analysis to be essential, but missing from the compilers under investigation. In PED, interprocedural analysis is found effective, but more advanced analysis such as interprocedural symbolic propagation is also needed.

Our evaluation is also distinguished because it examines the interactive parallelization process with outside users. The existence of an advanced interactive tool allowed us to go beyond the comments provided by the studies of automatic parallelizers to investigate the appropriate level for compiler and tool interaction. For instance, users deleted dependences in PED, as suggested previously [25, 33], but requested higher-level assertions and guidance. We also uncovered the need for new features such as access to compiler transformation algorithms and control flow simplification.

7 Conclusion

In an interactive system, the combination of user expertise with the sophisticated analysis and transformations used by parallelizing compilers requires powerful mechanisms and careful engineering. Through user evaluation of the ParaScope Editor, an interactive parallel programming tool, we have established several essential user requirements. Users prefer that the user interface tie the compiler analysis to the source code and provide facilities such as view filtering of source code and analysis results, navigational assistance, and transformation guidance. To assist users in refining program analysis for use in compilation, a facility that communicates high-level information to the tool in the form of assertions is needed. Advanced analysis, such as interprocedural array section analysis, symbolic analysis and array privatization, can substantially reduce the amount of work the user must perform. By continuing extensive evaluations, improvements and additions, the ParaScope Editor aspires to meet user requirements.

8 Acknowledgements

We would like to thank all of the researchers who participated in this study. We also thank the members of the ParaScope programming environment group, past and present, who participated in the implementation of PED and the infrastructure upon which it is built. We especially appreciate Scott Warren's implementation of the new user interface.

References

[1] F. Allen, M. Burke, P. Charles, R. Cytron, and J. Ferrante. An overview of the PTRAN analysis system for multiprocessing. In *Proceedings of the First International Conference on Supercomputing*. Springer-Verlag, Athens, Greece, June 1987.

[2] J. R. Allen, D. Bäumgartner, K. Kennedy, and A. Porterfield. PTOOL: A semi-automatic parallel programming assistant. In *Proceedings of the 1986 International Conference on Parallel Processing*, St. Charles, IL, August 1986. IEEE Computer Society Press.

[3] V. Balasundaram, K. Kennedy, U. Kremer, K. S. McKinley, and J. Subhlok. The ParaScope Editor: An interactive parallel programming tool. In *Proceedings of Supercomputing '89*, Reno, NV, November 1989.

[4] J. Banning. An efficient way to find the side effects of procedure calls and the aliases of variables. In *Conference Record of the Sixth Annual ACM Symposium on the Principles of Programming Languages*, San Antonio, TX, January 1979.

[5] A.J. Bernstein. Analysis of programs for parallel processing. *IEEE Transactions on Electronic Computers*, 15(5):757–763, October 1966.

[6] W. Blume and R. Eigenmann. Performance analysis of parallelizing compilers on the Perfect Benchmarks programs. *IEEE Transactions on Parallel and Distributed Systems*, 3(6):643–656, November 1992.

[7] D. Callahan. The program summary graph and flow-sensitive interprocedural data flow analysis. In *Proceedings of the SIGPLAN '88 Conference on Program Language Design and Implementation*, Atlanta, GA, June 1988.

[8] S. Carr. *Memory-Hierarchy Management*. PhD thesis, Rice University, September 1992.

[9] D. Cheng and D. Pase. An evaluation of automatic and interactive parallel programming tools. In *Proceedings of Supercomputing '91*, Albuquerque, NM, November 1991.

[10] K. Cooper, M. W. Hall, R. T. Hood, K. Kennedy, K. S. McKinley, J. M. Mellor-Crummey, L. Torczon, and S. K. Warren. The ParaScope parallel programming environment. *Proceedings of the IEEE*, To appear 1993.

[11] K. Cooper, K. Kennedy, L. Torczon, A. Weingarten, and M. Wolcott. Editing and compiling whole programs. In *Proceedings of the Second ACM SIGSOFT/SIGPLAN Software Engineering Symposium on Practical Software Development Environments*, Palo Alto, CA, December 1986.

[12] R. Eigenmann, J. Hoeflinger, G. Jaxon, Z. Li, and D. Padua. Restructuring Fortran programs for Cedar. In *Proceedings of the 1991 International Conference on Parallel Processing*, St. Charles, IL, August 1991.

[13] R. Eigenmann, J. Hoeflinger, Z. Li, and D. Padua. Experience in the automatic parallelization of four Perfect benchmark programs. In U. Banerjee, D. Gelernter, A. Nicolau, and D. Padua, editors, *Languages and Compilers for Parallel Computing, Fourth International Workshop*, Santa Clara, CA, August 1991. Springer-Verlag.

[14] D. C. Engelbart and W. K. English. A research center for augmenting human intellect. In *Proceedings of AFIPS 1968 Fall Joint Computer Conference*, San Francisco, CA, December 1968.

[15] J. Ferrante, K. Ottenstein, and J. Warren. The program dependence graph and its use in optimization. *ACM Transactions on Programming Languages and Systems*, 9(3):319–349, July 1987.

[16] K. Fletcher. Experience with ParaScope at NASA Ames Research Center. Presentation at the ParaScope Editor Workshop, July 1991.

[17] K. Fletcher, K. Kennedy, K. S. McKinley, and S. Warren. The ParaScope Editor: User interface goals. Technical Report TR90-113, Dept. of Computer Science, Rice University, May 1990.

[18] G. Goff. Practical techniques to augment dependence analysis in the presence of symbolic terms. Technical Report TR92-194, Dept. of Computer Science, Rice University, October 1992.

[19] G. Goff, K. Kennedy, and C. Tseng. Practical dependence testing. In *Proceedings of the SIGPLAN '91 Conference on Program Language Design and Implementation*, Toronto, Canada, June 1991.

[20] M. Haghighat and C. Polychronopoulos. Symbolic dependence analysis for high-performance parallelizing compilers. In *Advances in Languages and Compilers for Parallel Computing*, Irvine, CA, August 1990. The MIT Press.

[21] M. W. Hall. *Managing Interprocedural Optimization*. PhD thesis, Rice University, April 1991.

[22] M. W. Hall, S. Hiranandani, K. Kennedy, and C. Tseng. Interprocedural compilation of Fortran D for MIMD distributed-memory machines. In *Proceedings of Supercomputing '92*, Minneapolis, MN, November 1992.

[23] M. W. Hall, K. Kennedy, and K. S. McKinley. Interprocedural transformations for parallel code generation. In *Proceedings of Supercomputing '91*, Albuquerque, NM, November 1991.

[24] P. Havlak and K. Kennedy. An implementation of interprocedural bounded regular section analysis. *IEEE Transactions on Parallel and Distributed Systems*, 2(3):350–360, July 1991.

[25] L. Henderson, R. Hiromoto, O. Lubeck, and M. Simmons. On the use of diagnostic dependency-analysis tools in parallel programming: Experiences using PTOOL. *The Journal of Supercomputing*, 4:83–96, 1990.

[26] K. Kennedy, N. McIntosh, and K. S. McKinley. Static performance estimation in a parallelizing compiler. Technical Report TR91-174, Dept. of Computer Science, Rice University, December 1991.

[27] K. Kennedy, K. S. McKinley, and C. Tseng. Analysis and transformation in the ParaScope Editor. In *Proceedings of the 1991 ACM International Conference on Supercomputing*, Cologne, Germany, June 1991.

[28] K. Kennedy, K. S. McKinley, and C. Tseng. Interactive parallel programming using the ParaScope Editor. *IEEE Transactions on Parallel and Distributed Systems*, 2(3):329–341, July 1991.

[29] Kuck & Associates, Inc. *KAP User's Guide*. Champaign, IL 61820, 1988.

[30] K. S. McKinley. *Automatic and Interactive Parallelization*. PhD thesis, Rice University, April 1992.

[31] Pacific-Sierra Research. *Forge User's Guide, version 7.01*, December 1990.

[32] W. Pugh and D. Wonnacott. Eliminating false data dependences using the omega test. In *Proceedings of the SIGPLAN '92 Conference on Program Language Design and Implementation*, San Francisco, CA, June 1992.

[33] J. Singh and J. Hennessy. An empirical investigation of the effectiveness of and limitations of automatic parallelization. In *Proceedings of the International Symposium on Shared Memory Multiprocessors*, Tokyo, Japan, April 1991.

[34] D. C. Smith, C. Irby, R. Kimball, B. Verplank, and E. Harslem. Designing the Star user interface. *BYTE*, 7(4):242–282, April 1982.

[35] J. Stein. On outer-loop parallelization of existing, real-life Fortran-77 programs. Colloquium at Rice University, July 1991. In collaboration with M. Paul and G.C. Fox.

[36] R. C. Waters. Program editors should not abandon text oriented commands. *ACM SIGPLAN Notices*, 17(7):39–46, July 1982.

[37] N. Yankelovitch, N. Meyrowitz, and A. van Dam. Reading and writing the electronic book. *IEEE Computer*, 18(10):15–29, October 1985.

Perturbation Analysis of High Level Instrumentation for SPMD Programs

Sekhar R. Sarukkai*
Dept. of Computer Science
Indiana University, Bloomington, Indiana

Allen D. Malony†
Dept. of Computer and Information Science
University of Oregon, Eugene, Oregon 97405

Abstract

The process of instrumenting a program to study its behavior can lead to perturbations in the program's execution. These perturbations can become severe for large parallel systems or problem sizes, even when one captures only high level events. In this paper, we address the important issue of eliminating execution perturbations caused by high-level instrumentation of SPMD programs. We will describe perturbation analysis techniques for common computation and communication measurements, and show examples which demonstrate the effectiveness of these techniques in practice.

1 Introduction

Any measurement of a program's execution, no matter how non-intrusive, can perturb how the program behaves (important for debugging) and performs (important for performance evaluation). In contrast to perturbations of correct execution behavior, perturbations of performance behavior, although more tractable in theory, pose difficult problems for performance analysis in practice. For example, programs run on massively parallel systems with detailed performance measurement can have subtle perturbation effects that lead to large performance evaluation errors. In general, a balance exists between measurement detail and measurement perturbations that depends on the requirements of the performance evaluation problem being addressed. When perturbations lead to performance data that is too inaccurate to adequately evaluate a performance issue, measurements must be reduced, but this occurs at the risk of lost performance detail and, again, performance evaluation accuracy. Clearly, understanding perturbation effects of performance measurement is important for determining appropriate levels of instrumentation. However, improving the tradeoff of measurement detail and evaluation accuracy will come only from the incorporation of better perturbation analysis techniques in performance data processing.

The issue of perturbation analysis has been treated extensively by Malony [7, 8, 9]. However, that work dealt exclusively with shared memory programs and assumed the presence of fine-grained, low-level instrumentation. In this paper, we focus on source level instrumentation of programs based on the Single-Program, Multiple-Data (SPMD) execution model. Our aim is to determine the types of perturbations caused by high level instrumentation of SPMD programs and to devise analysis methods for removing perturbation effects.

The assumptions made regarding SPMD instrumentation are few. We assume that the un-instrumented parallel program is sequentially consistent (i.e., satisfies Lamport's sequential consistency criteria [5]). This implies that the instrumented program will be non-interfering and safe [1]. We assume that the instrumentation detects and records events independently in each processor. As such, the instrumentation does not

*Supported by the NSF New Technologies Program under grant NSF ACS 911616 and a contract from IBM. Current address: Recom Technologies, MS 269-3, NASA Ames Research Center, Moffett Field, California 94035.

†Supported in part by a contract from Rome Labs under Air Force contract no. AF 30602-92-C-0135.

4th ACM PPOPP,5/93/CA,USA
© 1993 ACM 0-89791-589-5/93/0005/0044...$1.50

affect the partial order of the original program. However, since the actual execution may have inherently nondeterministic behavior, a single performance measurement reflects only one possible execution scenario.

Section 2 discusses the characteristics of SPMD instrumentation, the effect of instrumentation on program performance, and the requirements for accurate perturbation analysis. Section 3 presents the perturbation analysis of several important instrumentation cases of interest in SPMD computations. In Section 4, we show experimental results that validate the use of perturbation analysis in practice.

2 Instrumentation

The SPMD execution paradigm offers the programmer a high level abstraction of parallel computation. In SPMD programs implemented using message passing, processors perform computations on local data, while executing local copies of the same code. When data from other processors are required, processors perform communication operations to obtain the data. This communication is also used for processor synchronization. Logically, there are no sequential regions in a SPMD program, since the whole program is executed in parallel by all the processors.[1]

From the perspective of the programmer, unless low level instrumentation is provided in the target system, the performance characteristics of a SPMD program execution must be determined through an analysis of high level, source code events. While it is clearly important to know if source code events alone are sufficient for performance evaluation, it is also important that the collected performance data accurately reflect the program's actual execution – perturbation effects introduced by the source instrumentation have to be eliminated or reduced to acceptable levels.

We assume that instrumentation inserted in a SPMD program generates data in the form of events that are stored in a trace file. There are a number of source level events that that might be captured during SPMD program execution. These can be broadly classified as:

- *Processor computation events:* These events occur in each processor and reflect local computation states. The events on a particular processor are dependent only on local computations. However, the timing of the events can be affected by the execution dependencies that exist between processors. The measurement of these events is necessary to capture timing information of local processor computations for reasons of execution profiling.
- *Message communication events*: Messages are used for different purposes such as data exchange, broadcast communication, and synchronization. Measurements of these events are needed to observe the performance of communication operations used to enforce data and control dependencies that exist in the SPMD computation.

The capture of processor computation or message communication events can perturb the execution of a program both directly and indirectly. Any event measurement will introduce a timing perturbation in a region of execution local to when the event occurred. However, perturbations can accumulate and can propagate through an execution, affecting the order and timing of events later captured.

As shown in Figure 1, the process of perturbation analysis takes the measured event trace and produces an event trace that is an approximation of the actual execution. It uses the execution semantics of the operations captured by the high-level events to reduce or eliminate the perturbations introduced in the measurement. The process of eliminating any perturbation effects must ensure that:

- causality is preserved (e.g., a message should not be received before it has been sent);
- partial order of the events is preserved (e.g., a new communication should not be initiated before a previous communication upon which it might depend has been completed); and
- deadlocks are not introduced.

Causality can be preserved by enforcing ordering and timing relationships between message

[1]The SPMD execution model is the basis for several programming languages targeting massively parallel systems [4, 6].

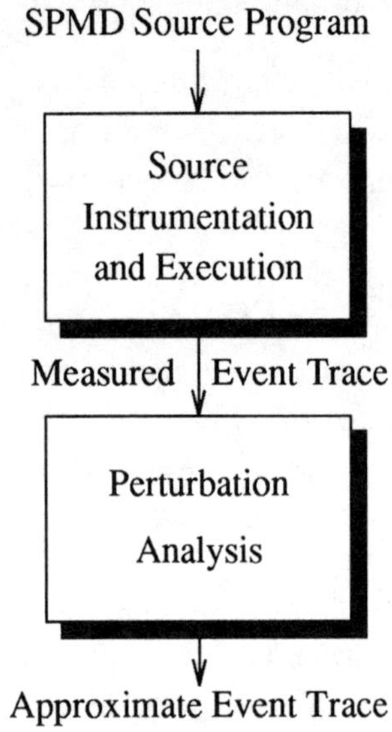

Figure 1: Perturbation Analysis Process

send and receive operations. Partial order is preserved on a single processor by guaranteeing that the time order of any two events is unchanged. By satisfying causality and partial order constraints during perturbation analysis, it follows that if no deadlock occurs in the observed execution of the program, none will be present in the approximated execution.

Our approach to perturbation analysis attempts to resolve the timing of measured events on each processor in sequence. The time of an event is approximated based on the perturbations introduced by events occurring prior to it and the timing relationships of events upon which it depends. It is our contention that perturbation effects of SPMD program instrumentation can be effectively analyzed by considering only the perturbations that result from instrumenting standard computation, communication, and synchronization primitives. Results from test studies of several applications run on different parallel systems show this approach is effective in practice; see Section 4. The following section describes the formal techniques involved in perturbation analysis for different SPMD program operations; a full description of the analysis and experimental results can be found in [10].

3 Perturbation Analysis

For the perturbation analysis discussion that follows, we consider as input a trace file consisting of a time ordered set of events. The time stamp of the ith event stored by a processor p in the trace file is represented by $t_m^p(i)$ ($p \leq P$, where P is the total number of processors that execute the program). The m indicates that the time stamp is a measured value. The perturbation analyzer generates a new trace file with the same number of events, but with recomputed time stamps. The time stamp of the events generated by the analyzer are represented as $t_a^p(i)$; the a subscript indicates that the time stamp is approximated.

If we let T represent the actual time taken to execute a SPMD program without instrumentation, T_m indicates the total time of the measured program and T_a the total approximated time after perturbation analysis. The difference between the measured and actual execution time of the program, $|T_m - T|$, gives an indication of the total amount of measurement error introduced into the program. The difference between the measured and approximated execution times, $|T_m - T_a|$, gives an indication of the amount of perturbation error that can be accounted for in the analysis. The aim of eliminating the perturbations is to ensure that $|T_a - T| \leq |T_m - T|$ and to minimize $\delta = \frac{|T_a - T|}{T}$.

3.1 Programs without Communication

Although somewhat unrealistic, a SPMD program without any inter-processor communication is the easiest to analyze. This case consists of a set of processors executing the same program on some local data, independent of each other. When instrumented, such a program produces a trace file containing processor computation events only. In this case, no communication occurs, so the perturbation analysis is all localized to the processors.

The effect of perturbation on such simple programs is an increase in the execution time on each processor. Although the perturbation effect for each processor is not dependent on the number of events captured in other processors, it is dependent on the number of events captured locally. Thus, one could see large perturbation effects for the SPMD computation in execution time due to the differences in the local perturbations on each processor.

The elimination of perturbation effects is performed incrementally, starting from the first event collected in each processor. Given $t^p_m(i)$, the approximated time stamp of the event, $t^p_a(i)$, is given by: $t^p_a(i) = t^p_m(i) - f(i-1)$ where $f()$ is an *instrumentation overhead* function. Assume that the time taken to store an event can be approximated by a constant α, then $f(i) = \alpha i$.

3.2 Programs with Global Synchronization

SPMD programs typically involve communication between processors for purposes of data exchange and synchronization. Different communication mechanisms require different perturbation analysis. Here we consider global synchronization. Global synchronization can manifest itself in SPMD programs in one of the following ways:

- barrier synchronization operations,
- global broadcast operations, or
- global reduction/combining operations.

Since the perturbation analysis for each case is similar, we concentrate on barrier synchronization.

A barrier is loosely defined as a point where all participating processors synchronize. Here, we treat the case where all P processors perform the barrier synchronization. The high level instrumentation of barrier synchronization involves capturing two events for each processor: barrier *entry* and barrier *exit*. Unless the barrier operation is explicitly coded at the source level, capturing low level communication events may be prohibitive. Thus, the high level semantics of barrier operation are all we can use in perturbation analysis.[2]

[2]We should note that global barriers act as boundaries to perturbation propagation. Because there is a point in time when all the processors are waiting for a single event to occur (i.e., the global synchronization), perturbation analysis errors occurring before that global synchronization point do not carry forward beyond that point in the approximation – the timings of all events following the synchronization point are relative to the time of the synchronization. Once the time of the barrier synchronization event is resolved, all following event times can be approximated.

Perturbation analysis of global synchronization must determine $t^p_a(entry)$ and $t^p_a(exit)$ for each processor p. Whereas $t^p_a(entry)$ can be calculated separately for each processor, $t^p_a(exit)$ depends on the time when the last processor arrives at the barrier as well as the barrier semantics concerning how processors exit. For sake of discussion, we assume that the processors leave the barrier sequentially in the reverse order of their arrival.

Figure 2 shows the measured and approximated execution for a SPMD program involving a barrier synchronization. Notice that, after the removal of the instrumentation overhead, it is possible that a different processor is the last to arrive at the barrier; in the figure, processor $P3$ is the last to arrive at the barrier in the measured execution whereas $P2$ is the last to arrive in the approximated execution. Once the approximated entry event times, $t^p_a(entry)$, are known, the exit event times, $t^p_a(exit)$, can be approximated by $t^p_a(exit) = t^l_a(entry) + (P - i + 1) * \beta$, where l is the last processor to enter the barrier (and the first processor to exit the barrier), processor p is the ith processor to enter the barrier, and β is the synchronization overhead per processor. Now all we have to do is approximate β. If F is the first processor to exit the barrier synchronization (in the measured execution) and L the last processor to exit the barrier synchronization (in the measured execution), β can be approximated from the measured data as $\beta = \frac{(t^L_m(exit) - t^F_m(exit))}{(P-1)}$.

In the case of logarithmic or sequentially scheduled barriers, the perturbation analysis is simpler because the order in which the processors exit from the synchronization is fixed. The analysis of these barrier cases and the cases of global communication operations (e.g., broadcast) and global reduction/combining operations can be found in [10].

3.3 Programs with Processor-pair Synchronization

Inter-processor communication in SPMD programs is most commonly performed by one processor writing data to another processor which reads the data. The read-write operations can be *blocking* or *non-blocking*. The most commonly used form of communication is blocking read-write. Invoking a blocking read operation causes

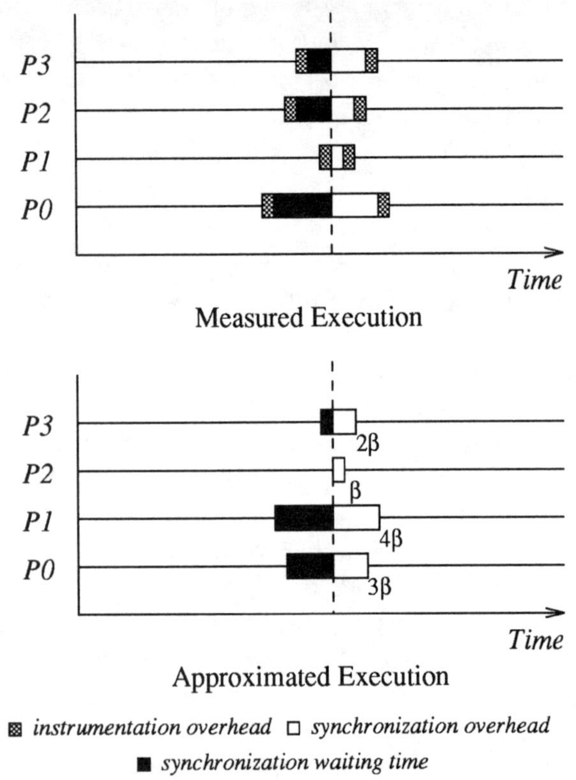

Figure 2: Perturbation analysis of barrier synchronization

the calling processor to block until the data has been received and copied into the program address space. Two mechanisms may be used for blocking writes: asynchronous and synchronous. Invoking a blocking write using some compilers, such as Fortran D [4], causes the calling process to block until the data has been copied out of the program address space into the system address space. However, this does not mean that the process must wait for the message to be actually received by another processor (i.e., the write blocks on buffer copy but is asynchronous to the receive). In other systems, blocked communications are implemented by ensuring that both the receiving and the sending processors have executed their respective communication calls before actually initiating the message transfer (i.e., blocking synchronous write).

Non-blocking messaging, supported in machines such as the iPSC/860, allow computation and message copying to be performed in parallel. The time to copy data into a system buffer is the amount of time that can be saved using non-blocking instead of blocking writes. However, in some cases, message startup time for non-blocking messages is higher than for blocking communication; hence, it is used selectively. In the blocking and non-blocking case, the high-level events captured in the SPMD program are assumed to be the begin and end of each of the communications, read or write.

The effects of perturbations in processor-pair synchronizations are more complex than in the global synchronization cases. Unlike the global synchronization cases, the approximated events must be resolved in sequence while carefully maintaining causality and partial order. Blocked synchronous communication is similar to a rendezvous between two processors followed by a message communication. The perturbation analysis for this case can be derived from that for global broadcasts where the number of processors is restricted to two. The non-blocked read-write case does not pose any problems for analysis per se, but it does includes a *busy wait* component, normally used in association with this call, that can lead to non-deterministic behavior. Although blocked asynchronous communications is more restrictive than the pure non-blocked case (since the read operation waits explicitly for the message), the perturbation analysis still must estimate message transfer times using communication timing models to improve perturbation resolution accuracy. We analyze this situation in detail below.

It is important to note that in some cases the processor that transmits the data may not be known to the receiving processor (e.g., when the receiving processor performs a "blind" receive). In such cases, the perturbation analyzer will have to determine which sending processor's data was actually read from the receiving processor's buffer. Unfortunately, it may be impossible to accurately determine this information without detailed knowledge of machine execution or access to lower level events. Instead, the perturbation analysis must assume the order in which the messages are read from the I/O buffer.

Perturbation analysis of blocked asynchronous read-write communications is complicated by the fact that the times the receiver and sender perform the read and write operations, respectively, can be reversed from the measured to the approximated execution. Consider the situation in Fig-

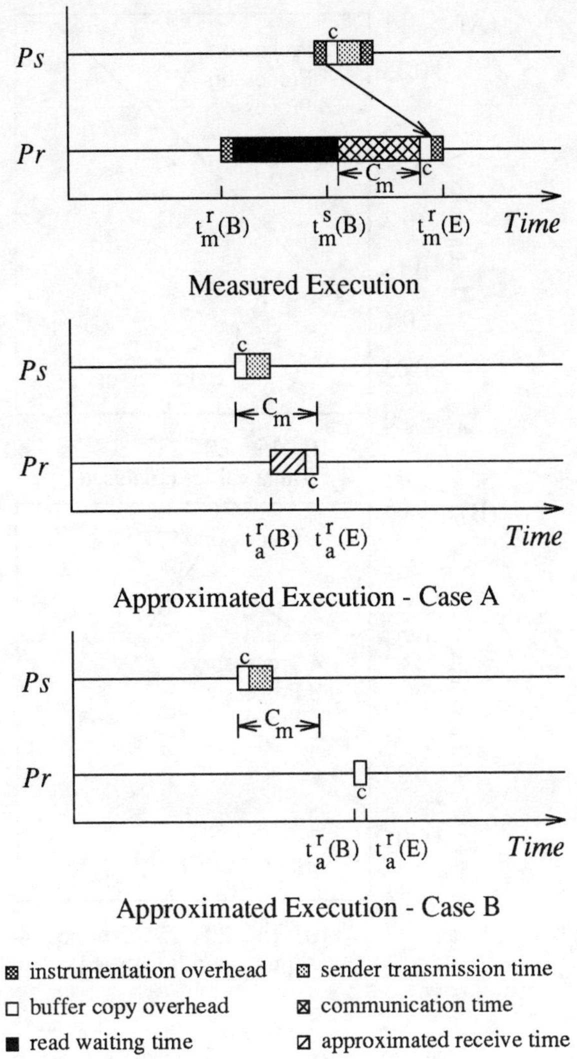

Figure 3: Perturbation analysis of blocked asynchronous communication – Scenario 1

ure 3. Here, processor Ps sends a message to processor Pr. In the measured execution, $P2$ arrives at the read earlier than the write and has to wait. Once Ps starts the write (at time $t^s_m(B)$), it begins sending the data to Pr which receives all the data by time $t^r(E)$; here, r refers to the receiver, s refers to the sender, B is the beginning event (send or receive), and E is the endinging event (send or receive). The difference in time between the initiation of the write and the completion of the read is the time taken to actually pass the data: communication time, C_m, plus the time to copy the data to and from system buffers, c. This time should be preserved in the approximated execution.

Now, let us look at the approximated execution. Suppose that perturbation analysis produces an approximation of the beginning read and write events such that $t^s_a(B) < t^r_a(B)$. There are two cases to consider. In Case A, the receiving processor performs the read after the sending processor performs the write, but before the communication has ended. In this case, the completion of the read operation will depend on when the write was initiated. The time of completion of the read is the sum of the approximated time of initiation of the send, $t^s_a(B)$, and the measured time for communicating the data, C_m, and buffer copy time, c, in the receiving processor. Case B illustrates the situation where the approximated time the read begins occurs after the communication finishes. Here, the time of completion of the read is the approximated time for read begin plus the buffer copy time.

In Figure 4, we see another scenario where, in the measured execution, the read operation is initiated after the write operation has completed. To apply the same perturbation analysis as above, the communication time must be determined. However, in this case, communication time cannot be exactly determined from source level instrumentation alone, because there is no event indicating when Pr received the data – only when the read operation completed. Rather, an estimation of the communication time must be used.

Figure 4 illustrates one of two situations that can arise in the approximated execution. Here, we see Pr beginning a read operation after the entire message has been transmitted; note, $t^r_a(B)$ does not depend on $t^s_a(E)$. However, how is $t^r_a(E)$ calculated? Since the time needed to transmit the data (represented by C_m) cannot actually be determined only from source level events, we have to approximate the communication time in one of two ways: 1) based on the length of the message in bytes n and the network bandwidth, or 2) based on lower and upper bound analysis. If the rate of transfer of a byte is γ, the start up time is S, and the per-hop delay is H, then the approximated communication time, C_a, can be estimated by: $C_a = S + n \times \gamma + h \times H$, where h is the number of hops.[3] The approximated time of the comple-

[3]The constant values can be determined by using a

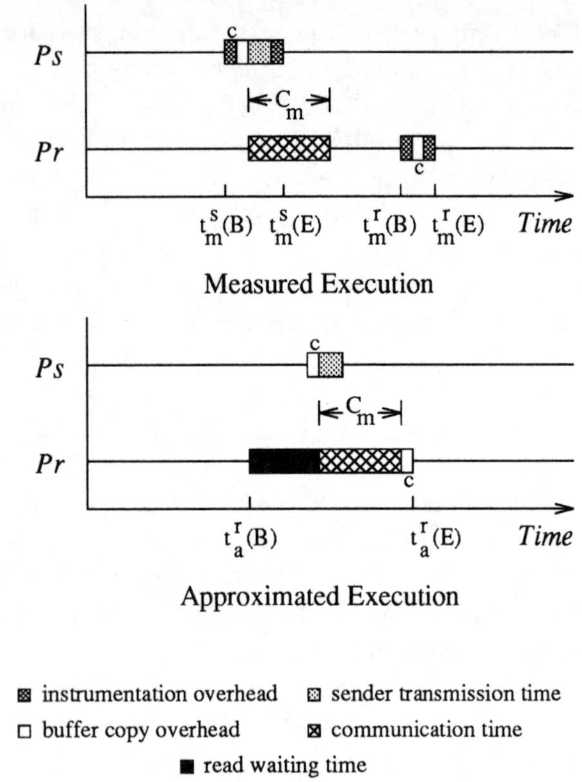

Figure 4: Perturbation analysis of blocked asynchronous communication – Scenario 2

tion of the read operation can then be expressed as:

$$t_a^r(E) = MAX\left\{ \begin{array}{l} t_a^s(B) + C_a + 2 \times c \\ t_a^r(B)) + c \end{array} \right.$$

Alternatively, we can use lower and upper bound values of the communication time to calculate $t_a^r(E)$. The lower bound assumes that the communication is infinitely fast (i.e., $C_a^l = 0$). The upper bound is assumes that the measured time between the write begin and the read end is the communication time (i.e., $C_a = C_m' = t_m^r(E) - t_m^s(B)$). The actual communication time will be between these two bounds.

linear-least square fit by experimenting with a number of different message sizes and processors. In [3], Dunigan estimates the constant values for messages > 100 bytes, for the iPSC/860 cube to be: $S = 136\mu$secs, $\gamma = 0.4\mu$secs and $H = 33\mu$secs.

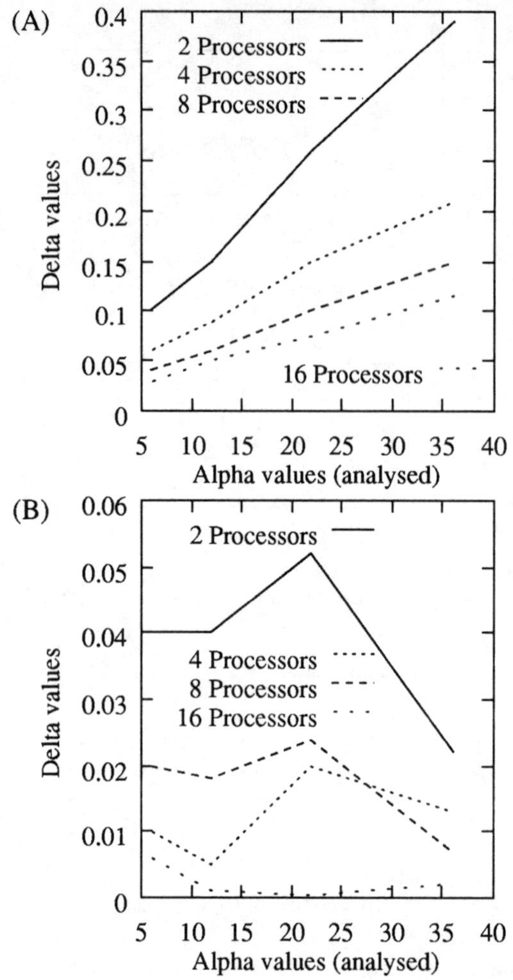

Figure 5: Perturbation analysis results from barrier synchronization experiments. (A): Measured versus Actual. (B): Approximated versus Actual.

4 Experimental Results

In this section, we present some experimental results to determine the efficacy of the perturbation analysis approach. All of the experiments were performed on an Intel iPSC/860 machine. Each experiment generated a trace file that was passed through a perturbation analyzer, producing a new trace file with approximated event orders and time stamps.

4.1 Barrier Synchronization

Our first experiment considers a program with global barriers. We use a simple test program that performs some local computation in each iteration of a loop and then synchronizes all the processors at the end of each iteration. A sequence of barrier executions result. The begin and end of each barrier is instrumented. We want to investigate the effect of the instrumentation overhead, α, on perturbation analysis. As α increases, the amount of intrusion introduced in the observed program execution also increases. Graph (A) in Figure 5 shows the difference in total execution time between the program's measured execution and its uninstrumented execution, δ_m, as a percentage of the uninstrumented time, for different number of processors and α values. The number of processors varies between 2 and 16, while α varies between 6 and 36 time units. The graph shows that α and δ_m are positively correlated, as expected. However, notice that the δ_m value changes are more significant for a smaller number of processors. This is due to the fact that the amount of time taken to execute the program increases as the number of processors increase (with the same number of events stored per processor), due to increase in synchronization time. This results in a reduction in percentage time spent in instrumentation overheads with increasing number of processors. For a program that scales well, however, we would tend to see the exact opposite effect, because the time to execute the program decreases with increase in number of processors, while the instrumentation time would remain constant.

Using perturbation analysis for barrier synchronization, we can determine δ_a values from the approximated execution derived from the measured trace. Graph (B) in Figure 5 we see that perturbation analysis can determine a total program execution time that is within 5 percent of the actual execution of the program, independent of α value and number of processors used.

4.2 Ocean Code

In general, measurement of an application program will involve capturing events from several different types of communication operations. For simplicity, the next experiment included events from blocked non-synchronous read-write communication only. We instrumented a parallel ocean circulation code [2] to capture communication between processors when transpose operations were performed on various matrices. In the code, each matrix is divided into slabs of columns. Each slab is divided into P blocks (for P processors), with the pth block communicated to processor p using a blocked non-synchronous read-write mechanism. We executed this program under two different scenarios: 1) the number of computation events stored by each processor decreases as the number of processors is increase, and 2) the number of computation events stored per processor is constant.

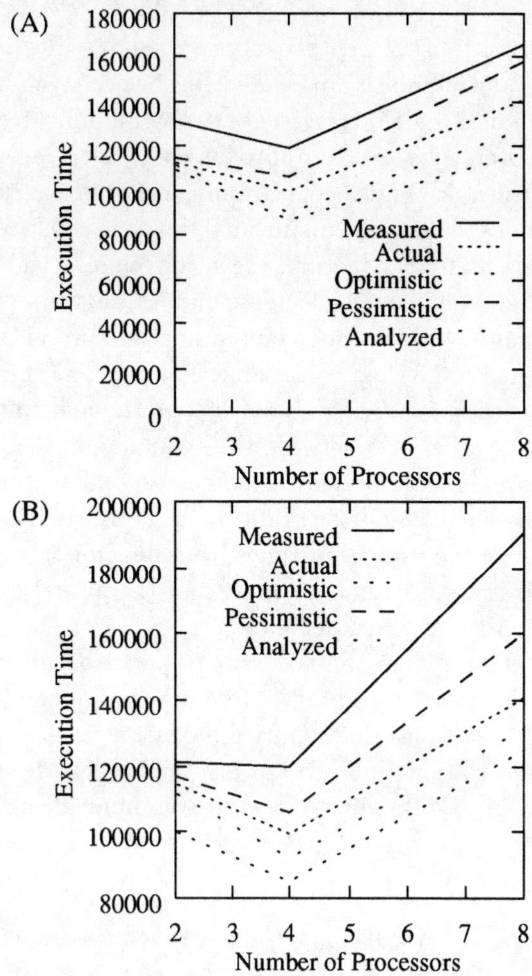

Figure 6: (A): Decreasing events per processor. (B): Equal events stored per processor.

Each case was analyzed using certain assumptions about the program execution. The cases we considered were:

- optimistic analysis
- pessimistic analysis

- analysis based on a communication model

Optimistic analysis corresponds to the lower bound analysis presented in Section 3.3 (i.e., we assume that messages are communicated infinitely fast in the approximated execution). As shown in Figure 6 (Graph (A)), the execution times from optimistic analysis are consistently less than the actual execution times. This is the expected result. Pessimistics analysis corresponds to the upper bound analysis presented in Section 3.3 (i.e., we assume that message communication times can always be determined from the time difference between the beginning of the write and the completion of the corresponding read in the measured execution). In Figure 6 (Graph (A)), the execution times from pessimistic analysis are consistently larger than the actual execution times, as expected.

To improve the accuracy of perturbation analysis, we must apply a communication model in the analysis that approximates the actual communication time. Following the model presented in [3], we assume that the communication time for a message of size n that traverses h hops is given by:

$$C_a = \begin{cases} 76 + n \times 0.4 + h \times 11 & n < 100 \\ 136 + n \times 0.4 + h \times 33 & n \geq 100 \end{cases}$$

Using this expression in the analysis results in an approximated execution more closely reflecting the actual execution for the different numbers of processors tested; see Figure 6 (Graph (A)). The fact that the analysis results in execution times that are lower than the actual execution times might be explained by the choice of constant factors in the model or by other errors in the perturbation analysis.

If the number of computation events stored is proportional only to the problem size, the number of computation events per processor reduces as the number of processors are increased, reducing per processor perturbation in turn. However, if the number of computation events collected per processor is constant, the total number of events collected increases in proportion to the number of processors. As shown in Figure 6 (Graph (B)), as the number of processors increase, the deviation between the observed and actual execution also increases. This implies that the execution time is not influenced only by the events stored in each processor independently. As in the analysis producing Graph A, we get lower and upper bound approximations on the actual execution time in Graph B using optimistic and pessimistic perturbation analysis. Similarly, the analysis based on modeled communication falls between the two bounds and consistently tracks the actual execution time of the program.

Now consider the same program but with all the receives replaced by a "blind" receive (i.e., the receiving processor can read any data that is present in its input buffer, without knowledge of the message's sending processor). Assume also that the events do not store information about the transmitting processor. In such a case, the analysis for the receiving processor will not be able to accurately match the processor whose value has been read from the receiving buffer. Rather, assumptions must be made in the perturbation analysis about the order in which the blind receives are satisfied. Possible strategies for perturbation analysis to follow include:

- Preserve communication order: The order of sends and receives in each processor is assumed to remain the same from the measured to the approximated execution. This is clearly a bad assumption for unbalanced instrumentation, since some processors may incur more perturbations than others, severely altering communication order in the measured execution.
- Last In First Out (*LIFO*): All sends in the approximated execution are stored in a stack. Each time the receiving processor performs a receive, it reads the last message written to its buffer (i.e., the most recently received message). Typically, this is not a good choice, since messages are most often written to a receiving queue.
- First In First Out (*FIFO*): All sends in the approximated execution are stored in a queue. The receiving processor reads data from its message queue, the next message read being the oldest one in the queue.

Executing the program with instrumentation that varies with the number of processors, we observed a 20% slowdown in actual execution time for 4 to 16 processors; see Figure 7. Using a

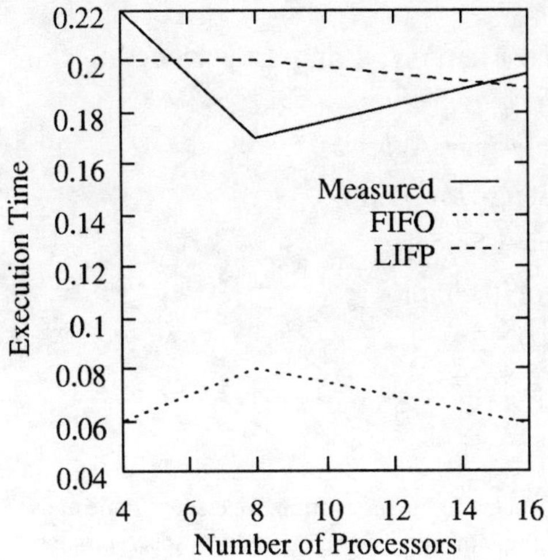

Figure 7: Perturbation analysis with communication order approximations

LIFO strategy in perturbation analysis, we notice that the error is not reduced. However, as expected, the *FIFO* strategy performs better than the *LIFO* strategy, significantly reducing the error in perturbation analysis.

The results of this experiment demonstrate that, even with simple assumptions regarding the execution characteristics at lower levels, the perturbation analysis can conservatively reduce perturbations using only high-level events.

5 Conclusion

Current and future performance analysis of SPMD programs requires the runtime measurement of program execution. Measurement issues concern the level of program instrumentation and the probe effect. In this paper, we have concentrated on high level source instrumentation of SPMD programs and have presented a practical approach to the systematic elimination of perturbation effects introduced by this instrumentation. The perturbation analysis techniques presented provide a means of generating a new set of events from a measured trace which more closely reflect the actual execution of the program. With the use of a few examples, we have shown that these techniques do help to reduce perturbation effects. Equally important, however, is the fact that the approach is based on high-level events.

References

[1] P. Bates and J. Wileden, "High-Level Debugging of Distributed Systems: The Behavioral Abstraction Approach," *Journal of Systems and Software*, April 1983.

[2] Z. Christidis, "Parallel Calculations on the Wind-Driven Oceanic Circulation Using Fourier Pseudospectral Methods," *Proceedings of Third Interrnational Conference on Supercomputing (ICS88)*, Boston, May 1988.

[3] T. Dunigan, "Performance of the Intel iPSC/860 and Ncube 6400 Hypercubes," *Technical Report ORNL/TM 11491*, Oak Ridge National Laboratory, 1991.

[4] G. Fox et al., "Fortran D Language Specification," *Technical Report 90-141*, Rice University, Dept. of Computer Science, 1990.

[5] L. Lamport, "How to make a Multiprocessor Computer that Correctly Executes Multiprocess Programs," *IEEE Transactions on Computers 28,9*, September 1979.

[6] J. Lee and D. Gannon, "Object Oriented Parallel Programming: Experiments and Results," *Supercomputing '91*, Albuquerque, pp. 273–282, November 1991.

[7] A. Malony, "Event Based Performance Perturbation: A Case Study," *Third ACM SIGPLAN Symp. on Principles and Practice of Parallel Programming*, pp. 201–212, Apr. 1991.

[8] A. Malony and D. Reed, "Models for Performance Perturbation Analysis," *Proceedings of the ACM/ONR Workshop on Parallel and Distributed Debugging*, Santa Cruz, May 1991.

[9] A. Malony and D. Reed, "Performance Measurement Intrusion and Perturbation Analysis," *IEEE Transactions on Parallel and Distributed Systems*, Vol.3, 4, July 1992.

[10] S. Sarukkai, "Performance Debugging Environments for Parallel Programs," *PhD Thesis*, Indiana University, December 1992.

Integrating Message-Passing and Shared-Memory: Early Experience

David Kranz, Kirk Johnson, Anant Agarwal,
John Kubiatowicz, and Beng-Hong Lim
Laboratory for Computer Science
Massachusetts Institute of Technology
Cambridge, MA 02139

Abstract

This paper discusses some of the issues involved in implementing a shared-address space programming model on large-scale, distributed-memory multiprocessors. While such a programming model can be implemented on both shared-memory and message-passing architectures, we argue that the transparent, coherent caching of global data provided by many shared-memory architectures is of crucial importance. Because message-passing mechanisms are much more efficient than shared-memory loads and stores for certain types of interprocessor communication and synchronization operations, however, we argue for building multiprocessors that efficiently support both shared-memory and message-passing mechanisms. We describe an architecture, Alewife, that integrates support for shared-memory and message-passing through a simple interface; we expect the compiler and runtime system to cooperate in using appropriate hardware mechanisms that are most efficient for specific operations. We report on both integrated and exclusively shared-memory implementations of our runtime system and two applications. The integrated runtime system drastically cuts down the cost of communication incurred by the scheduling, load balancing, and certain synchronization operations. We also present preliminary performance results comparing the two systems.

1 Introduction

Researchers in parallel computing generally agree that it is important to support a *shared-address space* or *shared-memory* programming model—programmers should not bear the responsibility for orchestrating all interprocessor communication through explicit messages. Implementations of this programming model can be divided into two broad areas depending on the target architecture. With message-passing architectures, the shared-address space is typically synthesized by low-level system software, while traditional shared-memory architectures offload this functionality into specialized hardware.

4th ACM PPOPP,5/93/CA,USA
© 1993 ACM 0-89791-589-5/93/0005/0054...$1.50

In the following section, we discuss some of the issues involved in implementing a shared-address space programming model on large-scale, distributed-memory multiprocessors. We provide a brief overview and comparison of conventional implementation strategies for message-passing and shared-memory architectures. We argue that the transparent, coherent caching of global data provided by many shared-memory architectures is of fundamental importance, because it affords low-overhead, fine-grained data sharing. We point out, however, that some types of communication are handled less efficiently via shared-memory then they might be via message-passing. Building upon this, we suggest that it is reasonable to expect that future large-scale multiprocessors will be built upon what are essentially message-passing communication substrates. In turn, this suggests that multiprocessor architectures might be designed such that processors are able to communicate with one another via either shared-memory or message-passing interfaces, using whichever is likely to be most efficient for the communication in question.

In fact, the MIT Alewife machine [1] does exactly that—interprocessor communication can be effected either through a sequentially-consistent shared-memory interface or by way of a messaging mechanism as efficient as those found in many present day message-passing architectures. The bulk of this paper relates early experience we've had integrating shared-memory and message-passing in the Alewife machine. Section 2 overviews implementation schemes for shared-memory. Section 3 describes the basic Alewife architecture, paying special attention to the integration of the message-passing and shared-memory interfaces. Section 4 provides results comparing purely shared-memory and message-passing implementations of several components of the Alewife runtime system and two applications. We show that a hybrid thread scheduler utilizing both shared-memory and message-based communication performs up to a factor of two better than an implementation using only shared-memory for communication. Section 5 discusses related work. Finally, Section 6 summarizes the major points of the paper and outlines directions for future research.

1.1 Contributions of this Paper

In this paper, we argue for building multiprocessors that efficiently support both shared-memory and message-passing mechanisms for interprocessor communication. We argue that efficient support for fine-grained data sharing is fundamental, pointing out that traditional message-passing architectures are unable to provide such support, especially for applications with irregular and dynamic communication behavior. Similarly, we point out that while shared-memory hardware can support such communication, it is not a panacea either—we identify several other communication styles which are handled less efficiently by shared-memory than by message-passing architectures. Finally, we (i) describe how shared-memory and message-passing communication is integrated in the Alewife hardware and software systems; (ii) present some preliminary performance data obtained with a simulator of Alewife comparing the performance of software systems using both message-passing and shared-memory against implementations using exclusively shared-memory; and (iii) provide analysis and early conclusions based upon the performance data.

2 Implementing a Shared-Address Space

Implementations of a shared-address programming model can be divided into two broad areas depending on the underlying system architecture. On message-passing architectures, a shared-address space is typically synthesized through some combination of compilers and low-level system software. In traditional shared-memory architectures, this shared-address space functionality is provided by specialized hardware. This section gives a brief comparison of these implementation schemes and their impact on application performance. We conclude that the efficient fine-grained data sharing afforded by hardware implementations is of fundamental importance for some applications, but also point out that some types of communication are handled less efficiently via shared-memory hardware then they could be via explicit message-passing. In either case, we assume that the physical memory is distributed across the processors.

2.1 Anatomy of a Memory Reference

When executing a multiprocessor application written assuming a shared-address space programming model, the actions indicated by the pseudocode in Figure 1 must be taken for *every* shared-address space reference. The pseudocode assumes that locally cached copies of locations can exist. (If shared-data caching is not supported, the first test is eliminated.) The most important parts of the code in Figure 1 are the two "local/remote" checks.

The local/remote check is the essence of the distinction between shared-memory and message-passing architectures. In the former, the instruction to reference memory is the same whether the object referenced happens to be in local or remote memory; the local/remote checks are facilitated by hardware support to determine whether a location has been cached (cache tags and comparison logic) or, if not, whether it resides in local or remote memory (local/remote address resolution logic). If the data is remote and not cached, a message will be sent to the remote node to access the data. Although the first test is unnecessary if local caching is disallowed,

```
shared-address-space-reference(location)
    if currently-cached?(location) then
        // satisfy request from cache
        load-from-cache(location)
    elsif is-local-address?(location) then
        // satisfy request from local memory
        load-from-local-memory(location)
    else
        // must load from remote memory; send remote
        // read request message and invoke any actions
        // required to maintain cache coherency
        load-from-remote-memory(location)
```

Figure 1: Anatomy of a shared-address space reference.

the second test is still required to implement a shared-address space programming model. Because shared-memory systems provide hardware support for detecting non-local requests and sending a message to fetch the data from the location, a single instruction can be used to access *any* shared-address space location, regardless of whether it is already cached, resident in local memory, or resident in remote memory.

Message-passing architectures, on the other hand, do not provide hardware support for these local/remote checks. Hence, they cannot use a single instruction to access locations in the shared-address space. Rather, they must implement the pseudocode of Figure 1 entirely in software.

The actions specified in Figure 1 may be performed by the programmer, compiler, runtime system, or hardware. For simplicity, assume that there are two types of applications: static and dynamic. In static applications, the control flow of the program is essentially independent of the values of the data being manipulated. Many scientific programs fit into this category. In dynamic applications, on the other hand, control flow is strongly dependent on the data being manipulated. Most real programs will lie somewhere between these two extremes, having some parts that are dynamic and others that are static. Data sharing in programs can also be fine- or coarse-grained.

Through a great deal of hard work, a programmer can often eliminate the overhead incurred by local/remote checks shown in Figure 1 by sending explicit messages. The fixed costs of such operations are typically high enough, however, that for efficient execution, the messages must be made fairly large. The result is that the granularity at which data sharing can be exploited efficiently is quite coarse. For static programs with sufficiently large-grained data sharing, these explicit messages are like assembly language: if done well, they always provide the best performance. However, as with assembly language, it is not at all clear that most programmers are better off if forced to orchestrate all communication through explicit messages. For static applications which share data at too fine a grain, even if overhead related to local/remote checks can be eliminated, performance suffers because messages typically aren't large enough to amortize any fixed overheads inherent in message-based communication. It is worth noting, however, that for architectures like iWarp [4] which in effect support extremely low overhead "messaging" for static communication patterns, this is not a problem.

Optimizations similar to those a programmer might use to eliminate the overhead of local/remote checks can be applied by a compiler. There has been a great deal of work in this area for scientific programs written in various dialects of FORTRAN and targeted at message-passing machines [5, 11, 14, 21, 24]. Of course, the constraints are the same as when the optimizations are programmer applied: applications must be primarily static and only coarse-grained data sharing can be exploited efficiently.

For dynamic applications, the compiler can't help much. It is usually not possible to know *a priori* (at compile time) whether or not a particular reference will be to local or remote memory. In such a case, the only way to achieve a shared-address space paradigm on message-passing architectures is essentially by executing something like the code in Figure 1 for every shared-address space reference in an application. This is typically done by having a low-level software layer that synthesizes a global address space, possibly also maintaining a cache of some sort. This software layer adds significant overhead to every shared-address space reference, *even when no communication is necessary*. Herein lies the primary advantage of shared-memory architectures: unlike shared-address space implementations on message-passing architectures, a shared-memory architecture will perform well on dynamic programs that re-use data because all data is automatically cached. If the data is not in the cache, but is in local memory, it will be automatically fetched into the cache. To get good performance on a message-passing architecture, the programmer or compiler must handle caching explicitly in order to generate the proper code, *i.e.* the program must be static. It is for these reasons that we believe that some hardware support for shared-memory programs is important; the fundamental hardware mechanism is coherent caching of global addresses.

Note that from this perspective, systems like [22] and Active Messages [23] provide just an efficient messaging interface—an implementation of a shared-address space programming model on top of such systems will face the same problems as those described above for implementations on message-passing architectures.

2.2 Defects of Shared-memory

The previous section discussed the aspects of application behavior that benefit from hardware support for shared-memory: dynamic memory reference behavior and fine-grain data sharing. The support for these behaviors have a cost, however, when the data sharing is coarse-grained or something is known statically about how shared data will be accessed. We enumerate below three scenarios in which we expect shared-memory to be less effective than message based communication:

Coarse granularity When a large chunk of data is to be shared, the cost of transferring the data from one processor to another must be incurred. The most efficient mechanism is a block transfer where all of the data is sent in a single message. If the copy is done with loads and stores of shared-memory, more network and memory bandwidth is required because of the fixed overhead associated with each shared-memory transaction. Section 4 contains several examples and suggests why it might be better sometimes to use shared-memory for copying in spite of these costs.

Known communication patterns Coherent caches on a multiprocessor work well when data is either read-only or is accessed many times on a single processor before being accessed by other processors. Frequent writes on different processors can cause poor performance because they make caching ineffective and lead to additional overhead due to invalidations or updates that must be sent over the network. Furthermore, in many cache coherence protocols, in order to acquire a cache line that is dirty in another processor's cache, that data must be communicated through a home or intermediate node instead of being passed directly to the requester. This is less efficient than communicating via direct point-to-point messages, as is possible when communication patterns are well known.

Combining Synchronization with Data Transfer A purely shared-memory implementation typically generates separate messages for communicating synchronization events and for transferring any associated data. Such transfers often occur during producer-consumer communication. While the latency associated with data transfer can often be tolerated through mechanisms like weak ordering and prefetching, the latency associated with the synchronization signal itself is hard to overlap. The central problem in overlapping the latency of synchronization signals lies in the inability of the consumer to predict exactly when to request a synchronization object; premature prefetching of the synchronization object can lead to even worse performance. A message from the producer to the consumer bundling both synchronization and data and informing the consumer of the availability of data is the natural mechanism in such situations. Section 4.3 provides an example of this.

We argue that to get good performance with a tractable programming model on a wide variety of applications, an architecture must integrate hardware support for both shared-memory *and* message-passing. The software system and/or programmer can then choose the appropriate mechanism based on cost. Such an architecture has been designed at MIT. The next section describes how shared-memory and message-passing are integrated in the Alewife machine. We then investigate the extent to which we can use Alewife's message-passing functionality to address the defects of shared-memory described above.

3 Architectural Interfaces for Messages

Most distributed shared-memory machines are built on top of an underlying message-passing substrate [1, 9, 13]. Therefore any additional cost to support both message-passing in addition to shared-memory must only be paid at the processor-network interface. In

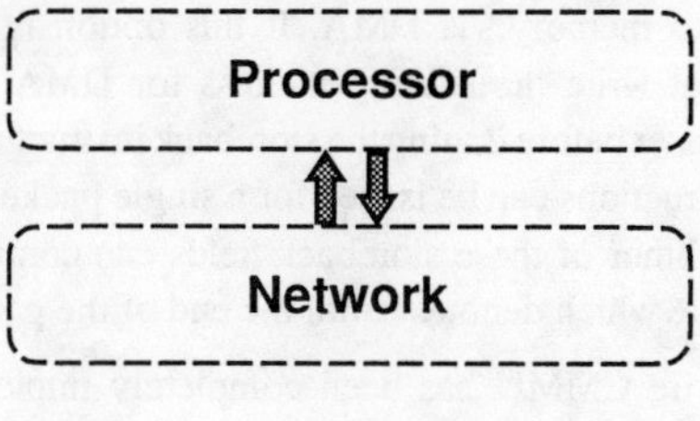

Figure 2: A message-passing interface.

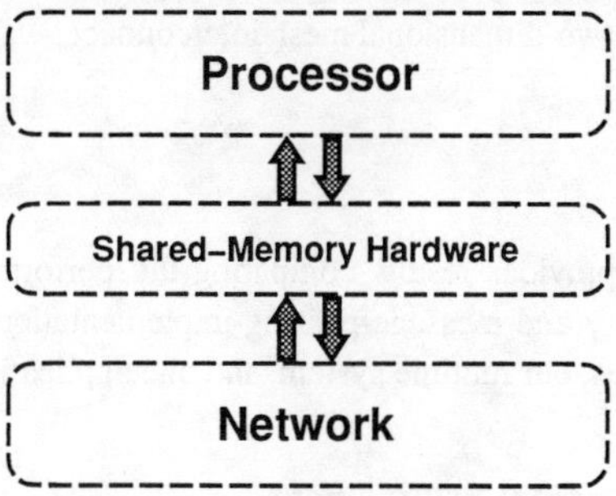

Figure 3: A shared-memory interface.

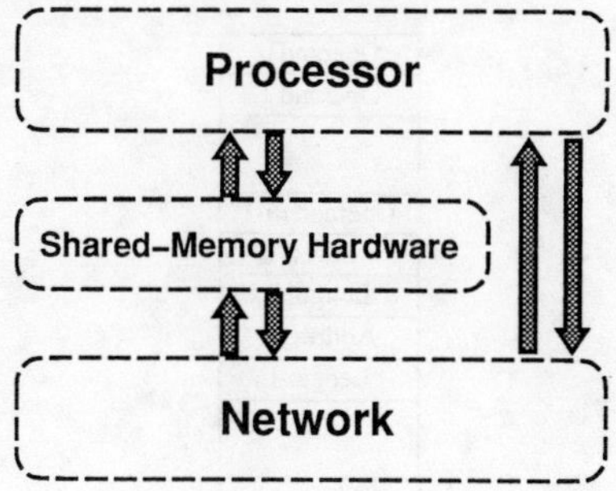

Figure 4: Alewife's integrated interface.

this section, we describe the manner in which Alewife integrates shared-memory and message-passing communication facilities; we provide this detail in part to demonstrate that the complexity of integrating both message-passing and shared-memory is not unreasonable. See [12] for additional details.

Figures 2 and 3 show typical interfaces provided by message-passing multicomputers and shared-memory machines, respectively. In the message-passing version, the processor has direct access to the network and can send (or receive) packets directly into (or from) the network. Messages from the network are placed into queues accessible by the processor; the contents of these queues can then be accessed via conventional loads and stores or register ops, depending on whether the queues are memory- or register-mapped.

Shared-memory interfaces, on the other hand, provide a hardware layer between the network and the processor. This layer typically translates certain loads and stores into messages to other nodes; it models the shared-memory programming paradigm by abstracting away the communication layer. The presence of this layer prevents the processor from directly accessing the network.

Recognizing that shared-memory machines are built on top of a message-passing substrate, Alewife integrates direct network access with the shared-memory framework as depicted in Figure 4. In a sense, the machine allows controlled *breaking of the shared-memory abstraction* by the programmer, runtime system, or compiler when doing so can yield higher performance. In fact, Alewife's coherence protocol, LimitLESS directories [6], relies on the processor's ability to directly send and receive coherence packets into the network.

With Alewife's integrated interface, a message can be sent with just a few user-level instructions. A processor receiving such a message will trap and respond either by rapidly executing a message handler or queuing the message for later consideration when an appropriate message handler gets scheduled. Scheduling and queuing decisions are made entirely in software.

The Alewife hardware provides the following high-level interface for integrating messages and coherent shared-memory to the software system. The runtime system provides other higher-level abstractions built upon this interface (*e.g.* remote thread invocation and barrier synchronization) to compiler writers and application programmers.

1. *Coherent shared-memory loads and stores:* These operations, implemented as single processor instructions, comprise the traditional shared-memory operations. They invoke suitable coherence actions when multiple cached copies of a memory location exist.

2. *Processor-to-processor message:* On the source side, this operation allows a processor to write packets directly into a network queue; it is implemented using a sequence of processor instructions described below. At the destination, message arrival interrupts the processor and invokes a handler which can examine the data in the packet. It takes 5 cycles to get into the message handler. These messages can be used for efficient register-to-register communication between processors.

3. *Source-and-destination-coherent data transfer:* A processor executing this operation describes a region of memory on the local (source) node to be sent in a single message to some region of memory on a remote (destination) node. The data transfer is achieved in a way that leaves the source and destination caches consistent with their respective local memories. Such a transfer takes no action on copies of the source or destination data present in other caches. These messages can be used for coarse-grained bulk (memory-to-memory) data transfer and invoke DMA facilities at the source and destination.

The processor-to-processor message and the data-transfer mechanisms are both implemented using a single low-overhead interface to the network. In fact, the interface describes a generic message with the combined characteristics of processor-to-processor messages and bulk data transfer.

Operand 0
Operand 1
⋮
Operand m-1
Address 0
Length 0
Address 1
Length 1
⋮
Address n-1
Length n-1

Figure 5: Packet descriptor format.

The network interface includes specifications at the source and at the destination. At the source, the network interface permits messages to be sent through a two phase process: *describe* then *launch*. Description proceeds by writing directly to registers on Alewife's network coprocessor, or *Communications and Memory-Management Unit* (CMMU). These writes proceed at the same speed as cached writes. The resulting descriptor, depicted in Figure 5, can be up to 16 words long. The descriptor consists of a variable number of explicit *operands* that will be placed at the head of the message followed by a number of address-length pairs describing data to be taken directly from memory and concatenated to the end of the packet. The first operand must specify the destination and a message type, while the remaining words are software defined.

Once a packet has been described, it is launched via an *atomic*, single-cycle instruction. The encoding of the launch instruction specifies both the number of explicit operands and the number of address-length pairs. Processor-to-processor messages specify only explicit operands, while bulk data transfer messages utilize only address-length pairs. The multiple address-length pairs allow multiple source regions of memory to be sent in a single packet. A single message with both explicit operands and multiple address-length pairs can also be sent. Both the user and supervisor are permitted to send messages.

On the destination side, for efficient reception of messages, the Alewife interface provides a 16-word, sliding window into the network input queue. On reception of a message, the CMMU interrupts the processor (unless the processor has masked message interrupts) while making the first 16 words of the packet visible in the reception window. The processor can examine words within this window by reading coprocessor registers; as with the output interface, these reads complete at the speed of a cached memory access.

Once the processor has examined the packet, it can execute a special coprocessor storeback instruction to remove data from the window. User code may dispose of user-generated messages. Two separate fields are encoded directly in the storeback instruction. First is the number of words to be discarded from the head of the window. Second is the number of words (following those discarded) to be stored to memory via DMA. If this option is chosen, the processor must write the starting address for DMA to a special controller register before issuing the storeback instruction. Multiple storeback instructions can be issued for a single packet to scatter it to memory. Either of these storeback fields can contain a special "infinity" value which denotes "until the end of the packet".

The Alewife CMMU has been completely implemented and is in the final stages of testing. We expect to have small prototype Alewife systems (four to 16 nodes) operational sometime this year. These systems will utilize nodes clocked at 33 MHz, coherent caches, and a two-dimensional mesh interconnect.

4 Results

This section provides results comparing the performance of the shared-memory and message-passing implementations of several library routines, our runtime system, and one application.

4.1 Experimental Environment

The results presented in this paper were obtained through the use of a detailed machine simulator. This simulator provides cycle-by-cycle simulation of all components of Alewife. Our original simulator implementation targeted desktop SPARC- and MIPS-based workstations; we have also developed a version of the simulator which runs on Thinking Machines' CM-5 multiprocessors. In the latter implementation, each CM-5 node simulates the processor, memory, and network hardware of one or more Alewife nodes. The CM-5 port of our simulator has proved invaluable, especially for running simulations of large Alewife systems (64 to 512 nodes).

4.2 Combining Tree Barriers

In order to implement barrier synchronization on Alewife, we use a *combining tree* scheme [16]. In such a scheme, a k-ary tree with n leaves is laid out across the n processors participating in the barrier such that exactly one tree leaf resides on each processor. Upon entering the barrier, a processor activates the leaf node of the tree, which in turn sends an *arrival* signal to its parent. Each internal node issues an arrival signal to its parent after arrival signals have been received from all its children. When the root of the tree has received arrival signals from all its children, it then issues *wakeup* signals to all its children. Internal nodes pass such wakeup signals on to all of their children. Once a wakeup signal arrives at a leaf node, the user thread which had been running on that processor before the barrier is allowed to continue execution.

In principle, only a single message need be sent to signal each combining tree arrival or wakeup. In a cache-coherent shared-memory implementation, arrivals and wake-ups are signaled via memory writes; even in a carefully tuned implementation, these writes require several messages each. By utilizing explicit messaging, the ideal of a single message per event is readily achieved. The benefit of doing so is substantial. On a 64-processor machine, our

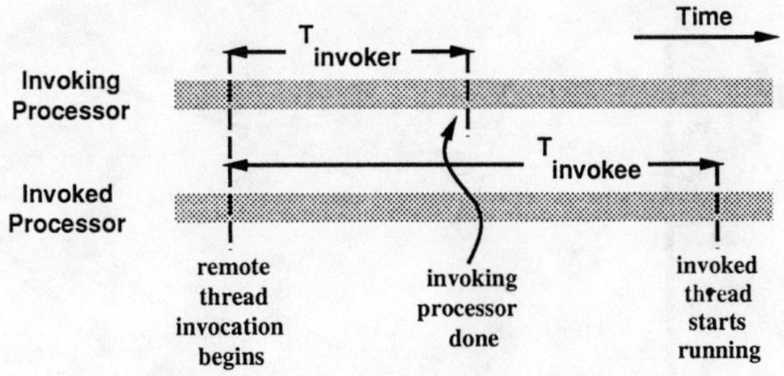

Figure 6: Remote thread invocation.

best shared-memory barrier implementation (utilizing a six-level binary tree carefully crafted to minimize the total number of message exchanges) executes in about 1650 cycles (50 μsec); a direct message-based implementation (utilizing a two-level eight-ary tree) takes only 660 cycles (20 μsec). By comparison, typical software implementations (e.g. Intel DELTA and iPSC/860, Kendall Square KSR1) take well over 400 μsec [9].

4.3 Remote Thread Invocation

To invoke a thread on a remote processor, a pointer to the thread's code and any arguments must be placed atomically on the task queue of another processor. To do so via shared-memory, the invoking processor must first acquire the remote task queue lock (which requires at least one network round-trip, if not more) and then modify and unlock the queue using shared-memory reads and writes, each of which can require multiple network messages. A message-based implementation is substantially simpler: all of the information necessary to invoke the thread is marshaled into a single message which is unpacked and queued atomically by the receiving processor. In this manner, we combine synchronization and data transfer in a single message, as suggested in Section 2.2.

We characterize the performance of these two implementation schemes by measuring two intervals: $T_{invoker}$, the time from when the invoking processor starts the operation until it is free to proceed with other work, and $T_{invokee}$, the time from when the invoking processor starts the operation until the invoked thread begins running (see Figure 6). With our best shared-memory implementation, these times are 353 and 805 cycles, respectively (10.7 and 24.4 μsec). With the message-based implementation, both times are reduced drastically, to 17 and 244 cycles, respectively (0.5 and 7.4 μsec). Note that for both implementations, these times were measured in the context of a complete thread scheduling and migration system; $T_{invokee}$ would be substantially smaller in a minimal system implementation.

4.4 Bulk Data Transfer

Memory-to-memory copy of data blocks between processors, as might be used to perform buffered disk I/O or when relocating large data objects, can be implemented using either shared-memory or message-passing. Figure 7 compares the performance of three

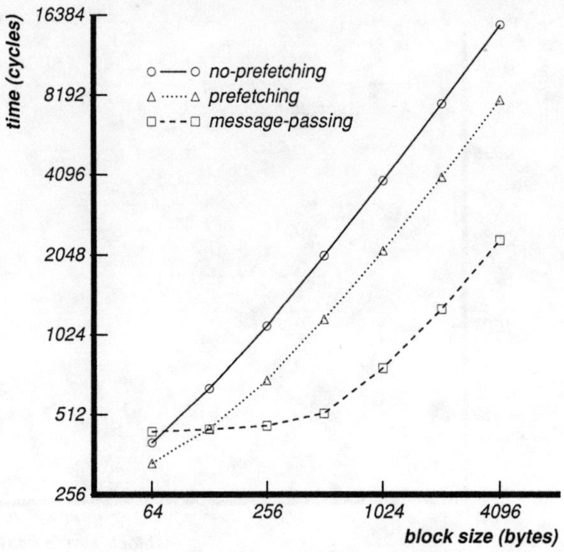

Figure 7: Memory-to-memory copy performance; see Section 4.4 for details.

different implementations of memory-to-memory copy. The first two implementations (*no-prefetching* and *prefetching*) utilize hand-coded inner loops to copy data between buffers using doubleword (eight byte) loads and stores through the shared-memory interface (*no-prefetching* uses a simple copy loop; *prefetching* uses essentially the same loop but also prefetches one cache block (16 bytes) ahead). The third implementation (*message-passing*) copies data between buffers using a single message and the CMMU's DMA facilities.

As expected, *message-passing* performs substantially better than *no-prefetching* or *prefetching*, even for relatively small block sizes. With 256-byte blocks, *message-passing* is roughly 1.5 and 2.4 times faster than *no-prefetching* and *prefetching*, respectively (17.3 vs. 11.7 and 7.3 Mbyte/sec). The benefit of message-passing grows with larger block sizes, reaching a peak rate with four-kilobyte blocks more than 3 and 6 times faster than *no-prefetching* and *prefetching*, respectively (55.4 vs. 16.4 and 8.6 Mbyte/sec).

In some situations, when an application fetches a large block of data from a remote node, it will immediately "consume" that data. A particularly simple example of this is accum, a toy application which computes the sum of a linear array of integers which resides on a remote node. Figure 8 compares the performance of shared-memory and message-passing implementations of accum. The shared-memory implementation uses a straightforward inner loop which prefetches one cache block ahead. The message-passing implementation first transfers the entire array into local memory (using the memory-to-memory copy mechanism described above) and then performs the necessary computation entirely out of local memory.

In this case, the message-passing implementation runs substantially slower than the shared-memory implementation—ranging from roughly twice as slow for small blocks to about 1.3 times slower for large blocks. Given that the message-passing implemen-

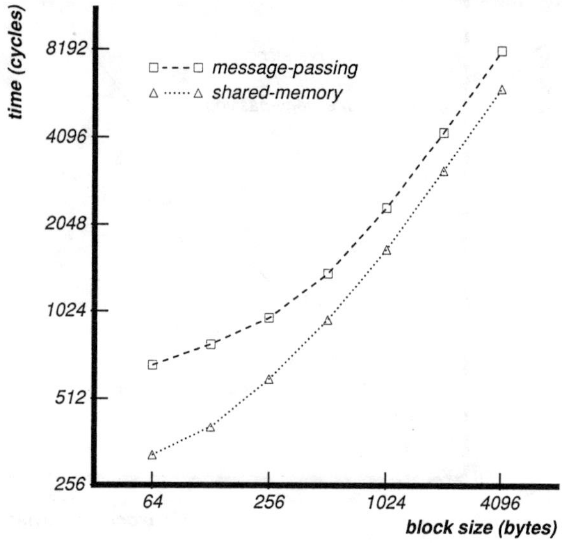

Figure 8: accum performance; see Section 4.4 for details.

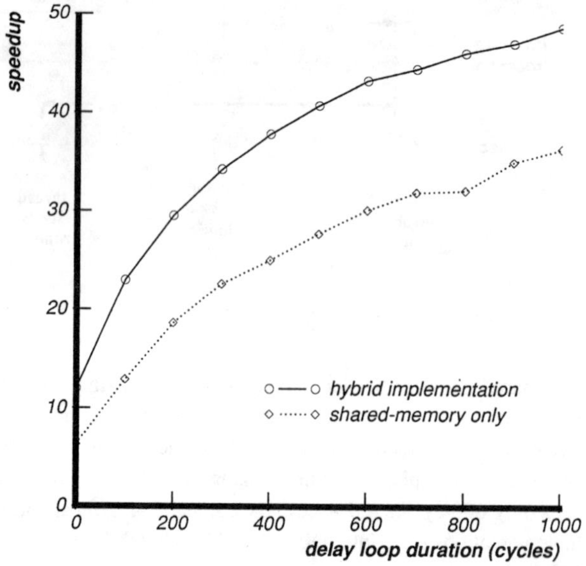

Figure 9: grain performance on 64 processors; see Section 4.5 for details.

tation serializes communication and computation, this is hardly surprising. To be fair, it might be reasonable to discount the time spent transferring data from the remote node, for during that time the local processor is idle and could be doing other useful work. Discounting this time amounts to subtracting the message-passing curve from Figure 7 from that in Figure 8; doing so provides a curve which rides just below the shared-memory curve in Figure 8. This is also not surprising, given that the "compute" phase of the message-passing implementation uses almost exactly the same inner loop as the shared-memory implementation—the only difference being that the shared-memory implementation has one additional instruction (a prefetch) per loop iteration.

From this last observation we can conclude that even if we were able to utilize the processor idle time during message transfer (perhaps by breaking large data blocks into smaller blocks and pipelining the transfer of and computation on those data blocks), the message-passing implementation might perform better than the shared-memory implementation, but only by a very small amount. We observe this effect with accum because:

- accum doesn't store the remote data it fetches for later use—array elements are only fetched such that they can be accumulated into the global sum.
- accum is a "static" application which accesses data in a particularly regular fashion—this allows data to be prefetched into the cache such that virtually all actual accesses to remote data hit in the cache, effectively hiding all communication latency.

4.5 Thread Scheduler

The Alewife runtime system is based on *lazy task creation* [17]. This system performs the tasks of load-balancing and dynamic partitioning of programs that cannot be statically partitioned effectively. As part of this research, we have implemented a version of this runtime system that uses message-based communication in both searching for work and thread migration. When compared to the original (shared-memory only) implementation, this hybrid (shared-memory + message-passing) implementation drastically cuts down on the communication overheads incurred by thread scheduling and load balancing operations. We benchmarked both the original shared-memory and the hybrid implementations using one synthetic application (grain) and an adaptive numerical integration code (aq).

As described in [17], the grain application enumerates a complete binary tree of depth n and sums the values found at the leaves using a recursive divide-and-conquer structure. Before obtaining the value found at each leaf, a delay loop of l cycles in duration is executed. Figure 9 compares the speedup for grain obtained with the two scheduler implementations running on 64 processors for $n = 12$ and a wide range of l. By choosing $n = 12$, we assure a sufficient amount of parallelism (4,096 leaf tasks for 64 processors); by varying l we can vary the "grain size" of that parallelism.

For very small grain size ($l = 0$, corresponding to a sequential running time[1] of 7.1 milliseconds), the lower searching and thread migration overheads afforded by the hybrid implementation scheme yield considerable benefit—grain runs almost twice as fast under the hybrid implementation (speedups of 12.0 vs. 6.3 for the hybrid and shared-memory implementations, respectively). As grain size l is increased, the relative benefit of the hybrid implementation decreases. This is as one would expect, since the fraction of time spent in "overhead" decreases with increased grain size. Even so, for relatively large grain size ($l = 1000$ cycles, corresponding to a

[1] In this paper, the sequential running time of an application is taken to be the running time of that application when compiled for and run on a single node. Thus sequential running time doesn't include any scheduler or runtime system overhead. The speedup results shown in Figure 9 and Figure 10 are computed with respect to sequential running time.

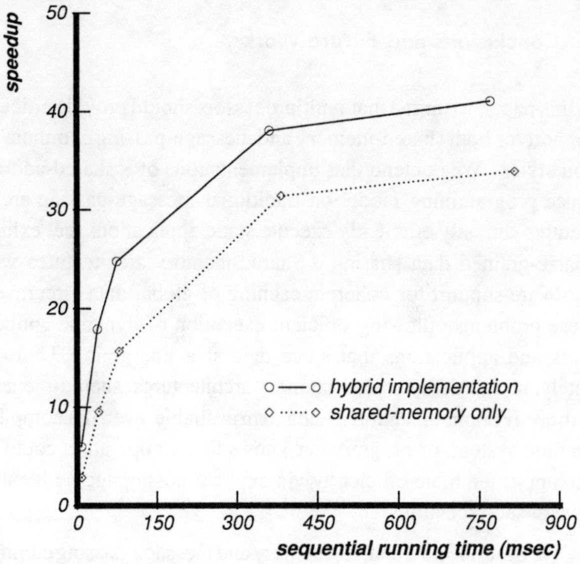

Figure 10: aq performance on 64 processors; see Section 4.5 for details.

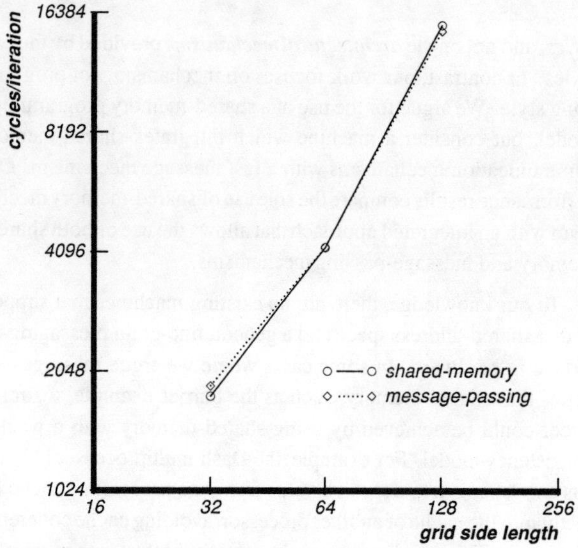

Figure 11: Jacobi SOR performance on 64 processors; see Section 4.6 for details.

sequential running time of 131.2 milliseconds) grain running under the hybrid scheme still runs around 33 percent faster than under the original shared-memory implementation (speedups of 48.6 and 36.4, respectively).

The aq application computes a numerical integration of a bivariate function over a rectangular domain. Like grain, aq utilizes a recursive divide-and-conquer structure, dividing space and recursing more deeply in those regions that are not sufficiently smooth at the current scale. Since the scale at which many integrands become sufficiently smooth can vary significantly across the domain of integration, the call tree resulting from this recursion is often relatively irregular. In the results presented here, we hold the integrand and domain of integration fixed; problem size is increased by changing the threshold for what is to be considered sufficiently smooth. Figure 10 compares the speedup for aq obtained with the two scheduler implementations running on 64 processors; sequential running time is used on the x-axis as a measure of problem size.

Once again, the hybrid scheduler implementation outperforms the shared-memory implementation by roughly a factor of two for small problem sizes. As problem size (and thus grain size) is increased, the relative advantage of the hybrid implementation decreases, although for the largest problem size shown in Figure 10 (sequential running time of around 800 milliseconds), the hybrid scheduler implementation still yields over 20 percent better performance than the original shared-memory implementation.

4.6 Jacobi SOR

Finally, we have developed both shared-memory and message-passing implementations of jacobi, a simple block-partitioned Jacobi SOR solver. In this application, processors only communicate with one another to exchange new values for their border elements. In the shared-memory implementation, this communication is effected through conventional shared-memory operations (without prefetching); in the message-passing implementation, all communication is accomplished through the message-based memory-to-memory copy mechanism described in Section 4.4. Figure 11 compares the performance obtained with both implementations for grid sizes of 32x32, 64x64, and 128x128 running on 64 processors.

In jacobi, the amount of data communicated with each neighboring processor on each iteration is proportional to the side length of the local grid block. Given the memory-to-memory copy and accum results from Section 4.4, it is not surprising that the performance of the shared-memory and message-passing implementations differs by such a small amount. With small grid sizes, the shared-memory implementation of jacobi performs slightly better than the message-passing implementation. Since only a small amount of data is transferred between neighboring processors when grid size is small, this follows directly from Figure 7, where we see that using shared-memory to copy small blocks of data between nodes is more efficient than using message-passing. For large grid sizes, the message-passing implementation of jacobi wins out by a small amount. In this case, much of the benefit of using messages to copy large blocks of data is masked by increasing computation-to-communication ratio—because computation-to-communication ratio in jacobi scales with problem size, efficient communication becomes less important for large problems.

5 Related Work

There have been several papers on comparing the performance of message-passing and shared-memory for particular applications. Martonosi and Gupta [15] compare the performance of a message-passing and a shared-memory implementation of a standard cell router. However, their comparison focused on the two *programming styles*, and not on the *architectural mechanisms* provided by the two styles. In contrast, our work focuses on mechanism, not programming style. We argue for the use of a shared-memory programming model, but consider a machine which integrates shared-memory communication mechanisms with a fast message mechanism. Our performance results compare the sole use of shared-memory mechanism with an integrated approach that allows the use of both shared-memory and message-passing mechanisms.

To our knowledge, there are no existing machines that support both a shared-address space and a general fine-grain messaging interface in hardware. In some cases where we argue messages are better that shared-memory, such as the barrier example, a similar effect could be achieved by using shared-memory with a weaker consistency model. For example, the Dash multiprocessor [13, 10] has a mechanism to deposit a value from one processor's cache directly into the cache of another processor, avoiding cache coherence overhead. This mechanism might actually be faster than using a message because no interrupt occurs, but a message is much more general.

Some shared-memory machines have implemented message-like primitives in hardware. For example, Beck, Kasten, and Thakkar [2] describe the implementation of SLIC—a system link and interrupt controller chip—for use with the Sequent Balance system. Each SLIC chip is coupled with a processing node and communicates with the other SLIC chips on a special SLIC bus that is separate from the memory system bus. The SLIC chips help distribute signals such as interrupts and synchronization information to all processors in the system. Although similar in flavor to this kind of interface, the Alewife messaging interface is built to allow direct access into the same scalable interconnection network used by the shared-memory operations.

Another example of a shared-memory machine that also supports a message-like primitive is the BBN Butterfly, which provides hardware support for block transfers. In an implementation of distributed shared-memory on this machine, Cox and Fowler [7] conclude that an effective block transfer mechanism was critical to performance. They argue that a mechanism that allows more concurrency between processing and block transfer would make a bigger impact. It turns out that Alewife's messages are implemented in a way that allows such concurrency when transferring large blocks of data. Furthermore, the Butterfly's block transfer mechanism is not suited for more general uses of fine-grain messaging because there is no support in the processor for fast message handling.

Finally, it is worth noting that some message-passing machines also provide limited support for the shared-address space programming model. For example, the J-machine [8] provides a global name space for objects and an object name cache which speeds up (but does not eliminate) the local/remote checks suggested in Figure 1.

6 Conclusions and Future Work

In this paper, we argue that multiprocessors should provide efficient support for both shared-memory and message-passing communication styles. We contend that implementations of a shared-address space programming model on traditional message-passing architectures can only efficiently execute static applications that exhibit coarse-grained data sharing. Shared-memory architectures with hardware support for coherent caching of global data circumvent these problems, allowing efficient execution of dynamic applications and applications that share data at a fine grain. Unfortunately, in traditional shared-memory architectures, shared-memory is the *only* communication mechanism available, even if a compiler, runtime system, or programmer knows that an operation could be accomplished more efficiently via explicit messaging; we identify several such scenarios.

We describe how shared-memory and message-passing communication are integrated in the Alewife hardware and software systems. We present preliminary results comparing the performance of various runtime system primitives and one complete application when implemented using exclusively shared-memory or a hybrid approach in which communication is effected through message-passing when appropriate. These results show performance gains on the order of two- to ten-fold for some of the runtime system primitives and up to a factor of two for applications running under the hybrid thread scheduler. We also show that in some cases message-based communication is not as efficient as that through shared-memory. From these observations, we draw the following general conclusions about the suggested "defects of shared-memory" of Section 2.2:

- When transferring large blocks of data between two nodes, using message-based communication to do so can yield a factor of three or more performance improvement over doing so via shared-memory, even if prefetching is used. If transferred data is consumed immediately in a regular fashion and not stored for later use (*e.g.* accum), judicious use of prefetching can eliminate any advantage of using messaging instead of shared-memory for data transfer.
- Message-based communication is only significantly more effective than shared-memory for applications with known communication patterns when (i) problem size can be scaled such that messages are large enough to amortize any (even modest) fixed messaging overhead and (ii) scaling problem size in such a manner does not increase the computation-to-communication ratio to the point where communication costs become insignificant (*e.g.* jacobi).
- When message-based communication can be used to bundle synchronization operations with data which must be operated on after successful synchronization, doing so is likely to yield substantial performance gains over shared-memory implementations of the same functionality (*e.g.* remote thread invocation).

As of this writing, we have only used explicit messaging in parts of the Alewife runtime system and software libraries. We plan to continue investigating further integration, including compile-time "communication optimizations" and programming systems which provide limited programmer access to both the shared-memory and message-passing interfaces. In addition, we note that a shared-object space with messages is the basis for implementing a parallel object-oriented language. In this sense shared-memory and message-passing might be integrated at the language level by integrating object-oriented and procedural programming as in T [18, 19], CLOS [3] and, more recently, Dylan [20].

7 Acknowledgments

The research reported on herein was funded in part by NSF grant # MIP-9012773, in part by DARPA contract # N00014-87-K-0825, and in part by a NSF Presidential Young Investigator Award. We would also like to thank Alan Mainwaring, Dave Douglas, and Thinking Machines Corporation for their generosity and assistance in porting our simulation system to the CM-5.

References

[1] Anant Agarwal, David Chaiken, Godfrey D'Souza, Kirk Johnson, David Kranz, John Kubiatowicz, Kiyoshi Kurihara, Beng-Hong Lim, Gino Maa, Dan Nussbaum, Mike Parkin, and Donald Yeung. The MIT Alewife Machine: A Large-Scale Distributed-Memory Multiprocessor. In *Proceedings of Workshop on Scalable Shared Memory Multiprocessors*. Kluwer Academic Publishers, 1991. An extended version of this paper has been submitted for publication, and appears as MIT/LCS Memo TM-454, 1991.

[2] Bob Beck, Bob Kasten, and Shreekant Thakkar. VLSI Assist for a Multiprocessor. In *Proceedings Second International Conference on Architectural Support for Programming Languages and Operating Systems (ASPLOS II)*, Washington, DC, October 1987. IEEE.

[3] Daniel G. Bobrow, Linda G. DeMichiel, Richard P. Gabriel, Sonya E. Keene, Gregor Kiczales, and David A. Moon. Common Lisp Object System Specification. *ACM SIGPLAN Notices*, 23, September 1988.

[4] S. Borkar, R. Cohn, G. Cox, T. Gross, H.T. Kung, M. Lam, M. Levine, B. Moore, W. Moore, C. Peterson, J. Susman, J. Sutton, J. Urbanski, and J. Webb. Supporting Systolic and Memory Communication in iWarp. In *Proceedings of the 17th Annual International Symposium on Computer Architecture*, pages 70–81, June 1990.

[5] David Callahan and Ken Kennedy. Compiling Programs for Distributed-Memory Multiprocessors. *Journal of Supercomputing*, 2(151-169), October 1988.

[6] David Chaiken, John Kubiatowicz, and Anant Agarwal. LimitLESS Directories: A Scalable Cache Coherence Scheme. In *Fourth International Conference on Architectural Support for Programming Languages and Operating Systems (ASPLOS IV)*, pages 224–234. ACM, April 1991.

[7] A. Cox and R. Fowler. The Implementation of a Coherent Memory Abstraction on a NUMA Multiprocessor: Experiences with PLATINUM. In *Proceedings of the 12th ACM Symposium on Operating Systems Principles*, pages 32–44, December 1989. Also as a Univ. Rochester TR-263, May 1989.

[8] William J. Dally et al. The J-Machine: A Fine-Grain Concurrent Computer. In *IFIP Congress*, 1989.

[9] Thomas H. Dunigan. Kendall Square Multiprocessor: Early Experiences and Performance. Technical Report ORNL/TM-12065, Oak Ridge National Laboratory, March 1992.

[10] K. Gharachorloo, D. Lenoski, J. Laudon, P. Gibbons, A. Gupta, and J. Hennessy. Memory Consistency and Event Ordering in Scalable Shared-Memory Multiprocessors. In *Proceedings 17th Annual International Symposium on Computer Architecture*, New York, June 1990. IEEE.

[11] K. Knobe, J. Lukas, and G. Steele Jr. Data Optimization: Allocation of Arrays to Reduce Communication on SIMD Machines. *Journal of Parallel and Distributed Computing*, 8(2):102–118, 1990.

[12] John Kubiatowicz and Anant Agarwal. Anatomy of a Message in the Alewife Multiprocessor. Submitted for publication. Also available as MIT Laboratory for Computer Science Tech Memo, 1993.

[13] D. Lenoski, J. Laudon, K. Gharachorloo, W. Weber, A. Gupta, J. Hennessy, M. Horowitz, and M. Lam. The Stanford Dash Multiprocessor. *IEEE Computer*, 25(3):63–79, March 1992.

[14] J. Li and M. Chen. Compiling communication-efficient programs for massively parallel machines. *IEEE Transactions on Parallel and Distributed Systems*, 2:361–376, July 1991.

[15] M. Martonosi and A. Gupta. Tradeoffs in Message Passing and Shared Memory Implementations of a Standard Cell Router. In *Proceedings of the 1989 International Conference on Parallel Processing*, pages III 88–96, 1989.

[16] John M. Mellor-Crummey and Michael L. Scott. Algorithms for Scalable Synchronization on Shared-Memory Multiprocessors. *ACM Transactions on Computer Systems*, 9(1):21–65, February 1991.

[17] E. Mohr, D. Kranz, and R. Halstead. Lazy Task Creation: A Technique for Increasing the Granularity of Parallel Programs. *IEEE Transactions on Parallel and Distributed Systems*, 2(3):264–280, July 1991.

[18] J. Rees and N. Adams. T: A Dialect of LISP. In *Proceedings of Symposium on Lisp and Functional Programming*, August 1982.

[19] J. Rees, N. Adams, and J. Meehan. The T Manual, Fourth Edition. Technical report, Yale University, Computer Science Department, January 1984.

[20] Apple Computer Eastern Research and Technology. *Dylan: an object-oriented dynamic language*. Apple Computer, Inc., 1992.

[21] Anne Rogers and Keshav Pingali. Process Decomposition through Locality of Reference. In *SIGPLAN '89, Conference on Programming Language Design and Implementation*, June 1989.

[22] Alfred Z. Spector. Performing Remote Operations Efficiently on a Local Computer Network. *Communications of the ACM*, 25(4), April 1982. Pages 246–260.

[23] Thorsten von Eicken, David Culler, Seth Goldstein, and Klaus Schauser. Active messages: A mechanism for integrated communication and computation. In *19th International Symposium on Computer Architecture*, May 1992.

[24] H. Zima, H.-J. Bast, and M. Gerndt. SUPERB: A tool for semi-automatic MIMD/SIMD parallelization. *Parallel Computing*, 6(1), 1988.

Using Scheduler Information to Achieve Optimal Barrier Synchronization Performance

Leonidas Kontothanassis and Robert W. Wisniewski

Abstract

Parallel programs frequently use barriers to synchronize successive steps in an algorithm. In the presence of multiprogramming the choice of spinning versus blocking barriers can have a significant impact on performance. We demonstrate how competitive spinning techniques previously designed for locks can be extended to barriers, and we evaluate their performance. We design an additional competitive spinning technique that adapts more quickly in a dynamic environment. We then propose and evaluate a new method that obtains better performance than previous techniques by using scheduler information to decide between spinning and blocking. The **scheduler information** technique makes optimal choices incurring little overhead.

1 Introduction

Although the decision between spinning and blocking at synchronization events is straightforward on a dedicated multiprocessor, multiprogramming introduces significant difficulties in many cases. Past work [3, 11, 14] has shown that on a multiprogrammed multiprocessor the best scheduling method is dynamic hardware partitioning. In such an environment it is not possible to determine *a priori* the number of processors on which an application will run. In fact, this number may vary over the execution of the program.

There are several techniques for barrier synchronization ranging from always spin to always block. In a dynamic environment the best techniques lie somewhere between the extremes. A competitive algorithm is an online algorithm whose worst-case performance is within a constant factor of the best offline algorithm. Competitive spinning for barriers tries to approximate the best offline algorithm by heuristically determining the overall distribution of spinning times. Competitive spinning uses this information to choose the appropriate policy and to minimize the expected cost over all executions of a barrier. Keeping track of this information is costly so there are several approximation algorithms that attempt to determine this distribution based on recent executions of the barrier.

The main difficulty in chosing an appropriate strategy in a hardware partitioned environment is that the number of processors devoted to a particular application varies with time. However, if the program could be made aware of how many processors it was allotted when it reached a particular barrier, a better performing choice could be made between blocking and spinning. We propose a method whereby the scheduler provides this information to the application. When the application is attempting to cross a barrier it will know how many processors are currently in its partition. A particular thread will block when it reaches a barrier if the number of threads not yet at the barrier is greater than the number of processors in its partition, else it will spin. A technique that decides either to block all threads or to have all threads spin, even if it does so very well, will not perform as well as possible. To perform well in a hardware partitioned environment, a method must allow some processes at a barrier to spin, and others to block. The **scheduler information** technique is optimal, meaning that, in addition to allowing the maximum possible number of processes to spin, it always chooses the correct action between blocking or spinning incurring only the small overhead needed to check the number of remaining threads against the number of processors in the partition.

The rest of this paper is organized as follows. Section 2 discusses related work and distinguishes our approach from previous ones. Section 3 presents the programming model used for the experiments, describes the competitive spinning techniques, and explains how scheduler information is used to perform barrier synchronization. Section 4 presents results comparing the **scheduler information** technique to other techniques. Finally, Section 5 summarizes our work, and suggests directions for future research.

This material is based upon work supported by DARPA grants MDA972-92-J-1012 and N000014-92-J-1801 and the National Science Foundation grant CDA-8822724. The Government has certain rights in this material.

4th ACM PPOPP,5/93/CA,USA

2 Related Work

Previous work on synchronization under multiprogramming has considered the performance effects of: multiprogramming on synchronization events, alternative implementations of synchronization data structures, and alternative scheduling strategies on synchronization events.

Early work by Tucker and Gupta [11] has shown that the main reason for performance degradation on a time-shared, multiprogrammed multiprocessor is the existence of more processes than physical processors. They have proposed a scheme of hardware partitioning that prevents the number of processes systemwide from exceeding the number of processors. However, this scheme requires applications to adjust the number of processes they use. For many programs it would be difficult to dynamically adjust the number of processes used, especially for the class of programs with coarse grained threads and barrier synchronization.

Using simulation, modeling, and experimentation, Crovella *et al* [3], Leutenegger and Vernon [7], and Zahorjan and McCann [14] have shown that dynamic hardware partitions are preferable to timesharing, co-scheduling, and static hardware partitions. Other work by Gupta *et al* [5] has studied the behavior of a multiprogrammed multiprocessor environment by simulating the concurrent execution of four applications. Their results indicate that hardware partitioning outperforms other policies most of the time.

Zahorjan, Lazowska, and Eager [12, 13] have determined the worst case performance degradation due to spinning in parallel systems when the number of processors available to the application varies with time. They have shown that although for locks, spinning introduces only moderate overhead, in the case of barriers spinning can degrade performance severely. They propose that processor allocation and individual thread scheduling be handled cooperatively by the system and the application.

Other work suggesting cooperation between the operating system scheduler and the runtime environment or the application includes the work of Black [2], Edler *et al* [4], Marsh *et al* [9], and Anderson *et al* [1]. Black has suggested that the application provide hints to the scheduler indicating which application thread to schedule next. Edler *et al* have suggested temporarily preventing a thread from being preempted while it is in a critical section. Marsh *et al* and Anderson *et al* have suggested that preemption information be communicated from the kernel to user space.

Markatos *et al* [8] have analyzed the suitability of alternative barrier data structures in a multiprogramming environment. They conclude that combination barriers, using blocking synchronization within a node and spinning across nodes, perform the best.

Karlin *et al* [6] have developed and tested a set of different competitive spinning techniques for a multiprocessor environment. Competitive spinning assumes that the behavior of a lock does not change rapidly with time, and that past behavior is an appropriate indicator of future behavior. While their techniques were developed for spinlocks, they can easily be extended to barriers. These techniques are most useful in a hardware partitioned environment where scheduling decisions are infrequent and many barriers are reached between scheduling decisions.

Our work extends previous work in several ways. Based on work by Karlin *et al*, we build and test several competitive spinning algorithms for barriers and conclude they have a significant performance benefit over always spinning or always blocking. Further, we propose that with only a little information (i.e. the size of the partition) from the kernel scheduler, it is possible to implement an efficient policy for barriers that performs better than all other policies. We verify this hypothesis on an Iris 4D/480 eight node multiprocessor using two real applications and a synthetic program.

3 Algorithms

As discussed in the previous sections, this work focuses on building barriers for a multiprogrammed environment. Since most researchers agree that the best way to multiprogram a multiprocessor is dynamic hardware partitions, this will be the environment assumed for the rest of the paper. It is unrealistic to assume that all programs can be written to dynamically adjust the number of processes they use to the number of processors provided. It is therefore not possible to obtain good barrier performance in these programs by always blocking or always spinning. Well performing barrier methods in a hardware partitioned environment must use a combination of spinning and blocking. The difficulty is dynamically determining the appropriate method for a particular thread in a particular instance of a barrier.

Patterned after the competitive spinning techniques used by Karlin *et al* [6] for locks, we built a set a competitive spinning techniques for barriers. These techniques decide whether to spin or block based on information from the last several barriers. The success of this technique stems from the fact that the hardware partition of an application will change considerably less frequently than the rate barriers are encountered. Pseudocode for the different competitive spinning algorithms is presented in the Appendix. These algorithms heuristically decide whether to block or spin based on their view of the hardware partition. Our final technique uses scheduler information. Instead of requiring the application to guess the partition configuration, this technique allows the size of the partition to be known, allowing the application to make a better decision than any technique limited to heuristically determining the partition. The rest of this section describes the different competitive spinning approaches and their motivation followed by the **scheduler information** technique.

All the competitive spinning techniques have a similar structure. They spin for a certain amount of time, and then block. Barriers that spin for a constant amount of time and then block are called fixed spinning barriers. Those that vary

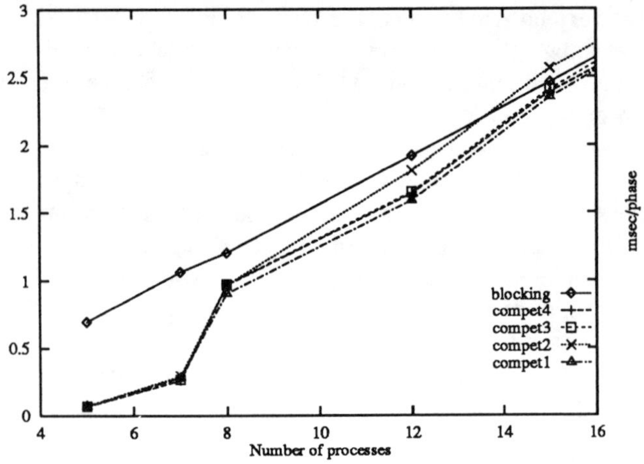

Figure 1: Competitive barriers for the synthetic program

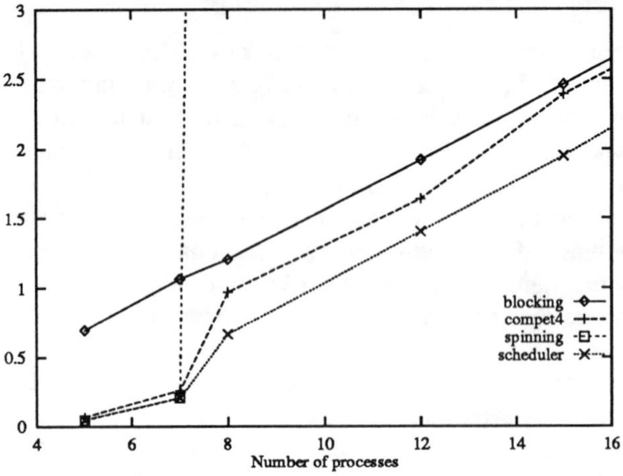

Figure 2: Scheduler information barrier for the synthetic program

the amount of time they spin before blocking are called adaptive. Without precise information of the hardware partition, adaptive techniques heuristically determine how the hardware partition is configured. The adaptive techniques estimate whether they spent longer or shorter at the barrier than expected. Based on this, they adjust their spin time for the next instance of the barrier. In the algorithms presented in the Appendix, whenever the command "block" occurs, the process that blocks will remain blocked until the last process enters the barrier and unblocks the other processes.

A complete description and motivation behind the **fixed spinning**, **last one**, and **average three** can be found in Karlin *et al* [6]. Briefly, **fixed spinning** implies that a process spins for a constant amount of time before blocking. It requires low overhead and is easy to implement. **Average three**, which adapts the spinning period based on the last three barrier episodes, avoids the excessive cost of storing the entire distribution while still maintaining the smoothing effect. **Last one** is patterned after **average three** but has lower overhead since it retains only information from one barrier. The pseudocode for these are in figures 9 through 11 respectively (in Appendix).

The last adaptive technique, **coarse adjustment** is similar to the **last one** in that it only uses data from the previous barrier. However instead of slowly moving the spin time up or down, it adjusts it entirely at once. The reasoning behind this strategy is that partition changes are infrequent and after a partition change the desired barrier behavior is fixed. Rapidly adjusting the spin time could lead to instability and poor performance if there are very few barriers per scheduling decision. However, for normal programs this proved to be an effective method. The pseudocode for **coarse adjustment** is in figure 12 (in Appendix).

With only a little bit of information about the size of the partition, it is possible to design a barrier with much better performance than the competitive spinning techniques. The scheduler was modified to constantly provide a shared variable containing the number of processors in a partition. The barrier was designed so that when any thread reached a synchronization point it compared the number of processors in the partition to the number of remaining threads needed to pass through the barrier. If the number of remaining threads was less than the number of processors in the partition, the checking thread chose spinning, else it blocked. This approach makes optimal choices and incurs only the little overhead required to check the number of processes left against the number of processors in the partition. Pseudocode for the **Scheduler Information** barrier appears in figure 13, and code for a process of a typical application using barriers can be seen in figure 14 (in Appendix).

In the general barrier case there are N processes trying to get through the barrier using P processors where $N \geq P$. If the `work` section is roughly the same for each thread, then all the threads can be separated into groups of size P, and the threads in each group can execute simultaneously. When those P threads reach the barrier point they can either spin for the remainder of their quantum or yield and let the next P threads run. Under these assumptions the optimal policy would force the first $N-P$ threads to block so that the remaining P can run. However blocking is not necessary for the last P threads since there is no remaining thread to perform any work. Blocking in this case would only incur the extra overhead of having to switch the thread back in when the barrier is completed. The **scheduler information** technique uses this method, yielding an optimal cost of $Cost_{sched} = \lceil \frac{N-P}{P} \rceil * c + overhead$, where *overhead* is the cost of checking the number of threads against the number of available processors, c is the cost of a context switch, and *Cost* is the amount of time spent at a barrier in spinning or context switching when useful work could have been done.

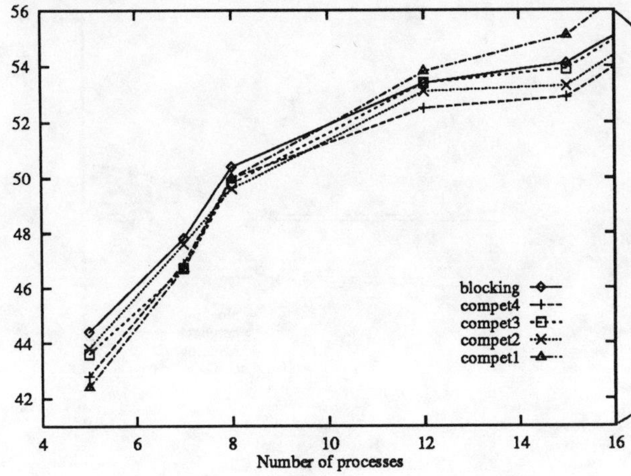

Figure 3: Competitive barriers for successive overrelaxation

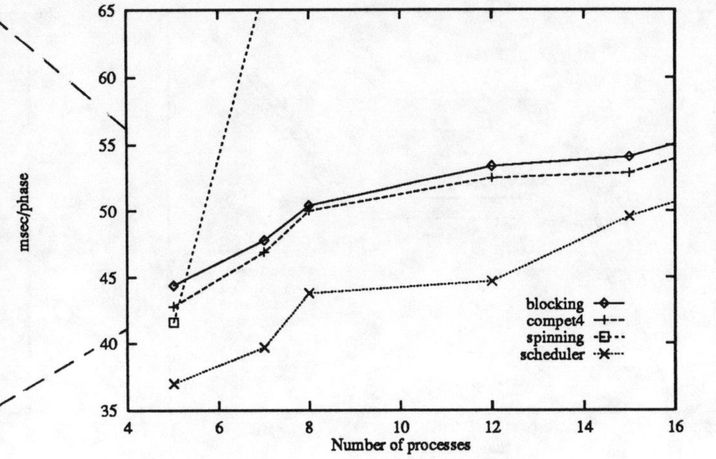

Figure 4: Scheduler information barrier for successive overrelaxation

4 Experiments and Results

We tested each technique on three different programs. The first was a synthetic program allowing us to isolate barrier performance. Each process of the synthetic program executes a loop that performs a controlled amount of work and then enters a barrier. The other two programs used were successive over-relaxation (SOR) and Gaussian elimination. These programs are the intensive portion of larger applications; thus, they represent a typical bottleneck in the performance of some important applications. This section shows results for each of these programs using the different barriers.

In order to verify our claims, a user level scheduler was developed and linked into all programs. The scheduler was prevented from interfering with the user program by restricting it to a single processor and disallowing other processes to run on that processor. A shared data structure between the scheduler and the program provided the application with the current number of processors in its partition. Processes were created using the Silicon Graphics parallel programming primitives, which are adequate for expressing coarse grain heavy-weight process parallelism. A production quality implementation of our ideas could be accomplished by using a shared data structure between the kernel scheduler and the user application, an approach suggested by some modern multiprocessor operating systems [1, 9, 10].

The different implementations of barrier synchronization that we tested were: plain blocking, plain spinning, different competitive strategies, and the scheduler information policy. Other parameters included the time between scheduling decisions and the minimum number of processors allotted to an application. Another parameter that might have been important in this analysis was the quantum of processes within a partition. However, since the experiments indicated that only the plain spinning approach was affected by this, and this effect is well understood, we have omitted results that explore this parameter. The default quantum size of thirty milliseconds was used in the experiments.

In many cases speedup is used to measure the effectiveness of tuning parallel programs. However, in a multiprogramming environment, speedup is not well defined. To best illustrate the comparative performance of different barriers, our results are presented on a time per phase basis. For the synthetic program, we factored out the work delay, thus the time presented represents solely barrier overhead. For Gauss and SOR, the time presented includes work and barrier overhead. Time was determined by measuring wall time on dedicated processors.

The graphs in figures 1 through 6 show the performance of a synthetic program and Gauss elimination and SOR applications as the number of processes varies. For clarity, a pair of graphs is presented for each application. The first graph compares the performance of the different competitive algorithms with blocking, and the second graph compares spinning, blocking, the best competitive strategy, and the **scheduler information** policy. All three applications use barrier synchronization between their phases. The scheduling policy makes decisions every eighty milliseconds, and gives the application seven processors for five percent of the time. The other 95% of the time the application is given between two and six processors with equal probability. This effectively simulates a hardware partitioned environment with applications arriving and leaving at the rate of the scheduling decision frequency. By collecting the history of scheduling decisions, it was verified that the average number of processors in a partition agreed with the statistically expected result computed from the probabilities stated above. As can be seen, the competitive approaches outperform both spinning and blocking in many cases, and deviate very little from

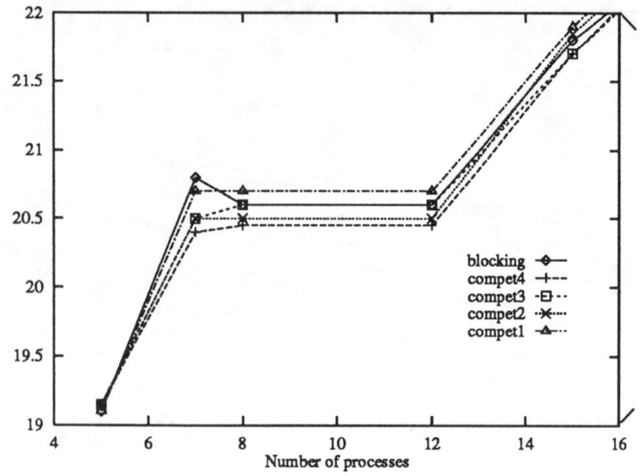

Figure 5: Competitive barriers for Gaussian elimination

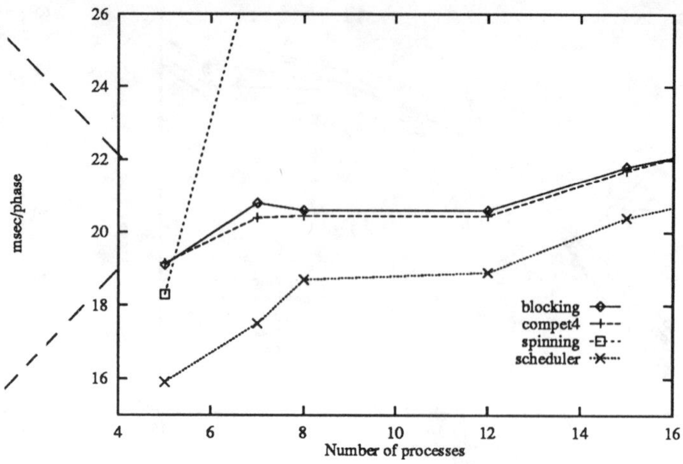

Figure 6: Scheduler information barrier for Gaussian elimination

the best of the two in the rest. Competitive spinning often outperforms both blocking and plain spinning in the cases of five and seven process applications because the scheduling policy will give the application anywhere between two and seven processors. When there are as many processors as processes, spinning outperforms blocking, otherwise the converse is true. Since the competitive approaches are able to adjust, they can outperform both plain spinning and blocking. When the number of processes increased to the point where there were always more processes than processors, the competitive approaches approximated blocking (with a small overhead) and were significantly better than spinning.

In addition to the above experiments, others were performed by varying the time between scheduling decisions from 80 to 800 milliseconds, by allowing the application full use of the multiprocessor for as little as five percent of the time or as much as fifty percent of the time, and by giving the application a small number of processors. While the results were quantitatively different, the qualitative behavior of the different barrier implementations remained the same. Thus, the graphs presented are representative of all our experiments.

The graphs in figures 7 and 8 show the performance of the barrier implementations across different periods of scheduling decisions. Varying times between scheduling decisions is different from varying the quantum of process execution, and that is why spinning is not affected as much as might be anticipated. As expected, the competitive approaches improve when the time between scheduling decisions increases. The reason is that the competitive approaches need a short period of time to adjust to the new environment after a scheduling action. When scheduling actions are in effect for longer periods of time, the adjustment cost is amortized over more barriers yielding better performance. Blocking is largely invariant to the time between scheduling decisions (figures 7 and 8). Spinning performs in a more complicated way. A possible explanation for this behavior is the interaction between scheduling decisions and quantum duration within a partition. This question wasn't pursued further, since spinning performs much worse than other policies and the qualitative analysis of a bad policy is not interesting.

The unexpected result was the small but steady improvement of the **scheduler information** policy when the time between scheduling decisions increased. While this policy should have been invariant to time between scheduling decisions, it is possible for the policy to err when a scheduling decision occurs at the same time the application is going through a barrier. In this case, some threads will use old information to guide their decision and thus may decide sub-optimally. When the time between scheduling decisions is large, this happens rarely, and is why the application has a small performance improvement. It is possible to correct this behavior by delaying scheduling decisions until the application has cleared the barrier but the performance benefit is too small to warrant this change.

5 Conclusion

We feel the work presented in this document has several interesting continuations. We are interested in examining the performance of scheduler information in conjunction with other synchronization primitives that may be adversely affected by multiprogramming, i.e., FIFO locks. We are also interested in studying the effect of scheduler information in systems where priorities are important, i.e., real-time applications. We believe that significant performance benefits can be achieved by sharing information between the kernel and application in such environments.

There are three primary contributions of this paper. We ex-

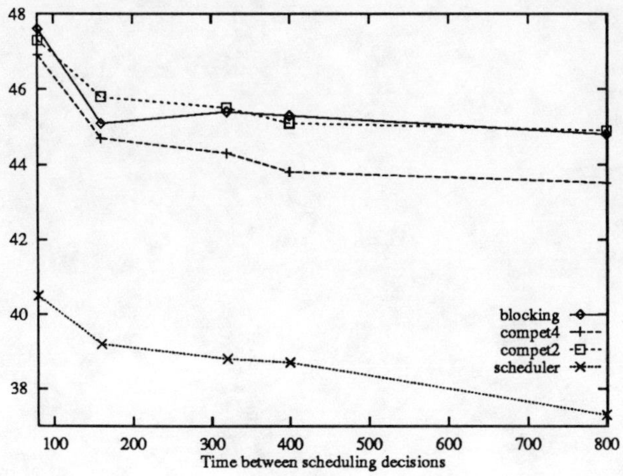

Figure 7: Effect of scheduling decision frequency on seven processors in SOR

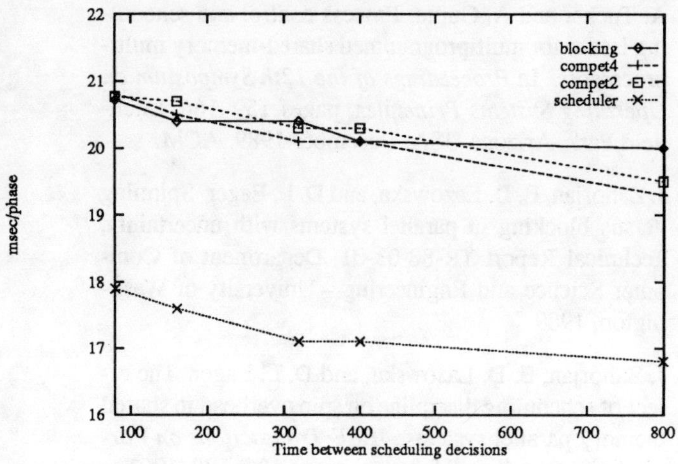

Figure 8: Effect of scheduling decision frequency on seven processors in Gaussian elimination

tended the work performed by Karlin *et al* on locks by showing these techniques perform well for barriers. We proposed **coarse adjustment**, another competitive spinning technique that performs better than the previous competitive spinning techniques applied to barriers. Finally, we proposed **scheduler information**, a new technique that outperformed all the previous techniques consistently and provided considerably better performance in many cases. This new technique is both optimal and easy to implement.

Acknowledgements

We would like to thank Michael Scott for his helpful comments on this document.

References

[1] T. E. Anderson, B. N. Bershad, E. D. Lazowska, and H. M. Levy. Scheduler activations: Effective kernel support for the user-level management of parallelism. *Transactions on Computer Systems*, pages 53–79, February 1992. Also presented at the Thirteenth Symposium on Operating Systems Principles.

[2] David L. Black. Scheduling support for concurrency and parallelism in the Mach operating system. *IEEE Computer*, 23(5):35–43, May 1990.

[3] M. Crovella, P. Das, C. Dubnicki, T. LeBlanc, and E. Markatos. Multiprogramming on multiprocessors. In *Proceedings of the Third IEEE Symposium on Parallel and Distributed Processing*, December 1991.

[4] J. Edler, J. Lipkis, and E. Schonberg. Process management for highly parallel Unix systems. In *Proceedings of the USENIX Workshop on Unix and Supercomputers*, September 1988.

[5] A. Gupta, A. Tucker, and S. Urushibara. The impact of operating system scheduling policies and synchronization methods on the performance of parallel applications. In *Proceedings of the 1990 ACM SIGMETRICS Conference on Measurements and Modeling of Computer Systems*, pages 120–132, May 1990.

[6] Anna R. Karlin, Kai Li, Mark S. Manasse, and Susan Owicki. Empirical studies of competitive spinning for a shared-memory multiprocessor. In *Proceedings of the 13th ACM Symposium on Operating Systems Principles*, pages 41–55, October 1991.

[7] Scott T. Leutenegger and Mary K. Vernon. Performance of multiprogrammed multiprocessor scheduling algorithms. In *Proceedings of the 1990 ACM SIGMETRICS conference in Measurements and Modeling of Computer Systems*, pages 226–236, May 1990.

[8] E. Markatos, M. Crovella, P. Das, C. Dubnicki, and T. LeBlanc. The effects of multiprogramming on barrier synchronization. In *Proceedings of the third symposium on parallel and distributed programming*, pages 662–669, December 1991.

[9] B. D. Marsh, M. L. Scott, T. J. LeBlanc, and E. P. Markatos. First-class user-level threads. In *Proceedings of the Thirteenth ACM Symposium in Operating System Principles*, pages 110–121, 1991.

[10] Michael Scott, Thomas LeBlanc, and Brian Marsh. Design rationale for Psyche, a general purpose multiprocessor operating system. In *In Proceedings of the 1988 International Conference on Parallel Processing*, August 1988.

[11] A. Tucker and A. Gupta. Process control and scheduling issues for multiprogrammed shared-memory multiprocessors. In *Proceedings of the 12th Symposium on Operating Systems Principles*, pages 159–166, Litchfield Park, Arizona USA, December 1989. ACM.

[12] J. Zahorjan, E. D. Lazowska, and D. L. Eager. Spinning versus blocking in parallel systems with uncertainty. Technical Report TR-88-03-01, Department of Computer Science and Engineering - University of Washington, 1989.

[13] J. Zahorjan, E. D. Lazowska, and D. L. Eager. The effect of scheduling discipline on spin overhead in shared memory parallel systems. *IEEE Transactions on Parallel and Distributed Systems*, pages 180–198, 1991.

[14] J. Zahorjan and C. McCann. Processor scheduling in shared memory multiprocessors. In *Proceedings of the 1990 ACM SIGMETRICS Conference on Measurements and Modeling of Computer Systems*, pages 214–225, May 1990.

Appendix

```
global_t gsense,bar_count,numb_procs;
global_t SpinThreshold;
local_t lsense,count;
SpinThreshold = switch_time;
bar_count = AtomicAdd(bar_count,1);
if bar_count < numb_procs then
   for count = 1 to SpinThreshold do
      if lsense == gsense then
         lsense = 1 - lsense;
         exit barrier;
else
   bar_count = 0;
   gsense = 1 - gsense;
   wakeup blocked threads;
   lsense = 1 - lsense;
```

Figure 9: **Fixed Time** Competitive Barrier

```
global_t gsense,bar_count,numb_procs;
global_t SpinThreshold;
global_t tcount[numbprocs];
global_t ttime[numbprocs][3];
local_t lsense,count,now,tblkd,id;
bar_count = AtomicAdd(bar_count,1);
if bar_count < numb_procs then
   for count = 1 to SpinThreshold do
      if lsense == gsense then
         tblkd = 0;
         goto exit_barrier;
   now = GetCurrentTime();
   block;
   tblkd = GetCurrentTime() - now;
 exit_barrier:
   ttime[id][tcount[id]%3] = tblkd;
   tcount[id] = tcount[id] +1;
   if Average(tcount[id]) < switch_time
     then
      SpinThreshold = min(switch_time,
                SpinThreshold+Adjust);
     else
      SpinThreshold = max(0,
               SpinThreshold - Adjust);
   lsense = 1 - lsense;
else
   bar_count = 0;
   gsense = 1 - gsense;
   wakeup blocked threads;
   lsense = 1 - lsense;
```

Figure 10: **Average Three** Competitive Barrier

```
global_t gsense, bar_count, num_procs;
global_t SpinThreshold;
local_t lsense, now, t_blkd, count;

bar_count = AtomicAdd(bar_count,1);
if bar_count < num_procs then
   for count = 1 to SpinThreshold do
      if lsense == gsense then
         tblkd = 0;
         goto exit_barrier;
   now = GetCurrentTime();
   block;
   tblkd = GetCurrentTime - now;
 exit_barrier:
   if tblkd < 2*switch_time
    then
      SpinThreshold = min(switch_time,
             SpinThreshold + Adjust);
    else
      SpinThreshold = max(0,
             SpinThreshold - Adjust);
   lsense = 1 - lsense;
else
   bar_count = 0;
   gsense = 1 - gsense;
   wakeup blocked threads;
   lsense = 1 - lsense;
```

Figure 11: **Last One** Competitive Barrier

```
global_t gsense, bar_count, num_procs;
global_t SpinThreshold;
local_t lsense, now, t_blkd, count;
bar_count = AtomicAdd(bar_count,1);
if bar_count < num_procs then
   for count = 1 to SpinThreshold do
       if lsense == gsense then
          tblkd = 0;
          goto exit_barrier;
   now = GetCurrentTime();
   block;
   tblkd = GetCurrentTime - now;
 exit_barrier:
   if tblkd < 2*switch_time ;
    then
      SpinThreshold = switch_time;
    else
      SpinThreshold = 0;
   lsense = 1 - lsense;
else
   bar_count = 0;
   gsense = 1 - gsense;
   wakeup blocked threads;
   lsense = 1 - lsense;
```

Figure 12: **Coarse Adjustment** Competitive Barrier

```
global_t gsense, bar_count, numb_procs;
global_t numb_blocked, numb_processors;
local_t lsense;

bar_count = AtomicAdd(bar_count,1);
if bar_count < numb_procs
   if (numb_procs - numb_blocked)
            <= numb_processors then
      while lsense <> gsense do
         Spin;
   else
      block;
   lsense = 1 - lsense;
else
   bar_count = 0;
   gsense = 1 - gsense;
   wakeup blocked threads;
   lsense = 1 - lsense;
```

Figure 13: **Scheduler Information** Barrier

```
for i:=0 to NUM_PHASES do
  begin
    work();
    barrier();
  end
```

Figure 14: Code for a typical process in a barrier application

This code is available via anonymous ftp from cayuga.cs.rochester.edu (/pub/barrier.src.tar.Z).

A Concurrent Copying Garbage Collector for Languages that Distinguish (Im)mutable Data

Lorenz Huelsbergen and James R. Larus*
University of Wisconsin–Madison†

Abstract

This paper describes the design and implementation of a concurrent compacting garbage collector for languages that distinguish mutable data from immutable data (*e.g.*, ML) as well for languages that manipulate only immutable data (*e.g.*, pure functional languages such as Haskell). The collector runs on shared-memory parallel computers and requires minimal mutator/collector synchronization. No special hardware or operating system support is required.

Our concurrent collector derives from sequential semi-space copying collectors. The collector requires that a heap object includes a ***forwarding pointer*** in addition to its data fields. An access to an immutable object can be satisfied either by the original or the forwarded copy of the object. A mutable object is always accessed through the forwarded copy, if one exists.

Measurements of this collector in a Standard ML compiler on a shared-memory computer indicate that it eliminates perceptible garbage-collection pauses by reclaiming storage in parallel with the computation proper. All observed pause times are less than 20 milliseconds. We describe extensions for the concurrent collection of multiple mutator threads and refinements to our design that can improve its efficiency.

*This work was supported in part by the National Science Foundation under grant CCR-9101035. L. Huelsbergen is supported by a DARPA fellowship in parallel processing.

†Authors's address: Department of Computer Sciences, 1210 West Dayton Street, Madison, Wisconsin 53706. Email: {lorenz,larus}@cs.wisc.edu

4th ACM PPOPP,5/93/CA,USA

1 Introduction

The convenience of programming languages with implicit storage allocation (*e.g.*, Lisp[19], ML [20], Haskell [17]) is tempered by the run-time cost of reclaiming discarded storage. Automatic recycling of storage is known as garbage collection. A garbage collector retains a program's data that are in-use (*live*) and reclaims data that are unreachable (*garbage*) by the program. Garbage collection is necessary since even large (virtual) memories are finite. In addition to reclaiming storage, a garbage collector can also restore ***locality*** to fragmented data by dynamically compacting it, thereby improving the performance of caches and virtual memory systems and reducing storage requirements [10, 12]. Automatic storage reclamation, however, introduces disruptive pauses into interactive programming environments and slows program execution.

Parallel computers offer the potential to remove much of the garbage-collection overhead by delegating storage reclamation to processors running in parallel with a program [24, 6, 14]. We show how programming languages such as ML and Haskell can harness parallel machines to make their implementations more responsive. This in turn enables programmers to use these languages to develop interactive systems (operating systems, editors, programming environments, *etc.*).

Our concurrent garbage collector uses a single thread, the *collector*, to reclaim storage for a single program, the *mutator*. This concurrent approach potentially reduces the collection overhead for sequential programs since the collector continually recycles the garbage that a program running on other processors creates. Hence, existing sequential programs can benefit directly from this approach. Furthermore, in an interactive programming environment, sequential program execution will not be disrupted by garbage collection if the concurrent processor reclaims garbage at least as quickly as the program creates it. To collect garbage in parallel systems, we describe extensions to our design that support multiple mutators.

Since a concurrent compacting collector relocates dynamic data and allows concurrent mutator access to these data, the cost of data access and allocation operations must be close to their cost with efficient sequential collection. To this end, we exploit the compile-time distinction between mutable and immutable data in some mostly-functional languages, such as ML. Pure functional languages (Pure Lisp, Haskell, *etc.*) can also be concurrently collected by this approach since they manipulate only immutable data.

Allocation in our design only requires initialization of an additional pointer in each object. Access to immutable data is as efficient as in a sequential implementation; since the data are immutable, they are constant, even if copied. The cost to access mutable data increases slightly in our design.[1] This is because a modification to a mutable datum requires that the modification always occur in the forwarded copy of the datum if one exists. If no copy exists, the mutator modifies the original. The modification of the original is followed by an additional check to ensure that the datum was not copied by the collector while the mutator performed the modification. If the collector's copy operation overlapped the mutator's modification, the modification is redone in the copy. Neither the mutator nor the collector explicitly lock the object since hardware and software locking is expensive; fine-grain synchronization based on a known order of memory operations is used instead.

We have implemented our design in the Standard ML of New Jersey (SML/NJ) optimizing ML compiler [7] on a shared-memory parallel computer. It successfully reduces mutator pause latency to a few milliseconds. Relative to simple sequential stop-and-copy collection [10, 12], our collector is very efficient. Its efficiency must, however, be further improved for it to outperform efficient sequential collectors based on generational scavenging [18, 26].

After stating the assumptions that underlie our design, we overview previous work on concurrent garbage collection (Section 2). Section 3 describes sequential copying collection before describing our concurrent copying collector. Section 4 describes an implementation of this collector in SML/NJ and Section 5 gives performance measurements of this implementation. Extensions to multiple mutators and further implementation improvements are in Section 6.

Assumptions

We assume that the mutator and collector share a common address space and that this common memory is *processor consistent* [13].[2] Reads and writes of machine-word quantities must be atomic. These assumptions allow ordered memory operations to implicitly perform fine-grain synchronization without explicit synchronization primitives (*cf.* lock-free synchronization [15]). The compiler must also distinguish mutable-data accesses from immutable-data accesses. This assumption allows the compiler to generate code for mutable accesses that implicitly synchronizes with the concurrent collector. Run-time separation of mutable and immutable data is not necessary. It is also assumed that the concurrent collector can inform the mutator that an event is pending via software interrupts or polling. This device is necessary since the mutator must periodically supply (upon collector request) its root set—the pointers that reach all live data. The mutator need not report its roots immediately, but may continue execution until gathering and reporting them is convenient. We assume that mutator allocation is heap based [1]. This simplifies the exposition of the collector's algorithms since it elides the details of stack management during collection. Finally, this design assumes that most mutator data accesses are to immutable data. This is often valid for programs written in a mostly-functional language and certainly valid for pure functional programs.

2 Previous Work

Various designs for concurrent garbage collectors have been proposed. Most of these require special hardware or operating system support; few have been implemented on parallel machines.

Our design is based on sequential copying collectors [10, 12]. Copying collectors are attractive since

[1] Depending on a language's object-equality semantics, equality testing (pointer comparison) may also incur a slight additional overhead if an extra indirection is required to correctly determine equality.

[2] Processor consistency guarantees that writes from a processor p appear to all other processors as occurring in the sequence in which p executes them. For example, if processor p_0 executes the sequence (`x ← 0; x ← 1; x ← 2`) and p_1 reads the value 1 for `x` then p_1 cannot subsequently read the value 0 for `x`. Processor consistency is weaker than sequential consistency.

they operate in time proportional to the amount of data in use by the system. They remove fragmentation and restore locality by compacting data as it is copied. Copying collectors are more efficient than reference-counting and mark-and-sweep collectors in theory and practice [8, 1]. Zorn provides analyses and simulations of mark-and-sweep and stop-and-copy collectors [27].

Sequential implementations of mostly-functional languages provide fast object allocation and access [4, 5, 1]. To retain efficiency, concurrent collectors must not substantially increase the costs of object allocation and access. Central to this goal is Brooks's idea that all dynamic heap objects contain an extra field for a forwarding pointer [9]. His approach sets the forwarding pointer of an object a to point to a itself if the object has not been copied. When the collector copies the object to a new object a', a's forwarding pointer is set to point to a'. Accesses to a simply indirect through a's forwarding pointer.

Our collector implements Brooks's forwarding pointer, but indirects through it only on access to mutable data. This is possible due to the assumption that the language being collected separates mutable data from immutable data at compile-time. In mostly-functional languages, indirection is rarely necessary. The Pegasus system's garbage collector [23] also employs Brooks's technique, but does not provide a concurrent implementation and the outlined concurrent design relies on the explicit locking of objects.

Real-time response is highly desirable in garbage-collected systems. Baker's algorithm [8] addresses this issue by interleaving allocation with collection, but his algorithm requires special hardware to run efficiently. Halstead [14] extended Baker's algorithm to shared-memory multiprocessors by using fine-grain synchronization on individual objects. Efficient implementation of Halstead's algorithm relies heavily on hardware support. A concurrent lock-free version of Halstead's algorithm is given by Herlihy and Moss [16]. Their algorithm never performs global synchronization. This, however, is achieved only at the cost of expensive object access and allocation. Again no implementation is provided.

Appel, Ellis, and Li implemented the first concurrent copying collector on a stock shared-memory multiprocessor [6]. It directly addresses the efficiency and response-time issues. The Appel-Ellis-Li collector uses operating-system memory-protection devices to detect mutator references to heap objects that have not been collected. Their collector does not require compiler cooperation. Response latency is on the order of hundreds of milliseconds—but, as noted by the authors, this is still too slow for some interactive applications. Efficiency of their concurrent collector is measured only in terms of a simple sequential stop-and-copy collector, not in relation to common generational collectors [18, 26] that provide very efficient sequential collection.

Doligez and Leroy implemented a hybrid concurrent collector for ML [11]. A copying collector reclaims storage in a processor's local memory and a mark-and-sweep algorithm collects shared global memory. Since mark-and-sweep collection fragments storage, the shared-memory objects in this design must eventually be relocated—the authors do not provide a concurrent relocation algorithm. Worst-case pause latencies of their collector, not including shared-data relocation costs, are on the order of hundreds of milliseconds.

Our collector provides excellent response; average response latency is a few milliseconds. Furthermore, our collector requires no hardware or operating system support and only minimal compiler co-operation. We provide empirical evidence that this collector is more efficient than sequential stop-and-copy collectors and describe refinements that can improve its efficiency to that of fast generational collectors [3] used in sequential implementations.

3 The Collector

In this section we describe the basic structure of sequential copying collection (§3.1) and then our concurrent copying collector (§3.2).

3.1 Sequential Copying Collection

A basic sequential copying collector [10, 12] requires two memory spaces of equal size. Denote these spaces as *From-Space* and *To-Space*. Figure 1 illustrates these spaces and the pointers that manage them. Mutator allocation of heap objects always occurs in *From-Space* at the next unused location (*New*). If allocation crosses a predetermined *Threshold*, *From-Space* is deemed full and garbage collection occurs. The *From-Space* in Figure 1a is full and requires collection.

At the beginning of a collection, *Scanned* and *Unscanned* point to the bottom of (empty) *To-Space*. *Scanned/Unscanned* form a queue for a breadth-first traversal of the live data in *From-Space*. *Scanned* points to the head of the queue

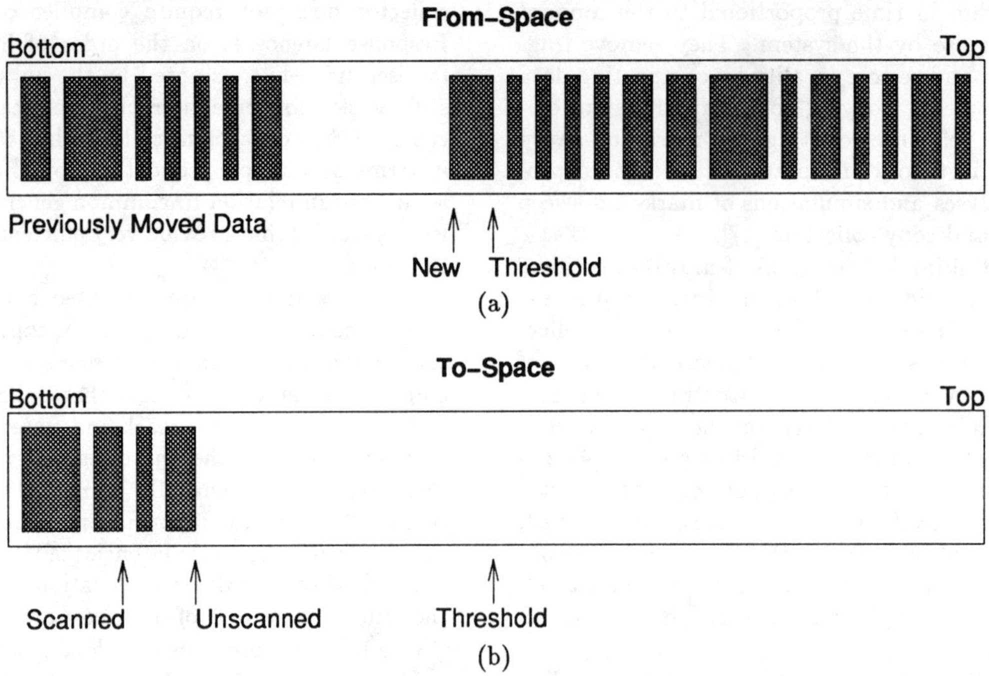

Figure 1: *From-Space* (a) and *To-Space* (b) and associated pointers for a sequential copying collector. After mutator allocation at *New* crosses *Threshold* in *From-Space*, the mutator halts and all live data are contiguously copied into *To-Space*. After copying, the spaces flip roles and mutator computation resumes.

and *Unscanned* to the tail. This queue is initialized with the objects pointed to by the *roots* of the mutator. Any pointer into the active heap (*From-Space*) that the mutator has access to (*e.g.*, registers) is a root and all such pointers constitute the mutator's root set. All live data available to the program is reachable via pointers from this root set. After an object's relocation in *To-Space*, the collector overwrites the original object in *From-Space* with the object's new location in *To-Space* (its *forwarding* pointer).

Objects in the initialized *Scanned/Unscanned* queue are scanned (from *Scanned* to *Unscanned*) for pointers into *From-Space*. A previously uncopied *From-Space* object is inserted into the queue and forwarded. A pointer to a previously copied object is translated to point to the copy using the forwarding pointer. All live data resides in *To-Space* when the queue of unscanned objects empties; that is, when *Scanned* = *Unscanned*. A *flip* operation then reverses the roles of the two spaces: *To-Space* becomes *From-Space* and *From-Space* becomes *To-Space*. The collection is now complete and the collector supplies an updated root set to the mutator. Mutator allocation proceeds anew from the top of the (empty) *From-Space*.

3.2 Concurrent Copying Collection

Our concurrent collector design is based on the sequential copying algorithm. It also copies live data between regions, but does not suspend mutator computation during the copying phase. Two modifications to the underlying data structures are required: objects contain an additional field, and the layout of *To-Space* is altered. First, every object r created by either the mutator or collector must contain an additional field f for a forwarding pointer. f is distinct from r's data fields. This is in contrast to implementations of the sequential algorithm that are free to overwrite r's data fields with forwarding information. We require an additional field since the contents of r and the contents of copies of r are simultaneously accessible to the mutator. Let A denote all address values for f. Distinguish four values in A: *Fresh, BeingTranslated, Translated, BeingCopied.* Partition A into mutator *inaccessible* and *accessible* state sets:

$$inaccessible = \{BeingTranslated, BeingCopied\}$$

$$accessible = A - inaccessible$$

An object r is always created with its forwarding pointer set to *Fresh.* Figure 2 shows the possible

Fresh → [*BeingTranslated*] → *Translated* ⇒ [*BeingCopied*] → *(forwarding address)*

Figure 2: Possible transitions an object can undergo. The ⇒ indicates that a flip occurs during this transition. A [*Boxed*] state is one in which an object is inaccessible to the mutator.

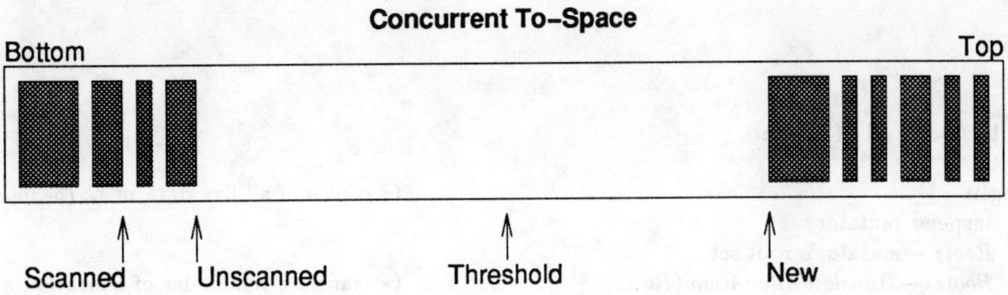

Figure 3: Concurrent *To-Space*. This *To-Space* is similar to the sequential *To-Space* (Figure 1b), but allows the mutator to allocate new data at *New* while the collector concurrently scans and inserts objects into the *Scanned/Unscanned* queue. The collector is also responsible for translating *From-Space* pointers in freshly-allocated data (from *New* to *Top*). Concurrent *From-Space* is identical to the sequential *From-Space* (Figure 1a).

transitions for *r*'s forwarding pointer. The mutator may access a mutable object only when it is in an accessible state. If the state of the object changes during the access, the mutator must redo the access. A change in state is easily detectable since the transitions can be implemented using a monotonic representation (*i.e.*, with reserved address values for the states). An access is performed in the forwarded copy if the state of the object is a true forwarding address. This synchronization is extremely fast—only two fetches from an immutable object are required in the expected case of no mutator/collector conflict. Figure 5 contains pseudo-code for mutator read and write operations to mutable data.

The other modification is to the heap's *To-Space*. Figure 3 illustrates the layout of the concurrent *To-Space*.[3] This change is also conceptual—mutator allocation occurs in *C.To-Space* and not in *C.From-Space* as per the sequential algorithm. This is necessary to properly identify and collect all live data while permitting concurrent mutator allocation.[4]

Figure 4 contains the concurrent copying collector.[5] As the **repeat** loop in *Collect* indicates, the collector runs continually. The algorithm divides into three logically-related parts: flipping (a)–(e), copying live data (f)–(m), and translating old *C.From-Space* pointers into their *C.To-Space* equivalents (n)–(p). We describe these parts in turn.

Lines (a)–(c) prepare the collector for interchanging *C.From-Space* and *C.To-Space*. Only during this part of the algorithm is the mutator inactive. It is, therefore, important that this section execute quickly. At line (a) it is known that all live data resides in *C.To-Space* (newly-allocated data is placed in *C.To-Space* at *C.New*). Pointers to *C.From-Space* may, however, still exist in the new allocation arena (from *C.New* to *C.To-Space.Top*). Since all live data has been copied out of *C.From-Space*, it is only necessary to translate these *C.From-Space* pointers in the allocation arena. This is accomplished at line (c). Since the new-data allocation arena may be large, it is not possible to translate it in its entirety without pausing the mutator for an exorbitant amount of time—overhead we are attempting to avoid in the first place. For this reason, most of the allocation arena is translated concurrently (lines (n)–(p)) with mutator allocation. We discuss this portion of the algorithm below. *TranslateAllocArena* at line (c) only translates a small piece of this arena, namely the data not translated after the last iteration of the loop at line (n). Line (d) performs the flip and repositions the pointers that govern the semi-spaces.

[3] We preface global identifiers used for sequential collection with *S.<identifier>* and global identifiers used for concurrent collection with *C.<identifier>*.

[4] If the mutator were to allocate in *C.From-Space*, it would be difficult to determine when all live data has been copied from *C.From-Space* since the mutator's root set continually changes.

[5] The predicate *Forwarded?(p)* is true if the object at *p* has been forwarded. *Forward(p,q)* forwards the object at *p* to location *q* and *Translate(p)* returns the forwarding address of the object at *p* if one exists, *p* otherwise. *SizeOf(p)* returns the number of fields in the object at *p*.

```
Collect()
    volatile Roots: set of pointers
    repeat
        begin                                               (* copies of all live data in C.To-Space *)
(a)         suspend mutator
(b)         Roots ←mutator's root set
(c)         Roots ←TranslateAllocArena(Roots)               (* translate remainder of allocation arena *)
(d)         Flip(C.From-Space, C.To-Space)                  (* all pointers are into C.To-Space before flip *)
(e)         release mutator                                 (* mutator allocates in (empty) C.To-Space *)
(f)         C.Scanned ←C.To-Space.Bottom                    (* initialize live-data queue *)
(g)         C.Unscanned ←C.Scanned
(h)         for all r ∈ Roots do                            (* Roots reach all live data in C.From-Space *)
(i)             r ←Copy&Forward(r)                          (* copy root objects into queue *)
(j)         while C.Scanned ≠ C.Unscanned do                (* perform breadth-first copy *)
                let object = object at C.Scanned
                    ptrs = set of pointers in object
                in
(k)                 Forward(object, BeingTranslated)        (* indicate impending modification to object *)
                    for all p ∈ ptrs do
                        p ←Copy&Forward(p)
                    C.Scanned ←C.Scanned + SizeOf(object)
(l)                 Forward(object, Translated)             (* modification done *)
(m)             end
(n)         while mutator still allocating do               (* translate pointers in allocation arena *)
(o)             Roots ←mutator's root set                   (* until mutator runs out of space *)
(p)             TranslateAllocArena(Roots)
        end

Copy&Forward(p : object pointer) : object pointer
(q) if not Forwarded?(p) then
        begin
(r)         Forward(p, BeingCopied)                         (* indicate copy operation to mutator *)
(s)         copy object at p to C.Unscanned
(t)         Forward(C.Unscanned, Fresh)                     (* new copy is not forwarded *)
(u)         Forward(p, C.Unscanned)                         (* inform mutator that copy is complete *)
(v)         C.Unscanned ←C.Unscanned + SizeOf(C.Unscanned)
(w)         return C.Unscanned − SizeOf(C.Unscanned)
        end
(x) else return Translate(p)
```

Figure 4: Concurrent copying collector. *Collect* runs continually. Lines (a)–(c) ensure that all pointers point into *C.To-Space*. Lines (f)–(m) perform the copying proper. Lines (k) and (l) indicate to the mutator that the object is undergoing modification. Lines (n)–(p) incrementally translate *C.From-Space* pointers in freshly-allocated data into their *C.To-Space* equivalents. *Copy&Forward* communicates to the mutator at line (r) that the object pointed to by *p* is about to be copied and at line (u) that the copy is complete.

```
Read(r : object pointer, i : integer) : value
    if Inaccessible(r) ∨ Forwarded?(r) then
        Read(Translate(r),i)
    else
        let  s = State(r)
             v = field i of r
        in
             if s ≠ State(r) then
                 Read(r,i)
             else v
        end
```

```
Write(r : object pointer, i : integer, v : value)
    if Inaccessible(r) ∨ Forwarded?(r) then
        Write(Translate(r),i,v)
    else
        let  s = State(r)
        in
             set field i of r to v
             if s ≠ State(r) then
                 Write(r,i,v)
        end
```

Figure 5: Mutator mutable-data access operations to *Read* (*Write*) field i of an object r. If the concurrent collector has forwarded r, the read (write) is performed in the copy. If the collector copies or updates r while the mutable access is underway, the access is redone.

Lines (f)–(m) perform the actual copying and forwarding of live data from *C.From-Space* to *C.To-Space*. *Copy&Forward* provides implicit synchronization information to the mutator (*cf.* Figure 5) by setting the object's state to *BeingCopied* before the actual copy ensues (r) and making it accessible after the copy is complete (line (u)). Similar synchronization is also performed during the scan of an object (line (k) and (l)).

All live data resides in *C.To-Space* when control reaches line (n); that is, all live data from *C.From-Space* has been copied and forwarded into *C.To-Space* and all data concurrently allocated by the mutator since the last flip is allocated in *C.To-Space*. However, pointers into *C.From-Space* may still exist in the fresh allocation arena (*C.New* to *C.From-Space.Top*) and possibly in the copied data (*C.To-Space.Bottom* to *C.To-Space.Unscanned*). This latter case occurs if the mutator updates a mutable location in this region *after* it was scanned and translated by the collector. These *C.From-Space* pointers in the copied area are identified by requiring the mutator to maintain a list of mutable locations into which it stores pointers.[6]

TranslateAllocArena is an incremental depth-first marking algorithm.[7] *TranslateAllocArena* is given a set of pointers to translate. It recursively translates all *C.From-Space* pointers reachable from its parameter into their *To-Space* equivalent and returns a translated version of its parameter. For synchronization, *TranslateAllocArena* uses the *BeingTranslated* and *Translated* states in a manner similar to the scanning and copying portions of the collector. The algorithm is incremental in that successive invocations of *TranslateAllocArena* do not reexamine objects that were previously translated. This insures only short pauses when translating reachable, yet untranslated, objects immediately before a flip (line (d)).

4 Implementation

We have implemented our concurrent collector in the SML/NJ 0.73 optimizing ML compiler [7]. ML has higher-order functions, parametric polymorphic types, statically-checked strong typing, and side-effecting operators that modify reference variables and perform IO [20, 21]. The SML/NJ implementation is garbage collected by an efficient generational stop-and-copy collector [3].

Our concurrent implementation runs on a Sequent Symmetry with 40MB of shared memory. Of the Sequent's 20 processors, we use only two—one to execute the program (the mutator) and one to collect the program's garbage (the collector). Each of the Sequent's 80386 processors is connected via a 64KB two-way set-associative cache to a bus to shared memory. The *sml2c* [25] backend to SML/NJ generates portable C code which is compiled with a native 80386 C compiler.

The compiler was modified to allocate an extra word as the forwarding pointer with all objects. Upon object allocation, this pointer is initialized to *Fresh*. The compiler's code generator was modified to include synchronization instructions on access to mutable data and to indirect through forwarding pointers when two object pointers are compared

[6] *Store lists* are used in generational collectors to detect pointers from older generations to younger ones [26, 3].

[7] The stack required for depth-first marking can be allocated explicitly or *threaded* through garbage objects in *C.From-Space*.

Knuth-Bendix (16MB)			
	Stop-&-Copy	Generational	Concurrent
Exec	200.7 s	200.4 s	270.9 s
GC	117.1	5.2	0.04
Sys	3.6	2.7	7.0
Elapsed	320.9	208.2	277.9
Max Pause	7380 ms	420 ms	10 ms
Avg Pause	2251	199	1

QuickSort (1MB)			
	Stop-&-Copy	Generational	Concurrent
Exec	32.3 s	32.4 s	40.0 s
GC	16.9	4.1	1.4
Sys	0.5	0.3	0.4
Elapsed	49.7	36.8	41.8
Max Pause	220 ms	180 ms	20 ms
Avg Pause	98	31	13

Table 1: Timing results for sequential and concurrent garbage collection schemes. *Stop-&-Copy* is a simple sequential collector. *Generational* is an efficient two-generation collector. *Concurrent* is the concurrent copying collector described in this paper. Resolution of the clock is ten milliseconds.

for equivalence. Since the backend of the compiler emits C code, these additions were implemented as C functions. Some of the performance degradation due to this implementation can be alleviated by performing these operations in line.

The collector is written in C. The SML/NJ runtime system, the concurrent collector, and the program (produced by *sml2c*) are linked into an executable image. Upon initiation, this image creates two parallel processes that concurrently execute the collector and mutator threads. Communication among the mutator and the collector occurs through shared memory. The collector acquires the mutator's roots by setting a single location. The mutator polls this location when it performs a check for sufficient heap space. Upon receiving such a request, the mutator copies its roots into a shared vector and communicates to the collector that the roots are in place. The collector communicates new root sets to the mutator via the same vector.

5 Results

This section presents performance measurements of the concurrent collector for two benchmark programs.[8] We compare the absolute performance of the concurrent collector to that of two sequential collectors: a simple stop-and-copy collector and a fast copying collector [3] that maintains two generations of live data. The heap size was fixed[9] for the entire execution of a program and was set to the smallest size in which the concurrent collector always completes its copying phase before the mutator exhausts its allocation arena.

The first benchmark implements the Knuth-Bendix completion algorithm processing some axioms of geometry (*cf.* [5]). It performs side effects in the form of IO. IO buffers are dynamically allocated heap objects in SML/NJ and subject to collection and hence require mutator synchronization when they are read or written. Table 1 gives times for collecting the garbage using the concurrent and the two sequential collectors. The concurrent collector performs extremely well in reducing the amount of time the mutator spends in the garbage collector (less than 1% of the stop-and-copy or generational times). It only creates low latency disruptions—average pause times almost two orders of magnitude smaller than the pauses exhibited by the Appel-Ellis-Li collector [6].

Our implementation of the concurrent algorithm does, however, adversely affect the overall efficiency of the program. A comparison of the total elapsed times shows the concurrent design to improve on the simple collector by 13%. However, the sequential generational scheme is almost 34% faster than the concurrent scheme even though it uses only one processor. The difference in elapsed times stems entirely from the difference in execution times. Reasons for these differences and possible solutions are discussed below (§6). The Appel-Ellis-Li collector [6] attained an 18% improvement over a simple stop-and-copy collector on a single benchmark, but was not compared to a generational collector.

The second program we timed is a QuickSort applied to a list of 1024 random integers (Table 1). Here concurrent collection is more efficient than in the Knuth-Bendix benchmark, but is still 12% slower than the sequential generational collector. As with Knuth-Bendix, concurrent collection of QuickSort exhibits low pause latencies: worst-case pause latency is 9 times lower than generational

[8] All timings were performed on a Sequent Symmetry with no load. The C program files produced by *sml2c* and the SML/NJ runtime system were compiled at the "-O" optimization level. When compiling the concurrent version, the compiler was also instructed to treat all variables as *volatile* since we use the Sequent's processor-consistent memory to synchronize mutator/collector interaction. Volatile variables restrict many compiler optimizations.

[9] SML/NJ normally resizes the heap dynamically.

pause latency and average pause latency is less than half as long. Mutator time in the collector is again very low for the concurrent collector when compared to both sequential collectors.

6 Future Work

This section addresses the concurrent collector's inefficiencies and extends the design to multiple parallel mutators.

Inefficiencies in the concurrent collector are due to two factors: (1) overhead incurred by the mutator to correctly cooperate with the collector, and (2) decreased locality inherent in distributing work among parallel processors. An inefficiency in our algorithm is mutator overhead due to forwarding pointer creation and manipulation. The additional forwarding pointer on every heap object increases the amount of mutator computation on allocation and decreases heap space available for program data.[10] Depending on the language's implementation, the forwarding pointer can be integrated with the object's usual fields. For example, in SML/NJ all object's carry a word of tag information. It is possible to merge the forwarding pointer with this tag (*cf.* [22]), thereby reducing object allocation costs and improving memory utilization.

Performance degradation due to disruption of locality is a more subtle point. For example, the concurrent collector disrupts mutator locality when it installs a forwarding pointer in an object that resides in the mutator's data cache. Furthermore, all data constantly moves between the mutator's and collector's caches. We suspect that this effect accounts for a large portion of the inefficiencies in our design. Incorporating generational techniques into this concurrent collector is paramount to improving its efficiency (*cf.* [6, 11]).

Our concurrent collector can be extended to reclaim the discarded storage of p parallel mutators as follows. On a flip, the collector partitions the new allocation arena (Figure 3) into m blocks of size k such that $m \gg p$. Each mutator is given a block in which to allocate. When a mutator exhausts the storage in its current block, it requests an additional block from the collector. In addition to dispensing heap blocks, the collector concurrently copies and translates live data (as in the case $p = 1$ described in this paper); the collector successively transmits requests for root sets to the p mutators. After dispensing $m - p$ blocks, the collector halts each mutator p_i in turn, completes the translation of p_i's untranslated reachable data, hands a fresh block to p_i (there are p unused blocks in the allocation arena since the collector only dispenses $m - p$ blocks), and finally releases p_i. The flip occurs after the collector processes all p mutators in this manner. No global synchronization is required under this scheme.

For a large number of parallel mutators, the collector must also be distributed among multiple processors.

[10] Objects in SML/NJ occupy approximately 2.9 words in the heap on average [2]. Adding an additional field to each object therefore reduces heap space by approximately one quarter.

7 Conclusion

We have designed and built a concurrent garbage collector. Our collector is derived from sequential copying collectors and exploits the compile-time separation of mutable and immutable data that some mostly-functional languages such as ML provide. The collector requires no special hardware or operating system support and is extensible to multiple parallel mutators. Experiments indicate that collector pause times are very short—less than 20 milliseconds. Our collector is more efficient than simple sequential collectors and we describe modifications to our design that potentially make it competitive with fast generational collectors.

Acknowledgement

Thanks to the anonymous referees for detailed suggestions.

References

[1] A. W. Appel. Garbage collection can be faster than stack allocation. *Information Processing Letters*, 25:275–279, 1987.

[2] A. W. Appel. Runtime tags aren't necessary. *Lisp and Symbolic Computation*, 2:153–162, 1989.

[3] A. W. Appel. Simple generational garbage collection and fast allocation. *Software Practice & Experience*, 19(2):171–183, February 1989.

[4] A. W. Appel. A runtime system. *Lisp and Symbolic Computation*, 3:343–380, 1990.

[5] A. W. Appel. *Compiling with Continuations.* University of Cambridge Press, 1992.

[6] A. W. Appel, J. R. Ellis, and K. Li. Real-time concurrent collection on stock multiprocessors. In *Conference on Programming Language Design and Implementation*, pages 11–20. Association for Computing Machinery, June 1988.

[7] A. W. Appel and D. B. MacQueen. A Standard ML compiler. *Functional Programming Languages and Computer Architecture*, 274:301–324, 1987.

[8] H. G. Baker. List processing in real time on a serial computer. *Communications of the ACM*, 21(4):280–294, April 1978.

[9] R. A. Brooks. Trading data space for reduced time and code space in real time garbage collection on stock hardware. In *Lisp and Functional Programming*, pages 256–262. Association for Computing Machinery, August 1984.

[10] C. J. Cheney. A nonrecursive list compacting algorithm. *Communications of the ACM*, 13(11):677–678, November 1970.

[11] D. Doligez and X. Leroy. A concurrent, generational garbage collector for a multithreaded implementation of ML. In *Symposium on Principles of Programming Languages*, pages 113–123. Association for Computing Machinery, 1993.

[12] R. R. Fenichel and J. C. Yochelson. A Lisp garbage-collector for virtual memory computer systems. *Communications of the ACM*, 12(11):611–612, November 1969.

[13] K. Gharachorloo, D. Lenoski, J. Laudon, P. Gibbons, A. Gupta, and J. Hennessy. Memory consistency and event ordering in scalable shared-memory multiprocessors. In *International Symposium on Computer Architecture*, pages 15–26. Association for Computing Machinery, May 1990.

[14] R. H. Halstead, Jr. Implementation of Multilisp: Lisp on a multiprocessor. In *Lisp and Functional Programming*, pages 9–17. Association for Computing Machinery, August 1984.

[15] M. P. Herlihy. Wait-free synchronization. *ACM Transactions on Programming Languages and Systems*, 13:124–149, January 1991.

[16] M. P. Herlihy and J. E. B. Moss. Lock-free garbage collection for multiprocessors. *IEEE Transactions on Parallel and Distributed Systems*, 3(3):304–311, May 1992.

[17] P. Hudak, S. P. Jones, P. Wadler, et al. Report on the programming language Haskell. *SIGPLAN Notices*, 27(5), May 1992.

[18] H. Lieberman and C. Hewitt. A real-time garbage collector based on the lifetimes of objects. *Communications of the ACM*, 26(6):419–429, June 1983.

[19] J. McCarthy. Recursive functions of symbolic expressions and their computation by machine. *Communications of the ACM*, pages 184–195, April 1960.

[20] R. Milner. A theory of type polymorphism in programming. *Journal of Computer and System Sciences*, 17:348–375, 1978.

[21] R. Milner, M. Tofte, and R. Harper. *The Definition of Standard ML*. MIT Press, 1990.

[22] S. Nettles and J. O'Toole. Replication-based real-time garbage collection. In *Conference on Programming Language Design and Implementation*. Association for Computing Machinery, 1993. (To appear).

[23] S. C. North and J. H. Reppy. Concurrent garbage collection on stock hardware. In Gilles Kahn, editor, *Functional Programming Languages and Computer Architecture*, pages 113–133. Springer-Verlag, 1987.

[24] Guy L. Steele Jr. Multiprocessing compactifying garbage collection. *Communications of the ACM*, 18(9):495–508, September 1975.

[25] D. Tarditi, A. Acharya, and P. Lee. No assembly required: Compiling Standard ML to C. Technical Report CMU-CS-90-187, School of Computer Science, Carnegie Mellon University, November 1990.

[26] D. Ungar. *The Design and Evaluation of a High Performance Smalltalk System*. MIT Press, 1987.

[27] B. Zorn. Comparing mark-and-sweep and stop-and-copy garbage collection. In *Proceedings of the 1990 ACM Conference on LISP and Functional Programming*, pages 87–98, Nice, France, June 1990.

Improving the Performance of Runtime Parallelization

Shun-tak Leung and John Zahorjan *
Department of Computer Science & Engineering
University of Washington

Abstract

When the inter-iteration dependency pattern of the iterations of a loop cannot be determined statically, compile time parallelization of the loop is not possible. In these cases, runtime parallelization [8] is the only alternative. The idea is to transform the loop into two code fragments: the *inspector* and the *executor*. When the program is run, the inspector examines the iteration dependencies and constructs a parallel schedule. The executor subsequently uses that schedule to carry out the actual computation in parallel.

In this paper, we show how to reduce the overhead of running the inspector through its parallel execution. We describe two related approaches. The first, which emphasizes inspector efficiency, achieves nearly linear speedup relative to a sequential execution of the inspector, but produces a schedule that may be less efficient for the executor. The second technique, which emphasizes executor efficiency, does not in general achieve linear speedup of the inspector, but is guaranteed to produce the best achievable schedule. We present these techniques, show that they are correct, and compare their performance to existing techniques using a set of experiments.

Because in this paper we are optimizing inspector time, but leaving the executor unchanged, the techniques we present have most dramatic effect when the inspector must be run for each invocation of the source loop. In a companion paper [3], we explore techniques that build upon those developed here to also improve executor performance.

*Support for this work was provided in part by the National Science Foundation (Grants CCR-8619663, CCR-9123308, and CCR-9200832), the Washington Technology Center, and Digital Equipment Corporation (Systems Research Center and External Research Program). Authors' addresses: Department of Computer Science & Engineering, University of Washington, Seattle, WA 98195; *shuntak@cs.washington.edu, zahorjan@cs.washington.edu.*

4th ACM PPOPP,5/93/CA,USA
© 1993 ACM 0-89791-589-5/93/0005/0083...$1.50

1 Introduction

Parallelizing compilers offer the parallel machine programmer the best of both worlds: the programming model is nearly identical to that of the familiar sequential programming language, while program execution makes use of the availability of multiple processors, resulting in good parallel performance. To achieve this goal, the compiler relies on a static dependency analysis in order to compute a valid parallel schedule for iteration execution. However, programs with complicated or data dependent array indexing expressions are not amenable to such static analysis, and so cannot be parallelized in this way. For these programs, runtime parallelization is an attractive alternative.

In this section, we introduce the basic mechanisms used to support runtime parallelization, as developed by Saltz and his colleagues [6, 7, 8]. We begin by presenting the basic scheme, and then examine a technique they have proposed for increasing its efficiency. Our improvements to these techniques are presented in subsequent sections.

1.1 The Basic Inspector/Executor Scheme of Saltz et al.

We call the loop being parallelized the *source loop*. A simplified representation of the form of the source loops on which we focus is shown in Figure 1. In it, each array element $a[i]$ in order is assigned a value that depends on other elements of a. Naturally, the loop body may contain other statements which do not lead to inter-iteration dependencies on a, or may be nested inside other sequential loops. These additional considerations are not shown for simplicity.

```
do i = 1 to n
  a[i] = F(a[g(i)], a[h(i)], ...)
enddo
```

Figure 1: Sequential Program Source Loop

The basic idea of runtime parallelization, as defined by Saltz et al. [6, 7, 8], is for the compiler to produce two pieces of customized code for each source loop . The first, called the *inspector*, calculates the values of the index functions used in each iteration of the loop, and from these values determines the inter-iteration dependencies. From these dependencies the inspector can produce a parallel execution schedule for the iterations. The second piece of code, called the *executor*, uses this schedule to achieve a parallel execution of the source loop.

The parallel schedule computed by the inspector is based on partitioning the set of iterations into subsets, called *wavefronts*. All iterations within the same wavefront can be executed concurrently. The wavefronts themselves are processed sequentially.

A schedule's *depth* is the number of wavefronts it has. There are many valid schedules for the same source loop, some with more wavefronts than others. As a rule of thumb, we prefer a schedule with minimal depth, as such a schedule is likely (but not guaranteed) to lead to minimal parallel execution time.

```
/* wf is initially all zeros */
do i = 1 to n
  wf[i] = max(wf[g(i)],wf[h(i)],...) + 1
enddo
```

Figure 2: Basic Inspector Structure

Figure 2 shows the structure of the basic Saltz et al. inspector, which is responsible for producing a schedule that respects flow (read-after-write) dependencies. If iteration l reads a value produced by iteration k, then because of the restrictions on the form of the source loop, l must be greater than k. Thus, when running the inspector, iteration k must have already been placed in a wavefront by the time iteration l is considered. The inspector looks up k's wavefront from wf and places l in a later wavefront, leading to a schedule that is correct with respect to flow dependencies.

On the other hand, because the inspector disregards both anti- (write-after-read) and output (write-after-write) dependencies, these must be enforced by the executor. The executor shown in Figure 3, first proposed by Saltz et al. [6, 8] and adopted for all work presented here, is sufficient to do this for the class of source loops under consideration. (Improvements to both executor efficiency and domain of applicability are developed in a companion paper [3].)

```
do w = 1 to depth
  pardo all i such that wf[i] = w
    if (g(i) < i) then a1 = anew[g(i)]
                  else a1 = aold[g(i)]
    endif
    ...
    anew[i] = F(a1, a2, ...)
  enddo
enddo
aold = anew
```

Figure 3: Basic Executor Structure

As written in Figure 2, the inspector is sequential. Because it processes as many iterations as the source loop itself, it requires time commensurate with that of a sequential source loop execution, defeating the purpose of runtime parallelization.

Saltz et al. have identified two techniques for reducing the overhead associated with running the inspector. The first is applicable when the source loop is contained inside one or more sequential loops, and when its dependency pattern does not change across iterations of these outer loops. In this case, a single execution of the inspector produces a parallel schedule that can be applied repeatedly, thus amortizing inspector overhead across repeated source loop executions.

The second technique used to reduce inspector overhead is to parallelize its execution. Saltz et al. do this using an alternative general runtime loop parallelization procedure, which they call the preprocessed doacross [7]. We explain this technique briefly in the following subsection.

1.2 Doacross Parallelization

Doacross parallelization [7] is a general runtime parallelization technique that is not in the class of inspector/executor approaches. Doacross is based on the use of an auxiliary array that specifies whether or not each data array element has already been written in the current invocation of the source loop. Processors are assigned iterations in a wrapped manner, and each spin waits until all operands necessary for its execution have been produced.

The advantages of doacross parallelization are that no inspector step is required for loops like the source loop we are considering, reducing overhead, and that a somewhat more general class of loop can be handled by introducing a preprocessing step. The disadvantages of doacross, though, are that it applies to only a restricted class of loop, and that it has potentially significantly suboptimal parallel efficiency. In fact, Saltz et al. find that while the doacross parallelization is preferable to sequential execution [7], it is not a viable alternative to the inspector/executor approach for loops amenable to the latter technique [8]. Thus, we will not consider doacross parallelization further for general runtime parallelization.

However, there is one case in which doacross parallelization can be applied usefully: parallelizing the computation of wavefronts in the inspector. As shown in Figure 2, the inspector is sequential, and so is very expensive. In [8] this expense is reduced by parallelizing the sequential inspector loop using the doacross technique.

There are in fact two variants of the parallel inspector used in [8]. Each employs doacross to parallelize the computation of the wavefronts. They differ, however, in how the iterations in each wavefront are assigned to processors for execution by the executor. The first method, *doacross-global*, appears to be inherently sequential [8], and so is expensive. However, it produces an iteration assignment that is as balanced as possible. In contrast, the second approach, *doacross-local*, is easily parallelized, but makes no guarantees about how balanced the resulting schedule will be. In the worst case, doacross-local can produce a schedule that is sequential in a situation where doacross-global would produce a schedule with perfect speedup.

1.3 Paper Goals and Organization

While the doacross technique does parallelize the inspector to some degree, performance may still be poor [8]. Saltz et al. reports an experiment in which, using sixteen processors, the inspector took 100 ms. while the executor required only 23 ms. In comparison, the source loop took 241 ms. when run sequentially, indicating that the efficiency of the inspector was less than 15%. While parallelizing the source loop in this case does significantly reduce the time to perform the computation (from 241 ms. to 123 ms.), the poor efficiency achieved by the inspector, which accounted for over 80% of the parallel execution time, indicates that there is much room for improvement. Our aim in this paper is to develop alternative inspector parallelization techniques that come as close as possible to the goal of perfect inspector speedup.

In Section 2 we present *sectioning*, a technique for parallelizing the inspector that achieves nearly linear speedup. In Section 3 we present *bootstrapping*, which is not quite as efficient but is guaranteed to produce a minimal depth schedule. In Section 4 we evaluate the performance of these techniques, and compare them to the doacross executions of the inspector. Finally, Section 5 summarizes our conclusions.

2 Parallelizing the Inspector: Sectioning

2.1 The Sectioning Algorithm

One way of parallelizing the inspector is by *sectioning*. The basic idea is simple. The entire range of iterations is partitioned into consecutive sub-ranges, which we call *sections*. Each section is assigned to a different processor. Each processor computes a valid parallel schedule for the iterations in its section by applying the sequential inspector algorithm and ignoring any dependencies on iterations outside of its section.

After all processors have finished, we have a schedule for each section. Every such schedule, which we call a *sub-schedule*, is a mapping from the iterations in the corresponding section to the wavefronts of that section. The overall schedule is formed by concatenating the sub-schedules in the order of the sections. In other words, in the overall schedule, the last wavefront of section s is immediately followed by the first wavefront of section $s+1$.

Figure 4 illustrates how fifteen iterations are divided into three sections and how the three sub-schedules are concatenated to form the overall schedule. (For simplicity, we have not shown the data dependencies that induce the particular sub-schedules shown.) This schedule is valid but, like all schedules computed by sectioning, it does not necessarily have the fewest possible wavefronts.

It is easy to show that sectioning produces a valid schedule. In particular, a valid schedule must satisfy the following condition: if there is a flow dependence from iteration k to iteration l (remember that the inspector needs to consider only flow dependencies), then l's wavefront is after k's. There are two cases to consider. If iterations k and l belong to different sections, the concatenation of sub-schedules guarantees this condition by putting all the wavefronts of l's section behind those of k's section. If the two iterations are in the same section, they are handled by a single processor running the sequential inspector algorithm. The algorithm ensures that the condition is satisfied.

Given the mapping from iterations to wavefronts, the final step is to assign iterations to processors in a way that respects these wavefronts. This assignment is done in the inspector. Each processor is responsible for scheduling its own section, thus yielding good parallelism. The iterations of each wavefront are assigned in a wrapped manner among the processors, thus giving good executor load balance.

2.2 Comparison with the Doacross Inspector

There are two criteria by which we can compare the different inspectors: execution time and quality of the schedule produced.

In terms of execution time, the key consideration is how efficiently each approach is able to make use of multiple processors. In this respect, both of the doacross-based techniques are at a disadvantage. To begin with, the efficiency of the basic doacross scheme is data dependent. While it is probably fairly good in many cases, there are certain to be a large number of others in which it is quite poor. Additionally, doacross-global has a large, basically sequential component in forming the schedule for the executor from the wavefront information.

In contrast, our parallel inspector should exhibit nearly perfect speedups[1]: each processor works on a subproblem in a way that is completely independent of the others. There is no need for any kind of locking as no shared data structures are modified. Nor is there any need for synchronization, other than a barrier to detect when all the processors have finished.

In terms of the quality of the schedule produced, the situation is less clear. Intuitively, a good schedule is one that has minimum depth and is load balanced. Of the three inspectors we are considering, only doacross-global has this property: doacross-local produces a minimum depth schedule, but it may be very load imbalanced, while sectioning produces a load balanced schedule, but its depth may be somewhat greater (up to a factor of the number of sections) than the minimum possible.

In Section 4, we use experimental results to assess the impact of schedule depth on performance. In the next section, we show how to compute a minimal depth schedule in a highly parallelizable way, but at the cost of a second pass over the iterations.

3 Parallelizing the Inspector: Bootstrapping

When we parallelize the inspector by sectioning, we achieve perfect speedup at the cost of a schedule that is deeper than necessary. In this subsection we

[1]Technically, speedup is an inappropriate term as the output of our inspector, like that of doacross-local, depends on the number of processors assigned to the problem. However, the intuitive notion of speedup captures the running time considerations important here.

section	1	2	3
iterations	1 2 3 4 5	6 7 8 9 10	11 12 13 14 15

(a) Partitioning iterations into sections

section	1		2		3		
wavefront number in sub-schedule	1	2	1	2	1	2	3
wavefront number in overall schedule	1	2	3	4	5	6	7
iterations in wavefront	1 2 5	3 4	6 7 9	8 10	11 14	12	13 15

(b) Concatenating sub-schedules

Figure 4: Example of Parallelizing the Inspector by Sectioning

present a method of parallelizing the inspector that costs more inspector execution time but that guarantees that the schedule generated is identical to the minimal depth schedule produced by the sequential inspector. We call this method ***bootstrapping***.

Bootstrapping is based on the observation that the sequential inspector (Figure 2) is itself a loop, and that it has the same inter-iteration dependency pattern as the source loop (Figure 1). Comparing the two loops, we see that the inspector loop is simply the source loop with the general function $F(.)$ replaced by $max(.) + 1$ and a by wf. It therefore follows that any parallel schedule valid for the source loop is also valid for the inspector loop. This observation forms the basis of the boostrapping technique.

To bootstrap, we first generate a valid source loop schedule using sectioning. Then we use this schedule to run the sequential inspector loop in a wavefront-by-wavefront (i.e., parallel) manner. We call this second step ***refinement***. The final schedule thus computed is the same as what a sequential inspector would compute, for the same reason that the executor yields the same results as the sequential source loop. Thus, bootstrapping must produce the same minimum depth schedule as the sequential inspector.

Having computed the minimum depth schedule, the inspector must assign iterations to processors for execution in the executor. This is done in two steps. First, when a processor running the inspector assigns an iteration to a wavefront, it tentatively assigns execution of that iteration to itself. The schedule resulting from this procedure could be imbalanced. Therefore, in the second step, overloaded processors reassign iterations to underloaded ones. This too is done in parallel.

4 Performance Comparison

In this section, we compare the speeds of the various inspector algorithms and their performance impacts on the executor. We use successive over-relaxation as a concrete example.

4.1 Successive Over-Relaxation

Successive over-relaxation (SOR) [1, 5] is a numerical technique that can be used to obtain the solution of a sparse linear system. Given a non-singular $n \times n$ matrix A and an n-dimensional vector b, we want to solve the system of linear equations $Ax = b$ for the unknown n-dimensional vector x. The SOR algorithm starts with an initial guess of the solution vector, x^0, and repeatedly computes a new estimate x^{t+1} from the previous estimate x^t using the formula:

$$x_i^{t+1} = (1-\gamma)x_i^t - \frac{\gamma}{A_{ii}}\left(\sum_{j<i} A_{ij}x_j^{t+1} + \sum_{j>i} A_{ij}x_j^t - b_i\right)$$

where the subscripts represent indexing and where γ is a manually chosen non-zero scalar called the relaxation parameter. The algorithm terminates when the estimates converge or after some predetermined number of iterations have been performed.

Figure 5 shows a sequential implementation of SOR when the matrix A is sparse. (For concreteness, it is shown in actual C code rather than pseudo-code.) Because A is sparse, only non-zero coefficients are stored: $nzCoeffs$ holds the coefficients used by the algorithm (*not* elements of A), while *nzColumns* records the columns to which they belong. Element $firstNz[i]$ indicates where the information for row i starts in $nzCoeffs$ and *nzColumns*.

For this program, the outer loop is our source loop. Each iteration reads and writes elements of x. Only iteration i writes $x[i]$ and hence there are no inter-iteration output dependencies. The flow dependencies and anti-dependencies cannot be determined at compile time because the contents of *nzColumns* depend on input data and are not known until runtime. However, the dependencies do not depend on computation performed within the source loop, and so runtime parallelization is possible.

In our experiments, the source loop was manually transformed into its corresponding inspector and executor because we did not have compiler support for this conversion.

4.2 Results

We applied the SOR technique to solve the global balance equations [2] corresponding to a queueing network model with blocking [4]. The model itself consists of a number of service centers in series, each with a finite capacity queue. This sort of model is commonly used to evaluate the performance of communication networks built from switches with finite buffer space.

Measurements were taken on a Sequent Symmetry shared memory multiprocessor running Mach 3.0. All programs were written in C using Cthreads and compiled with the *gcc* compiler. In each case studied, we made several measurements and observed only insignificant variations among the measured times.

We tried a number of different parameterizations of the queueing model, leading to different sets of linear equations to be solved. We present two examples here. Problem A has a 17577×17577 coefficient matrix with about 100000 non-zero elements. A sequential execution of a single iteration of SOR for this problem takes 1.58 seconds. Problem B has a 45676×45676 matrix with about 250000 non-zero elements. A sequential execution of a single iteration of SOR for this problem takes 4.03 seconds.

Figure 6 shows the achieved inspector and executor efficiencies for the two problems. For the inspector, efficiency is measured against the sequential inspector of Figure 2. For the executor, efficiency is measured against a true sequential execution of the loop.

Considering the inspectors first, we see that only the sectioning approach achieves good efficiency[2]. For the doacross inspectors, efficiency drops off rapidly with number of processors. For bootstrapping, efficiency is more nearly constant, but is half that of sectioning, reflecting the two pass nature of this technique.

Examining executor efficiency, we note first they are uniformly much lower than would be desired (although they still represent a considerable improvement over the sequential execution that would be the only option if compile time parallelization were employed). This is due in part to the overheads involved in the executor (Figure 3) relative to the sequential loop, as evidenced by the poor executor efficiency when running on a single processor. Because our focus in this paper is on improving the inspector phase, we have not attempted to address these executor inefficiencies here, but leave them for a companion paper [3].

Since we ran identical executor code with each inspector, any differences observed in their efficiencies must stem from differences in the schedules the inspectors produce. We make two observations in this regard. First, the doacross-local technique distinguishes itself with slightly lower efficiency than the others. This is a reflection of that policy's imbalanced assignment of iterations to processors within each wavefront.

[2]Because the various inspectors in fact compute different results than the sequential inspector, the term "efficiency" does not strictly apply. However, the efficiencies as we have computed them do convey the proper sense of reduction in elapsed time due to parallelization.

```
for (i = 0; i < n; i++) {
   sum = constant[i];
   for (nz = firstNz[i]; nz < firstNz[i+1]; nz++) {
      sum += nzCoeffs[nz] * x[nzColumns[nz]];
   }
   x[i] = sum;
}
```

Figure 5: Sequential Implementation of SOR for Sparse Linear Systems

Second, we note that, perhaps surprisingly, the increase in schedule depth caused by sectioning does not necessarily have a great impact on performance. Table 1 shows the number of wavefronts produced by the sectioning inspector. The minimum possible depth schedule (which is produced by the other three inspectors) corresponds to the sectioning result when run on a single processor. Examining Figure 6, we observe that a doubling of the schedule depth has little or no effect on executor performance.

Number of Processors	Number of Wavefronts	
	Problem A	Problem B
1	9	12
2	14	18
4	15	18
8	16	20
16	21	24

Table 1: Number of Wavefronts in Schedule Produced By Sectioning

A look at the parallel schedules tells us why sectioning does not necessarily slow down the executor. Take problem B (the larger problem) as an example. The sequential inspector generates a schedule with 12 wavefronts, giving an average of about 3800 iterations per wavefront. In contrast, the schedule computed using 16 sections has 24 wavefronts, for an average of 1900 iterations each. Although the schedule is deepened by a factor of two, there is more than enough work in each wavefront to keep all 16 processors busy. Thus, the difference in schedule depth does not translate into a difference in execution time. Clearly, if the minimal depth schedule had been much deeper because of the dependencies, doubling the schedule depth could have meant under-utilized processors and added synchronization overhead, leading to degraded executor performance.

As a final test of the effect that a deeper schedule obtained by sectioning has on performance, we examined a single queueing model and varied the number of customers in it, producing a set of related systems of linear equations of varying sizes. In Figure 7 we plot the number of invocations of the executor required for sectioning and bootstrapping to have identical total execution times against the average number of iterations per processor per sectioning wavefront. If SOR takes more than the plotted number of iterations to converge, the greater efficiency of the executor under the bootstrapping schedule more than compensates for the added expense of the refinement step required to produce that schedule; below the line, sectioning is cheaper overall.

We see from Figure 7 that when the average number of iterations executed by each processor per sectioning wavefront is small, bootstrapping is advantageous even for very small numbers of invocations of the executor. However, this breakeven point grows quite rapidly, and in general it appears that sectioning is the method of choice for loops where the number of iterations per wavefront greatly exceeds the number of processors.

4.3 Combining Bootstrapping with Sectioning

The relationship of schedule depth to executor execution time motivates the following heuristic technique. We first generate a schedule by sectioning. Given this schedule, we can easily determine how many iterations there are on average in each wavefront. If this number is *not* much greater than the

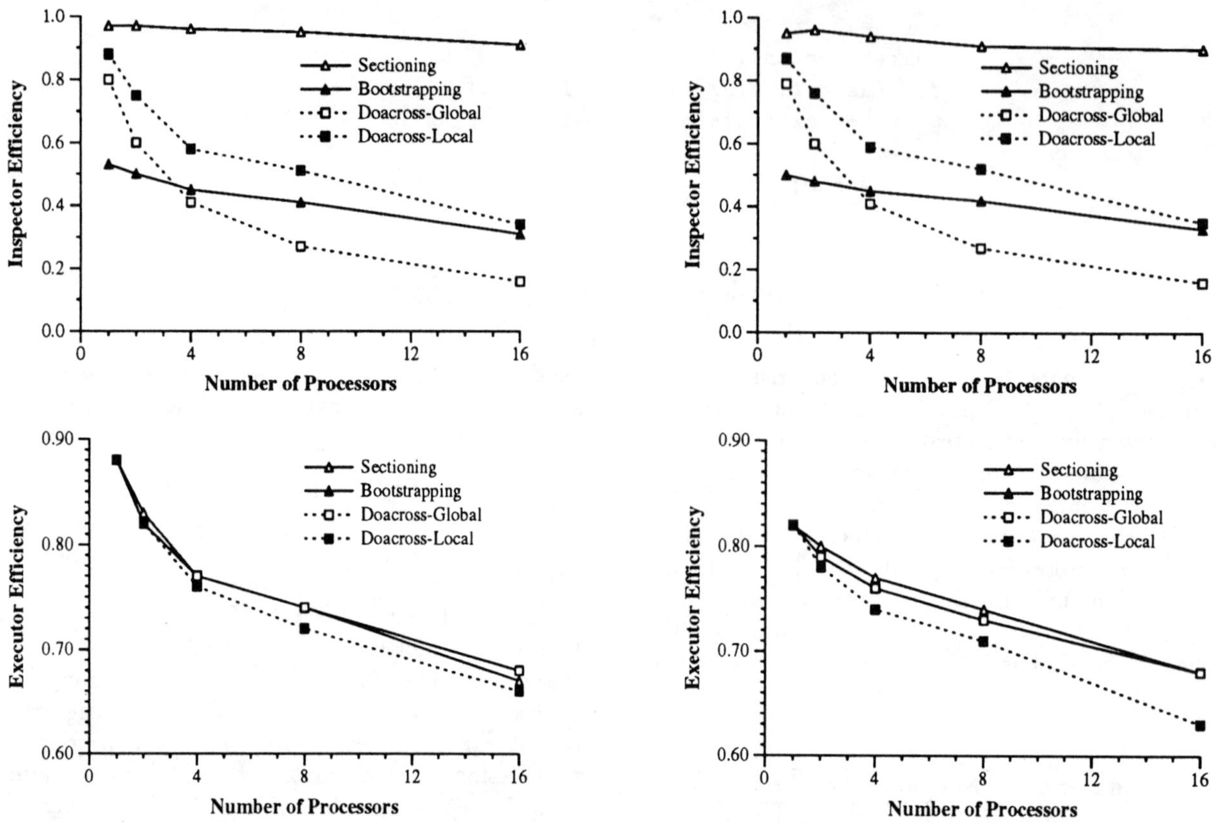

Model A (17577 × 17577)   Model B (45676 × 45676)

Figure 6: Observed Inspector and Executor Efficiencies

number of processors that the executor can use, it is likely that the processors will be under-utilized. In this case, the refinement step is performed to obtain a schedule with a minimum number of wavefronts. Otherwise, there is no need to do so. How many times the executor will be run can also be taken into account, if it is known or can be reasonably estimated: the larger the estimated number of executor invocations, the greater the tendency to choose boostrapping over sectioning.

5 Conclusions

Saltz et al. [6, 8, 7] have made important contributions to the area of runtime parallelization. Our work builds on theirs. The purpose of the work described here is to improve the efficiency of the inspector phase of runtime parallelization through its parallel execution.

We have discussed two approaches to achieving this: sectioning and bootstrapping. Sectioning is a divide-and-conquer strategy that has nearly perfect speedup. On the other hand, the schedule it produces may contain more wavefronts than necessary. While it is unlikely that this would result in a noticeable degradation in executor efficiency unless the average number of iterations per wavefront per processor is quite low, this cannot be guaranteed.

Our second technique, bootstrapping, addresses this potential drawback of sectioning, trading some inspector time for a schedule that is guaranteed to have minimal depth. Bootstrapping is based on the observation that the sequential inspector loop itself can be parallelized using the same schedule as

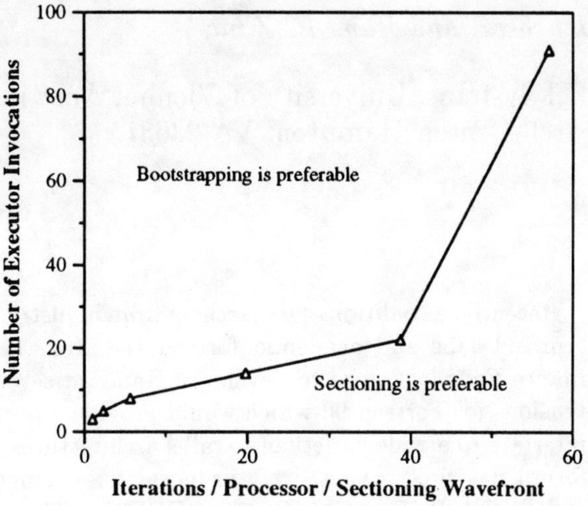

Figure 7: Number of Executor Invocations Required for Equal Sectioning and Boostrapping Total Execution Time

the source loop. Thus, we first compute a schedule by sectioning, producing a potentially suboptimal parallel schedule, and then use this schedule to execute the parallelized version of the sequential inspector, which is known to produce a minimal depth schedule.

We performed a number of experiments to compare these methods. We saw that our new techniques can significantly reduce the overhead of running the inspector. We noted that while sectioning can increase the depth of the schedule, that this has little impact on executor performance if there are enough iterations per wavefront to keep all processors busy. Finally, we noted that in cases where the number of iterations per wavefront is modest relative to the number of processors, and the executor will be executed many times with the same schedule, that the additional cost of bootstrapping can be paid for by a reduction in executor times.

The techniques presented in this paper and the old techniques represent an array of options from which the compiler can choose when it generates code for the inspector. Which one is best in terms of overall execution time (which is the ultimate bottom line) depends on the size and dependency pattern of the source loop, as well as the number of times it is executed. We believe that in many situations, sectioning and bootstrapping are appropriate choices.

Acknowledgements

Derek Eager, Ed Felten, Ed Lazowska, and Radika Thekkath provided valuable comments on the content and presentation of this material.

References

[1] Dimitri P. Bertsekas and John N. Tsitsiklis. *Parallel and Distributed Computation: Numerical Methods.* Prentice Hall, Englewood Cliffs, NJ, 1989.

[2] Edward D. Lazowska, John Zahorjan, G. Scott Graham, and Kenneth C. Sevcik. *Quantitative System Performance.* Prentice Hall, Englewood Cliffs, NJ, 1984.

[3] S. Leung and J. Zahorjan. Extending the domain and improving the execution performance of runtime parallelization. Technical Report , in preparation, Department of Computer Science & Engineering, University of Washington, October 1992.

[4] Raif O. Onvural. Survey of closed queueing networks with blocking. *ACM Computing Surveys*, 22(2):83–121, June 1990.

[5] William H. Press, Brian P. Flannery, Saul A. Teukolsky, and William T. Vetterling. *Numerical Recipes: The Art of Scientific Computing.* Cambridge University Press, Cambridge, 1986.

[6] J. Saltz, H. Berryman, and J. Wu. Multiprocessors and runtime compilation. In *Proc. International Workshop on Compilers for Parallel Computers*, Paris, 1990.

[7] J. Saltz and R. Mirchandaney. The preprocessed doacross loop. In *Proc. 1991 International Conference on Parallel Processing*, August 1991.

[8] J. Saltz, R. Mirchandaney, and K. Crowley. Runtime parallelization and scheduling of loops. *IEEE Transactions on Computers*, 40(5):603–612, May 1991.

High Performance Fortran Without Templates: An Alternative Model for Distribution and Alignment[1]

Barbara M. Chapman[a], *Piyush Mehrotra*[b] *and Hans P. Zima*[a]

[a]Department for Software Technology and Parallel Systems, University of Vienna, Austria.
[b]ICASE, MS 132C, NASA Langley Research Center, Hampton, VA 23681.

Abstract

Language extensions of Fortran are being developed which permit the user to map data structures to the individual processors of distributed memory machines. These languages allow a programming style in which global data references are used. Current efforts are focussed on designing a common basis for such languages, the result of which is known as High Performance Fortran (HPF). One of the central debates in the HPF effort revolves around the concept of templates, introduced as an abstract index space to which data could be aligned. In this paper, we present a model for the mapping of data which provides the functionality of High Performance Fortran distributions without the use of templates.

1 Introduction

Much current research activity is concentrated on providing suitable programming tools for distributed-memory architectures. One focus is on the provision of appropriate high-level language constructs to enable users to design programs in much the same way as they are accustomed to on a sequential machine. Several proposals have been put forth in recent months for a set of language extensions to achieve this [3, 4, 5, 6, 10], in particular (but not only) for Fortran.

[1]Research supported by the National Aeronautics and Space Administration under NASA contract NAS1-18605 while the authors were in residence at ICASE, Mail Stop 132C, NASA Langley Research Center, Hampton, VA 23681, and also by the Austrian Research Foundation (FWF) and the Austrian Ministry for Science and Research.

This paper is partially based on Chapter 3 of the Version 0.2 draft HPF specification [8].

4th ACM PPOPP,5/93/CA,USA
© 1993 ACM 0-89791-589-5/93/0005/0092...$1.50

Recently, a coalition of researchers from industry, government labs and academia formed the High Performance Fortran Forum to develop a standard set of extensions for Fortran 90 which would provide a portable interface to a wide variety of parallel architectures. The forum has produced a draft proposal for a language, called High Performance Fortran (HPF), which focuses mainly on issues of distributing data across the memories of a distributed memory multiprocessor.

High Performance Fortran (HPF) adds directives to Fortran 90 to allow the user to advise the compiler on the allocation of data objects to processor memories. The three basic elements of the model are:

- **abstract processors**,
- **distributions**, which are mappings of objects to abstract processors,
- **alignments**, which are mappings of data objects to other objects.

The **distribution** of an object (usually an array) specifies a mapping of the index domain associated with the object to the index domain of a set of abstract processors. This may be specified by the user: a) **directly**, by explicitly specifying suitable directives, or b) **indirectly**, by using an **alignment** that relates the index domain of the array to the index domain of another object whose distribution is known.

The HPF directives provide a way to direct the compiler to ensure that certain data objects will reside in the same processor. The underlying motivation is that an operation on two or more data objects is likely to be carried out much faster if they all reside in the same processor, and, furthermore, it may be possible to carry out several such operations concurrently if they can be performed on different processors.

Alignment can serve as a *bundling mechanism*: once many arrays are aligned to the same object, then they can be distributed onto a processor arrangement with a single statement.

In general, arrays are aligned to other arrays. However, HPF has introduced the concept of templates to be used as an alignment base. As stated in the HPF language specification [8]:

> *Sometimes it is desirable to consider a large index space with which several smaller arrays are to be aligned, but not to declare any array that spans the entire index space. HPF provides the notion of a TEMPLATE, which is like an array whose elements have no content and therefore occupy no storage; it is merely an abstract index space that can be distributed and with which arrays may be aligned.*

The problem with this approach is that even though it is useful in some special situations, the concept of templates necessarily complicates the whole underlying semantic model. Since templates are not first class objects in the language (they can occur only in directives), they cannot be passed across procedure boundaries, and thus cannot be used to describe the distributions and alignments of procedure arguments. Also, as currently defined, the size of templates has to be a specification expression and hence templates cannot be used for describing the alignment of Fortran 90 allocatable arrays.

In this paper, we show that the HPF distribution and alignment model can be defined in a clear and concise manner without templates, while retaining the intended functionality.

The major differences between the current HPF draft [8] and the language proposed in this paper are as follows. The model has been **simplified** by:

1. Removing template directives.
2. Limiting the height of alignment trees to 1.
3. Clarifying the role of processors by establishing a language defined mapping to an implementation-specific abstract processors arrangement.
4. Passing of arguments to procedures has been simplified by eliminating the INHERIT attribute, matching alignments, and the TO-clause for dummy arguments.

At the same time, the language has been significantly **generalized** with the objective of improving object program performance. In particular:

1. Arrays may be distributed to processor sections.
2. The set of distribution functions has been extended by including GENERAL_BLOCK. This allows the specification of irregular block distributions, which are important for the support of load balancing, and can be implemented efficiently [13].
3. The concept of *distribution functions* has been defined in a general way so that future language standards may easily incorporate more general mappings.

The paper is organized as follows. In the next section we describe the model and terminology underlying our proposal. The subsequent sections introduce the main language extensions – processors, distribution directives and alignment directives. Issues involving allocatable arrays and procedures are treated separately. We then discuss the issues arising due to HPF templates and conclude with a discussion of related work.

2 Model

2.1 Index Domains

An **index domain I of rank (dimension)** n is an ordered set of subscript tuples that can be represented by a subscript-triplet-list of length n (see Fortran 90 specification, R619). Each element of an index domain is called an **index**; it represents an n-dimensional arrangement of values. **I** is called a **standard index domain** iff the stride in each subscript triplet is 1.

Let A denote a declared data array (or processor array) that has been created. Then A is associated with a standard index domain which we denote by $\mathbf{I}^A$.

2.2 Distributions

A **distribution** of an array maps each array element to one or more processors which become the **owners** of the element and, in this capacity, store the element in their local memory. We model distributions by mappings between the associated index domains.

Definition 1 Index Mappings
Let $\mathbf{I}, \mathbf{J}$ *denote two index domains. An* **index mapping** *from* **I** *to* **J** *is a total function* $\iota : \mathbf{I} \rightarrow \mathcal{P}(\mathbf{J}) - \{\phi\}$, *where* $\mathcal{P}(\mathbf{J})$ *denotes the powerset of* **J** .

Definition 2 Distributions
Let A denote an array, and R a processor array. An index mapping δ_R^A from $\mathbf{I}^A$ to $\mathbf{I}^R$ is called a **distribution function** *for A with respect to R.*

A distribution function δ_R^A – which is a mapping between index domains – induces an associated **element-based distribution** that maps elements of A to one or more abstract processors.[1]

Note that scalars can easily be accommodated in our model by treating them as if they were associated with an index domain consisting of exactly one element.

[1]Note that replication can be modeled as a special case of distribution, since every array element can be distributed to an arbitrary (positive) number of processors.

2.3 Alignment

Definition 3 *Let A, B denote arbitrary arrays. An index mapping α_B^A from $\mathbf{I}^A$ to $\mathbf{I}^B$ is called an* **alignment function** *for A with respect to B.*

Definition 4 Construction of a distribution
If A, B, δ_R^B, and $\alpha_B^A : \mathbf{I}^A \to \mathcal{P}\ (\mathbf{I}^B) - \{\phi\}$ are given as above, then δ_R^A can be determined as follows: For each $\mathbf{i} \in \mathbf{I}^A$:

$$\delta_R^A(\mathbf{i}) := \bigcup_{\mathbf{j} \in \alpha(\mathbf{i})} \delta_R^B(\mathbf{j})$$

We will express this relationship below in the form

$$\delta_R^A = CONSTRUCT(\alpha, \delta_R^B).$$

This can be verbally described as follows: if $\mathbf{i}$ is an index of A which is mapped to an index $\mathbf{j}$ of B via the alignment function α, then $A(\mathbf{i})$ and $B(\mathbf{j})$ are guaranteed to reside in the same processor under any given distribution for B.

2.4 The Alignment Relation

For the following discussion, we consider the data space $\mathcal{A}$ of all arrays that are accessible in a given scope, and have been created, at a given time during the execution of a program unit.

An **alignment directive** (see Section 5) establishes an **alignment** from an array A_1, the **alignee**, to an array A_2, the **alignment base**. It defines an alignment function for A_1 with respect to A_2.

An HPF program must satisfy the following constraints:

1. Each array occurring as an alignment base must not be aligned to another array. For such an array, a distribution must be specified directly.

2. Each array occurring as an alignee can be aligned with only one alignment base.

This enables us to represent $\mathcal{A}$ as an **alignment forest**, consisting of a set of **alignment trees**. The nodes in the alignment forest represent arrays, and there is a directed edge from B to A if and only if A is aligned to B. The height of alignment trees may be either 1 or 0. An alignment tree of height 0 is called **degenerate**: it consists of exactly one node that represents an array which is not aligned to any other array, and to which no other array is aligned.

Each alignment tree T has a uniquely defined root, which is called the **primary array** of T. All other nodes of T are called **secondary arrays**.

Let B denote a primary array. Then there is either a directive which explicitly specifies a distribution for B or B is implicitly distributed by the compiler. Primary arrays are the only arrays with this property.

Let A denote an arbitrary secondary array of a tree with primary array B . Then there exists an alignment function α, describing the alignment from A to B. If δ_R^B is the distribution of B, the distribution of A satisfies $\delta_R^A = CONSTRUCT(\alpha, \delta_R^B)$.

After the specification part of a unit has been completely processed, the alignment forest can be constructed for the set of all arrays that are accessible and have already been created. This is the initial state for the **actual alignment forest** associated with the processing of the executable part of the program. The structure of the forest may change dynamically during execution as a result of executing REDISTRIBUTE and REALIGN directives, ALLOCATE and DEALLOCATE statements, and procedure calls.

For the details of these manipulations see Sections 4.2, 5.2, and 7. Distribution and alignment functions are explained in Sections 4 and 5, respectively.

3 The Processors Directive

Each implementation of HPF determines uniquely an **implicit abstract processor arrangement**, AP, which specifies a linear numbering scheme for the physical processors of the underlying machine.

The PROCESSORS directive declares one or more processor arrangements, each of which may be either a **processor array arrangement** or a conceptually **scalar processor arrangement**.

The specification of a processor arrangement determines the name and, in the case of a processor array arrangement, a non-empty index domain. It must appear in the specification part of a program unit.

Each processor arrangement is mapped to AP in the same way as storage association is defined for the Fortran 90 EQUIVALENCE statement, with abstract processors playing the role of the storage units (see Fortran 90 specification, 5.5.1). The sharing of an abstract processor implies the sharing of the associated physical processor.

Depending on the target architecture, data distributed to a (conceptually) scalar processor arrangement may reside in a single control processor (if the machine has one), or may reside in an arbitrarily chosen processor, or may be replicated over all processors. The language does not specify a relationship between different scalar processor arrangements.

4 Distribution Directives

The DISTRIBUTE directive specifies the distribution (Section 2.2) of one or more arrays, the **distributees**, by establishing for each distributee a mapping between its index domain and the index domain of the **distribution target**, which is either a processor array or a section thereof. The distribution target is specified, after the keyword TO, in a TO-clause. The mapping between distributee and processor array can be specified either **explicitly**, as a **distribution format list**, or as an **inherited distribution**. The elements in the distribution format list are associated with the dimensions of the distributee; each element is one of the following:

1. BLOCK
2. GENERAL_BLOCK(restricted-expression)
3. CYCLIC[(specification-expression)]
4. ":"

The meaning of these elements will be discussed below. Inherited distributions will be discussed in Section 7.

Examples:

```
!HPF$ DISTRIBUTE A(BLOCK)
!HPF$ DISTRIBUTE B(CYCLIC) TO Q(1:NOP:2)
!HPF$ DISTRIBUTE C(GENERAL_BLOCK(S))
!HPF$ DISTRIBUTE (BLOCK,:) :: E,F
```

4.1 Determining an Array Distribution

Let A denote an array of rank n which is not a dummy argument, and assume that R is the associated *distribution target* (explicitly or implicitly specified). The distribution of A is specified by a list of *distribution formats*. The length of this list must be n. A *distribution format* ":" specifies that the corresponding array dimension is not being distributed. The rank of R must be n, reduced by the number of colons in the *distribution format-list*. The non-colon entries in the *distribution format list* are matched from left to right to the dimensions of R. For each such entry, a distribution function is determined according to the rules defined below. Here we assume both the array and the processor array are one-dimensional, with index domains $\mathbf{I}^A = [1 : N]$ and $\mathbf{I}^R = [1 : NP]$. We will define the functions associated with the *distribution formats* by specifying the associated distributions, which will be simply denoted by δ.

4.1.1 Block Distributions

The block distribution function is specified by the *distribution format* BLOCK; it divides the array into contiguous blocks whose sizes are identical, except possibly for the last block, which may be of a smaller size. More precisely, let $q := \lceil \frac{N}{NP} \rceil$. Then:

- $\delta(i) = \{j\}$ for all $i, 1 \leq i \leq N$, where $j = \{\lceil \frac{i}{q} \rceil\}$.
- The local index associated with element $A(i)$ in processor $R(j)$ is $i - (j-1) * q$.

4.1.2 General Block Distributions

A *distribution format* for a general block distribution is of the form GENERAL_BLOCK(G), where G is an integer array with index domain [1:M], where $M \geq NP-1$.

A is partitioned into NP contiguous blocks. For all $i, 1 \leq i < NP$, $G(i)$ specifies the upper bound of block i. The index range associated with block 1 is $[1 : G(1)]$; for $1 < i < NP$, $[G(i-1)+1 : G(i)]$ is the index range of block i; and $[G(M-1)+1 : N]$ is the index range of block NP.

4.1.3 Cyclic Distributions

Block-cyclic distributions are specified by the *distribution format* CYCLIC(k), with an argument, $k \geq 1$, of type integer. CYCLIC(k) defines contiguous segments of length k and maps them cyclically to the processors. The distribution function is given as follows:

$\delta(i) = \{MODULO(\lceil \frac{i-1}{k} \rceil, NP+1)\}$ for all $i, 1 \leq i \leq$N

Cyclic distributions are specified by the *distribution format* CYCLIC. This is equivalent to CYCLIC(1).

4.2 The REDISTRIBUTE Directive

The REDISTRIBUTE directive is syntactically similar to the DISTRIBUTE directive but may appear only in the execution part of a program unit. It is used for dynamically changing the distribution of an array and may only be used for arrays that have been declared as DYNAMIC.

If an array B is redistributed, then every array A that is aligned to B is redistributed in such a way that the relationship expressed by the alignment function linking A to B is kept invariant (see Section 2.4). If B is a secondary array at the time of redistribution, then the actual alignment forest changes as follows: B is disconnected from A and made into a new degenerate tree with primary array B.

5 Alignment Directives

The ALIGN directive is used to distribute data objects indirectly, by specifying one or more direct alignment relationships and the associated alignment functions (see Sections 2.3 and 2.4).

Every axis of the alignee is specified as either ":" or "*" or an *align-dummy*, which is a scalar integer variable. If it is ":", then positions along that axis will be spread out across the matching axis of the alignment base; if it is "*", then that axis is collapsed: positions along that axis make no difference in determining the corresponding position of the alignment base. (Replacing the "*" with an align-dummy not used anywhere else in the directive would have the same effect; thus this notation is a convenience only). An align-dummy is considered to range over all valid index values for that dimension of the alignee.

Each element of the alignee is aligned with all corresponding positions of the alignment base.

5.1 Determining the Alignment Function

This section describes how an ALIGN directive specifies the alignment function associated with the direct alignment relationship between alignee and alignment base. Let

- A denote the alignee, and $\mathbf{I}^A = [L_1 : U_1, \ldots, L_n : U_n]$
- B denote the alignment base, and $\mathbf{I}^B = [L'_1 : U'_1, \ldots, L'_m : U'_m]$

The alignment function mapping $\mathbf{I}^A$ to the power set of $\mathbf{I}^B$ will be denoted by α.

Assume that the directive has the form

ALIGN $A(s_1, \ldots, s_n)$ WITH $B(t_1, \ldots, t_m)$

where

- each s_i is ":", "*", or an *align-dummy*)
- each t_j is a *base-subscript*. This can be any of the following cases:
  - a *dummyless-expr*, i.e., a scalar integer expression in which no *align-dummy* occurs
  - a *dummyuse-expr*, i.e., a scalar integer expression in which exactly one *align-dummy* occurs
  - a *subscript-triplet*
  - "*"

We explain the construction of α by first applying a sequence of transformations to the directive which eliminate ":" and "*" in the alignee, and subscript-triplets as well as "*" in the *base-subscript-list*. The transformations are specified as follows:

- Assume that s_i =":" matches the subscript triplet $t_j = [LT : UT : ST]$. Then $U_i - L_i + 1 \leq MAX(INT(UT{-}LT{+}ST)/ST, 0)$ must hold. The positions in axis i of the alignee are spread out across axis j of the alignment base:

  s_i is replaced by a new align-dummy J, and t_j is replaced by the expression $(J - L_i) * ST + LT$. (This is analogous to array assignment).

- Assume that s_i ="*". Then axis i of the alignee is collapsed:

  s_i is replaced by a new align-dummy J which occurs nowhere else.

- Assume that t_j ="*". This denotes replication:

  $B(t_1, \ldots, t_{j-1}, *, t_{j+1}, \ldots, t_m)$ is replaced by the set $\{B(t_1, \ldots, t_{j-1}, k, t_{j+1}, \ldots, t_m) \mid L'_j \leq k \leq U'_j\}$.

By applying these transformations until neither the alignee nor the alignment base contain positions with either ":" or "*" we obtain:

- a *reduced alignee* of the form $A(J_1, \ldots, J_n)$, where the J_i are distinct *align-dummies*. The range of J_i is given by $[L_i : U_i]$.
- an *alignment base set ABS*, every element of which has the form $B(y_1, \ldots, y_m)$, where each y_j is either a *dummyless-expr* or a *dummy-use-expr*. The operators "+", "-", and "*" may be applied to form expressions which are linear in the *align-dummy*. Since linear expressions cannot handle some frequently occurring cases, such as truncation at either end of the alignment, we also allow the intrinsic functions MAX, MIN, LBOUND, UBOUND, and SIZE to be used in alignment functions. Each J_i may occur in at most one y_j (this excludes the possibility to specify skew alignments).

The basic rules for determining α are now as follows:

1. Select an arbitrary tuple $\mathbf{j} = (j_1, \ldots, j_n)$, where each j_i is a value in the range of J_i, and substitute j_i for each occurrence of J_i in ABS.
2. Evaluate all expressions in the modified set ABS; this evaluation is performed modulo the extent of the associated dimension of the alignment base: the value y associated with dimension j is replaced by $\hat{y} = MIN(U'_j, y)$.

Example:

```
      REAL A(1:N), D(1:N,1:M)
!HPF$ ALIGN A(:) WITH D(:,*)
```

aligns a copy of A with every column of D. The reduced alignee has the form $A(J)$, where the range of J is $[1 : N]$. For the alignment base set we obtain:

$ABS=\{D(J,k) \mid 1 \leq k \leq M\}$. Hence, $\alpha(J) = \{(J,k) \mid 1 \leq k \leq M\}$ for each $J \in [1:N]$.

Example:

```
      REAL B(1:N,1:M), E(1:N)
!HPF$ ALIGN B(:,*) WITH E(:)
```

Here, the reduced alignee has the form $B(J_1, J_2)$, where the range of J_1 is $[1:N]$ and the range of J_2 is $[1:M]$. For the alignment base set we obtain:$ABS=\{E(J_1)\}$. Thus, $\alpha(J_1, J_2) = \{(J_1)\}$ for each $J_1 \in [1:N]$ and $J_2 \in [1:M]$.

5.2 The REALIGN Directive

The REALIGN directive is syntactically similar to the ALIGN directive but may appear only in the execution-part of a program unit. It is used for dynamically changing the alignment of an array and again may only be used for arrays that have been declared as DYNAMIC.

Assume that A is the alignee, B the base array, with distribution δ_R^B, and α the alignment function determined by the REALIGN directive. Then the actual alignment forest is modified as described by the steps below:

1. If A is a primary array at the root of a non-degenerate tree immediately before execution of the REALIGN directive, then all secondary arrays associated with A are disconnected from A and made into primary arrays of degenerate trees with their current distribution.

   If A is a secondary array with associated primary array B', then A is disconnected from B'. (Note that $B' = B$ is possible).

2. A is made a new secondary array of B.

3. The distribution of A is determined as $\delta_R^A = CONSTRUCT(\alpha, \delta_R^B)$

6 Allocatable Arrays

Distribution and alignment for variables with the ALLOCATABLE attribute may be specified using DISTRIBUTE or ALIGN directives. These directives may occur in the specification-part of a program unit just as for other arrays: the associated attributes are propagated to each associated ALLOCATE statement. Such variables may also be used in REDISTRIBUTE and REALIGN directives.

In the following example, distributions are specified for the allocatable arrays A, C and D which are valid for each allocation instance. When C is allocated in the instance shown, it is given a cyclic distribution in the executable REDISTRIBUTE directive. At the time ALLOCATE is applied to an array B, the array is created according to the alignment given in the executable REALIGN statement. The actual alignment forest is modified by entering B as a new element in the position determined by the alignment relationships involving B. At the time DEALLOCATE is applied to B, the array is removed from the alignment forest and each array A directly aligned to B is made into a new tree with primary A. Note that a local array which is not declared ALLOCATABLE cannot be aligned in the specification-part of a program unit to an allocatable array.

Example:

```
      REAL,ALLOCATABLE(:,:) :: A,B
      REAL,ALLOCATABLE(:) :: C,D
!HPF$ PROCESSORS PR(32)
!HPF$ DISTRIBUTE A(CYCLIC,BLOCK)
!HPF$ DISTRIBUTE(BLOCK) :: C,D
!HPF$ DYNAMIC B,C
      ...
      READ 6,M,N
      ALLOCATE(A(N*M,N*M))
      ALLOCATE(B(N,N))
!HPF$ REALIGN B(:,:) WITH A(M::M,1::M)
      ALLOCATE(C(10000), D(10000))
!HPF$ REDISTRIBUTE C(CYCLIC) TO PR
```

7 Procedures

The distribution of dummy arguments can be specified as shown below; it can also be specified by giving an alignment to another dummy argument or a local data object in the usual way. Further, a local data object may be aligned to a dummy argument.

The alignment tree, as defined in Section 2.4, is local to a procedure. Thus, an array which is the actual argument of a procedure call is not connected with its alignment tree in the calling unit during execution of the called procedure.

If a dummy argument is redistributed or realigned during execution of the procedure, then the original distribution must be restored on procedure exit.

The distribution of a dummy argument A can be specified in four different ways:

1. **explicitly** by providing a distribution specification of the form:

   DISTRIBUTE A *d* [TO *r*]

   where *d* is a parenthesized *distribution format-list*, and *r* is the *distribution target*. Here, the distribution of the actual argument is changed, if necessary, to the distribution determined by the specification (see Section 4.1). If necessary, the distribution of A before the call has to be restored upon exit from the procedure.

2. by **inheritance**, syntactically expressed by:

   DISTRIBUTE A *

   In this case, the distribution of the actual argument is transferred into the procedure and **inherited** by A.

3. by **inheritance matching**, syntactically expressed by:

   DISTRIBUTE A * *d* [TO *r*]

   A specification of this form indicates that the distribution of the actual argument is transferred into the procedure and inherited by A. However, if this distribution does not match the above specification, then the program is not HPF-conforming.

   If this distribution attribute of the dummy is known within the calling routine (through the use of interface blocks, for example), then the language processor will arrange for remapping the actual argument to the specified distribution (and mapping it back on return from the subprogram, if necessary). If the distribution attribute of the dummy is not made available when the caller is compiled, the onus is on the programmer to arrange for proper distribution of the actual argument.

4. **implicitly**: No explicit distribution is specified (directly or indirectly). In this case, the compiler provides an implicit distribution specification.

8 The Template Directive in High Performance Fortran

In the above sections, we have presented a model for mapping of data to processor memories without using templates. We claim that the HPF template directives are limited in their applicability and give rise to serious problems in the specification of the language, without adding any significant functionality.

Template directives, which may occur only in the specification part of a (sub)program, result in the creation of a **template**. Although the language definition states that "templates are just abstract index spaces", it postulates in other places that distinct definitions of templates in the same or different scopes are to be considered as different, independent of their associated index domain. As a consequence, each template created in a program execution must be interpreted as a *tagged index domain.*

The discussion in the rest of this section does not include the so-called "natural templates" of HPF: they represent the index domain associated with an array and are thus implicitly part of our proposal. In fact, our claim could be rephrased as saying that "natural templates" are sufficient to describe all features related to distribution and alignment.

8.1 The Usefulness of Templates

Templates have been perceived to have two separate uses within the language. We discuss each of these briefly.

8.1.1 Alignment of Staggered Grids

The first use of templates is to enable the specification of alignment between arrays where there is no appropriate common index domain: this can occur whenever two or more arrays are each associated with different parts of a physical grid which do not completely overlap.

Before we discuss the general case, we consider the example posted on the HPFF Distribution mailing list by C. A. Thole:

```
      REAL U(0:N,1:N), V(1:N,0:N), P(1:N,1:N)

!HPF$ TEMPLATE T(0:2*N,0:2*N)
!HPF$ ALIGN P(I,J) WITH T(2*I-1,2*J-1)
!HPF$ ALIGN U(I,J) WITH T(2*I,2*J-1)
!HPF$ ALIGN V(I,J) WITH T(2*I-1,2*J)

      P=U(0:N-1,:)+U(1:N,:)+V(:,0:N-1)+V(:,1:N)
```

For the above code, the claim was made that:

1. *Only a template with a larger index domain than any of the arrays involved represents the nature of the physical grid structure correctly.*
2. *Therefore the template T is required to specify the relationship between the data objects precisely: in particular, it is supposed to express the fact that P(I,J) is a neighbor of U(I,J) and U(I-1,J), but not of U(I+1,J), and similarly for P and V.*
3. *The actual distribution of the template (which is deliberately omitted) is irrelevant and will be chosen in a machine-dependent manner.*

Now, note that whenever two data objects in HPF are aligned with the *same* element of a template, then the language guarantees that these objects will be mapped to the same physical processor. But in the above example, all arrays are aligned with *disjoint* elements of the template. As a consequence, only the *distribution* of the template decides the actual, physical neighborhood relation. For example, the distribution

```
!HPF$ DISTRIBUTE(CYCLIC,CYCLIC)::T
```

results in the worst possible effect, viz. different processor allocations for any two neighbors.

While an alignment relation between *arrays* in a program's data space is a relatively natural concept, the template-based code above does not establish one. Hence, this example is misleading at best, and would seem to point out a danger associated with the template concept rather than a use for it.

However, the user will certainly desire to specify a collocation of the arrays in the above code or similar codes, which can be accomplished by declaring a template of size (N+1,N+1). It is indeed not possible to correctly specify an HPF alignment (without a template) in this situation. Our extension of the HPF alignment directive (which allows restricted usage of MAX and MIN), will suffice to permit explicit alignment directives for many cases which occur in practice, including this one. Otherwise, the distributions must be specified explicitly. Given a suitable definition of the block distribution, one way to perform the required distributions is the following:[2]

```
      REAL U(0:N,1:N), V(1:N,0:N), P(1:N,1:N)
!HPF$ DISTRIBUTE (BLOCK,BLOCK):: U,V,P

      P=U(0:N-1,:)+U(1:N,:)+V(:,0:N-1)+V(:,1:N)
```

The language proposal contained in this paper offers a much more general solution, by providing a generalized form of block distribution.

8.1.2 Passing Array Sections to Subroutines

The second perceived use for a template directive was to permit the explicit declaration of mappings of array sections in subroutines:

```
      REAL A(1000)
!HPF$ DISTRIBUTE A (CYCLIC(3))

      CALL SUB(A(2:996:2))
       ...

      SUBROUTINE SUB(X)
      REAL X(:)  !X inherits its distribution
```

We assume that the dummy argument in subroutine SUB inherits its distribution from the actual argument. The question raised here is:

how can the mapping of X be declared in SUB if one wants to specify it explicitly?

[2]Here the Vienna Fortran definition of BLOCK is assumed. With the HPF definition, this will cause a problem if and only if the number of processors divides N exactly.

Now one will, in general, *not* want to explicitly specify such a distribution: the relatively high cost associated with data movement on the current generation of parallel computers means that a subroutine will usually be written so that it is invoked with distributed arguments and the dummy arguments will indeed inherit the distribution from the actual argument as above. However, just as we write one subroutine to handle arrays of different sizes, so one expects such a subroutine to accept arrays with different distributions. In those cases where a subroutine is important enough to warrant a specific redistribution of its arguments, or if this should be necessary for some reason, then the language provides the constructs required to prescribe the mappings.

Templates were seen as a solution to the problem of providing distributions such as that of X above explicitly, should it be deemed necessary:

```
      SUBROUTINE SUB(X)
!HPF$ TEMPLATE T(1000)
!HPF$ ALIGN X(I) WITH T(2*I)
!HPF$ DISTRIBUTE T (CYCLIC(3))
```

The template does help to specify this distribution in the example, but at the above-mentioned cost of a loss of generality for the entire subroutine. Note, further, that the same effect can be achieved by passing the entire array A to the subroutine and either using the array section explicitly or, if it is passed as a separate argument, repeating the alignment of the argument as above:

```
      SUBROUTINE SUB(A,X)
!HPF$ REAL A(1000)
!HPF$ ALIGN X(I) WITH A(2*I)
!HPF$ DISTRIBUTE A *(CYCLIC(3))
```

(The asterisk indicates that the distribution of A is inherited). But recall that if there is another call site for this subroutine with a different actual argument for X, then neither of these solutions will be of any use. Instead, inquiry functions must be used to determine the properties of alignments and/or distributions passed into the subroutine.

The current definition of HPF further attempts to facilitate the manipulation of the distributions of sections of arrays passed to subroutines by introducing the INHERIT directive, which further removes the need for explicit use of templates in this situation (albeit at the cost of introducing a host of new syntactic and semantic difficulties).

The main reason for this problem is that the current HPF language specification has an unfortunate shortcoming: HPF **cannot** (in contrast to, for example, Kali or Vienna Fortran, which include the concept of *user-defined distribution functions*), describe explicitly every distribution that it can actually generate.

8.2 Language Problems with Templates

We now reiterate the two major problems caused by templates in the HPF language definition. Note that templates are **not** first-class objects of the language: in particular, **templates cannot** be defined as being **ALLOCATABLE**. Furthermore, they cannot be passed as arguments to subroutines.

1. Templates cannot handle allocatable arrays:

   While the shape of templates is determined at entry to a program unit and cannot be changed afterwards, an allocatable array may be subject to multiple ALLOCATE and DEALLOCATE statements, where the extents of the dimensions associated with each instance may depend on run-time and input values. There is no way in which HPF can establish a direct relationship between the shape of an instance of an allocatable array, and the shape of an associated template.

   Methods to avoid this dilemma would include the definition of allocatable templates, or of infinite templates (neither of which are a serious alternative).

2. Templates cannot be passed across procedure boundaries:

   A data object whose distribution is described by a template may be passed to a subprogram in such a way that the dummy inherits the distribution. If we need to describe the distribution of the dummy argument, then we must be able to refer to the template of the actual (see above example). In HPF this would require the passing of templates to the subprogram as well. The **INHERIT** option for dummy arguments in the current HPF definition tries to achieve exactly that, introducing an element of *maximum surprise* for the user. The above example could be written as follows:

```
      REAL A(1000)
!HPF$ DISTRIBUTE A (CYCLIC(3))

      CALL SUB(A(2:996:2))
       ...

      SUBROUTINE SUB(X)
      REAL X(:)

!HPF$ INHERIT::X
!HPF$ DISTRIBUTE X *(CYCLIC(3))
```

   The idea here is that the distribution specified for X is not the distribution of the dummy argument, i.e., the distribution of the array section A(2:996:2), but that of the array associated with the actual argument.

   In contrast, the distributions defined in the language proposal of this paper (as well as in Vienna Fortran) are considered to be an attribute of an array, and they are handled that way as well. Even in the case of inherited distributions which cannot be explicitly specified, inquiry functions can be used to determine every aspect of the distribution passed into the procedure.

9 Related Work

Many of the concepts and constructs used in the above language proposal, and in the HPF specification, are not new. Processor arrays and the distribution of data to them were first used for distributed memory machines in the Kali programming language [9]. They were further refined in the Vienna Fortran language, where processor arrays could also be reshaped, now expressed by means of the HPF VIEW attribute. A major difference in the handling of processor arrays is, however, that Vienna Fortran supports the mapping of data to subsets of processor arrays and provides a canonical mapping of processor arrays to a linear processor array, to facilitate the portability of code.

The Vienna Fortran language [1, 3, 12] is based both upon Kali and upon experience gained with the SUPERB parallelization system ([7, 11, 13]); it provides the user with a wide range of facilities for mapping data structures to processors, including those proposed in this paper and user-defined distributions. Vienna Fortran was the first language in which the issues of distribution handling at subroutine boundaries were investigated in depth. It introduced the concept of inheriting and of enforcing distributions and provided an attribute to enable the user to make assertions about the distributions of actual arguments. This language was also the first to make the distinction between static and dynamic distributions.

Among other things, the mapping of data to subsets of processors and the inheritance of distributions have been implemented within the framework of the Vienna Fortran Compilation System. Two variants of the general block distribution used in this paper, but not included in HPF, have also been implemented.

The programming language Fortran D [6] proposes a Fortran language extension in which the programmer specifies the distribution of data by aligning each array to a decomposition, which corresponds to a template, and then specifying a distribution of the decomposition to a virtual machine. These are executable statements, and array distributions are dynamic only.

The Yale Extensions [4] specify the distribution of arrays in three stages: alignment, partition and a physical map. Because all these stages are modeled as bijective functions between index domains, data replication is not possible. By restricting the scope of layout directives to phases, a block structure is imposed on Fortran 90.

Cray Research Inc. has announced a set of language extensions to Cray Fortran (cf77) [10] which enable the user to specify the distribution of data and work. They provide intrinsics for data distribution and permit redistribution at subroutine boundaries. Further, they permit the user to structure the executing processors by giving them a shape and weighting the dimensions. Several methods for distributing iterations of loops are provided.

10 Conclusions

An approach which substantially reduces the cost of developing codes for distributed memory parallel machines is to provide a set of extensions for sequential languages (in particular, Fortran and C). These extensions should be portable across a wide range of architectures and should suffice for a wide variety of algorithms. The methods by which the user may distribute data to the processors are the central feature of such a language, and should be as natural and as flexible as possible. In this paper, we have presented in detail such a model for distribution and alignment of data. This model is both simpler and more general than the current High Performance Fortran model. In particular, it does not require a template directive and has simplified the passing of distributed arguments to subroutines. On the other hand, the concept of distribution functions has been generalized. A full description of the model described in this paper can be found in [2].

References

[1] S. Benkner, B. Chapman, and H. Zima. Vienna Fortran 90. In *Proceedings of the Scalable High Performance Computing Conference 1992*, IEEE Computer Society Press, Los Alamitos, April 1992, pages 51–59.

[2] B.M. Chapman, P. Mehrotra, and H. Zima. High Performance Fortran Without Templates: An Alternative Model for Distribution and Alignment, Technical Report, University of Vienna, 1993.

[3] B. Chapman, P. Mehrotra, and H. Zima. Programming in Vienna Fortran. *Scientific Programming*, 1(1):31–50, 1992.

[4] M. Chen and J. Li. Optimizing Fortran 90 programs for data motion on massively parallel systems. Technical Report YALE/DCS/TR-882, Yale University, January 1992.

[5] *CM Fortran Reference Manual, Version 5.2.* Thinking Machines Corporation, Cambridge, MA, 1989.

[6] G. Fox, S. Hiranandani, K. Kennedy, C. Koelbel, U. Kremer, C. Tseng, and M. Wu. Fortran D language specification. Department of Computer Science Rice COMP TR90079, Rice University, March 1991.

[7] H. M. Gerndt. *Automatic Parallelization for Distributed-Memory Multiprocessing Systems.* PhD thesis, University of Bonn, December 1989. Reprinted as Tech. Report TR90-1, Austrian Center for Parallel Computation, January 1990.

[8] High Performance Fortran Forum. *DRAFT High Performance Fortran Language Specification. Version 1.0 Draft*, January 25,1993. Technical Report, Rice University.

[9] P. Mehrotra and J. Van Rosendale. Programming distributed memory architectures using Kali. In A. Nicolau, D. Gelernter, T. Gross, and D. Padua, editors, *Advances in Languages and Compilers for Parallel Processing*, pages 364–384. Pitman/MIT-Press, 1991.

[10] D. Pase. MPP Fortran programming model. In *High Performance Fortran Forum*, Houston, TX, January 1992.

[11] H. Zima, H. Bast, and M. Gerndt. Superb: A tool for semi-automatic MIMD/SIMD parallelization. *Parallel Computing*, 6(1):1–18, 1988.

[12] H. Zima, P. Brezany, B. Chapman, P. Mehrotra, and A. Schwald. Vienna Fortran – a language specification. ICASE Internal Report 21, ICASE, Hampton, VA, 1992.

[13] H. P. Zima and B. M. Chapman. Compiling for distributed-memory systems. *Proceedings of the IEEE, Special Section on Languages and Compilers for Parallel Machines (To appear 1993).* Also: Technical Report ACPC/TR 92-16, Austrian Center for Parallel Computation (November 1992).

Implementation of a Portable Nested Data-Parallel Language*

Guy E. Blelloch[1] Siddhartha Chatterjee[2]
Jonathan C. Hardwick Jay Sipelstein Marco Zagha
School of Computer Science
Carnegie Mellon University
Pittsburgh, PA 15213

Abstract

This paper gives an overview of the implementation of NESL, a portable nested data-parallel language. This language and its implementation are the first to fully support nested data structures as well as nested data-parallel function calls. These features allow the concise description of parallel algorithms on irregular data, such as sparse matrices and graphs. In addition, they maintain the advantages of data-parallel languages: a simple programming model and portability. The current NESL implementation is based on an intermediate language called VCODE and a library of vector routines called CVL. It runs on the Connection Machine CM-2, the Cray Y-MP C90, and serial machines. We compare initial benchmark results of NESL with those of machine-specific code on these machines for three algorithms: least-squares line-fitting, median finding, and a sparse-matrix vector product. These results show that NESL's performance is competitive with that of machine-specific codes for regular dense data, and is often superior for irregular data.

*This research was sponsored by the Avionics Laboratory, Wright Research and Development Center, Aeronautical Systems Division (AFSC), U.S. Air Force, Wright-Patterson AFB, Ohio 45433-6543 under Contract F33615-90-C-1465, ARPA Order No. 7597. Cray Y-MP C90, Connection Machine CM-2 and Connection Machine CM-5 time was provided by the Pittsburgh Supercomputing Center (Grant ASC890018P).

[1] Partially supported by a Finmeccanica chair and an NSF Young Investigator award.

[2] RIACS, Mail Stop T045-1, NASA Ames Research Center, Moffett Field, CA 94035

The views and conclusions contained in this document are those of the authors and should not be interpreted as representing the official policies, either expressed or implied, of the U.S. government.

4th ACM PPOPP,5/93/CA,USA

1 Introduction

The high cost of rewriting parallel code has resulted in significant effort directed toward developing high-level languages that are efficiently portable among parallel and vector supercomputers. A common approach has been to add data-parallel operations to existing languages, as exemplified by the High Performance Fortran (HPF) effort [23] and various extensions to C [35, 34, 4]. Such data-parallel extensions offer fine-grained parallelism and a simple programming model, while permitting efficient implementation on SIMD, MIMD, and vector machines. On the other hand, it is generally agreed that although these language extensions are ideally suited for computations on dense matrices or regular meshes, they are not as well suited for algorithms that operate on *irregular structures*, such as unstructured sparse matrices, graphs or trees [21]. Languages with control-parallel constructs are often better suited for such problems, but unfortunately these constructs do not port well to vector machines, SIMD machines or MIMD machines with vector processors.

Nested data-parallel languages [45, 7, 22] combine aspects of both strict data-parallel languages and control-parallel languages. Nested data-parallel languages allow recursive data structures, and also the application of parallel functions to multiple sets of data in parallel. For example, a sparse array can be represented as a sequence of rows, each of which is a subsequence containing the nonzero elements in that row (each subsequence may be a different length). A parallel function that sums the elements of a sequence can be applied in parallel to sum all the rows of our sparse matrix. Because the nested calls are to the same function, a technique called *flattening nested parallelism* [13] allows a compiler to convert them into a form that runs on vector and SIMD machines. Nested data-parallel languages therefore, in theory, maintain the advantages of data-parallel languages (fine-grained parallelism, a simple programming model, and portability) while being well suited

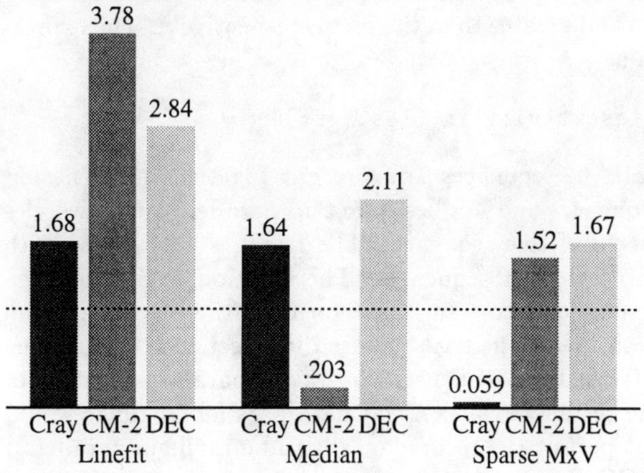

Figure 1: Performance summary for the three benchmarks. The numbers given are the ratio of the times taken by the NESL and native code versions of the benchmark (smaller numbers are therefore better). The problem size was the largest that fit in physical memory. Full performance results are given in Section 5.

for describing algorithms on irregular data structures. Their efficient implementation, however, has not previously been demonstrated.

As part of the Carnegie Mellon SCAL project, we have completed a first implementation of a nested data-parallel language called NESL. This implementation is based on an intermediate language called VCODE and a library of vector routines called CVL. The implementation runs on the Connection Machine CM-2, the Cray C90, and serial workstations. (We are currently working on a version for the Connection Machine CM-5.) In this paper we describe the language and implementation, provide benchmark numbers, and analyze the benchmark results. These results demonstrate that it is possible to get both efficiency and portability on a variety of parallel machines with a nested data-parallel language.

The three benchmarks we use are a least-squares line-fitting algorithm, a median-finding algorithm and a sparse-matrix vector product. Figure 1 summarizes the benchmark timings. For each machine we give direct comparisons to well-written native code compiled with full optimizations. All the NESL benchmark times given in this paper use the interpreted version of our intermediate language (as discussed in Section 5, a compiled version is likely to be significantly faster). The line-fitting benchmark measures the interpretive overhead in our implementation: it contains no nested parallelism and therefore generates near-optimal code from FORTRAN 77 (vectorized) and CM Fortran. The other two benchmarks demonstrate the efficiency of dynamic memory allocation and nested-parallel code.

The paper is organized as follows: Section 2 describes NESL and illustrates how nested parallelism can be applied to some simple algorithms on sparse matrices. (A description of how NESL can be used for a wider variety of algorithms, including computing the minimum-spanning-tree of sparse graphs, searching for patterns in strings, and finding the convex-hull of a set of points, is given elsewhere [12].) Section 3 outlines the different components of the current NESL implementation. Section 4 describes our benchmarks and Section 5 discusses the running times of the benchmarks.

2 NESL and Nested Parallelism

NESL is a high-level language designed to allow simple and concise descriptions of nested data-parallel programs [8]. It is strongly typed and applicative (side-effect-free). Sequences are the primitive parallel data type and the language provides a large set of built-in parallel sequence operations. Parallelism is achieved through the ability to apply functions in parallel to each element of a sequence. The application of a function over a sequence is specified using a set-like notation similar to *set-formers* in SETL [37] and *list-comprehensions* in Miranda [44] and Haskell [26]. For example, the NESL expression

```
{negate(a): a in [3,-4,-9,5] | a < 4}
```

can be read as "in parallel, for each `a` in the sequence `[3, -4, -9, 5]` such that `a` is less than `4`, negate `a`". The expression returns `[-3, 4, 9]`. The parallelism is applied both to the expression to the left of the colon (`:`) and to the subselection to the right of the pipe (`|`). This parallel subselection can be implemented with packing techniques [5]. NESL also supplies a set of parallel functions that operate on sequences as a whole. Figure 2 lists several of these functions; a full list can be found in the NESL manual [8]. These are similar to operations found in other data-parallel languages.

NESL supports nested parallelism by permitting sequences as elements of a sequence and by permitting the parallel sequence functions to be used in the apply-to-all construct. For example, a sparse matrix can be represented as a sequence of rows, each of which is a sequence of `(column-number, value)` pairs. The matrix

$$m = \begin{bmatrix} 2.0 & -1.0 & \\ -1.0 & 2.0 & -1.0 \\ & -1.0 & 2.0 \end{bmatrix}$$

is represented with this technique as

```
m = [[(0, 2.0), (1, -1.0)],
     [(0, -1.0), (1, 2.0), (2, -1.0)],
     [(1, -1.0), (2, 2.0)]].
```

Operation	Description
#a	*Length of sequence* a.
a[i]	i^{th} *element of sequence* a.
sum(a)	*Sum of sequence* a.
plus_scan(a)	*Parallel prefix with addition.*
permute(a,i)	*Permute elements of sequence* a *to positions given in sequence* i.
get(a,i)	*Get values from sequence* a *based on indices in sequence* i.
a ++ b	*Append sequences* a *and* b.

Figure 2: Seven of NESL's sequence operations.

Sum values in each row:
```
{sum({v : (i,v) in row}): row in m};
```
Delete elements less that eps:
```
{{(i,v) in row | v < eps}: row in m};
```
Add a column j of all 1's:
```
{[(j,1.0)] ++ row : row in m};
```
Permute the rows to new positions p:
```
permute(m,p);
```

Figure 3: Some simple operations on sparse matrices. Note that the last operation permutes whole rows.

This representation can be used for matrices with arbitrary patterns of non-zero elements. Figure 3 shows examples of some useful operations on matrices. In these operations there is parallelism both within each row and across the rows. The parallelism is therefore proportional to the total number of non-zero elements, rather than the number of rows (outer parallelism) or average row size (inner parallelism). Graphs can be represented similarly to sparse matrices, using each subsequence to keep an adjacency list.

Nested parallelism is also very useful in divide-and-conquer algorithms. As an example, consider a parallel quicksort algorithm (Figure 4). The three assignments

```
function qsort(s) =
if (#s < 2) then s
else
  let pivot = s[rand(#s)];
      les = {e in s| e < pivot};
      eql = {e in s| e = pivot};
      grt = {e in s| e > pivot};
      result = {qsort(v):v in [les, grt]}
  in result[0] ++ eql ++ result[1];
```

Figure 4: A nested data-parallel quicksort in NESL.

for les, eql and grt select the elements less than, equal to, and greater than the pivot, respectively. The expression

```
{qsort(v):v in [les, grt]}
```

puts the sequences les and grt together into a nested sequence, and applies qsort in parallel to the two elements of this sequence. The result is a sequence with two sorted subsequences. The function ++ appends the three sequences. In this algorithm, there is parallelism both within the pack required to select each of the three intermediate sequences and in the parallel execution of the recursive calls. A flat data-parallel language would not permit the recursive calls to be made in parallel.

We decided to define a new language instead of adding nested parallel constructs to an existing language for two main reasons. First, we wanted a small core language, to allow us to guarantee that everything that is expressed in parallel compiles into a parallel form. Second, we wanted a side-effect-free language, due to the difficulty of implementing nested data-parallelism when nested function calls can interact with each other through side-effects. This problem can probably be overcome with aggressive compiler analysis to determine places where there is the possibility of interaction.

3 System Overview

Our implementation of NESL consists of an intermediate language called VCODE [9], a compiler [15, 16] and interpreter for VCODE, and a portable library of parallel routines called CVL [10]. Figure 5 illustrates how the implementation is organized. We split our system along these lines so that we could concentrate on different aspects of the system in isolation. This section gives an overview of the various components of the system: a more detailed description can be found in the full version of this paper [11].

VCODE: VCODE is a stack-based intermediate language where the objects on the stack are vectors of atomic values (integers, floats, or booleans). VCODE instructions act on these vectors as a whole, performing such operations as elementwise adding two vectors, summing a vector, or permuting the order of elements within a vector. To provide support for nested parallelism, VCODE supplies the notion of *segment descriptors* [7]. These objects, also kept on the stack, describe how vectors are partitioned into segments. For example, the segment descriptor [2, 3, 1] specifies that a vector of length 6 should be considered as 3 segments of lengths 2, 3 and 1, respectively (segments are contiguous and never overlap). The VCODE representation of the segment descriptor is machine-dependent: our serial

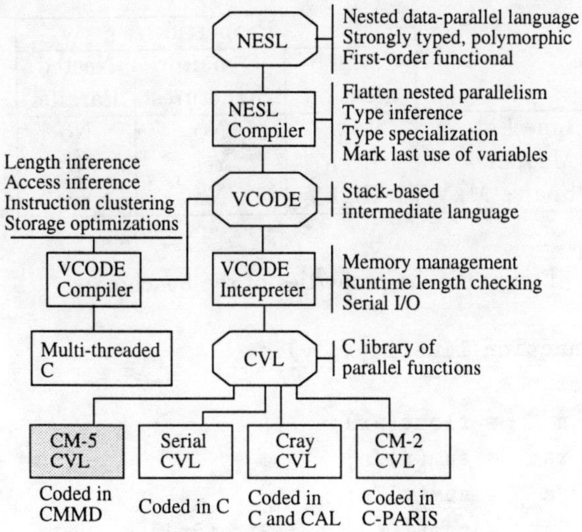

Figure 5: The parts of the SCAL project and how they fit together. CAL stands for Cray Assembly Language, and C-PARIS is the C interface to the Connection Machine Parallel Instruction Set. CM-5 CVL is under development.

implementation uses a sequence of the lengths of each segment, while our implementations on the Connection Machine CM-2 and Cray also use flags to mark boundaries between segments. Most of the non-elementwise VCODE instructions require both a vector and a segment descriptor as arguments. Each instruction then operates independently over each segment of the vector. For example, the `+_scan` instruction will perform a parallel prefix operation on each segment, starting from zero on each segment boundary. The segmented versions of the instructions are critical for the implementation of nested parallelism. The notion of segments also appears in some of the library routines of the Connection Machines CM-2 and CM-5 [43, 42] and has been adopted in the PREFIX and SUFFIX operations of High Performance Fortran.

NESL compiler: The NESL compiler translates NESL code into VCODE. The most important compilation step is the use of a technique called *flattening nested parallelism* [13, 7]. This process converts nested sequences into sets of flat vectors and translates the nested operations into segmented VCODE operations on the flattened representation. The flattening of nested sequences is achieved by converting all sequences into a pair: a `value` vector and a `segdes` (segment descriptor). For example, the sequence `[2, 9, 1, 5, 6, 3, 8]` would be represented by the pair

```
segdes = [7]
value  = [2, 9, 1, 5, 6, 3, 8]
```

and the nested sequence `[[2, 1], [7, 0, 3], [4]]` would be represented as

```
segdes1 = [3]
segdes2 = [2, 3, 1]
value   = [2, 1, 7, 0, 3, 4]
```

In these examples, a `segdes` with only one value specifies that the whole vector is one segment (the use of this seemingly redundant data is critical when implementing nested versions of user-defined functions). In the second example, `segdes1` describes the segmentation of `segdes2`, not of `value`. Sequences that are nested deeper are represented by additional segment descriptors. Sequences of fixed-sized structures (such as pairs) are represented as multiple vectors (one for each slot in the structure) that each use a single segment descriptor.

Using this representation, nested versions of NESL operations with VCODE counterparts can be directly converted into the corresponding segmented VCODE instruction. Nested versions of user-defined functions are implemented by using program transformations called *stepping-up* and *stepping-down*. These transformations convert all the substeps of a nested call into segmented operations or into calls to other functions that have already been transformed. With these transformations, when a user function is called in parallel, each subcall gets placed in a separate segment, and the computations on these segments can proceed independently.

The most complex part of flattening nested parallelism is transforming conditional statements. There are two main parts of this transformation. The first part inserts code for packing out all the subcalls that do not take a branch, and then reinserts this data when that branch is completed. This guarantees that work is only done on the subcalls that take the branch, and is similar to a technique used by vectorizing compilers to vectorize loops with conditionals. It also results in proper load balancing on parallel machines. The second part inserts code to test if any of the subcalls are taking the branch, and to skip the branch if none are. This is important for guaranteeing termination. The communication costs involved in doing the packing and unpacking can be quite high, and one area of our ongoing research is to see how the communication can be minimized by only packing when there is a significant load imbalance among processors [38].

CVL: To enable us to quickly implement VCODE on new machines, we designed CVL (C Vector Library), a library of low-level segmented vector routines callable from C. These are used by a VCODE interpreter, described below. Our implementations of CVL on the Connection Machine CM-2, Cray and serial workstations are highly optimized. We originally tried to implement these operations in a high-level language, but to attain high efficiency, we were forced to use Cray Assembly Language (CAL) on the Cray and the Parallel Instruction Set (PARIS) on the Connection Machine CM-2. This was particularly important on the Cray, since we could not get the C or FORTRAN compilers to vectorize the segmented code (some of these issues are discussed in [17]). We might have achieved better performance on the Connection Machine CM-2 by going one level closer to the machine and using CMIS, but time did not permit this. Our implementation of CVL on workstations uses ANSI C and can therefore be ported easily to most serial machines.

VCODE interpreter: The two main requirements for the VCODE interpreter are portability and efficient management of the vector memory. The actual vector instructions supplied by VCODE are mapped into CVL calls in a fairly straightforward manner via table-lookup. The VCODE interpreter imposes a constant per executed instruction overhead on VCODE programs. Hence, efficient execution of these primitives within CVL guarantees efficient evaluation of VCODE programs for large vectors. The most interesting part of the interpreter is how it manages memory. The interpreter uses free lists of varying sized blocks of memory and reference counting on vectors in order to create and destroy vectors of differing and dynamically determined sizes. The algorithm used is fully described in [11].

VCODE compiler: Chatterjee's doctoral dissertation [15] discusses the design, implementation, and evaluation of an optimizing VCODE compiler for shared-memory MIMD machines. There is, of course, a trivial implementation of VCODE on a MIMD machine: each VCODE instruction is written as a parallel loop, and the processors synchronize between instructions. This is precisely how the VCODE interpreter works. However, such an implementation of data parallelism on a MIMD machine has several performance bottlenecks that limit both the asymptotic performance and the performance for small problem sizes. The VCODE compiler addresses these problems through a set of program optimization techniques that cluster computation into larger loop bodies, reduce intermediate storage, and relax synchronization constraints. These techniques do not require compile-time knowledge of data sizes or the number of processors.

The compiler accepts VCODE as input and outputs C code with thread extensions targeted at shared-memory multiprocessors. The native C compiler is then invoked to produce the final machine code. This makes the compiler portable and allows the use of the best compiler technology available for the machine.

	Properties		
	Communication	Dynamic Structures	Nested Parallel
Line Fit	Low	No	No
Median	High	Yes	No
Sparse MxV	High	No	Yes

Figure 6: The properties of the benchmarks.

```
function linefit(x, y) =
let
  n    = float(#x);
  xa   = sum(x)/n;
  ya   = sum(y)/n;
  Stt  = sum({(x - xa)^2:  tmp});
  b    = sum({(x - xa)*y:  tmp; y})/Stt;
  a    = ya - xa*b;
  chi2 = sum({(y-a-b*x)^2:  x; y});
  siga = sqrt((1.0/n + xa^2/Stt)*chi2/n);
  sigb = sqrt((1.0/Stt)*chi2/n)
in
  (a, b, siga, sigb);
```

Figure 7: NESL code for fitting a line using a least-square fit. The function takes sequences of x and y coordinates and returns the intercept (a) and slope (b) and their respective probable uncertainties (siga and sigb).

4 Benchmarks

This section describes three benchmarks: a least-squares line-fit, a generalized median find, and a sparse-matrix vector product. The particular benchmarks were selected for their diverse computational requirements (summarized in Figure 6). They are each simple enough that the reader should be able to fully understand what the algorithm is doing, but are more complex than bare kernels such as the Livermore Loops [31]. The performance of these benchmarks demonstrate many of the advantages and disadvantages of our system. The results of these benchmarks will be analyzed in Section 5.

Our first benchmark is a least-squares line-fitting routine using the algorithm described in Press *et al.* [33, section 14.2] (the version we use assumes all points have equal measurement errors). This is a straightforward algorithm that requires very little communication and has no nested parallelism. Furthermore, all vectors are of known size at function invocation and can be allocated statically. It is therefore well suited for languages such

```
function select_kth(s, k) =
let pivot = s[#s/2];
    les = {e in s | e < pivot}
in
  if (k < #les) then
    select_kth(les, k)
  else
    let grt = {e in s | e > pivot}
    in if (k >= #s - #grt) then
         select_kth(grt, k - (#s - #grt))
       else pivot;

function median(s) = select_kth(s, #s/2);
```

Figure 8: NESL code for median finding. The function select_kth returns the kth smallest element of s. This is used by median to find the middle element.

```
function MxV(Mval, Midx, Mlen, Vect) =
let v = get(Vect, Midx);
    p = {a * b:  a in Mval; b in v}
in
  {sum(row) :  row in nest(p, Mlen)};
```

Figure 9: Sparse-matrix vector product. Mval holds the matrix values, Midx holds the column indices, Mlen holds the length of each row, and Vect is the input vector. The function nest takes the flat sequence p and nests it using the lengths in Mlen (the sum of the values in Mlen must equal the length of p).

as FORTRAN 90. We use this benchmark to measure the overhead incurred by our interpreter-based implementation. The NESL code for the benchmark is given in Figure 7.

Our second benchmark is a median-finding algorithm. To implement median-finding we use a more general algorithm that finds the $\mathtt{k}^{th}$ smallest element in a set. The algorithm is based on the quickselect method [24]. This method is similar to quicksort, but calls itself recursively only on one of the two partitions, depending on which contains the result (the recursion was removed in the FORTRAN version). This algorithm requires dynamic memory allocation (also removed in the FORTRAN version) since the sizes of the less-than-pivot and greater-than-pivot sets are data dependent. In order to obtain proper load balancing, the data must be redistributed on each iteration. The NESL code for the algorithm is shown in Figure 8. This algorithm was selected to demonstrate the utility and efficiency of dynamic allocation.

Our third benchmark multiplies a sparse matrix by a dense vector, and demonstrates the usefulness of nested parallelism. Sparse-matrix vector multiplication is an important supercomputer kernel that is difficult to vectorize and parallelize efficiently because of its irregular data structures and high communication requirements. While there are many algorithms for special classes of sparse matrices, we are interested in supporting operations for arbitrary sparse matrices. This is a challenge since the matrices used in a number of different scientific and engineering disciplines often have average row lengths of less than 10. These row lengths are significantly less than the start-up overhead for vector machines ($n_{1/2}$) and are far too small to divide among processors in an attempt to parallelize row by row. On the other hand, dividing rows among processors makes load balancing difficult since each row can have a different length and the longest rows could be very long. Our implementations (in NESL, C, and FORTRAN) use a compressed row format containing the number of nonzero elements in each row, and the values of each nonzero matrix element along with its column index [20]. Figure 9 shows the NESL implementation.

5 Results

Running times for all benchmarks with a variety of data sizes are given in Table 1. Times are given for both interpreted NESL code and for native code. For native code we used FORTRAN 77 on the Cray C90, CM Fortran [42] on the Connection Machine CM-2, and C on the DECstation 5000/20 (using the gcc compiler). In all cases we used full optimization, and in the case of the median-finding code on the Cray we had to include compiler directives (ivdep) to force vectorization. The full listing of the native code we used is given in [11]. NESL timings are for the code shown in the previous section run using the VCODE interpreter. All Cray C90 benchmarks were run on one processor of a C90/16 with 256 Mwords of memory. All Connection Machine CM-2 benchmarks were run on 16K processors of a CM-2, each with 256 Kbits of memory. All DECstation benchmarks were run on a DECstation 5000/20 with 16 Mbytes of memory.

We now discuss three main issues exhibited by the timings: the advantage of nested parallelism in the implementation of the sparse-matrix vector product, the overhead incurred by our interpreter, and the need for dynamic load-balancing in the median-finding code on the Connection Machine CM-2.

Nested Parallelism: The sparse-matrix vector multiplication benchmark demonstrates the advantages and efficiency of nested data parallelism. Figure 10 gives running times on the Cray for a variety of degrees of

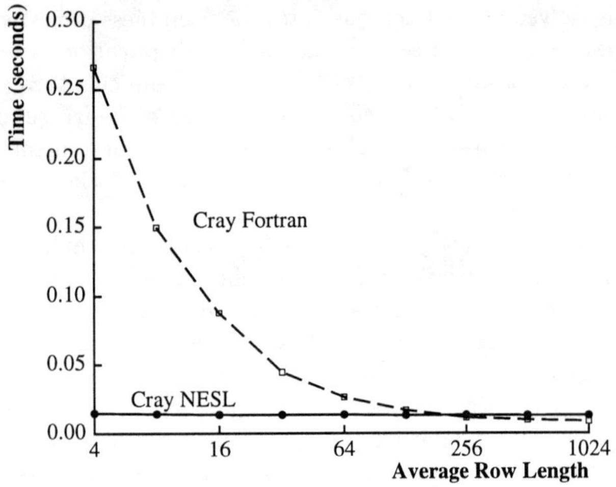

Figure 10: Running times of the sparse-matrix vector product for varying levels of sparseness. The number of nonzero entries in each sparse matrix is fixed at 10^6.

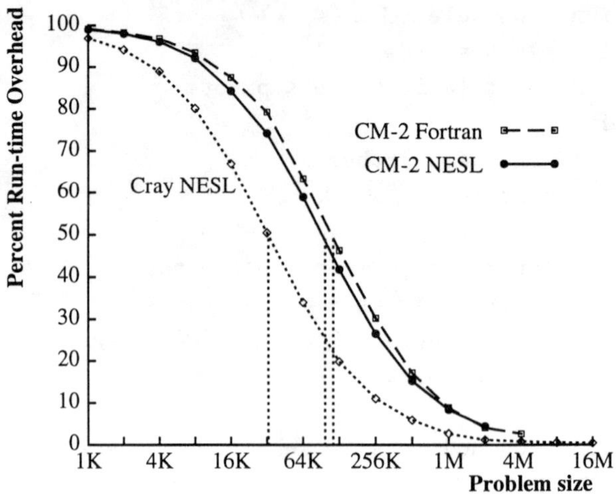

Figure 11: Interpreter overhead for the line-fitting benchmark. The vertical lines indicate the points at which overhead accounts for 50% of the running time. The percentage overhead for the CM-2 NESL implementation is comparable to that for the CM Fortran implementation. The Cray FORTRAN overhead is insignificant for the data sizes in the graph and is not shown.

sparseness. For very sparse matrices, the NESL version outperforms the native version by over a factor of ten. This is because the compilation of nested data parallelism described in Section 3 generates code with running time essentially independent of the size of the subsequences. The full efficiency (vectorization on the Cray and high data-to-processor ratio on the CM-2) of executing on the full input data is achieved by the nested code. The result is consistently high performance regardless of how sparse the matrix is. Note, however, that as the matrix density increases, the Cray FORTRAN performance improves. Eventually, FORTRAN achieves superior performance because of the extra per-element cost of interpretation relative to compilation.

Interpretive overhead: The main source of inefficiency in our system is the interpretation of the VCODE generated by the NESL compiler. The cost of interpretation can be analyzed by studying the line-fitting benchmark since this benchmark requires very little communication and the native-code implementations compile to almost perfect code.

There are two main sources of interpretive overhead in our system. First, there is the cost of executing the interpreter itself. For the line-fitting benchmark, this is constant, independent of input size (since the interpreter executes a fixed number of VCODE steps), and so may be computed by examining the running times for small input. Figure 11 shows the percentage of run time accounted for by this overhead for varying input sizes, as well as the $n_{1/2}$ value at which the implementations attain half of their asymptotic efficiency. As the figure shows, NESL sometimes requires fairly large input in order to attain close to its peak efficiency. This overhead is not a problem on the CM-2; here, since there are 16K processors, the loss of efficiency when working with small vectors ($n < 16\text{K}$) overwhelms the interpretive overhead.

The second major deficiency of an interpreter-based system is that the granularity of the operations performed by the library is too fine. Each operation on a collection of data is performed by a distinct call to the CVL library. In a compiled system, the loops performing the separate parallel operations could be fused together. This optimization would result in much better memory locality (quantities could be kept in registers and reused, instead of being loaded from memory, acted on, and written back) and would also allow chaining on the Cray. These inefficiencies adversely affect the peak performance of NESL programs, and the effects can be seen in the performance of line-fitting for large data sizes (see Table 1).[1]

Dynamic load balancing: We now consider why the native code for the median algorithm does poorly compared to the NESL code on the CM-2. The median algorithm reduces the number of active elements on each step. In our CM Fortran implementation, as these elements get packed to the bottom of an array, they become more imbalanced across the processors. Although

[1]On the CM-2 there is an additional important source of inefficiency: CM-2 CVL is built on top of the Paris instruction set [43]. Although working with Paris has many advantages, it forces use of the older "fieldwise" representation of data, instead of the more efficient "slicewise" representation generated by the CM Fortran compiler.

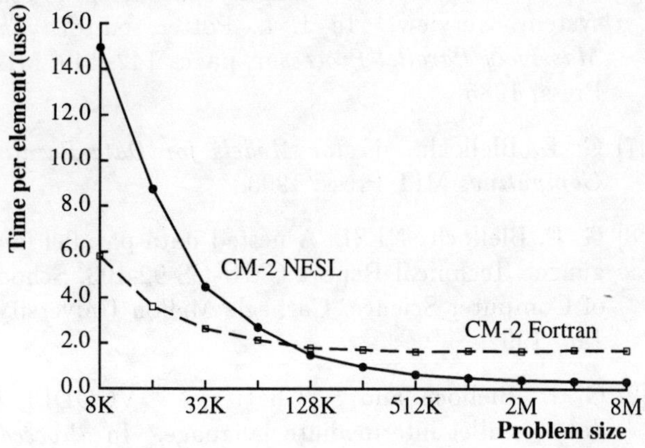

Figure 12: CM-2 median: NESL vs. CM Fortran.

n	DEC C	DEC NESL	C90 F77	C90 NESL	CM-2 CMF	CM-2 NESL
			Line Fit			
2^{10}	0.0048	0.0156	0.0001	0.0012	0.0018	0.0061
2^{14}	0.1094	0.2969	0.0004	0.0018	0.0019	0.0061
2^{18}	1.7500	4.9844	0.0058	0.0122	0.0055	0.0208
2^{22}			0.0927	0.1551	0.0633	
			Median			
2^{10}	0.0024	0.0156	0.0001	0.0059	0.0266	0.1009
2^{14}	0.0508	0.1094	0.0005	0.0092	0.0592	0.1432
2^{18}	1.0156	2.1406	0.0080	0.0233	0.4479	0.2515
2^{22}			0.1276	0.2099	7.1841	1.4565
			Sparse Matrix-Vector Multiply			
2^{10}	0.0156	0.0156	0.0002	0.0003	0.0043	0.0137
2^{14}	0.0469	0.0625	0.0037	0.0006	0.0072	0.0161
2^{18}	0.8750	1.4688	0.0589	0.0038	0.0541	0.0823
2^{22}			0.9436	0.0557	0.8020	

Table 1: Running times (in seconds) of the benchmarks for NESL and native code. The sparse-matrix vector product uses a row length of 5 and randomly-selected column indices.

it is possible to pack the elements into a smaller array, this would require dynamically allocating a new vector on each step, which is awkward in CM Fortran. In NESL, vectors are dynamically allocated with the data automatically balanced across the processors. Although the median algorithm requires $O(\log n)$ steps on average, the NESL implementation only requires a total of $O(n)$ work because on each step the amount of data processed is cut by a constant factor. Since the CM Fortran implementation requires $O(n)$ work on each step, it is a factor of $O(\log n)$ slower for large inputs, as illustrated in Figure 12.

6 Comparison to Other Systems

Numerous flat data-parallel languages have been proposed for portable parallel programming, such as C* [35], MPP-Pascal [6], *Lisp [29], UC [4], and FORTRAN 90 [2]. Section 2 explained some of the expressibility and efficiency limitations imposed by this type of language. These problems are also discussed elsewhere [7, 21, 39, 22, 8].

There are two existing languages that permit the user to describe nested data-parallel operations: Connection Machine Lisp [45] and Paralation Lisp [36]. However, the implementations of these languages are only able to exploit the bottom level of parallelism; for the sparse matrix example, this results in a parallel sum for each row, and a serial loop over the rows. Both these languages are data-parallel extensions to Common Lisp [40]. The large number of features in Common Lisp, and the difficulty of extending their semantics to parallel execution, preclude the implementation of full nested data parallelism. This is the main reason why we wanted a simple core language.

The parallel languages ID [32], SISAL [30], and Crystal [18], although not explicitly data parallel, do support fine-grained parallelism. They also support nested data structures, although there has been little research on implementing nested parallelism for these languages. There are also several serial languages that supply data-parallel primitives and nested structures. These include SETL [37], APL2 [28], J [27], and FP [3]. For a discussion of these languages from the perspective of supporting data parallelism see [39].

Another approach to architecture-independent parallel programming is control-parallel languages that provide asynchronous communicating serial processes. Examples include CSP [25], Linda [14], Actors [1], and PVM [41]. These languages are well suited for problems (including irregular problems) that can be specified in terms of coarse-grained sub-tasks. Unfortunately, high overhead in the implementation makes efficiency too dependent on finding a decomposition into reasonably sized blocks [14]. As a result, these systems are not well suited for exploiting fine-grained parallelism. The large grain size renders programs less likely to be efficient on most parallel supercomputers because they won't vectorize well and don't expose enough parallelism to take advantage of large numbers of processors. Extending this model to capture fine-grained parallelism is an area of active research [19].

7 Conclusions

The purpose of nested data-parallel languages is to provide the advantages of data parallelism while extending their applicability to algorithms that use "irregular" data structures. The main advantages of data parallelism that should be preserved are the efficient implementation of fine-grained parallelism and the simple synchronous programming model.

We have described the implementation of a nested data-parallel language called NESL. NESL was designed to allow the concise description of parallel algorithms on both structured and unstructured data. It has been used in a course on parallel algorithms and has allowed students to quickly implement a wide variety of programs, including systems for speech recognition, ray-tracing, volume rendering, parsing, maximum-flow, singular value decomposition, mesh partitioning, pattern matching, and big-number arithmetic [12].[2] The benchmark results in this paper have shown that it is possible to get good efficiency with a nested data-parallel language, across a variety of different parallel machines. NESL runs within a local interactive environment that allows the user to execute programs remotely on any of the supported architectures. This portability depends crucially on the organization of the system and the use of an intermediate language.

The efficiency of NESL on large applications still requires further study. Some other issues that we plan to examine: (1) getting good efficiency on nested parallel code with many conditionals, (2) the specification of data layout for irregular structures, (3) tools for profiling nested parallel code, (4) the interaction of higher-order functions with nested parallelism, and (5) porting the system to other architectures.

References

[1] G. Agha. Concurrent object-oriented programming. *Communications of the ACM*, 33(9):125–141, Sept. 1990.

[2] ANSI. *ANSI Fortran Draft S8, Version 111.*

[3] J. Backus. Can programming be liberated from the von Neumann style? A functional style and its algebra of programs. *Communications of the ACM*, 21(8):613–641, Aug. 1978.

[4] R. Bagrodia and S. Mathur. Efficient implementation of high-level parallel programs. In *Fourth International Conference on Architectural Support for Programming Languages and Operating Systems*, pages 142–52, Apr. 1991.

[5] K. E. Batcher. The flip network of STARAN. In *Proceedings International Conference on Parallel Processing*, pages 65–71, 1976.

[2] A full implementation of NESL is available from blelloch@cs.cmu.edu.

[6] K. E. Batcher. The massively parallel processor system overview. In J. L. Potter, editor, *The Massively Parallel Processor*, pages 142–149. MIT Press, 1985.

[7] G. E. Blelloch. *Vector Models for Data-Parallel Computing.* MIT Press, 1990.

[8] G. E. Blelloch. NESL: A nested data-parallel language. Technical Report CMU-CS-92-103, School of Computer Science, Carnegie Mellon University, Jan. 1992.

[9] G. E. Blelloch and S. Chatterjee. VCODE: A data-parallel intermediate language. In *Proceedings Frontiers of Massively Parallel Computation*, pages 471–480, Oct. 1990.

[10] G. E. Blelloch, S. Chatterjee, J. C. Hardwick, J. Sipelstein, and M. Zagha. CVL: A C vector library. Technical Report CMU-CS-93-114, School of Computer Science, Carnegie Mellon University, Feb. 1993.

[11] G. E. Blelloch, S. Chatterjee, J. C. Hardwick, J. Sipelstein, and M. Zagha. Implementation of a portable nested data-parallel language. Technical Report CMU-CS-93-112, School of Computer Science, Carnegie Mellon University, Feb. 1993.

[12] G. E. Blelloch and J. C. Hardwick. Class notes: Programming parallel algorithms. Technical Report CMU-CS-93-115, School of Computer Science, Carnegie Mellon University, Feb. 1993.

[13] G. E. Blelloch and G. W. Sabot. Compiling collection-oriented languages onto massively parallel computers. *Journal of Parallel and Distributed Computing*, 8(2):119–134, Feb. 1990.

[14] N. Carriero and D. Gelernter. How to write parallel programs: A guide to the perplexed. *ACM Computing Surveys*, 21(3):323–357, Sept. 1989.

[15] S. Chatterjee. *Compiling Data-Parallel Programs for Efficient Execution on Shared-Memory Multiprocessors.* PhD thesis, School of Computer Science, Carnegie Mellon University, Oct. 1991.

[16] S. Chatterjee, G. E. Blelloch, and A. L. Fisher. Size and access inference for data-parallel programs. In *ACM SIGPLAN '91 Conference on Programming Language Design and Implementation*, pages 130–144, June 1991.

[17] S. Chatterjee, G. E. Blelloch, and M. Zagha. Scan primitives for vector computers. In *Proceedings Supercomputing '90*, pages 666–675, Nov. 1990.

[18] M. Chen, Y. Choo, and J. Li. Crystal: Theory and pragmatics of generating efficient parallel code. In B. K. Szymanski, editor, *Parallel Functional Languages and Compilers*, chapter 7. Addison-Wesley, Reading, MA, 1991.

[19] A. A. Chien and W. J. Dally. Experience with concurrent aggregates (CA): Implementation and programming. In *Proceedings of the Fifth Distributed Memory Computers Conference*. SIAM, Apr. 1990.

[20] I. S. Duff, R. G. Grimes, and J. G. Lewis. Sparse matrix test problems. *ACM Trans. Math. Software*, 15:1–14, 1989.

[21] G. C. Fox. The architecture of problems and portable parallel software systems. Technical Report SCCS-134, Syracuse Center for Computational Science, Syracuse University, 1991.

[22] P. Hatcher, W. F. Tichy, and M. Philippsen. A critique of the programming language C*. *Communications of the ACM*, 35(6):21–24, June 1992.

[23] High Performance Fortran Forum. *High Performance Fortran Language Specification*, Jan. 1993.

[24] C. A. R. Hoare. Algorithm 63 (partition) and algorithm 65 (find). *Communications of the ACM*, 4(7):321–322, 1961.

[25] C. A. R. Hoare. Communicating sequential processes. *Communications of the ACM*, 21(8):666–677, Aug. 1978.

[26] P. Hudak and P. Wadler. Report on the functional programming language HASKELL. Technical report, Yale University, Apr. 1990.

[27] R. K. W. Hui, K. E. Iverson, E. E. McDonnell, and A. T. Whitney. APL\? In *APL 90 Conference Proceedings*, pages 192–200, Jan. 1990.

[28] IBM. *APL2 Programming: Language Reference*, first edition, Aug. 1984. Order Number SH20-9227-0.

[29] C. Lasser. *The Essential *Lisp Manual.* Thinking Machines Corporation, Cambridge, MA, July 1986.

[30] J. McGraw, S. Skedzielewski, S. Allan, R. Oldehoeft, J. Glauert, C. Kirkham, B. Noyce, and R. Thomas. *SISAL: Streams and Iteration in a Single Assignment Language, Language Reference Manual Version 1.2.* Lawrence Livermore National Laboratory, Mar. 1985.

[31] F. H. McMahon. The Livermore Fortran kernels: A computer test of the numerical performance range. Technical Report UCRL-53745, Lawrence Livermore National Laboratory, Dec. 1986.

[32] R. S. Nikhil. ID Version 90.0 Reference Manual. Computation Structures Group Memo 284-1, Laboratory for Computer Science, Massachusetts Institute of Technology, July 1990.

[33] W. H. Press, B. P. Flannery, S. A. Teukolsky, and W. T. Vetterling. *Numerical Recipes.* Cambridge University Press, Cambridge, 1986.

[34] M. J. Quinn and P. J. Hatcher. Data-parallel programming on multicomputers. *IEEE Software*, 7(5):69–76, Sept. 1990.

[35] J. R. Rose and G. L. Steele Jr. C*: An extended C language for data parallel programming. In *Proceedings Second International Conference on Supercomputing, Vol. 2*, pages 2–16, May 1987.

[36] G. W. Sabot. *The Paralation Model: Architecture-Independent Parallel Programming.* The MIT Press, Cambridge, Massachusetts, 1988.

[37] J. T. Schwartz, R. B. K. Dewar, E. Dubinsky, and E. Schonberg. *Programming with Sets: An Introduction to SETL.* Springer-Verlag, New York, 1986.

[38] J. Sipelstein. *Data Representation Optimizations for Collection-Oriented Languages.* PhD thesis, School of Computer Science, Carnegie Mellon University, Pittsburgh, PA, To appear.

[39] J. Sipelstein and G. E. Blelloch. Collection-oriented languages. *Proceedings of the IEEE*, 79(4):504–523, Apr. 1991.

[40] G. L. Steele Jr., S. E. Fahlman, R. P. Gabriel, D. A. Moon, and D. L. Weinreb. *Common LISP: The Language.* Digital Press, Burlington, MA, 1984.

[41] V. S. Sunderam. PVM: A framework for parallel distributed computing. *Concurrency: Practice and Experience*, 2(4):315–339, Dec. 1990.

[42] Thinking Machines Corporation, Cambridge, MA. *CM Fortran Reference Manual*, July 1991.

[43] Thinking Machines Corporation, Cambridge, MA. *Paris Reference Manual*, Feb. 1991.

[44] D. Turner. An overview of MIRANDA. *SIGPLAN Notices*, Dec. 1986.

[45] S. Wholey and G. L. Steele Jr. Connection Machine Lisp: A dialect of Common Lisp for data parallel programming. In *Proceedings Second International Conference on Supercomputing*, May 1987.

An Equational Language for Data-Parallelism

Pushpa Rao
Dartmouth College
Hanover, NH 03755
pushpa@cs.dartmouth.edu

Clifford Walinsky
The Portland Group
Wilsonville, OR 97070
cliffw@pgroup.com

Abstract

Data-parallelism provides a clean conceptual framework for parallel programming. We are developing two programming languages: a high level equational language, called EL*, and a low-level implementation language. Both languages exploit data-parallelism instead of control-parallelism. EL* is a declarative data-parallel language. EL* programs are high-level equational specifications that use extensive pattern-matching and recursion. The language's syntax and semantics are intended to be clear and simple. Recursive forms are restricted to enable translation to efficient data-parallel operations. EL* programs are compiled into FP*, a variant of Backus's FP, where parallel operations are more explicit and low-level. The target language has a rich set of functions for performing communication, and computation. It also has a powerful set of combining forms that generate large highly-parallel functions from smaller program units. Prototype compilers have been implemented for both languages, and they demonstrate good performance. Several linear algebra and non-numeric problems have been programmed with relative ease using EL*. We are currently developing compilation techniques for a wider range of scientific problems that have more complex parallel solutions, and are continuing to expand the language's scope.

1 Overview

Data-parallelism [8] provides a clean simple conceptual model for parallel programming. It has been observed that a vast number of problems can be formulated naturally in this framework. Since a single thread of control exists within data-parallel programs, they are easy to understand and debug. Design of programming languages and tools that promote software development using data-parallelism, is an active area of research.

We are developing two declarative programming languages: a high-level equational language called EL*, and a low-level implementation language called FP* [3, 16, 17, 18]. Declarative languages have a side-effect free operational semantics which promotes parallel execution. Hence, these languages are a promising choice as languages for specifying data-parallel activities. In EL*, recursion is the only means of specifying parallel activities. Like other functional languages, EL* promotes development of reusable program libraries, since all program units may be called from within other units, and side-effects are not present to impose sequential ordering on procedure activations. EL*, like other functional languages, is compiled to a combinator-based language, in this case a data-parallel dialect of Backus's FP [2]. FP* has a rich set of routing functions for performing communication. It also has a powerful set of combining forms for constructing highly parallel programs from smaller program units. Many optimizations are performed during EL* compilation so that the resulting FP* programs exhibit expected parallel performance.

An optimizing compiler [3] compiles FP* into efficient IL (intermediate language) in which the `forall` construct is the only parallel construct. IL can easily be mapped to many of the imperative data-parallel languages that are available. We currently generate CM Fortran [15] (a dialect of Fortran 90 for the Connection Machine CM-2 and CM-5) and MPL (a dialect of C for the MasPar MP-2). Efficiency is achieved mainly by extensive compile-time analysis and evaluation of FP* data-independent communication functions. These optimizations minimize communication overhead and also prevent the formation of large intermediate data structures at run time.

2 Related Work in Parallel Functional Languages

Development of parallel functional languages and systems has been ongoing for many years. Most systems developed and proposed so far consist of heterogeneous (MIMD) processes. There are fewer functional languages for SIMD and SPMD architectures. SISAL is a stream-oriented language with a preliminary implementation for the Connection Machine [7]. Language constructs tailored to data-parallelism include a parallel loop, similar to `forall`, and 16 reduction operators, e.g., sum and product. Due to the presence of side-effects within SISAL, modularity and algebraic properties are difficult to achieve. There are two data-parallel variants of Lisp, Connection Machine Lisp [14] and *Lisp. The combining forms of FP* (Apply-all and Insert) have analogous forms in CM-Lisp. However, CM-Lisp's support of other Lisp constructs detracts from its overall performance. *Lisp is more efficient, but gains this efficiency by relying on architecture-specific features of the Connection Machine.

ParAlfl [10] programs contain explicit statements directing the mapping of processes to physical processors. This

4th ACM PPOPP,5/93/CA,USA

mapping problem is substantially reduced in data-parallel systems because processes are always mapped to distinct virtual processors, and the mapping of virtual to physical processors is performed automatically according to problem size. Much work has been conducted in the development of CM-Fortran [15], determining proper physical layout of data to reduce inter-processor communication [11]. At this early stage in its development, the Connection Machine FP compiler generates CM-Fortran programs enabling it to obtain reasonably good layout of data structures.

Mou and Hudak have developed a data-parallel functional language, called Divacon [12]. Functions designated for parallel evaluation are evaluated in a divide-and-conquer manner. With two communication functions, "mirror" and "correspondence," PDC schemas can be compiled into efficient code suitable for evaluation on data-parallel architectures. Additional communication primitives would make programs easier to comprehend and produce, but may complicate compilation.

Blelloch presents "scan primitives" to replace memory access operations in PRAM models, resulting in more realistic performance analysis [5]. Blelloch also demonstrates how scan can simplify algorithm description. Scans can be implemented as recursive functions in EL*. Languages such as Crystal [6] decompose problems by specifying values of individual computational elements with recursion equations.

3 EL*: Syntax, Semantics, and Examples

An EL* program is a set of equations, possibly mutually recursive. Problems are specified in a divide-and conquer style, using a restricted form of recursion. Parker *et. al* also use recurrence equations in their SVP language to describe divide-and-conquer style algorithms [13]. Though SVP contains a larger variety of data types than FP*, many SVP programs are compatible with EL* and can be compiled to FP*.

Figure 1 presents a BNF for the EL* language. This BNF describes the core of the language, and is quite compact. Tokens include variables, function symbols, constant symbols, and numeric and Boolean constants. The language is strongly-typed, and a type inference system deduces types for variables and functions that are not explicitly assigned types. All examples in this paper omit explicit type declarations.

As with other equational languages, the operational semantics of the language are based on pattern matching and term-rewriting. Evaluation is described with a rewriting relation $\rightarrow$ on terms, possibly annotated with a matching substitution σ. If a term cannot be rewritten further, it is in *normal form*. The following rules describe when $e_1 \rightarrow e_2$—that is, term e_1 is rewritten to term e_2.

1. $f(e) \xrightarrow{\sigma} e'\sigma$ if (a) e is in normal form, and (b) $f(x) = e'$ is the first program equation for which there is a substitution σ such that $e = x\sigma$.

2. $f(\ldots, e_i, \ldots) \rightarrow f(\ldots, e_i', \ldots)$ if (a) every term e_j (for $j < i$) is in normal form, and (b) $e_i \rightarrow e_i'$.

3. $e_1 \rightarrow e_3$ if $e_1 \rightarrow e_2$ and $e_2 \rightarrow e_3$.

Conditions (1a) and (2a) above ensure evaluation is strict. Furthermore, in every program and for every term e, the rules are stated so that whenever e has a normal form, it is unique.

The matching algorithm is enhanced to accomplish splitting of vectors. While pattern `[x]` matches a vector of length 1 (with x bound to the vector's sole element), the pattern `v1++v2` matches any vector of length greater than 1. When used in a pattern, ++ is the splitting operator, while ++ used in an expression is the concatenation operator. A vector v that matches the pattern `v1++v2` is split as follows. Let $v = [x_1, \ldots, x_m]$, where $2 \leq m \leq 2^{k+1}$ and $k \geq 0$. Then `v1` is set to $[x_1, \ldots, x_{2^k}]$ and `v2` is set to $[x_{2^k+1}, \ldots, x_m]$ in the matching substitution σ.

For example, the program below defines a `broadcast` function in a divide-and-conquer style.

```
broadcast([x],y) = [(x,y)].
broadcast(v1++v2,y) =
      broadcast(v1,y) ++ broadcast(v2,y).
```

Arguments applied to the ++ operator, such as `v1` and `v2` above, are called *inductive arguments* of a function. Other arguments, such as `y` in the `broadcast` program, are *non-inductive* arguments. `v1` is the *left sub-vector* and `v2` is the *right sub-vector* of the inductive argument. A *combining function* combines results of recursive calls. The combining function for `broadcast` is ++, the concatenation operator. `broadcast([1,2,3], 100)` is evaluated as follows:

```
broadcast([1,2,3],100) →
  broadcast([1,2],100) ++ broadcast([3],100) →
  (broadcast([1],100) ++ broadcast([2],100))
    ++ broadcast([3],100) →
  [(1,100), (2,100)] ++ [(3,100)] →
  [(1,100), (2,100), (3,100)].
```

EL* functions can have multiple inductive arguments, as in the inner-product function definition below.

```
ip([x],[y]) = x*y.
ip(v1++v2,w1++w2) = ip(v1,w1) + ip(v2,w2).
```

The `ip` function is the simplest form of divide-and-conquer program, since the recursive calls refer exclusively either to left sub-vectors or right sub-vectors. In more complex problems, each recursive call may have any combination of left and right sub-vectors as arguments.

In SVP [13], results of recursive calls can be combined only through a fixed set of combining functions. In Divacon [12], activities carried out during combining of sub-vectors must be expressed explicitly in terms of combine functions, pre-morphisms and post-morphisms. In contrast, combine functions in EL* can be programmer-defined. Also, the programmer does not need to separate the components of a divide-and-conquer problem into the separate components of Divacon.

Higher-order functions are implemented through parameterization. The BNF of Figure 1 is extended for this facility. Given below is a parameterized `map` function. The function `f` is a parameter to the `map` function and is applied to each element of an input array when `map` is executed. Our optimizations ensure that `map<f>` applies `f` to all elements simultaneously.

```
map<f>([x]) = [f(x)].
map<f>(u++v) = map<f>(u) ++ map<f>(v)
```

EL* has a well-defined operational semantics. For its model-theoretic semantics, many theories have been developed that treat arrays as structured data types and define

```
<Program> ::=              <Equation_1>. ··· <Equation_n>.
<Equation> ::=             <LHS> = <Expression>
<LHS> ::=                  Symbol (<Top-level Pattern_1>, ..., <Top-level Pattern_n>)
<Top-level Pattern> ::= <Pattern> | Variable1 ++ Variable2
<Pattern> ::=              Variable | Constant | <Vector Pattern> | <Tuple Pattern>
<Vector Pattern> ::=       [ <Pattern1>, ..., <Patternn> ]
<Tuple Pattern> ::=        ( <Pattern1>, ..., <Patternn> )
<Expression> ::=           Constant | Variable | <Tuple Expression> | <Vector Expression>
                           | if <Expression> then <Expression_1> else <Expression_2>   (Conditional)
                           | Symbol <Tuple Expression>                                  (Function Application)
                           | Variable <Vector Expression>                               (Vector Selection)
                           | <Expression> where                                         (Local Equations)
                               Variable1 = <Expression_1>;
                               ...
                               Variablen = <Expression_n>
<Vector Expression> ::=[ <Expression_1>, ..., <Expression_n> ]
<Tuple Expression> ::= ( <Expression_1>, ..., <Expression_n> )
```

Figure 1: BNF for EL*

legal operations on them. Banger [4] defines arrays as categorical data types, constructed from infinite sequences of a base type. Arrays of arbitrary dimensions (over a given base type) are freely generated algebras. Catamorphisms are homomorphisms from initial algebras. Catamorphisms over freely generated data types can always be factored into composition of a mapping function and a reduction. Coincidentally, recursive EL* functions qualify as catamorphisms and operate on arrays which are freely generated. This theory therefore provides the basis for the compilation schema presented in Section 4.2.

The theory needs further refinement. Infinite sequences always generate regular arrays but infinite sequences cannot be used in a strict language like EL*. To guarantee formation of regular arrays at compile-time, constraints on dimensionality and lengths of arrays are needed. Hence, a theory that classifies arrays based on their base type as well as dimensionality is required.

4 EL* Compilation

Compilation of EL* programs into efficient FP* programs is a challenging task. The EL* compiler extracts parallelism that is available in the divide-and-conquer structure of EL* functions and expresses it in terms of data-parallel operations of FP*. The compiler also recognizes instances of data-communication in EL* programs and generates appropriate FP* communication functions. A complete description of the FP* language and its compiler is presented in [3, 16, 17, 18]. A concise description of the implementation language and the compilation scheme follow.

4.1 FP* Overview

In order to make this paper self-contained, a brief overview of the FP* language is presented in this section. FP* is a low-level data-parallel functional language that is used to implement EL*. All FP* functions are monadic and act on data objects as a whole. There are three kinds of data objects in FP*:

Scalars are numbers and boolean constants, e.g., "1" and "true".

Arrays are sequences of objects of the same type and size, e.g., $[1, 11, 15]$. Higher-dimensional arrays are denoted by lists of arrays of rank one lower. For example: $[[11, 13, 15], [1, 3, 5]]$ denotes a 2×3 matrix.

Tuples are sequences of objects of different types (and sizes). For example, $\langle 1, [3, 5], \text{true} \rangle$.

Further, we use $\perp$ to describe the error object. $\perp$ may not appear within arrays or tuples, *i.e.*,

$$[\ldots, \perp, \ldots] = \langle \ldots, \perp, \ldots \rangle = \perp.$$

On the Connection Machine CM-2, and other massively parallel computer systems, memory allocation of FP* data objects to distributed memory is similar to the default allocation strategy employed by many Fortran implementations. A vector (of scalars) is allocated across processors, with each element residing in a distinct virtual processor. A tuple (of scalars) is allocated with each element residing on a single processor. This default allocation scheme can be overridden by the programmer by coercing vectors to tuples, or vice versa.

All expressions in FP* are functions. If f is an FP* expression and x is an FP* object, $f : x$ denotes application of x to f. FP* has a fixed set of primitive functions. Primitives fall into two categories.

- Computational primitives perform the standard arithmetic, logical and relational operations.
- Communication primitives, also called *routing functions*, copy elements of inputs to outputs in a data-independent manner. For example, the `distr` primitive broadcasts an FP* data object to all elements of an array. The elements of the output array are 2-tuples containing the original input element and the data that was broadcasted. By contrast, a sorting function is data-dependent; hence, it is not a routing function.

Table 1 describes primitive routing functions that will appear later. For brevity, error cases are omitted from the

Function	Syntax	Description
Copy	(copy)	$\texttt{copy} : x = x.$
Distribute-from-right	(distr)	$\texttt{distr} : \langle[x_1, \ldots, x_n], y\rangle = [\langle x_1, y\rangle, \ldots, \langle x_n, y\rangle]$
Select k^{th}	(k_n)	$k_n : \langle x_1, \ldots, x_n\rangle = x_k$, for $1 \leq k \leq n$.
Transpose-tuple	($\texttt{trans}_k$)	$\texttt{trans}_k : \langle[x_{11}, \ldots, x_{1n}], \ldots, [x_{k1}, \ldots, x_{kn}]\rangle = [\langle x_{11}, \ldots, x_{k1}\rangle, \ldots, \langle x_{1n}, \ldots, x_{kn}\rangle]$

Table 1: Primitive FP* Routing Functions

Function	Syntax	Description
Constant	$(\bar{c})$	$\bar{c} : x = \begin{cases} c, & \text{if } x \neq \perp; \\ \perp, & \text{otherwise.} \end{cases}$
Composition	(o)	$f \circ g : x = f : (g : x)$
Construction	$([\cdots])$	$[f_1, \ldots, f_n] : x = \langle f_1 : x, \ldots, f_n : x\rangle$
Apply-All	(α)	$\alpha f : [x_1, \ldots, x_n] = [f : x_1, \ldots, f : x_n]$
Insert	$(/)$	$/f : [x_1, \ldots, x_n] = \begin{cases} f : \langle /f : [x_1, \ldots, x_{2^k}], /f : [x_{2^k+1}, \ldots, x_n]\rangle, & \text{if } 1 \leq 2^k < n \leq 2^{k+1}; \\ x, \text{if } n = 1; \\ \perp, \text{otherwise.} \end{cases}$

Table 2: Higher-Order FP* Functions

table. If the form of an input to one of the primitive functions does not match the form presented in the table, $\perp$ is returned.

Programs are constructed by combining primitive functions with higher-order functions. FP*'s higher-order functions are similar to FP's. Some higher-order functions of FP* are shown in Table 2.

The Apply-All and the Insert higher-order functions are valuable from a data-parallel programming point of view. Function f in αf is applied to each element of an input array in parallel. $/f$ is evaluated through a binary tree of depth $\lceil \lg n \rceil$, where n is the length of an input array to $/f$. Also optimizations of the FP* compiler remove the intermediate data values that may be generated by the naïve evaluation of *routing expressions*. An FP* expression f is a routing expression if:

- f is a primitive routing function; or
- $f = \alpha f_1$ where f_1 is a routing expression; or
- $f = [f_1, ..., f_n]$ where each f_i is a routing expression; or
- $f = f_1 \circ f_2$ where f_1 and f_2 are routing expressions.

The FP* compiler's abilities are illustrated in the compilation of the following FP* program that computes the inner-product of two vectors.

```
def ip = /(+) o α(*) o trans₂
```

From this program the following CM-Fortran program (absent variable declarations) is produced:

```
FORALL (I=1:N) C(I) = A(I)*B(I)
D = SUM(C,RANK(C))
```

To generate this Fortran program from IL, optimizations are needed to reduce the number of copy statements present in the code [19]. Table 3 demonstrates the impact of these optimizations on an FP* matrix multiply program, which uses the ip function. This data was produced on an 8K-processor CM-2.

4.2 Compilation Scheme

The EL* compiler is defined inductively as a function of two arguments, based on the possible expressions of the language. An *environment* is a possibly nested structure describing the location in the runtime stack of formal parameters and local variables. In the compilation rules, environ-

Result Size	No Copy Prop. (Secs)	Copy Prop. (Secs)
16×16×16	0.113	0.015
32×32×32	0.278	0.021
64×64×64	2.045	0.062
80×80×80	———	2.490

Table 3: Matrix multiplication performance comparing copy propagation.

ments are denoted by ρ. The FP* expression that accesses a variable **x** from an environment ρ is emitted by the compiler function *access*, applied to **x** and ρ. Representatives of the compilation rules are presented below:

$\mathcal{C}[\![c]\!]\rho = \bar{c}$, where c is a constant.

$\mathcal{C}[\![\mathbf{x}]\!]\rho = access(\mathbf{x}, \rho)$, where **x** is a variable.

$\mathcal{C}[\![e_1 + e_2]\!]\rho = + \circ [f_1, f_2]$, where:
$f_1 = \mathcal{C}[\![e_1]\!]\rho$, and
$f_2 = \mathcal{C}[\![e_2]\!]\rho$.

$\mathcal{C}[\![x[e]]\!]\rho = \mathtt{sel} \circ [f_1, f_2]$, where:
$f_1 = \mathcal{C}[\![e]\!]\rho$, and
$f_2 = \mathcal{C}[\![x]\!]\rho$.

$\mathcal{C}[\![e \ \mathtt{where}\ (\mathbf{x} = e_1)]\!]\rho = f \circ [f_1, \mathrm{copy}]$, where:
$f_1 = \mathcal{C}[\![e_1]\!]\rho$, and
$f = \mathcal{C}[\![e]\!][\mathbf{x}, \rho]$.

$\mathcal{C}[\![f(e)]\!]\rho = f_1 \circ f_2$, where:
$f(x) = e'$ is an equation,
$f_1 = \mathcal{C}[\![e']\!][x]$,
($[x]$ is the environment describing the location of variable(s) x), and
$f_2 = \mathcal{C}[\![e]\!]\rho$.

One of the rules above pertaining to compilation of vector selections uses a function **sel** that is not present within the original definition of FP. This function has been added within FP* to support use of arrays. Its definition follows.

$$\mathtt{sel} : \langle i, [x_1, \ldots, x_n] \rangle = \begin{cases} x_i, & \text{if } 1 \le i \le n; \\ \bot, & \text{otherwise.} \end{cases}$$

Recursive divide-and-conquer EL* functions have one or more equations for the base and inductive cases. The activities that take place when these functions are applied to actual arguments can be divided into three phases:

Divide Phase The inductive arguments are divided recursively into smaller and smaller sub-vectors until every sub-vector has the size that is specified in the base case of recursion. Our compilation scheme at present requires that lengths of all inductive vectors in the base case be 1.

Apply-All Phase If n is the length of the inductive arguments, then there are n invocations of the base case of recursion at the end of the **Divide** phase. Each invocation also has a copy of all non-inductive argument. Since each invocation can be evaluated simultaneously, this phase gives rise to an **Apply-All** form of parallelism.

Combine Phase The combine phase then recursively combines the set of values produced from the **Apply-All** phase in a tree-like fashion using the combining function. This phase has the operational semantics of the Insert operation and logarithmic-time performance.

Recursive functions, exhibit the three phases described above. Hence, they generate FP* expressions that conform to the following schematic structure:

$$/(F) \circ \alpha(B) \circ \alpha(C) \circ (\mathtt{distr} \circ [\mathtt{trans}_k \circ 1_2, 2_2]) \circ A \circ R$$

In this schema, F, B, C, A, and R are FP* expressions that are specific to the particular recursive EL* function being compiled. R reverses every inductive vector argument whose right sub-vector is referenced within a recursive call along with other left sub-vector arguments.[1] Expression A regroups input arguments into a tuple consisting of non-inductive and inductive arguments. Corresponding elements of inductive arguments are grouped into k-tuples (via $\mathtt{trans}_k \circ 1_2$), and the non-inductive arguments are broadcast to each k-tuple via **distr**. C undoes the tupling of arguments performed by A so that argument values are arranged as they appear in the EL* function definition. B is the base case emitted by the compilation function $\mathcal{C}$. F is code emitted just for the combine function. Since $\alpha(C) \circ (\mathtt{distr} \circ [\mathtt{trans}_k \circ 1_2, 2_2]) \circ A \circ B$ is a routing expression, no intermediate data structures are produced during its evaluation.

There are two expressions within the general schema where parallel activities take place. The expression $\alpha(B)$ evaluates function B simultaneously on all processors. Expression $/(F)$ evaluates F in a tree-like fashion obtaining logarithmic-time performance (subject to availability of processors).

This general schema is able to generate the FP* program **ip** of Section 4.1 from the EL* function definition in Section 3. In this program R is the identity function, as left and right sub-vectors are referenced in their proper positions by the combine function.

In the **broadcast** program of Section 3, R is again the identity function. In addition, the reduction step, $/(F)$, is not produced, since the combining function is $+\!\!+$ (concatenation), and reduction by $+\!\!+$ with only left sub-vectors in the left-side argument and right sub-vectors in the right-side argument is the identity function.

Almost all of the primitive functions of FP* can be directly reproduced with EL*. For example, the **broadcast** program of Section 3 compiles to the primitive **distr** (see Table 1).

5 Performance Evaluation

To date, we have written and compiled large-scale EL* programs for Gaussian Elimination with partial pivoting on

[1] At this point in development, vector reversal is only valid if all inductive arguments are the same length, which is a power of 2.

dense matrices, and finite difference computation. The resulting FP* programs were compiled into CM-Fortran, and exhibit the performance shown in Table 4. We have also hand-coded programs solving identical problems and compare the results in the same table. These running times were produced on an 8K-processor section of a Connection Machine CM-2. The EL* finite difference program attains roughly 26 MFLOPS (209 MFLOPS if scaled to 64K processors). Sample functions from these applications are illustrated next.

`maxloc` presented below, is an important function in Gaussian Elimination. `maxloc` has four arguments:

A: An $m \times n$ matrix of numbers.

c: A column number in the range 1 up to n.

B: A vector of Boolean values of length m.

I: A vector of integers ranging from 1 up to n.

This function locates the maximum value within a column of array A. More formally, `maxloc` returns a pair consisting of an element $I[i]$ and row number i such that $B[i]$ is true, and for all $1 \leq j \leq m$ for which $B[j]$ is true: $A[i] \geq B[j]$. Notice that the combining function of `maxloc` is a conditional expression, rather than a fixed arithmetic or logical primitive.

```
maxloc([r],col,[false],[row]) = (r[col],row).
maxloc([r],col,[true],[row]) = (−∞,row).
maxloc(a1++a2,col,f1++f2,i1++i2) =
        if (m1 > m2) then (m1,row1) else (m2,row2)
        where (m1,row1) = maxloc(a1,col,f1,i1);
              (m2,row2) = maxloc(a2,col,f2,i2).
```

The finite-difference computation takes as input a 2-dimension array and returns an array, in which every interior element has a value that is the average of four of its nearest neighbors. The main averaging functions are provided below.

```
finite-dif(A) =
  map4<map4<avg4>>(shiftl(A),
                   shiftr(A),
                   map<shiftl>(A),
                   map<shiftr>(A)).
avg4(w,x,y,z) = 0.25 * (w + x + y + z).
map4<f>([w],[x],[y],[z]) = [f(w,x,y,z)].
map4<f>(w1++w2,x1++x2,y1++y2,z1++z2) =
  map4<f>(w1,x1,y1,z1) ++ map4<f>(w2,x2,y2,z2).
```

The stencil (a 4-element cross in this example) can be varied in size by performing additional shifts, and changing the averaging function. The compiler is able to recognize that logarithmic reduction is unnecessary, due to use of the `map` (see Section 3) and `map4` functions. Also, the `shift` primitives generate efficient CM-Fortran grid communication.[2] Table 4 demonstrates linear slowdown in performance with linear increase in data size.

[2] In the CM-Fortran implementation, without a number of primitives like shift that compile directly to similar CM-Fortran primitives, performance would suffer dramatically.

6 Future Work: Language Enhancements

We are currently engaged in producing more extensive applications in EL*. We are also expanding the scope of the language by incorporating nested sequences that overcome the length restrictions of arrays. Nested sequences are important in applications, like quicksort, where dynamic allocation of data to processes is required. Nested sequences are currently implemented in the NESL language [5].

Both EL* and FP* compilers are specified functionally. It is tempting to compose the two compilers as functions, thereby omitting an intermediate compilation step. With this composition two important enhancements are possible.

- With FP*, the input to every function must be explicitly passed to it. This constrains FP* functions to operate only on local data. However, without the FP* compilation step, global data can be referenced without expensive copying.
- FP* data values exclude functional expressions. Without the FP* compilation step, we can expand the range of data values to include functions. With functions as data values, they can be passed as arguments to other functions. Currently, functional arguments are only passed as macro-like parameters. Macro expansion of functional arguments prohibits references to variables, because scope information is lost during the expansion. When functional values are represented as closures, consisting of function-pointer/environment pairs, scope information is retained. In particular, the `broadcast` and `map` functions of Section 3 could be rewritten as follows.

```
broadcast(v,x) = map(f,v)
  where f(y) = (y,x).
map(f,[y]) = [f(y)].
map(f,v1++v2) = map(f,v1) ++ map(f,v2).
```

Acknowledgments

This work would not have been possible without the efforts of Deb Banerjee who conceived and implemented the FP* compiler and motivated this project. Thanks also to Z. George Mou for his encouragement and guidance, and to the referees for their helpful comments. Time on the Connection Machine was furnished by DARPA. The research was conducted under the sponsorship of Dartmouth College.

References

[1] S. Akl, *Parallel Sorting Algorithms*, Academic Press, 1985.

[2] J. Backus, "Can programming be liberated from the von Neumann style? A functional style and its algebra of programs," *CACM*, 21(8), pp. 613–641 (Aug. 1978).

[3] D. Banerjee & C. Walinsky, "An Optimizing Compiler for FP* — A Data-Parallel Dialect of FP," *3rd International Symposium on Parallel and Distributed Processing*, Dallas (Dec. 1991).

# Eqns.	Compiled (Secs)	Hand-coded (Secs)
24	0.5	0.4
48	1.3	0.6
100	3.7	2.2
200	10.5	9.5
400	56.0	30.9
800	286	214

Matrix Dim.	Compiled (Secs)	Hand-coded (Secs)
64 × 64	0.002	0.001
64 × 128	0.002	0.002
250 × 250	0.016	0.015
500 × 500	0.054	0.047
1000 × 1000	0.191	0.166

Table 4: Performance of Gaussian Elimination and finite difference method

[4] C. Banger, "Arrays with Type Constructors," *ATABLE-92: 2nd Int'l Workshop on Array Structures,* Montreal, 1992.

[5] G.E. Blelloch, "Scans as Primitive Parallel Operations," *IEEE Transactions on Computers,* 38(11), pp. 1526–38 (Nov. 1989).

[6] M.C. Chen, "A Parallel Language and Its Compilation to Multiprocessor Machines or VLSI," *13th Annual ACM Symposium on Principles of Programming Languages,* pp. 131–39 (Jan. 1986).

[7] J.T. Feo, D.C. Cann & R.R. Oldehoeft, "A Report on the Sisal Language Project," *Journal of Parallel and Distributed Computing,* 10: 349–66 (1990).

[8] W.D. Hillis, *The Connection Machine,* MIT Press, 1985.

[9] W.D. Hillis & G.L. Steele, Jr., "Data Parallel Algorithms," *CACM,* 29(12), pp. 1170–83 (Dec. 1986).

[10] P. Hudak, "Para-Functional Programming," *IEEE Computer,* 19(8), pp. 60–70 (Aug. 1986).

[11] K. Knobe, J.D. Lukas & G.L. Steele, Jr., "Data Optimization: Allocation of Arrays to Reduce Communication on SIMD Machines," *Journal of Parallel and Distributed Computing,* 8, pp. 102–18 (1990).

[12] Z.G. Mou & P. Hudak, "An Algebraic Model for Divide-and-Conquer and Its Parallelism," *The Journal of Supercomputing,* vol. 2, pp. 257–78 (1988).

[13] D.S. Parker, E. Simon & P. Valduriez, "SVP—A Model Capturing Sets, Streams, and Parallelism," *Proceedings of the 18th VLDB Conference,* Vancouver, British Columbia, Canada (1992).

[14] G.L. Steele, Jr. & W.D. Hillis, "Connection Machine Lisp: Fine Grained Parallel Symbolic Processing," *1986 ACM Conference on Lisp and Functional Programming,* Cambridge, pp. 279–97 (Aug. 1986).

[15] *CM-Fortran Reference Manual (Version 5.2–0.6),* Thinking Machines Corporation, Cambridge, Massachussets.

[16] C. Walinsky & D. Banerjee, "A Functional Programming Language Compiler for Massively Parallel Computers," *1990 ACM Conference on Lisp and Functional Programming,* Nice, pp. 131–38 (June 1990).

[17] C. Walinsky & D. Banerjee, "Compiling FP for Data-Parallel Systems (Extended Abstract)," *Workshop on Compiling (Symbolic) Languages for Parallel Systems at the 1991 International Logic Programming Symposium,* San Diego (Oct. 1991).

[18] C. Walinsky & D. Banerjee, "A Data-Parallel FP Compiler," to appear in *Journal of Parallel and Distributed Computing.*

[19] C. Walinsky, D. Banerjee & P. Rao, "Array Definition Propagation Across Data-Parallel Loops," submitted for publication.

Transforming High-Level Data-Parallel Programs into Vector Operations†

Jan F. Prins and Daniel W. Palmer
Department of Computer Science
University of North Carolina
Chapel Hill NC 27599-3175
{prins,palmerd}@cs.unc.edu

Abstract

Efficient parallel execution of a high-level data-parallel language based on nested sequences, higher order functions and generalized iterators can be realized in the vector model using a suitable representation of nested sequences and a small set of transformational rules to distribute iterators through the constructs of the language.

1. Introduction

Currently, the development of parallel programs primarily takes place in low-level machine-specific programming languages since these are typically the only languages supported on parallel machines. In this setting, prototyping is a painful process, since small changes in the high-level approach precipitate a flood of changes in low-level details. To make things worse, little or none of this effort may be portable to other settings.

Proteus[1] is a high-level language designed for the prototyping of parallel computations [MNP+91, NP92]. A *Proteus* program specifies parallelism in a high-level and machine-independent fashion. The parallel semantics of such a program can be simulated sequentially, to observe its behavior and make measurements of machine-independent characteristics such as total work and available concurrency. Actual parallel execution on a parallel machine can be obtained by *directed transformation* of the prototype to place it in a restricted form that can then be translated directly to a low-level (possibly machine specific) programming language. We use the KIDS [Smith90] interactive program development system to manage the transformation and translation process. In this fashion, a high-level prototype parallel computation can be experimentally developed and subsequently refined into a parallel program executing on a parallel machine.

In this paper, we are concerned with the directed transformation of *data-parallel Proteus* programs. The data-parallel constructs of *Proteus* permit the construction and manipulation of aggregate values (e.g. sets and sequences) and, in particular, include the ability to apply an arbitrary function to each element of an aggregate value to yield an aggregate result.

High-level programming languages like APL [Iver62] and SETL [Schw70] pioneered the inclusion of data-parallel constructs to gain expressive power by bringing the languages closer to familiar and powerful mathematical notations. The aggregate in the original APL language was the *flat* array, an array whose elements are all scalar values. To obtain fully general data-parallelism, in which *any* function including data-parallel functions can be applied in a data-parallel fashion, requires *nested* aggregates, in which elements may themselves be aggregates. A nested array foundation for APL was described by [More79], and can be found in NIAL, APL2, J, SETL and FP [Back78]. Although fully general data-parallel programs are conveniently specified in these languages, they are not executed in parallel. This is due to implicit serial dependencies in the specification of apply-to-each operations and the apparent requirement for complex and fine-grain MIMD control of execution. Thus these languages are not parallel programming languages.

Languages in which data-parallelism is the mechanism used to specify actual parallel computation such as *Lisp, MPL, and DAP-Fortran have historically targeted specific SIMD parallel computers. More recent languages like CMFortran and C* are portable across various SIMD and MIMD machines. The aggregates in these languages are restricted to flat arrays distributed in a regular manner over processors in an effort to predict and minimize communication requirements in execution [KLS+90, Prin90]. Because aggregates are flat, only a limited class of arithmetic and logical operations may be applied in a data-parallel fashion.

Consequently, using these languages, it is not possible to directly express *nested parallelism* –the data-parallel application of a function which is itself data-parallel.

---

†This work supported in part by DARPA/ISTO,monitored under ONR Contract N00014-91-C-0114

[1]The *Proteus* language is a component of the DARPA Prototech effort.

4th ACM PPOPP,5/93/CA,USA

For example, a data-parallel sort function can not be applied in parallel to every sequence in a collection of sequences. Yet this is the key step in several parallel divide-and-conquer sorting algorithms. Indeed, there is extensive evidence that nested data-parallelism is an important component in the compact expression of efficient parallel computations [Blel90, Skil90, MNP+91]. The difficulty is not in the languages, since general data-parallel languages can easily express nested parallel computations. Rather the problem lies in the difficulty of translating nested parallelism to achieve efficient parallel execution.

A major step in this direction was taken in [Blel90] where it was shown that for nested sequence aggregates subject to a restricted set of operations, an equivalent *vector model* program operating on segmented flat sequences can be derived. The vector model is efficiently executed on a wide class of parallel machines. Building on these techniques, the transformations presented in this paper give a simple mechanism to transform the fully general data-parallelism available in *Proteus* programs into the vector model.

1.1 Related work

The problem of deriving parallel programs by transformation has received wide attention. In this paper, we are concerned specifically with the translation of data-parallelism, so we restrict our review of related work to that concerned with the implementation of nested parallelism.

CM Lisp [SH86] and Paralation Lisp [Sabo88] are fully-general data-parallel languages implemented as high-level programming languages for the Connection Machine. However, implementations of these languages apply nested data-parallel operations in a serial fashion. McCrosky [McCr87] describes a way to represent the nested arrays of APL and gives implementations for APL primitives on a SIMD execution model, but nested parallel execution is not addressed. Philippsen [PTH91] describes an implementation of nested parallelism in Modula-2* for a SIMD computer, but Modula-2* has no data-parallel nested aggregates. So while data parallel operations may be nested the programmer must orchestrate their parallel access to the appropriate portions of a shared global variable. This requires extensive bookkeeping and use of low-level facilities; thus, we believe that the expressive utility of nested parallelism in this setting is limited.

In [BS90] it was shown how to compile a subset of Paralation LISP into vector model code. More recently, the nested vector model language NESL [Blel92] has used similar techniques to target the portable vector model intermediate language CVL. Compared to these approaches, the translation of *Proteus* includes translation of function values (which are critical elements of the higher-order data-parallel style), and starts from a more general definition of the data-parallel construct (the iterator in *Proteus*) based on a shared memory view. A key contribution of this paper, consistent with our aims for parallel program development by refinement, is the transformational approach to the translation problem.

The remainder of this paper is organized as follows. The next section describes a subset of the *Proteus* notation. Section 3 details language transformations to remove iterators from a *Proteus* expression. Section 4 describes the vector model representation of nested sequences and a translation rule that replaces parallel functions operating on nested sequences with simple vector model functions. Section 5 demonstrates the rules on a simple example. We conclude with implementation status, and a discussion of results.

2. Data-Parallel Expression Language

We describe a subset $\mathcal{P}$ of *Proteus* that can be transformed for vector-model execution. This subset is a restriction of *Proteus* in three ways. First, we restrict ourselves to the expression language; thus the Proteus notion of state is not considered. Second, we require that the types of all expressions be static and monomorphic; *Proteus* expressions in general may exhibit dynamic and polymorphic types. Since overloading is permitted in $\mathcal{P}$, a polymorphic *Proteus* function can be instantiated with several different monomorphic argument types. Finally, the types of values and operations available are restricted to simplify the exposition. For example, function values must be fully-parameterized, set-valued aggregates are not considered, the set of scalar types is limited, and only a small number of operations on sequences are provided. Extension of this last restriction should be relatively simple. To achieve programs that meet all of these restrictions, prior directed transformation steps may be required. The restrictions are not overly limiting because the subset is highly expressive.

The types of $\mathcal{P}$ include scalar types, arbitrarily nested sequences, tuple types and function types generated by the following CFG:

$$T ::= Int \mid Bool \mid Seq(T) \mid (T \times \ldots \times T) \mid (T \rightarrow T)$$

In contrast to data-parallel languages that do not distinguish between tuples and sequences, the sequences in $\mathcal{P}$ are *homogeneous*. This requirement is needed to statically type all expressions.

Expressions in $\mathcal{P}$ are composed using the constructs in Table 1. A small number of *basic functions* predefined in $\mathcal{P}$ are given in Table 2; other functions can be constructed in terms of these basic functions. We note that we have deviated somewhat from the usual *Proteus* syntax.

construct	meaning
$(e_f)\,(e_1,...,e_n)$	application of function value e_f to arguments $(e_1,...,e_n)$
fun $(x_1, ... ,x_n)$ e	λ–abstraction of body e with parameters $x_1, ... ,x_n$
let $x = e_1$ **in** e_2	value of e_2 with x bound to value of e_1
if b **then** e_1 **else** e_2	yields e_1 if b is true else yields e_2

Table 1. Basic constructors of $\mathcal{P}$

The index origin for sequences is 1, hence `V[1][2]` is the second element of the first sequence in the nested sequence V. The operation `restrict(`V,M`)` with $\#V = \#M$ yields V with all elements corresponding to false values in M removed. If R = `combine(`M,V,U`)` where $\#M = \#V + \#U$, then `restrict(`R,M`)` $= V$ and `restrict(`$R, \sim M$`)` $= U$ (here $\sim M$ denotes the element-wise complement of M).

The dist operation replicates values in the first sequence by the corresponding value in the second sequence. For example, `dist`([3,4,5],[3,2,1]) yields [[3,3,3],[4,4],[5]].

The remaining construct in $\mathcal{P}$ is the *iterator* which is the source of all data-parallelism. Its form is:

```
[x ← d: e]
```

where x is an identifier, d is a sequence-valued expression of type $Seq(\alpha)$ called the domain of the iterator, and e is an expression of type β under the assumption that free occurrences of identifier x have type α. The iterator yields a value of type $Seq(\beta)$ defined as follows (e^x_y is the syntactic replacement of every free occurrence of x in e by the expression y):

$$\forall k \in 1..\#d:\quad [x \leftarrow d\colon e][k] \equiv (e)^x_{d[k]}$$

This definition gives the value of an arbitrary element of the result independent of the values of the other elements, hence a natural implementation is to evaluate all elements of the result in parallel.

It is often convenient to restrict the set of values for which e will be evaluated to elements from d satisfying a predicate b in which there are free occurrences of x. Thus we define

```
[x ← d | b : e]  ≡
  let
     T = restrict(d, [x ← d : b])
  in
     [t ← T: e^x_t]
```

The subset $\mathcal{P}$ is a flexible and comprehensive notation that can be used to express scalar functions,

```
fun odd(a) = (1 == (a mod 2))
```

data-parallel functions,

```
fun sqs(n) = [i ← [1..n]: i*i]

fun concat(V,W) =
   [i ← [1..(#V+#W)]:
        if (i≤#V)
        then V[i]
        else W[i-(#V)] ]
```

higher-order data-parallel functions,

name	notation	signature
scalar functions	+, -, ==, etc.	$\alpha \to \beta$ (where $\alpha, \beta \in \{Bool, Int\}$)
tuple_cons	$(e_1, ..., e_n)$	$\alpha_1 \times ... \times \alpha_n \to (\alpha_1 \times ... \times \alpha_n)$
tuple_extract	$e_t.i$	$(\alpha_1 \times ... \times \alpha_n) \times Int \to \alpha_i$
seq_cons	$[e_1, ..., e_n]$	$\alpha \times ... \times \alpha \to Seq(\alpha)$
seq_index	$e_s[e_1]\,[e_2]\,...\,[e_k]$	$Seq^k(\alpha) \times Int^k \to \alpha$
seq_update	$(e_s;\ [e_1]\,...\,[e_k] : e_v)$	$Seq^k(\alpha) \times Int^k \times \alpha \to Seq^k(\alpha)$
length	$\#e_s$	$Seq(\alpha) \to Int$
range	$[e_1\ ..\ e_2]$	$Int \times Int \to Seq(Int)$
restrict	restrict (e_s, e_b)	$Seq(\alpha) \times Seq(Bool) \to Seq(\alpha)$
combine	combine $(e_b\, e_1, e_2)$	$Seq(Bool) \times Seq(\alpha) \times Seq(\alpha) \to Seq(\alpha)$
distribute	dist (e_1, e_2)	$Seq^k(\alpha) \times Seq^k(Int) \to Seq^{k+1}(\alpha)$

Table 2. Basic functions of $\mathcal{P}$

```
fun reduce(f,V) =
  if (#V = 1)
  then V
  else
    let
      W = [i ← [1..(#V) div 2]:
                f(V[(2*i)-1],V[2*i])]
    in
      if (odd(#V))
      then reduce(f,
              concat(W,[V[#V]]))
      else reduce(f,W)
```

and nested data-parallel functions,

```
fun oddsq(n) =
  [i ← [1..n] | odd(i): sqs(i)]
```

```
fun flatten(V) =
  reduce(concat,V)
```

We now turn to the transformation of $\mathcal{P}$.

3. Transforming $\mathcal{P}$ to data-parallel form

The expressive utility of the iterator construct comes from its ability to give a per-element specification of an aggregate result. In this view, an iterator sits at the head of a syntax tree that is repeatedly evaluated with different values for the bound variable to yield successive elements of the result. This per-element view of the computation is, however, rather different from a data-parallel computation in which operations are applied to aggregates of data, instead of single elements.

To place an arbitrary expression involving iterators into a form suitable for data-parallel execution, we use transformation rules that distribute the iterators through the constructs of $\mathcal{P}$ toward the leaves of the syntax tree. When fully distributed through all the internal nodes of a syntax tree, iterators enclose leaves that are simple constants or references to variables. These iterators can then be replaced by sequence-valued expressions that directly generate the equivalent result. An expression transformed in this manner is data-parallel: it contains no iterators and operates on sequence aggregates rather than individual elements.

In order to simplify the presentation of the transformations, we introduce some definitions. Let α be an arbitrary type of $\mathcal{P}$, let d be some non-negative integer. A *depth d frame* of elements of type α is a nested sequence of type $Seq^d(\alpha)$. For a given function

$$g: \alpha_1 \times \ldots \times \alpha_n \rightarrow \beta,$$

the *depth d parallel extension* of g is defined to be the function

$$g^d: Seq^d(\alpha_1) \times \ldots \times Seq^d(\alpha_n) \rightarrow Seq^d(\beta)$$

that applies g to each element in a depth d frame of arguments, yielding a depth d frame of results. Note that under this definition, $g^0 = g$. All arguments of g^d must be *conformable* at depth d, meaning that each argument exhibits the same nesting structure within the depth d frame.

If g is defined as **fun** g($x_1, \ldots, x_n$) = e, for some arbitrary body e, then g^d can be derived from g by enclosing e within d iterators that enumerate the elements of the arguments at depth d. That is,

```
fun gd(V1, ... , Vn) =                                  (R0)
  [i1 ← [1..#V1]:
    [i2 ← [1..#(V1[i1])]:
      ...
      [id ← [1..#(V1[i1]..[id-1])]:
        let
          x1 = V1[i1]..[id],
          ...
          xn = Vn[i1]..[id]
        in
          e
      ]
      ...
    ]
  ]
```

The conformability requirement permits selection of corresponding elements from all arguments based on the nesting structure of one argument (the first argument in this case).

Definitions of g^d will be overloaded to permit particular arguments to omit the depth d frame. Semantically, such arguments are considered to be replicated into a depth d frame to be conformable with the remaining arguments. This is a generalization of scalar extension found in the operations of many data-parallel languages.

To explain the transformation, consider placing the expression

```
[i ← [1..N]: g(i)]                                      (3.1)
```

into data-parallel form where **fun** g(x) = e is some arbitrary function with type $Int \rightarrow Int$. The iterator can be distributed through the function application of g in (3.1) by replacing g with the depth 1 parallel extension g^1 to obtain

```
g1([i ← [1..N]: i])                                     (3.2)
```

where

```
fun g1(V) =
  [j ← [1..#V]:  let
                   x = V[j]
                 in
                   e
  ]
```

The iterator introduced in g^1 can in turn be eliminated by application of the transformation rules to the body of g^1. The iterator `[i ← [1..N]: i]` remaining in expression (3.2) encloses a simple reference to the bound variable *i* and can be replaced by the sequence valued expression `[1..N]` to yield

$$g^1([1..N]) \tag{3.3}$$

and this is the form of (3.1) that is suited for data-parallel execution (after g^1 is transformed).

The most challenging problem is the construction of sequence-valued expressions to replace simple references inside nested iterators. Each enclosing iterator increases the combinations of values of the bound variables for which the expression can be evaluated simultaneously. Iterators enclosing a constant or a free occurrence of a variable may be replaced directly by the constant or variable since we rely on parallel extensions of functions to replicate such single values to the appropriate depth. For an occurrence of a variable bound in one of the enclosing iterators (variables introduced in iterators or in **let** statements enclosed within iterators), the sequence-valued expression will depend on the iterators between its definition and its use.

If we restrict the form of the iterator domain to [1..*e*] where *e* may be an arbitrary expression, then the basic operations `range1` and `dist` and their parallel extensions suffice to build all required sequence-valued expressions. The definitions of these two functions are

```
range1(n)  = [1..n]
dist(c,r)  = [i ← [1..r]: c]
```

The general form of a collection of iterators enclosing a bound occurrence of a variable is

$$[i_1 \leftarrow [1..e_1]: \ \dots\ [i_d \leftarrow [1..e_d]: i_k] \ \dots\ ]$$

where i_k is bound in iterator *k*. The expression replacing the iterator nest must yield elements arranged in a depth *d* frame. Generally speaking, the transformation of the upper bound expression e_k of the domain in iterator $k \le d$ yields a depth *k*-1 frame of upper bounds $\tau(e_k)$, hence the values assumed by i_k are given by $V = range1^{k-1}(\tau(e_k))$. To expand this value to a depth *d* frame, we must replicate the values in *V* according to the domain sizes of the iterators *k*+1 ... *d*. Since the size of the domain in iterator *j* on each nested invocation is given by the upper bound expression e_j, this can be accomplished with the expression

$$dist^{d-1}(dist^{d-2}(\dots dist^{k+1}(dist^{k}(V, \tau(e_{k+1})), \tau(e_{k+2})), \dots, \tau(e_{d-1})), \tau(e_d))$$

For example, in the following two iterators

```
[i ← [1..N]: [j ← [1..i]: i]]
[i ← [1..N]: [j ← [1..i]: j]]
```

we have $\tau(e_1)$ = `N` and $\tau(e_2)$ = `range1`^{0}`(N)` = `[1..N]`. These iterators can be replaced by the expressions

$$dist^1(range1^0(\tau(e_1)), \tau(e_2)) = dist^1(range1^0(N), range1^0(N))$$

and

$$range1^1(\tau(e_2)) = range1^1(range1^0(N))$$

respectively. In the syntax-directed transformation rules that follow, the expressions replacing iterator nests are constructed incrementally, with the depth of all bound variables increased each time an iterator is encountered.

We now outline the transformations to eliminate iterators from arbitrary programs in $\mathcal{P}$. A program in $\mathcal{P}$ consists of a set of function definitions. The transformations are applied to the body of each of function *f* defined in the program as well as to each of the parallel extensions of *f* introduced as a result of the transformations. The number of parallel extensions of *f* that are introduced is a static property of the program. A subsequent translation step provides a single flat-vector implementation that can be used for all depth $d \ge 1$ parallel extensions of functions.

3.1. Iterator canonical form

We first transform a program so that each iterator is in a *canonical* form. An iterator is in canonical form if its domain is a range of consecutive integers starting with 1. An arbitrary iterator can be placed in this form using the rule

$$[x \leftarrow e_1: e_2] \equiv \textbf{let}\ V = e_1\ \textbf{in}\ [i \leftarrow [1..\#V] : (e_2)^{x}_{V[i]}] \tag{R1}$$

3.2 Iterator elimination

For each function definition `f(x1, ..., xn) = e`, we eliminate all iterators from the body of the definition by replacing *e* with the syntax-directed transformation $\tau(e, 0)$ defined as follows:

$$\tau(«id», j) = id \tag{R2a}$$

$$\tau(«const», j) = const \tag{R2b}$$

$$\tau(«e_f(e_1, \dots, e_n)», j) = (\tau(e_f, j))^j\ (\tau(e_1, j), \dots, \tau(e_n, j)) \tag{R2c}$$

```
τ(«[i ← [1..e1]: e2]»,j) =                      (R2d)
  let
    ib = τ(e1),
    i  = range1^j(ib)
    v  = dist^j(v, ib)
           for all v that occur in e2 and are
           bound in enclosing iterators
  in
    τ(e2, j+1)
```

```
τ(«if e1 then e2 else e3»,j) =                  (R2e)
  let
    M = τ(e1,j)
  in
    let
      R2 =
        if restrict^j(M,M) ≠
                empty_frame^j(M)
          then
            let
              v = restrict^j(v,M)
                for all v that occur in e2
                bound in enclosing iterators
            in τ(e2,j)
          else
            empty_frame^j(M)
      R3 =
        if restrict^j(M,not^j(M)) ≠
                empty_frame^j(M)
          then
            let
            v = restrict^j(v,not^j(M))
                for all v that occur in e3
                bound in enclosing iterators
            in τ(e3,j)
          else
            empty_frame^j(M)
    in
      combine^j(M,R2,R3)
```

```
τ(«let v = e1 in e2»,j) =                       (R2f)
  let
    v = τ(e1,j)
  in
    τ(e2,j)
```

```
τ(«fun (x1, ... ,xn) e »,j) =                   (R2g)
  fun (x1, ... ,xn) e
```

where `empty_frame`^{j}`(V)` creates a depth d frame that has the same structure as V but contains no elements at depth d. Since all function definitions are fully parameterized, a function definition is independent of any surrounding iterators and reduces to the case of an iterator surrounding a simple constant.

The transformations have the potential to create a large number of function definitions, since each function may be called in a variety of iteration depths d and with a variety of depth 0 and depth d argument frames. However, as we shall see in the next section, all depth 0 argument frames can be converted to depth d argument frames in a uniform way, and all depth $d>1$ parallel extensions of a function can be implemented by using the depth 1 parallel extension.

4. Translation of $\mathcal{P}$ to $\mathcal{V}$

Iterator free data-parallel expressions in $\mathcal{P}$, as produced by the transformations of the previous section, can be translated to an implementation of vector-model parallelism [Blel90] such as C with the C Vector Library of [BCS+90]. Here, we characterize such an implementation, $\mathcal{V}$, as a flat, low-level data-parallel notation that may be viewed as a further restriction of $\mathcal{P}$.

The types of $\mathcal{V}$ are scalar types, flat sequence types, tuple types and function types that are generated by the following CFG:

$$T ::= Int \mid Bool \mid Seq(Int) \mid Seq(Bool) \mid Seq(T \rightarrow T) \mid (T \times \ldots \times T) \mid (T \rightarrow T)$$

The basic constructors of $\mathcal{V}$ include the constructors given in Table 1. Note that $\mathcal{V}$ does not include the iterator construct. The operations of $\mathcal{V}$ are the operations given in table 2, and the depth 1 parallel extensions of each of these functions.

4.1 Representation of Nested Sequences

All values of $\mathcal{P}$, with the exception of nested sequences and sequences of tuples, can be directly represented in $\mathcal{V}$. A sequence value in $\mathcal{P}$ with type $Seq^d(\alpha)$ for some type α in $\mathcal{P}$ and $d \geq 1$ has a *vector representation* in $\mathcal{V}$ as follows. A collection of k vectors $V_1, \ldots, V_k$ are used, where $V_1,..,V_d$ are *descriptor* vectors, V_1 is always a singleton vector and $V_{d+1},..,V_k$ are *value* vectors, If α is a scalar type then $k = d+1$, but if α is a tuple type then $k > d+1$. A vector representation and its equivalent *nesting tree* representation are shown in figure 1. Each descriptor vector indicates the partitioning for the vector on the level below. An important characteristic of this representation is that:

$$\forall\ 1 \leq i \leq d\ \ \#V_{i+1} = \Sigma\, V_i$$

Only adjacent descriptor vectors are directly related to each other, so maintaining a consistent representation when performing sequence operations is relatively simple. Note that empty sequences at the leaves of the nesting tree are represented by a zero index in the lowest-level descriptor vector.

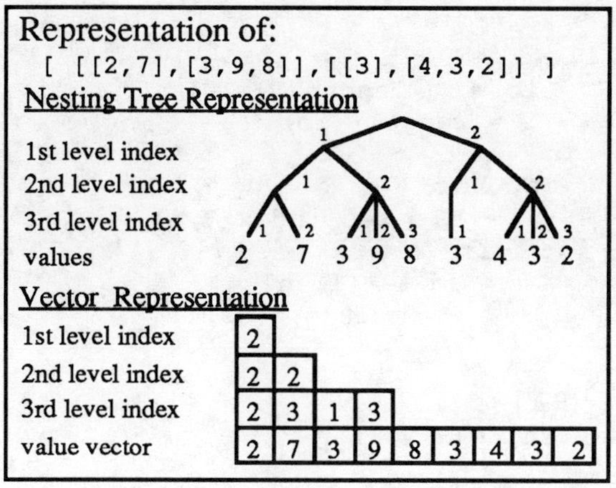

figure 1

4.2 Operations on Vector Representation of Nested Sequences

There are two operations that directly manipulate the representations of nested sequences: *extract* and *insert*. For V a sequence of depth $d+k$, *extract*(V,d) flattens the top d-1 nesting levels (see figure 2) and can be implemented by replacing the top d-1 descriptors by the singleton vector $V_1 = [\ \Sigma V_d]$.

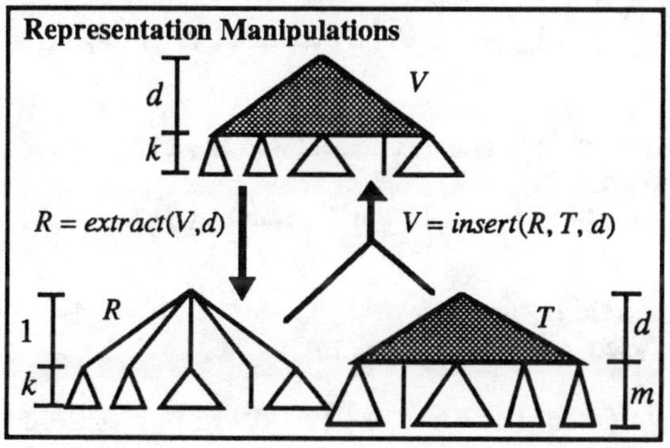

figure 2

The *insert* operation forms a depth $d+k$ sequence from a sequence of depth k+1 and another sequence of depth greater than d. In our translation, the second sequence is always the same as the sequence used in an *extract* operation, but this is not required. *Insert*(R,V,d) removes the top descriptor from R and replaces it with the top d descriptors from V (see figure 2). We require that $\#T_d = R_1[1]$. This insures that the result of an *insert* operation is a consistent nested sequence representation. Note that $V = insert(extract(V,d),V,d))$ for any $d \leq$ depth of V.

4.3 Translation of Functions on Nested Sequences

A depth d parallel extension of f, operates on values at depth d without altering the frame, hence it suffices to use f^1, the simple depth 1 parallel extension of f, to be used in all contexts. To achieve the effect of $f^d(e)$, we flatten the frame around values in e, apply f^1, and restore the frame around the result of this application.

This is accomplished by using the *extract* operation to remove the nesting frame of a sequence so the simple data-parallel function can be applied. The result is then re-attached to a frame using the *insert* instruction as shown in figure 3.

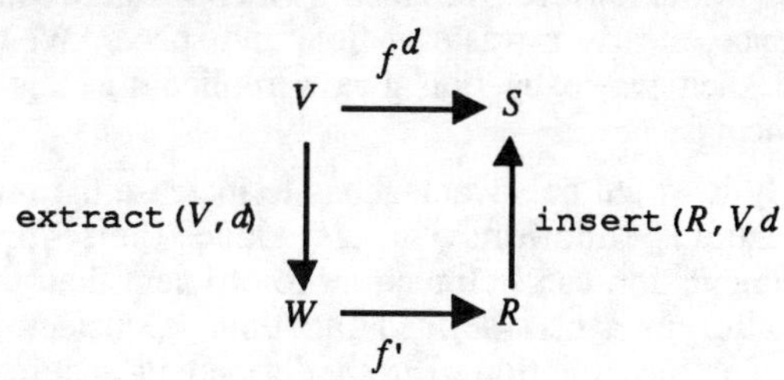

figure 3

This principle is the basis for our translation rule. It eliminates the need for the higher depth parallel extensions of functions. The translation rule for application of f^d with $d > 1$ is:

```
fd (e1, e2, ...,en) ≡                                  (T1)
    let V1=e1, V2=e2,...,Vn=en
    in
      Insert
        (f'   (Extract(V1,d),
               Extract(V2,d),...
               Extract(Vn,d)),
      V1,d)
```

If f is a function-valued parameter to a function g, it is necessary to pass f in invocations of g as a pair (f, f^1), so that the correct version can be used in a given context.

4.4 Implementation of Functions of $\mathcal{P}$

After application of the translation rule, all expressions in $\mathcal{P}$ are in terms of the basic functions of $\mathcal{V}$. To realize parallel execution, $\mathcal{V}$ is in turn translated to some executable notation. In our case this is C with the vector operations provided by CVL. The details of the implementation in CVL of the operations in table 2 and their depth 1 parallel extensions is beyond the scope of the current paper. With these implementations and the translation rule, we can claim that all possible expressions in $\mathcal{P}$ can be represented and executed using only constructs in $\mathcal{V}$.

4.5 Vector Level Optimizations

Because they are so frequently applied, it is critically important that the *insert* and *extract* operations have minimal overhead. The selection of the tree vector representation for nested sequences was chosen specifically because those operations can be implemented inexpensively on this representation.

Certain functions may have parameters that should not be extracted and inserted. Consider the function *seq_index*. If the source parameter is fixed relative to the surrounding iterators, there is no need to replicate it when using iterator transformations. If the replication is applied in these cases, the result is that each set of index values would retrieve from their own copy of the source sequence, clearly a waste of time and space. We can avoid such waste by not always replicating depth 0 argument frames.

Clearly it would be advantageous to increase the set of predefined functions in $\mathcal{V}$ since their direct implementation can be much more efficient than their evaluation as a user-defined function. Consider, for example, the function *flatten* defined in section 2. *Flatten* can be implemented simply by creating a new descriptor vector for the values rather than by creating a new value using the *reduce* and *concat* function definitions.

5. Example

We illustrate the transformations and translations described in the previous two sections on the simple expression

```
[k ← [1..5]: sqs(k)]
```

using the function *sqs* defined in section 2:

```
fun sqs(n) = [j ← [1..n]:mult(j,j)]
```

The top level expression is transformed to

```
let
  kb = 5
  k  = range1⁰(kb)
in
  sqs¹(k)
```

Since the resultant expression has introduced $\texttt{sqs}^1$, we must define this function using `sqs` and transform it to remove iterators.

```
  {R0}
fun sqs¹(V) =

   τ(«[i ← [1..length(V)] :
      let
         n = seq_index(V,i)
      in
         [j ← [1..n]: mult(j,j)] ]»,0)


  {R2d}
τ(«[i ← [1..length(V)] :
   let
      n = index(V,i)
   in
      [j ← [1..n]: mult(j,j)] ]»,0) =

let
   ib = τ(«length(V)»,0)
   i = range1⁰(ib)
in
  τ(«let
       n = seq_index(V,i)
     in
       [j ← [1..n]
          :mult(j,j)]»,1)


  {R2c}
τ(«length(V)»,0) =

  τ(«length»,0)⁰(τ («V»,0))


  {R2a}
τ(«length»,0)⁰(τ («V»,0)) =

  length⁰(V)


  {R2f}
τ(«let
     n = index(V,i)
  in
       [j ← [1..n]:mult(j,j)]»,1) =

  let
    n = τ(«seq_index(V,i)»,1)
  in
    τ(«[j ← [1..n] :mult(j,j)]»,1)


  {R2c.}
τ(«seq_index(V,i)»,1) =

  τ(«seq_index»,1)¹(τ («V»,1),τ («i»,1))


  {R2a}
τ(«seq_index»,1)¹(τ («V»,1),τ («i»,1)) =

  seq_index¹(V,i)


  {R2d}
τ(«[j ← [1..n] :mult(j,j)]»,1) =

  let
    jb = τ(«n»,1)
    j = range1¹(jb)
  in
    τ(«mult(j,j)»,2)
```

{R2a}

```
τ(«n»,1) = n
```

{R2d}

```
τ(«mult(j,j)»,2) =

   τ(«mult», 2)2 (τ («j»,2), τ («j»,2))
```

{R2a}

```
τ(«mult», 2)2 (τ («j»,2), τ («j»,2)) =

   mult2(j,j)
```

Combining all the results yields the transformed version of the function sqs^1:

```
fun sqs1(V) =
   let
      ib = #V
      i  = range10(ib)
   in
      let
         n = seq_index1(V,i)
      in
         let
            jb = n
            j  = range11(jb)
         in
            mult2(j,j)
```

The translation rule must be applied to both the top level expression and the transformed function. The expression remains unchanged, but the invocation of *mult* is translated.

{T1}

```
mult2(j,j) =

   insert(mult1(extract(j,1),
                extract(j,1),J,1) )
```

C code can be generated directly from this final transfomed sqs^1 program by the KIDS system. The code produced for this example is:

```
nseq sqs_1(nseq s)
   { nseq q =
         range1_1(
            index_1(s,
               range1_0(length(s))
            )
         )
     return
        insert(mult_1(extract(q,1),
                      extract(q,1)
              ),q,1);
   }
```

With CVL implementations of the primitves of $\mathcal{V}$ this code can be directly executed on a wide variety of parallel computers.

6. Discussion

Implementation Status

Most of the primitives of $\mathcal{V}$ have been implemented in CVL at the time of this writing. The transformations have been implemented by our colleagues at Kestrel Institute on the KIDS system. Combing these efforts gives us an end-to-end system that can automatically transform and execute *Proteus* programs. We are currently executing using the sequential version of the vector library, but attaining actual parallel execution only requires recompilation on parallel hardware. We are currently implementing the remaining language primitives and investigating improvements to the transformations that yield more efficient code.

Implications for sequential execution

In addition to providing a route to parallel execution of high-level data-parallel programs, the transformations can also be of use in a sequential setting. One of the objections often raised to the iterator construct is that it incurs substantial overhead in the repeated evaluation of the iterator body. The transformation rules suggest, however, that by replacing the iterators with vector primitives, the overhead of repeated calls can be eliminated.

Conclusions

We have described a simple transformational framework for achieving parallel execution of high-level, data-parallel programs. We have implemented these transformations on *Proteus* programs using the KIDS system and can execute the results.

Acknowledgments

We would like to thank Stephen Westfold of the Kestrel Institute for his implementation efforts and improvement of the transformation rules.

Bibliography

[Back78] Backus, J., "Can Programming be Liberated from the VonNeumann Style? A Functional Style and its Algebra of Programs", *Communications of the ACM*, 1978.

[BCS+90] Blelloch, G., Chatterjee, S., Sipelstein, J., Zahga, M., "CVL: A C Vector-Library", Draft Technical Note, Carnegie Mellon University, 1990.

[Blel90] Blelloch, G., *Vector Models for Data-Parallel Computing*, MIT Press, 1990.

[Blel92] Blelloch, G., "NESL: A Nested Data-Parallel Language", Technical Report

CMU-CS-92-103, Carnegie Mellon University, January 1990.

[BS90] Blelloch, G., Sabot, G., "Compiling Collection-Oriented Languages onto Massively Parallel Computers", *Journal of Parallel and Distributed Computing*, 8(2), February 1990.

[Iver62] Iverson, K., *A Programming Language*. Wiley, New York, 1962.

[KLS+90] Knobe, K., Lukas, J., Steele, G., "Data Optimization: Allocation of Arrays to Reduce Communication on SIMD Machines", *Journal of Parallel and Distributed Computing* 8, 1990.

[McCr87] McCrosky, C., "Realizing the Parallelism of Array-based Computation", *Parallel Computing 10* 1989.

[MNP+91] Mills, P., Nyland, L., Prins, J., Reif, J., Wagner, R.,"Prototyping Parallel and Distributed Programs in *Proteus*", *Proceedings Symposium on Parallel and Distributed Processing 92*. 1992.

[MNP+92] Mills, P., Nyland, L., Prins, J., Reif, J., "Prototyping N-body Simulations in *Proteus*", *Proceedings IPPS 92*, IEEE, 1992.

[More79] More, T., "The Nested Rectangular Array as a Model of Data" *APL79 Conference Proceedings*. ACM 1979.

[NP92] Nyland, L., Prins, J., "Prototyping Parallel Programs", Proceedings *1992 Dartmouth Institute for Advanced Graduate Studies in Parallel Computing Symposium*, 1992.

[Prin90] Prins, J., "A Framework for Efficient Execution of Array-Based Languages on SIMD Computers", *Proceedings Frontiers 90*, IEEE 1990.

[PTH91] Philippsen, M., Tichy, W., Herter, C., "Modula-2* and its Compilation", *Proceedings Austrian Conference on Parallel Computing*, 1991.

[Sabo88] Sabot, G., *The Paralation Model : Architecture-Independent Parallel Programing*, MIT Press, 1988.

[Schw70] Schwartz, J., "Set Theory as a Language for Program Specification and Programming", Technical Report Computer Science Department, Courant Institute of Mathematical Sciences, New York University, 1970.

[Skil90] Skillicorn, D., "Architecture-Independent Parallel Computation", *IEEE Computer 11*, Vol.23 No. 12 (Dec.), 1990.

[Smit90] Smith, D., "KIDS - A Semi-automatic Program Development System", IEEE *Transactions on Software Engineering Special Issue on Formal Methods in Software Engineering* Vol. 16, No. 9, 1990.

[SH86] Steele, G. L., Hillis, W., "Connection Machine LISP: Fine-grained Parallel Symbolic Processing ", *Proceedings 1986 ACM Conference on Lisp and Functional Programming* ACM, 1986.

Non-concurrency Analysis.

Stephen P. Masticola (masticol@cs.rutgers.edu)
Barbara G. Ryder (ryder@cs.rutgers.edu)

Department of Computer Science
Rutgers University, New Brunswick, NJ 08903

Abstract. Non-concurrency analysis is a set of techniques for statically identifying pairs (or sets) of statements in a concurrent program which can never happen together. This information aids programmers in debugging and manually optimizing programs, improves the precision of data flow analysis, enables optimized translation of rendezvous, facilitates dead code elimination and other automatic optimizations, and allows anomaly detection in explicitly parallel programs. We present a framework for non-concurrency analysis, capable of incorporating previous analysis algorithms [CS88, DS91] and improving upon them. We show general theoretical results which are useful in estimating non-concurrency, and examples of non-concurrency analysis frameworks for two synchronization primitives: the Ada rendezvous and binary semaphores. Both of these frameworks have a low-order polynomial bound on worst-case solution time. We provide experimental evidence that static non-concurrency analysis of Ada programs can be accomplished in a reasonable time, and is generally quite accurate. Our framework, and the set of refinement components we develop, also exhibits dramatic accuracy improvements over [DS91], when the latter is used as a stand-alone algorithm, as demonstrated by our experiments.

1 Introduction.

Parallel and concurrent programs are often explicitly divided into tasks by the programmer. The tasks may synchronize with each other at various points, to request services or information from each other, or to prevent races. If the synchronization structure is complex, it may be difficult to determine *a priori* which parts of the program may, or may not, execute in parallel. Taylor showed that determining this exactly is NP-hard [Tayl83b]; our objective, rather, is to obtain a close underestimate of non-concurrency, in a time polynomial in the number of program statements.

4th ACM PPOPP,5/93/CA,USA

1.1 Applications.

Information about guaranteed non-concurrency has a variety of uses in compilation and debugging. Specifically, it is useful for program understanding tools, data flow analysis [RS90, LC91], rendezvous optimization, dead code elimination, and synchronization anomaly detection.

Debuggers and program understanding tools. While debugging concurrent programs, or tuning their performance, it may be valuable to know that some pair of code segments can never happen together. For example, if the code segments that access a shared resource are non-concurrent, the programmer can safely delete any locks that are protecting the resource.

We envision a debugger that includes a structured source code editor. On the user's command, the editor would highlight all code that might be concurrent with the code at the current cursor position. Alternately, the debugger could answer queries about whether two statements may be concurrent. Thus, non-concurrency analysis may become a valuable addition to program understanding tools.

Data flow analysis. If tasks pass data to each other during rendezvous, non-concurrency information can eliminate some infeasible def-use pairs. Statements which are non-concurrent cannot rendezvous with each other; no definitions can reach uses via rendezvous which can never occur. Similar examples exist for other classic data flow problems.

Optimizing rendezvous. Rendezvous can be optimized by choosing the proper implementation for a particular statement instance. In a simple form of rendezvous synchronization, signaling tasks call an accepting task; both wait until the call is completed. Each signaling task may call the accepting task from more than one call point; the accepting task may also accept the calls at any of several entry points.

Entries might be implemented in two alternate ways: by polled flags or by call queues. Polling will be more efficient when few call points can execute simultaneously with the entry; beyond some threshold, the time to poll will be greater than the overhead for queue management. Non-concurrency analysis might determine that this threshold has not been reached for a particular entry, even though the total number of call points is greater than the threshold. If so, we can gain speed by using polling.

Dead code elimination. Dead code can also be detected using non-concurrency information. If some statement in a task can never happen together with *any* other statement in the program (including the beginning and end of the program), then it can never happen at all. The code may thus be eliminated from the program. If the code is dead because some `accept` alternative of an entry can never rendezvous, then the entry may also be optimized by removing the alternative.

In some cases, the code may be dead because some predecessor in the same task *must* starve or deadlock; here, the dead code is only a symptom of a more serious anomaly.

Synchronization anomalies. More commonly, non-concurrency analysis has been applied to static detection of synchronization anomalies, including races and deadlocks.

A *race* occurs whenever two tasks may simultaneously access the same shared object (variable or resource), and if at least one of those accesses changes the state of the resource (e.g., advances a stream or writes a variable).[1] If we can prove that two accesses are non-concurrent, then there can be no races between them. Callahan and Subhlok [CS88] apply this methodology to post/wait synchronization in programs without loops.[2]

A *deadlock* occurs when several tasks mutually wait on each other to advance. The statements at which these tasks wait are the *head* statements of the deadlock. Given a proposed head statement s, we can often decide that all proposed deadlocks which might contain s must also contain statements that are non-concurrent with s, and thus do not represent actual deadlocks. This allows us to prune s as a possible member of any deadlock [MR90, MR91b].

[1] To guarantee that the program produces determinate results, we must usually also guarantee that conflicting statement instances are *totally ordered*, rather than just non-concurrent.

[2] Their later work [CKS90] incorporated loops, but the methodology they used there is only tangentially related to non-concurrency analysis.

1.2 Previous work.

Callahan and Subhlok [CS88] presented a method for polynomial-time static non-concurrency analysis in programs which use post/wait synchronization. Later, Duesterwald and Soffa [DS91] used similar methods in the rendezvous model. Our technique can use these as components to refine non-concurrency information; we adapted [DS91] as part of our empirical model. We show experimental evidence that for Ada programs, an algorithm based only on [DS91] would miss much non-concurrency information that a broader range of refinements can extract.

Bristow, et. al. [BDER79] presented some early ideas related to non-concurrency analysis; we describe the relation of their work to ours further in Sections 2 and 4.

2 Framework for non-concurrency analysis.

Figure 1 shows the general framework used in non-concurrency analysis. The framework must be specialized for a particular tasking model and set of synchronization primitives.

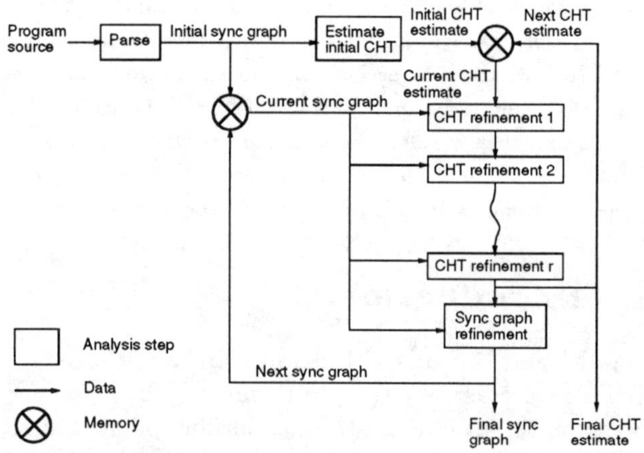

Figure 1: General framework of iterative non-concurrency analysis.

The program is parsed, and a *sync graph* representation of the program's synchronization behavior is generated. The sync graph represents only synchronizations and control flow between synchronization statements, and omits instruction timing and priorities, if they exist in the source language. Non-concurrency results are thus conservative with respect this information; knowledge of timing and priorities could add to non-concurrency information, but could never invalidate a non-concurrency relationship between statements.

Each node in the sync graph represents a synchronization statement in the program. Directed *control edges* are placed from node m to n if there is a control path from m to n that contains no tasking statements other than m and n. *Sync edges* represent synchronizations, and are placed between all nodes that may synchronize with each other. Sync edges may be directed, undirected, or multi-ended, depending on the synchronization model.

The non-concurrency relation is labeled *CHT*, for *can't happen together*. For each node n in the sync graph, $CHT(n)$ is a set of nodes which have no instances that can ever occur simultaneously with any instance of n, in any execution of the program. Note that $CHT(n)$ need not be the complete set of such nodes; the latter is denoted $CHT_{perf}(n)$. We obtain an initial estimate $CHT_0(n)$ of $CHT(n)$. If task instances are not created dynamically, we may use $CHT_0(n) = Task(n) - \{n\}$ as the initial estimate, where $Task(n)$ is the set of nodes in the task containing n.

We refine each estimate CHT_i of CHT to an estimate $CHT_{i+1} = r_i(CHT)$ by applying one of a set of conservative refinement analyses r_i. We require that all refinements be *monotone*, *inflationary*, and *conservative*, i.e.:

$$\begin{aligned}\forall r_i, n: \quad & [\forall m : CHT(m) \subseteq CHT'(m)] \\ & \Rightarrow [r_i(CHT)(n) \subseteq r_i(CHT')(n)] \\ \wedge \quad & CHT(n) \subseteq r_i(CHT)(n) \\ \wedge \quad & [\forall m : CHT(m) \subseteq CHT_{perf}(m)] \\ & \Rightarrow [r_i(CHT)(n) \subseteq CHT_{perf}(n)].\end{aligned}$$

As an example of a refinement, we may be able to decide, from the construction of the sync graph and CHT_i information currently available, that all instances of m happen before any instance of n, as is done in [CS88] and [DS91]. Thus, $m \in CHT_{i+1}(n)$ and $n \in CHT_{i+1}(m)$. Other forms of analysis are also possible; these must be specialized to the tasking model being analyzed.

While refining *CHT*, we also eliminate *extraneous* sync edges from the sync graph. A sync edge is extraneous if it cannot correspond to an executable synchronization. *CHT* information can be used to find extraneous sync edges; eliminating extraneous sync edges can, in turn, improve *CHT* information. Therefore, the sync graph and the *CHT* relation are refined in the same loop.

When no refinement can add any node to any of the *CHT* sets, we have reached a fixed point in the process of refinement. We then terminate refinement, returning the final *CHT* set and sync graph. As long as the refinements satisfy our requirements, they may be done in arbitrary order within the loop, and the same fixed point will be reached [Mast93]. The refinements need not be commutative for this guarantee to hold.

The refinement process terminates after performing at most $r|N|^2$ refinements, where N is the set of nodes in the sync graph and r is the total number of refinements available. This can be seen by a simple argument on the height of the lattice of *CHT* relations. Thus, if each refinement terminates in time polynomial in the size (nodes plus all edges) of the sync graph, then the entire *CHT* process also terminates in polynomial time.

Bristow, et. al. [BDER79] first mentioned the idea of iterative refinement of information similar to *CHT*, using a graph representation of programs similar to our sync graphs. Their work concerned only post/wait/clear synchronization, and they limited themselves to a single refinement. Our work thus generalizes their theory; in addition, we provide experimental evidence of the effectiveness of the technique.

2.1 Widening and pseudotransitivity of the *CHT* relation.

The *CHT* relation is not generally transitive; however, it admits two useful properties, which we call *widening* and *pseudotransitivity*. We will use these properties extensively in designing the refinements.

We can sometimes discover a set of nodes S for node n, such that whenever n is executing, some node(s) in S are executing as well. For example, n may be a node inside a remote procedure and S the set of nodes that call the remote procedure. Note that we do not require that a single node in S execute throughout the entire duration of n; the executing members of S may change during n's execution. We can then improve our $CHT(n)$ information using S as shown in Theorem 1:

Theorem 1 (Widening.) *If there exists a set of nodes S such that some member(s) of S must always execute together with n, and $CHT(n) \subseteq CHT_{perf}(n)$, then the nodes in $\bigcap_{n' \in S} CHT(n')$ cannot happen together with n.*

In general, a small S yields the greatest chance for adding information to *CHT*. We can sometimes also expand *CHT* by finding S *within CHT itself*:

Corollary 1 (Pseudotransitivity.) *The nodes in the set*

$$\bigcap_{n' \in N - CHT(n) - \{n\}} CHT(n')$$

cannot happen together with n, where N is the set of all nodes in the sync graph and $CHT(n) \subseteq CHT_{perf}(n)$.

Pseudotransitivity is especially useful in cases where widening is being done to refine *CHT*, but some nodes have no set S. If we are manipulating relations as Boolean matrices, we may refine *CHT* by pseudotransitivity at the same time, by using $N - CHT(n) - \{n\}$ as a default value of S for node n. Doing this incurs little additional computation cost, may increase precision, and eliminates complicated handling of special cases. Furthermore, we can sharpen the accuracy of Corollary 1 by considering pseudotransitivity on a task-wise basis:

Corollary 2 (Task-wise pseudotransitivity.) *For any node n, and for any task $T, n \notin T$ that must execute concurrently with n, the nodes in the set*

$$\bigcap_{n' \in T - CHT(n)} CHT(n')$$

cannot happen together with n, where $CHT(n) \subseteq CHT_{perf}(n)$.

3 Rendezvous.

The Ada rendezvous model is quite complex. We will give here a simplified version of the complete model, with only the detail needed to illustrate *CHT* computation. For a more thorough treatment of the Ada rendezvous model, see [ANSI83]; for complete details of *CHT* detection in a larger subset of Ada, see [Mast92, Mast93].

In the Ada model, any task may signal other tasks, using a statement of the form `<acceptingTask>.<signalName>`. The signaler blocks until the accepting task has accepted, and completed processing of, the signal.

The accepting task accepts the signal at statements of the form, `accept <signal> [do <block>; end <signal>;]`. If no task has signaled, the accepting task blocks until one does; if multiple tasks have signaled, one is selected arbitrarily[3]. The optional `do` block is then executed; it may also contain rendezvous statements. While the `do` block executes, the signaling task remains suspended at the signaling statement. The `do` block is often used to implement a remote procedure call.

We exclude dynamic task creation and task access variables from our Ada subset model. Thus, the set of task instances, and the program statements which rendezvous with each other, are known precisely at compile time. In our work on Concurrent C [Mast93], we propose a non-concurrency analysis for the Concurrent C language [GR86], which includes dynamic task creation.

3.1 Ada sync hypergraphs.

Figure 2 shows a simple Ada program, and its *sync hypergraph* representation [MR91b]. Signaling statements are represented by a single *signaling node*; `accept` statements are represented by an *accept-in* node and an *accept-in* node, with the subgraph for their `do` block (if any) embedded between them.

```
int stop = 0;

task t1 is begin
  while !stop loop
    t2.s2;              -- 1
    accept s1 do        -- 2
      t3.call3;         -- 3
      t3.exit3;         -- 4
    end accept;         -- 5
    t2.s2;              -- 6
  end loop;
end t1;

task t2 is begin
  while !stop loop
    accept s2;          -- 7,8
    t1.s1;              -- 9
    accept s2;          -- 10,11
  end loop;
end t2;

task t3 is begin
  while !stop loop
    accept call3;       -- 12,13
    accept exit3;       -- 14,15
  end loop;
end t3;

begin
  for i in 1..100000 loop
    t3.call3;           -- 16
    t3.exit3;           -- 17
  end loop;
  stop := 1;
end;
```

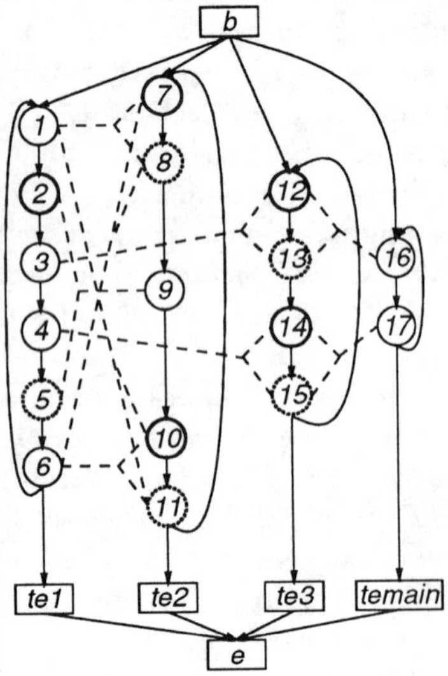

Figure 2: An example Ada program and its sync hypergraph.

Nodes *b* and *e* represent, respectively, the beginning and end of the program. In addition, a *task end* node is included for each task, to distinguish the end of each task from the end of the program. Doing so helps to eliminate special cases in certain analyses (Section 3.2.1), and enables the use of the task-wise pseudotransitivity of Corollary 2.

Control flow is represented conventionally by directed edges between nodes in the same task. Rendezvous are represented by three-ended *sync hyperedges*, connecting each signaling node with each accept-in/accept-out pair of the same signal type. A more detailed explanation of the sync hypergraph representation may be found in [Mast92, Mast93].

In our execution model, all program statements other than rendezvous are assumed to execute instantaneously. *CHT* remains conservative under this assumption [MR90].

3.2 Computation of *CHT*.

We exploit four refinements for *CHT* information. Each of these is described briefly in the following sections. In [Mast92, Mast93], we give more complete details of each refinement, and prove the correctness of each refinement given here, as well as polynomial worst-case time bounds.

3.2.1 Pinning analysis.

Pinning analysis is a general *CHT* refinement, based on widening the *CHT* relation using Theorem 1. Ex-

[3] This is a simplification of the true Ada model, which uses priority queues.

perimentation has shown that pinning analysis yields a wealth of *CHT* information.

Pinning analysis is best described by an example. Referring to Figure 2, node 2 cannot begin execution until its predecessor, node 1, has finished. Node 1 can rendezvous only with the pairs $(7,8)$ and $(10,11)$; thus, either node 8 or node 11 must complete immediately before node 2 starts. The successor of node 8 is node 9; the successors of node 11 are nodes 7 and and *te2*. Thus, one of these must start at the same time node 2 does. We call nodes 7, 9, and *te2* the *partners* of node 2.

Node 9 can rendezvous only with node 2; node *te2* cannot rendezvous with any other nodes. Node 7 can only rendezvous with nodes 1 and 6; neither of these may execute together with node 2, since they are in the same task as node 2. Thus, the partners of node 2 must continue executing at least as long as node 2 does, and node 2 is said to *pin* its partners. The set $\{7, 9, te2\}$ can thus be used as the set S of Theorem 1 to refine the *CHT* information for node 2.

Nodes may have the task end nodes of other tasks as partners. Including the task end nodes in the sync hypergraph helps to eliminate a troublesome special case in pinning analysis, which would occur if node e represented the end of each task, as well as the end of the program.

3.2.2 Remote procedure calls.

The nodes embedded inside a remote procedure, and the accept-out node for the procedure, may execute only while a signaling node that calls the remote procedure is executing. For instance, nodes 3, 4, and 5 of Figure 2 may execute only while node 9 is executing. Thus, the set $\{9\}$ can be used as the set S of Theorem 1 to refine the *CHT* information for nodes 3, 4, and 5.

3.2.3 Critical section analysis.

A *critical section structure* is a program construct which is often used to enforce mutual exclusion between tasks, without blocking the calling task as the remote procedure call does. In Figure 2, node pairs $(3,4)$ and $(16,17)$ delineate *call bodies* of a critical section structure, while node pair $(12,15)$ delineates the *critical section body* of the structure[4].

Both call bodies and critical section bodies are single entry, single exit regions of the control flow subgraph, with additional restrictions detailed in [Mast92, Mast93]. The call bodies and critical section bodies exclude their entry nodes, but include their exit nodes.

[4] While the structure shown has only one critical section body, multiple critical section bodies are possible, with appropriate restrictions. See [Mast92, Mast93] for details.

Knowledge about critical section structures can be used to derive *CHT* information in the following ways:

- No two call bodies of the same structure can execute simultaneously. Thus, every node in one call body for the structure may be placed in the *CHT* set of all nodes in other call bodies.
- The critical section body must execute concurrently with some call body. Thus, the set of nodes in all call bodies may be used as the set S of Theorem 1, for each node in any critical section body.
- Likewise, the call body must execute concurrently with some critical section body. Thus, the set of nodes in the critical section bodies form the set S of Theorem 1, for each node in any call body.

A more precise explanation of the behavior of critical section structures may be found in [Mast92, Mast93]. Empirical work indicates that this type of critical section structure is moderately common in practice (Table 1).

3.2.4 *B4* analysis.

B4 analysis attempts to discover pairs of nodes (m, n) such that all instances of m must occur before any instance of n. We denote this relation as $m \in B4(n)$. If $m \in B4(n)$, then $m \in CHT(n)$, and $n \in CHT(m)$[5].

Our approach in computing *B4* sets is, in principle, similar to that of [DS91]; however, there are differences in the set of Ada constructs addressed, the graph representation, and the propagation of *B4* information between tasks. We adapt the *B4* computation to the sync hypergraph model, as a *CHT* refinement, and also construct a lattice framework for iterative calculation of *B4*.

Computation of *B4* is done iteratively. We may place $m \in B4(n)$ if any of the following is true:

- There is a control path from m to n, but not from n to m.
- m is in the intersection of the *B4* sets of all control predecessors of n.
- m is in the intersection of the *B4* sets of all nodes that can rendezvous with the *completors* of n, i.e., the most immediate control ancestors of n that can complete a rendezvous. The completors of any node may include signaling and accept-out nodes, and the program begin node b. Figure 3 illustrates the concept of completors; the completors of x are s^5, a_o^3, and s^6.

These rules sketch the basics of *B4* computation.

[5] [MR91b] detailed an extension of *B4* analysis to produce *CHT* information within loop bodies. This extension was later shown to be potentially unsafe, although no problems occurred in practice.

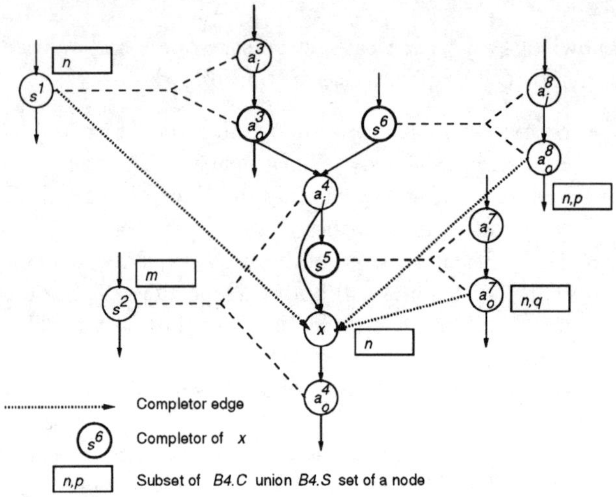

Figure 3: Completors of node x and completor edges to x.

$B4$ lattice framework. Lattice frameworks are a more complete encoding than the set of data flow equations used in [CS88] or [DS91], and can be used to deduce precision and convergence time properties. We present here the lattice framework we use for $B4$ calculations; a similar framework is also used in a different concurrency analysis problem in Section 4.2.3. This provides a simple illustration of how data flow problems can be encoded as lattice problems, when information enters nodes through edges in different classes. Each edge class denotes a different source of information; therefore, a separate meet must be taken with respect to each edge class. To accomplish this, we represent information as a k-tuple, where k is the number of edge classes.

The lattice framework used for $B4$ analysis is a quadruple $D = (G, L, F, M)$. $G = (N, E_C, E_{Completors})$, where N and E_C are as they were for the sync hypergraph, and $E_{Completors}$ is the set of pairs (m, n) such that m can rendezvous with a completor of n. $E_{Completors}$ is called the set of *completor (pseudo)edges*. In Figure 3, the completor edges to x are (s^1, x), (a_o^7, x), and (a_o^8, x).

L is a lattice of pairs of sets of nodes, (C, S); the meet operation is element-wise set intersection. Intuitively, if the framework has a pair (C, S) at node n, then C is the set of nodes in $B4(n)$ due to *control flow* into n, and S is the set of nodes in $B4(n)$ because of *synchronization* at the completors of n. Thus, $B4(n) = C \cup S$. For all $m \in B4(n)$, $m \in CHT_{perf}(n)$ and $n \in CHT_{perf}(m)$.

$F : L \rightarrow L$ contains the set of edge functions, and is the closure of the set of all possible edge functions under meet and function composition. $M : (E_C \cup E_{Completors}) \rightarrow F$ is a mapping from the edges of G to functions of F.

Let $CReach(m)$ denote the set of nodes q such that there is a control path from q to m, possibly of length zero. If $m \in CReach(n)$ and $n \notin CReach(m)$, then there is a control path from m to n, but not from n to m; thus, $m \in B4(n)$.

We map a control or completor edge $e = (m, n)$ to a function $f_e \in F$ as follows:

$$f_e((C, S)) = (C \cup S \cup K_e, N)$$

if e is a control edge, or

$$f_e((C, S)) = (N, C \cup S \cup K_e),$$

if e is a completor edge. For either edge type,

$$K_e = CReach(m) \cup \{m\} - \{p : m \in CReach(p)\},$$

i.e., the set of nodes q such that there is a control path from q to m (possibly of zero length), but no control path of length > 0 from m to q.

We have shown in [Mast92, Mast93] that the functions of F are monotone and inflationary, and are therefore *1-semibounded* [MR91a]. However, the framework is not Kam-Ullman *rapid* [KU76] because the edge functions are not, in general, distributive.

3.2.5 Iterative refinement of CHT sets.

In the four refinements listed above, CHT sets are refined iteratively through two mechanisms. The most direct mechanism is seen in the refinements that use widening (i.e., all except $B4$). Since widening propagates CHT sets between nodes, improvements in CHT will also be propagated.

Eliminating extraneous sync hyperedges is also important for all four refinements. Suppose that a hyperedge includes signaling node s and accept-in node a_i, and that $s \in CHT(a_i)$. Then the hyperedge represents an unexecutable rendezvous. Such hyperedges introduce imprecision in each of the refinements to CHT, and can be safely eliminated from the refinements once we know that $s \in CHT(a_i)$.

4 Binary semaphores.

Binary semaphores, a specialization of integer-valued semaphores [Dijk68], are essentially Boolean flags. Since rendezvous can be implemented using a number of binary semaphores proportional to the number of rendezvous signal types, binary semaphores are at least as powerful a synchronization mechanism as rendezvous. (This is in contrast to post-wait-clear synchronization, in which the number of event flags must also increase with the number of signaling tasks.)

Binary semaphores are accessed only through the

special commands p and v. A task executing the instruction $p(X)$ suspends execution until semaphore $X = 1$, then atomically decrements x to 0. If several tasks execute $p(X)$ simultaneously, only one can proceed until x is again set to 1. $v(X)$ sets the value of X to 1.

We assume that semaphores are declared to be either initially *set* (i.e, equal to 1) or *clear* (i.e., equal to 0). We will label initially set semaphores as S_i, and initially clear semaphores as C_i.

4.1 Binary semaphore sync graphs.

Figure 4 shows a program using binary semaphores, and its sync graph representation. $p(X)$ and $v(X)$ statements are represented by p and v nodes, respectively; task end nodes, and the program begin and end nodes b and e, are also included. Control paths between synchronization statements are represented by directed control edges; a directed sync edge is drawn from each $v(X)$ node to each $p(X)$ node for the same semaphore x. For such a set semaphore S, a sync edge is also drawn from the program begin node b to all $p(S)$ statements.

```
bool stop = false;
ClearSemaphore C1, C2;
SetSemaphore S;

task t1 is begin
  while !stop loop
    p(S);               -- 1
    v(C1)               -- 2
    p(C2);              -- 3
    v(S);               -- 4
  end loop;
end t1;

task t2 is begin
  while !stop loop
    p(S);               -- 5
    v(C1);              -- 6
    p(C2);              -- 7
    v(S)                -- 8
  end loop;
end t2;

task t3 is begin
  while !stop loop
    p(C1);              -- 9
    v(C2);              -- 10
  end loop;
end t3;

begin
  for i in 1..100000 loop
    null;
  end loop;
  stop := true;
end;
```

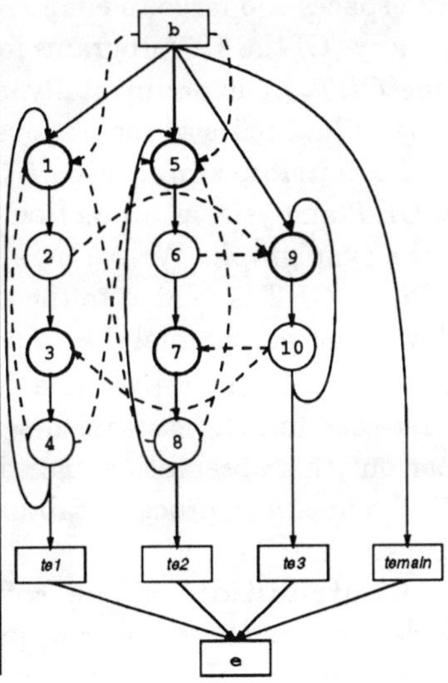

Figure 4: An example program which uses binary semaphore synchronization, and the sync graph of the program.

4.2 Computation of *CHT*.

We use three refinement analyses to estimate *CHT*: critical section and *B4* analysis, as with Ada, plus a new *mutex* analysis technique. Each of these is detailed in the sections below.

In the binary semaphore model, pinning does not occur, at least not at the abstraction level of semaphores, since a v node does not wait for a p node to clear the semaphore it sets. Therefore, we cannot perform pinning analysis. Also, since critical sections can be used to implement remote procedure calls in the binary semaphore model, we do not separate these two refinements.

4.2.1 Mutex analysis.

Set semaphores can easily be used to implement mutual exclusion. In Figure 4, the set semaphore S is used to implement mutual exclusion between node sets $\{2, 3, 4\}$ and $\{6, 7, 8\}$. If we can detect program structures that enforce mutual exclusion, we can use these structures as a source of *CHT* information.

Mutual exclusion is commonly enforced by embedding the exclusive code in a single-entry, single-exit region, with a $p(S)$ statement as the entry and a $v(S)$ statement as the exit, for some set semaphore S. As with critical section structures, some additional restrictions are also required, both on the node types and connectivity of the regions, and on the use of $p(S)$ and $v(S)$ statements throughout the program. If a set semaphore S obeys these restrictions, the p and v statements acting on it define a *mutex structure.*

The *mutex bodies* of a mutex structure are the regions bracketed by $p(S)$ and $v(S)$ statements, excluding the entry node. If a node n is in a mutex body, then all nodes in other mutex bodies of the same structure are in $CHT(n)$.

4.2.2 Critical section analysis.

Critical section structures in a binary semaphore program are intended to function like those in a rendezvous program. One variant of critical section structures uses a pair of clear semaphores to signal calls to, and returns from, critical section bodies. In the program of Figure 4, semaphore $C1$ signals the call, and $C2$ signals the return. The call bodies of the critical section structure are delineated by entry/exit node pairs $(2, 3)$ and $(6, 7)$; the critical section body is delineated by node pair $(9, 10)$.

Note that call bodies $(2, 3)$ and $(6, 7)$ are enclosed in mutex structures. If they were not, then both call bodies could simultaneously call the critical section body. We require, as a condition of structural correctness, that all call bodies be in each others' *CHT* sets, since mutual exclusion of the call bodies could not otherwise be enforced. However, the entry nodes of the critical section bodies may be concurrent, since only one critical section body can be entered when a single semaphore is set.

Other variants of binary semaphore critical section structures exist; empirical work must determine which variants are the most common in practice. Then, frameworks can be devised for recognizing them and extracting *CHT* information. For at least some variants, *CHT* information is needed to determine whether a candidate critical section structure is recognizable. Thus, refining *CHT* information can reveal further critical section structures, which can in turn propagate *CHT* information.

4.2.3 *B4* analysis and the semaphore kill problem.

B4 sets in the binary semaphore model are generated and propagated much as they are in the rendezvous model. To iteratively refine *B4* information, we must eliminate extraneous sync edges, as we did in the rendezvous model.

There is an important difference between the rendezvous and binary semaphore models, which affects the elimination of extraneous sync edges. In the rendezvous model, sync edges may be eliminated solely on the basis of *CHT* information. In the binary semaphore model, however, the sync edges have different semantics; completion of the tail node represents an event that may enable the head node to complete execution, even when the head node executes later than the tail node.

To eliminate extraneous sync edges, we have to prove that the *definition* of the semaphore at the tail cannot reach the *use* of the semaphore at the head. This is called the *semaphore kill* problem; we say that $m = v(X) \in SemKill(n)$ if no definition of semaphore X by m can reach a use at n. This is true in at least two special cases:

- $n \in B4(m)$; or,
- Between any instance of m and any later instance of n, there must be another statement instance that sets or clears X. As in widening, the statement instances that modify X need not correspond to any single statement.

Bristow, et. al. [BDER79] showed a special case solution of this problem for post/wait/clear synchronization, but they limited themselves to problems in which the instances of a single statement modified X.

Our *SemKill* analysis for binary semaphores is similar to reaching-definitions analysis, in that we attach "generate" and "propagate" sets to control and synchronization edges [Mast93]. We use a lattice framework with multiple classes of edges, similar to the *B4* framework described in Section 3.2.4.

We briefly outline a set of conditions sufficient to determine that $m = v(X)$ is killed when n completes. Our *SemKill* lattice framework is based on these conditions.

- $n \in B4(m)$; or,
- $n \neq m$, and either $n = p(X)$ or $n = v(X)$; or,
- For all sync edges (n', n) such that n' is not killed at the top of n, either:
  - $m \in B4(n')$ and m is killed at n'; or,
  - $m = n'$;

  or,
- For all control predecessors n' of n, m is killed at the bottom of n' and $m \in CHT(n)$.

If m is killed at the top of n and $m \in CHT(n)$, then m is killed at the bottom of n.

5 Experimental work.

An experimental *CHT* analyzer was constructed for Ada, as part of a static deadlock analysis tool. The experiments were conducted on a Sun Sparc-2 processor with 225 megabytes of virtual memory. A total of 138 programs were successfully analyzed, using the polynomial-time analysis techniques of Section 3. We also were able to obtain CHT_{perf} sets for 127 of these programs by exhaustive state enumeration, in a manner similar to [Tayl83]. The remaining 11 programs had state spaces too large to enumerate within the available memory. Of the 127 programs for which we could determine CHT_{perf} experimentally, a total of 115 programs actually had pairs of rendezvous nodes in CHT_{perf}.

Execution time. Figure 5 shows the time taken by *CHT* analysis, as a function of the number of nodes in the sync graph. We see here that the actual time to estimate *CHT* is related to the size of the sync graph by a low-order polynomial (i.e., a polynomial whose degree in $|N|$ is ≤ 5, since $|N|^5$ is a factor of the theoretical worst-case limit); least-mean-square curve fittings also bear out this observation. For all programs tested, the *CHT* refinement process stabilized in five or fewer iterations.

Contribution of the refinement techniques. Table 1 shows the number of programs for which each refinement of *CHT* contributed to the total solution, and for which sync edges were pruned by *CHT*. From the table, we find that the great majority of programs have some *CHT* information; those that do not are quite simple in structure (i.e., one node per task). Pinning analysis disclosed at least some *CHT* information in 71.0% of the programs. The *B4* refinement was also of use in a sizable minority of the programs tested.

Figure 6 shows the relative contributions of each of the four techniques, as a percentage of the total number of ordered pairs (m, n) such that $m \in CHT(n)$. Pinning analysis and initialization are clearly the greatest contributors to the total *CHT* information, though the other techniques catch additional special cases that can seriously affect the accuracy of analyses which use *CHT* (e.g., deadlock detection). For instance, critical

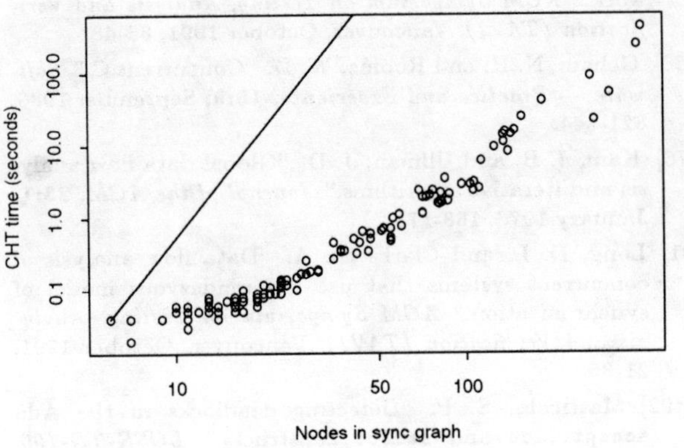

Figure 5: Time to estimate *CHT* (in user CPU seconds on a Sparc-2 processor), versus number of nodes in the sync hypergraph. The line indicates the $\mathcal{O}(|N|^5)$ factor of the theoretical time bound. The scale is log-log for clarity; a straight line on a log-log plot indicates a polynomial relation between x and y.

Refinement	Programs	Percent
Total programs	138	
Initial	126	91.3
Pinning	98	71.0
B4	24	17.4
Remote proc. calls	11	8.0
Critical sections	9	6.5
Pruned sync edges	25	18.1

Table 1: Number of programs with *CHT* contributions from each refinement, and for which sync edges were pruned. Note that a single program may have *CHT* contributions from more than one refinement.

section structures can cause incorrect reporting of potential deadlocks, unless they are recognized and their contribution to *CHT* is reported.

Accuracy of *CHT* estimation. Figure 7 (left) details the accuracy of the *CHT* estimate versus CHT_{perf}. For the vast majority of programs seen, the estimate was quite accurate. The plot shows that, for 92 of the 115 programs which had any pairs in CHT_{perf}, at least 95% of all pairs were found.

Comparison with [DS91]. Table 1 and Figures 6 and 7 (right) show that, while the *B4* analysis of [DS91] (and, by implication, [CS88]) are valuable as refinements, they clearly miss a large component of non-concurrency information in most programs. The other refinements we have presented are needed to obtain the majority of *CHT* information in the majority of programs.

Effectiveness of *CHT* in deadlock detection.

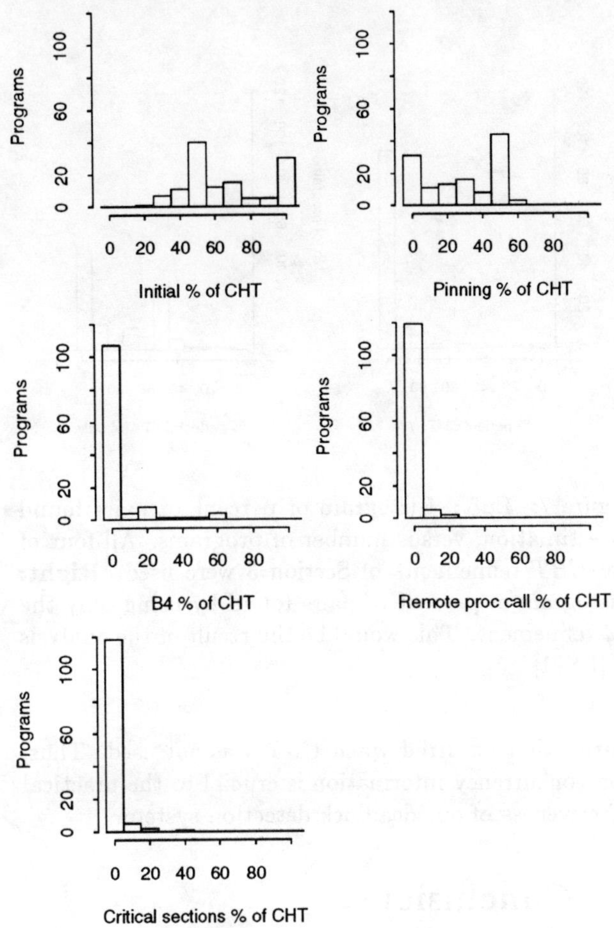

Figure 6: Histograms of the relative number of ordered *CHT* pairs contributed by initialization, pinning, *B4*, remote procedure call, and critical section analyses. The x axis is the percent of pairs contributed by the refinement shown. The y axis is the number of programs in which the specified percent of pairs was contributed by the refinement. The 12 programs with no *CHT* pairs are omitted.

CHT information has proven vital in static polynomial-time deadlock detection [MR91b, Mast92, Mast93]. To find deadlocks, we detect (but do not enumerate) cycles in the sync graph that might correspond to deadlocks. In such cycles, the nodes which represent deadlocked statements must be able to happen concurrently. We use *CHT* to prune away some spurious cycles, which helps to eliminate "false alarm" reports of deadlock.

To determine the effectiveness of *CHT* in preventing false alarms, we compared the false-alarm rate with, and without, *CHT* pruning. False alarms were found by comparing the results of our polynomial analysis against those of full concurrency state enumeration; we could thus detect false alarms in 127 candidate programs. We found that the use of *CHT* information prevented 34 false alarms, i.e., 87.2% of the 39 false

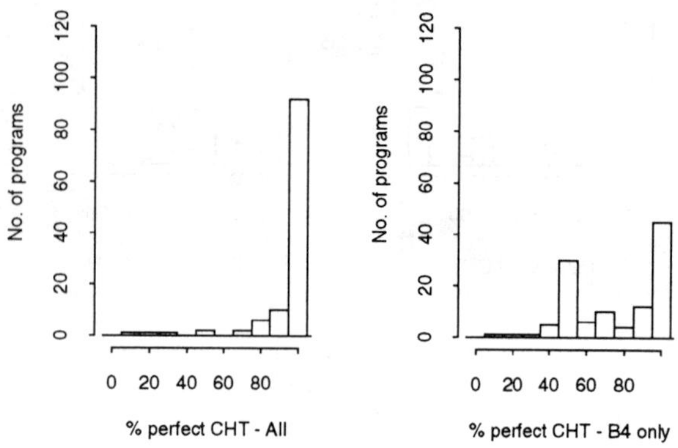

Figure 7: **Left:** Histogram of percent of pairs found by estimation, versus number of programs. All four of the *CHT* refinements of Section 3 were used. **Right:** Histogram of percent of pairs found by using only the *B4* refinement. This would be the result of the analysis of [DS91].

alarms that occurred when *CHT* was not used. Thus, non-concurrency information is crucial to the practical effectiveness of our deadlock detection system.

6 Conclusions.

Non-concurrency information about concurrent programs has a variety of uses in program analysis, optimization, and anomaly detection. It is possible to estimate non-concurrency information in time polynomial in the number of synchronization statements in the program. Experimental work has shown that these estimates are quite accurate, and that obtaining them takes little time in practice.

References

[ANSI83] American National Standards Institute. "ANSI/MIL-STD 1815A (1983) reference manual for the Ada programming language." United States Government Printing Office, Washington DC, 1983.

[BDER79] Bristow, G., Drey, C., Edwards, B., and Riddle, W. "Anomaly detection in concurrent programs." *Fourth IEEE International Conference on Software Engineering*, Munich, 1979, 265-273.

[CS88] Callahan, D. and Subhlok, J. "Static analysis of low-level synchronization." *SIGPLAN/SIGOPS Workshop on Parallel and Distributed Debugging*, 1988, 100-111.

[CKS90] Callahan, D., Kennedy, K., and Subhlok, J. "Analysis of event synchronization in a parallel programming tool." *2nd ACM SIGPLAN Symposium on Principles and Practice of Parallel Programming*, 1990, 21-30

[Dijk68] Dijkstra, E. W. "Co-operating sequential processes." In *Programming Languages*, F. Genuys, ed., Academic Press, 1968, 43-112.

[DS91] Duesterwald, E. and Soffa, M. L. "Concurrency analysis in the presence of procedures using a data-flow framework." *ACM Symposium on Testing, Analysis and Verification (TAV4)*, Vancouver, October 1991, 36-48.

[GR86] Gehani, N. H. and Roome, W. D. "Concurrent C." *Software — Practice and Experience*, **16:9**, September 1986, 821-844.

[KU76] Kam, J. B. and Ullman, J. D. "Global data flow analysis and iterative algorithms." *Journal of the ACM*, **23:1**, January 1976, 158-171.

[LC91] Long, D. L. and Clarke, L. A. "Data flow analysis of concurrent systems that use the rendezvous model of synchronization." *ACM Symposium on Testing, Analysis and Verification (TAV4)*, Vancouver, October 1991, 21-35.

[Mast92] Masticola, S. P. "Detecting deadlocks in the Ada `accept...do` and `select` constructs." *LCSR-TR-190*, Laboratory for Computer Science Research, Rutgers University, 1992.

[Mast93] Masticola, S. P. "Static detection of deadlocks in polynomial time." Ph.D. thesis, Department of Computer Science, Rutgers University, 1993. In preparation.

[MR90] Masticola, S. P. and Ryder, B. G. "Static infinite wait anomaly detection in polynomial time." *1990 International Conference on Parallel Processing*, Chicago, August 1990, 2:78-87. ISBN 0-271-00728-1.

[MR91a] Marlowe, T. J. and Ryder, B. G. "Properties of data flow frameworks: a unified model." *Acta Informatica*, **28:2**, 1991, 121-164.

[MR91b] Masticola, S. P. and Ryder, B. G. "A model of Ada programs for static deadlock detection in polynomial time." *1991 ACM/ONR Workshop on Parallel and Distributed Debugging*, Santa Cruz, CA, May 1991, 91-102. Also *ACM SIGPLAN Notices* **26:12**, December 1991, 97-107.

[RS90] Reif, J. H. and Smolka, S. A. "Data flow analysis of distributed communicating processes." *International Journal of Parallel Programming*, **19:1**, 1990, 1-30.

[Tayl83] Taylor, R. N. "A general-purpose algorithm for analyzing concurrent programs." *Communications of the ACM*, May 1983, 362-376.

[Tayl83b] Taylor, R. N. "Complexity of analyzing the synchronization structure of concurrent programs." *Acta Informatica*, **19**, 1983, 57-84.

Explicit Data Placement (XDP): A Methodology for Explicit Compile-Time Representation and Optimization of Data Movement

Vasanth Bala   Jeanne Ferrante   Larry Carter

IBM T.J. Watson Research Center

P.O. Box 218, Yorktown Heights, NY 10598

{vas, ferrant, carterl}@watson.ibm.com

Abstract

The ability to represent, manipulate and optimize data movement between devices such as processors in a distributed memory machine, or between global memory and processors in a shared memory machine, is crucial in generating efficient code for such machines. In this paper we describe a methodology for representing and manipulating data movement explicitly in a compiler. Our methodology, called Explicit Data Placement (XDP), consists of extensions to the compiler's intermediate program language, as well as run-time structures that allow certain operations to be performed efficiently. We also illustrate one of the unique features of the XDP methodology: the ability to manipulate the run-time transfer of data ownership between processors.

1 Introduction

Many program representations used in compilers represent data movement and partitioning only partially, and in an implicit manner. Explicit Data Placement (XDP) is a methodology for the explicit representation and treatment of data movement and placement in a compiler. The key ideas behind the XDP methodology are:

1. Separation of data transfer from local computation, enabling the compiler to control their overlap.
2. Language- and machine-independent representation of data transfer operations, allowing their incorporation into existing optimizations such as code motion and redundant code elimination.
3. Unified and explicit treatment of data and ownership transfer enabling optimizations specific to these operations.
4. Generalized compute rules which allow the compiler freedom to go beyond the "owner-computes" rule.
5. Delayed binding of communication primitives to the transfer operations.

The XDP methodology can be incorporated into compilers that use a high-level compiler intermediate language in the SPMD (Single Program Multiple Data) execution model; the program will be loaded onto every processor of the target machine that is assigned to the program. While SPMD programs are commonly used in a distributed memory setting, the XDP methodology can also be used for compiling shared memory (sequential or parallel) programs to a distributed memory SPMD node program. The original shared memory program can be considered to be an SPMD node program that is replicated along with all its data, on every node. The compiler can then use data partitioning to transform the intermediate representation into the eventual distributed memory SPMD node program desired. At present, the XDP methodology does not apply to languages with pointer variables; the addition of pointers is the subject of future work.

The rules governing execution allow non-determinism and do not guarantee coherence or freedom from deadlock. The XDP approach is to expose the power of manipulating data ownership and transfer to a compiler allowing the loosest possible semantics for a variety of implementations. While XDP could be used as a programming language, it has been designed for use by the compiler, which can use XDP's unsafe operations with care.

Our thesis is that if a compiler is to optimize data movement, it needs a methodology with the key ideas 1-5 noted above. The XDP operations and structures provide a convenient platform for this optimization. In this paper, we give a syntax and an operational semantics for the XDP language constructs, outline an imple-

4th ACM PPOPP,5/93/CA,USA

mentation of the data structures and routines to support the constructs at run-time, briefly discuss optimization and code generation, and give examples that illustrate one of XDP's unique features: the ability to specify dynamic transfer of data ownership.

2 XDP Language Constructs

The Explicit Data Placement (XDP) methodology can be used to extend an existing compiler Intermediate Language (IL) to obtain an SPMD program representation. Henceforth, we will use "IL+XDP" to denote a compiler intermediate language that has been extended with the XDP constructs and support structures. Before giving the formal definition of the XDP constructs, we first give some underlying assumptions and illustrate some of its features with an example.

2.1 Preliminaries

In this paper, we assume every variable is either a scalar or an array[1]. Each variable consists of *elements*; a scalar has only a single element.

XDP assumes the distribution of elements of all variables among processors: every element of a variable is either *exclusively owned* by a single processor or *universally owned* by all processors. It is possible to transfer the ownership of exclusively owned elements between processors. If an element is universally owned, each processor has a copy, and the values at each processor can be different.

A *section* of a variable is either a scalar variable or some subset of an array's elements. The form of possible sections is determined by IL; in this paper, we assume that sections are defined by Fortran 90 triplet notation. We say that a section of a variable is *exclusive* if every element of the section is exclusively owned; a section is *universal* if every element is universally owned. It is possible for one section of an array to be universal and another section of the same array to be exclusive.

We say that a section of a variable is *owned* by a processor if the processor exclusively or universally owns every element of the section. We distinguish between references to the *value* and the *name* of a section of a variable. A value cannot be used unless it is owned by the processor, names in XDP statements can be any section of any variable.

In XDP an exclusive section can be in one of three states with respect to a given processor p: unowned by p; `accessible`, meaning owned by p, and p has not initiated a receive that hasn't completed for that section; and `transitional`, meaning owned by p and p has initiated an uncompleted receive for that section. The value of a transitional section is unpredictable, and yet XDP does not automatically check the state of a variable at run-time (except by use of the `accessible( )` and `await( )` predicates described later). This allows optimizations to remove run-time checks when it can be determined they are unnecessary.

[1] Adding structures is an easy extension, pointers would be harder.

2.2 A Simple Example

Consider the program fragment:

```
do i = 1, n
  A[i] = A[i] + B[i]
enddo
```

It can be straightforwardly translated into the IL+XDP SPMD program:

```
do i = 1, n
  iown(B[i]) : { B[i] -> }
  iown(A[i]) : {
                 T[mypid] <- B[i]
                 await(T[mypid])
                 A[i] = A[i] + T[mypid]
               }
enddo
```

This translation follows the "owner-computes" rule. The variable `mypid` is an intrinsic which evaluates on each processor to a unique integer. Here, we assume that the elements of arrays `A`, `B` and `T` are all exclusively owned and processor `mypid` owns the `mypid`-th element of `T`. The variable `i` is universally owned, so each processor has its own copy of `i`.

In the example, each iteration of the loop is executed on every processor. On a given iteration of the loop, the execution of the first statement of the loop will be executed only by the exclusive owner of `B[i]`; this is insured by guarding the statement with the intrinsic predicate `iown(B[i])`. The use of `iown` is an example of a *compute rule*, which can be used to guard any XDP statement. Similary, only the exclusive owner of `A[i]` will execute the second statement on any iteration of the loop.

Following "`iown(B[i]):`" is a data transfer statement, where the exclusive owner of `B[i]` sends its value to another, unspecified processor. The notation "`->`" denotes the initiation of a data transfer operation in which the executing processor sends both the name and the value of a section of a variable to an unspecified processor. The statement "`T[mypid] <- B[i]`" is a data receive statement, where the executing processor receives the message with name `B[i]`, putting the value into `T[mypid]`. It is the responsibility of the compiler to only generate programs in which all sends have matching receives. The `await( )` intrinsic ensures the sum is not computed until the received value is available.

Optimization can be applied by the compiler to this straightforward translation, based on its knowledge of ownership. For instance, if the same processor that exclusively owns `A[i]` also owns `B[i]`, then the data transfer statments can be eliminated. Even if they cannot be eliminated, the compiler may be able to move them out of the computation loop and combine or *vectorize* [8] the messages. In either case, if the loop bounds can be adjusted so that each reference to `A[i]` is local, then the ownership test on the remaining body of the loop can also be eliminated, yielding a much more efficient SPMD program.

An important feature of XDP is that other strategies than "owner-compute" can be expressed. For instance, the compiler might determine that it would save future communication if ownership of each element of the `A` array were moved to the same processor as the corresponding element of the `B` array. The following IL+XDP program fragment shows the result of this optimization:

```
do i = 1, n
   iown(A[i]) : { A[i] -=> }
   iown(B[i]) : { A[i] <=- }
   await(A[i]): { A[i] = A[i] + B[i] }
enddo
```

Here, the "-=>" and "<=-" notation indicates that both the ownership and value of `A[i]` is moved to the processor that owns `B[i]`. Only the processor that is the new owner of `A[i]` will perform the addition.

We next discuss the XDP language constructs and their semantics, which are also summarized in Figure 1.

2.3 Intrinsics

The first argument of an intrinsic is a *name* of an exclusive section, but it need not be owned by the executing processor. Thus, intrinsics can be evaluated on any processor.

XDP assumes each processor has a unique *processor id* denoted `mypid`.

The routine `mylb(X,d)` returns the smallest index in the `d`th dimension of any element of the exclusive section `X` owned by the invoking processor. If no element is owned, `MAXINT`, the largest representable integer, is returned. A similar routine `myub(X,d)` can be used to get the upper bound.

The `iown( )` predicate returns `true` iff the processor executing it is the owner of all elements of the named section.

The `accessible( )` predicate returns `true` iff the section is accessible on the calling processor. It can be used to allow a processor to perform a background computation while awaiting data from another processor.

The `await( )` intrinsic returns `false` if the section is unowned, otherwise it blocks until the section becomes

NOTATION	
X	Any exclusive Section.
E	Exclusive section owned by p.
U	Exclusive section, all elements unowned by p.
INTRINSICS	
mypid	Returns the unique identifier of p.
mylb(X,d)	If any element of X is owned by p, returns the smallest index in dimension d, `MAXINT` otherwise.
myub(X,d)	If any element of X is owned by p, returns the largest index in dimension d, `MININT` otherwise.
iown(X)	Returns `true` if X is owned by p, `false` otherwise.
accessible(X)	Returns `true` if X is owned by p and its data is accessible, `false` otherwise.
await(X)	Returns `false` if X is unowned by p, otherwise blocks until X is accessible, then returns `true`.
SEND STATEMENTS	
E ->	Initiate send of the name and value of E.
E -> S	Initiate sends of the name and value of E to processors specified by set S.
E =>	Blocks until E is accessible, then initiate send of the ownership of E.
E -=>	Blocks until E is accessible, then initiate send of ownership and value of E.
RECEIVE STATEMENTS	
E <- X	Blocks until E is accessible, then initiate receive of the value named X into E.
U <=	Initiate receive of the ownership of U.
U <=-	Initiate receive of ownership and value of U.
STATES OF A SECTION	
accessible	Entire section is owned by p and p has no uncompleted receives involving any element of the section.
transitional	Entire section is owned by p and an uncompleted receive involving any element of the section has been initiated by p.
unowned	Some element of section is not owned by p. If a section is not unowned, we say it is owned.

Figure 1: Rules governing execution on processor p

accessible, at which time it returns `true`. Thus, `await` is a synchronization primitive.

All of the intrinsics can be implemented as a lookup into the processor's local run-time symbol table, discussed in section 3.1.

2.4 Compute Rules

A compute rule is any expression, including uses of intrinsics, that evaluates to `true` or `false`. However, compute rules may not have side effects, so in particular they may not include send or receive statements. Compute rules are used to govern execution of XDP statements. Only if the compute rule evaluates to `true` will the statement it guards be executed [3].

In a compute rule, any reference to a section (other than as the first argument of an intrinsic) which is not owned by the processor causes the entire compute rule to evaluate to `false`. Thus, a compute rule can always be executed on any processor without error.

Compute rules are syntactically distinct from the other IL+XDP statements so they can be treated separately, allowing the compiler to optimize them more easily. A typical optimization is compute rule elimination — the removal of a compute rule that always evaluates to true. Compute rule elimination can often be performed after the loop bounds are adjusted so that the computation within the loop only references owned sections [21, 4, 17].

XDP generalizes the notion of compute rule used in previous work by allowing general Boolean valued expressions to be used by the compiler.

2.5 Statements

Statements are executed only if the compute rule guarding them evaluates to `true`; in the absence of a compute rule, statements are executed by each processor that reaches the statement.

XDP augments IL with data and ownership transfer statements. These are either *send* or *receive* statements, and have an *initiation* and a subsequent *completion.*

XDP does not check whether a section used by a statement is transitional. Thus, the compiler must guard statements with appropriate synchronizing compute rules to ensure the program's correctness. This choice has been made to allow the compiler to remove run-time checks when it determines they are unnecessary.

We now discuss the send and receive statements in turn. Since these operations are distinct from the other operations in XDP+IL, they can be separately optimized.

2.6 Send Statements

Here, E always denotes an exclusively owned section of a variable by the executing processor.

Send statments come in several flavors. The statement "E `->`" denotes the initiation of a data transfer operation in which the executing processor sends the name[2] and the value of E it exclusively owns to another unspecified processor. The restriction of data sends to exclusively owned sections of variables can always be overcome by copying the value of a universally owned section to an exclusive section. We impose the restriction here to simplify the semantics of our data transfer operations.

We also allow statements of the form E `->` S, where S is some set of processor id's. This statement denotes the initiation of a set of data transfer operations in which the executing processor sends the value and name of E it exclusively owns to the specified locations. This statement can be used with S containing only one processor id as a way for the compiler to annotate which processor will be the recipient of the section. It can also be used for a broadcast or multicast operation.

A novel feature of XDP is its treatment of data ownership. Ownership in XDP is a transferable object, just as a data value can be transferred from one processor to another through communication. The statement "E `-=>`" denotes the initiation of an ownership send in which the executing processor relinquishes the exclusive ownership of E as well as its value to an unspecified processor. The statement "E `=>`" indicates the transfer of only the ownership of E, and not the value. The compiler may be able to determine that only the ownership, and not the value, needs to be transferred, and use the latter operation. Owner send operations block until the section is accessible.

There are various uses that can be made of XDP's ability to transfer ownership. First, when ownership of a section is transferred out of a processor, the storage it had occupied can be reused for a newly acquired section. This conserves address space and reduces paging. Second, it provides a wealth of possibilities for redistributing computation among the processors. Normally, one implements load balancing by migrating processes between processors. However, in XDP, load balancing can be implemented by migrating ownership of data while still running the same SPMD program on each processor. Since ownership dictates which SPMD program statements are executed by each processor, the ability to transfer data ownership allows the computation done on each processor to be altered dynamically

[2] The name is used as a tag to associate a send with a corresponding receive. It will be unnecessary to actually send the name if either the association between sender and receiver can be made at compile time, or if the hardware can make the association as on a shared address space machine.

without migrating any code. Thirdly, it opens up the possibility of new uses. For instance, a debugger could allow the user to input an ownership transfer command that moves exclusive ownership of a variable (and hence the permission to execute certain SPMD code segments, such as a print command that outputs the value of local data structures to the user's screen) from one processor to another. Thus, processors can be selectively monitored by simply transferring ownership of this variable.

2.7 Receive Statements

Here, X always denotes an exclusive section (but not necessarily one owned by the executing processor p), E always denotes a section exclusively owned by p, and U denotes an exclusive section, no element of which is owned by p.

The statement "E <- X" denotes the initiation of a data receive operation, in which the executing processor assigns to the variable E the received value of X. If the section is transitional, the statement blocks until it becomes accessible. "U <=-" denotes the initiation of an ownership and value receive from an unspecified processor, in which the executing processor accepts the exclusive ownership and value of U. The statement "U <=" indicates the initiation of only the transfer of ownership of U, and not the value of U. Ownership of a section can only be received if the section was unowned.

Upon initiation of a receive of a section on a processor, the section must be put in state `transitional`; upon completion of the receive, the section is returned to state `accessible`. This can be implemented by an update to the processor's run-time symbol table, as discussed in section 3.1.

It is incorrect usage of XDP if the sections transferred in send and receive operations do not match. The results of such a communication are unpredictable. XDP restricts the left hand side of a receive statement to an exclusive section so that the run-time symbol table need not contain entries for universally owned variables.

It is legal to have several processors initiate receive statements for the same section concurrently. For simplicity, a particular compiler may choose not to use this construct. However, it can be used to advantage, for instance to facilitate load balancing. This could be accomplished by having the owner of a particular variable initiate a sequence of sends of values of the variable, each value representing a certain job to be performed. Meanwhile, any processor that was otherwise idle could initate a receive of that variable, and then perform the indicated job. Depending on the load at run-time, there might be multiple outstanding sends or outstanding receives.

3 Implementation

While XDP language constructs are designed to be used by a compiler, it is entirely possible that the compiler will not be able to remove *all* ownership or accessibility tests, and so `iown( )`, `await( )` and `accessible( )` predicates may need to be evaluated at run-time [17]. In addition, ownership transfers result in run-time changes in ownership and so may need to be tracked at run-time. To support this, the XDP methodology supplies both a compile-time symbol table, and a run-time, per-processor symbol table for exclusive sections, discussed in detail in the next section.

The XDP language constructs allow ownership transfers to occur at the granularity of a single element. However, for efficiency's sake, a compiler may use a *coarser granularity* of ownership transfer. The use of segments in the implementation given here is an example.

Whether the symbol table is simple or complex depends on such choices as whether the number of processors is fixed and known at compile-time, and what partitioning of arrays into sections are allowed. These choices also affect what optimizations can be performed. In our example implementation, we assume a fixed, known processor grid and and partitioning as allowed in HPF [5].

3.1 Symbol table

An important structure required for incorporating the XDP methodology is the symbol table. The XDP symbol table structure is used at compile-time by the compiler, as well as at run-time by all the processors that execute the output SPMD code. Each processor must maintain and update its own local copy of the XDP symbol table structure at run-time, unless all uses of the table have been optimized away. In contrast to a regular symbol table, the run-time XDP symbol table only contains information about exclusive sections.

Figure 2 illustrates the XDP symbol table structure for two array variables `A[1:4,1:8]` and `B[1:16,1:16]`, partitioned over 4 processors, which are assumed to be indexed as a 2x2 processor grid. The `symtab index`, `symbol name`, `rank`, and `global shape` fields are self-explanatory. The `partitioning` field indicates the partitioning scheme of the array. The partitioning scheme, together with the shape of the processor grid, are used by the compiler and the XDP run-time system to determine ownership of array sections.

For efficiency's sake, the compiler can logically divide each processor's local partition of an array into *segments* of a size and shape chosen by the compiler. A processor can transfer the ownership of each segment individually. The last three fields of the symbol table describe the partitioning. They specify how many segments comprise the processor's partition, the shape of each seg-

symtab index	symbol name	rank	global shape	partitioning	segment shape	#segments	segment descriptor
1	A	2	(4,8)	(*,BLOCK)	(2,1)	4	→ ptr to segdesc
2	B	2	(16,16)	(BLOCK,CYCLIC)	(4,2)	8	→ ptr to segdesc

Figure 2: XDP symbol table structure, showing the entries for two arrays `A` and `B`, partitioned over a 2x2 processor grid. The shaded entries are filled in at run-time by each processor.

ment (which must have the same rank as the array variable), and finally an array of segment descriptors, which record, for each segment, the array elements contained in the segment and the current state (`unowned`, `transitional`, or `accessible`). In our implementation, the segment descriptor data structure was declared as:

```
struct SegmentDesc {
  int  status;      /* accessibility status  */
  int  lbound[rank]; /* lower bound indices */
  int  ubound[rank]; /* upper bound indices */
  int  stride[rank]; /* strides             */
  ...               /* other relevant info  */
  long segptr;      /* pointer to segment   */
} segdesc [#segments];
```

The last two fields of the XDP symbol table are shaded dark in Figure 2, to indicate that these entries are filled in only at run-time. When ownership is transferred or receives are initiated or completed, the symbol table must be updated.

Either at the start of program execution or dynamically, each processor allocates local storage for its segments in contiguous chunks whose sizes are determined by the `segment shape` field. The number of such segments allocated depends on the number of array elements the processor owns. Figure 3 illustrates two different partitioning schemes for a 4x8 array, and for each partitioning scheme, two possible logical segmentations are shown.

The use of segments allows the pipelining of a transfer of a section, either ownership or data. A processor can transfer each segment individually, requiring only enough synchronization to ensure that the transfer is legal in XDP. In many cases, this can effectively reduce the total time by allowing a processor to overlap one segment's transfer with computation on another segment. This will be illustrated the 3-D FFT example.

If the code running on a processor executes an `iown( )` intrinsic at run-time, the section described in the query is intersected with all the segment bounds corresponding to the named array variable. If the union of all the results is equal to the queried section, and no segment that has a non-null intersection is `unowned`, then the `iown( )` query returns `true`. Otherwise it returns `false`. For example, consider an array `C[1:4,1:8]`, distributed as `(BLOCK,BLOCK)` over a 2x2 processor grid, and 2x1 segmented (as shown in Figure 3 (a)). Suppose processor P3 executes the operation `iown(C[1,5:7])`. Intersecting the bounds of the section `(1,5:7)` with the bounds of the four 1x2 segments owned by P3 yields: {`(1,5)`, `(1,6)`, `(1,7)`, `null`}. The union of these is `(1,5:7)`, which is equal to the section specified in the `iown( )` query. Now, if none of the non-null intersecting segments are `unowned`, the operation returns `true`, and it returns `false` otherwise. The other intrinsics are handled similarly. Although the algorithm we described for evaluating `iown( )` involves examining the entire segment descriptor array, more efficient algorithms could be developed.

When any receive is initiated or completed on a segment, the `status` field of the segment needs to be updated as well. When any ownership transfer is initiated, the processor must update the `segment descriptor` fields of its symbol tables to reflect the data that is currently owned. The `partitioning` field may need to be updated as well.

We have chosen *not* to supply in the XDP methodology a mechanism for testing which processor owns an arbitrary section at run-time. A compiler using the XDP methodology could itself provide such a mechanism. If such information is unavailable at compile-time and needs to be repeatedly computed at run-time, the techniques such as [20] can be used to improve efficiency. Note, however, that it may be unsafe to compute owner information on an array that is undergoing incremental ownership transfer, until the transfer of all segments has been finished.

3.2 Optimization and Code Generation

Compiler optimizations that affect data movement and storage issues can be represented as transformations to the IL+XDP code. After the optimization phase is complete, the IL+XDP program is translated to executable code by the compiler's back end.

The translation needs to map XDP constructs to operations provided by the target computer's hardware and operating system. For instance, on a shared-address

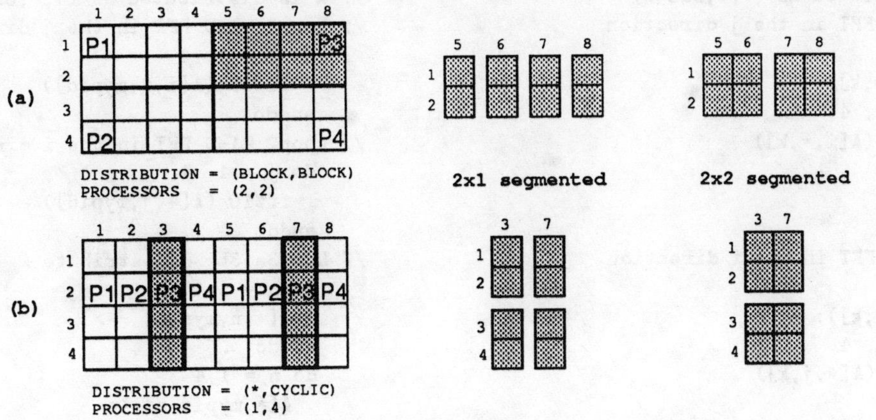

Figure 3: Example distributions and local segmentations of a 4x8 array, shown for processor P3.

computer such as the KSR1 [16], receives and sends might be translated as prefetch and poststore instructions. On a message-passing machine, they would become calls to the communication primitives. The XDP data and ownership transfer operations allow the compiler to delay until code generation time, the actual binding of communication primitives to the data transfer operations. The advantage of this delayed binding for optimization is noted in [7].

Some optimizations, such as compute rule elimination, are independent of the target computer. Other optimizations need to be modified depending on various architectural and system considerations. For instance, if the communication primitives generated by the compiler are non-blocking, then it is generally desirable to move the XDP receive statements as early in the program as possible (consistent with the data dependence constraints) to give the maximum opportunity of overlapping communication with computation. However, if the communication primitives are blocking, then the optimizations must be careful not to introduce deadlock.

To perform optimizing transformations and code generation, the compiler may need information about the IL+XDP program in addition to the usual data structures such as a control flow graph and data flow information. For instance, it may be useful for optimizations (and essential for code generation) to annotate an XDP send statement with the id of the receiving processor. Other aspects of XDP code can be handled by traditional techniques. For instance, if no use-def chains from a use of `X` in an `accessible(X)` intrinsic lead back to a receive statement, then it may be possible to eliminate the `accessible(X)` call.

The set of optimizations on XDP code, as well as details of XDP itself, are the subject of current research. For instance, aggregating a set of separate data transfers into a single message can reduce overhead on some systems. It might be desirable to allow this aggregation to be expressed in XDP, for instance by allowing the left-hand side of XDP send and receive statements to be a set of sections, rather than a single section.

4 An Example: 3-D FFT

We now illustrate a use of XDP, using a 3-dimensional Fast Fourier Transform (3-D FFT) application as an example. The 3-D FFT code considered here operates on an array `A[1:4,1:4,1:4]` which is assumed to be initially distributed as `(*,*,BLOCK)` over a linear array of 4 processors `P1-P4`. Thus, processor `i` owns the section `A[1:4,1:4,i]`. We assume that the compiler has chosen to divide each processor's local storage into segments containing 4 consecutive array elements each. The 3-D algorithm employs a 1-D FFT routine, `fft1D( )`, that is successively applied along each line of the second dimension of the array, then the first and finally the third dimensions to compute the 3-D FFT. The initial `(*,*,BLOCK)` distribution of the array allows the first two dimensions to be handled with no interprocessor communication. The array is then redistributed to a `(*,BLOCK,*)` scheme in order that the 1-D FFT along the third dimension can be done independently on each processor without communication. The two partitioning schemes, and the actual data layout in each processor's local storage is shown in Figure 4.

The following programs illustrate the steps involved in the optimization of the redistribution operation. In order to keep the illustration compact, we start with the IL+XDP code after some compiler optimizations have been finished. These initial optimizations include the insertion of `iown( )` guards based on the data distribution of the array `A`, and generating the appropriate XDP ownership transfer operations to do the redistribute operation to change the partitioning scheme of `A` from `(*,*,BLOCK)` to `(*,BLOCK,*)`.

```
// A is distributed as (*,*,BLOCK)
// Loop1: 1-D FFT in the j direction
  do k = 1, 4
    iown(A[*,*,k]): {
      do i = 1, 4
        fft1D (A[i,*,k])
      enddo
    }
  enddo
// Loop2: 1-D FFT in the i direction
  do k = 1, 4
    iown(A[*,*,k]): {
      do j = 1, 4
        fft1D (A[*,j,k])
      enddo
    }
  enddo
// Loop3: Redistribute A as (*,BLOCK,*)
    do p = 1,4
      iown(A[*,*,p]): {
        do n = 1,4
          A[*,n,p] -=>
        enddo
        do n = 1,4
          A[*,p,n] <=-
        enddo
      }
    enddo
// Loop4: 1-D FFT in the k direction
  do j = 1, 4
    await(A[*,j,*]): {
      do i = 1, 4
          fft1D (A[i,j,*])
      enddo
    }
  enddo
```

Loop 3 in the above code is one possible way of performing the desired array redistribution using the XDP ownership transfer operations. Although not shown here, an auxillary data structure is created by the compiler that links the -=> and <=- statements. This is used for communication binding at code generation time and to generate matching message types for these communications. Another data structure is used to bind the local segment that will hold the received ownership (and associated values) upon termination of an ownership transfer.

A typical optimization step is compute rule elimination. This is achieved by adjusting the outer loop bounds so that each processor only does those iterations for which it owns the data. In our example, the result is each processor has to execute only one outer loop iteration for each of the loops shown above. By replacing all references to the loop's induction variable in the body of the loop by mypid, these single iteration outer loops can also be removed as a further optimization. The resulting code is:

```
// A is distributed as (*,*,BLOCK)
// Loop1: 1-D FFT in the j direction
    do i = 1, 4
      fft1D (A[i,*,mypid])
    enddo
// Loop2: 1-D FFT in the i direction
    do j = 1, 4
      fft1D (A[*,j,mypid])
    enddo
// Loop3a,3b: Redistribute A as (*,BLOCK,*)
    do n = 1,4
      A[*,n,mypid] -=>
    enddo
    do n = 1,4
      A[*,mypid,n] <=-
    enddo
// Loop4: 1-D FFT in the k direction
    await(A[*,mypid,*]): {
      do i = 1, 4
        fft1D (A[i,mypid,*])
      enddo
    }
```

Dependence analysis of Loops 2 and 3a indicates that they can be fused together. Note that the analysis for validity of fusion must also check to make sure that between any -=> and its corresponding <=- operation, no ownership queries are performed on the associated data, and that these data are not accessed by computation in the interim. The potential benefit of the loop fusion is that it allows the ownership transfer to be "pipelined" so that the redistribute latency can be partially covered by the computation.

A second transformation is also illustrated: moving the await statement *into* Loop 4. Although this might incur a greater run-time overhead, it can allow the FFT operations to proceed while other data is still being transferred. The resulting program is:

```
// A is distributed as (*,*,BLOCK)
// 1-D FFT in the j direction
    do i = 1, 4
      fft1D (A[i,*,mypid])
    enddo
// 1-D FFT in the i direction
    do j = 1, 4
      fft1D (A[*,j,mypid])
      A[*,j,mypid] -=>
    enddo
// Loop3b
    do n = 1,4
      A[*,mypid,n] <=-
    enddo
// 1-D FFT in the k direction
    do i = 1, 4
      await(A[i,mypid,*]): {
        fft1D (A[i,mypid,*])
      }
    enddo
```

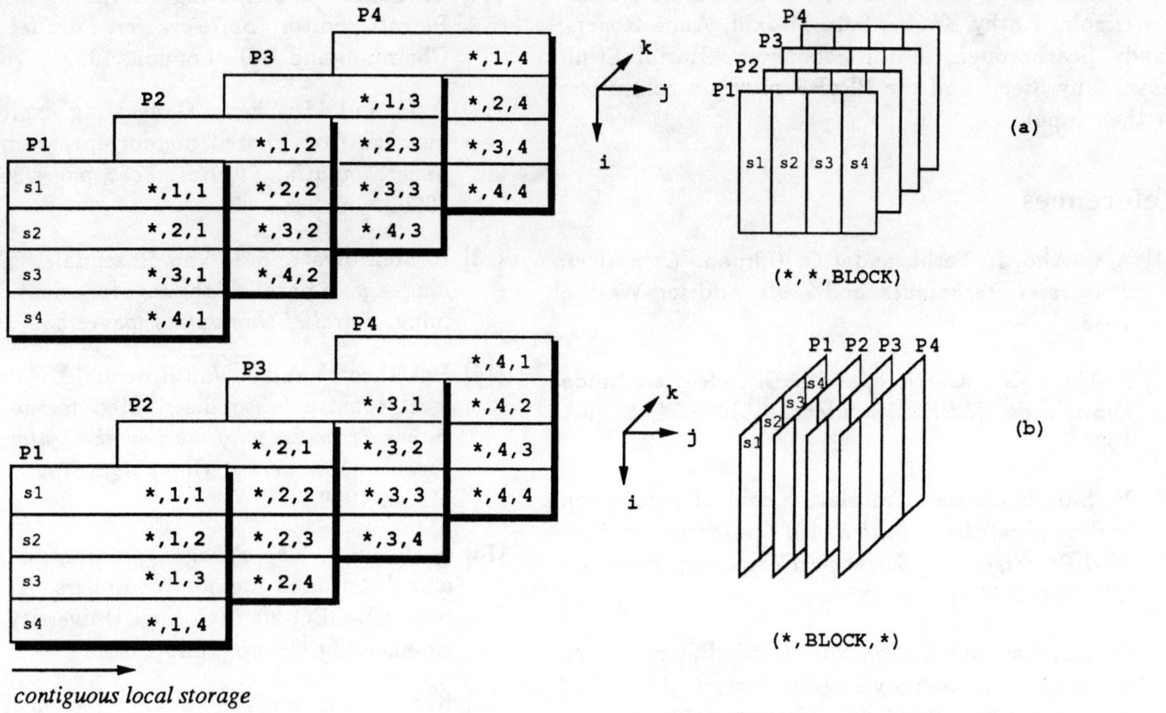

Layout of array values in local memory **Array partitioning scheme**

Figure 4: 3-D FFT example. The column on the left shows how the array data are assigned to logical segments on each processor. The column on the right illustrates the conceptual partitioning scheme of the 3-D array geometry.

The actual performance improvements of these optimizations depend largely on the capabilities of the run-time communication library of the target machine.

5 Related Work

Traditional optimizing compilers [1] use relatively language- and machine-independent intermediate program representations, but do not represent data movement and placement in an explicit manner, as done in XDP. Compilers being developed for distributed-memory multiprocessors [2, 4, 6, 8, 9, 19, 12, 13, 14, 15, 17, 18, 21] represent data movement in terms of communication primitives available on the target machine. Lake [11] has cited the importance of annotating programs with data placement, and suggested its insertion into imperative languages. Ownership transfer at the operating system level is considered by systems such as [10].

6 Conclusion

The XDP methodology has been designed to expose the power of manipulating data transfer and ownership to the compiler. We have given rules governing the use of its constructs; the compiler must supply adequate synchronization to satisfy these rules. Coherence and freedom from deadlock must also be ensured by the compiler.

The key ideas behind the XDP methodology are its separation of data transfer from local computation, its non-blocking semantics to allow overlapping of communication with computation, and its unified treatment of data and ownership transfer. In addition, XDP offers the compiler a convenient platform for doing optimizations involving data movement by providing mechanisms for delayed communication binding and generating generalized compute rules. The run-time symbol table given here to support XDP is implementable as an extension to most high-level compiler intermediate languages. The applicability of XDP is quite general, and is not restricted to the optimization of communication for distributed memory machines. For instance, it can be used to optimize data transfers across different levels of a memory hierarchy.

Acknowledgments

We would like to thank Manish Gupta for participating in several discussions with us and also helping us with a preliminary implementation. We are also grateful to Fran Allen, Guang Gao, Dave Gelernter, Francois Irigoin, Kathy Knobe, Sam Midkiff, Anne Rogers, Randy Scarborough, Edith Schonberg, Harini Srinivasan, Guy Steele and the PPoPP program committee for their input.

References

[1] A.V. Aho, R. Sethi, and J.D. Ullman. *Compilers: Principles, Techniques, and Tools.* Addison-Wesley, 1986.

[2] S. Ahuja, N.J. Carriero, and D.H. Gelernter. Linda and friends. *IEEE Computer*, 19(8):26–34, August 1986.

[3] V. Balasundaram. Translating control parallelism to data parallelism. *Fifth SIAM Conference on Parallel Processing for Scientific Computing*, Houston, TX, March 1991.

[4] D. Callahan and K. Kennedy. Compiling programs for distributed-memory multiprocessors. *Journal of Supercomputing*, 2:151–169, October 1988.

[5] HPF Forum. High Performance Fortran language specification. *Version 1, available from Rice University, Houston TX*, January 1993.

[6] M. Gupta and P. Banerjee. Automatic data partitioning on distributed memory multiprocessors. *Proceedings of the Sixth Distributed Memory Computer Conference (DMCC6), Portland, Oregon*, April 1991.

[7] Mary Hall, Seema Hiranandani, Ken Kennedy, and Chau-Wen Tseng. Interprocedural compilation of Fortran D for MIMD distributed-memory machines. *Proceedings of Supercomputing '92*, pages 522–534, November 1992.

[8] Seema Hiranandani, Ken Kennedy, and Chau-Wen Tseng. Compiling Fortran D for MIMD distributed-memory machines. *Communications of the ACM*, 35(8):66–80, August 1992.

[9] K. Ikudome, G. Fox, A. Kolawa, and J.W. Flower. An automatic and symbolic parallelization system for distributed memory parallel computers. *Proceedings of the Fifth Distributed Memory Computing Conference, Charleston, S. Carolina*, April 1990.

[10] E. Jul, H. Levy, N. Hutchinson, and A. Black. Fine-grained mobility in the Emerald system. *ACM Transactions on Computer Systems*, 6(1):109–133, February 1988.

[11] T. Lake. Distributing computations. In R.H. Perrott, editor, *Software for Parallel Computers.* Chapman and Hall, London, 1992.

[12] J. Li and M. Chen. Generating explicit communication from shared memory program references. *Supercomputing 90, New York*, pages 865–877, Nov 1990.

[13] P. Mehrotra and J. Van Rosendale. The BLAZE language: a parallel language for scientific programming. *Parallel Computing*, pages 339–361, 1987.

[14] P. Mehrotra and J. Van Rosendale. Compiling high level constructs to distributed memory architectures. *Proceedings of the Fourth Conference on Hypercube Concurrent Computers and Applications*, March 1989.

[15] A. Reeves. The Paragon programming paradigm and distributed memory compilers. Technical Report EE-CEG-90-7, Cornell University, Computer Engineering Group, June 1990.

[16] Kendall Square Research. Technical summary. Technical report, Kendall Square Research, 1992.

[17] A. Rogers and K. Pingali. Process decomposition through locality of reference. *ACM SIGPLAN 89 Conference on Programming Language Design and Implementation*, pages 69–80, June 1989.

[18] M. Rosing, R. Schnabel, and R. Weaver. The DINO parallel programming language. *Journal of Parallel and Distributed Computing*, 13(9):30–42, September 1991.

[19] R. Rühl and M. Annaratone. Parallelization of Fortran code on distributed memory parallel processors. *Proceedings of the ACM International Conference on Supercomputing*, 1990.

[20] J. Wu, J. H. Saltz, S. Hiranandani, and H. Berryman. Runtime compilation methods for multicomputers. *Proceedings of the 1991 International Conference on Parallel Processing, St. Charles, IL*, August 1991.

[21] H.P. Zima, H.J. Bast, and M. Gerndt. SUPERB: A tool for semi-automatic SIMD/MIMD parallelization. *Parallel Computing*, 6:1–18, 1988.

Generating Local Addresses and Communication Sets for Data-Parallel Programs

Siddhartha Chatterjee * John R. Gilbert † Fred J. E. Long ‡ Robert Schreiber * Shang-Hua Teng §

Abstract

Generating local addresses and communication sets is an important issue in distributed-memory implementations of data-parallel languages such as High Performance Fortran. We show that for an array A affinely aligned to a *template* that is distributed across p processors with a *cyclic*(k) distribution, and a computation involving the regular section $A(\ell : h : s)$, the local memory access sequence for any processor is characterized by a finite state machine of at most k states. We present fast algorithms for computing the essential information about these state machines, and extend the framework to handle multidimensional arrays. We also show how to generate communication sets using the state machine approach. Performance results show that this solution requires very little runtime overhead and acceptable preprocessing time.

1 Introduction

Languages such as Fortran D [4] and High Performance Fortran [5] allow the programmer to annotate programs with *alignment* and *distribution* statements that describe how to map arrays to processors in a distributed-memory environment. Both languages introduce an auxiliary Cartesian grid called a *template*; arrays are aligned to templates, and templates are distributed across the processors. The alignment of an array to a template and the distribution of the template determine the final *mapping* of the array. The compiler must partition the arrays and produce "node code" for execution on each processor of a distributed-memory parallel computer.

Consider an array A of size n aligned to a template such that array element $A(i)$ is aligned to template cell $ai + b$. The template is distributed across p processors using a *cyclic(k)* distribution, in which template cell i is held by processor $(i \text{ div } k) \bmod p$. (We number array elements, template cells, and processors starting from zero.) Thus the array A is split into p local arrays residing in the local memories of the processors. Consider a computation involving the *regular section* $A(\ell : h : s)$, *i.e.*, the set of array elements $\{A(\ell + js) : 0 \le j \le (h - \ell)/s\}$, where $s > 0$. (Table 1 summarizes the notation.) In this paper we consider the following problems:

Symbol	Meaning
A	a distributed array
n	size of array A
a	stride of alignment of A to the template
b	offset of alignment of A to the template
p	number of processors to which the template is distributed
k	block size of distribution of the template
ℓ	lower bound of regular section of A
h	upper bound of regular section of A
s	stride of regular section of A
m	processor number

Table 1: Symbols used in this paper.

- What is the sequence of local memory addresses that a given processor m must access while performing its share of the computation?
- What is the set of messages that a given processor m must send while performing its share of the computation?

The *cyclic*(k) distributions generalize the familiar *block* and *cyclic* distributions (which are *cyclic*($\lceil n/p \rceil$) and *cyclic*(1) respectively). Dongarra *et al.* [3] have shown these distributions to be essential for efficient dense matrix algorithms on distributed-memory machines. High Performance Fortran includes directives for multidimensional *cyclic*(k) distribution of templates.

Many special cases of these problems have been solved, but the general solution does not appear in the literature or (to the best of our knowledge) in any implementation. Koelbel and Mehrotra [8] treat special cases where the array is mapped using a *block* or a *cyclic* mapping, and the regular section has unit stride. Koelbel [7] handles non-unit-stride regular sections with *block* or *cyclic* mappings. MacDonald *et al.* [9] discuss the problem in the context of Cray Research's MPP Fortran, and conclude that a general solution requires unacceptable address computation overhead in inner loops. They therefore restrict block sizes and number of processors to powers of two, allowing the use of bit manipulation in address computation. Experimental implementation of our solution shows

---

*Research Institute for Advanced Computer Science, Mail Stop T045-1, NASA Ames Research Center, Moffett Field, CA 94035-1000 (sc@riacs.edu, schreibr@riacs.edu). The work of these authors was supported by the NAS Systems Division via Cooperative Agreement NCC 2-387 between NASA and the Universities Space Research Association (USRA).

†Xerox Palo Alto Research Center, 3333 Coyote Hill Road, Palo Alto, CA 94304-1314 (gilbert@parc.xerox.com).

‡Department of Computer and Information Science, University of California, Santa Cruz, CA 95064 (flong@cse.ucsc.edu). This work was performed while the author was a summer student at RIACS.

§Department of Mathematics, Massachusetts Institute of Technology, Cambridge, MA 02139 (steng@theory.lcs.mit.edu). This work was performed while the author was a postdoctoral scientist at Xerox PARC.

4th ACM PPOPP,5/93/CA,USA

that address computation and interprocessor communication can be performed efficiently without these restrictions.

The paper is organized as follows. Section 2 solves the problem for a one-level mapping ($a = 1, b = 0$). Section 3 reduces the problem for two-level mappings to combining the solutions from two subproblems involving one-level mappings. Section 4 extends the framework to handle multidimensional arrays, and Section 5 extends it to handle generation of communication sets. Section 6 discusses performance results, and Section 7 presents conclusions.

2 One-level mappings

We first consider the problem where a one-dimensional array A is aligned to a template with $a = 1$ and $b = 0$. This is called a *one-level mapping*. In this case, the array and the template are in one-to-one correspondence, and we specify the problem by the pair (p, k) describing the distribution of the template across the processors. As shown in Figure 1(a), we visualize the layout of the array in the processor memories as courses of blocks. Three functions $\mathcal{P}$, $\mathcal{C}$, and $\mathcal{O}$ describe the location of array element $A(i)$. $\mathcal{P}(i; p, k)$ is the processor holding $A(i)$, $\mathcal{C}(i; p, k)$ is the course of blocks within this processor holding $A(i)$, and $\mathcal{O}(i; p, k)$ is the offset of $A(i)$ within the course. The layout of array elements in the local processor memories is as shown in Figure 1(b).

These functions are defined as follows.

$$\mathcal{P}(i;p,k) = (i \bmod pk) \operatorname{div} k = (i \operatorname{div} k) \bmod p \qquad (1)$$
$$\mathcal{C}(i;p,k) = i \operatorname{div} pk = (i \operatorname{div} k) \operatorname{div} p \qquad (2)$$
$$\mathcal{O}(i;p,k) = i \bmod k \qquad (3)$$

Therefore, we have

$$i = pk \cdot \mathcal{C}(i;p,k) + k \cdot \mathcal{P}(i;p,k) + \mathcal{O}(i;p,k).$$

The following function gives the local memory location (with respect to the base of the local array) where element $A(i)$ is stored within processor $\mathcal{P}(i; p, k)$:

$$\mathcal{M}(i;p,k) = k \cdot \mathcal{C}(i;p,k) + \mathcal{O}(i;p,k). \qquad (4)$$

We are interested in the sequence of local memory locations that an individual processor, numbered m, accesses while performing its share of the computation on the regular section $A(\ell : h : s)$. We specify the sequence of accesses by its starting location and by the differences $\Delta\mathcal{M}(i_1, i_2) = \mathcal{M}(i_2; p, k) - \mathcal{M}(i_1; p, k)$, where i_1 and i_2 are two successive indices of the part of the regular section mapped to processor m. As the examples in Figure 2 illustrate, the spacing $\Delta\mathcal{M}$ is not constant.

The key insight is that (for a particular p, k, and stride s) the offset $\mathcal{O}(i_1; p, k)$ of one element of the regular section determines the offset $\mathcal{O}(i_2; p, k)$ of the next element of the regular section in the same processor, and also determines the spacing $\Delta\mathcal{M}(i_1, i_2)$. Thus we can represent the offset sequence and the $\Delta\mathcal{M}$ sequence as a simple table indexed by offset. We visualize this table as the transition diagram of a finite state machine (FSM) whose k states are the offsets. This FSM is particularly simple because it has no input, and each state has only one outgoing transition; in fact, it is just a union of state-disjoint cycles. Thus the sequence of $\Delta\mathcal{M}$'s is periodic, with period at most k.

The contents of the table, or the transitions of the FSM, depend on p, k, and s, but not on the section bounds ℓ and h or the processor number m. The same FSM describes the offsets for every processor, though each processor sees at most one cycle of the FSM. The first memory location used by the section in processor m (and its offset, which is the "start state" for that processor's view of the FSM) depends on ℓ and m as well as p, k, and s.

Following equation (4), we can write $\Delta\mathcal{M}$ in terms of the differences in course and offset:

$$\Delta\mathcal{M}(i_1, i_2) = k \cdot \Delta\mathcal{C}(i_1, i_2) + \Delta\mathcal{O}(i_1, i_2), \qquad (5)$$

where the definitions of $\Delta\mathcal{C}$ and $\Delta\mathcal{O}$ are analogous to that of $\Delta\mathcal{M}$.

Here are some examples. We assume that $\ell = 0$ and that h is large.

Example 1 $k = 4, p = 4, s = 3$. The distribution is shown in Figure 2(a). The transition table T is as follows. For convenience, we also tabulate $\Delta\mathcal{C}$ and $\Delta\mathcal{O}$. This shows a simple case where all processors access local memory with constant stride.

STATE	NEXT	$\Delta\mathcal{M}$	$\Delta\mathcal{C}$	$\Delta\mathcal{O}$
0	3	3	0	3
1	0	3	1	−1
2	1	3	1	−1
3	2	3	1	−1

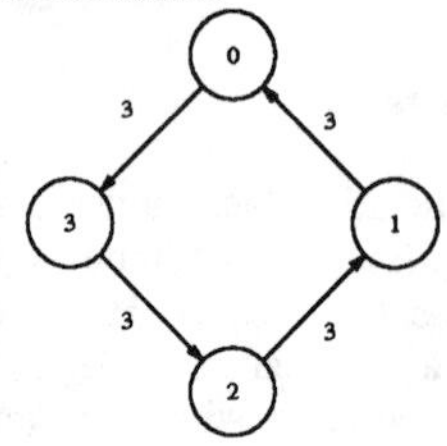

Example 2 $k = 4, p = 3, s = 3$. The distribution is shown in Figure 2(b). The transition table T is as follows. This demonstrates that the FSM for a problem can consist of disjoint cycles. Each processor sees at most one cycle of the FSM, depending on its start state.

STATE	NEXT	$\Delta\mathcal{M}$	$\Delta\mathcal{C}$	$\Delta\mathcal{O}$
0	3	3	0	3
1	1	4	1	0
2	2	4	1	0
3	0	1	1	−3

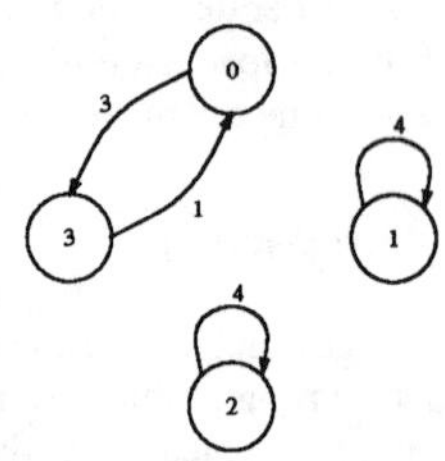

Example 3 $k = 4, p = 3, s = 5$. The distribution is shown in Figure 2(c). The transition table T is as follows. The $\Delta\mathcal{M}$ sequence has period k, and local memory accesses vary in stride.

STATE	NEXT	$\Delta\mathcal{M}$	$\Delta\mathcal{C}$	$\Delta\mathcal{O}$
0	3	7	1	3
1	2	9	2	1
2	0	2	1	−2
3	1	2	1	−2

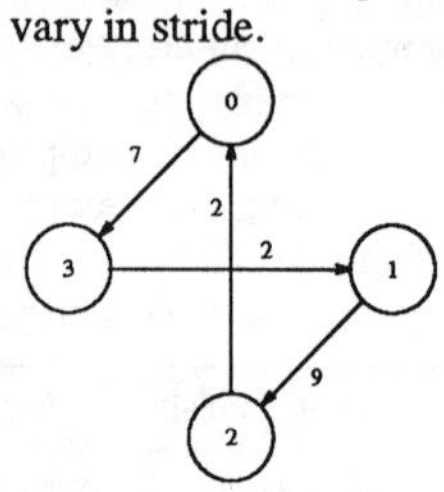

2.1 The algorithm

Preparatory to finding a processor's $\Delta\mathcal{M}$ sequence, we solve the problem of finding its starting memory location. Given a processor number m, regular section $A(\ell : h : s)$, and layout parameters p and k, we wish to find the first element (if any) of the regular section that resides on that processor. This is equivalent to finding the smallest nonnegative integer j such that $\mathcal{P}(\ell + sj; p, k) = m$.

Substituting the definition of $\mathcal{P}$ from equation (1), we get

$$((\ell + sj) \bmod pk) \operatorname{div} k = m.$$

This reduces to

$$km \leq (\ell + sj) \bmod pk \leq k(m+1) - 1$$

Course	Processor 0			Processor 1			...	Processor $p-1$		
0	0	...	$k-1$	k	...	$2k-1$	...	$(p-1)k$	...	$pk-1$
1	pk	...	$(p+1)k-1$	$(p+1)k$	...	$(p+2)k-1$	...	$(2p-1)k$	...	$2pk-1$
⋮	⋮	⋮	⋮	⋮	⋮	⋮	⋮	⋮	⋮	⋮
Offset	0	...	$k-1$	0	...	$k-1$	...	0	...	$k-1$

(a)

Local memory location	0	...	$k-1$	k	...	$2k-1$	...
Array index (processor 0)	0	...	$k-1$	pk	...	$(p+1)k-1$	...
Array index (processor 1)	k	...	$2k-1$	$(p+1)k$	...	$(p+2)k-1$	...
Array index (processor $p-1$)	$(p-1)k$	...	$pk-1$	$(2p-1)k$	...	$2pk-1$	...

(b)

Figure 1: A one-level mapping. (a) Layout parameters. Processors run across the page, while memory is organized as a two-dimensional array of courses and offsets. Each box represents a memory cell, and the number in the cell indicates the array element it holds. (b) Layout of array elements in local processor memories. Each processor's memory is one row of the diagram.

(a)

Proc. 0				Proc. 1				Proc. 2				Proc. 3			
0	1	2	**3**	4	5	**6**	7	8	**9**	10	11	**12**	13	14	**15**
16	17	**18**	19	20	**21**	22	23	**24**	25	26	**27**	28	29	**30**	31
32	**33**	34	35	**36**	37	38	**39**	40	41	**42**	43	44	**45**	46	47

(b)

Proc. 0				Proc. 1				Proc. 2			
0	1	2	**3**	4	5	**6**	7	8	**9**	10	11
12	13	14	**15**	16	17	**18**	19	20	**21**	22	23

(c)

Proc. 0				Proc. 1				Proc. 2			
0	1	2	3	4	**5**	6	7	8	9	**10**	11
12	13	14	**15**	16	17	18	19	**20**	21	22	23
24	**25**	26	27	28	29	**30**	31	32	33	34	**35**
36	37	38	39	**40**	41	42	43	44	**45**	46	47
48	49	**50**	51	52	53	54	**55**	56	57	58	59

Figure 2: One-level array mappings. The corresponding state tables are shown in Examples 1–3. (a) $k = 4, p = 4, s = 3$. (b) $k = 4, p = 3, s = 3$. (c) $k = 4, p = 3, s = 5$.

which is equivalent to finding an integer q such that

$$km - \ell \leq sj - pkq \leq km - \ell + k - 1. \qquad (6)$$

We rewrite inequality (6) as a set of k linear Diophantine equations in the variables j and q,

$$\{sj - pkq = \lambda : km - \ell \leq \lambda \leq km - \ell + k - 1\}. \qquad (7)$$

The equations in this set are to be solved independently (rather than simultaneously). Solutions exist for an individual equation if and only if λ is divisible by GCD(s, pk).

The general solution to the linear Diophantine equation $sj - pkq = \lambda$ is found as follows. Let $d = \text{GCD}(s, pk) = \alpha s + \beta pk$, with $\alpha, \beta \in \mathbb{Z}$. The quantities α, β, and d are determined by the extended Euclid algorithm [6, page 325]. Then the general solution of the equation is the one-parameter family $j = (\lambda\alpha + pk\gamma)/d$ and $q = (-\lambda\beta + s\gamma)/d$, for $\gamma \in \mathbb{Z}$.

For each solvable equation in set (7), we find the solution having the smallest nonnegative j. The minimum of these solutions gives us the starting index value $\ell + js$, which we then convert to the starting memory location using equation (4). We compute the ending memory location similarly, by finding the largest solutions no greater than h, and taking the maximum among these solutions.

Now we extend this idea to build the $\Delta\mathcal{M}$ sequence for the processor. A sorted version of the set of smallest positive solutions determined above gives us the sequence of indices that will be successively accessed by the processor. A linear scan through this sequence is sufficient to generate the $\Delta\mathcal{M}$ sequence for the cycle of the FSM visible to processor m. If the FSM has multiple cycles, the local $\Delta\mathcal{M}$ sequences may be different for different processors; otherwise, the sequences are cyclic shifts of one another. To avoid following the NEXT pointers at runtime, the $\Delta\mathcal{M}$ table we compute contains the memory spacings in the order seen by the processor.

All of these elements are combined in Algorithm 1, which provides the solution for the memory address problem for a one-level mapping. The running time of Algorithm 1 is $O(\log \min(s, pk)) + O(k \log k)$, which reduces to $O(\min(k \log k + \log s, k \log k + \log p))$. As the output can be of size k in the worst case, any algorithm for this problem takes $\Omega(k)$ time. Finding an algorithm with $O(k)$ running time remains an open problem. Our implementation recognizes the following special cases that can be handled more quickly: $p = 1$, s divides k, $k = 1$, pk divides s, a single course of blocks, and s divides pk.

Algorithm 1 can be simplified by noting that the right hand sides of successive solvable equations differ by d, and that the identity of the first solvable equation is easily determined from the value of $(km - \ell) \bmod d$. This removes the conditional from the loop in lines 5–12. Similar incremental computations can also be used to simplify the floor and ceiling computations in that loop.

The node code for each processor consists of the following loop.

base $\leftarrow$ *startmem*; *i* $\leftarrow$ *0*
while (*base* $\leq$ *lastmem*) **do**
  compute with address *base*
  base $\leftarrow$ *base* + $\Delta\mathcal{M}$[*i*]
  i $\leftarrow$ (*i* + *1*) mod *length*
enddo

Algorithm 1 (Memory access sequence for a one-level mapping.)

Input: Layout parameters (p, k), regular section $A(\ell : h : s)$, processor number m.

Output: The $\Delta\mathcal{M}$ table, the length of the table, starting memory location, ending memory location, and $\sum \Delta\mathcal{M}$ for processor m.

Method:

1 **integer** $\Delta\mathcal{M}$[*k*], *length*
2 **integer** λ, *i, start, end, d*, α, β, *lcourse, loffset, course, offset*
3 **integer** *loc*[*k*+*1*], *sorted*[*k*+*1*]

4 $(d, \alpha, \beta) \leftarrow$ EXTENDED-EUCLID(s, pk); *length* $\leftarrow$ *0*;
  start $\leftarrow h + 1$; *end* $\leftarrow \ell - 1$
5 **for** $\lambda = km - \ell$ **to** $km - \ell + k - 1$ **do**
6   **if** $\lambda \bmod d = 0$ **then** /* Solvable equation */
7   *loc*[*length*] $\leftarrow \ell + \frac{s}{d}(\lambda\alpha + pk\lceil\frac{-\lambda\alpha}{pk}\rceil)$
8   *start* $\leftarrow$ min(*start, loc*[*length*])
9   *end* $\leftarrow$ max(*end*, $\ell + \frac{s}{d}(\lambda\alpha + pk\lfloor\frac{(h-l)d-\lambda\alpha s}{pks}\rfloor)$)
10   *length* $\leftarrow$ *length* + *1*
11   **endif**
12 **enddo**
13 **if** *length* = *0* **or** *start* > *h* **then**
14   **return** $\Delta\mathcal{M}, \bot, \bot, \bot, \bot$ /* No work for processor */
15 **endif**
16 *sorted* $\leftarrow$ SORT (*loc, length*)
17 *sorted*[*length*] $\leftarrow$ *sorted*[*0*] $+pks/d$; *lcourse*
  $\leftarrow \mathcal{C}$(*sorted*[*0*]; *p, k*); *loffset* $\leftarrow \mathcal{O}$(*sorted*[*0*]; *p, k*)
18 **for** *i* = *0* **to** *length* − *1* **do**
19   *course* $\leftarrow \mathcal{C}$(*sorted*[*i* + *1*]; *p, k*); *offset*
    $\leftarrow \mathcal{O}$(*sorted*[*i* + *1*]; *p, k*)
20   $\Delta\mathcal{M}$[*i*] $\leftarrow$ *k*·(*course* − *lcourse*) + (*offset* − *loffset*)
21   *lcourse* $\leftarrow$ *course*; *loffset* $\leftarrow$ *offset*
22 **enddo**
23 **return** $\Delta\mathcal{M}$, *length*, $\mathcal{M}$(*start*; *p, k*), $\mathcal{M}$(*end*; *p, k*), $sk/\text{GCD}(s, pk)$

We illustrate the actions of Algorithm 1 on Example 3 for processor 0. Here, $p = 3$, $k = 4$, and $s = 5$. The extended Euclid algorithm returns $d = 1$, $\alpha = 5$, and $\beta = -2$. Since each linear Diophantine equation is solvable, the loop in lines 5–12 is executed four times. At the end of this loop, *loc* = [0, 25, 50, 15], *length* = 4, *start* = 0, and *end* = 50. After line 17, *sorted* = [0, 15, 25, 50, 60]. At the end of the loop in lines 18–22, $\Delta\mathcal{M}$ = [7, 2, 9, 2].

3 Two-level mappings

Two-level mappings are solved by two applications of Algorithm 1. As an example, let A be an array with element $A(i)$ aligned with template cell $3i$, let the template be mapped with $p = k = 4$, and let the regular section be $A(0:42:3)$, which we abbreviate to B. The picture is shown in Figure 3(a). The boxes represent template cells, the number j indicates the location of $A(j)$, and numbers in squares are part of the regular section $A(0:42:3)$. Two-level mappings encompass all mappings possible with the linguistic constructs of nested sections, affine alignment, and *cyclic*(k) distribution.

Unlike the one-level case, all template cells do not contain array elements. However, we allocate local storage only for the *occupied* cells of the template. Thus, the local memory storage for A in the example above is as shown in Figure 3(b). We handle this complication by first doing all our computations with respect to the template (the *local template space*), and then switching back to the local memory space in the final step. The picture in local template space is shown in Figure 3(c).

Note that A and B are both aligned to "regular sections" of the template: $A(i)$ is aligned to template cell $3i$, and $B(i)$ is aligned to template cell $9i$. We therefore create state tables for A and B with respect to the local template space using Algorithm 1. The "$\Delta\mathcal{M}$" entries returned by the algorithm are actually spacings in local template space; we therefore rename this column $\Delta\mathcal{T}$. This gives the tables for A and B shown below.

T_A =

STATE	NEXT	$\Delta\mathcal{T}$	$\Delta\mathcal{M}$
0	3	3	?
1	0	3	?
2	1	3	?
3	2	3	?

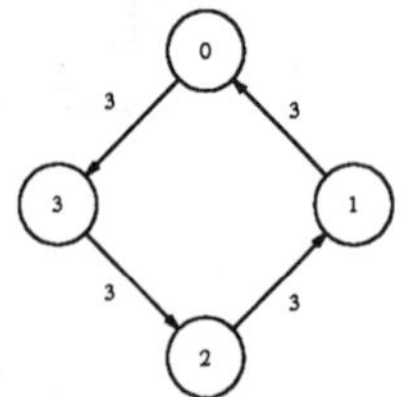

T_B =

STATE	NEXT	$\Delta\mathcal{T}$	$\Delta\mathcal{M}$
0	2	6	?
1	3	6	?
2	1	15	?
3	0	9	?

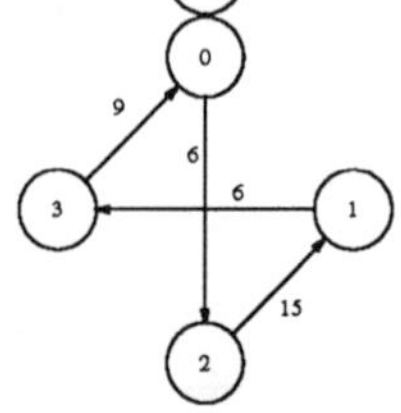

Now all we need is to switch back to local memory space and fill in the $\Delta\mathcal{M}$ entries.

As we traverse the state table T_A for any processor m, we access each element of A stored on that processor, in order. But since storage is allocated based on A, this translates to accessing consecutive locations in local memory. Thus the $\Delta\mathcal{M}$ entries for T_A are all unity. Now it is a simple matter to find the $\Delta\mathcal{M}$ entries for the desired section B. For instance, the first line of T_B says that if we are at an element of the section that has offset 0, the next element has offset 2 and is 6 template cells away. To find the corresponding $\Delta\mathcal{M}$, we start in state 0 of T_A, and walk the state table, accumulating $\Delta\mathcal{T}$ and $\Delta\mathcal{M}$ counts. We stop when we have accumulated the desired $\Delta\mathcal{T}$ count. (It is easy to show that at this point we will have arrived at the correct offset as well.) The accumulated $\Delta\mathcal{M}$ value is the desired entry for that line of T_B. This procedure results in the following table for B.[1]

STATE	NEXT	$\Delta\mathcal{T}$	$\Delta\mathcal{M}$
0	2	6	2
1	3	6	2
2	1	15	5
3	0	9	3

The algorithm as presented above requires $O(k)$ time to compute each $\Delta\mathcal{M}$ entry of T_B. Two optimizations reduce this complexity to $O(1)$, allowing the final fixup phase to run in $O(k)$ time.

[1] In this case, $\Delta\mathcal{M}$ turns out to be $\Delta\mathcal{T}$ divided by the alignment stride $a = 3$, but this is not true in general. Try the following case: $a = 3, b = 0, p = 3, k = 8, s = 3$.

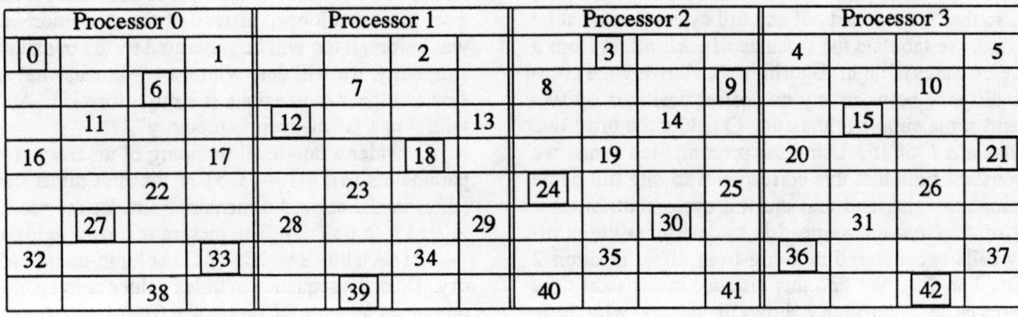

(b)

Local memory location	0	1	2	3	4	5	6	7	8	9	10
Processor 0	0	1	6	11	16	17	22	27	32	33	38
Processor 1	2	7	12	13	18	23	28	29	34	39	
Processor 2	3	8	9	14	19	24	25	30	35	40	41
Processor 3	4	5	10	15	20	21	26	31	36	37	42

(c)

Local template cell	0	1	2	3	4	5	6	7	8	9	10	11	...
Processor 0	0			1			6			11			...
Processor 1			2			7			12			13	...
Processor 2		3			8			9			14		...
Processor 3	4			5			10			15			...

Figure 3: A two-level mapping of an array A aligned to the template with stride 3. (a) Layout of template cells. Numbers are array elements; boxed numbers are in the regular section $A(0:42:3)$. (b) Local memory storage for array. (c) Local template space for array.

Processor (0, 0)				Processor (0, 1)			
(0, 0)	(0, 1)	(0, 4)	(0, 5)	(0, 2)	(0, 3)	(0, 6)	(0, 7)
(1, 0)	(1, 1)	(1, 4)	(1, 5)	(1, 2)	(1, 3)	(1, 6)	(1, 7)
(2, 0)	(2, 1)	(2, 4)	(2, 5)	(2, 2)	(2, 3)	(2, 6)	(2, 7)
(9, 0)	(9, 1)	(9, 4)	(9, 5)	(9, 2)	(9, 3)	(9, 6)	(9, 7)
(10, 0)	(10, 1)	(10, 4)	(10, 5)	(10, 2)	(10, 3)	(10, 6)	(10, 7)
(11, 0)	(11, 1)	(11, 4)	(11, 5)	(11, 2)	(11, 3)	(11, 6)	(11, 7)
Processor (1, 0)				**Processor (1, 1)**			
(3, 0)	(3, 1)	(3, 4)	(3, 5)	(3, 2)	(3, 3)	(3, 6)	(3, 7)
(4, 0)	(4, 1)	(4, 4)	(4, 5)	(4, 2)	(4, 3)	(4, 6)	(4, 7)
(5, 0)	(5, 1)	(5, 4)	(5, 5)	(5, 2)	(5, 3)	(5, 6)	(5, 7)
(12, 0)	(12, 1)	(12, 4)	(12, 5)	(12, 2)	(12, 3)	(12, 6)	(12, 7)
(13, 0)	(13, 1)	(13, 4)	(13, 5)	(13, 2)	(13, 3)	(13, 6)	(13, 7)
(14, 0)	(14, 1)	(14, 4)	(14, 5)	(14, 2)	(14, 3)	(14, 6)	(14, 7)
Processor (2, 0)				**Processor (2, 1)**			
(6, 0)	(6, 1)	(6, 4)	(6, 5)	(6, 2)	(6, 3)	(6, 6)	(6, 7)
(7, 0)	(7, 1)	(7, 4)	(7, 5)	(7, 2)	(7, 3)	(7, 6)	(7, 7)
(8, 0)	(8, 1)	(8, 4)	(8, 5)	(8, 2)	(8, 3)	(8, 6)	(8, 7)
(15, 0)	(15, 1)	(15, 4)	(15, 5)	(15, 2)	(15, 3)	(15, 6)	(15, 7)
(16, 0)	(16, 1)	(16, 4)	(16, 5)	(16, 2)	(16, 3)	(16, 6)	(16, 7)
(17, 0)	(17, 1)	(17, 4)	(17, 5)	(17, 2)	(17, 3)	(17, 6)	(17, 7)

Figure 4: Mapping a two-dimensional array. Layout of array elements on processor arrangement with $p = k = 3$ in the vertical dimension and $p = k = 2$ in the horizontal dimension. The boxed pairs are $A(0:17:2, 0:7:3)$.

First, we compute the sum of the $\Delta\mathcal{T}$ and the $\Delta\mathcal{M}$ around the state machine cycle, so that we can cast out any full cycles that must be traversed. Second, we tabulate the distance of each offset from a fixed origin (the *numarcs* table in Algorithm 2), allowing the computation of the distance between any two offset positions by two table lookups and some simple arithmetic. Consider the third line of T_B, which has a $\Delta\mathcal{T}$ of 15. Using the precomputed sums, we determine in constant time that this corresponds to one full cycle plus 3 more template cells, and that the full cycle contributes a memory offset of 4. Now all we need is to determine the number of memory cells encountered in going from offset position 2 to offset position 1 in T_A. We find this distance in constant time using the *numarcs* table. Algorithm 2 shows the method with these optimizations incorporated.

Algorithm 2 (Memory access sequence for a two-level mapping.)
Input: Alignment parameters (a, b), layout parameters (p, k), array length n, regular section $A(\ell : h : s)$, processor number m.
Output: The $\Delta\mathcal{M}$ table, length of the table, starting memory location, ending memory location, and the length of A in processor m.
Method:

```
integer i, mm, numarcs[k]
integer ΔM[k], length, startmem, lastmem
integer ΔM1[k], length1, startmem1, lastmem1, memcycle1
integer ΔM2[k], length2, startmem2, lastmem2, memcycle2

function residual(x) =
    length1 · ⌊ (x−startmem1)/memcycle1 ⌋
function major(x) = (numarcs[x mod k] −
    numarcs[startmem1 mod k]) mod length1
function realmem(x) = major(x) + residual(x)

(ΔM1, length1, startmem1, lastmem1, memcycle1)
    ← Algorithm 1(b, a(n − 1) + b, a, p, k, m)
(ΔM2, length2, startmem2, lastmem2, memcycle2)
    ← Algorithm 1(aℓ + b, ah + b, as, p, k, m)
if length1 = ⊥ or length2 = ⊥ then
    return ΔM, ⊥, ⊥, ⊥, 0 /* No work for processor */
endif
mm ← startmem1
for i = 0 to length1 − 1 do
    numarcs[mm mod k] ← i
    mm ← mm + ΔM1[i]
enddo
mm ← startmem2
for i = 0 to length2 − 1 do
    ΔM[i] ← realmem(mm + ΔM2[i]) − realmem(mm)
    mm ← mm + ΔM2[i]
enddo
return ΔM, length2, realmem(startmem2),
    realmem(lastmem2), realmem(lastmem1) −
    realmem(startmem1)+1
```

4 Multidimensional arrays

So far, we have characterized the access sequence of a single processor by a start address and a memory stride pattern, the latter being generated by the transitions of a FSM. For a multidimensional array, each dimension will be characterized by a (p, k) pair and have a FSM associated with it, and each processor will execute a set of nested loops. Instead of the start address being fixed as it was before, it too will be generated by the transitions of a FSM. For simplicity, we will deal with a two-dimensional array. The extension to higher dimensions is straightforward. An array dimension with $p = 1$ is "mapped to memory".

Consider a one-level mapping of an array $A(0:17, 0:7)$ with parameters $(p_1, k_1) = (3, 3)$ in the first dimension and $(p_2, k_2) = (2, 2)$ in the second dimension, and let the section of interest be $A(0:17:2, 0:7:3)$. The picture is shown in Figure 4.

Let each block be laid out in column-major order in local memory. Thus, the sequence of index values corresponding to successive memory elements of processor (0,0) is {(0,0), (1,0), (2,0), (9,0), (10,0), (11,0), (0,1), ...}. Such a decomposition is used by Dongarra *et al.* for dense linear algebra codes on distributed-memory machines [3]. Then the tables corresponding to the two dimensions of A are

$T_1 =$

STATE	NEXT	$\Delta\mathcal{M}$
0	2	2
1	0	2
2	1	2

and

$T_2 =$

STATE	NEXT	$\Delta\mathcal{M}$
0	1	30
1	0	6

.

(Had the section been larger in the second dimension, the column accessed by processor $(0, 0)$ immediately after column 0 would be column 9. The elements $(0, 0)$ and $(0, 9)$ would be 30 locations apart in local memory. This explains the $\Delta\mathcal{M}$ entry in the first row of T_2.)

The FSM T_2 is used to generate memory spacings for successive base addresses, while the FSM T_1 is used to generate memory spacings between successive elements with the same base address. Algorithm 3 computes these FSMs.

Algorithm 3 (Memory access sequence for a multidimensional array with a two-level mapping.)
Input: Number of dimensions d; alignment parameters (a_j, b_j), layout parameters (p_j, k_j), dimension length n_j, regular section $A(l_j : h_j : s_j)$, processor number m_j, for each dimension j $(1 \le j \le d)$.
Output: $\Delta\mathcal{M}_j$, length$_j$, startmem$_j$, lastmem$_j$ $(1 \le j \le d)$.
Method:

```
integer j, mem, m, k

mem ← 1
for j = 1 to d do
    (ΔM_j, length_j, startmem_j, lastmem_j, m)
        ← Algorithm 2(a_j, b_j, p_j, k_j, n_j, l_j, h_j, s_j, m_j)
    startmem_j ← startmem_j · mem
    lastmem_j ← lastmem_j · mem
    for k = 0 to length_j − 1 do
        ΔM_j[k] ← ΔM_j[k] · mem
    enddo
    mem ← mem · m
enddo
return ΔM_j, length_j, startmem_j, lastmem_j
    (1 ≤ j ≤ d)
```

For the two-dimensional case, each processor executes the following doubly-nested loop. Higher-dimensional cases follow the same pattern, with one loop for each dimension.

```
base2 ← startmem2
i2 ← 0
while base2 ≤ lastmem2 do
   base1 ← startmem1
   i1 ← 0
   while base1 ≤ lastmem1 do
      compute with address base2 + base1
      base1 ← base1 +ΔM1[i1]
      i1 ← (i1 + 1)mod length1
   enddo
   base2 ← base2 +ΔM2[i2]
   i2 ← (i2 + 1)mod length2
enddo
```

5 Generating communication sets

The set of messages that a given processor m must send while performing its share of the computation is called its *communication set*. We now extend the FSM approach to generate communication sets for regular communication patterns such as shifts and stride changes. In this section, we assume a one-dimensional array with a single-level mapping. Extensions to multilevel and multidimensional cases are as in the address generation problem.

We adopt Koelbel's execution model for parallel loops [7], in which a processor goes through four steps:

1. Send those data items it holds that are required by other processors.
2. Perform local iterations, *i.e.*, iterations for which it holds all data.
3. Receive data items from other processors.
4. Perform nonlocal iterations.

We combine the final two steps into a receive-execute loop.

Our approach puts all the intelligence on the sending side, keeping the receive-execute loop simple. We wish to minimize the number of messages sent and maximize cache benefits. To this end, each processor makes a single pass over the data in its local memory using the FSM technique described above, figuring out the destination of each data element and building messages. The messages contain (address, value) pairs which the receiving processor uses to perform its computations. All the data that must go from processor i to processor j are communicated in a single message. The data items corresponding to the local iterations are conceptually sent by the processor to itself. Of course, this message is never sent; rather, the local iterations are performed out of the message buffer. The idea is similar to the inspector-executor model [10] for irregular loops.

5.1 Shifts

Consider the computation

$$A(0\colon h\colon s) = A(0\colon h\colon s) + A(\ell\colon \ell + h\colon s),$$

where the regular section $A(\ell\colon \ell + h\colon s)$ is to be moved to align with $A(0\colon h\colon s)$. (For simplicity, assume $\ell > 0$.) In this case, a processor communicates with at most two processors. We show how to augment the FSM with a $\Delta\mathcal{P}$ and a $\Delta\mathcal{L}$ column, such that adding these quantities to the processor and memory location of the current element gives the remote processor number and the memory location in the remote processor of the element with which it interacts.

Suppose we know that element $A(i)$ is located on processor m at memory location $\mathcal{M}(i;p,k)$ with offset $O_i = \mathcal{O}(i;p,k)$. Then the problem is to find the processor and local memory location of the element $A(i-\ell)$. Let $\ell = q\cdot pk + r$, and $\Delta\mathcal{P} = \lceil (r - O_i)/k \rceil$. Then $\mathcal{P}(i-\ell;p,k) = (m - \Delta\mathcal{P} + p) \bmod p$. Since $0 \le O_i < k$, $\Delta\mathcal{P}$ can assume only two values as the offset O_i varies.

We also define the quantity $\Delta\mathcal{L}$ such that $\mathcal{M}(i-\ell;p,k) = \mathcal{M}(i;p,k) + \Delta\mathcal{L}(O_i)$.

$$\begin{aligned} \Delta\mathcal{L}(O_i) &= ((O_i - r) \bmod k) - O_i - kq - \eta, \\ \eta &= \begin{cases} k & \text{if } (mk - r + O_i) < 0, \\ 0 & \text{otherwise.} \end{cases} \end{aligned}$$

5.2 Stride changes

Now consider the communication required to move the regular section $A(0\colon s_2 n\colon s_2)$ to align with the regular section $A(0\colon s_1 n\colon s_1)$. This is harder than a shift; there is no simple lookup technique for generating the communication sets. The problem is that the pattern of destination processors can have period longer than k. The only fact that appears to be true in this case is that the sum of the periods over all processors divides pk. We therefore resort to a simple technique.

We generate the FSM to reflect the storage properties of the s_2-section. Now, the jth element of this section interacts with index $i = j \cdot s_1$ of A. Let $q_1 = i \text{ div } pk$, $r_1 = i \bmod pk$, $q_2 = r_1 \text{ div } k$, and $r_2 = r_1 \bmod k$. Then the desired element is stored in memory location $q_1 \cdot k + r_2$ on processor q_2.

Many modern RISC microprocessors perform integer division and remainder operations in software, which are rather slow. The equations above can be rewritten to require only two integer divisions, which substantially speeds up the implementation. If either p or k is a power of two, the computation can be sped up further by using shifts and bit masks instead of the division operations. Our implementation incorporates these optimizations.

5.3 Termination

Each processor must determine when it has completed all its operations. As we do not send messages between every pair of processors, we cannot use the number of messages to determine termination. However, it is easy to figure out the total number of operations that processor m will execute (by a variant of Algorithm 1). A simple termination test initializes a counter to this value, decrements it by the number of array elements received in each message, and exits when the counter reaches zero.

6 Experimental results

In this section we present experimental results of implementing the algorithms above. We measure both the preprocessing cost of table generation and the runtime loop overhead.

Our computational kernel is the DAXPY operation

```
y(1:n:s) = y(1:n:s) + a*x(1:n:s).
```

The ratio of memory operations to computation is high in this kernel, making it unfavorable for our algorithms. The overhead due to irregular memory access patterns would decrease with more computation in the loop. All experiments reported in this section were done on a Sparcstation 2, for which Dongarra [2] reports a 100×100 double-precision LINPACK performance of 4.0 Mflops. (We measured 3.3 Mflops.) (A repetition of the experiments on a single processor of an iPSC/860 showed similar characteristics.) We used the GNU C compiler, with optimization at the -O2 level.

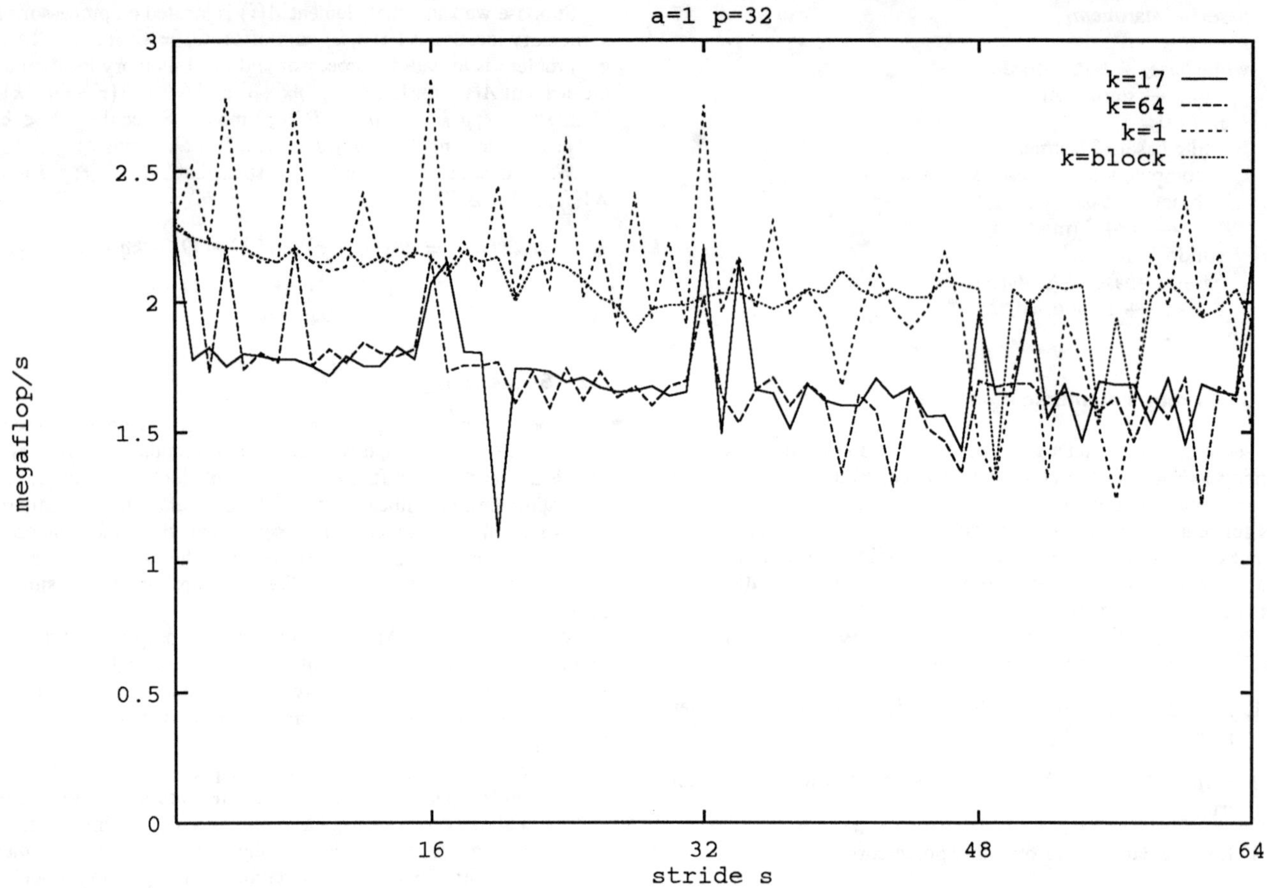

Figure 5: Performance of DAXPY for various block sizes k.

A higher optimization level increased compilation time without improving the quality of the generated code. With $s = 1$ the loop compiled into 9 instructions, while the general case with table lookup compiled into 17 instructions. Our measured performance for the $s = 1$ case was 2.0 Mflops for long vectors.

6.1 Local address generation

We have seven parameters for a one-dimensional array: two alignment parameters a and b, two layout parameters p and k, and three section parameters ℓ, h, and s. This is too large a space over which to present results. We now explain how we reduce the number of variables.

- **Alignment stride a:** For any constant c, the memory layout for parameters ca and ck is exactly the same as that for a and k. Thus we experiment only with $a = 1$; the effect of changing a can be simulated by changing k instead.
- **Alignment offset b:** This is irrelevant for large sections. For small sections where end effects could be important, we observed that changes in b affected results by less than 5%. We therefore take $b = 0$.
- **Section lower bound ℓ:** Again, this is irrelevant for large sections and has negligible effect even for small sections. We therefore take $\ell = 0$.
- **Section upper bound h:** This affects the number of elements in the DAXPY, which in turn affects the tradeoff between loop startup and iteration time in a single processor. We vary h along with s, keeping h/s fixed, so that all our experiments do the same amount of work regardless of stride.
- **Section stride s:** This is the x-axis of our plots, as one of the two independent variables.
- **Number of processors p:** We run our experiments with a fixed number of processors. Varying the number of processors has the effect of scaling the plots.
- **Block size k:** This varies from plot to plot, as the second of the two independent variables.

We use the execution time per element of the DAXPY loop as our measure of performance. For a given set of parameters, we compute the tables for each processor and time the execution of the distributed loop. Let τ_m be the time taken by processor m to execute the n_m iterations it receives. Then the execution time per element is

$$t_e = \max_m \frac{\tau_m}{n_m}.$$

This factors out the effect of load imbalance.

We plot $2/t_e$ (the megaflops per second per processor) against stride s for various block sizes k. The plots are shown in Figure 5. The curves are the sum of two effects.

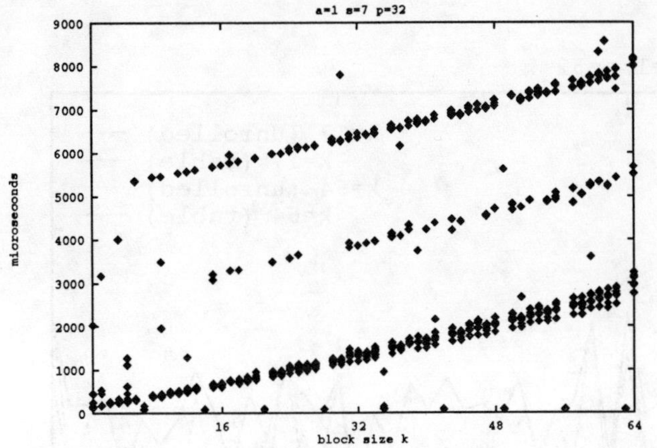

Figure 6: Preprocessing overhead for memory stride computations. The graph corresponds to an alignment stride of 1. The multiple points for each block size show the processing times for each of 32 processors.

1. **Baseline:** The lower envelope is a smooth, relatively flat function of s. The value of the envelope is approximately the asymptotic performance for the single-processor DAXPY.

2. **Jiggles:** The plot jiggles up and down some, presumably due to cache stride effects [1].

Although the general loop has almost twice as many instructions as the unit-stride loop, the difference in performance is much less. This is because the execution time is dominated by the floating-point operations and references to operands in memory. The references to the $\Delta\mathcal{M}$ array usually hit in cache, and the additional loop control instructions probably execute in overlapped fashion.

The preprocessing time required to compute the $\Delta\mathcal{M}$ tables is shown in Figure 6, where we plot the running time of Algorithm 1 against block size k. The running time is approximately $O(k)$, with certain special cases being handled much faster. Experimental observation confirmed that the running times for Algorithm 2 were no more than twice those of Algorithm 1.

If the $\Delta\mathcal{M}$ sequence is known at compile time, unrolling the loop bodies avoids the indirection into the $\Delta\mathcal{M}$ array. Figure 7 shows that the benefits of this are mixed. While loop unrolling removes the indirection, it also increases the size of the loop body; thus the benefits of a simpler loop body may be undone by misses in the instruction cache caused by the larger loop body. This is a factor for larger block sizes, since the amount of unrolling may be as large as k. We recommend unrolling only if the $\Delta\mathcal{M}$ sequences are short, or can be compacted, *e.g.*, by run-length encoding.

6.2 Communication set generation

For the communication set generation algorithms, we measured the time required to generate the FSM tables and the time required to marshal the array elements into messages. We did not measure the actual communication time, since that varies widely among machines. The results are presented in Table 2.

(a)

k	s	ℓ	FSM gen. time (μs)	Run time/elt (μs)
1	3	10	360	3.3
17	3	10	1831	3.1
17	3	40	1870	3.1
64	3	10	6632	3.2
64	3	100	6508	3.2
blk	3	10	408	3.2

(b)

k	s_1	s_2	FSM gen. time (μs)	Run time/elt (μs)
1	3	5	360	5.3
17	3	5	1891	14.3
64	3	5	6542	5.4
blk	3	5	400	11.3

Table 2: Performance of communication set generation algorithms. All numbers are for 32 processors. (a) Shift communication: the shift distance is ℓ. (b) Change of stride: the stride is changed from s_2 to s_1.

7 Conclusions

Our table-driven approach to the generation of local memory addresses and communication sets unifies and subsumes previous solutions to these problems. The tables required in our method are easy to compute, and the runtime overheads due to indirect addressing of data are small. Our data access patterns exploit temporal locality and make effective use of cache. We also support blocking of messages to reduce message startup overheads.

Our prototype implementation has demonstrated our performance claims. An optimized implementation of our techniques should deliver close to maximum performance for general *cyclic*(k) distributions of arrays.

Our algorithms are fully parallel in that each processor of a parallel machine can generate its tables independently. Finding a fully parallel algorithm running in $O(k)$ parallel time or with $O(p+k)$ total work remains an open problem.

Acknowledgments

J. Ramanujam proofread an early draft and suggested the simplifications to Algorithm 1. We also thank the referees for their helpful comments.

References

[1] BAILEY, D. H. Unfavorable strides in cache memory systems. RNR Technical Report RNR-92-015, Numerical Aerodynamic Simulation Systems Division, NASA Ames Research Center, Moffett Field, CA, May 1992.

[2] DONGARRA, J. J. Performance of various computers using standard linear equations software. *Computer Architecture News 20*, 3 (June 1992), 22–44.

[3] DONGARRA, J. J., VAN DE GEIJN, R., AND WALKER, D. W. A look at scalable dense linear algebra libraries. In *Proceedings of the Scalable High Performance Computing Conference* (Williamsburg, VA, Apr. 1992), IEEE Computer Society Press, pp. 372–379. Also available as technical report ORNL/TM-12126 from Oak Ridge National Laboratory.

[4] FOX, G. C., HIRANANDANI, S., KENNEDY, K., KOELBEL, C., KREMER, U., TSENG, C.-W., AND WU, M.-Y. Fortran D language specification. Tech. Rep. Rice COMP TR90-141, Department of Computer Science, Rice University, Houston, TX, Dec. 1990.

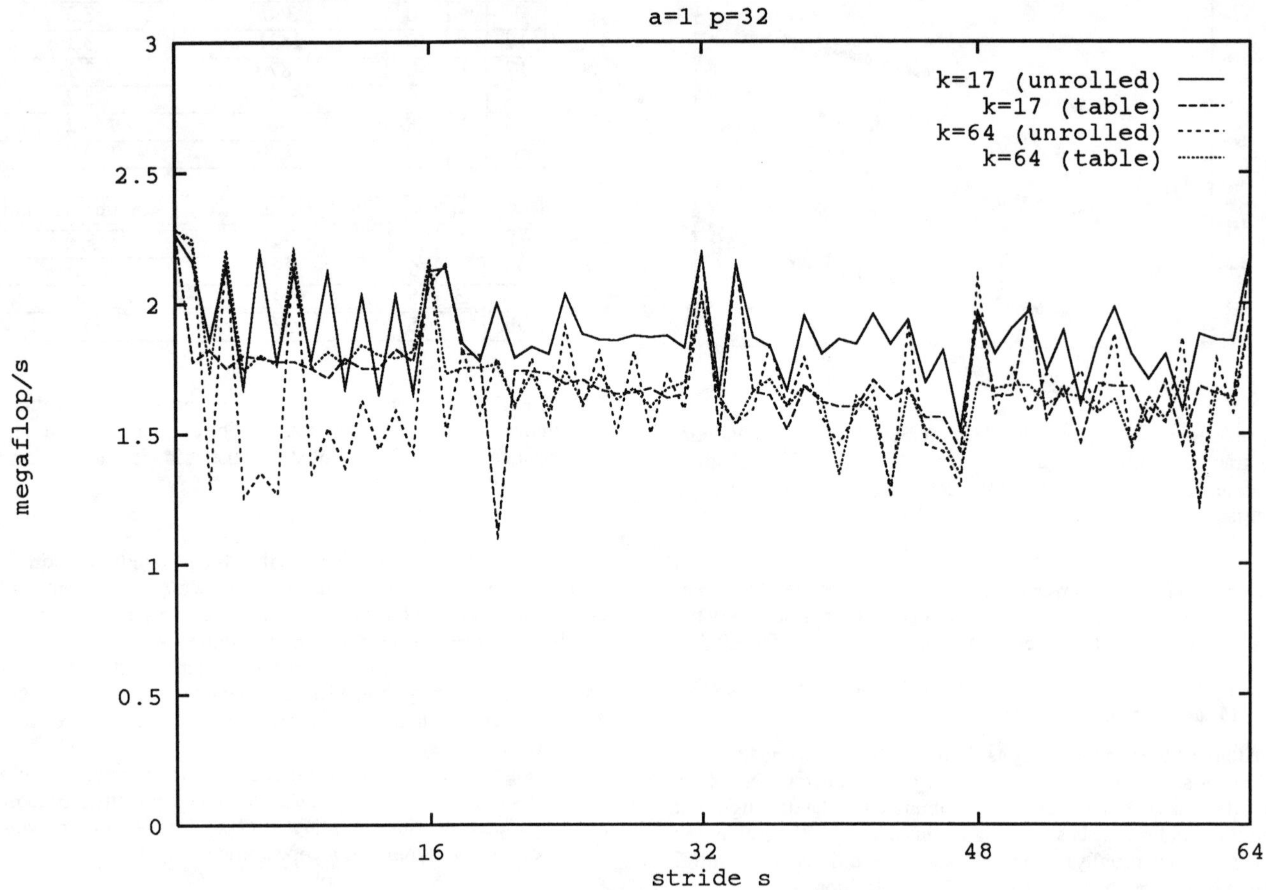

Figure 7: Effect of loop unrolling on performance of DAXPY for various block sizes k.

[5] HIGH PERFORMANCE FORTRAN FORUM. High Performance Fortran language specification version 0.4. Draft, Nov. 1992. Also available as technical report CRPC-TR 92225, Center for Research on Parallel Computation, Rice University.

[6] KNUTH, D. E. *Seminumerical Algorithms*, second ed., vol. 2 of *The Art of Computer Programming*. Addison-Wesley Publishing Company, Reading, MA, 1981.

[7] KOELBEL, C. Compile-time generation of regular communication patterns. In *Proceedings of Supercomputing'91* (Albuquerque, NM, Nov. 1991), pp. 101–110.

[8] KOELBEL, C., AND MEHROTRA, P. Compiling global namespace parallel loops for distributed execution. *IEEE Transactions on Parallel and Distributed Systems* 2, 4 (Oct. 1991), 440–451.

[9] MACDONALD, T., PASE, D., AND MELTZER, A. Addressing in Cray Research's MPP Fortran. In *Proceedings of the Third Workshop on Compilers for Parallel Computers* (Vienna, Austria, July 1992), Austrian Center for Parallel Computation, pp. 161–172.

[10] MIRCHANDANEY, R., SALTZ, J. H., SMITH, R. M., CROWLEY, K., AND NICOL, D. M. Principles of runtime support for parallel processors. In *Third International Conference on Supercomputing* (July 1988), ACM Press, pp. 140–152.

Data Flow Equations for Explicitly Parallel Programs

Dirk Grunwald and Harini Srinivasan
grunwald@cs.colorado.edu harini@cs.colorado.edu
Department of Computer Science
University of Colorado at Boulder
Campus Box 430
Boulder, CO - 80309

Abstract

We present a solution to the reaching definitions problem for programs with explicit *lexically specified* parallel constructs, such as cobegin/coend or parallel_sections, both with and without explicit synchronization operations, such as Post, Wait or Advance. The reaching definitions information for sequential programs is used to solve many standard optimization problems. In parallel programs, this information can also be used to explicitly direct communication and data ownership. Although work has been done on analyzing parallel programs to detect data races, little work has been done on optimizing such programs.

We show how the memory consistency model specified by an explicitly parallel programming language can influence the complexity of the reaching definitions problem. By selecting the "weakest" memory consistency semantics, we can efficiently solve the reaching definitions problem for correct programs.

1 Introduction

In this paper, we describe a *data flow framework* [1] for computing reaching definition information in parallel programs. The reaching definitions are the set of definitions reaching each use of a variable in a program. This information is used in optimizations such as constant propagation, induction variable analysis, common subexpression elimination, dead code elimination etc. on sequential programs.

Although we use the parallel extensions to FORTRAN specified by the Parallel Computing Forum [21], our analysis is applicable to any program using *lexical parallelism*, such as cobegin and coend, where sections of the parallel construct are *data independent* except when appropriate synchronization mechanism is used. The performance of parallel programs on existing and future high performance architectures depends on the ability to perform aggressive code optimizations. Most existing compilers for parallel programs do not perform optimizations across parallel constructs. Instead, they restrict optimizations to specific sequential sections of code in the parallel program [6].

4th ACM PPOPP,5/93/CA,USA


```
L = 1
do I = 1, N
   Parallel Section
   Section A
       Q = h(I)
       L = L + 1
       do J = 1, N
           X = f(J, L * 4 )
           Advance(EV1, J)
           Wait(EV2, K)
         end do
   Section B
       do K = 1, N
           Y[K] = g(I,K)
           Wait(EV1, K)
           Z[K] = Y[K] + X + Q
           Advance(EV2, K)
       end do
   End Parallel Section
end do
```

Figure 1: Example Parallel Program.

Though extensive work has been done on analyzing parallel programs for potential *races* [2, 4, 8, 10, 20], little work has been done on optimizing those programs. Midkiff and Padua [17] point out the difficulties in optimizing explicitly parallel programs. Earlier papers have considered the problem of optimizing parallel programs without event synchronization [24, 25, 26]. This paper includes explicit synchronization and uses a dataflow framework. Chow and Harrison [5] present a general framework for analyzing parallel programs but consider only cobegin/coend parallelism without explicit synchronization. Long and Clarke [16] give a data flow framework for Ada programs with task parallelism and rendezvous synchronization, but do not handle shared variables. They use interprocedural analysis methods between tasks that synchronize and assume the rendezvous graph is always acyclic. Our work addresses cyclic synchronization structures.

Consider the parallel program in Figure 1. It's clear that 'L' is a linear induction variable since it is incremented in Section A, and both Section A and B always execute in each iteration of the outer loop. This implies that the expression L * 4 can be strength reduced and hoisted from the inner loop. Each of these optimizations require reaching definition information across the `parallel_sections` construct.

Furthermore, synchronization is used to coordinate passing the value of 'X' between sections A and B. If the use in B is the only use of the definition in A, then, on some architectures, we may be able to pass the value between the processors executing sections A and B without globally updating memory. Likewise, section A does not use the value of 'Q' after it is computed, but it is used by section B. On some architectures, we may be able to *post-store* the update immediately, reducing cache miss latency, or transfer ownership by some other method.

In section 2, we describe data flow analysis and how the reaching definition information is computed in sequential programs. Section 3 describes the the semantics of the parallel constructs considered in this paper, and §4 describes the data structures we use to represent such constructs. Section 5 describes equations for computing reaching definition information to handle parallel constructs, and in §6 we extend these equations to handle synchronization. We conclude with a detailed example in §7.

2 Global Data Flow Analysis

The problem of global data flow analysis can be explained as follows [19]: given the control flow structure, we must discern the nature of the data flow (which definitions of program quantities can affect which uses) within the program. Data flow problems are often posed as a system of equations based on the Control Flow Graph of the program. A Control Flow Graph, CFG, of a program is a directed graph, $\langle N, E, N_0 \rangle$, where N is the set of nodes representing basic blocks in the program, E is the set of edges representing flow of control in the program and N_0 is the unique entry node. The set of edges define predecessor and successor relations on the nodes. A node P is a predecessor of node Q ($P \in \text{pred}(Q)$) if there is an edge in the CFG from P to Q; Q is a successor of P.

In a sequential program, a definition of a variable 'v' *reaches* a point p in the program if there is a definition-free path in the CFG from that definition to p[1]. The *reaching definitions* problem determines the definitions that can reach a given point in a program. We uniquely number each definition and find $In(n)$, the set of definitions that reach the beginning of node n.

A definition d for a variable 'v' in node n ('v_n') is *downward-exposed* if no other definition of 'v' occurs in node n. A downward-exposed definition reaches node m if there is a path from n to m on which no other definition of 'v' occurs. For node n, $Gen(n)$ is the set of downward-exposed definitions and $Kill(n)$ is the set of definitions for 'v' in nodes other than n. $Gen(n)$ and $Kill(n)$ are used to to compute $In(n)$ for a CFG using a dataflow framework:

$$Out(n) = In(n) - Kill(n) \cup Gen(n)$$
$$In(n) = \bigcup_{p \in \text{pred}(n)} Out(p).$$

$Out(n)$ is the set of definitions that reaches the *end* of node n. We are interested in the meet-over-paths (MOP) solution to these equations, and typically solve them iteratively until a fixpoint is reached. This particular set of equations and the iterative algorithm form a monotone dataflow system.

```
(0)     event( ev )
(0)     x = 2
(0)     y = 5
(1)     loop
(2)         Parallel Sections
(3)         Section A
(3)             if (condition) then
(4)                 x = 7; Advance(ev)
                else
(5)                 x = 8; Advance(ev)
(6)             endif
(6)             z = y * 7
(7)         Section B
(7)             Parallel Sections
(8)             Section B1
(8)                 Wait( ev ); x = x * 32
(9)             Section B2
(9)                 z = y * 54
(10)            End Parallel Sections
(11)        End Parallel Sections
(12)        y = x * z
(13)    endloop
```

Figure 2: Parallel Program with `parallel_sections` and event synchronization

3 Parallel Constructs

We are concerned with determining the reaching definitions in a language with `cobegin/coend` or the `parallel_sections` construct of PCF FORTRAN [21]; later papers address parallel loops. In the remainder of this paper, we will use the notation and descriptions of the PCF Fortran parallelism constructs, because it a well documented standard, provides labeled sections and supports synchronization. The `parallel_sections` construct specifies parallel execution of explicitly identified sections of code. Each section of a `parallel_section` is a separate thread. All threads in a `parallel_section` construct must be data independent except where an appropriate synchronization mechanism is used to exchange data values. The `parallel_sections` construct can also be nested, appear in the body of a loop and so on. Threads can be explicitly synchronized using *wait clauses* or *event variables*. A section can wait for other labeled sections to complete execution. The `Post`, `Advance` and `Wait` operations are used to explicitly synchronize concurrent threads. Our analysis considers `Post` and `Advance` to be equivalent, because both can cause a waiting thread to continue execution. For expository simplicity, we use `Post` to refer to either construct.

An example parallel program with `parallel_sections` and event synchronization is shown in Figure 2. Sections `A` and `B` execute in parallel. Section `B` contains a nested `parallel_-sections` construct. Sections `B1` and `B2` may also execute in parallel. The event '`ev`' is posted in one of the branches of the if-construct, depending on the value of '`condition`'. Section `B1` can not proceed until at least one `post` occurs. We refer to this example in §7 to show the interaction of loops and synchronization variables. Note that the figure contains a `parallel_sections` inside a *sequential* loop; analysis of parallel loops is a topic of future papers.

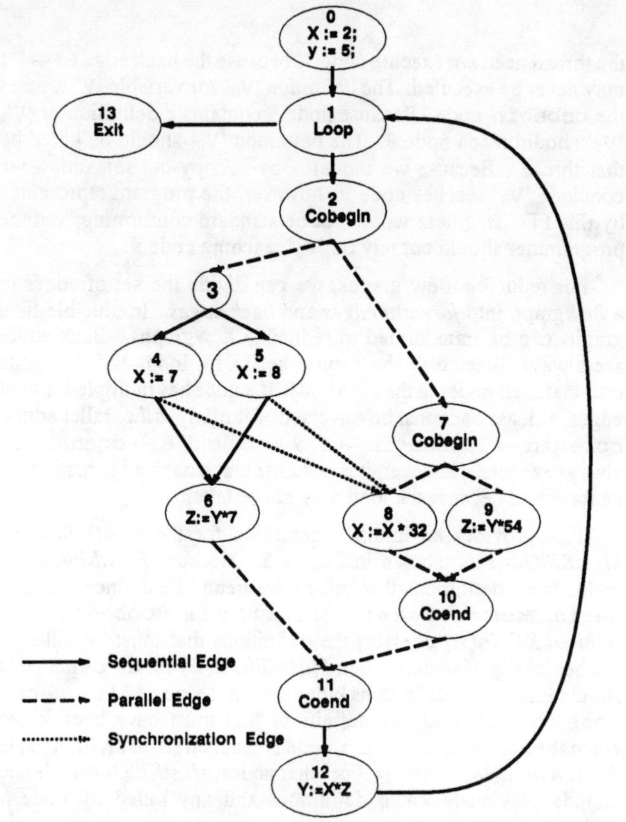

Figure 3: Parallel Flow Graph for the Example Parallel Program in Figure 2

4 Parallel Flow Graph

We use a *Parallel Flow Graph* (PFG)[24], analogous to the Control Flow Graph, to represent parallel programs. A PFG is similar to a Synchronized Control Flow Graph [4] or Program Execution Graph [2]. A PFG is a directed graph $\langle N, E, N_0 \rangle$ where N is the set of nodes representing extended basic blocks in the program, E is the set of edges representing either sequential control flow, parallel control flow or synchronization and N_0 is the unique entry point into the program. An *extended basic block* is a basic block with at most one `Wait` statement at the start of the basic block and at most one `Post` or branch statement at the end. A `cobegin` or `parallel_sections` statement is denoted by a `cobegin` node, and a `coend` or `end_parallel_sections` statement is denoted by a `coend` node. `cobegin` and `coend` nodes contain no definitions or statements.

A *sequential control flow edge* represents sequential flow of control within sequential parts of the program. A *parallel control flow edge* represents parallel control flow. Successors of `cobegin` and predecessors of `coend` are connected via parallel control flow edges. Each successor of a `cobegin` node must have the `cobegin` as a single, unique predecessor; empty basic blocks can be inserted if necessary. Finally, a *synchronization edge* is an edge from a `Post` statement to a corresponding `Wait` statement. Wait clauses are modeled using explicit `Post` and `Wait` operations. The PFG for the parallel program in Figure 2 is shown in Figure 3. Nodes (2) and (7) are `cobegin` nodes and nodes (11) and (10) are the respective `coend` nodes. Sequential, parallel and synchronization edges are identified in this figure.

The PCF FORTRAN standard states that each thread should be data independent; threads exchange values using explicit synchronization operations. The standard states "the appropriate shared variables are made consistent" at a synchronization point, and all "standard conforming" programs must follow these restrictions. Statically detecting conformance is undecidable because some definitions may be the result of conditional execution.

Compiler dataflow analysis can not omit a definition that can possibly reach a synchronization point to avoid incorrect optimizations. The definition of memory consistency in PCF FORTRAN permits a range of memory consistency models, such as strong, program or weak consistency models [9, 15]. Increasingly, proposed parallel architectures rely on weak memory consistency models to improve system performance. In a system with weak memory consistency, updates to memory may occur out of order and explicit memory barrier instructions are needed to insure that all reads or writes have completed. On an architecture with weak memory consistency, synchronization operations imply that the processors executing different threads have a common, or consistent, view of memory when a synchronization completes. This simplifies the task of dataflow analysis. If we assume strong memory consistency, the compiler needs to consider all possible interactions between parallel threads. This is difficult for all but the most simple programs [18, 5].

We believe it is unlikely that explicitly parallel languages will require strongly consistent memory, because it is difficult to implement strongly consistent memory on a scalable architecture. Weaker memory semantics provide more opportunity for optimizations because each thread is free to copy variables to registers, disregarding the actions of other threads except at synchronization points. Previous research on dataflow analysis of parallel programs have considered copy-in/copy-out memory semantics[25]. Any "standard conforming" PCF FORTRAN program should work correctly on systems using strong, weak or copy-in/copy-out memory semantics; thus, a compiler may assume any of these memory semantics.

The memory semantics modeled by the compiler directly determines the complexity of the dataflow equations. Consider Figure 3. If the compiler assumes copy-in/copy-out memory semantics, synchronization implies that only certain threads explicitly exchange values. The programmer has not synchronized the action of node 8 with those of 4,5 and 6 – node 8 *may* execute before or after these nodes. Thus, although definitions in nodes 4 and 5 *may* reach node 8, we do not consider definitions in node 8 to reach nodes 4,5 or 6.

If the compiler assumes weakly consistent memory semantics, each thread must indicate where memory barriers are needed. Thus, nodes 4, 5 and 8 would contain explicit "memory barrier" operations. In this model, the compiler must assume that definitions in node 8 may be visible in node 6, and definitions in 3, 4 and 5 may be visible in node 8. To compute reaching definitions for a strongly consistent memory model, we need to assume that definitions in each node may be visible to uses that may execute concurrently, leading to a significantly more complicated problem.

The language standard implies that a "standard conforming" program must be correct using *any* of these memory semantics. Modeling strong or weak memory semantics is computationally more difficult than modeling copy-in/copy-out semantics, but may be more accurate when analyzing incorrect programs. In this paper, we are only interested in optimizing correct, standard conforming programs. Threads in programs not using explicit synchronization have fewer interactions than threads in programs using ex-

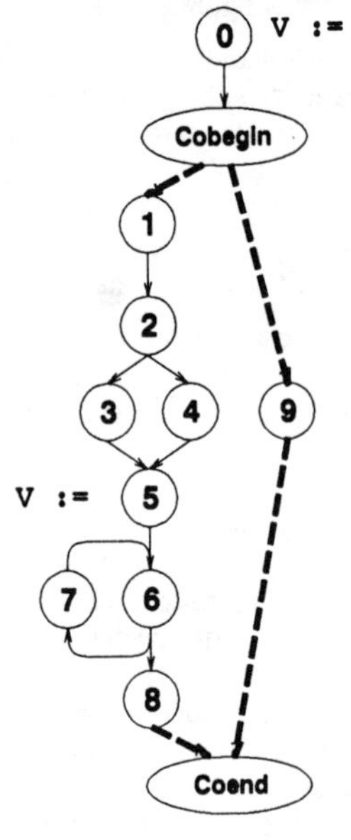

Figure 4: Example for Parallel Sections

plicit synchronization. Our analysis for programs without explicit synchronization correctly models both weak and copy-in/copy-out memory semantics, while our analysis for explicit synchronization only models copy-in/copy-out memory semantics.

5 Parallelism Without Explicit Synchronization

We first describe dataflow equations to analyze `parallel_sections` construct without synchronization operations, and then provide additional equations that model synchronization. Reaching definitions outside of a `parallel_sections` construct are computed using the standard sequential dataflow equations. Each basic block, or node, lexically enclosed in a `parallel_section` belongs to a specific *thread.* We define a function *InFork*(n) that identifies the lexically enclosing `cobegin` node for node n. In Figure 4, there are two parallel threads. One contains nodes 1 through 8 and the other contains only node 9. For each node n, excluding the `cobegin` node and node 0, *InFork*(n) = `cobegin`.

Intuitively, any definition for a variable 'v' that reaches a `cobegin` node should reach a lexically enclosed node n unless 'v' is redefined by nodes executed before n. For each node n in a thread, we compute reaching definitions that arise from local definitions in the current thread, and then add definitions from the `cobegin` node that have not been killed by redefinitions. We use the *LocalIn* and *LocalOut* sets to record the local definitions, and the *MustKillIn* and *MustKillOut* sets to record the definitions redefined by a thread. We will now describe the final dataflow equations, shown in Figure 5, in more detail.

Computing `MustKill`**:** The sets *MustKillIn* & *MustKillOut* are sets of definitions that *must have been killed* since the lexically enclosing `cobegin`. The set *MustKillIn*(n) includes all definitions that must have been killed by the beginning of node n, and *MustKillOut*(n) includes all definitions killed by the end of node n.

In Figure 4, the left thread *must* execute nodes 1, 2, 5 6 and 8 and one of 3 or 4 for control to reach node 8. However, the thread need *not* execute node 7, because the back edge 6 $\rightarrow$ 7 may never be executed. The definition 'V_0' for variable 'V' reaches the `cobegin` node. Because node 5 contains a definition of 'V', 'V_5' should reach node 8. The definition 'V_0' should be killed by that thread. Because we model copy-in/copy-out semantics, we conclude 'V_0' reaches node 9; however, the program represented by this PFG fragment would not be standard conforming, and the programmer should not rely on 'V_0' reaching node 9.

For reducible flow graphs, we can divide the set of edges in a flowgraph into *forward edges* and *back edges.* Irreducible flow graphs can be transformed to reducible flowgraphs. Back edges are always directed to the natural head of a loop, and that node dominates all nodes in the loop body. If a node has multiple forward edges, at least one must be traversed. Similarly, *all* parallel edges, `cobegin` $\rightarrow$ 1, `cobegin` $\rightarrow$ 9, 9 $\rightarrow$ `coend`, 8 $\rightarrow$ `coend`, must always execute. However, it is possible that a back edge may never be traversed because the loop may not be taken.

This provides an intuitive definition for the *MustKillIn* and *MustKillOut* sets, shown in Figure 5. Because *MustKillOut*(n) includes all definitions that must have been killed since the `cobegin`, *MustKillOut*(n) must be empty for a `cobegin` node. If *MustKillIn*(n) contains the definitions that must be killed at the beginning of node n, then *MustKillOut*(n) for a `coend` node should include all definitions killed within the `parallel_sections` construct *and* any definitions that must have been killed when the matching `cobegin` node is reached (*MustKillIn*(n) $\cup$ *MustKillIn*(*InFork*(n))). For other nodes, *MustKillOut*(n) should include previously killed definitions and any killed by node n (*Kill*(n)).

To compute *MustKillIn*(n), we divide the predecessors of node n into sets of predecessor nodes that reach via parallel edges ($Pred_p(n)$), and those that reach by sequential edges ($Pred_s(n)$). We further divide $Pred_s(n)$ into two sets containing predecessors reached by a forward sequential edge ($Pred_f(n)$) and predecessors reached by a sequential back edge ($Pred_b(n)$). We know that every parallel edge is executed; any definition killed by $Pred_p(n)$ will have been killed by the time we reach node n, $\bigcup_{p \in Pred_p} MustKillOut(p)$. We also know that not more than *one* sequential forward edge is traversed at the same time, and a definition killed by a node in $Pred_f(n)$ will only be killed if it is killed in *each* node in $Pred_f(n)$, $\bigcap_{p \in Pred_f} MustKillOut(p)$. This gives the definitions in equation (2) of Figure 5. Because the *MustKillIn* and *MustKillOut* sets ignore back edges, there are no cycles in the equations and we can compute *MustKillIn* and *MustKillOut* for each thread by elimination rather than iteration.

Computing ***LocalIn*** **and** ***LocalOut*****:** We compute two sets of local reaching definitions, *LocalIn* & *LocalOut*. These sets are analogous to the standard *In* and *Out* sets but only contain reaching definitions defined since the most recent `cobegin` node. The *LocalOut* set for `cobegin` nodes is empty, because a `cobegin` node contains no definitions. For other nodes, we use the standard computation for *Out* sets. When computing *LocalIn*, definitions may reach via parallel *or* sequential edges, but all such edges are treated similarly because any predecessor may execute. To avoid incorrect optimizations, a compiler must be conservative and not omit any possible reaching definitions. The only complication is for `coend` nodes, where we must propagate any definitions that reached the corresponding `cobegin` node but were not killed by any of the threads.

$$MustKillOut(n) = \begin{cases} \emptyset & \text{(cobegin)} \\ MustKillIn(n) \cup MustKillIn(InFork(n)) & \text{(coend)} \\ MustKillIn(n) \cup Kill(n) & \text{(otherwise)} \end{cases} \quad (1)$$

$$MustKillIn(n) = \bigcup_{p \in Pred_p} MustKillOut(p) \cup \bigcap_{p \in Pred_f} MustKillOut(p) \quad (2)$$

$$LocalOut(n) = \begin{cases} \emptyset & \text{(cobegin)} \\ LocalIn(n) - Kill(n) \cup Gen(n) & \text{(otherwise)} \end{cases} \quad (3)$$

$$LocalIn(n) = \bigcup_{p \in pred(n)} LocalOut(p) \cup \begin{cases} LocalIn(InFork(n)) - MustKillIn(n)) & \text{(coend)} \\ \emptyset & \text{(otherwise)} \end{cases} \quad (4)$$

$$Out(n) = LocalOut(n) \cup \left(Out(InFork(n)) - MustKillOut(n)\right) \quad (5)$$

$$In(n) = LocalIn(n) \cup \left(In(InFork(n)) - MustKillIn(n)\right) \quad (6)$$

Figure 5: Dataflow Sets for Lexical Parallelism

Computing *In* and *Out*: The dataflow equations reflect the lexical structure of the parallelism. The scope of modified values is lexically constrained and threads can not interact except at `cobegin` and `coend` nodes. However, `parallel_sections` construct can be nested, complicating equations (1) and (4) of Figure 5 for `coend` nodes. For each node n, we now have the sets of new definitions that may reach n and the set of all definitions that must have been killed since the last lexically enclosing `cobegin`. As stated earlier, the set of reachable definitions for nodes in a parallel construct are either those that arise within the thread *or* those that reach the lexically enclosing `cobegin` that have not been killed by a more recent definition. This leads to the definitions in equations (6) and (5) of Figure 5.

Because the *MustKillIn* and *MustKillOut* sets do not need to be solved by iteration, the complexity of these dataflow equations is similar to the traditional equations for reaching definitions.

An alternative method for analyzing parallel programs would be to *linearize* them[11, 12, 23], i.e. convert them to sequential programs, and then use standard dataflow analysis techniques. However, linearization is not a simple process, and our data flow analysis for parallel programs has the same complexity as data flow anlysis for sequential programs. Since we avoid the overhead implied by linearization, our technique is in fact simpler.

6 Synchronization

Modeling synchronization is more difficult than modeling simple `cobegin/coend` parallelism. Threads can interact at numerous points using synchronization. To maintain consistency for data independent threads, the actions of individual threads must be communicated to other threads. With simple `cobegin/coend` parallelism, such interaction can only occur at `coend` nodes. Figure 6 illustrates some of the problems encountered with a PFG representing a single `parallel_sections` construct. There are two threads ($2 \rightarrow 3 \rightarrow 4$ and $5 \rightarrow 6 \rightarrow 7 \rightarrow 8$). There are synchronization edges from $1 \rightarrow 3$, $2 \rightarrow 6$, $3 \rightarrow 8$ and $8 \rightarrow 4$ and four definitions for variable 'X' ('X_1', 'X_2', 'X_4' and 'X_7').

The semantics for the synchronization edge $1 \rightarrow 3$ is fundamentally different than that for $2 \rightarrow 6$. There is no need to insure that memory is made consistent, because nodes 1 and 3 can never execute concurrently. This typically indicates that the `Post` is sim-

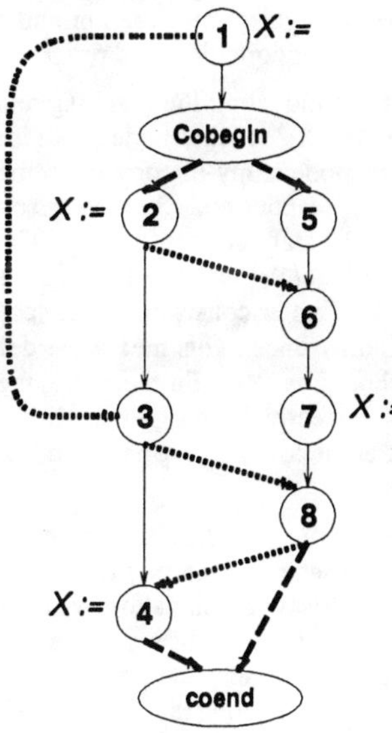

Figure 6: Problems Encountered in Synchronization

$$Synch(n) = \bigcap_{p \in Pred_{sy}} Out(p) \cup \bigcup_{p \in Pred_p} Synch(p) \cup \bigcap_{p \in Pred_s} Synch(p) \cup \bigcup_{p \in (Pred_{sy} \cap Pres(n))} Out(p) \quad (7)$$

$$AKillOut(n) = \begin{cases} AKillIn(n) \cap Synch(n) & \text{(cobegin)} \\ AKillIn(n) \cup (AKillIn(InFork(n)) - Out(n)) & \text{(coend)} \\ (AKillIn(n) \cup Kill_s(n) \cup (Kill_p(n) \cap Synch(n))) - Gen(n) & \text{(otherwise)} \end{cases} \quad (8)$$

$$AKillIn(n) = \bigcup_{p \in Pred_p(n)} AKillOut(p) \cup \bigcap_{p \in Pred_s(n)} AKillOut(p) \cup \bigcap_{p \in Pred_{sy}(n)} AKillOut(p) \quad (9)$$

$$Out(n) = (In(n) - Kill(n)) \cup Gen(n) \quad (10)$$

$$In(n) = \bigcup_{p \in pred(n)} Out(p) - AKillIn(n) \quad (11)$$

Figure 7: Extensions to handle synchronization constructs

ply initializing an event variable. By comparison, nodes 2 and 6 are in different threads, and the $2 \rightarrow 6$ edge implies synchronization and consistency operations. We disregard the effect of event initialization edges such as $1 \rightarrow 3$ to increase the accuracy of reaching definitions. Simple analysis can remove most such edges.[1] If we include these edges in our analysis, the reaching definitions is still correct, but not as accurate. For example, if we did not ignore the $1 \rightarrow 3$ edge, we would conclude that 'X_1' may reach node 3. We believe a concurrent programming language should provide separate mechanisms to distinguish initialization and synchronization, to avoid this ambiguity for compilers and programmers.

Dataflow equations modeling the reaching definitions for Figure 6 must indicate that 'X_2' reaches node 6, but is then superceded by 'X_7'. Because we model copy-in/copy-out semantics, we would also conclude that 'X_2' reaches node 3, although programs depending on this would not be standard conforming. The equations must also avoid indicating that 'X_2' reaches node 8 via the $3 \rightarrow 8$ edge. A variable should be "made consistent" (i.e. copied, in a copy-in/copy-out model) only once. This means the definition reaching the `coend` node should be 'X_4'. Furthermore, the dataflow equations need to work correctly for programs where synchronization occurs between different concurrent `parallel_sections` constructs, as in Figure 2.

Our previous equations relied on the precedence relations implied by the lexical structure of the `parallel_sections` construct. To model arbitrary synchronization, we use the *accumulated kill sets*, *AKillIn* and *AKillOut*. These sets are a refinement of the *MustKillIn* and *MustKillOut* sets, and are used to accumulate definitions that are *always* killed along distinct parallel branches within a `parallel_sections` construct. The *MustKillIn* and *MustKillOut* sets include definitions that must have been killed since the lexically enclosing `cobegin`. However, programs with explicit synchronization can propogate values between threads at points other than `cobegin` or `coend` nodes. The *AKillIn* and *AKillOut* sets *are* the *MustKillIn* and *MustKillOut* sets with the addition of definitions of variables that have been propogated via synchronization edges and later killed.

[1] We can disregard the edge if the posting node p and the waiting node w are *not* in different branches of some common `parallel_sections` construct, i.e. p and w can not execute concurrently.

Our previous equations also did not account for definitions reaching via synchronization edges. We use the *Synch* set to propagate definitions that *must reach* from posting nodes to waiting nodes. The *Synch* set is used to compute $AKillIn(n)$ and $AKillOut(n)$, and programs may have "synchronization cycles." Thus, because *Synch* can not be computed by elimination, *AKillIn* and *AKillOut* can not be computed by elimination, unlike *MustKillIn* and *MustKillOut*. This means it is computationaly more difficult to compute reaching definitions information for parallel programs if they use explicit synchronization.

Our eventual goal is to define $AKillOut(n)$, which is used to define the actual $In(n)$ and $Out(n)$ sets for each node n as given in equations (11) and (10) of figure 7. Figure 7 summarizes the dataflow equations we introduce. We discuss each equation in turn, motivating each term in the equations.

Computing ***Synch*****:** The set $Pred_{sy}(n)$ denotes all "interesting" nodes that may `Post` to a `Wait` node. Some post statements simply initialize event variables, and are not included in $Pred_{sy}$. For the graph in Figure 6, $Pred_{sy}(6) = \{2\}$, $Pred_{sy}(8) = \{3\}$ and $Pred_{sy}(4) = \{8\}$; however, $1 \notin Pred_{sy}(3)$. The set *Synch* includes definitions that *must* reach via nodes in $Pred_{sy}$. A thread waiting at node n can proceed if *any* matching post in $Pred_{sy}(n)$ is executed. Thus, only definitions that reach each node in $Pred_{sy}(n)$ will be guaranteed to reach node n. Since `Post` statements must occur at the end of a node and the set $Out(n)$ includes all definitions that reach the end of a node, *Synch* will include $\bigcap_{p \in Pred_{sy}} Out(p)$.

For some programs, the compiler may be able to determine that some nodes in $Pred_{sy}(n)$ will always execute before node n. Callahan *et al* define the *Preserved* (*Pres*(x)) set [3]

> A node y is in *Pres*(x) *iff* for all parallel executions of the program, if x and y are both executed then, y is completed before x is begun.

In general, computing $Pres(n)$ is Co-NP Hard [3], but a conservative approximation can be computed using a dataflow framework. However, simple hueristics using the structure of the PFG can also determine a large, yet conservative subset of $Pres(n)$[14]. If this additional information about the PFG is available, the *Synch* set is updated to include the *Out* sets of those synchronization predecessors that are in *Pres*(n): $\bigcup_{p \in (Pred_{sy}(n) \cap Pres(n))} Out(p)$. If this information is not available, or it is too expensive to compute accurately, this term can be omitted from the computation of *Synch*(n). Its presence simply makes the results more accurate.

The *Synch* set should also include reaching definitions that were previously posted and then propogated via sequential or parallel edges. For example, in Figure 6, node 2 passes 'X_2' to node 6, and node 6 must pass 'X_2' to node 7. Values of *Synch* that reach any parallel predecessor, $\bigcup_{p \in Pred_p} Synch(p)$, and values that reach all sequential predecessors, $\bigcap_{p \in Pred_s} Synch(p)$, will be included in *Synch*(n). Again, we use different meet operators because all parallel edges are traversed, but not all sequential edges are traversed. As shown in equation (7) of Figure 7, each of these terms contributes to the sum of *Synch*(n).

Computing *AKillIn* and *AKillOut*: The dataflow equations for *AKillIn* and *AKillOut*, equations (9) and (8) in Figure 7, are very similar to those for *MustKillIn* and *MustKillOut*, Figure 5(2) and (1), with slight additions. The set *AKillIn*(n) is the set of definitions that must be killed at the beginning of node n. Previously, we divided the predecessors of node n into sets of predecessors reached by parallel edges ($Pred_p(n)$), and those reached by sequential edges ($Pred_s(n)$). Now, we must also include information reached via synchronization edges ($Pred_{sy}(n)$). For a definition to be killed, it must be killed along each incoming synchronization edge or each incoming sequential edge or any of the parallel edges. We use different meet operators because all parallel edges are traversed, but not all sequential or synchronization edges are traversed.

For simple `cobegin`/`coend` parallelism, we can break the set of reaching definitions into a local contribution and a contribution that is "copied in" (i.e. $In(InFork(n)) - MustKillIn(n)$). By comparison, the equations for synchronization can include contributions from different portions of the program. Rather than have *AKillOut* be a monotonically increasing set like *MustKillOut*, it must also exclude generated definitions, *i.e.* $Gen(n)$. The *AKillIn* and *Synch* sets are initialized to the set of all definitions for all nodes in the PFG execept for the entry node, where they are initialized to the empty set, because nothing is killed prior to or reaches the entry node.

Recall that *Gen* and *Kill* are empty for `cobegin` and `coend` nodes. Thus, because *AKillOut*(n) includes all definitions that must have been killed since the `cobegin` node, at a `cobegin` node, it must be the set of definitions that are propagated via synchronization edges from other threads and that are always killed by the time the `cobegin` node executes ($AKillIn(\texttt{cobegin}) \cap Synch(\texttt{cobegin})$) (Figure 7, equation (8)). If *AKillIn*(n) are the definitions that must be killed at the beginning of node n, then *AKillOut* for a `coend` node should include all definitions killed within the `parallel_-sections` structure *and* any definitions we know must have been killed when the matching `cobegin` node was reached, *except* for definitions that reach the `coend` node.

For other nodes, we need to model copy-in/copy-out memory consistency, and must distinguish the actions of the current thread from the actions of other threads. We divide the set $Kill(n)$ into two sets, $Kill_s(n)$ and $Kill_p(n)$, where $Kill(n) = Kill_s(n) \cup Kill_p(n)$. For a each variable 'V' generated by node n, $Kill_p(n)$ contains definitions of 'V' in other concurrent nodes. Since we already know how to compute $Kill(n)$, we can define $Kill_s(n) = Kill(n) - Kill_p(n)$. For example, in Figure 6, $Kill_s(2) = \{'X_1', 'X_4'\}$, and $Kill_p(2) = \{'X_7'\}$. When node n in thread P is executed, a definition for variable 'v' in node n kills all definitions for 'v' that occur in the same thread ($Kill_s(n)$). Definitions in thread P should only kill definitions in a thread Q if those definitions are propogated from Q to P via synchronization ($Kill_p(n) \cap Synch(n)$). Furthermore, any definitions generated by the current node ($Gen(n)$) are obviously no longer killed, and should be removed from *AKillOut*(n).

Computing *In* and *Out*: As stated previously, the definitions for *In* and *Out* are:

$$Out(n) = (In(n) - Kill(n)) \cup Gen(n)$$

$$In(n) = \bigcup_{p \in \text{pred}(n)} Out(p) - AKillIn(n)$$

Essentially a definition reaches the beginning of a block via any edge in the PFG, but is not killed along some set of the edges. The computation of *AKillOut*(n) relies on *Synch*(n), which in turn relies directly or indirectly on the set $Out(p)$. Thus, we can not solve *AKillOut*(n) or *Synch*(n) by elimination, and must compute them iteratively, as is normally done for $In(n)$ and $Out(n)$. We have shown that these and similar equations form a monotone dataflow system [13] with complexity on the same order as dataflow analysis for sequential programs. As with lexical parallelism, it is possible to solve these more general equations for a subset of the Parallel Flow Graph. However, that subset must include all nodes containing `Post` or `Wait` statements as well as nodes contained within a `parallel_sections` construct.

7 An Example with Synchronization

Figure 8 is an enlargement of Figure 3, providing detailed information about the fixpoint values of the dataflow sets for programs with explicit synchronization. Some sets are elided for clarity; we omit the *In* set for nodes with a single predecessor, since they are equal to the *Out* set of the predecessor, as well as empty sets. Some dataflow sets are not needed by certain nodes; for example, nodes outside the `cobegin/coend` construct only use the *In* and *Out* sets.

For the PFG in figure 8, the data flow equations converge to a fixed point in the third iteration. Figure 8 shows the data flow sets at the end of the third iteration. Also note that $Kill_s(8) = \{'X_0'\}$, $Kill_p(8) = \{'X_4', 'X_5'\}$, and $Pres(8) = \{0, 1, 2, 3, 4, 5, 7\}$. This does not imply that e.g., nodes 4 and 5 *always* execute before node 8. Node 4 should be in *Pres*(8) because if *both* node 8 and node 4 execute, then node 4 must execute before node 8; similarly, if node 8 and node 5 execute, then node 5 must preceed node 8.

This solution assumes we have computed *Pres*(8); these nodes will always execute before node 8 if they execute at all. If we could not compute this information, we would assume that definitions 'X_4', 'X_5' and 'X_8' reach node 11. Although this is correct reaching definitions information, it is less precise; however, there is an efficient way to calculate this *Pres*(8) [14]

The definitions, 'X_4' and 'X_5' do not each the `coend` node because 'X_8' always kills 'X_4' and 'X_5'; this information is propogated to other nodes via *AKillOut*(8). *Synch*(8) contains 'X_4' and 'X_5' because they are in *Out*(4) and *Out*(5); these definitions are then killed by 'X_8'. The variable 'Z' is defined in both branches of the outer parallel construct. Both the definitions reach the corresponding `coend` (node 11), indicating a potential anomaly in the program.

The reaching definitions information could be used to optimize use of the variable 'X'. The definitions 'X_4' and 'X_5' are only used

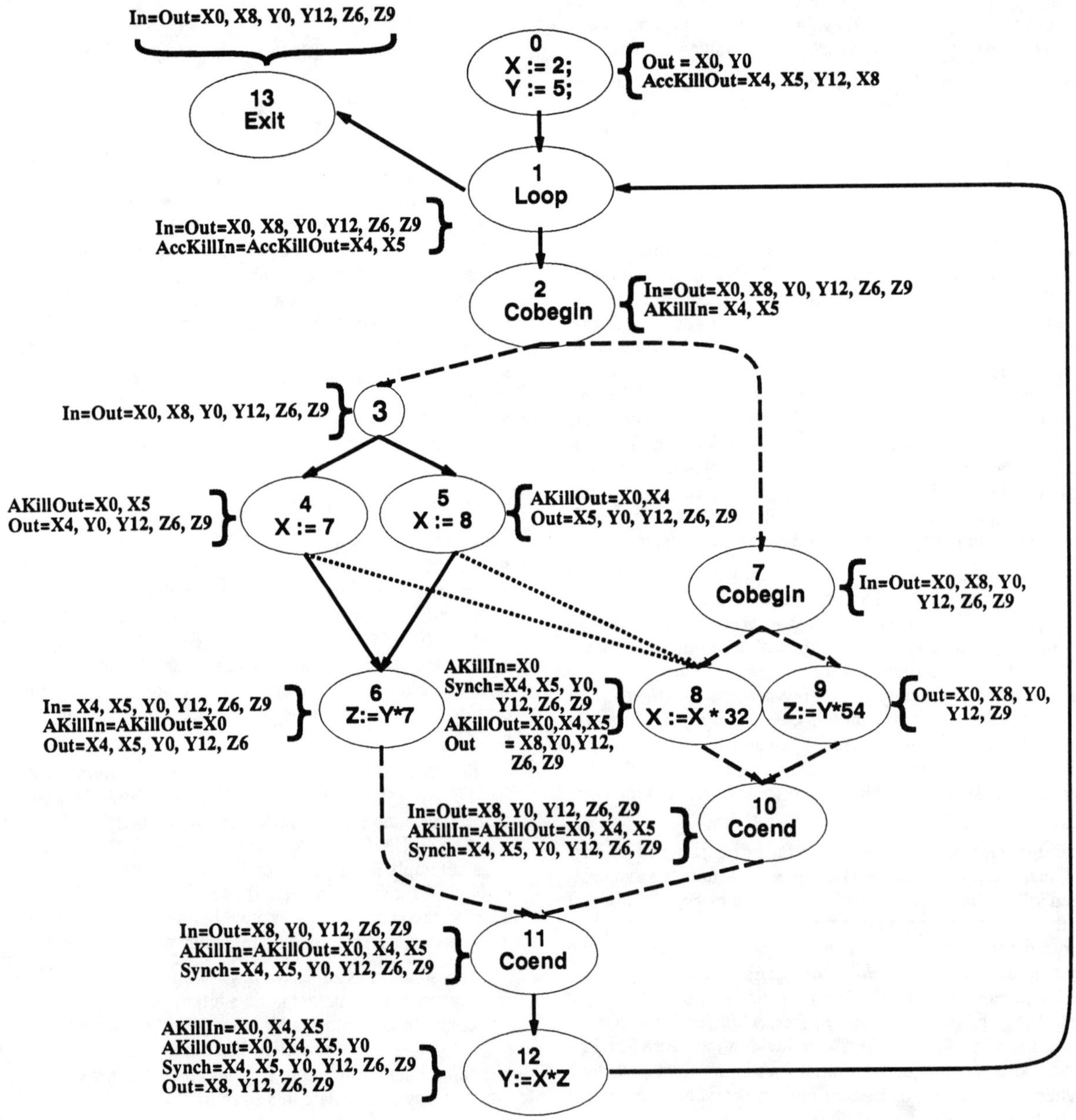

Figure 8: Detailed Example of Reaching Definitions Computation, with Certain Sets Elided For Clarity.

by node 8. In some architectures, ownership of the variable 'X' may be transferred explicitly (e.g., via message passing), avoiding memory coherence overhead. Likewise, 'Y' is never modified, but is used in both branches of the `parallel_sections`; thus, 'Y_0' could be *post-stored* to the processors executing sections A, B1 and B2 to reduce cache miss latencies.

8 Conclusion & Future Work

This work has considered the `parallel_sections` or `cobegin/coend` construct and event synchronization in languages such as PCF FORTRAN. We have presented data flow equations to compute the reaching definition information at any point in an explicitly parallel program, both with and without event synchronization.

We have shown that it is simpler to compute reaching definitions information for programs without synchronization than for programs with explicit synchronization. Our algorithm for reaching definitions in programs with simple `cobegin/coend` parallelism has the same complexity as for computing reaching definitions in sequential programs. When explicit synchronization (`Post/Wait`) is introduced, more sets are used in the dataflow equations, making the solution slightly more complicated. The reaching definitions for programs with explicit synchronization can be more precisely determined if we used the preserved sets notion of Callahan *et al*, but the method does not require this information. We can also use less costly methods to determine a precedence information[14].

We assumed it was only important to optimize correct programs, and found it easier to compute dataflow information when using copy-in/copy-out memory consistency semantics. In future work, we will quantify the complexity introduced by different memory consistency semantics, such as strong or weak consistency. We believe that the complexity of a programming language can be measured to some extent by the difficulty of computing the reaching definitions for programs in that language. Ideally, programmers know what definitions reach particular points in a programs execution. In the future, we propose to extend the data flow equations to handle `Parallel Do`, another parallel construct specified by PCF FORTRAN. We anticipate the use of some technology from data dependence analysis to analyze these constructs. Earlier work [25, 24] has looked at optimizing programs with lexical parallelism using the Static Single Assignment intermediate representation [7], a more efficient dataflow representation. We are applying the experience of our current work to develop efficient SSA algorithms for explicit synchronization.

Acknowledgements This work was supported in part by the National Science Foundation under NSF Grant CCR-9010624 and an IBM Graduate Fellowship. We would like to thank Jeanne Ferrante and Michael Wolfe for their comments and guidance.

References

[1] A. V. Aho, R. Sethi, and J. D. Ullman. *Compilers: Principles, Techniques, and Tools*. Addison-Wesley, Reading, MA, 1986.

[2] Vasanth Balasundaram and Ken Kennedy. Compile-time detection of race conditions in a parallel program. In *Proc. 3rd International Conference on Supercomputing*, pages 175–185, June 1989.

[3] D. Callahan and J. Subhlok. Static analysis of low-level synchronization. In *Proc. of the ACM SIGPLAN and SIGOPS Workshop on Parallel and Distributed Debugging*, pages 100–111, Madison, WA, May 1988.

[4] David Callahan, Ken Kennedy, and Jaspal Subhlok. Analysis of event synchronization in a parallel programming tool. In *Second ACM SIGPLAN Symposium on Principles and Practice of Parallel Programming* [22], pages 21–30.

[5] Jyh-Herng Chow and Williams Ludwell Harrisson. Compile time analysis of parallel programs that share memory. In *Conf. Record 19th Annual ACM Symp. Principles of Programming Languages*, pages 130–141, 1992.

[6] Kendall Square Computers. User orientation. (private communication), August 1992.

[7] Ron Cytron, Jeanne Ferrante, Barry K. Rosen, Mark N. Wegman, and F. Kenneth Zadeck. Efficiently computing Static Single Assignment form and the Control Dependence Graph. *ACM Trans. on Programming Languages and Systems*, 13(4):451–490, October 1991.

[8] Anne Dinning and Edith Schonberg. An empirical comparison of monitoring algorithms for access anomaly detection. In *Second ACM SIGPLAN Symposium on Principles and Practice of Parallel Programming* [22], pages 1–10.

[9] Michel Dubois, Christoph Scheurich, and Faye Briggs. Memory access buffering in multiprocessors. In *Conf. Proc. 13th Annual International Symp. on Computer Architecture*, pages 434–442, June 1986.

[10] Perry Emrath, Sanjoy Ghosh, and David A. Padua. Event synchronization analysis for debugging parallel programs. In *Proc. Supercomputing 89*, pages 580–588, Reno, NV, November 1989. IEEE Computer Society Press.

[11] J. Ferrante and M. E. Mace. On linearizing parallel code. *Conf. Rec. Twelfth ACM Symp. on Principles of Programming Languages*, pages 179–189, January 1985.

[12] Jeanne Ferrante, Mary Mace, and Barbara Simons. Generating sequential code from parallel code. *Proceedings of the ACM 1988 International Conference on Supercomputing*, pages 582–592, July 1988.

[13] Dirk Grunwald and Harini Srinivasan. A Monotone Data Flow System for Analyzing Explicitly Parallel Programs. Technical Report CU-CS-614-92, University of Colorado at Boulder., October 1992.

[14] Dirk Grunwald and Harini Srinivasan. Efficiently Computing Preserved Sets. Technical Report (In Preperation), University of Colorado at Boulder., February 1993.

[15] John Hennessy Kourosh Gharachorloo, Anoop Gupta. Performance evaluation of memory consistency models for shared memory multiprocessors. In *Proceedings of the 4th International Conf. on Architectural Support for Programming Languages and Operating Systems*, pages 245–257, Santa Clara, CA, April 1991.

[16] Douglas Long and Lori A. Clarke. Data Flow Analysis of Concurrent Systems that use the Rendezvous Model of Synchronization. Technical Report COINS 91-31, Univ. Mass. Amherst, July 1991.

[17] Samuel P. Midkiff and David A. Padua. Issues in the optimization of parallel programs. In David Padua, editor, *Proc. 1990 International Conf. on Parallel Processing*, volume II, pages 105–113, St. Charles, IL, August 1990. Penn State Press.

[18] Samuel P. Midkiff, David A. Padua, and Ron Cytron. Compiling programs with user parallelism. In David Gelernter, Alexandru Nicolau, and David A. Padua, editors, *Languages and Compilers for Parallel Computing*, Research Monographs in Parallel and Distributed Computing, pages 402–422. MIT Press, Boston, 1990.

[19] Steven S. Muchnick and Neil D. Jones. *Program Flow Analysis: Theory and Applications*. Prentice Hall, Englewood Cliffs, NJ, 1981.

[20] Robert Netzer. *Race Condition Detection for Debugging of Shared-Memory Parallel Programs*. PhD thesis, University of Wisconsin - Madison, 1991.

[21] Parallel Computing Forum. PCF Parallel FORTRAN Extensions. *FORTRAN Forum*, 10(3), September 1991. (special issue).

[22] *Second ACM SIGPLAN Symposium on Principles and Practice of Parallel Programming*, Seattle, Washington, March 1990. ACM Press.

[23] Barbara Simons, David Alpern, and Jeanne Ferrante. A foundation for sequentializing parallel code. *Proceedings of the ACM 1990 Symposium on Parallel Algorithms and Architecture*, July 1990.

[24] Harini Srinivasan and Dirk Grunwald. An Efficient Construction of Parallel Static Single Assignment Form for Structured Parallel Programs. Technical Report CU-CS-564-91, University of Colorado at Boulder., December 1991.

[25] Harini Srinivasan, James Hook, and Michael Wolfe. Static Single Assignment form for explicitly parallel programs. In *Conf. Record 20th Annual ACM Symp. Principles of Programming Languages*, Charleston, South Carolina, January 1993.

[26] Harini Srinivasan and Michael Wolfe. Analyzing programs with explicit parallelism. In Utpal Banerjee, David Gelernter, Alexandru Nicolau, and David A. Padua, editors, *Languages and Compilers for Parallel Computing*, pages 405–419. Springer-Verlag, 1992.

Implementing an Irregular Application on a Distributed Memory Multiprocessor*

Soumen Chakrabarti   Katherine Yelick

Computer Science Division

University of California at Berkeley

Email: soumen@cs.berkeley.edu, yelick@cs.berkeley.edu

Abstract

Parallelism with irregular patterns of data, communication and computation is hard to manage efficiently. In this paper we present a case study of the Gröbner basis problem, a symbolic algebra application. We developed an efficient parallel implementation using the following techniques. First, a sequential algorithm was rewritten in a *transition axiom* style, in which computation proceeds by non-deterministic invocations of guarded statements at multiple processors. Next, the algebraic properties of the problem were studied to modify the algorithm to ensure correctness in spite of locally inconsistent views of the shared data structures. This was used to design data structures with very little overhead for maintaining consistency. Finally, an application-specific scheduler was designed and tuned to get good performance. Our distributed memory implementation achieves impressive speedups.

1 Introduction

In this paper we present a case study of an irregular symbolic algebra application, the Gröbner basis problem.

Computing the Gröbner basis of a set of multivariate polynomials has applications in solving systems of non-linear equations, implicitizing parametric equations and automating geometry proofs. Efforts have been made to develop parallel algorithms for this problem on shared memory machines, but efficiency and scalability have not been encouraging. Here we describe a distributed memory implementation of the Buchberger [2] algorithm that equals and often surpasses shared memory performance and scales to a larger number of processors.

This symbolic algebra application is different in many aspects from the most frequently parallelized numerical scientific computations.

- It involves irregular data structures rather than arrays.
- No well-marked computation and communication phases can be identified.
- The amount of computation is unpredictable. The problem resembles search in that running time may vary widely depending on heuristic choice.
- The amount and pattern of communication is unpredictable for conceivable parallelizations.

Our preliminary profiling experiments on a sequential implementation (from CMU [7]) suggested that the problem has significant parallelism: a large fraction of running time is spent in relatively independent polynomial arithmetic with hardly any data dependencies preventing their parallelization.

The following list summarizes our contributions.

- A distributed memory algorithm has been developed for computing Gröbner bases.
- An efficient program has been implemented. It runs on the CM-5 distributed memory multiprocessor (described in more detail in §7).
- Properties of the problem have enabled the use of distributed data structures with relaxed, software controlled consistency mechanisms to minimize synchronization and communication overhead.
- Processor utilization has been improved by application level *thread* scheduling. Computations are effectively suspended by storing and retrieving state information in an application level data structure.
- From a sequential algorithm, the parallel program has been derived in a sequence of successively refined *transition axioms*, starting from the most abstract description and modifying it to a distributed memory program.

The paper is organized as follows. We introduce the

---

*This work was supported in part by the Advanced Research Projects Agency of the Department of Defense monitored by the Office of Naval Research under contract DABT63-92-C-0026, by AT&T, and by a National Science Foundation Infrastructure Grant (number CDA-8722788). The information presented here does not necessarily reflect the position or the policy of the Government and no official endorsement should be inferred.

4th ACM PPOPP,5/93/CA,USA

problem in §2. A non-deterministic specification of the algorithm using *transition axioms* is developed and refined in §3. Design of the necessary distributed data structures is described in §4. Code organization and scheduling to improve processor utilization are addressed in §5. A summary of implementation details is in §6. Performance for some standard benchmarks is presented in §7. Related work is reviewed in §8. Conclusions are drawn in §9.

2 Problem Statement

Roughly speaking, Buchberger's algorithm is a symbolic form of Gaussian elimination. Given a set of polynomials, it produces another set of polynomials with the same roots and additional properties that make it easier to compute those roots. The new set, called the Gröbner basis, is analogous to a triangular set of linear equations, which can be solved by substitution. The two basic operations in computing a Gröbner basis are to take two polynomials and eliminate one of their terms, and to simplify a polynomial by subtracting multiples of other polynomials.

Polynomials are defined by a set of coefficients, such as the rational numbers, and a set of variables. The reader may safely consider the special case, used in the examples, in which coefficients are rationals on which exact arithmetic is performed. A more general formulation is presented next; it occurs when the coefficients form an arbitrary field and is important in some applications.

Let K be a field and $x_1, ..., x_n$ be variables, then $K[x_1, ..., x_n]$ denotes a ring of polynomials under standard polynomial arithmetic. To define a canonical form for the polynomials, an (arbitrary) ordering is chosen on the variables and extended to an ordering on monomials. Either a lexicographic or total degree ordering is typically used on monomials. A polynomial is canonicalized as a sequence of terms, each containing a coefficient and a monomial, written in decreasing order of the monomials. We can therefore speak of the leading or *head* term, monomial or coefficient of a polynomial.

Example. Given variables $x > y > z$ and lexicographic ordering on monomials, polynomial $p = 2x^2yz^3 - 7xy^{10} + z$ is in canonical form with $\textsc{Hterm}(p) = 2x^2yz^3$, $\textsc{Hmono}(p) = x^2yz^3$ and $\textsc{Hcoef}(p) = 2$.

Polynomial r can *reduce* polynomial p if $\textsc{Hmono}(r)$ divides $\textsc{Hmono}(p)$. The act of reducing p by r involves subtracting a multiple of r from p so that the head term of p is cancelled.

Example. If $p = 2x^2yz^3 - 7xy^{10} + z$ and $r = 5xyz - 3$ then r reduces p to $p' = p - \boxed{\frac{2}{5}xz^2} \cdot r = -7xy^{10} + \frac{6}{5}xz^2 + z$.

A polynomial p is reduced by a set S of polynomials by looking for some $s \in S$ that reduces p. If none is found, p is in *normal form* with respect to S, which is denoted by $\textsc{Normal}(p, S)$. Otherwise p is reduced by s and the process is repeated. For any general set S a polynomial p may end up in many normal forms; the collection of all possible normal forms is denoted $\mathrm{NF}_S(p)$. The zero polynomial, 0, is in normal form with respect to any S. Given monomials $m_1 = x_1^{i_1} \cdots x_n^{i_n}$ and $m_2 = x_1^{j_1} \cdots x_n^{j_n}$, their *highest common factor* is defined as

$$\textsc{Hcf}(m_1, m_2) = x_1^{\min(i_1, j_1)} \cdots x_n^{\min(i_n, j_n)}.$$

Let p_1 and p_2 be polynomials with $\textsc{Hterm}(p_1) = k_1 m_1$ and $\textsc{Hterm}(p_2) = k_2 m_2$, where $k_1, k_2 \in K$ and m_1 and m_2 are monomials. The *s-polynomial* of p_1 and p_2 is defined as

$$\textsc{Spol}(p_1, p_2) = p_1 \frac{k_2 m_2}{\textsc{Hcf}(m_1, m_2)} - p_2 \frac{k_1 m_1}{\textsc{Hcf}(m_1, m_2)}.$$

The *ideal* generated by a set S of polynomials is denoted by $\textsc{Ideal}(S)$. Given a set P of polynomials, a Gröbner basis of P is a set G of polynomials satisfying the following:

- $\textsc{Ideal}(G) = \textsc{Ideal}(P)$ and
- For each $p \in \textsc{Ideal}(P)$, $\mathrm{NF}_G(p) = \{0\}$.

The original sequential algorithm for computing a Gröbner basis was given by Buchberger [2]. A survey of the theory can be found in Mishra [5].

```
Input: F, a finite set of polynomials.
Initially:
    G = F
    gpq = { {f,g} : f,g ∈ G, f ≠ g }
while gpq ≠ ∅ {
    let {f,g} be any pair in gpq
    gpq = gpq \ {{f,g}}
    h = SPOL(f,g)
    h' = REDUCE(h,G)
    if h' ≠ 0 {
        gpq = gpq ∪ {{f,h'} : f ∈ G}
        G = G ∪ h'
    }
}
```

Figure 1: Sequential Algorithm S [Buchberger]. G is initialized to the input set F and grows to become a Gröbner basis. Elements in G are never modified. gpq is the set of pairs of polynomials. The function $\textsc{Reduce}(h, G)$ returns some element $h' \in \mathrm{NF}_G(h)$, i.e., it reduces h completely to normal form.

3 Basic Algorithm

In this section we develop the parallel algorithm from the sequential one by Buchberger. The data structures are described first and then the transition axioms are introduced.

3.1 Abstractions

The sequential algorithm has two important data structures (figure 1). The set G is initialized to input set

F and, in course of time, grows to a Gröbner basis of F. Reduction prevents two identical polynomials from entering G, so G is a set. However, the data type implementing G does not itself prevent duplicates, so it is specified as a (monotonically growing) multiset.

Pairs of polynomials for s-polynomial computation are kept in *gpq* (global pair queue). The reason for specializing *gpq* from a multiset to a queue is that *selection* of a pair in the **while** loop is sensitive. Correctness is ensured regardless of the selection, but heuristics exist to dramatically improve performance. Thus, priority ordering is necessary in *gpq*, so that heuristic merit can be encoded into priority.

The central problem in our design is understanding the algebraic properties of the problem and exploiting them to design suitable data structures and communication protocols. We *encapsulate* the data structures so that the semantics and consistency are exposed through a specified interface to the higher level. We can therefore reason about correctness (safety and liveness properties) using these specifications [4], without having to use the specifics of implementation. The details of the data structure implementations are in §4.

Input: F, a finite set of polynomials.
Initially:
$grq = \emptyset$, $G = F$,
$gpq = \{\ \{f,g\}:\ f,g \in G,\ f \neq g\ \}$.
<u>S-POLYNOMIAL</u>
$\exists\{p,q\} \in gpq \Rightarrow$
$gpq = gpq \setminus \{\{p,q\}\}$
$grq = grq \cup \{\mathrm{SPOL}(p,q)\}$
<u>AUGMENT BASIS</u>
$\exists r \in grq : \mathrm{NORMAL}(r,G),\ r \neq 0 \Rightarrow$
$grq = grq \setminus \{r\}$
$gpq = gpq \cup \{\{s,r\}:\ s \in G\}$
$G = G \cup \{r\}$
<u>REDUCE</u>
$\exists r \in grq :\ \neg\mathrm{NORMAL}(r,G) \Rightarrow$
$r = \mathrm{REDUCE}(r,G)$

Figure 2: G-1: Transition Axiom formulation with one copy of G. Data structures G and *gpq* as before. Unlike in Algorithm S, $\mathrm{REDUCE}(r,G)$ need not return a normal form; a partially reduced form will do.

3.2 Transition Axiom Specifications

Transition axioms [9, 11] are a means to exploit nondeterminism in an algorithm description. They help decompose the computation into independently schedulable chunks, so that scheduling decisions are deferred as much as possible. This means that significant performance tuning can be done late in the design process without major design changes.

Given the basic sequential algorithm by Buchberger, we transform it in a series of refinements to a transition axiom style parallel algorithm for a distributed memory machine. As we proceed from one axiom system to the next, the effort is to convert a formal algorithm to an efficient implementation for a distributed memory machine, in our case, the CM-5 multiprocessor.

Input: F, a finite set of polynomials.
Initially:
$grq = \emptyset$,
$gpq = \{\ \{f,g\}:\ f,g \in F, f \neq g\ \}$.
$\forall i:\ 1 \leq i \leq P, G_i = F, G'_i = \emptyset$
Processor i, $1 \leq i \leq P$.
<u>VALIDATE</u>
$(gpq \neq \emptyset$ **or** $grq \neq \emptyset)$ **and** $\exists g \in G'_i \Rightarrow$
$G'_i = G'_i \setminus \{g\}$
$G_i = G_i \cup \{g\}$
<u>S-POLYNOMIAL</u>
$\exists\{p_i,q_i\} \in gpq:\ p_i,q_i \in G_i \Rightarrow$
$gpq = gpq \setminus \{\ \{p_i,q_i\}\ \}$
$grq = grq \cup \{\mathrm{SPOL}(p_i,q_i)\}$
<u>AUGMENT BASIS AND INVALIDATE</u>
$G'_i = \emptyset$, $\exists r_i \in grq : r_i \neq 0$, **and** $\mathrm{NORMAL}(r_i,G_i) \Rightarrow$
$grq = grq \setminus \{r_i\}$
$gpq = gpq \cup \{\ \{s,r_i\},\ \forall s \in G_i\ \}$
$G_i = G_i \cup \{r_i\}$
$\forall j: 1 \leq j \leq P, i \neq j$
$G'_j = G'_j \cup \{r_i\}$
<u>REDUCE</u>
$\exists r_i \in grq:\ \neg\mathrm{NORMAL}(r_i,G_i) \Rightarrow$
$r_i = \mathrm{REDUCE}(r_i,G_i)$

Figure 3: G-P: Transition axioms using P copies of G, one for each processor. *gpq*, *grq* as before. Each processor i has a local copy G_i of the basis.

Replicating the Basis

Figure 2 is a transition axiom specification (named G-1) of the sequential algorithm in figure 1. While G-1 uses essentially the same data structures as the sequential algorithm, the next version G-P (figure 3) has P copies of the basis, one with each processor. We justify replicating the basis in §4. Consistency is managed explicitly at the application level to exploit algebraic properties.

Formally, we regard invalidations as updating a *shadow set* at each processor. A processor can access elements in the shadow set only after moving them explicitly from the shadow set to its local replica. To model our consistency mechanism, suppose each processor i has a (possibly incomplete) copy of G called G_i. To incorporate invalidations and validations, we use the shadow set G'_i. Say processor i adds a new element g. This involves adding g to G_i and invalidating all other copies by adding g to $G'_j, j \neq i$. If processor k has $G'_k = \emptyset$ then G_k is a valid copy, otherwise it can validate its copy by moving the elements in G'_k to G_k. Processor k can inspect element g only after moving it to G_k. All the transition axioms are written in terms of these abstractions.

Of course, for this technique to be practically useful, the algorithm must have the following properties.

- The representation of elements in G'_i is significantly smaller than in G_i. For polynomials, which are typically several hundreds to thousands of bytes large, the elements in G'_i are only eight byte unique identifiers.
- The properties of the algorithm permit a processor to do a significant amount of work with an incomplete basis. In particular, no reduction "goes to waste". This allows us to update local copies lazily upon demand, which reduces communication expense and obviates stringent synchronization of the critical section style.

Input: F, a finite set of polynomials.
Initially:
$\forall i : 1 \le i \le P, lpq_i = lrq_i = \emptyset$
$gpq = \{ \{f, g\} : f, g \in F, f \ne g \}$.
$\forall i : 1 \le i \le P, G_i = F, G'_i = \emptyset$
Processor i, $1 \le i \le P$.

TRANSFER
$\exists \{p_i, q_i\} \in gpq \Rightarrow$
$gpq = gpq \setminus \{\{p_i, q_i\}\}$
$lpq_i = lpq_i \cup \{\{p_i, q_i\}\}$

VALIDATE
$(lpq_i \ne \emptyset$ **or** $lrq_i \ne \emptyset)$ **and** $\exists g \in G'_i \Rightarrow$
$G'_i = G'_i \setminus \{g\}$
$G_i = G_i \cup \{g\}$

S-POLYNOMIAL
$\exists \{p_i, q_i\} \in lpq_i : p_i, q_i \in G_i \Rightarrow$
$lpq_i = lpq_i \setminus \{ \{p_i, q_i\} \}$
$lrq_i = lrq_i \cup \{\text{SPOL}(p_i, q_i)\}$

AUGMENT BASIS AND INVALIDATE
$G'_i = \emptyset$, $\exists r_i \in lrq_i : r_i \ne 0$, **and** $\text{NORMAL}(r_i, G_i) \Rightarrow$
$lrq_i = lrq_i \setminus \{r_i\}$
$gpq = gpq \cup \{ \{s, r_i\}, \forall s \in G_i \}$
$G_i = G_i \cup \{r_i\}$
$\forall j : 1 \le j \le P, i \ne j$
$G'_j = G'_j \cup \{r_i\}$

REDUCE
$\exists r_i \in lrq_i : \neg\text{NORMAL}(r_i, G_i) \Rightarrow$
$r_i = \text{REDUCE}(r_i, G_i)$

Figure 4: GL-P: Transition Axioms with P copies of G and local pair and reduct queues lpq and lrq to buffer work.

Local Threads

To hide the latency of remote operations across the network, we implement application level "threading" by packaging up state into application level data structures: local queues holding pairs of polynomial pointers and partially reduced polynomials. The version incorporating these is GL-P (figure 4).

REDUCE/AUGMENT
$\exists r \in lrq_i,\ r \ne 0 \Rightarrow$
if $\neg\text{NORMAL}(r, G_i)$
$r = \text{REDUCE}(r, G_i)$
else {
if $G'_i = \emptyset$ {
$lrq_i = lrq_i \setminus \{r\}$
$gpq = gpq \cup \{\{s, r\},\ \forall s \in G_i\}$
$G_i = G_i \cup \{r_i\}$
$\forall j : 1 \le j \le P,\ i \ne j$
$G'_j = G'_j \cup \{r\}$
}
}

Figure 5: Axioms REDUCE and AUGMENT BASIS are combined into REDUCE/AUGMENT to eliminate redundant computation of the expensive guard $\text{NORMAL}(r, G_i)$.

Stuttering Axioms

Certain transitions have complicated guards that are expensive to evaluate. For instance, $\text{NORMAL}(f, S)$ requires checking divisibility of $\text{HMONO}(f)$ by $\text{HMONO}(s)$ for all $s \in S$. We collapse the axioms REDUCE and AUGMENT BASIS into a single axiom in figure 5 to cut down redundant computation of NORMAL.

However, in an execution of the resulting set of transition axioms, it is possible for the new axiom REDUCE/AUGMENT to fire repeatedly without making any progress in the state of computation. It is called a *stuttering* axiom. To ensure termination, the scheduler must prevent infinite sequences of invocations of stuttering axioms.

These axioms can be interpreted as specifying an interleaving of axioms without any real concurrency. Few axioms actually interfere by sharing data. Using little serialization we can enable the axioms to fire concurrently in the implementation. In [4] we have shown that the transition axiom specifications correctly compute a Gröbner basis; we omit the proofs.

4 Data Structure Design

In this section we describe the design and implementation of the two aggregate data structures used in the algorithm.

4.1 The Basis

A major decision was the representation of the basis, the choices being essentially to replicate or partition. A parallel algorithm employing a ring of reducers with the basis partitioned among them was proposed by Buchberger [7]. A slight variant using a reducing pipeline has been implemented by Siegl [6]. We believe that partitioning has less available parallelism and more communication overhead. It is useful only if available memory is too small to replicate the basis.

4.1.1 To Replicate or Partition

The following analysis shows that replication of basis polynomials, if permitted by memory capacity, can be expected to give better performance. We demonstrate the following problems in using a partitioned scheme: poor load balance, insufficient parallelism and high communication overhead.

Input	Pipeline			Max Single Reduction Step (μs)
	Max Stage Time (μs)	Maximum Parallelism	Efficiency (Percent)	
arnborg4	51208	3.55	35	1771
arnborg5	6226476	15.0	26	19983
katsura4	6092409	6.03	30	11410
lazard	12355072	8.02	24	95935
morgen-	10259753	2.88	15	15495
pavelle4	3680064	4.99	36	14324
robbiano	533431	2.65	9	3143
rose	29213252	3.31	16	174201
trinks1	2343233	6.03	35	14242
trinks2	545874	5.58	27	17621

Table 1: The potential parallelism using a replicated basis is inherently larger than that using a partitioned basis.

Poorly Balanced Pipeline

Partitioning means that reduction will have to be done in a pipeline as in [6]. The basic requirement for a pipelined computation to be efficient is that there should be a large number of stages, each taking about the same time (i.e., no bottlenecks exist). To measure the limitations of pipelining, assume the machine has an unlimited number of processors, instantaneous communication and no dependencies between reduction events. Place one reducer at each pipeline stage (processor). The maximum achievable parallelism is limited by the ratio of the total time for reduction to the maximum time spent by one pipeline stage. Table 1 shows that this upper bound on parallelism is rather low for most standard benchmarks. Typical efficiency is only 20–30%.

Granularity

A possible way to increase efficiency is to exploit statistical averaging, by putting several basis polynomials (reducers) in each stage of the pipeline. The parallelism obtained from a pipelined approach is already limited by the the number of reducers; in this case it will decrease further. In contrast, the work can be decomposed into much finer grain units by replicating the basis. The time for a single reduction step (which is the minimum possible grain size permitted by our design) is also shown in table 1. It is about two orders of magnitude less than a pipeline stage time.

Communication Overhead

Let us make a rough estimate of the number of polynomials that get reduced to zero and the number added to the basis. Consider algorithm S (figure 1). Suppose a problem starts with ℓ polynomials and $\binom{\ell}{2}$ pairs, finishing with $m \geq \ell$ polynomials. When we add the i-th polynomial to G, we make $i-1$ new pairs. Thus $\ell, \ell+1, \ldots, m-1$ pairs are added at those times when the basis is grown. How many pairs are generated in all?

$$\binom{\ell}{2} + \sum_{\ell \leq i \leq m-1} i = \binom{\ell}{2} + (m-\ell)\frac{m+\ell-1}{2}.$$

If $m \gg \ell$, as often is the case for large problems, the number of polynomials added is $\Theta(m)$ while the number reduced to zero is $\Theta(m^2)$.

It has been pointed out that with a good implementation of pruning criteria a large number of pairs are eliminated quickly and only about m instead of m^2 pairs have to be actually reduced. However,

- A formal proof of this fact exists in [3], but it only works for restricted inputs with *two* symbols ($n = 2$). No such result is known for general inputs.
- Our sequential prototype with Buchberger's criteria shows the performance presented in table 2 which shows a much larger (at least 5 times) number of reductions to zero.
- Eliminating pairs using criteria, while not as expensive as reduction, still lead to computations involving potentially all basis polynomials ([2],page 197). Thus the number of pairs generated is still a reasonable measure of communication expense.

What is the impact of this analysis? In a partitioned scheme, partially reduced polynomials go around the pipeline, several times in general, perhaps to get reduced to zero, thus incurring communication overhead. On the contrary, suppose the basis is replicated. Then communication involves only those polynomials which have gone through (local) reduction and actually entered the basis. Communication is thus undertaken only *once* for *added* polynomials and not polynomials reduced to zero. Table 2 clearly indicates reduction to zero as the common case to be optimized.

Our assumption of large memory resources might not be justified under all circumstances. As we note in §7, there exist long-running problem instances we could not run owing to limited memory capacity. In such cases, a hybrid strategy using both replication and partitioning may be useful.

Input	Added	Zeroed	Ratio
arnborg5	53	511	9.64
morgenstern	14	117	8.36
pavelle4	10	57	5.70
robbiano	26	158	6.07
trinks1	11	83	7.55

Table 2: Typical number of polynomials added and reduced to zeroes in a sequential implementation.

4.1.2 Interface

The basis of polynomials, G, is implemented as a multiset abstraction with operations **AddToSet**, **Validate**, predicate **Valid?** and iterator **ForAll** (used for reduction). The specifications we give are based on the abstractions in the transition axioms (figure 3): local replicas G_i and shadow sets G'_i on processor i.

AddToSet(G, g):
$G_i = G_i \cup \{g\}$
$\forall j: 1 \leq j \leq P, j \neq i : G'_j = G'_j \cup \{g\}$
Validate(G):
$G'_i = G'_i \setminus \{g\}$
$G_i = G_i \cup \{g\}$ for some $g \in G'_i$.
Valid?(G):
Return 1 if $G'_i = \emptyset$, 0 otherwise.
ForAll(g, G) [**Stmt**]:
Execute **Stmt** iteratively for each $g \in G_i$
(G_i might be incomplete.)

Note that the abstraction in itself does not guarantee any consistency (for example, for a read-only semantics a program need never validate its copy). The application must use the operations so as to implement the nature of consistency it needs. Thus the abstraction provides a software controlled *weak consistency* mechanism (see [1], for example).

4.2 The Pair Queue

The algorithm needs a priority queue for pairs of polynomials. The priority corresponds to the heuristic merit of a pair. Since this is only a heuristic, it need not be adhered to exactly. In the parallel algorithm, *gpq* is as much a scheduling control as a data structure.

The *distributed task queue* by Wen *et al*, described in [10], is designed for applications that can be broken down into *tasks*. The suggested paradigm is that the task queue starts with some number of tasks, processors dequeue tasks and perform them, possibly generating more tasks. Our parallel algorithm naturally fits into this model.

4.2.1 Implementation

The queue is partitioned, so there is only one copy of each element and each processor has a local portion of the queue. Processors are logically organized in a ring. **Enqueue** adds the given element to the local queue. **Dequeue** attempts to dequeue work off the local queue; if it is empty remote queues are tested. Protocols execute in the background to sense load imbalance and redistribute tasks more evenly. Priority is ensured only within each local queue and not across processors. Termination detection, a non-trivial problem in distributed queues, is provided to detect global completion of tasks.

4.2.2 Interface

The task queue creation operation **Create** expects as argument a function **Idle?** which is a function in the application that returns true if and only if the calling processor has no work (at the moment). This is used for termination detection, and is necessary because tasks may be in transit on the communication network or buffered in local variables of busy processors. **Enqueue** adds the given element to the queue. **Dequeue** can either remove and return some element or signal *empty* or *terminated*. *Empty* is only a hint: it says that the local queue is empty. *Terminated* is a stable property, true only if the total number of enqueued tasks equals the total number of dequeued tasks, and all processors are idle. Formal specifications are omitted.

5 Scheduling

We now describe how computation is organized. The basic principles are as follows.

- The work is decomposed into basic units called *tasks* that can be dynamically created, scheduled and executed.
- To overlap local and remote computation, suitable state is maintained at each processor to get the benefit of threading.
- Split phase data transfer is used to pipeline communication.

Task Queue

A task in our implementation is a pair of polynomial ID's. Solving a task involves finding both polynomials, computing their s-polynomial and reducing the s-polynomial by the basis. If the s-polynomial does not reduce to zero it is added to the basis, generating new tasks in the form of pairs between old basis polynomials and the new one. Tasks are used to implement parallelism and to balance load. The distributed pair queue contains only unique polynomial ID's, not polynomials so polynomials are not transferred when tasks move about.

Local Threads

Efficient implementation of the transition axioms should avoid having processors wait for a response from a remote computation, using some form of threading. Since threading is not as yet available on the CM-5, we implemented a special purpose application level threading.

There are two places where this might be necessary. First, when an s-polynomial must be computed, one or both of the polynomials of the pair might be missing. Instead of fetching the polynomial(s) immediately, we put the pair "on hold" (by representing it as a suspended thread) and look for other pairs whose polynomials can be found locally. Second, since **Invalidates** cannot be overlapped, we arbitrate using a mutex lock. If a processor fails to get the lock, it suspends the current thread and proceeds with other activity, such as other s-polynomial computations or reductions.

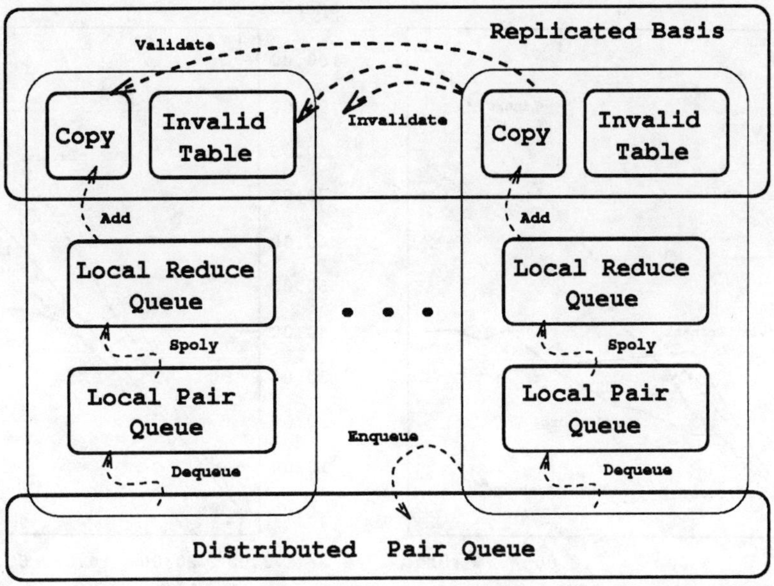

Figure 6: Sketch of data structures and transition axioms in our implementation.

Split Phase Operations

Another optimization in programming a machine like the CM-5 is to pipeline communication. In *split phase* data transfer, a processor can do useful work between initiating data transfer and responding to the other party. For example, in reading an integer from each of the other processors it is better to initiate all reads together and then wait until all the data arrives.

We use this principle in invalidations and validations. During invalidations, the broadcasting processor sends out invalidates all at once and then waits for acknowledgements (acknowledgements are necessary for correctness). During validations, the processor sends out requests for all necessary polynomials that are missing and then waits for all data transfer to complete.

The CM-5 currently does not support significant overlap of communication and computation since the nodes do not have DMA's. It can, however, support overlap of computation with delays for remote acknowledgements. Pipelined communication would be more valuable if true overlap were possible.

6 Sketch of Implementation

Figure 6 sketches the general organization of our implementation. Each processor has local pair and reduce queues and access to the distributed pair queue and basis. Data transfer paths induced by the transition axioms are shown as thin broken arrows.

Communication for *gpq* occurs mostly in a ring pattern. Invalidations follow a star pattern. Validations involve bulk transfer. To balance communication load over the network, for each polynomial added to the basis, a tree is embedded into the network with the processor adding it at the root. Any processor in search of a polynomial knows the tree structure implicitly from the unique ID of the polynomial. It traverses up the tree along its ancestors until it finds the polynomial.

One processor, the *coordinator* (not shown), is reserved for running a termination detection protocol and managing a lock to arbitrate invalidations. We used simple, centralized methods to keep the prototype simple. Being centralized, these protocols will not scale to thousands of processors. However, a large variety of relatively decentralized protocols are available. We have never observed this centralization to be a bottleneck: less than 2% of running time is spent in mutual exclusion and termination detection.

7 Performance

In this section we present the performance of our implementation.

The Environment

We used a CM-5 multiprocessor. Each node is a 33 MHz (15–20 MIPS) Sparc processor with 8 MB of memory. The network is a fat-tree supporting at most 20 MB/s data transfer. For our purpose we ignored the topology. Communication was done using the *active message* layer [8]. The implementation is in C; we used `gcc-2.2.2` with optimization `"-O2"` for our measurements.

Measurement and Fluctuation

The sequential algorithm S is under-specified, even though a sequential program could be designed to be deterministic. In the parallel algorithms we exploit this loose specification, resulting in highly non-deterministic behavior.

- Lock serializations and message ordering by the communication network are unpredictable.
- Since the heuristic priority on pairs is weakly enforced, there is more uncertainty in pair selection.
- Because polynomials may be added to copies of the

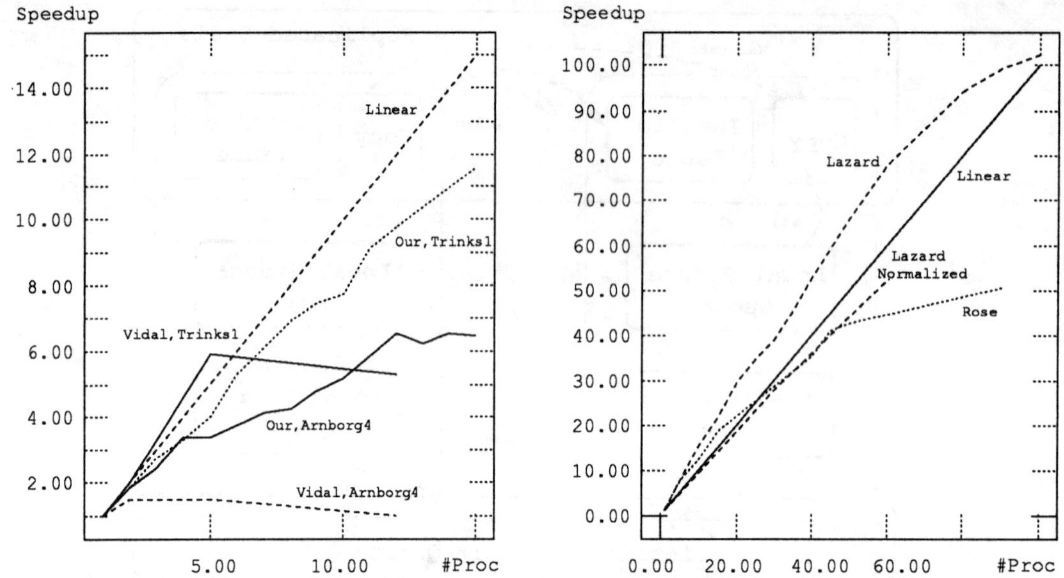

(a) (b)

Figure 7: Speedups (based on raw running time) for some standard benchmarks. Our implementation scales better than the best shared memory performance reported by Vidal even for very small examples (a). For large inputs (Lazard = 5 copies of `lazard`; Rose = 2 copies of `rose`) in (b) we get near-linear speedups up to 100 processors (see text for an explanation about the anomaly of superlinear speedup in (b)).

basis in various orders, the choice of reducers can differ across processors and over different invocations of the program on the same input.

- Pairs in the task queue can migrate in complicated ways and get dequeued by an arbitrary processor at an unpredictable time.

Apart from these nondeterminism issues, factors like code optimization and message protocol tuning are important. Although we have been able to demonstrate the benefits of parallelism without too much noise in the data, slight perturbations of such nature *can* make significant differences to performance.

Speedup Baseline

Given the irregular nature of this problem, it is difficult to define a fair baseline for computing speedups. If we wish to define speedup traditionally as the ratio of running times of the parallel to a sequential algorithm, the sequential algorithm must be the best known — but

Input	Time (s) $P = 1$	Time (s) $P = 10$	Time (s) Best Seq.
arnborg4	0.27	0.06	0.28
arnborg5	486	15	46
katsura4	29.2	3.1	11
lazard	55.5	2.6	1009
morgenstern	5.5	1	6.17
pavelle4	5.17	0.7	4.5
rose	12.5	1	15
trinks1	6.44	1	4

Table 3: Sample times for benchmarks for a sequential algorithm and our parallel implementation.

what is *best* is not known. There is a wide spectrum of opinion about the efficacy of various pair selection and elimination heuristics, whether interreduction helps or not, whether to reduce only head terms or all terms, etc. As might be expected, no single heuristic does well all the time.

Thus we had two choices for the speedup baseline: the parallel program running on one processor or a sequential implementation. The latter choice exposes the overhead of parallelization, but has the disadvantage that the "speedup" for the parallel algorithm running on one processor is generally different from 1. This is counter-intuitive. We decided to scale all speedups to pass through the point (1,1), and also provide the ratio of absolute running times of the two choices to demonstrate that there is true parallelism (table 3). There are cases where the one processor parallel version outperforms the sequential program and vice versa.

It is clear from the discussion that an exact characterization of speedup using speedup curves has relatively little meaning when the basic sequential algorithm is heuristic guided and quite sensitive to minor perturbations. The point we wish to make is that the problem, while not as amenable to scalable parallelization as, say, matrix multiplication, *does* have usable parallelism which even a distributed memory multiprocessor can exploit.

Benchmarks

We have used the set of standard benchmarks collected by Vidal [7]. On one processor they run for about half a second to a few minutes, with total degree ordering[1]. The smaller inputs are solved too quickly to

[1] Ties are resolved by lexicographic order.

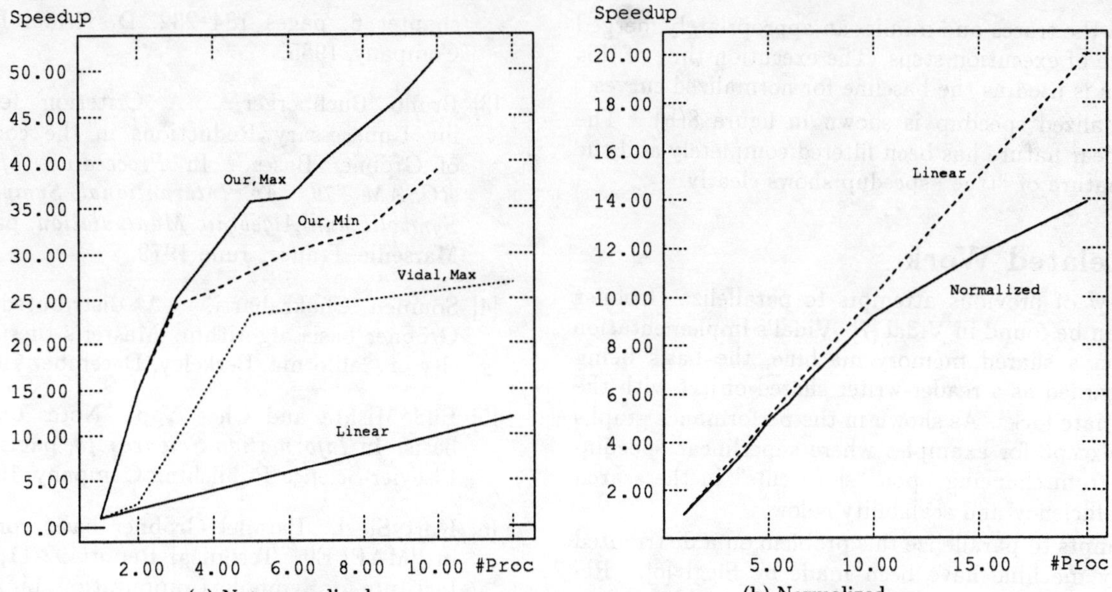

(a) Not normalized (b) Normalized

Figure 8: Superlinear speedup (`lazard`). Figure (a) shows our best and worst performance over 5 runs and the best shared memory performance. All are superlinear. When speedup is determined by normalizing running time using a simulator, near-linear "true" speedup is seen in figure (b).

make accurate speedup measurements.

In figure 7(a) we give performance on two small examples, **`arnborg4`** and **`trinks1`**. The best speedups over 5 runs are shown for our implementation. In comparison, the best curve from Vidal [7] show less scalable speedup. These speedups were computed as the ratio between P processor running time (excluding input, output and initialization) and 1 processor running time, both for the parallel algorithm. We used the pair elimination criteria in [3] and the traditional pair selection in [2].

Inspection of execution profiles indicated that for small problems, parallelism was limited by underutilization of processors during startup and termination transients. The total number of tasks is too small to saturate all processors with work for a large fraction of the running time. To see if this is an inherent limitation of the design, we needed synthetic long-running workloads. For this we started the program with multiple copies of a benchmark with variables named apart. Note that this construction is only for evaluating the *potential* performance and not necessarily representative of realistic large examples. These examples run for hours on one processor. Performance (in terms of running time) for two of these are shown in figure 7(b) (best over 3 runs). Impressive scalability is observed.

An input instance can be "large" in the sense of running time or memory requirements or both. Although our implementation scales well in *time*, replication of the basis presents a limit to scalability in *space*. We have come across long-running instances that might show highly scalable speedups, but all of them exceed the current memory capacity. We are designing a more flexible abstraction that performs this space-time tradeoff on a continuum using a hybrid of partitioning and replication. This extension should enable us to run large interesting examples.

Superlinear Speedup

Parts of the speedup curves in figure 7(b) are *above* the ideal linear speedup, a phenomenon arising from our definition of speedup. It is a well-known phenomenon in problems with nondeterministic or heuristic scheduling that it is possible to solve a problem with P processors in less than $1/P$ of the time needed for one processor, because some of them may find "short cuts" to the solution whereas a single processor may be misled by an inaccurate heuristic. Backtracking search, branch and bound, and some pattern matching problems belong to this category. To get around this difficulty the notion of speedup is often modified. In the 8-queen problem, for instance, the time to find *all* solutions as against just one has been considered.

For the Gröbner basis problem, superlinear speedup occurs when certain "magic" polynomials get added to the basis that reduce many other polynomials quickly to zero. Consider figure 8(a). We get superlinear speedup according to the prior definition of speedup, with a similar effect reported by Vidal for the shared memory implementation [7].

This indicates that the heuristic is not sufficiently discerning for these inputs, so that exploring a few of the best pairs (as against *the* best) in parallel pays off[2].

To make sure that the speedup curves indicate the benefit of parallelism and not fortuitous choice of polynomials we also calibrated speedups after getting rid of the non-determinism. For this, the parallel version accumulates *traces* of activity at each processor. A sequential program running on only one node of the CM-5

[2]The heuristic favors the pair $\langle f, g\rangle$ with the smallest $\text{HMONO}(f) \times \text{HMONO}(g)/\text{HCF}(\text{HMONO}(f), \text{HMONO}(g))$.

reads in the traces and mimics an appropriately merged sequence of execution steps. The execution time of this program is used as the baseline for normalized curves.

Normalized speedup is shown in figure 8(b). The superlinear nature has been filtered completely and the linear nature of "true" speedup shows clearly.

8 Related Work

A review of previous attempts to parallelize Gröbner basis can be found in Vidal [7]. Vidal's implementation [7] is on a shared memory machine, the basis being still regarded as a reader-writer shared object with the appropriate locks. As shown in the performance graphs in §7, except for examples where superlinear speedup results from chancing upon "short-cuts" in the search space, efficiency and scalability is low.

Attempts to parallelize this problem on a distributed memory machine have been made by Siegl [6]. Reduction of a polynomial is done by a pipeline of processes across which the current basis is partitioned. As discussed earlier, communication costs are an order of magnitude higher. The implementation was ported to a network of SUN workstations, a transputer and a (shared memory) Sequent, but performance figures are available only for the Sequent. These do not appear to be significant improvements over Vidal's performance.

9 Conclusion

In conclusion, we outline our results. We have successfully parallelized an irregular application using interesting techniques: introducing non-determinism using transition axioms, minimizing synchronization and communication overhead by designing distributed data structures with weak consistency and improving efficiency using application level state and schedule management. The speedup and scalability of our distributed memory implementation equals and often surpasses performance on shared memory machines.

Acknowledgements

We are grateful to Steve Schwab for providing the packages for *bignum* and polynomial arithmetic and a shared memory Gröbner basis program developed at CMU. Professor Richard Fateman made valuable comments on the work. Chih-Po Wen contributed the task queue.

References

[1] Sarita V. Adve and Mark D. Hill. Weak ordering–a new definition. In *17th International Symposium on Computer Architecture*, April 1990.

[2] Bruno Buchberger. Gröbner basis: an algorithmic method in polynomial ideal theory. In N. K. Bose, editor, *Multidimensional Systems Theory*, chapter 6, pages 184–232. D. Reidel Publishing Company, 1985.

[3] Bruno Buchberger. A Criterion for detecting Unnecessary Reductions in the construction of Gröbner Bases. In *Proceedings of the EUROSAM '79, An International Symposium on Symbolic and Algebraic Manipulation*, pages 3–21, Marseille, France, June 1979.

[4] Soumen Chakrabarti. A distributed memory Gröbner basis algorithm. Master's thesis, University of California, Berkeley, December 1992.

[5] Bud Mishra and Chee Yap. Notes on Gröbner basis. In *Information Sciences 48*, pages 219–252. Elsevier Science Publishing Company, 1989.

[6] Kurt Siegl. Parallel Gröbner basis computation in ||MAPLE||. Technical Report 92-11, Research Institute for Symbolic Computation, Linz, Austria, 1992.

[7] Jean-Philippe Vidal. The computation of Gröbner bases on a shared memory multiprocessor. Technical Report CMU-CS-90-163, School of Computer Science, Carnegie Mellon University, Pittsburgh, PA 15213, 1990.

[8] Thorsten von Eicken, David E. Culler, Seth Copen Goldstein, and Klaus Erik Schauser. Active messages: A mechanism for integrated communication and computation. In *Proceedings of the 19th Annual International Symposium on Computer Architecture*, pages 256–266, 1992.

[9] Katherine Yelick. Using abstraction in explicitly parallel programs. Technical Report MIT/LCS/TR-507, Massachusetts Institute of Technology, 545 Technology Square, Cambridge, MA 02139, July 1991.

[10] Katherine Yelick. Programming models for irregular applications. In *Proceedings of the Workshop on Languages, Compilers and Run-Time Environments for Distributed Memory Multiprocessors*, October 1992. To appear in SIGPLAN notices.

[11] Katherine A. Yelick and Steven J. Garland. A parallel completion procedure for term rewriting systems. In *Conference on Automated Deduction*, Saratoga Springs, NY, 1992.

Parallelizing Algorithms for Symbolic Computation using ||MAPLE||*

Kurt Siegl
Research Institute for Symbolic Computation (RISC-Linz)
Johannes Kepler University
A-4040 Linz, Austria

e-mail: siegl@risc.uni-linz.ac.at
voice: (Austria) 7236 3231 66
fax: (Austria) 7236 3231 30

Abstract

||MAPLE|| (speak: parallel Maple) is a portable system for parallel symbolic computation. The system is built as an interface between the parallel declarative programming language Strand and the sequential computer algebra system Maple, thus providing the elegance of Strand and the power of the existing sequential algorithms in Maple.

The implementation of different parallel programming paradigms shows that it is fairly easy to parallelize even complex algebraic algorithms using this system. Sample applications (among them algorithms solving multivariate nonlinear equation systems) are implemented on various parallel architectures. For example a straightforward parallelization of the complex and important problem of real root isolation has been parallelized using a generic Strand program of fewer than 20 lines of code and a slight modification of 5 lines in the original sequential Maple source. Even with such a simple modification we gained a speed-up of 5 times, that is better than those reported by others in the literature.

Keywords: Programming Methods for Parallel Symbolic Computation, Computer Algebra Systems, Logic Programming.

1 Introduction

Symbolic computation is an important part of applied mathematics, physics, engineering and other areas. Nowadays sequential computer algebra systems like Maple, Mathematica and Reduce are widely used. But currently it is only possible to solve small examples, because of the inherent complexity of the problems in symbolic computation. In particular, a lot of problems involving non-linear equation systems cannot be solved symbolically within a reasonable amount of time using today's computers. Furthermore, for a lot of algorithms it is not even possible to predict their runtime and memory demands for a given input.

How should we deal with such problems? An obvious solution is parallelization. Todays fast parallel computers are theoretically able to solve huge problems, but for solving large problems, we face the following situation:

- Sequential computer algebra systems have big sequential libraries and fast implementations of the basic algorithms but are not yet suitable for parallel computers.
- Parallel programming languages are well suited for parallel programming, but have no libraries for solving problems in symbolic computation.

Thus our goal should be to reuse the huge library in existing computer algebra systems and, additionally, to get easy access to the power of today's parallel computers.

Several attempts at parallelizing Maple have been made before. In [Watt, 1986] the UNIX fork and join primitives were used for parallelism. The programmer had to develop his parallel algorithm on a very low level. An improvement was done in [Char, 1990] where Linda is used. Linda is more hardware independent, but programmers still have to worry about creation of parallel processes and communication between them. The system was implemented on a shared memory machine but still had problems with communication and job creation overhead.

There are also several parallelizations of other computer algebra systems available: the C based SAC algebra library has been parallelized for shared memory machines only. An implementation by [Kuechlin, 1990] (called PARSAC) uses MACH thread routines for parallelization. A parallelization by [Hong *et al.*, 1992, Schreiner and Hong, 1993] (called PACLIB) includes several high level functions for communication and process generation. These systems provide the best efficiency but are not available for distributed memory machines.

*Supported by: Austrian Science Foundation (FWF), ESPRIT-III POSSO project

4th ACM PPOPP,5/93/CA,USA

By contrast, ||MAPLE|| [Siegl, 1993] is especially designed for distributed memory architectures and is kept absolutely portable. ||MAPLE|| programs may run on different hardware without any modification or recompilation. All necessary communication is done automatically by the system without any additional programming effort. Since ||MAPLE|| uses implicit parallelism, it allows writing parallel programs without any expert knowledge in parallel programming.

A disadvantage compared to the shared memory systems, our design introduces a higher overhead for communication. Additionally, we have a bigger memory overhead due to the need of copying the required data between the Maple and Strand heaps.

To achieve this goal we developed an interface between Maple [Char *et al.*, 1983] with the parallel programming language Strand [Foster and Taylor, 1989]. The result is a parallel programming system with the full functionality of Maple and parallel power of Strand. This method allows easy writing and porting of parallel algorithms.

We give several sample programs describing different techniques for a quick parallelization of algorithms in ||MAPLE||. All our experiments are done on a 20 processor Sequent shared memory machine and tested on a network of SUN workstations as well as on a 16-processor Transputer distributed memory machine where they showed a good speedup for a minimal programing effort.

2 The ||MAPLE|| System

The ||MAPLE|| system has two layers (Figure 1). The top layer is the parallel declarative programming language Strand which controls the parallel execution of an algorithm. For performing sequential tasks we may call arbitrary Maple functions or sequences of Maple statements in the underlying Maple system.

This method combines the advantages of Strand as well as of Maple.

2.1 Strand

Strand is a parallel programming language of the guarded Horn clause type.

That means that the basic construct is a clause of the form:

$$H : -G_1, ..., G_n | B_1, ..., B_m. \qquad (n, m \geq 0)$$

where the bodies B_j are executed in parallel as soon as all the guards G_i are fulfilled.

In Strand pattern matching is used instead of unification, and assignments are used to describe output bindings to increase the performance. Data dependencies can be expressed by data-flow synchronization and stream communication. Additionally Strand allows the use of arbitrary sequential subroutines written in C or Fortran as guards or body calls.

To describe the basic communication features, we give an short example of a program of the type "Producer - Consumer Parallelism with Request". The interested reader may find more details about Strand in [Foster and Taylor, 1989]

```
main():-
  producer(Channel),
  consumer(Channel)@fwd.

producer([X|Xs]):-  % Get empty variable X
  create(X),        % Generate value for X
  producer(Xs).

consumer(Out):-
  Out:=[X|Xs],      % Generate empty var X
  use(X),           % Use the value of X
  consumer(Xs).

-mode create(^).    % Generate an value
-mode use(?).       % Take an action.
```

A mode declaration for a procedure says that the argument annotated by "?" is used for input matching and arguments annotated by "^" should be used for output bindings. This declaration must be used if a pattern is used as output to allow data-flow synchronization. The "@fwd" annotation means that the annotated goal should be executed on the next processor.

Starting the main procedure generates two parallel subtasks (producer, consumer). Both are connected via a shared stream variable (Channel). The consumer process sends out a request for data (instantiating the first cons cell of the stream). This tells the producer to create a value for the stream element (X). As soon as it finished the consumer process can use the value.

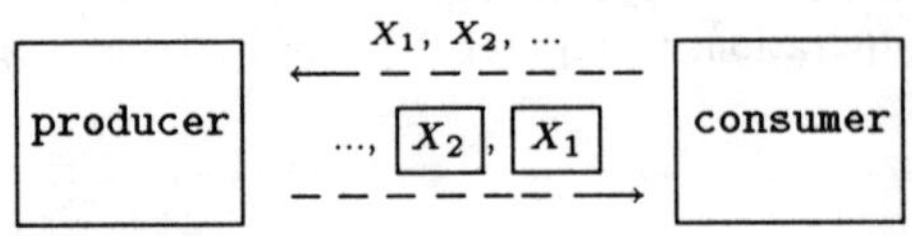

2.2 Maple

Maple is a well known computer algebra system with one of the biggest libraries available. Most of the known algorithms for symbolic computation are already implemented in Maple. Maple has its own programming language that supports functional as well procedural programming styles in a Pascal-like syntax. Maple has a Kernel written in C which can be linked as a subroutine to C programs. Input and output may be handled via strings representing Maple expressions. Further information may be found in [Char *et al.*, 1983, Char *et al.*, 1988]

2.3 ||MAPLE|| Kernel

The main task for the Kernel of the system was to find a minimal set of interface routines combining the syntactic and

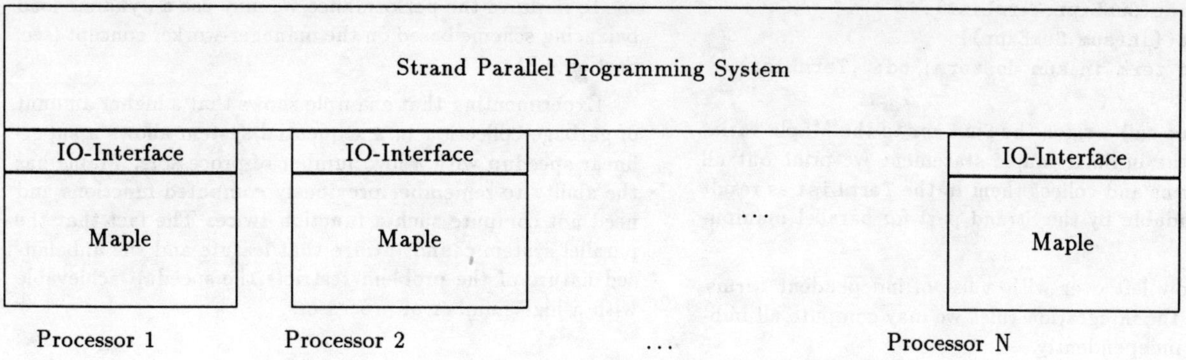

Figure 1: Structure of the ||MAPLE|| system

semantic features of the parallel, declarative programming language Strand with the imperative, sequential language of Maple. Finally we came up with an interface consisting of one new Strand guard and two bodies.

- A `maple` body call takes an arbitrary Maple function and its arguments as input and returns the result computed by Maple. This procedure covers most of the sequential calls to Maple used in a parallelized program. Using that call a sequential ||MAPLE|| program for symbolic integration for example would look like:

```
int(F,X,Result):- maple(int(F,X),Result).
```

- To extend the non-deterministic guard check over Maple expressions, we need an `m_test` guard that takes a boolean Maple function and succeeds if the function evaluates to true and fails otherwise.

  Now we are able to write a Strand program finding the maximum of arbitrary Maple data structures by the statements:

```
max(X,Y,Z):- m_test(less(X,Y)) | Z:=Y.
max(X,_,Z):- otherwise | Z:=X.
```

  Since we can also use the guard operation for solving arbitrary constraints in the guard, ||MAPLE|| may also be used as a constraint logic programming language.

- For complex sequential operations, involving several input and output arguments we use an `inline` operation allowing the inclusion of a sequence of arbitrary Maple statements. Additionally we may specify which variables should be used as input and which ones as output. Here a tuple of the form `in(mvar,Svar)` means that the content of the Strand variable `Svar` will be assigned to the Maple variable `mvar` before the Maple program is executed. On the contrary an `out(mvar,Svar)` tuple stands for the assignment of the Maple expression denoted by `mvar` to the Strand variable `Svar` after the computation. The procedure collects all output expressions and returns them in a list as result.

  If one finally finds symbolic expression as the result and wants to generate an executable C program evaluating the result the ||MAPLE|| program looks like:

```
generate_C(Expr,C-prog):-
    inline({in(tmp,Expr)},
      "readlib(C):C(tmp,optimized);",C-prog).
```

A critical part in the interface is the data type used for communication. It should be possible to manipulate the data within Strand as well as in Maple. Additionally an efficient communication between parallel tasks require a structure that may be packed in an array easily, because all communication primitiva on distributed systems may only transfer arrays in a single step. So we decided to use strings containing Maple expressions in legible form for communication between Strand and Maple.

In experiments we found out that this method allows easy porting and developing parallel algorithms used in symbolic computation.

3 Parallel Programming in ||MAPLE||

We describe the most important programming concepts necessary to parallelize algorithms in symbolic computation with ||MAPLE||. The reader should have some basic knowledge in parallel logic programming to understand the given programming examples.

3.1 Generating Parallel Tasks

At the beginning of a parallel program we will split several tasks from a single incoming expression. In ||MAPLE|| this can be done with the help of the `inline` function.

As example we consider the problem of integrating an sum expression symbolically. The integral may be easily parallelized by computing all individual terms in parallel. In ||MAPLE|| we generate the independent tasks by the following procedure:

```
split_int(SumExpr,TermList):-
  inline({in(sum,SumExpr)},
    "for term in sum do term; od;",TermList).
```

The `inline` call assigns the `SumExpr` to the Maple variable `sum`. In the in-lined Maple statement we print out all individual terms and collect them in the `TermList` as result list understandable by the Strand part for parallel manipulation.

We are now left over with a list of independent terms. According to the integration rules we may compute all individual terms independently.

3.2 Parallel Evaluation

As the simplest parallel program, we consider the case where we may compute all tasks independently in parallel.

To continue our integration example, we give the program for distributing the data in a parallel shell. For simplicity we assume that our integral has to be solved in the variable x.

```
-mode par_int(Input?,Output^).
par_int([],[]).
par_int([T|Ts],[Y|Ys]):-
   maple(int(T,x),Y),
   par_int(Ts,Ys)@fwd.
```

As first step, we split the list into the single elements and return a list of unbound variables as result immediately. The individual values of these variables are not known at this stage. Then we integrate all the terms of the input list in parallel. The result values are bound to the corresponding variables of the result list as soon as the individual processes integrating the single terms are finished.

3.3 Combining the Result

Finally we have to combine all individual subexpressions to a single expression. In our example this is done by the following procedure.

```
combine_int(ResultList,ResultExpr):-
   list_to_maple(ResultList,MapleList),
   maple(convert(MapleList,"`+`"),ResultExpr).
```

The builtin ||MAPLE|| call `list_to_maple` synchronizes the `ResultList` and converts its elements to a Maple list expression. Finally we have to convert the list back to a sum expression using the corresponding Maple function.

The whole parallel integration program now looks like:

```
sum_int(SumExpr,Result):-
   split_int(SumExpr,TermList),
   par_int(TermList,ResultList),
   combine_int(ResultList,Result).
```

To improve the performance we may use a dynamic load balancing scheme based on the manager-worker concept (see: Section 4.3).

Experimenting that example shows that a higher amount of garbage collection in a sequential system allows a super-linear speedup with a low number of processors. Maple has the ability to remember previously computed functions and need not compute such a function twice. The fact that the parallel system cannot utilize that feature and the unbalanced nature of the problem restricts the speedup achievable with a high number of processors.

3.4 Meta Programming Methods

Maple has the ability to return partially evaluated functions. We use that fact if we already have a sequential program available and would like to parallelize it with a minimum of effort.

Instead of immediately evaluating all functions, we just return them with evaluated arguments. A control process picks up all partially evaluated functions and distributes them to the parallel processors.

As an example, we consider a parallelization of the following Maple procedure:

```
seq_prog:=proc()
  var:= do_something();
  [p1(var),p2(var),p3(var)]
end;
```

This procedure generates some value for `var` and returns a list of the three elements computed by the independent sub procedures $p_{1..3}$.

For parallelizing this procedure, we use a generic parallel evaluation procedure that takes a list of Maple statements as input and returns a list of results.

```
-mode par_list(Input?,Output^).
par_list([],[]).
par_list([Expr|ExprList],[Y|Ys]):-
   inline([],Expr,Y),
   par_list(ExprList,Ys)@fwd.
```

The parallelized Maple program looks like:

```
par_prog:=proc()
  var:= do_something();
  print('p1'(var));
  print('p2'(var));
  print('p3'(var));
end;
```

Now Maple evaluates only the variable *var* and returns the independent sub procedures $p_{1..3}$ unevaluated.

To complete the program we have to combine the Strand and Maple part.

```
example(Result):-
  inline([],"par_prog():",WorkList),
  par_list(WorkList,ResultList),
  maple_to_list(ResultList,Result).
```

For an efficient parallelization of more complicated Maple programs we have also implemented generic versions of the parallel evaluation and a generalized divide and conquer (see: Section 4.1) method based on dynamic load balancing using the manager-worker scheme (see: Section 4.3).

4 Main Parallelization Techniques

We describe several programing techniques used for parallelizing algorithms in ||MAPLE||. Each technique is explained on an example of an important algorithm used in symbolic computation.

4.1 Divide&Conquer: Real Root Isolation

An important problem in symbolic computation is the real root isolation problem. The goal is a procedure for finding rational intervals around all real roots of polynomials with real coefficients, where each interval contains only a single root. In Maple this is done with the Uspensky procedure [Collins and Loos, 1982]. The algorithm is of the divide and conquer style.

The idea of parallelizing a divide-and-conquer algorithm is clear. The input is split into independent subproblems of the same type and the subproblems are solved on different nodes. On each of them we recursively solve the subproblem again until a base case is reached. This leads to a tree structure of parallel processes.

The Uspensky procedure splits the range of roots into two pieces and calls itself recursively until we found an isolating interval. Since roots normally are not equally balanced, only one half is worth for further search. Because of this fact we do not expect a high speedup for that problem.

For parallelizing that algorithm we used a generic divide and conquer algorithm (Figure 2), based on the meta programming technique (3.4). We modified the original Maple algorithm in the way that Maple returns the recursive calls unevaluated instead of computing the result. These calls are distributed to the parallel processors for further computation.

In more detail a Maple routine (Mcall) called by the generic divide and conquer algorithm (divconq) simply has to print out all recursive calls unevaluated. They are collected in the Strand list Parts. Additionally the global Maple variable compose_fun has to be assigned with a function for composing the evaluated parts again. In case of the base case compose_fun has to be assigned to 0. Until the base case is not yet reached, the split_comp procedure collects all the results of the recursive calls (split procedure) and transfers them to a Maple list (Mlist). Finally the composition function (compose_fun), returning the result, will be executed.

```
divconq(Mcall,Result):-
    inline(out("compose_fun",Comp),
        Mcall,Parts),                          % divide
    split_comp(Comp,Parts,Result).

-mode split_comp(?,?,^).
split_comp('0',[X],X):-   % Base case: 0 function
split_comp(Comp,Parts,Result):-
    otherwise |
        split(Parts,Results),
                           % Wait for sub-proc be comp
        list_to_maple(Results,Mlist),
                              % Compose partial results
        inline(in("in_args",Mlist),Comp,Res),
        strip_list(Res,Result).

-mode split(?,^).
split([X|Xs],[Y|Ys]):-
    divconq(X,Y)
    split(Xs,Ys)@fwd
split([],[]).
```

Figure 2: Generic Divide&Conquer Algorithm

This function has access to the results of the recursive calls over the Maple list variable in_args.

An improved version of that algorithm uses a dynamic load balancing algorithm based on the manager-worker scheme for the recursive calls.

We give the results on instances of the Chebyshev polynomials $T_n(x)$ on a 20 processor Sequent shared memory machine. Times are given in seconds of total execution time, including time for garbage collection and loading the required modules. The numbers in parentheses denote the speedup gained.

n	Maple V	||MAPLE|| on	
		4 Proc.	16 Proc.
20	16	13 (1.2)	12 (1.3)
40	252	98 (2.6)	71 (3.5)
50	956	365 (2.6)	190 (5.0)

As we expected by the analysis of the program, the speedup gained is not very high. But compared with parallelizations reported by the literature ([Char, 1990]) where a maximum speedup of 1.7 with the same examples was achieved, we found ourselves rather successful. The better performance comes mainly from a lower communication and programming overhead in our system.

4.2 Pipelining: Gröbner Bases Computation

The Gröbner bases algorithm invented by [Buchberger, 1965] is one of the most important and time intensive algorithm in symbolic computation. It is used for solving many problems in polynomial ideal theory. In particular, it can be used for the symbolic solution of arbitrary nonlinear multivariate polynomial equations. The parallel implementation of the Gröbner bases algorithm described in [Siegl, 1990, Siegl, 1991] uses a pipeline principle for polynomial reduction. Here we give only a sketch of the overall method. All details and proofs are given in [Siegl, 1990].

In a pipeline algorithm we have to test or modify the input with respect to a set of properties. After the test modify part we may (like in the well known Concurrent Prolog implementation of the Sieve of Eratosthenes [Shapiro, 1987]) append some of the tested values to our set in order to use it for testing the rest of the input. In some cases the result of a test has to be used for generating new input values. Typical examples are all Critical Pair Completion procedures. Here a set of critical pairs is built and tested with respect to a given set of properties. Pairs that are not canceled are appended to the test set and new critical pairs are built.

For parallelizing this method, we assign each element of the test set to one parallel process connected in a pipe. The input values are driven subsequently through the pipe. Each intermediate process takes the first element from its previous neighbor and tests, modifies or cancels it. The result is sent to the next process. Then it waits for the next input for computing the result. Whenever a value reaches the end of the pipe-line it is possible to extend the test set by simply creating a new process holding the new value at the end of the pipe. Thus, the future input values will be tested with respect to the new value, too.

If necessary, we have to send the computed values back through the pipe for generating new input. In each intermediate pipe process, we generate new input values and send them back to the front end. The front end process takes the new values coming back from the pipe and sends them through the pipe again.

The sequential Gröbner bases algorithm is a Critical Pair Completion algorithm. Given a set of input polynomials as initial basis, one computes critical polynomials and reduces them with respect to the basis polynomials. The resulting polynomials are added to the basis and new critical pairs are formed.

In the parallel version we have a pipeline of processes reducing the input polynomials with respect to an increasing set of basis polynomials. The irreducible input values are appended to the reduction processes. For generating new critical polynomials (called S-polynomials) as input, the new polynomials joining the basis are sent back through the pipe building the S-polynomials with the earlier computed basis polynomials. The process at the front of the pipe only needs to collect the computed S-polynomials and sends them to the reduction processes again.

As a result we get a bidirectional pipe forming a dynamically expandable ring. The organization of the pipe to compute the Gröbner basis is shown in (Figure 3):

```
-mode main(InPoly?,Basis^).
main(InPoly,Basis):-                          % Main loop
    append_spol(InPoly,Spol,Testpoly),        % Top end
    sieve(Testpoly,Spol,Basis)@fwd.           % Back end

-mode sieve(Test-polys?,S-polys^,Basis-polys^).
sieve([BP|TPs],[sp(BP,[])|SPs1],[BP|BPs]):-
    BP =\= '0' |                              % New basis poly
      filter(BP,TPs,SPs,RPs,SPs1),
      sieve(RPs,SPs,BPs)@fwd                  % Extend pipe
sieve(['0'|TPs],SPs,B):-                      % Zero reduction
    sieve(TPs,SPs,B).
```

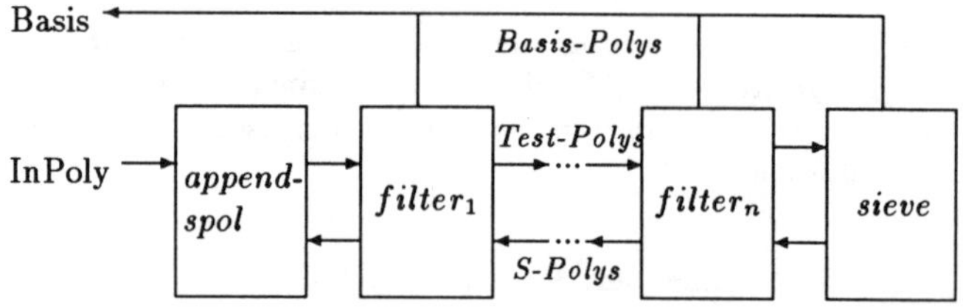

Figure 3: Organization of the Pipe for Computing Gröbner Bases

In more detail the main procedure generates the top end (append_spol) and the back end (sieve) process of the pipe. The top end process collects the newly generated S-polynomials (Spol) from the pipe, appends them to the initial input polynomials (InPoly) and sends the whole to the pipe again. The intermediate (filter) processes take each polynomial, reduces it with respect to its basis polynomial and returns the result to the next pipe process. As soon the back end receives a non zero polynomial it extends the pipe by a new intermediate (filter) process and sends that new basis polynomial (BP) back through the pipe for generating new S-polynomials. Polynomials reducing to zero are canceled out. As soon there will be no further polynomials flowing in the pipe the algorithm terminates.

The benchmarks are done with standard example from the literature ([Boege *et al.*, 1986]) computed with different term orderings (total degree, pure lexicographic term order).

Example	Order	||MAPLE|| on		
		1 Proc.	4 Proc.	16 Proc.
Trinks2	tdeg	125	53 (2.4)	28 (4.5)
Robbiano	tdeg	156	73 (2.1)	31 (5.0)
Katsura3	plex	147	38 (3.9)	11 (13.4)
Katsura3	tdeg	196	51 (3.8)	14 (14.0)
Trinks2	plex	272	62 (4.4)	16 (17.0)

The Gröbner bases algorithm has a nondeterministic behavior. It is not possible to decide in advance which order of reduction should be chosen. In our implementation polynomials flowing through the pipe are allowed to overtake each other if they will be reduced faster. In general it turns out that using faster generated and therefore simpler polynomials earlier reduces the overall computation time. This may lead to a super-linear speedup.

4.3 Manager/Worker: Parallel Interactive User Interface

||MAPLE|| may not be used for developing parallel algorithms only. It is even possible to parallelize Maple's interactive user interface, in a way that several user queries can be fullfiled simultaneously. The user interface of ||MAPLE|| is internally parallelized, using a manager worker scheme of parallelism.

```
shell(N):-                          % Shell with N workers
    merger(Workers,Request),        % Merge streams
    init_worker(N,Workers),         % Spawn N workers
    manager(Work,Request),          % Initialize manager
    shellinput(Work).               % Get user request

-mode init_worker(?,^).
init_worker(0,[]).
init_worker(N,[merge(Request)|Rs]):- N>0 |
    worker([],Request)@N,           % Place worker
    N1 is N-1,
    init_worker(N1,Rs).

manager([],_).
manager([{Mexpr,Res}|Work],[m(Expr,Mres)|Request]):-

    Expr:=Mexpr,                    % Send expr. to worker
    Res:=Mres,                      % Send result to user
    manager(Work,Request).

-mode worker(?,^).
worker(X,[m(Mexpr,Result)|Request]):-
    data(X) |                       % 1 instance per proc.
      maple(Mexpr,Result),          % Compute request
      worker(Result,Request).
```

Figure 4: Parallel User Shell

The manager-worker approach is used for parallelizing algorithms where a big set of independent parts and a limited number of nodes is used. The computing time of the various parts may vary and the load should be equally distributed among the nodes.

Many problems that may be parallelized with other methods may also be parallelized using the manager-worker approach. In practice, the method is very often used for avoiding load balancing problems.

In the shell, each user request is processed on a different node. The computing time of each request will vary greatly.

For parallelizing the user interface (Figure 4), we use a set of worker processes which subsequently solve one query. Each worker requests a piece of work from the manager process. The manager responds to the request with the next user query. Whenever one worker has finished its job it sends the result back to the manager and receives a new query. This allows the user to make queries without having to wait for the results.

In more detail, we spawn a set of workers (init_worker) and a manager process. Whenever a worker is idle it sends a request for new work (m(Mexpr,Result) tuple with empty variables). A merger combines the individual requests of the workers to a single stream connected to the manager. Whenever the manager gets new input to compute ({Mexpr,Mres}) and finds a worker requesting new work, it sends the work to the corresponding worker (Expr:=Mexpr) and returns the location of the result to the I/O-process (Res:=Mres). The worker may compute now the user request. As soon it is ready the result is sent directly to the I/O-process and a new request for work is sent to the manager.

In the actual implementation of the ||MAPLE|| user interface, we may also describe dependencies between parallel tasks.

The parallelized user interface has the advantage that the user may type in one query after the other and never be blocked waiting for the results. One can not give objective values for the performance gained by such an user interface. As soon one can type in queries faster than the whole system can solve, one will gain up to a linear speed-up. But the subjective performance due to the non blocking behavior will be much higher than the measurements will tell. This gives a significant speedup in the problem solving capacity.

5 Conclusion

We showed the usage of a system for parallelizing algorithms in symbolic computation in a simple and elegant way. Several programming techniques are given for developing and parallelizing algorithms. We found out that even with a quick parallelization it is possible to get up to a linear speedup as long as there is enough inherent parallelism and the grain size is large enough.

Due to the high level approach used in ||MAPLE|| we could keep our algorithms portable across different parallel architectures. Since ||MAPLE|| is available on many parallel computers ranging from shared memory systems over several distributed memory systems up to workstation networks we are able to develop algorithms on one machine architecture and test them on different others without any modification. Utilizing the whole sequential library of Maple enabled us to parallelize rather complicated algorithms.

In various tests we found that the main problem in achieving a high speedup is to find a proper division strategy of the algorithm to exploit the inherent parallelism. For algorithms for symbolic computation, an efficiency of 50 percent may be a very successful result. While utilizing only coarse grain parallelism, the actual communication time in the system has a minor influence on the performance.

Currently, the interface uses strings for communication which introduces a small linear overhead for parsing. Parsing and transferring for example the factorial of 1000, which is an 2568 digits long number, from Strand to Maple and back again requires approximately 0.3 sec on an i386 processor, whereas just squaring this number in Maple requires around 3 seconds. Independent operations in the sequential Maple kernel should be large enough to cover this overhead for parsing the expressions to strings suitable for the interface. In later releases, we will use a linearized form of the internal data structure for communication to allow a finer granularity.

We will also investigate various algorithms in more detail and try to find better parallelization strategies for a better efficiency.

References

[Boege *et al.*, 1986] W. Boege, R. Gebauer, and H. Kredel. Some Examples for Solving Systems of Algebraic Equations by Calculating Gröbner Bases. *Journal of Symbolic Computation*, 2(1):83–96, 1986.

[Buchberger, 1965] Bruno Buchberger. *Ein Algorithmus zum Auffinden der Basiselemente des Restklassenringes nach einem nulldimensionalen Polynomideal (An Algorithm for Finding a Basis for the Residue Class Ring of a Zero-dimensional Polynomial Ideal) (In German).* PhD thesis, University of Innsbruck, Department of Mathematics, Austria, 1965.

[Char *et al.*, 1983] Bruce W. Char, Keith O. Geddes, W. Morven Gentleman, and Gaston H. Gonnet. The Design of Maple: A Compact, Portable and Powerful Comuter Algebra System. In *EUROCAL '83, Proceedings of the International Symposium on Symbolic and Algebraic Computation*, pages 101–115. Springer, Berlin, 1983.

[Char *et al.*, 1988] Bruce W. Char, Keith O. Geddes, Gaston H. Gonnet, Michael B. Monagan, and Stephen M. Watt. *MAPLE — Reference Manual.* Symbolic Computation Group, Department of Computer Science, University of Waterloo, Ontario, Canada, 5th edition, March 1988.

[Char, 1990] Bruce W. Char. Progress Report on a System for General-Purpose Parallel Symbolic Algebraic Computation. In *Proceedings of the ISSAC'90, Tokyo, Japan, August 20–24*, pages 96–103, Department of Computer Science, University of Tennessee, Knoxville, TN 37996-1301, 1990. ACM Press, New York.

[Collins and Loos, 1982] G.E. Collins and R. Loos. Real zeros of polynomials. *Comuter Algebra, Symbolic and Algebraic Computation*, pages 83–94, 1982.

[Foster and Taylor, 1989] Ian Foster and Stephen Taylor. *Strand — New Concepts in Parallel Programming.* Prentice-Hall, Englewood Cliffs, New Jersey, 1989.

[Hong *et al.*, 1992] Hoon Hong, Wolfgang Schreiner, Andreas Neubacher, Kurt Siegl, Hans-Wolfgang Loidl, Tudor Jebelean, and Peter Zettler. PACLIB User Manual. Technical Report 92-32, RISC-Linz, Johannes Kepler University, Linz, Austria, May 1992. Also: Technical Report 92-9, ACPC Technical Report Series, Austrian Center for Parallel Computation, July 1992.

[Kuechlin, 1990] Wolfgang Kuechlin. A Parallel SAC-2 Based on Threads. Technical report, Computer and Information Sciences, Ohio State University, Columbus, Ohio, April 1990.

[Schreiner and Hong, 1993] Wolfgang Schreiner and Hoon Hong. PACLIB — A Library for Parallel Algebraic Computation on Shared Memory Computers. In *Parallel Systems Fair at the Seventh International Parallel Processing Symposium*, Newport Beach, CA, April 13–16, 1993.

[Shapiro, 1987] Ehud Shapiro, editor. *Concurrent Prolog, Collected Papers, Volumes 1 and 2.* MIT Press, Cambridge, Massachusetts, 1987.

[Siegl, 1990] Kurt Siegl. Gröbner Bases Computation in STRAND: A Case Study for Concurrent Symbolic Computation in Logic Programming Languages. Master's thesis, Johannes Kepler University, Linz, Austria, 1990. Also: Technical Report 90-54, RISC-Linz, Johannes Kepler University, Linz, Austria, 1990.

[Siegl, 1991] Kurt Siegl. Parallel Gröbner Bases Computation in ||MAPLE||. Technical Report 92-11, RISC-Linz, Johannes Kepler University, Linz, Austria, 1991. Also: Technical Report 92/13, Austrian Center for Parallel Computation, July 1992.

[Siegl, 1993] Kurt Siegl. ||MAPLE|| — A System for Parallel Symbolic Computation. In *Parallel Systems Fair at the Seventh International Parallel Processing Symposium*, Newport Beach, CA, April 13–16, 1993.

[Watt, 1986] Stephen Michael Watt. Bounded Parallelism in Computer Algebra. Research Report CS-86-12, Faculty of Mathematics, University of Waterloo, Ontario, Canada, 1986.

Experience with Fine-Grain Synchronization in MIMD Machines for Preconditioned Conjugate Gradient

Donald Yeung and Anant Agarwal
Laboratory for Computer Science
Massachusetts Institute of Technology
Cambridge, MA 02139

Abstract

This paper discusses our experience with fine-grain synchronization for a variant of the preconditioned conjugate gradient method. This algorithm represents a large class of algorithms that have been widely used but traditionally difficult to implement efficiently on vector and parallel machines. Through a series of experiments conducted using a simulator of a distributed shared-memory multiprocessor, this paper addresses two major questions related to fine-grain synchronization in the context of this application. First, what is the overall impact of fine-grain synchronization on performance? Second, what are the individual contributions of the following three mechanisms typically provided to support fine-grain synchronization: language-level support, full-empty bits for compact storage and communication of synchronization state, and efficient processor operations on the state bits?

Our experiments indicate that fine-grain synchronization improves overall performance by a factor of 3.7 on 16 processors using the largest problem size we could simulate; we project that a significant performance advantage will be sustained for larger problem sizes. We also show that the bulk of the performance advantage for this application can be attributed to exposing increased parallelism through language-level expression of fine-grain synchronization. A smaller fraction relies on a compact implementation of synchronization state, while an even smaller fraction results from efficient full-empty bit operations.

1 Introduction

This paper describes an in-depth investigation of the impact of fine-grain synchronization in MIMD machines on the performance of the preconditioned conjugate gradient method. The method uses the modified incomplete Cholesky factorization of the coefficient matrix to form the preconditioner (we will henceforth refer to this application as MICCG3D). An application study of this sort is important because it tells architects not only how programmers will use the mechanisms provided in parallel machines, but also the relative usefulness of various mechanisms provided in the system as evidenced by their impact on end application performance.

4th ACM PPOPP,5/93/CA,USA
© 1993 ACM 0-89791-589-5/93/0005/0187...$1.50

One of the challenges in such a design methodology lies in finding appropriate applications which will provide meaningful information concerning a specific set of mechanisms. The problem of finding an application that is both important and suitable for investigating fine-grain synchronization is particularly difficult because most parallel application studies for MIMD multiprocessors have focused on problems that are uninteresting from the standpoint of synchronization. One of the reasons for this lack of benchmarks is the lack of machines that support fine-grain synchronization. The MICCG3D application meets our criteria because it is an important application with challenging synchronization requirements.

Our investigation of fine-grain synchronization has two major aspects. First, we investigate how fine-grain synchronization can be gainfully employed in MICCG3D and determine quantitatively the resulting performance benefits. We analyze the benefits both with a fixed problem size and when problem size is scaled with machine size. Our study uses a simulator of Alewife, a distributed memory multiprocessor that provides hardware support for the shared-memory abstraction [1]. Our first result is that applications for which synchronization is challenging do exist. Furthermore, implementations on MIMD machines can achieve good performance by employing fine-grain synchronization.

Second, through a sequence of experiments, we try to understand exactly where the "muscle" of fine-grain synchronization lies. A common conception of fine-grain synchronization – one which has contributed to the preference for coarse-grain approaches – has been that its success relies on efficient, but expensive, hardware-supported synchronization primitives. We demonstrate that the most significant contributions of fine-grain synchronization for MICCG3D do not rely on hardware acceleration; rather, they arise from the expressiveness and flexibility of language-level support.

The rest of this paper proceeds as follows. Section 2 discusses the different styles of synchronization, and identifies the levels of support for fine-grain synchronization that machines can provide. Section 3 describes the MICCG3D application and motivates the need for fine-grain synchronization by discussing why MICCG3D is difficult to parallelize. Section 4 discusses how we actually parallelize MICCG3D using coarse- and fine-grain synchronization. Section 5 describes our experimental environment. Section 6 presents our results and discusses their significance. Finally, Section 7 summarizes our work and makes some concluding remarks.

2 Synchronization

Synchronization in shared-memory MIMD multiprocessors ensures correctness by enforcing two conditions: read-after-write data dependency and mutual exclusion. Read-after-write data dependency is a contract between a producer and a consumer of shared data. It ensures that a consumer reads a value only *after* it has been written by a producer. Mutual exclusion enforces atomicity. When a data object is accessed by multiple threads, mutual exclusion allows the accesses of a specific thread to proceed without intervening accesses by the other threads. Because the MICCG3D application uses the producer-consumer style of synchronization, the rest of this paper will only address read-after-write data dependency.

A coarse-grain solution to enforcing read-after-write data dependency is barrier synchronization. Barriers are typically used in programs involving several phases of computation where the values produced by one phase are required in the computation of subsequent phases. Parallelism is realized within a single phase, but between phases, a barrier is imposed which requires that all work from one phase be completed before the next phase is begun. Under the producer-consumer model, this means that all the consumers in the system must wait for all the producers at a common synchronization point. In contrast, a fine-grain solution provides synchronization at the data level. Instead of waiting on all the producers, fine-grain synchronization allows a consumer to wait only for the data that it is trying to consume. Once the needed data is made available by the producer(s), the consumer is allowed to continue processing.

Fine-grain synchronization provides two primary benefits over coarse-grain synchronization.

- Unnecessary waiting is avoided because a consumer waits only for the data it needs.
- Global communication is eliminated because consumers communicate only with those producers upon which they depend.

The significance of the first benefit is that parallelism is not artificially limited. Barriers impose false dependencies and thus inhibit parallelism because of unnecessary waiting. The significance of the second benefit is that each fine-grain synchronization operation is much less costly than a barrier. This means that synchronizations can occur more frequently without incurring significant overhead.

It is important to emphasize that these benefits are manifested by the expressiveness of fine-grain synchronization; they will be felt regardless of the underlying hardware implementation. This observation is important because it underscores the fact that fine-grain expression of synchronization and the implementation of synchronization primitives are orthogonal issues.

In this paper, we identify three mechanisms to support fine-grain synchronization. They are:

- Language-level support for the expression of fine-grain synchronization.
- Memory hardware support to compactly store synchronization state.
- Processor hardware support to operate efficiently on synchronization state.

The first component of support provides the programmer with a means to express synchronization at a fine granularity resulting in increased parallelism. Another attractive consequence is simpler, more elegant code [3]. The second component of support addresses the fact that an application using fine-grain synchronization will need a large synchronization name space. Providing special synchronization state can lead to an efficient implementation from the standpoint of the memory system. We refer to this benefit as *memory efficiency*. Finally, the last component of support addresses the fact that synchronizations will occur frequently. Therefore, support for the manipulation of synchronization objects can reduce the number of processor cycles incurred. We refer to this benefit as *cycle efficiency*.

3 Preconditioned Conjugate Gradient

The Conjugate Gradient (CG) algorithm is a semi-iterative method for solving a system of linear algebraic equations expressed in matrix notation as $Ax = b$. The rate of convergence of the CG method can be improved substantially by preconditioning the system of equations with a matrix K^{-1} and then applying the CG method to the preconditioned system. The idea is to choose a preconditioner such that $K^{-1}A$ is close to the identity matrix I [5].

Since the operations in the basic CG method consist of vector updates, inner products, and sparse matrix-vector multiplies, efficient parallel versions of the algorithm have been demonstrated on many vector machines and MIMD multiprocessors [4, 6]. Preconditioned CG methods, however, have not enjoyed the same success. In many of the most popular preconditioning techniques, the preconditioner steps involve recurrence relations which do not vectorize or parallelize easily. Algorithmic solutions have been proposed which use different preconditioning techniques to obtain better parallel performance [8, 11, 13, 14]; however, these approaches commonly suffer from reduced convergence rates. Also, some of these algorithms target a specific number of processors and are too complex to generalize to arbitrary machine configurations.

In this paper, we study the preconditioned CG method known as the Modified Incomplete Cholesky Factorization Conjugate Gradient in 3-Dimensions (MICCG3D). Although our study centers around a particular implementation, the general problem being addressed involves increasing parallel performance through the recurrence relations in the preconditioner steps, a problem that is common to almost all preconditioned iterative methods. Therefore, our solution using fine-grain synchronization has general consequences for the large number of algorithms that MICCG3D represents.

3.1 MICCG3D

MICCG3D is a preconditioned conjugate gradient method that assumes the coefficient matrix A in the system $Ax = b$ is sparse, and symmetric positive definite (SPD). Such a matrix commonly arises from the discretization of elliptic partial differential equations. In this paper, we use MICCG3D to solve Laplace's equation in three dimensions.

Discretizing Laplace's equation in three dimensions using a standard 7-point discretization results in a SPD coefficient matrix A that has 7 non-zero diagonals; all other elements are zero. Since matrix A is symmetric, we can write $A = L + diag(A) + L^T$ where L is a lower triangular matrix. Using the incomplete Cholesky

Vector Operation	Cycles	%
Vector Update	10589	6.17
Sparse Matrix-Vector Multiply	56099	32.7
Inner Product	6212	3.62
Vector Update	9295	5.41
Vector Update	9288	5.41
Solver	74058	43.1
Inner Product	6212	3.62

Table 1: Cycle breakdown of one iteration of MICCG3D.

factorization method, we obtain an approximate L-U factorization of matrix A which we denote as K. K can be computed as follows and is given in [13].

$$K = (L + D)D^{-1}(D + L^T) \tag{1}$$

In this expression, L is the same lower triangular matrix mentioned above, and D is a diagonal matrix which can be easily computed from matrix A (see [13]). Since K is an approximate factorization of A, we use K^{-1} as the preconditioning matrix and apply the conjugate gradient method to the preconditioned system.

As mentioned earlier, the challenge of MICCG3D lies in parallelizing the vector solution step involving the preconditioner (which we shall refer to as the "solver operation"). Table 1 shows a cycle breakdown for one iteration of MICCG3D on a problem size of $8 \times 8 \times 8$, where the problem size $n_x \times n_y \times n_z$ signifies the degree of discretization in the x, y, and z dimensions, respectively. The numbers were acquired from a single processor simulation of the Alewife machine which will be described in Section 5. Notice the solver is the most costly vector operation. If poor parallel performance is suffered in this part of the application, the potential parallel performance of the entire application will be severely limited.

3.2 Parallelization Issues

MICCG3D is difficult to parallelize because the recurrence relations in the solver operation impose data dependencies which are numerous and complex. The solver computes w_i, the residual vector in the preconditioned system. w_i is given by

$$\begin{aligned} w_i &= K^{-1}b - K^{-1}Ax_i \\ &= K^{-1}r_i \end{aligned} \tag{2}$$

where x_i is the solution vector of the current iteration step and $r_i = b - Ax_i$ is the residual vector in the original system without preconditioning. Although K^{-1} is the preconditioner, actually calculating it is infeasible because it is the inverse of a sparse matrix (and thus will be dense). Therefore, instead of solving equation 2, we solve

$$Kw_i = r_i \tag{3}$$

Since we have the factorization of K as the product of a lower triangular matrix and an upper triangular matrix (equation 1), we can solve for w_i by first employing back substitution followed by forward substitution. As an example, the backward substitution step can be expressed as follows.

$$w_i = (r_i - l_{i-1,2}w_{i-1} - l_{i-n_x,3}w_{i-n_x} - l_{i-n_xn_y,4}w_{i-n_xn_y})/l_{i,1} \tag{4}$$

where L is the lower triangular factor in K and $l_{i,j}$ is the ith element in the jth non-zero diagonal away from the center diagonal in matrix

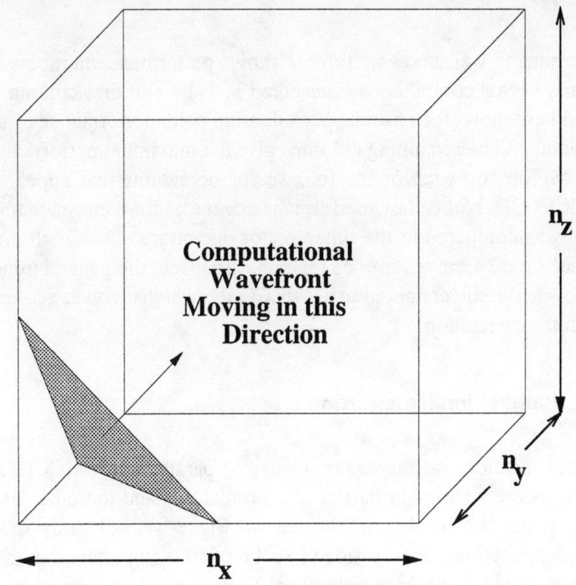

Figure 1: Computational wavefront at an instant in time. n_x, n_y, and n_z denote the discretization degree in the x, y, and z dimensions, respectively.

Machine	Peak MFlops	Vector Update	Inner Product	Sparse MxV	2-Term Recur
CRAY-1	160	46	75	54	10
CRAY-2	1951	71	88	77	8.5
CRAY X-MP	941	166	166	178	5.7
CYBER 205	400	200	100	100	2.9
ETA-10P	333	167	83.3	83.3	1.6
IBM 3090	800	21	29	27	6.5
NEC SX/2	1300	548	905	843	21
Alliant FX/80	188	17.1	30.5	16.8	3

Table 2: Performance of vector operations in MICCG3D on vector machines. The last column is for the solution of a 2-term recurrence relation.

L. Because of the recurrence in w, it is not possible to perform the entire backward substitution step in parallel. A similar problem exists for the forward substitution step. The dependencies imposed by the recurrence relation in equation 4 result in what is known as "wavefront computation." This form of computation derives its name from the fact that the solutions which can be computed in parallel at any instant in time form a wavefront in the solution space which propagates forward as time elapses. Figure 1 shows a snapshot of the wavefront in the three-dimensional solution space of MICCG3D.

Wavefront computation in MICCG3D is difficult to parallelize for two reasons. First, the parallelism is not uniform. While there is sufficient parallelism in the middle of the computation, there is very little parallelism at the beginning and the end of the computation. Second, the dependencies exist across all three spatial dimensions. That is, an element can be computed only if all the elements to the left of it, behind it, and below it have been computed. Consequently, it is impossible to choose any cartesian axis in the solution space along which to partition work for the different processors and simultaneously avoid heavy dependencies.

The difficulty in performing computations involving recurrence relations is well known. Table 2 shows performance numbers on some vector computers as presented in [4]. The first column of numbers shows the absolute peak floating point performance of the machine. The remaining columns give the maximum performance in MFlops on each of the four vector operations that appear in MICCG3D. Notice how performance degrades for recurrence relations as compared to the other vector operations. Although only results for 2-term recurrence relations are given, the general trends apply to the solver operation in MICCG3D (which involves a 3-term recurrence relation).

4 Parallel Implementation

In this section, we discuss two ways of parallelizing MICCG3D. One uses coarse-grain barrier synchronization and the other uses fine-grain data-level synchronization. Since we will study these implementations side-by-side in Section 6, it is important that they are in some sense a fair comparison. We believe our two implementations present a fair comparison based on the fact that both require equal programming effort. We do not claim that either implementation is *the best* that can be done; however, we are confident that they are both reasonable implementations.

4.1 Coarse-Grain MICCG3D

In the coarse-grain approach, we partition the solution space along the z dimension and assign n_z/P contiguous planes in the solution space to each processor, where P is the number of processors. To maximize physical locality of data reference, we ensure that all planes assigned to a processor are allocated in that processor's local memory. For this partitioning of the data, communication occurs only in the sparse matrix-vector multiply and solver operations. Furthermore, communication occurs only between adjacent processors and only when computing elements in the solution space which reside in planes at partition boundaries.

Barriers are placed in between vector operations to ensure that results are fully completed before being used in subsequent computation. For all but the solver operation, this is sufficient to guarantee correctness. Dependencies arising from the recurrence relation in the solver require further use of barriers. Computation in the solver is further sectioned into k parts along the x dimension. Each processor computes all the results in one block and enters a barrier before it is allowed to move on to the next block. Dependencies between blocks across processors must be enforced by staggering the computation. This process is illustrated in Figure 2 on an example that has been partitioned for four processors with k equal to four. The blocks that are computed in parallel between barriers are filled with the same hash pattern. Staggering the blocks results in a staircase-like propagation of computation.

Notice this scheme suffers from limited parallelism. At the beginning of the solver operation, when processor P0 computes its first block, processors P1, P2, and P3 must remain idle. After the first barrier, P0 moves on to its second block, but only P1 is allowed to start computing; P2 and P3 are still idle, and so on. Not until P0 is on its 4th block are all processors busy (note the same problem occurs at the end of the solver operation). The degree to which parallelism is limited depends on the value of k. The larger k is, the finer the grain of data associated with each synchronization and thus the smaller the amount of serialization. For all the simulations reported in Section 6, we used $k = P$.

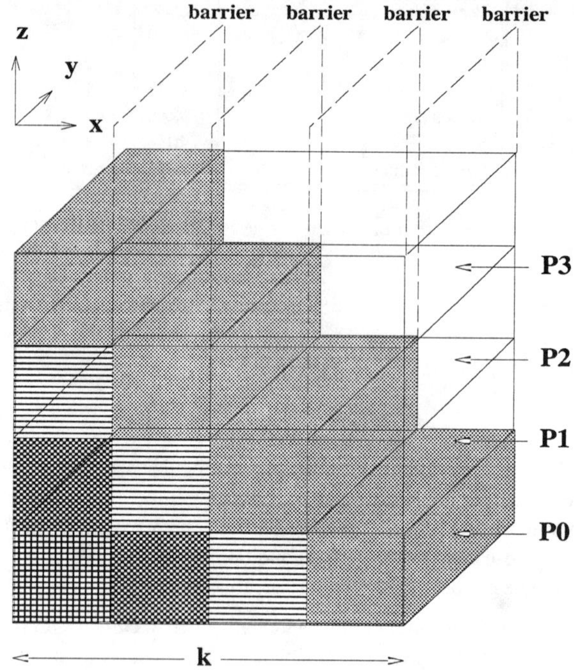

Figure 2: Coarse-grain parallel implementation of the solver operation for 4 processors. Similarly shaded blocks are computed in parallel. Pi denotes processor i, and k is the number of computational blocks in the x-dimension.

To find an upper bound on speedup in the solver computation, we observe that sequential execution time is proportional to kP, the total number of blocks. Parallel execution time is proportional to the number of blocks per processor, k, added to the number of intervals between barriers each processor spends idling, $P - 1$. Taking the ratio of sequential to parallel execution time gives the upper bound on speedup.

$$S_{upper} = \frac{kP}{k + P - 1} \tag{5}$$

Notice this is only an upper bound because it ignores the overhead of barrier operations which becomes more significant as k increases.

4.2 Fine-Grain MICCG3D

Like the coarse-grain implementation, each processor is assigned n_z/P planes partitioned along the z dimension; however, in the fine-grain implementation, these planes are not contiguous. Instead, processors are allocated planes modulo P. This scheme is illustrated in Figure 3. Notice that compared to the coarse-grain implementation, this partitioning scheme results in substantially more communication in the sparse matrix-vector multiply and solver operations because the computation of every element in the solution space depends on a value belonging to a remote processor.

Synchronization is done at the word-level using fine-grain synchronization. The need for barriers is completely eliminated except in the inner product where an implicit barrier occurs in the accumulate of all the individual scalar multiplies. Word-level synchronization automatically enforces the recurrence dependencies in

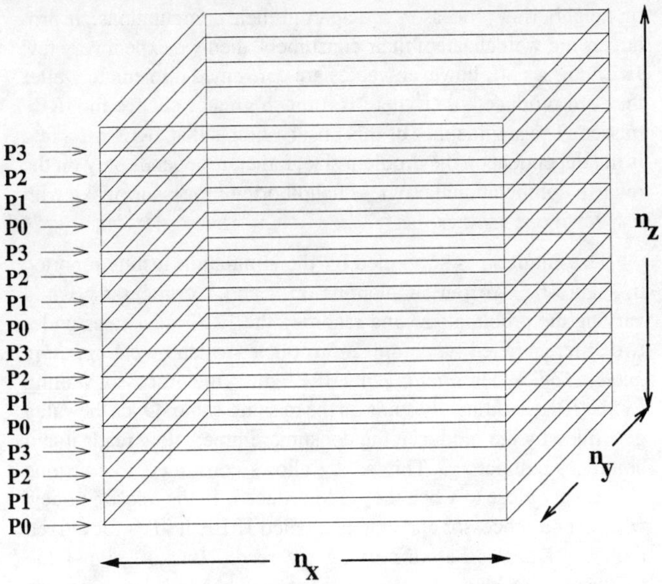

Figure 3: Fine-grain parallel implementation of the solver operation for 4 processors. n_x, n_y, and n_z denote the discretization degree in the x, y, and z dimensions, respectively.

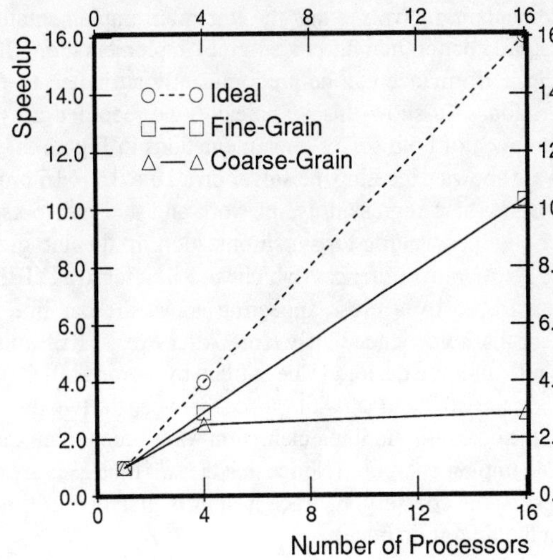

Figure 4: Coarse-grain and fine-grain speedups on MICCG3D. Problem Size = 16 × 16 × 16.

the solver operation. In the fine-grain version of the solver, each processor can compute results as fast as possible. If a thread tries to read a value that has not yet been computed, the semantics of the data-level synchronization force that thread of execution to stop and wait until the value becomes available. Therefore, processors never wait unnecessarily.

For this implementation, the theoretical speedup is linear (*i.e.*, $S_{upper} = P$).

5 Implementation Environment

The results we report in Section 6 are in the context of the Alewife Machine. Alewife consists of a scalable number of homogeneous processing nodes connected in a 2-D mesh topology. The network channels are bidirectional; end-around connections do not exist at the edges of the network. Each Alewife node consists of a 32-bit RISC processor, a floating point unit, 64K bytes of cache memory, 8M bytes of dynamic RAM, and a network routing chip. Although the memory is distributed across processors, a shared-memory abstraction is implemented in hardware which includes support for maintaining cache coherence.

Alewife supports the fine-grain synchronization capabilities described in Section 2. At the language level, L-structure and J-structure constructs allow the expression of synchronization at data-level granularity. L-structures enforce mutual exclusion and J-structures provide producer-consumer synchronization (a detailed discussion on language-level support for fine-grain synchronization in Alewife appears in [7]). Memory efficiency and cycle efficiency as discussed in Section 2 are facilitated by full-empty bits in the memory hardware and fast operations on full-empty bits in the processor hardware, respectively.

Alewife facilitates memory efficiency by allocating a full-empty bit for every word in memory. Each full-empty bit acts as a dedicated hardware synchronization variable. The memory efficiency benefit has two consequences. First, the memory overhead for synchronization objects is low. Without full-empty bits, a programmer would have to explicitly allocate extra memory for every synchronization variable. Second, memory efficiency reduces communication. A synchronized data access on Alewife brings both the datum and the synchronization variable to the processor in one memory system transaction. If the datum and synchronization variable were stored in separate memory locations, two memory transactions would be needed.

Alewife facilitates cycle efficiency by providing special processor hardware that enables the manipulation of a full-empty bit simultaneously with the load or store of its associated data. Thus, a synchronized data access costs no more than a normal load or store. Without hardware support, a synchronized access would take at least three instructions: one to access the full-empty bit, another to test the bit, and a third to access the datum. Alewife uses the result of full-empty tests to conditionally trap the processor. This trapping mechanism is used to identify exceptional cases such as failed synchronizations so they can be handled by software trap handlers. This approach provides efficient hardware support for successful synchronization operations, but relegates the processing of failed synchronizations to less efficient software handlers. The philosophy driving this approach is that successful synchronization operations will be the common case when using fine-grain synchronization.

In Section 6, we will compare the importance of cycle efficiency, memory efficiency, and the benefit of increased parallelism offered by language-level support.

6 Results

Simulation results were obtained for both the coarse-grain and fine-grain implementations on 1, 4, and 16 processor Alewife configurations. A problem size of 16 × 16 × 16 was used.

Figure 4 shows the speedups calculated by normalizing execution times against the uniprocessor execution time of the coarse-grain implementation. We see that the fine-grain implementation does consistently better than the coarse-grain implementation. The difference in performance can be predominantly attributed to the solver operation. To show this graphically, we recorded a synchronization trace of both solver implementations in Figure 5. 16 processors are shown executing the solver on a $16 \times 16 \times 16$ problem size. Black bars represent useful work and the interspersed white space signifies waiting for synchronization. In the fine-grain trace, failed J-structure references (which we will refer to as "JREF misses") are traced by a cross appearing above the bar line of the processor that experienced the event. After every JREF miss, processors idle until the desired value is filled by a producer. Comparing the amount of idle time (white space) between the two traces, we see that the coarse-grain implementation waits much more than the fine-grain implementation. (Notice that the two time axes are on different scales; the coarse-grain trace is approximately four times longer than the fine-grain trace).

Table 3 shows a cycle breakdown of the $16 \times 16 \times 16$ problem size simulation for both implementations. There are three sources of overhead: waiting for the memory system labeled "cache", waiting for JREFs labeled "JREF", and waiting at barriers. Barrier overhead is split into two components. The first, "Bar Time," is the number of cycles from when the last thread enters the barrier until the last thread leaves the barrier. The second is "Bar Skew" which is the number of cycles from when the first thread arrives at the barrier until the last thread arrives at the barrier. "Bar Time" is a measure of the cost of the barrier operation after all threads have arrived, and "Bar Skew" is a measure of skew between the runtimes of the threads. Both are totals across all barriers averaged for each processor.

In the next three sections, we discuss each of these sources of overhead and their significance. In particular, we try to extrapolate the behavior as problem size and machine size are increased beyond what we are able to simulate in a reasonable amount of time.

6.1 Memory System Overhead

The overhead of the memory system is consistently one of the smallest overheads in Table 3, and we expect the effect of the memory system to be even less at larger problem sizes. In the coarse-grain implementation, the number of remote accesses will grow with the surface area of each processor partition while the number of local accesses will grow with the volume. Thus, as problem size is increased, the overall cost of memory system overhead will decrease. In the fine-grain implementation, a new J-structure is allocated on each iteration thereby bypassing the need to reset the J-structure in between iterations. This results in no data reuse. In a real implementation, J-structures will be reset between iterations and reused thus giving rise to better cache performance. Moreover, because of the static nature of the computation, we expect very naive prefetching to be effective in hiding most of the memory latency in both implementations.

6.2 Controlling J-Structure Synchronization Overhead

In the fine-grain implementation of the solver, processor P_i consumes values produced by processor P_{i-1}. We expect the number of JREF misses to be related to how far producers and consumers on neighboring processors are apart in their computations. If producers are well ahead of their consumers, then we expect very few JREF misses. If, however, values are consumed immediately after they are produced, then there is a much greater chance for JREF misses. The significance of this observation is that JREF miss rate is not dependent on the problem size; rather, it depends only on the relative computational progress neighboring processors make with respect to one another.

This intuition is supported by the simulation results reported in Figure 6. We ran simulations on 4 and 16 processors while varying the problem size and recorded the JREF miss rates under two different failed synchronization policies which we call *spinning* and *backoff*. When *spinning* on a JREF miss, the processor waiting for the JREF continually spins on the missing value. Once the value gets filled by the producer, the consumer immediately reads it and continues computing. This policy allows consumers to consume values very close to when they are produced. In the *backoff* policy, whenever a processor encounters a failed JREF, it idles for a fixed number of cycles before retrying the read. Backoff allows the producer to make computational progress ahead of the consumer. Figure 6 verifies that backoff achieves a dramatically lower JREF miss rate and also confirms that for non-trivial problem sizes, the miss rate is constant with respect to problem size. Along with a lower JREF miss rate, backoff has the added benefit of reducing false sharing effects in the cache.

6.3 Barrier Overhead

The most serious barrier overhead reported in Table 3 appears in the coarse-grain implementation of the solver where barriers are used to enforce the dependencies caused by the recurrence relations. To better understand how this overhead effects performance as a function of problem size and machine size, we rederive the theoretical speedup in the coarse-grain solver operation, equation 5, to include barrier overhead. With barrier overhead (but still ignoring communication costs), the time to execute the solver in parallel, T_{par}, is

$$T_{par} = \frac{T_{seq}}{S_{upper}} + Bn_B \tag{6}$$

where T_{seq} is the sequential execution time, S_{upper} is the theoretical solver speedup, B is the average cost of a barrier synchronization (includes skew), and n_B is the number of barriers encountered per processor. Using equation 5, we get

$$T_{par} = \frac{T_{seq}(k+P-1)}{kP} + B(k+P-1) \tag{7}$$

where we have used $n_B = k + P - 1$ by recognizing that n_B is equivalent to the number of blocks encountered by each processor as discussed in Section 4.1. The solver speedup including barrier overhead $S(k, P) = T_{seq}/T_{par}$ is

$$\begin{aligned} S(k,P) &= \frac{T_{seq}}{\frac{T_{seq}(k+P-1)}{kP} + B(k+P-1)} \\ &= \left(\frac{kP}{k+P-1}\right)\left(\frac{T_{seq}}{T_{seq}+BkP}\right) \end{aligned} \tag{8}$$

From Figure 2, we see that the run-length between barriers is proportional to a single block of computation. If we define this run-length as r_l, then we can express T_{seq} as $T_{seq} = r_l kP$ since there are kP

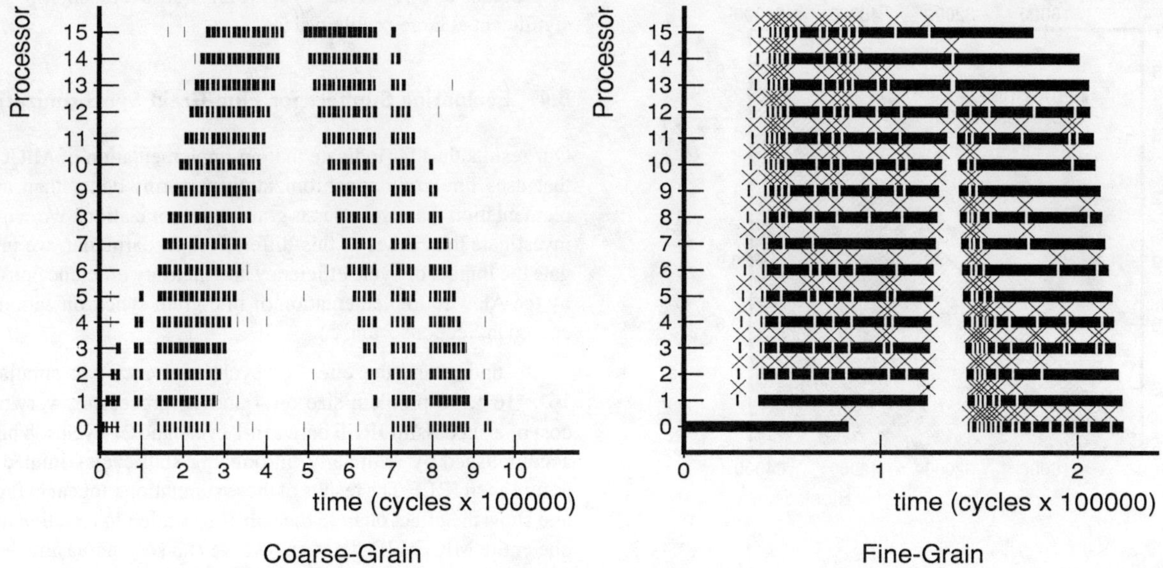

Figure 5: Traces in the solver operation of MICCG3D. Problem size = 16 × 16 × 16. Bar lines show useful work, and white space shows waiting for synchronization. Crosses indicate JREF misses. The staircase shape is the signature of the back and forward substitution steps.

Coarse-Grain MICCG3D.										
Processors	Total	Cache	%	JREF	%	Bar Time	%	Bar Skew	%
1	6943004	568540	8.19	N/A	N/A	17921	0.258	0	0.0
4	2769725	85157	3.07	N/A	N/A	73799	2.66	946855	34.19
16	2428515	179888	7.41	N/A	N/A	945195	38.92	735474	30.28

Fine-Grain MICCG3D.									
Processors	Total	Cache	%	JREF	%	Bar Time	%	Bar Skew	%
1	6831696	472287	6.91	0	0.0	1270	0.019	0	0.0
4	2328728	305456	13.12	111627	4.79	11636	0.50	57288	2.46
16	662230	65929	9.96	36301	11.55	12496	1.89	68996	10.42

Table 3: Cycle breakdown for simulations. Problem size = 16 × 16 × 16. "Cache" is waiting on the memory system, "JREF" is waiting on failed J-structure references, "Bar Time" is the cost of all the barriers (without skew), and "Bar Skew" is the total skew between the runtimes of the threads at all the barriers.

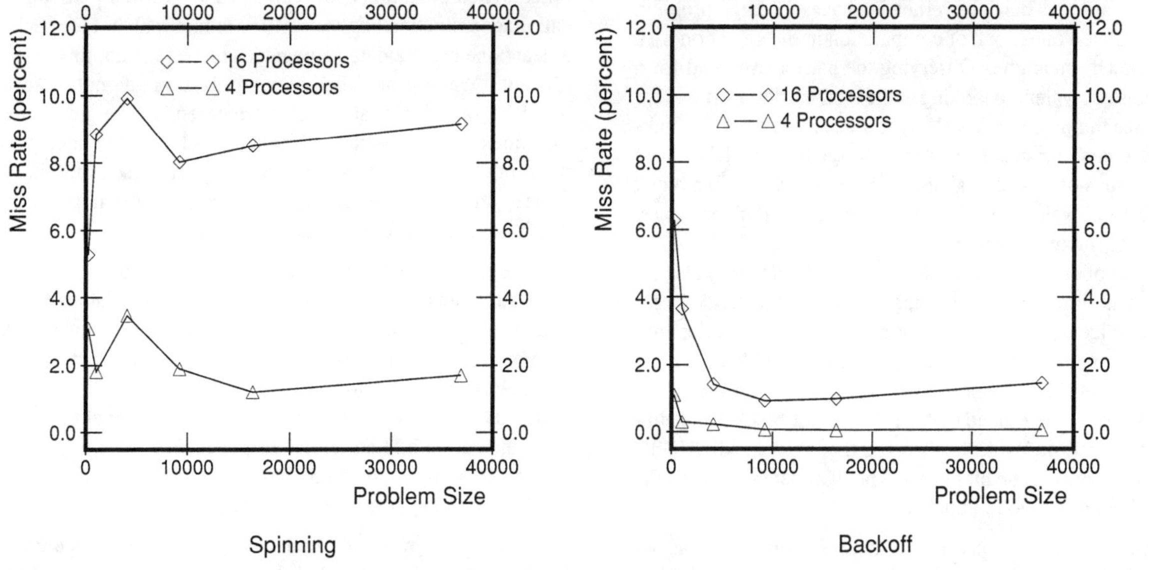

Figure 6: JREF miss rate as a function of problem size in the Spinning and Backoff synchronization failure policies. Problem size is given by $n_x \times n_y \times n_z$ where n_x, n_y, and n_z are the degree of discretization in the x, y, and z dimensions, respectively.

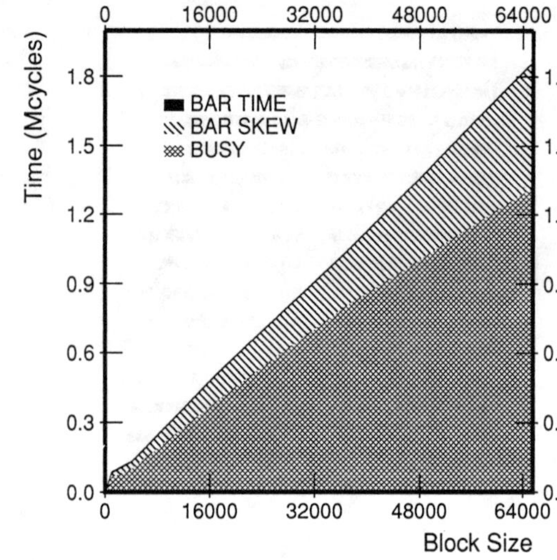

Figure 7: Barrier overhead as a function of block size for 16 processors. Block size is given by $n_x \times n_y \times n_z$ where n_x, n_y, and n_z are the number of elements in one block in the x, y, and z dimensions, respectively.

blocks in total. Therefore, we can rewrite equation 8 as

$$S(k, P) = \left(\frac{kP}{k + P - 1}\right)\left(\frac{r_l}{r_l + B}\right) \tag{9}$$

Equation 9 is the product of the ideal theoretical solver speedup and the overhead of a barrier operation in comparison to the average run-length between barriers. Notice that both these terms cannot be optimized simultaneously. Making k large increases the theoretical speedup term; however, it reduces the run-length between barriers, r_l, which makes the barrier overhead B more significant. Similarly, decreasing k helps the overhead term but lowers the theoretical speedup term.

To understand how barrier overhead behaves for large problem sizes, we simulated one block of computation in the solver on a 16 processor Alewife machine. Observing the barrier overhead for a single block is equivalent to looking at the total barrier overhead for a problem size that is a factor kP larger since there are kP blocks in the entire coarse-grain solver operation (see Section 4.1). Even for modest values of P and k, simulating the largest feasible block size is in fact equivalent to looking at fairly large problem sizes. The result of this experiment appears in Figure 7 which shows the average barrier operation cost (appearing as "BAR TIME") and the average skew in thread runtimes (appearing as "BAR SKEW") for various block sizes. Since the cost of a barrier operation depends only on the number of processors, it is constant with respect to block size and is trivial for most block sizes. Skew, however, is a significant source of overhead even at the largest block sizes simulated (roughly 30%). We have observed that skew in MICCG3D is due to nonuniform cache hit rates and network latency across the machine and not due to load imbalance.

We draw two conclusions from Figure 7. First, the barrier overhead of 68% reported for our 16 processor simulation in Table 3 is pessimistic and is due to the fact that we can only simulate small problem sizes. Second, although we expect better performance as problem size is scaled, synchronization overhead will still be significant at large problem sizes.

6.4 Evaluating Support for Fine-Grain Synchronization

Our results thus far indicate that an implementation of MICCG3D that uses fine-grain synchronization performs better than an implementation that uses coarse-grain synchronization. We will now investigate the causes of this difference. In particular, we investigate the impact of cycle efficiency and memory efficiency provided by the Alewife implementation of fine-grain synchronization (discussed in Sections 2 and 5).

To understand the effect of cycle efficiency, we simulated a $16 \times 16 \times 16$ problem size on 4 and 16 processors, varying the cost of a successful JREF between 1 cycle and 21 cycles. This was accomplished by artificially introducing stall cycles immediately before each JREF. The results of these simulations appear in Figure 8 and show the effect on both the solver operation in isolation and on one entire MICCG3D iteration. As we can see, increasing the cost of a successful JREF does not dramatically impact overall runtime. We simulated the cost out to 21 cycles only to show extreme effects. We expect any realistic JREF implementation to cost less than 10 cycles. Notice the 4 processor simulation is more sensitive to the cost of a successful JREF than the 16 processor simulation (exhibited by a steeper slope). This is because for a fixed problem size, there are more JREFs in the critical path of execution for smaller machine sizes; thus, a greater increase in execution time will result from a given increase in the cost of each JREF.

The degree to which performance is affected by the cost of a successful JREF depends on the frequency of JREFs. The more frequent JREFs are, the greater the effect increasing successful JREF cost will have. For MICCG3D on 16 processors, we have observed frequencies of approximately 1 JREF every 80 cycles. We were surprised to find such a low JREF frequency.

The frequency of JREFs is determined by three factors: the amount of computation between JREFs, the amount of waiting on the memory system between JREFs, and the amount of waiting on failed synchronizations between JREFs. For this particular application, computation between JREFs is minimal, but for each JREF, at least one remote data value needs to be fetched; this cost is significant. Waiting on failed synchronization attempts also lowers the JREF rate significantly. This effect tends to be greater on large machines since the number of failed JREF attempts increases with more processors. We expect greater synchronization failure rates to be a trend as machine size grows; therefore, on larger machines, it will be more difficult to sustain high JREF rates.

The effect of memory efficiency can be measured by implementing J-structures with explicit synchronization variables for each J-structure element in place of the full-empty bits. This doubles the memory requirement and forces two memory transactions to occur for each JREF. We performed this modification to the solver operation and compared its performance with the original full-empty bit implementation of J-structures in simulations of 4 and 16 processors on $16 \times 16 \times 16$ and $32 \times 32 \times 32$ problem sizes each. The results of this experiment appear in Figure 9.

In the left graph of Figure 9, we compare execution times. For each machine size and problem size, there is a group of three bars. The "H" bar (for Hardware) uses the Alewife support for J-structures. The "S1" bar (for Software1) uses explicit synchroniza-

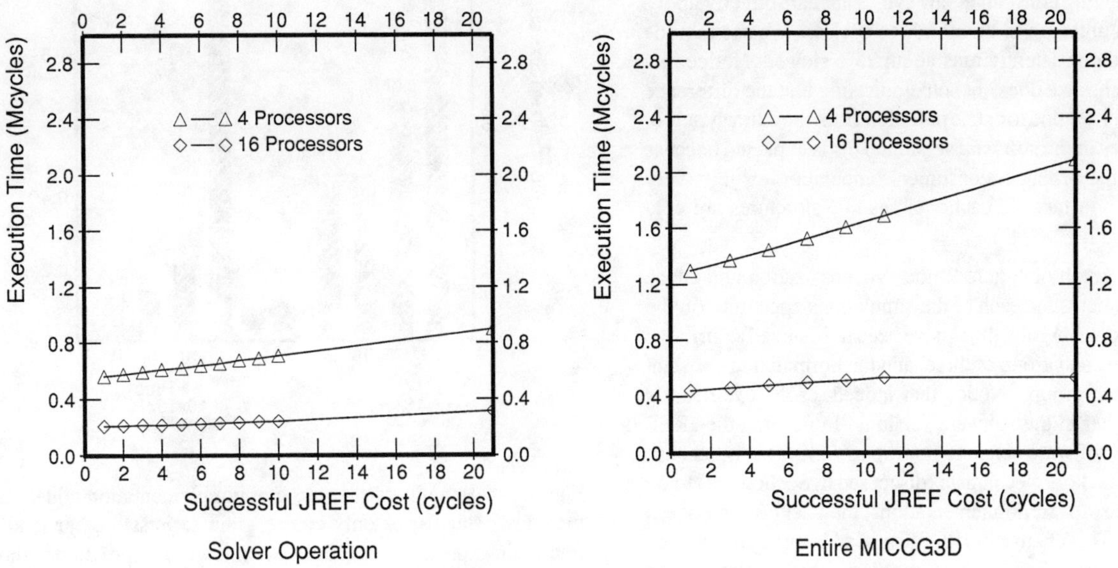

Figure 8: Effect of increasing successful JREF cost in both the solver operation and an entire MICCG3D iteration. Problem size = $16 \times 16 \times 16$.

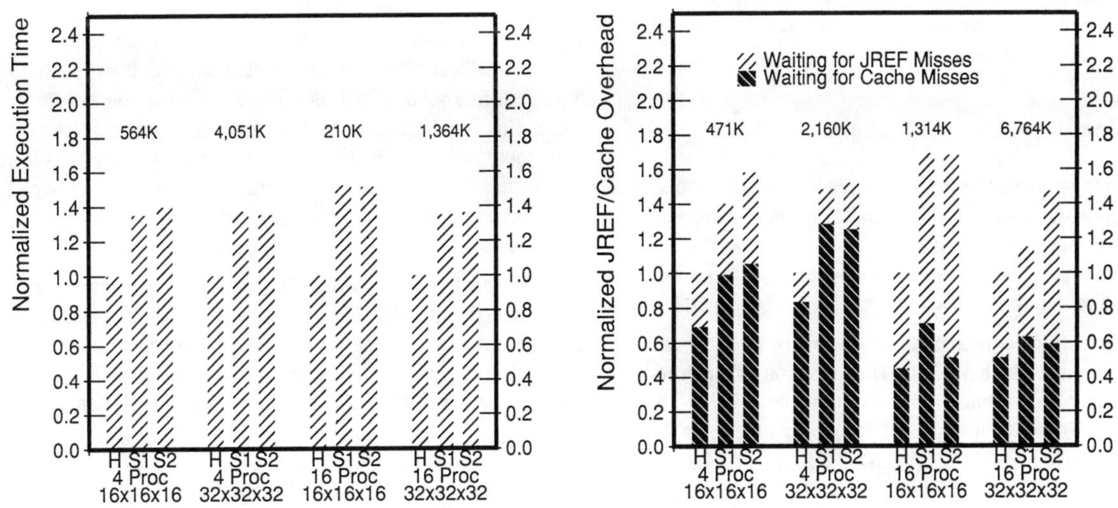

Figure 9: Execution times and overheads in hardware versus software implementations of J-structures in the solver operation. The "H" bars (for "Hardware") use full-empty bit support, the "S1" bars (for "Software1") use explicit software variables, and the "S2" bars (for "Software2") use the same implementation as the "S1" bars except cache size has been doubled to study the effects of cache pollution.

tion variables for each J-structure element, and "S2" (for Software2) uses the same J-structure implementation as "S1" except the cache size has been doubled from 64K bytes to 128K bytes. All three bars in the group have been normalized against the "H" execution time; the normalizing constant in raw cycles appears directly above each group (the units are in thousands of cycles). We see that the software version consistently runs about 35% slower. Notice that doubling the cache size does not help, indicating that the difference in performance is not due to cache pollution from the extra synchronization variables in the software version. This is expected because in MICCG3D, the producer-consumer computation exhibits very little data reuse. In fact, all cache misses to J-structures are cold start misses.

In the right graph of Figure 9, the synchronization and cache overhead components for each of the simulations appearing on the left graph are shown. Again, times have been normalized against the hardware time in each group of three, and the normalizing constant appears over each group. Notice that indeed, cache overhead is significantly higher in the software versions. In general, the JREF overhead for the software versions goes up as well. This is because in order for the backoff mechanism (discussed in Section 6.2) to be effective for the software implementations, the backoff time needs to be increased. This change in JREF overhead is most pronounced in the 16 processor, $16 \times 16 \times 16$ problem size simulation. In this simulation, because of the relatively small problem size for the relatively large machine size, total execution time is very short. This means the JREF overhead is dominated by the JREF misses which occur at the beginning and end of the back and forward substitution steps. In these phases of the solver step, JREF misses are frequent, so the increase in backoff time for the software implementation has a significant impact on total JREF overhead. For more realistic problem sizes, this "JREF cold start" effect will not be significant and instead, we should see a "steady state" JREF overhead. This trend is already visible in the 4 processor $32 \times 32 \times 32$ simulation. Since the JREF miss rate is independent of problem size (shown in Section 6.2), the asymptotic overhead for real problem sizes will be dominated by the cache overhead.

6.5 Interpreting the Fine-Grain Performance Gains

The discussion in the previous section examined in detail the impact of two components of support for fine-grain synchronization on application performance, those two which involve hardware-level support. In this section, we consider the essential results of this study and relate it to the importance of language-level support.

We collect data from earlier parts of the paper to show the increase in performance of the MICCG3D application as the components of support for fine-grain synchronization are added incrementally. Figure 10 shows normalized execution times for the $16 \times 16 \times 16$ problem size of MICCG3D. Two sets of data are shown, one for 4 processors and one for 16 processors. In each set, bar I shows the execution time of MICCG3D implemented with coarse-grain barriers. Bar II shows the execution time when J-structure style synchronization is used; however, the J-structures are implemented purely in software without the benefit of cycle efficiency and memory efficiency. Bar III shows the execution time when the J-structures are supported by full-empty bits that can be accessed in 5 cycles thus providing memory efficiency (but not cycle efficiency). Finally, bar IV shows the addition of cycle efficiency by allowing single cycle access to full-empty bits (*i.e.*, full Alewife support for fine-grain synchronization).

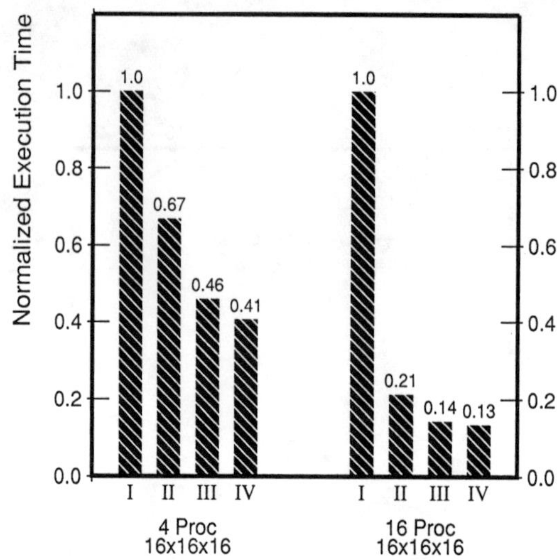

Figure 10: Benefits of the fine-grain implementation added incrementally. Bar I uses only coarse-grain expression, bar II allows fine-grain expression, bar III allows fine-grain expression with full-empty bit support, and bar IV allows fine-grain expression with full-empty bits and fast bit operations.

The impact of cycle efficiency is quantified by the difference in execution times between bars III and IV. In both sets of data, this performance gain is small, on the order of 10%. The impact of memory efficiency is quantified by the difference between bars II and III, and indicates a more significant performance improvement of about 40%. But by far the largest gain in performance comes from increased parallelism due to the expressiveness of fine-grain synchronization as quantified by the difference between bars I and II. The two sets of data together also show that as machine size is scaled, fine-grain expression of synchronization becomes even more critical in improving application performance in comparison to memory and cycle efficiency. Notice that 16 processors is still a very modest machine size. With further machine scaling, we expect that the sharp difference in performance gains observed for the 16 processor data set will be even more pronounced.

There are two issues which help define the bounds within which this conclusion is valid. First, we recognize that this discussion has only considered machine scaling on a fixed problem size. This is important if we are interested in running a *given problem* as fast as possible. What if we are interested in scaling problem size while keeping machine size fixed? We expect that a larger problem size will improve the execution time of the coarse-grain implementation more than the fine-grain implementation, so the dramatic difference between bars I and II should decrease with problem size scaling. The question is, how much will it decrease? Recall from Section 6.3 that even for fairly large problem sizes, barrier overhead will remain significant due to skew in the runtimes of threads. Therefore, we predict that limited parallelism will remain a problem in the MICCG3D application and fine-grain expression of synchronization will continue to be important.

Second, we recognize that the importance of memory and cycle efficiency ultimately depends on the frequency of JREFs (recall the discussion in Section 6.4). JREF frequency is determined by the amount of computation, memory system latency, and synchronization failure latency between every JREF. Therefore, the JREF frequency can be increased by employing the following optimizations. More aggressive compiler optimizations can reduce the cost of the computation, prefetching can reduce the overhead of the memory system, and multithreading combined with fast context switching can hide the latency of synchronization failures. The extent to which these optimizations will influence the importance of memory and cycle efficiency relative to fine-grain expression requires further study.

7 Summary

Previous application studies have dealt with problems which do not present a challenge for synchronization. To obtain a better understanding of what the synchronization needs of programmers will be, a more comprehensive look into how applications synchronize is needed. MICCG3D, a preconditioned conjugate gradient algorithm using the incomplete Cholesky factorization of the coefficient matrix as a preconditioner, is an application for which synchronization is a challenging problem. It is an important application having received much attention in previous work [8, 11, 13, 14], and it represents a larger class of preconditioned iterative methods which have traditionally been hard to parallelize. By implementing MICCG3D using both a coarse- and fine-grain approach, we have discovered that the application benefits greatly from fine-grain synchronization.

In problem sizes that we simulated, we observe that the implementation using fine-grain synchronization executed 3.7 times faster than the coarse-grain implementation on a 16 processor Alewife machine. Since JREF overhead does not depend on problem size, we expect the fine-grain version to maintain its performance as problem size is scaled. Although the barrier overhead in the coarse-grain implementation will improve as problem size is scaled, simulations show that skew in the runtimes of threads will remain significant for realistic problem sizes. Fundamentally, this is due to the fact that an increase in problem size only affects an increase in run-length between barriers that is kP times smaller. Even for modest machine sizes, and especially for large machines, we expect run-lengths to be small enough on realistic problem sizes that skew at the barriers will remain significant. Therefore, we anticipate that the fine-grain implementation will sustain a significant performance advantage over the coarse-grain implementation at large problem sizes.

After evaluating the performance of MICCG3D implemented with both coarse- and fine-grain synchronization, we extended our study to understand how fine-grain synchronization achieves its performance advantage. First, we identified three components of support for fine-grain synchronization and enumerated the benefits they provide for applications: increased parallelism through expressiveness, cycle efficiency, and memory efficiency. Next, we ascertained the degree to which each of these benefits were responsible for the performance gains we observed in the fine-grain implementation of MICCG3D. Our conclusion is that for the MICCG3D application, cycle efficiency has the least impact while memory efficiency provides a more significant 40% increase in performance. But by far the most important benefit for MICCG3D is the ability to increase parallelism by expressing synchronization at a fine granularity. By employing optimizations to reduce the cost of the computation, memory system, and synchronization failures, we expect the contributions of memory and cycle efficiency to become more significant, but further study is needed to quantify this effect.

8 Acknowledgments

This research was funded in part by NSF grant # MIP-9012773, in part by DARPA contract # N00014-87-K-0825, and in part by a NSF Presidential Young Investigator Award. We would also like to acknowledge Norm Rubin [10] for inspiring us to use the MICCG3D application for our study.

References

[1] Anant Agarwal, David Chaiken, Kirk Johnson, David Kranz, John Kubiatowicz, Kiyoshi Kurihara, Beng-Hong Lim, Gino Maa, and Dan Nussbaum. The MIT Alewife Machine: A Large-Scale Distributed-Memory Multiprocessor. *MIT/LCS/TM 454*, MIT Laboratory for Computer Science, June 1991.

[2] Gail Alverson, Robert Alverson, and David Callahan. Exploiting Heterogeneous Parallelism on a Multithreaded Multiprocessor. *Workshop on Multithreaded Computers, Proceedings of Supercomputing '91*, ACM Sigraph & IEEE, November 1991.

[3] Arvind, and Rishiyur S. Nikhil. I-Structures: Data Structures for Parallel Computing. *ACM Transactions on Programming Languages and Systems*, pp. 598-632, Vol. 11, No. 4, October 1989.

[4] Jack J. Dongarra, Iain S. Duff, Danny C. Sorensen, and Henk A. van der Vorst. Solving Linear Systems on Vector and Shared Memory Computers. *SIAM*, Philadelphia. 1991.

[5] Gene H. Golub and Charles F. van Loan. Matrix Computations. *Johns Hopkins University Press*, Baltimore, Maryland. 1983.

[6] Louis A. Hageman and David M. Young. Applied Iterative Methods. *Academic Press*, New York. 1981.

[7] David Kranz, Beng-Hong Lim, and Anant Agarwal. Low-Cost Support for Fine-Grain Synchronization in Multiprocessors. Multithreading: A Summary of the State of the Art, *Kluwer Academic Publishers*, 1992. Also available as *MIT/LCS/TM 470*, 1992.

[8] Gerard Meurant. Multitasking the Conjugate Gradient Method on the CRAY X-MP/48. *Parallel Computing*, Vol 5, pp 267-280, 1987.

[9] G. M. Papadopoulos and D. E. Culler. Monsoon: An Explicit Token-Store Architecture. *Proceedings of the 17th Annual International Symposium on Computer Architecture*, pp. 82-91, New York, June 1990.

[10] Norman Rubin. Data Flow Computing and the Conjugate Gradient Method. *MCRC-TR-25*, Motorola Cambridge Research Center, 1992.

[11] Youcef Saad and Martin H. Schultz. Parallel Implementations of Preconditioned Conjugate Gradient Methods. *Research Report YALEU/DCS/RR-425*, Yale University, Department of Computer Science, October 1985.

[12] B. J. Smith. Architecture and Applications of the HEP Multiprocessor Computer System. *SPIE*, 298:241-248, 1981.

[13] Henk A. van der Vorst. High Performance Preconditioning. *SIAM Journal of Scientific Statistical Computing*, Vol. 10, No. 6, pp. 1174-1185, November 1989.

[14] Henk A. van der Vorst. The Performance of FORTRAN Implementations for Preconditioned Conjugate Gradients on Vector Computers. *Parallel Computing*, Vol 3, pp 49-58, 1986.

Procs and Locks: A Portable Multiprocessing Platform for Standard ML of New Jersey*

J. Gregory Morrisett
Carnegie Mellon University
jgmorris@cs.cmu.edu

Andrew Tolmach
Portland State University
apt@cs.pdx.edu

Abstract

We have built a portable platform for running Standard ML of New Jersey programs on multiprocessors. It can be used to implement user-level thread packages for multiprocessors *within* the ML language with first-class continuations. The platform supports experimentation with different thread scheduling policies and synchronization constructs. It has been used to construct a Modula-3 style thread package and a version of Concurrent ML, and has been ported to three different multiprocessors running variants of Unix. This paper describes the platform's design, implementation, and performance.

1 Introduction

Many concurrent and parallel computations can be expressed elegantly and efficiently using collections of lightweight threads. Both kernel-level and user-level thread packages have become a common part of computing environments. User-level packages can offer substantially better performance than kernel facilities, because thread operations do not require expensive system calls [2, 15, 23].

A user-level thread package can also provide flexibility in choosing scheduling mechanisms and synchronization primitives, especially if the package is implemented within a powerful higher-level language. Wand [36] enumerated three essential mechanisms for language-based multithreaded computation on a uniprocessor: process saving (i.e., the ability to remember the state of a paused thread), elementary exclusion, and data protection. He showed that first-class continuations can be used to implement process saving elegantly and simply. Elementary exclusion is trivial to achieve on a uniprocessor, and the thread package's internal data can be protected if the implementation language provides an abstract data type mechanism. Wand used Scheme [10] as his implementation language.

Standard ML of New Jersey (SML/NJ) is another suitable language system for building continuation-based uniprocessor thread packages [13, 28, 30]. Standard ML [26] is a mostly functional programming language that provides first-class functions (closures), compile-time typing, polymorphism, exceptions, garbage collection, and a powerful module facility. The SML/NJ implementation [6, 7] supports type-safe, first-class continuations [16] and provides asynchronous exception handling facilities in the form of signal handlers [29].

Continuation-based mechanisms can also be used to build language-based *multi*processor thread packages that support true parallelism. To make this possible in ML, we have extended the SML/NJ runtime system to include a multiprocessing platform, called **MP**, that makes parallel hardware resources directly available to ML code. Our primary design goal was to provide a platform that could be easily ported to different architectures and/or operating systems. To this end, we kept the interface as simple as possible. Efficiency and elegance were also important goals.

From the point of view of a thread system, or *client*, **MP** consists of a processor abstraction `Proc` and a mutex lock abstraction `Lock`. Together with first-class continuations, these facilities suffice to implement multiprocessor thread packages in a machine-independent fashion. **MP** has been used to build an enhanced and portable version of ML Threads [13], a Modula-3 style thread package, and this in turn has served as a basis for experimentation with concurrent debugging [34, 35], a transaction system [38], and general systems programming [11]. **MP** has also been used to construct a multiprocessor prototype of Concurrent ML (CML) [30, 31], an ML dialect supporting threads, channels, synchronous communication events (e.g., send, receive), and powerful event combinators (e.g., CSP-style nondeterministic choice).

MP is intended for shared-memory multiprocessors running Unix-like operating systems. Porting **MP** to a new machine involves implementing only a small number of system-dependent routines. **MP** has been implemented for the Mips R3000-based Silicon Graphics (SGI) 4D/380S running Irix, the Motorola 88100-based Omron Luna88k running Mach, and the Intel 80386-based Sequent Symmetry running Dynix. In addition, a trivial uniprocessor implementation works on all processors that run SML/NJ, including VAX, SPARC, and Motorola 68000.

*This research was sponsored in part by the Defense Advanced Research Projects Agency, CSTO, under the title "The Fox Project: Advanced Development of Systems Software", ARPA Order No. 8313, issued by ESD/AVS under Contract No. F19628-91-C-0168. The research was conducted in part while the authors were visiting AT&T Bell Laboratories, Murray Hill, NJ. The first author was supported in part by a NSF Graduate Fellowship. The work of the second author was conducted in part at Princeton University with support from NSF grant CCR-9002786.

4th ACM PPOPP,5/93/CA,USA
© 1993 ACM 0-89791-589-5/93/0005/0198...$1.50

```
signature THREAD =
sig
    val fork : (unit -> unit) -> unit    (* start new thread *)
    val yield : unit -> unit             (* yield processor to another thread *)
    val id : unit -> int                 (* return own thread id *)
end

signature QUEUE =
sig
    type 'a queue
    val create : unit -> '1a queue
    val enq : 'a queue -> 'a -> unit    (* enqueue *)
    val deq : 'a queue -> 'a            (* dequeue *)
    exception Empty                     (* raised on dequeue when empty *)
end

functor UniThread (Queue : QUEUE) : THREAD =
struct
    val ready : (unit cont * int) Queue.queue = Queue.create ()
    val current_id = ref 0
    val next_id = ref 1

    fun reschedule (cont,id) = Queue.enq ready (cont,id)
    fun dispatch () = let val (cont,id) = Queue.deq ready
                      in current_id := id;
                         throw cont ()
                      end

    fun fork (child : unit -> unit) =
        callcc (fn parent =>
                (reschedule (parent,!current_id);
                 current_id := !next_id;
                 next_id := !next_id + 1;
                 child ();
                 dispatch()))

    fun yield () =
        callcc(fn cont =>
               (reschedule (cont,!current_id);
                dispatch()))

    fun id () = !current_id
end
```

Figure 1: Implementing Threads in Uniprocessor SML/NJ. Some ML syntax: The keyword `signature` declares a module interface specification; `functor` declares a parameterized module. `A.x` refers to element `x` of module `A`. `unit` denotes the void type; `unit->unit` is the type of a procedure that takes no arguments and returns no results, and is thus executed only for its effects. `ref x` constructs a mutable data object with initial contents `x`; its contents are fetched by the explicit dereferencing operator `!` and changed by the assignment operator `:=`. `callcc(fn c => body)` binds the "current continuation" (i.e., the continuation of the `callcc` invocation) to `c` and executes *body*; `throw c ()` invokes continuation `c`. `'a` and `'1a` are type variables; they appear in the types of polymorphic functions.

2 User-Level Threads in SML/NJ

Figure 1 shows the specification and implementation of a simple user-level thread package in uniprocessor SML/NJ. An ML module interface is called a `signature`. A simple module implementation is a `structure`; an implementation parameterized by another interface is a `functor`. Our `THREAD` signature exports three functions: `fork` creates a thread to execute a specified function and assigns it a new integer thread identifier, and sets it running in parallel with its parent; `yield` temporarily yields control of the processor to another thread; and `id` returns the integer identifier of the current thread. A thread inherits the environment of its parent, which may contain both mutable and immutable identifiers. This environment forms a shared memory; any variable accessible from two threads is implicitly shared by them. Shared access to mutable variables (`ref` cells) requires a suitable mutual exclusion protocol (not shown here).

The key aspect of the implementation shown in Figure 1 is the representation of waiting threads by a queue of first-class continuations. Making the queue explicit gives us great flexibility in managing threads. The thread module we present is a functor parameterized by a `QUEUE` structure whose implementation is straightforward and is not shown here. The `QUEUE` signature does not specify the queuing discipline; for example, FIFO and randomized queue implementations will both match the signature. Thus, thread scheduling policy can be changed simply by varying the functor's argument.[1]

A more realistic implementation would use timer alarm signals to preempt compute-bound threads periodically, preventing them from monopolizing the processor. To implement preemption, we can set up an alarm signal handler to invoke `yield` asynchronously. For brevity, preemption has been omitted from the examples in this paper.

This continuation-based implementation is particularly efficient in SML/NJ because creating and invoking continuations is as fast as function invocation. In a system where closures (i.e., procedure-frames) are stack allocated, capturing continuations (via `callcc`) generally requires that the stack be copied, since continuations might be invoked (via `throw`) multiple times. SML/NJ allocates all closures on the heap instead of on a stack and the closures are reclaimed by the garbage collector. Thus, `callcc` simply allocates and initializes a new closure without having to copy anything; the same work is required to call an arbitrary procedure.[2]

On the other hand, allocating closures on the heap may slow down ordinary execution compared to a stack-based implementation. Although Appel has shown that heap allocation can be as fast as stack allocation with respect to instruction counts [3], he ignores memory effects. This allocation scheme is likely to be slower than a stack-based implementation for systems with small first-level caches. Thus, while thread operations built on top of SML/NJ's continuations should be efficient relative to the rest of the ML computation, thread applications may not perform as well overall under SML/NJ as under stack-based systems.

The heap-based approach has another significant advantage over systems, such as C threads [12], that require a stack to be allocated explicitly for each thread. Since SML/NJ threads do not use a stack, no stack space needs to be reserved for them. Consequently, we support the use of hundreds or even thousands of continuation-based threads. Since closures are garbage collected as heap objects, threads that are unreachable can also be garbage collected.

[1] Many useful scheduling policies would require minor changes to the signature; for example, priority queues would need a priority to be passed to the enqueue operation.

[2] Functions whose call sites are all statically known can sometimes be called with less overhead.

```
signature PROC =
sig
    type proc_datum
    datatype proc_state =
        PS of (unit cont * proc_datum)

    val acquire_proc: proc_state -> unit
    exception No_More_Procs
    val release_proc: unit -> 'a

    val initial_datum : proc_datum
    val get_datum     : unit -> proc_datum
    val set_datum     : proc_datum -> unit
end

signature LOCK =
sig
    type mutex_lock
    val mutex_lock: unit -> mutex_lock
    val try_lock : mutex_lock -> bool
    val lock     : mutex_lock -> unit
    val unlock   : mutex_lock -> unit
end
```

Figure 2: The `PROC` and `LOCK` Interfaces

3 MP Specification

We have extended SML/NJ to support multiprocessing by adding new primitive facilities for processor management and for locking. Figure 2 shows ML signatures for these facilities. A structure `Proc` that implements the signature `PROC` provides operations for managing processors and their state. A structure `Lock` that implements `LOCK` provides mutual exclusion among processors.

3.1 Procs

A *proc* is a language-level view of a kernel thread executing on a physical processor. `Proc` does not define a proc datatype; rather, it contains functions that an executing proc can call to alter itself, or to start a new proc. Initially, a single root proc is executing on a single processor. An existing proc can start a new proc executing in parallel by invoking `acquire_proc` with the continuation to be executed and a client-defined `proc_datum`, described below.

Typically, `Proc` is implemented so that the number of available procs is equal to the number of physical processors on the machine; after this limit is reached, calls to `acquire_proc` will raise the exception `No_More_Procs`. However, the number of physical processors available to an SML/NJ image can change without warning during a computation, as a result of activity by other users and by the operating system itself. Thus, as is usual with kernel threads, the correspondence between procs and available physical processors is only an approximate one.

Function `release_proc` causes the calling proc to stop executing, and releases the current physical processor to the operating system. If the client wishes to save the execution state of the proc before releasing it, it does so by capturing a continuation using callcc. Since acquire_proc and release_proc require communication with the operating system, clients will wish to invoke them sparingly. To obtain good performance (at the expense of other system users) a client can call acquire_proc repeatedly when it starts up, acquiring as many procs as possible, and hold on to them for the duration of the computation.

3.2 Per-Proc Data

Often, a proc needs some small amount of private state. For example, consider the ref cell containing the current_id of the executing thread in Figure 1. In a multiprocessor setting in which all ref cells are shared by various processors, it is not possible to store a unique id in a single ref; instead, each processor requires a private copy of current_id.

Proc provides a single, programmer-defined proc_datum for each proc. The operations get_datum and set_datum allow a proc to read and write its private datum. The initial datum value for the root proc is specified by initial_datum.

Specific requirements for private data vary from client to client. For the thread system of Figure 1, a single integer thread identifier suffices; this integer can be stored directly in the proc_datum slot. Clients needing to store more complex state information can define proc_datum to be a record or array.

3.3 Memory Management and Mutual Exclusion

All heap memory is implicitly shared among all procs; in particular, a proc can freely read or write into heap locations allocated by another proc. To prevent access conflicts on shared mutable variables, **MP** provides *mutex locks* to achieve mutual exclusion. Mutex locks are one-bit shared memory locations that can be atomically tested and set. They are often used as spin locks. More elaborate synchronization constructs such as reader/writer locks, semaphores, channels, etc., can be synthesized from mutex locks, refs, and first-class continuations.

Function mutex_lock returns a fresh lock in unlocked state. try_lock attempts to lock the specified mutex lock and immediately returns a bool indicating whether the operation was successful. unlock releases a mutex lock; it may be called by any proc (not necessarily the one that set the lock). lock is equivalent to the following function:

```
fun lock sl = while not(try_lock sl) do ()
```

It is included in the interface because some operating systems may provide a more efficient spin than the one shown above (e.g., by using backoff techniques [1]).

Mutex locks are directly supported in hardware on most current multiprocessors, typically in the form of a test-and-set primitive. Implementations of Lock use hardware support where available to make locks as efficient as possible.

The current **MP** specification does not address the underlying memory consistency model provided by the hardware architecture; maintaining the desired degree of consistency is the responsibility of the **MP** client. For the machines on which it is currently implemented, **MP** does expose enough of the low-level architecture to allow clients to control consistency. However, lack of a common consistency model can be a major problem in designing efficient, portable client code.

3.4 I/O and Signals

In addition to the explicit addition of Proc and Lock facilities, we must specify the behavior of existing SML/NJ I/O and signal handling facilities on multiprocessors.

The major I/O problem posed by multiprocessing is that two procs may may perform I/O operations simultaneously, possibly accessing the same runtime-system data structures. **MP** takes no specific steps to prevent such conflicts since different clients may have different locking needs. For instance, our CML implementation protects the data structures by a single global lock. Other clients may wish to use finer-grained locking.

We use the existing SML/NJ signal interface [29], adding suitable conventions for multiprocessing. Signal handlers are installed on a global basis, i.e., all procs share the same signal-handling functions, and all procs receive each delivered signal. However, masking and unmasking of signals is controlled on a per-proc basis. There is no **MP** facility for procs to signal, control, or alert one another, primarily because we found it difficult to provide a semantically uniform interface that could be ported easily. Fortunately, these operations may be simulated using timer-driven polling in the target proc.

4 MP Applications

This section illustrates the use of **MP** facilities by describing some simple client packages.

4.1 A Thread Package

Figure 3 shows a multiprocessor implementation of the simple thread signature from Figure 1.

Changes from the uniprocessor version are few and simple. When a thread is forked, the multiprocessor kernel first attempts to allocate a new proc on which to continue running the parent thread; only if this attempt fails is the parent blocked on the ready queue. Conversely, a proc calling dispatch releases itself if there are no threads available in the ready queue. The ready queue and next_id reference must be protected by mutex locks to avoid race conditions between competing procs. The current_id number is stored in the per-proc datum, as suggested above.

4.2 A Selective Communication Facility

A real thread package also requires a mechanism for communication and synchronization between threads. A fairly complicated example of such a mechanism is CSP-style selective communication, described by the SELECT signature of Figure 4. It specifies dynamically created, polymorphic channels ('a chan), a send operation that sends a value to a channel (blocking until the value is received), and a receive operation that takes a list of channels and "nondeterministically" chooses to receive a value from one of them.

Figure 5 shows how SELECT can be implemented using **MP**, refs, and continuations. The protocol is similar to one used in our multiprocessor CML prototype. A channel consists of a queue sndrs of sender states and a queue rcvrs of receiver states, jointly protected by a mutex lock ch_lock. A sender's state consists of its continuation, its id, and the value that it is sending. A receiver's state consists of its continuation, its id, and a mutex lock, committed, that serves as a flag to indicate when a sender has been determined.[3]

[3]This mechanism is similar to the one proposed by Ramsey [28].

```
functor MPThread(structure Proc  : PROC
                 structure Lock  : LOCK
                 structure Queue : QUEUE
                 sharing type Proc.proc_datum = int) : THREAD =
struct
    val ready : (unit cont * int) Queue.queue = Queue.create ()
    val ready_lock = Lock.mutex_lock()
    val next_id = ref 1
    val next_id_lock = Lock.mutex_lock()

    fun reschedule (cont,id) = (Lock.lock ready_lock;
                                Queue.enq ready (cont,id);
                                Lock.unlock ready_lock)

    fun dispatch () = (Lock.lock ready_lock;
                       let val (cont,id) = Queue.deq ready
                       in Lock.unlock ready_lock;
                          Proc.set_datum id;
                          throw cont ()
                       end handle Queue.Empty => (Lock.unlock ready_lock;
                                                  Proc.release_proc()))

    fun fork child =
        callcc (fn parent =>
                 (let val current_id = Proc.get_datum()
                  in Proc.acquire_proc (Proc.PS(parent,current_id))
                         handle Proc.No_More_Procs =>
                                 reschedule (parent,current_id)
                  end;
                  Lock.lock next_id_lock;
                  Proc.set_datum (!next_id);
                  next_id := !next_id + 1;
                  Lock.unlock next_id_lock;
                  child ();
                  dispatch()))

    fun yield () =
        callcc (fn cont =>
                 (reschedule (cont,Proc.get_datum());
                  dispatch()))

    fun id () = Proc.get_datum ()
end
```

Figure 3: **MP** Threads. More ML syntax: *expr* **handle** *exn* **=>** *body* installs *body* as the handler for exception *exn* during the execution of *expr*.

```
signature SELECT =
sig
  type 'a chan

  val chan : unit -> '1a chan            (* create a channel *)
  val send : ('a chan * 'a) -> unit      (* send a value to a channel *)
  val receive : '1a chan list -> '1a     (* receive a value from one channel *)
end
```

Figure 4: Selective Communication

```
type 'a sndr = {kont : unit cont, id : Proc.proc_datum, value: 'a}

type 'a rcvr = {kont : 'a cont, id : Proc.proc_datum, committed : Lock.mutex_lock}

type 'a chan = {ch_lock : Lock.mutex_lock,
                sndrs : 'a sndr Queue.queue,
                rcvrs : 'a rcvr Queue.queue}

fun send ({ch_lock, sndrs, rcvrs}, v) =
   (Lock.lock ch_lock;
    let fun loop () =
            let val {kont,id,committed} = Queue.deq rcvrs
            in if (Lock.try_lock committed) then
                  (Lock.unlock ch_lock;
                   reschedule_thread (kont,v,id))
               else
                  loop()
            end
    in loop()
    end handle Queue.Empty =>
          callcc (fn c =>
                  (Queue.enq sndrs {kont = c, id = Proc.get_datum(), value = v};
                   Lock.unlock ch_lock;
                   dispatch ())))

fun receive (chans: '1a chan list) =
    callcc (fn c =>
      let val committed = Lock.mutex_lock ()
          val r = {kont = c, id = Proc.get_datum(), committed = committed}
          fun loop [] = dispatch ()
            | loop ({ch_lock, sndrs, rcvrs}::rest) =
              (Lock.lock ch_lock;
               let val {kont,id,value} = Queue.deq sndrs
               in if Lock.try_lock committed then
                     (Lock.unlock ch_lock;
                      reschedule (kont,id);
                      value)
                  else
                     (Lock.unlock ch_lock;
                      dispatch ())
               end handle Queue.Empty =>
                     (Queue.enq rcvrs r;
                      Lock.unlock ch_lock;
                      loop rest))
      in
          loop (randomize chans)
      end)
```

Figure 5: Implementing Send and Receive. Function `reschedule_thread`, not shown here, converts the receiver's `'1a cont` and `'1a value` to a `unit cont` that can be rescheduled as in Figure 3.

When a thread wants to send a value to a channel, it first checks to see if a receiver is available for that channel. If so, the sender must check that no other sender has already delivered a value to that receiver; it does so by trying to lock the receiver's `committed` lock. If the sender is successful in obtaining the lock, it effects the communication by rescheduling the receiver's continuation and id along with the value. If the sender fails to lock the receiver's `committed` lock, it looks for another receiver; if there are no more, the sender enqueues its current state and the value it is sending onto the channel's `sndrs` queue, and passes control of the proc to another thread by calling `dispatch`.

When a thread wants to receive a value from a list of channels, it creates a single receiver state, including a `committed` lock. It then loops through the channels in pseudo-random order, trying to find a blocked sender. If it finds a sender, the receiver attempts to lock its own `committed` lock; if successful, it effects the communication by reading the sender's value and rescheduling the sender for execution. If the receiver cannot acquire its own `committed` lock, some sender must have already effected the communication and re-scheduled the receiver's continuation, so this invocation of the receiver abandons its computation and passes control of the proc to another thread by calling `dispatch`. If the receiver cannot find a sender on the channel, it inserts its state into the channel's `rcvr` queue, and tries another channel on its list; when all channels have been processed, the receiver calls `dispatch`.

5 MP Implementation

The implementation of the **MP** platform is divided into a generic system-independent layer, and a system-dependent layer. The generic layer makes up the bulk of the implementation, allowing the platform to be ported easily. In adding **MP** support, we attempted to minimize changes to the existing SML/NJ implementation. Internally, SML/NJ supports a range of mechanisms for access to the underlying hardware and operating system [5, 6]. The compiler generates generic machine code, which is then translated into machine-specific instruction sequences. The generic machine model includes general-purpose registers and transfer operations, and a set of primitive operators (primops) for arithmetic and logic functions and specialized tasks such as `callcc`; primops are translated to in-line machine-specific code. Assembly-level functions are used for common code sequences, such as string allocation and built-in arithmetic functions, that are too lengthy to generate in line. The SML/NJ runtime system is written in C and uses a coroutine interface with machine code generated from ML. ML code obtains runtime services, such as garbage collection or I/O, by passing control to C code. This code executes on the ordinary C stack, accesses C global variables containing runtime flags and values, and can invoke the underlying operating system using standard system calls.

In our **MP** implementation, each proc is allowed to execute both ML and C code. The obvious alternative—restricting C execution to a single server thread—would introduce unnecessary synchronization delays. Most of the runtime system's global variables have become per-proc variables; a few remaining globals are shared under protection of (internal) mutex locks.

`acquire_proc` and `release_proc` are implemented as C functions. Since the ML runtime system must statically allocate data structures for each process, a compile-time constant determines the maximum number of procs that the runtime system can provide. When a client calls `acquire_proc` (and the proc limit has not yet been reached), the runtime system normally obtains a new kernel thread from the operating system and sets it executing the specified continuation. Alternatively, the runtime system may choose to re-use a previously released kernel thread and avoid creating a new one.

The Luna port maps procs onto kernel threads, which are provided directly by Mach. Irix and Dynix do not provide kernel threads *per se*, but do provide the ability for Unix-style processes to share a common address space (though by somewhat different mechanisms). Thus, for the SGI and Sequent, each **MP** proc is mapped onto a distinct process.

To implement the `proc_datum`, we modified the SML/NJ generic machine model to include a new dedicated virtual register. Two primops corresponding to `get_datum` and `set_datum` were added to read and write the register. On RISC machines that have 32 or more registers, like the MIPS-based SGI, dedicating a register for per-proc data scarcely affects performance [6, page 189], so the virtual register is implemented by an actual register. On architectures with fewer registers, the datum is stored on the stack and accessed indirectly through the stack pointer.

Mutex lock implementation is heavily dependent on underlying hardware support. The Motorola 88100 provides an atomic exchange instruction on any word in memory. Thus, on the Luna, mutex locks are implemented as ML boolean `refs` and an exchange instruction is used to implement the `try_lock` routine. The Sequent has a similar facility. The MIPS R3000 does not have a test-and-set instruction. However, the SGI provides a limited number of hardware locks, which are implemented by a separate lock memory and bus. The runtime system uses these to control an extensible set of software locks implemented as ML `ref` cells. On all machines, the mutex lock operations `try_lock` and `unlock` are implemented as assembly language subroutines.

Our present **MP** implementation uses a modification of SML/NJ's existing two-generation, copying garbage collector [4]. SML/NJ allocates heap storage very frequently (approximately one word per every 3-7 instructions [6, page 196]), and thus depends on allocation being fast. Allocation is performed by in-line code; heap overflow checks are made at "clean" points where the location of all live roots is known. In adapting this system to a multiprocessor, it is important to avoid proc synchronization during allocation. This means that each proc must allocate into a separate part of the total allocation region; all regions can be read or updated by the other procs, however. When one proc fills its share of the allocation region, it can "steal" spare memory from other procs. When the allocation region is completely filled and a garbage collection (GC) is required, the procs are synchronized at clean points, the collection is performed by one of them, and the allocation region is redivided.

6 Evaluation

To judge **MP**'s portability, we counted the number of lines of code (including whitespace and comments) that make up the system-dependent routines of each **MP** implementation. The SGI system-dependent code consists of 144 lines of C code and 15 lines of assembly. The Sequent system-dependent code consists of 267 lines of C code and 10 lines of assembly; 115 of these lines implement restart of exported images. The Luna system-dependent code consists of 630 lines of C code and 34 lines of assembly. However, 214 lines of the Luna code, which implement routines needed

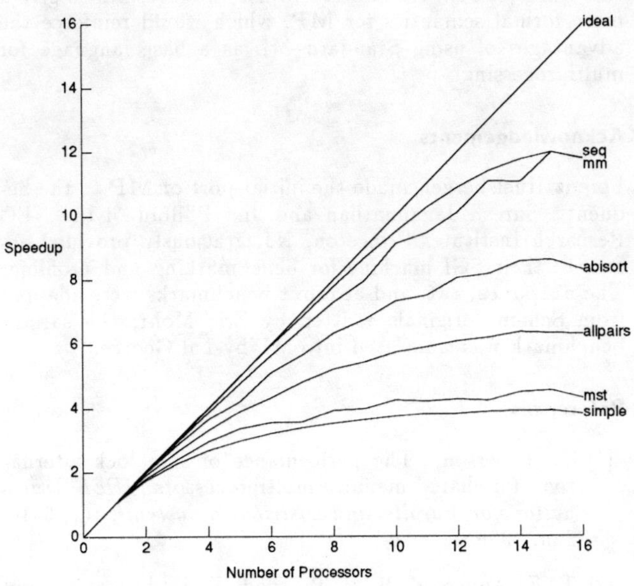

Figure 6: Self-Relative Speedup for ML Threads Benchmarks (Sequent)

to export restartable images, replace a 600 line machine-independent module in the original SML/NJ runtime. An additional 280 lines of the code, which emulate signals for Mach kernel threads, replace a 101 line operating system-independent module. For comparison, the entire SML/NJ runtime system (version 0.75 including **MP** support) for a MIPS machine, consists of approximately 6,750 lines of C code and 650 lines of assembly.

Another indication of portability is the time it takes to complete an implementation of the platform for a new architecture or operating system. After the initial port to the SGI, the Luna implementation was completed within two days by the first author. An initial Sequent implementation was completed within a week by someone familiar with SML/NJ but unfamiliar with **MP**. The current Sequent implementation took longer, primarily because of complications involved in exporting restartable images which could have been avoided by taking the machine-specific approach of the Luna port.

To evaluate the performance of our **MP** implementations, we measured benchmarks running on top of a complete thread package running on top of **MP**. The package was similar to that shown in Figure 3, with the addition of a distributed run queue and a signal-based preemption mechanism. Shared memory locations were protected with user-level mutex locks built on top of `Lock` mutex locks. Tests used a 16-processor Sequent Symmetry S81 with 16MHz Intel 80386 processors, running Dynix V3.1.4. Tests used 100 MB of main memory; all measurements include garbage collection time.

Figure 6 shows the *self-relative* speedup curves for five applications:

- `allpairs`: Floyd's algorithm for computing all shortest paths between two nodes of a 75 node graph [27].
- `mst`: Computes the minimum spanning tree on 200 randomly distributed points using Prim's algorithm [27].
- `abisort`: An adaptive bitonic sorting algorithm [9] run on an input of 2^{12} integers [27].
- `simple`: The Simple hydrodynamics benchmark [14], which solves a set of differential equations across a grid of size 100×100, run for one time step.
- `mm`: Matrix multiply of two 100×100 integer matrices.

One application, `mm`, shows excellent self-relative speedup, which appears to be limited primarily by main-memory bus contention due to SML/NJ's heap allocation. Separate measurements indicate that the bus has a maximum achievable bandwidth of about 25 MB/sec; with 16 processors `mm` generates about 20 MB/sec of bus traffic in allocation alone. Evidence that lock contention and other parallelism issues are not at fault is given by the curve labeled `seq`, which represents the speedup obtained on p processors by running p independent copies of a simple SML/NJ application; `mm` does almost as well.

Speedup for the other benchmarks is limited by other factors, especially our sequential garbage collection strategy; if garbage collection time were omitted, the maximum speedups for `abisort` and `allpairs` would be considerably higher, although the rough shape of their curves would be the same. The applications with the poorest speedups lack enough available parallelism; they leave processors idle much of the time. For example, `simple`, the worst case, has average processor idle rates above 50% for 10 processors or more. `simple` also displays moderate contention for access to the run queues and data locks; none of the other applications showed any significant lock contention. Sequential garbage collection, idle time and lock contention were not significant factors in earlier experiments we conducted on the SGI 4D/380S machine, which has much faster processors but only slightly larger bus bandwidth;[4] on that machine, main-memory contention problems swamped all other effects.

7 Related Work and Conclusions

Although multi-threaded extensions to symbolic computing languages already exist on several multiprocessors, our approach is distinctive because we continue to rely on first-class continuations to represent thread state (a la Wand), and because we stress portability of the multiprocessor platform. The former aspect of our approach is attractive for SML/NJ because continuations play a central role in the existing SML/NJ implementation; the latter aspect is consistent with SML/NJ's commitment to supporting multiple target architectures. Using continuations allows us to describe important aspects of the thread system, such as scheduling policies and synchronization mechanisms, within ML itself rather than burying them in the runtime system. Machine portability allows us to take advantage of a wide variety of hardware, to compare platform performance, and to make the system more readily available for others to use.

Most existing multiprocessor implementations of symbolic languages have been based on Lisp. Multilisp [19] and Qlisp [17] provide concurrency extensions to Lisp and have been implemented for various multiprocessors [18, 22, 25, 32]. These systems have served as the basis for substantial research on problems such as efficient thread scheduling and avoiding excess parallelism. However, they tend to support only one primary synchronization model (e.g., futures

[4] Approximately 30MB/sec. To illustrate the difference in processor speed, locking and unlocking an MP mutex takes only 6μsec on the SGI versus 46μsec on the Sequent.

in Multilisp) and rely on sophisticated runtime system support; they don't attempt to be extensible or portable.

The Lisp-based system most closely resembling ours is STING [20, 21], a concurrent dialect of Scheme specifically intended as a substrate for building higher-level parallel computing environments. STING's basic data types are threads and virtual processors; the system provides flexibility in scheduling, storage allocation and thread migration policies while attempting not to compromise efficiency. The thread data type is simultaneously lower-level and more complex than an SML/NJ continuation; for example, it includes a thread control block with associated stack, heap segment, saved registers, genealogy information, and other state. Threads are therefore expensive to create, and STING includes several optimizations, such as "thread stealing," to avoid creating new threads when possible. In SML/NJ, threads are represented by simple continuations, which cost almost nothing until they begin executing, so there is no need or opportunity for such optimizations. Similarly, **MP** has no processor data type; clients can emulate any of STING's scheduling options by explicitly varying queuing disciplines. By using an explicitly stack-based thread model, STING implementations may be able to offer better performance than our continuation-based approach. However, we believe **MP** presents a simpler view of the multiprocessing environment, which will be easier to port to new hardware and operating system platforms.

Matthews [24] describes several implementations of a concurrent extension to Poly/ML using CSP-style communication operators [8]. He describes several implementations, including one for the DEC Firefly multiprocessor. Support for the thread and communication model is hard-wired into the Poly/ML runtime system, and is not designed for easy porting to different thread models or hardware platforms.

Some existing concurrent systems do stress portability at the runtime-system level. The Portable Common Runtime system (PCR) [37] offers portable and language-independent facilities for threads, storage management, and other runtime-system features. PCR's implementation of threads is similar to ours: user-level threads are multiplexed on top of kernel threads. However, PCR does not allow the thread package or its scheduling policy to be customized.

Although we have stressed simplicity and portability in our **MP** implementation, better performance is also important. One critical task for the future is to improve the present system's poor locality of reference and consequent memory bus contention. One cause of this problem is SML/NJ's heap-based allocation strategy for procedure frames, which makes `callcc` and `throw` cheap relative to ordinary computation but re-uses memory only after garbage collections. When the size of the collector's *from* and *to* spaces exceed the size of a processor's cache, this strategy insures a cache-miss on almost every allocation. Potentially better strategies include using a multi-generational collector with very small young generations that can fit in the cache, or using a stack to allocate "non-escaping" procedure frames. We also need to provide more efficient access to hardware locking facilities, though doing so will unfortunately make the code generator sensitive to the target's operating system as well as its architecture.

Other important areas to address include concurrent garbage collection, compiler-level support for different memory consistency models, and improved I/O interfaces and processor utilization using an operating system based on scheduler activations [2]. Finally, some progress has recently been made in the exploration of a semantics for a multiprocess SML [8, 31]. We hope to to use these results to give a more formal semantics for **MP**, which would reinforce the advantages of using Standard ML as a base language for multiprocessing.

Acknowledgements

Lorenz Huelsbergen made the initial port of **MP** to the Sequent. Suresh Jagannathan and Jim Philbin of the NEC Research Institute, Princeton, NJ, graciously provided access to their SGI machine for benchmarking and profiling. The `allpairs`, `mst`, and `abisort` benchmarks were adapted from Scheme originals written by Eric Mohr; the `simple` benchmark was translated into ML by Lal George.

References

[1] T. Anderson. The performance of spin lock alternatives for shared memory multiprocessors. *IEEE Transactions on Parallel and Distributed Systems*, 1(1):6–16, Jan. 1990.

[2] T. E. Anderson, B. N. Bershad, E. D. Lazowska, and H. M. Levy. Scheduler activations: Effective kernel support for the user-level management of parallelism. In *Proc. 13th ACM Symposium on Operating Systems Principles*, pages 95–109, Oct. 1991.

[3] A. W. Appel. Garbage collection can be faster than stack allocation. *Information Processing Letters*, 25(4):275–279, June 1987.

[4] A. W. Appel. Simple generational garbage collection and fast allocation. *Software—Practice & Experience*, 19(2):171–183, Feb. 1989.

[5] A. W. Appel. A runtime system. *Journal of Lisp and Symbolic Computation*, 3(4):343–380, Nov. 1990.

[6] A. W. Appel. *Compiling with Continuations*. Cambridge University Press, 1992.

[7] A. W. Appel and D. B. MacQueen. Standard ML of New Jersey. In M. Wirsing, editor, *Third Int'l Symp. on Prog. Lang. Implementation and Logic Programming*, pages 1–13, New York, Aug. 1991. Springer-Verlag.

[8] D. Berry, R. Milner, and D. Turner. A semantics for ML concurrency primitives. In *Proceedings of the Nineteenth ACM Symposium on Principles of Programming Languages*, pages 119–129, Jan. 1992.

[9] G. Bilardi and A. Nicolau. Adaptive bitonic sorting: An optimal parallel algorithm for shared-memory machines. *SIAM Journal of Computing*, 18(2):216–228, Apr. 1989.

[10] W. Clinger and J. Rees. Revised[4] report on the algorithmic language Scheme. *LISP Pointers*, IV(3):1–55, July-Sep. 1991.

[11] E. Cooper, R. Harper, and P. Lee. The Fox project: Advanced development of systems software. Technical Report CMU-CS-91-178, School of Computer Science, Carnegie Mellon University, Aug. 1991.

[12] E. C. Cooper and R. P. Draves. C Threads. Technical Report CMU-CS-88-154, Computer Science Department, Carnegie Mellon University, June 1988.

[13] E. C. Cooper and J. G. Morrisett. Adding threads to Standard ML. Technical Report CMU-CS-90-186, School of Computer Science, Carnegie Mellon University, Dec. 1990.

[14] W. P. Crowley, C. P. Hendrickson, and T. E. Rudy. The SIMPLE code. Technical Report UCID 17715, Lawrence Livermore Laboratory, Livermore, CA, Feb. 1978.

[15] T. W. Doeppner Jr. Threads: A system for the support of concurrent programming. Technical Report CS-87-11, Department of Computer Science, Brown University, June 1987.

[16] B. F. Duba, R. W. Harper, and D. B. MacQueen. Typing first-class continuations in ML. In *Conference Record of the 18th Annual ACM Symposium on Principles of Programming Languages*, pages 163–173, Jan. 1991.

[17] R. Gabriel and J. McCarthy. Qlisp. In J. Kowalik, editor, *Parallel Computation and Computers for Artificial Intelligence*, pages 63–89. Kluwer Academic Publishers, Boston, 1988.

[18] R. Goldman and R. P. Gabriel. Preliminary results with the initial implementation of Qlisp. In *Proceedings of the 1988 ACM Conference on Lisp and Functional Programming*, pages 143–152, July 1988.

[19] R. H. Halstead, Jr. Multilisp: A language for concurrent symbolic computation. *ACM Trans. Prog. Lang. Syst.*, 7(4):501–538, Oct. 1985.

[20] S. Jagannathan and J. Philbin. A customizable substrate for concurrent languages. In *Proc. ACM SIGPLAN '92 Conference on Programming Language Design and Implementation*, pages 55–67, June 1992. Published as *SIGPLAN Notices*, 27(7), July 1992.

[21] S. Jagannathan and J. Philbin. A foundation for an efficient multi-threaded Scheme system. In *Proc. 1992 ACM Conference on Lisp and Functional Programming*, pages 345–357, June 1992.

[22] D. A. Kranz, R. H. Halstead, Jr., and E. Mohr. Mul-T: A high-performance parallel Lisp. In *ACM SIGPLAN '89 Conference on Programming Language Design and Implementation*, pages 81–90, June 1989. Published as *SIGPLAN Notices*, 24(7), July 1989.

[23] B. D. Marsh, M. L. Scott, T. J. LeBlanc, and E. P. Markatos. First-class user-level threads. In *Proc. 13th ACM Symposium on Operating Systems Principles*, pages 110–121, Oct. 1991. Published as *Operating Systems Review*, 25(5), Oct. 1991.

[24] D. C. J. Matthews. A distributed concurrent implementation of Standard ML. Technical Report ECS-LFCS-91-174, Laboratory for Foundations of Computer Science, Dept. of Computer Science, University of Edinburgh, Aug. 1991.

[25] J. Miller. *MultiScheme: A parallel processing system based on MIT Scheme.* PhD thesis, Massachusetts Institute of Technology, Aug. 1987.

[26] R. Milner, M. Tofte, and R. Harper. *The Definition of Standard ML.* MIT Press, 1990.

[27] E. Mohr. *Dynamic Partitioning of Parallel Lisp Programs.* PhD thesis, Yale University, Aug. 1991.

[28] N. Ramsey. Concurrent programming in ML. Technical Report CS-TR-262-90, Department of Computer Science, Princeton University, Apr. 1990.

[29] J. H. Reppy. Asynchronous signals in Standard ML. Technical Report TR 90-1144, Department of Computer Science, Cornell University, Aug. 1990.

[30] J. H. Reppy. CML: A higher-order concurrent language. In *Proceedings of the ACM SIGPLAN '91 Conference on Programming Language Design and Implementation*, pages 293–305, June 1991.

[31] J. H. Reppy. *High-order Concurrency.* PhD thesis, Computer Science Department, Cornell University, Ithaca, NY, Jan. 1992. Also Cornell Univ. Computer Science Dept. Tech. Report 92-1285.

[32] M. R. Swanson, R. R. Kessler, and G. Lindstrom. An implementation of Portable Standard Lisp on the BBN Butterfly. In *Proceedings of the 1988 ACM Conference on Lisp and Functional Programming*, pages 132–141, July 1988.

[33] D. Tarditi, A. Acharya, and P. Lee. No assembly required: Compiling Standard ML to C. Technical Report CMU-CS-90-187, School of Computer Science, Carnegie Mellon University, Nov. 1990.

[34] A. P. Tolmach. *Debugging Standard ML.* PhD thesis, Princeton University, Oct. 1992. Also Princeton Univ. Dept. of Computer Science Tech. Rep. CS-TR-378-92.

[35] A. P. Tolmach and A. W. Appel. Debuggable concurrency extensions for Standard ML. In *Proc. ACM/ONR Workshop on Parallel and Distributed Debugging*, pages 120–131, May 1991. Published as *SIGPLAN Notices* 26(12), December 1991. Also Princeton Univ. Dept. of Computer Science Tech. Rep. CS-TR-352-91.

[36] M. Wand. Continuation-based multiprocessing. In *Proceedings of the 1980 LISP Conference*, pages 19–28, Aug. 1980.

[37] M. Weiser, A. Demers, and C. Hauser. The portable common runtime approach to interoperability. In *Proceedings of the 12th ACM Symposium on Operating Systems Principles*, pages 114–122, Dec. 1989.

[38] J. M. Wing, M. Faehndrich, J. G. Morrisett, and S. Nettles. Extensions to Standard ML to support transactions. In *Proceedings of the ACM SIGPLAN Workshop on ML and its Applications, San Francisco*, pages 104–118, June 1992.

Leapfrogging: A Portable Technique for Implementing Efficient Futures

David B. Wagner Bradley G. Calder*
Department of Computer Science
Campus Box #430
University of Colorado, Boulder 80309–0430

Abstract

A *future* is a language construct that allows programmers to expose parallelism in applicative languages such as MultiLisp [5] with minimal effort. In this paper we describe a technique for implementing futures, which we call *leapfrogging*, that reduces blocking due to load imbalance. The utility of leapfrogging is enhanced by the fact that it is completely platform-independent, is free from deadlock, and places a bound on stack sizes that is at most a small constant times the maximum stack size encountered during a sequential execution of the same computation. We demonstrate the performance of leapfrogging using a prototype implementation written in C++.

1 Introduction

A *future* is a language construct that enables programmers to identify parallelizable computations in an otherwise sequential program. Rather than waiting for the result of such a computation, the program receives a "placeholder" for that result and is able to continue executing. The placeholder behaves just like any other variable until an attempt is made to use its value; at that point, if the computation is not finished then the thread of execution trying to obtain the value will be blocked until the value is ready.

The principal design rationale behind futures is that "the programmer takes on the burden of identifying *what* can be computed safely in parallel, leaving the decision of exactly *how* the division [of work] will take place to the runtime system" [6].

*Authors' email address: {wagner,calder}@cs.colorado.edu.

4th ACM PPOPP,5/93/CA,USA

Another nice feature of futures is that all synchronization is implicit. The programmer never explicitly checks to see if the value of a computation is ready; if it is not, the thread of control trying to use that value is transparently blocked. Because of this, futures are much easier to use than e.g., fork-join.

There are significant challenges to making a futures runtime system efficient when the emphasis is on *minimal programmer effort*. For example, the programmer might identify very fine-grained computations as candidates for parallel execution. Actually executing each of these computations as a separate task might be counterproductive, since the overhead of creating tasks and synchronizing might overwhelm the time saved by parallelization.

Another potential problem is that of unbalanced computation graphs. The computation graph might be structured such that the result of a future is almost never ready when called for; this leads to extra overhead, either in the form of idle processor time or context switching. Even worse, a careless implementation can lead to very subtle deadlock problems in realistic (not contrived) computations.

A very elegant, but complicated, solution to these problems was presented by Mohr, Krantz and Halstead [6]. Their system, which we will explore in more detail in the next section, is based on *continuations*.

In this paper we present an alternative technique for implementing efficient futures, *leapfrogging*, that also is very portable. Our testbed system is currently implemented in C++, although the leapfrogging technique is completely language- and platform-independent. The crucial point is that leapfrogging provides efficiency similar to that of more complex techniques such as LTC, but can be ported with very little effort to any system that provides process creation, shared memory, and lock synchronization primitives.

2 Performance Issues

2.1 Basic issues

The Mul-T function **psum-tree** [6] shown below provides a good illustration of how difficult it is to get good load distribution and minimal blocking using futures, because it contains a plethora of potential parallelism:

```
(define (psum-tree tree)
  (if (leaf? tree)
      (leaf-value tree)
      (+ (future (psum-tree (left tree)))
         (psum-tree (right tree)))))
```

A naive approach to parallelizing **psum-tree** would use a separate task for each future, so that the number of tasks used would be equal to the number of leaves in the tree. This excessive task creation will greatly diminish the speedup of the parallelized program, since the granularity of task creation will certainly be much larger than the granularity of a leaf computation.

In order to avoid excessive task creation, the programmer could limit the creation of tasks to a fixed depth in the algorithm itself. Below that depth the algorithm would execute the recursive calls directly, rather than futurizing them. In this way, the programmer takes responsibility for matching the granularity of the tasks to the overheads of the runtime system. Unfortunately, it is frequently the case that the only way to find the optimal cut-off depth is through experimentation.

One possible attack on the granularity problem is called *load-based inlining*. The idea is to dynamically monitor the load and create a new task to compute a future only when processors are idle. Otherwise, the future is executed inline by the task that creates it. This keeps the number of tasks created close to the number of processors available. Qlisp [3, 4] provides the programmer with primitives that inspect the state of the system, and allows the programmer to specify an arbitrary predicate to control the inlining of futures.

One problem with any type of inlining is that a decision to inline a future cannot be revoked. This could result in some processors sitting idle while others work on large tasks, especially if the task granularity is unpredictable. Another problem is that keeping track of processor availability creates extra overhead for the task scheduler.

Thus, there appears to be a fundamental tradeoff between achieving good task granularity and achieving good load balance.

2.2 WorkCrews

The "obvious" solution to the granularity vs. load balancing dilemma is to note that there is really no need to create a separate task for every future. Instead, a WorkCrew-style approach can be adopted [7]: a future is implemented as a passive object that contains enough information to carry out the computation. These passive objects are then picked up by worker tasks and executed. The number of workers is fixed and is equal to the number of processors. The advantage of using passive futures and active workers is that the overhead of creating a future is reduced so much that inlining, with its associated load balancing problems, rarely is required for good performance.

Unfortunately, there are other performance problems with a WorkCrew-style implementation. Foremost among these is that of workers blocking to wait for an unfinished future. In the one-task-per-future implementation, either (a) the blocked task can idle its processor until the desired result is available, or (b) it can context switch to some other task. The former lowers processor utilization, thus the latter alternative would be preferred unless futures were of extremely small granularity. Unfortunately, in the WorkCrew approach there is no other task to switch to!

We conclude that a naive WorkCrew approach would be considerably faster than the one-task-per-future approach for balanced computations, but could be arbitrarily bad for unbalanced computations.

2.3 Lazy Task Creation

Mohr et al. [6] have devised a clever scheme that they call *Lazy Task Creation* (LTC) that solves the problems just discussed. Their technique is built into a compiler for Mul-T, a parallel dialect of Scheme.

In Mul-T, `(K (future X))` is interpreted to mean, "Start evaluating X in the current task, but save enough information so that its continuation K can be moved to a separate task if another processor becomes idle" [6]. This effectively makes the decision to inline any future a revocable one, so the default behavior is that every future is inlined. Continuations may be *stolen* (i.e., moved to another task) when another task becomes idle.

LTC is implemented by maintaining a list of continuations on the producer task's stack. Then when a continuation is stolen, the scheduler cuts the stack apart and replaces the inlined future's stack frame with a placeholder. The continuation-based strategy also provides a strategy for dealing with the problem of a task blocking on some unfinished future. When such a case arises, the scheduler selects another continuation from the blocked task's stack to work on and cuts the stack again. The authors claim that the costs of doing this are low enough to meet their performance goals. For more details see [6].

Obviously, LTC is a completely general approach with the potential for very good performance. If the load is well-balanced, continuation-stealing will happen infrequently, if at all, and the computation will proceed much faster than if the futures had not been inlined. On the other hand, if the computation is seriously unbalanced, then it is crucial that the implementation make the time required to steal a continuation competitive with having created a separate future in the first place.

The principal drawback to the LTC alternative, as we see it, is that it requires some very intricate implementation. Using a traditional call-stack implementation, continuation stealing requires the copying of stack frames, which is platform-dependent as well as expensive. To solve the latter problem, Mohr et al. implemented a linked-list call-stack, which exacerbates the former problem. Practically speaking, this will likely limit the use of LTC to a narrow community of users.

Our experience in [8] has convinced us that futures have a much wider domain of application than they have usually been credited with, and our motivation is thus to "spread the word" about them to as wide a community of users as possible. The main contribution of this research is a new technique, *leapfrogging*, that provides very good performance while being extremely easy to implement.

2.4 Leapfrogging

The leapfrogging technique is built into a WorkCrew-style implementation. In this implementation, futures are passive objects rather than active tasks. The number of worker tasks is fixed and equal to the number of processors, and each worker has a corresponding FIFO work queue into which futures are inserted and removed. A worker can remove a future from any work queue, but by default inserts futures only into its own.

When a worker finishes evaluating a future and has nothing in its work queue, it looks in other workers' work queues in order to find work. This is termed *stealing*. Since futures typically are not inlined (because the cost of creating them is so small), if there is work available anywhere in the computation, an idle worker eventually will find it.

Stealing futures is the principal way of balancing the load among the workers, but it does not solve the problem of workers blocking on unresolved futures. *Leapfrogging* is our solution to the problem of worker blocking. A prototypical leapfrogging scenario is depicted in Figure 1.

Suppose that a worker, X, creates a future F1 and begins executing its continuation K1 (Figure 1(a)). Now worker Y steals F1 and the scenario becomes that of Figure 1(b). (In the figure, the clear nodes represent uncomputed futures, and the opaque nodes represent work that has been or is currently being executed. The current position of each worker is marked with an arrowhead, and the flow of control of each worker is differentiated by line styles.)

Sometime later, the computation might appear as shown in Figure 1(c). Both workers have created additional futures and are further down in the computation tree. At this point, suppose that X returns to the next higher level in the tree and requires the value of F2, which has not yet been computed. Since no other worker has claimed F2, X would inline it (Figure 1(d)).

Eventually, X will return to the root of the tree and require the value of F1. If the load is unbalanced, it may be the case that F1 is not ready. Rather than block itself, X takes the first future in Y's work queue that is descended from F1 (F3) and starts executing it. The result is shown in Figure 1(e).

The motivation for leapfrogging is that X cannot proceed until Y has completed evaluating F1, so X is indirectly helping itself if it evaluates F3. The assumption implicit in this statement is that F1 depends on the value of F3; in other words, that a future does not create other futures unless it is going to use their values. Although it is not difficult to write programs that violate this assumption,[1] it holds for many applications of practical interest.

Of course, it is perfectly plausible that after X leapfrogs Y but before X finishes F3, Y might require the value of F3. In this case, if X had created yet another future (F4) then Y could leapfrog over X, leading to the situation depicted in Figure 1(f). This can continue for the entire depth of the tree, if necessary; by now it should be apparent why we chose the term "leapfrog" to describe this mechanism.

Given the assumption stated above, our implementation guarantees that all of the futures on a worker's stack always lie on a single path from the root of the computation tree to a leaf, although there may be any number of "gaps" along the way. This implies that (a) the computation cannot deadlock unless there is a cycle in the dependence graph, and (b) no worker's stack will ever exceed the maximum stack size that a sequential execution of the program would cause.

It might seem to be more beneficial in the long run

[1] For example, OR-parallel search algorithms.

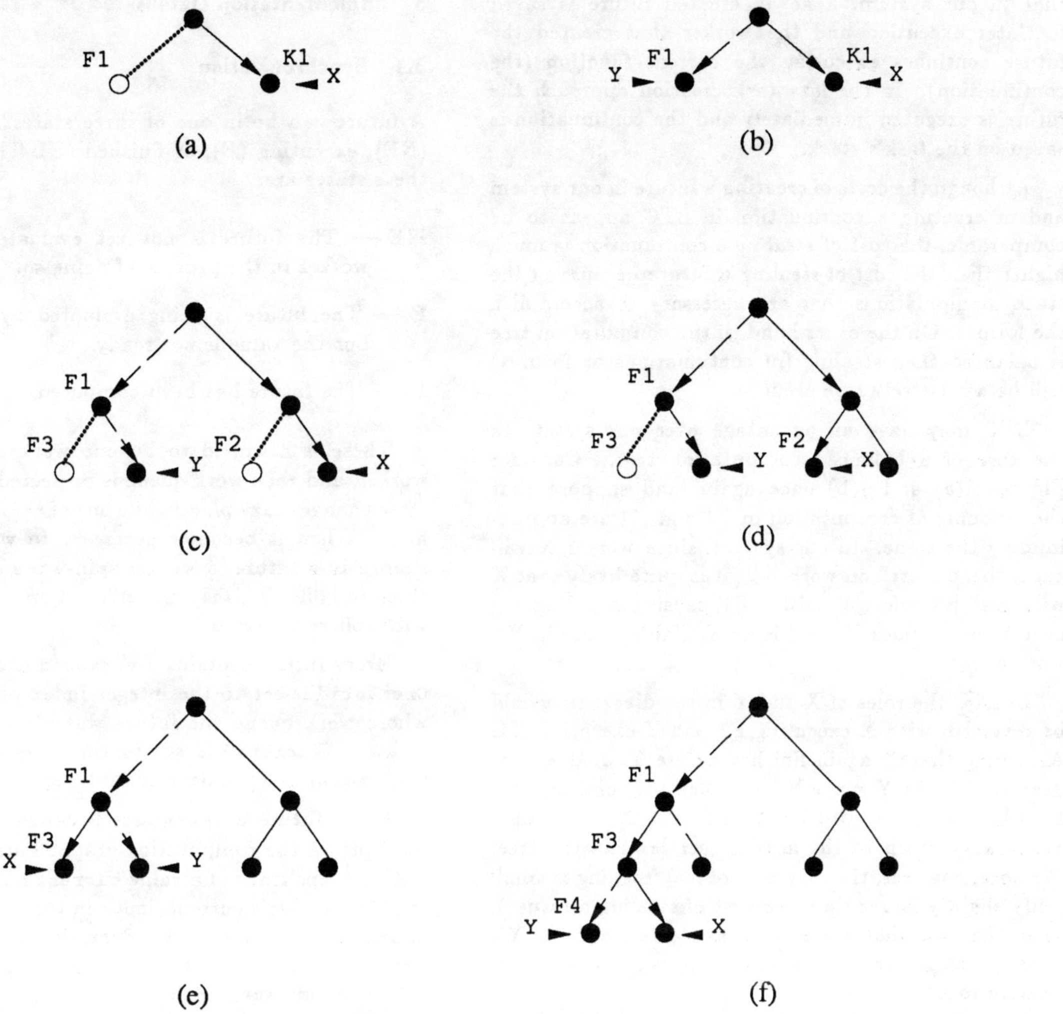

Figure 1: Typical leapfrogging scenario.

to allow workers to leapfrog onto a future as high up in the computation tree as possible, because it would likely have a larger granularity. However, this would violate the conditions necessary to ensure the bounded stack property.

The action of leapfrogging prevents workers from idling when there is work to do. The difference between stealing and leapfrogging is that the former is done by an idle worker (with an empty stack), whereas the latter is done by a worker that is trying to resolve a future (whose stack is in some intermediate stage of a computation).

The time required to create a future and the time required to leapfrog are each[2] approximately 58 microseconds on a Sequent Symmetry multiprocessor, a machine whose individual processors are rated at about 3 MIPS.

2.5 Comparison with Lazy Task Creation

The creating of a future in our system is similar to Mohr et al. idea of creating a continuation because our futures are just passive objects on a work queue, and if no other processor steals the futures the worker that created them executes them. The main differences are

[2] The fact that these times are nearly the same is pure coincidence; there is no similarity at all between the two actions.

that in our system, a newly created future is saved for later execution and the worker that created the future continues executing the current function (the continuation). In the lazy task creation approach the future is executed immediately and the continuation is saved on the task's stack.

Although the costs of creating a future in our system and of creating a continuation in LTC appear to be comparable, the cost of *stealing* a continuation is much higher than the cost of stealing a future because of the stack manipulations that are necessary to accomplish the former. On the other hand, if the computation tree is balanced then stealing (of continuations or futures) will be a relatively rare event.

LTC may have an advantage over our system in the case of a balanced computation tree. Consider Figures 1(a) and 1(b) once again, and suppose that the amounts of computation in F1 and K1 are approximately the same. In our system, since worker X will get a "head start" on worker Y, it is quite likely that X will finish K1 before Y finishes F1, causing X to leapfrog over Y, or to block if there is no available future in Y's work queue.

In LTC the roles of X and Y in the diagrams would be reversed, with X executing F1 and Y executing K1. Assuming that X again finishes before Y, X does not need to wait for Y, since Y has stolen the continuation. In other words, it will be Y, and not X, that must eventually return to the next higher level in the tree. We note, however, that the cost of leapfrogging is small (only slightly larger than the cost of stealing a future), so in the case that there is an available future in Y's work queue, leapfrogging is really not at a disadvantage relative to LTC.

On the other hand, if the computation tree were unbalanced it might transpire that Y would finish before X. Using leapfrogging, this would free Y to look for work elsewhere. But the LTC strategy in this case is to have Y steal a continuation *from itself*. Although not very obvious, this behavior is possible when futures are passed as arguments to functions.

In some sense, the two scenarios described above are the dual of each other. Overall, the two approaches seem to have complementary strengths and weaknesses, and their performance is comparable. Of course, LTC is more general than leapfrogging, since leapfrogging constrains the structure of the computation in order to guarantee freedom from deadlock (LTC is always deadlock free). Our main motivation for proposing leapfrogging as an alternative to LTC is that leapfrogging is much easier to implement and, as a corollary, is more portable.

3 Implementation Details

3.1 Synchronization

A future can be in one of three states: not executing (NE), executing (E), or finished (F). The meanings of these states are:

NE — The future is not yet evaluated, nor is any worker in the process of doing so.

E — The future is being evaluated by some worker, but the value is not ready.

F — The future has been computed.

There is assumed to be one work queue for each worker, and each work queue is protected by a lock. All state changes take place while one of these locks is being held. When it becomes necessary to wait for a state change in a future, a worker spin-waits on the future's state variable. This is quite efficient on a multiprocessor with coherent caches.

Every future contains a `workerid` and a `creatorid`. `Creatorid` is set to the integer index of the worker in whose work queue the future was placed when it was created. `Workerid` is set to the integer index of the worker that is evaluating the future, if any.

Every future also contains a `depth` field indicating its depth in the computation graph. Furthermore, each worker keeps track of a value `current_depth`, representing that worker's current depth in the graph.The depth of the main routine is by definition 0. Each time a worker creates a new future, it sets the depth of that future to `current_depth` + 1. [3]

When a worker executing a future `f` tries to resolve a future `q`, the action taken depends on the state of `q`:

- If `q.state` is NE, the worker finds the work queue in which `q` resides using the `q.creatorid` field, and locks that work queue. If `q.state` is still NE, the worker dequeues `q`, sets `q.workerid` to its own id, sets `q.depth` to `max(q.depth, current_depth+1)`, sets `q.state` to E, and unlocks the work queue. If not, it proceeds to the appropriate case.
- If `q.state` is E, the worker attempts to leapfrog worker `q.workerid`. The worker is allowed to

[3] Note that it is necessary for a worker to increment current_depth each time a call to a futurized function is made, even if the call is statically inlined. One way to implement this (in C++) is to have the programmer encapsulate the futurized function in a subclass of a special base class, which in turn overloads the *member selection operator* [2]. This enables the base class to track every call to the function.

leapfrog if it can find some future `g` in worker `q.workerid`'s work queue with a depth that is *strictly greater* than `max(f.depth, q.depth)`. If so, it attempts to dequeue `g` and evaluate it. It continues this behavior until `q.state` changes to F.

- If `q.state` is F, the worker obtains the value.

The constraint `g.depth > max(f.depth, q.depth)` in the leapfrogging case is called the *leapfrog depth rule*. We emphasize this because it is a necessary condition to guarantee freedom from deadlock and bounded stack sizes.

3.2 Deadlock freedom and stack size bounds

Given two very simple (and reasonable) assumptions about program behavior, we can guarantee the following desirable properties about our implementation:

P1: The computation will be deadlock-free.

P2: The maximum stack size (measured in stack frames) of any worker will be at most a constant factor times the maximum depth of any node in the computation graph.

The reason for the "constant factor" disclaimer in P2 is that, while the maximum number of activations of a futurized function on a worker's stack will never exceed the maximum depth of the computation graph, there may be an extra stack frame or two *per activation* because of calls to runtime system utility functions (function wrappers, type coercion operators, etc.).

The assumptions that allow us to guarantee P1 and P2 are:

A1: The precedence graph for the computation is acyclic.

A2: If `f1` creates `f2` then `f1` depends upon f2.

The necessity of A1 is obvious; however A2 is more subtle. A2 implies that a future does not create "dangling" futures, i.e., futures that are still unevaluated when their creator returns. This assumption is true of many computations of practical interest.

Space constraints prevent us from including any proofs here; the full proofs can be found in [8]. We show that, under the assumptions given, the leapfrog depth rule not only is a sufficient condition for P1 and P2 to hold, but also is a necessary one.

3.3 Portability

It should be clear from the discussion in this section that our techniques are not platform- or language-dependent. In particular, we do not require knowledge of stack-frame layout.

The parallel processing requirements of the software are satisfied by any system that provides a mechanism for thread creation (Cthreads, Posix threads, even heavyweight processes with shared memory such as are provided by Dynix's `m_fork()`) and locks. Our current implementation is based on Cthreads [1].

The techniques are most efficient using spin-waiting locks, but the implementation can be modified easily to work with blocking locks. All lock routines are accessed indirectly through macros that are declared in a single header file. For example, on the Sequent we changed the macros to allow the program to use native Dynix spinlocks rather than the slower locks provided by our Cthreads runtime system. This took only a few minutes and resulted in a noticeable improvement in performance.

The prototype was implemented in `C++`. Some syntactic issues of the implementation are discussed in the appendix.

4 Experimental Results

The results presented in this section were obtained from executions of our benchmark programs on a Sequent Symmetry model B. We recorded the timings for each benchmark using 1, 2, 4, 8 and 16 processors. In doing multiple timings for each run we found that the timings were very consistent on all benchmarks.

We graph the speedup of our futurized implementations relative not only to a sequential implementation (denoted by (S) on the graphs), but also relative to the futurized implementation running with one worker on one processor (denoted by (F) on the graphs).

We have found that recursive programs can benefit from load-based inlining, using a work queue limit of around two to four. A small work queue limit is reasonable because our recursive programs create futures at a steady rate. If future creation were extremely bursty then such a small work queue limit could cause poor performance. The only way to *guarantee* good performance with load-based inlining is through experimenting with some work queue limits until one is found that best fits the application.

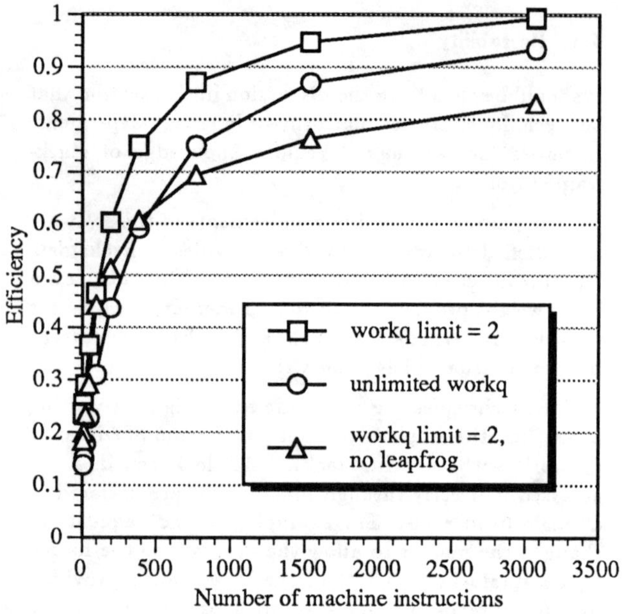

Figure 2: Efficiency vs. granularity on the synthetic benchmark.

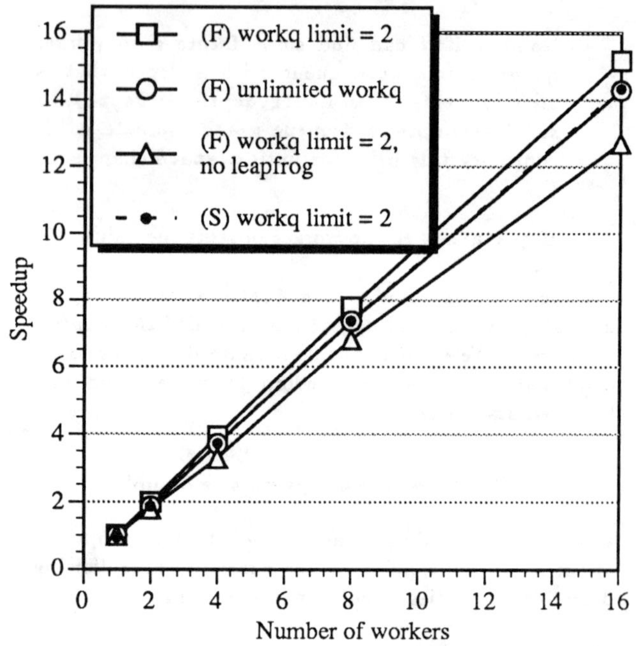

Figure 3: Speedup for Gamma.

4.1 A synthetic benchmark

To gauge the effect of future granularity on performance, we ran a synthetic benchmark similar to the one in [6].

The synthetic benchmark is a modification of the `psum-tree` program. The only difference is that before a leaf returns its value, a for loop is executed that delays the leaf node for a specified number of machine instructions. The average number of machine instructions per future is actually half of this number, because the loop is executed only in the leaf futures and they account for only half of the futures in the computation tree.

The granularity benchmark was run with 16 processors (and thus 16 workers). Efficiency is the *sequential* (not one-processor parallel) time divided by the product of the number of processors and the parallel time. As can be seen in Figure 2, small granularities lead to poor efficiency because of the overhead associated with creating futures, although load-based inlining yields a substantial improvement. Even more striking is the substantial difference in performance between the runs with leapfrogging enabled and the run with it disabled.

Our best performance is comparable to but not quite as good as the Encore implementation of Lazy Task Creation reported in [6]. However, this is somewhat misleading, because certain futures-related overheads, which are built into the Mul-T compiler, are present in the sequential times reported in that paper; these overheads reportedly cause dilations of the execution times of sequential programs in the range of 1.4 to 2.2 [6, Table 1].

4.2 Gamma

Gamma is a recursive, adaptive quadrature algorithm that computes the gamma function:

$$\Gamma(n) = \int_0^\infty x^n e^{-x} dx$$

The basic subroutine in Gamma computes the area under the integrand over a given interval using trapezoidal rule. If the curvature of the integrand in the interval is above a certain threshold, the interval is bisected and recursive calls are made. Because the integrand in the gamma function has widely varying curvature, the computation tree is highly unbalanced, leading to a great deal of leapfrogging. Thus, Gamma is a good test of the efficiency of leapfrogging.

Figure 3 shows the performance of this benchmark computing $\Gamma(6)$ to six decimal places of accuracy. The curves marked (F) show speedup relative to a 1-processor execution of the futurized code, and the curve marked (S) shows speedup relative to a purely sequential implementation in one particular case. In general we get close to linear speedup, and the futurized implementation does not suffer much in comparison to the sequential implementation.

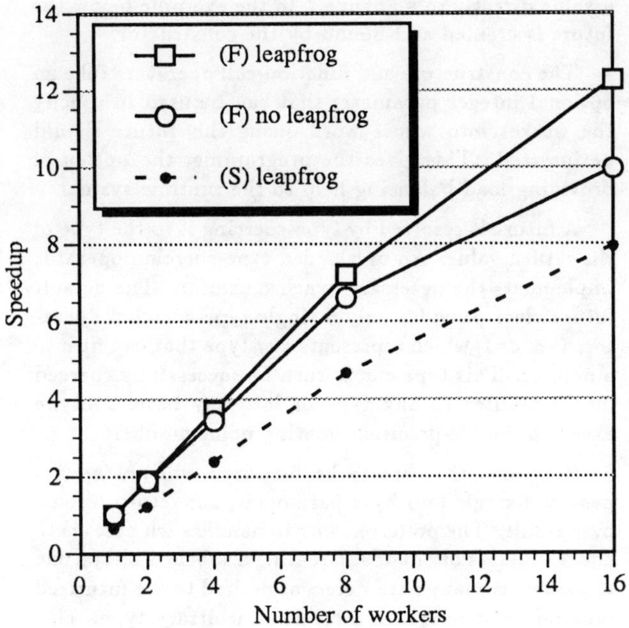

Figure 4: Speedup for Queens(10).

In the graph there are three different futurized executions being compared: one using load-based inlining[4] and leapfrogging, another that uses load-based inlining but no leapfrogging, and another that uses only leapfrogging. A comparison among these curves provides additional evidence that leapfrogging has a much larger effect on performance than does load-based inlining.

4.3 Queens

Our next benchmark, Queens(10), recursively counts all the possible solutions to the problem of placing 10 queens on an 10x10 chess board without any queen attacking another.

The Queens problem is challenging because the granularity of the futures near the bottom of the computation tree is extremely small. In order to get reasonable performance on the Queens(10) benchmark, we coded the program so that it would not create any futures below level 7 in the tree. We found this to be more effective than dynamic load-based inlining.

Figure 4 shows the speedup of the queens program. The futurized code when compared with itself (F) gets almost linear speedup up to eight processors. Again, leapfrogging has a substantial impact on performance.

[4] For the load-based inlining we fixed the work queue sizes at two, a number we arrived at through trial and error.

The poor performance compared to the sequential execution (S) indicates that our implementation is creating a lot of overhead even in the absence of parallel execution. The probable reason for this is that the computation tree for Queens has a much larger average fanout than in either of the previous two examples. Thus, futures are being created unnecessarily.

5 Conclusions

The principal contribution of this research is *leapfrogging*, a portable, efficient implementation technique for futures. Leapfrogging handles the problem of worker blocking, balances the load well and is completely platform-independent. In addition, it is provably free from deadlocks and worker stack sizes are kept within a constant factor of the maximum stack size that a sequential execution of the computation would encounter.

We have demonstrated the performance of leapfrogging using a prototype system implemented in C++ using Cthreads [1] to manage parallelism and synchronization. However, the implementation is easily portable to any platform that provides thread creation primitives, shared memory, and mutual-exclusion locks.

Additional information on our implementation and our experiences using futures on a variety of parallel program structures can be found in the unabridged version of this paper [8].

6 Acknowledgements

The authors would like to thank Mike Fox for working out some of the syntax design issues in embedding futures in C++; the Computer Science Department at the University of Washington for allowing us access to its Sequent multiprocessor; and the anonymous referees for their many valuable comments.

The authors also would like to acknowledge the National Science Foundation, which supported this research under award #CCR-9010672.

References

[1] Cooper, E., and Draves, R. C-Threads. Tech. Rep. CMU-CS-88-154, Carnegie-Mellon University, Feb. 1988.

[2] Ellis, M. A., and Stroustrup, B. *The Annotated C++ Reference Manual.* Addison-Wesley, Reading, MA, 1990.

[3] Goldman, R., and Gabriel, R. Preliminary results with the initial implementation of Qlisp. In

Proc. 1989 Conf. on Lisp and Functional Programming (July 1989), ACM SIGPLAN, ACM, pp. 143–152.

[4] GOLDMAN, R., AND GABRIEL, R. Qlisp: Parallel procesing in Lisp. *IEEE Software* (July 1989), 51–59.

[5] HALSTEAD, JR., R. Multilisp: A language for concurrent symbolic computation. *ACM Transactions on Programming Languages and Systems 7*, 4 (Oct. 1985), 501–538.

[6] MOHR, E., KRANZ, D., AND HALSTEAD, JR., R. Lazy task creation: A technique for increasing the granularity of parallel programs. *IEEE Transactions on Parallel and Distributed Systems 2*, 3 (July 1991), 264–280.

[7] VANDEVOORDE, M. T., AND ROBERTS, E. S. Workcrews: An abstraction for controlling parallelism. *Int. Journal of Parallel Programming 17*, 4 (1988), 347–366.

[8] WAGNER, D. B., AND CALDER, B. G. Portable, efficient futures. Computer Sci. Dept. Tech. Rep. #CU-CS-609-92, University of Colorado, Boulder, CO, Aug. 1992.

A Prototype Details

Our entire implementation of futures is encapsulated in a single C++ class called, not surprisingly, `Future`. The syntax is not very elegant and could certainly benefit from a simple preprocessor; however, in its current form it is not difficult to use, and syntactic issues are not the main focus of this research.

To begin a futurized parallel computation, the program issues a call to `Future::begin()`, in which it specifies the number of workers to use and, optionally, a limit on the work queue sizes. After calling `begin()` and creating one or more futures, the main thread simply continues executing. If and when it references some unresolved future it will automatically start executing as a worker until that future is resolved. On the other hand, if it never references an unresolved future then it does not wait for the computation to finish. To terminate the other workers, the main thread calls `Future::end()`.

A `Future` can be created and bound to a computation in a single step by the constructor functions. Alternatively, creation and binding can be decoupled: class `Future` provides a constructor that takes no arguments to create an unbound `Future`, and overloaded function-call operators to bind such a future to a computation. There is also an overloaded assignment operator to bind a value directly to a `Future`.[5] In the example below the future is created and bound by the constructor.

The constructors and function-call operators take an optional integer parameter that can be used to specify the worker into whose work queue this future should be inserted. This gives the programmer the *option* of providing load-balancing help to the runtime system.

A future is resolved by type-coercing it to the type of the return value. An overloaded type-coercion operator implements the necessary synchronization. The default future class provides only a single type-coercion operator, `(void*)`, which represents any type that can fit into a pointer. This type can in turn be successfully coerced into a pointer to any type or into any basic subtype except a double-precision floating point number.

Programs that are to be futurized will not always pass in a single four byte parameter, nor return a four-byte result. The preferred way to handle such cases is to add a subclass of `Future`. Creating a subclass allows one to pass in as many parameters as desired to the futurized function, and to return a result of arbitrary type. This means the declaration of the futurized function can remain unchanged.

As a concrete example, suppose the leaves of the tree in the `psum_tree` example contained double-precision floating point numbers; then clearly we would want `psum_tree` to return a value of that type. Figure 5 shows a subclass of future that futurizes the hypothetical double-precision `psum_tree` function. Note that we have hard-coded the function to be called into the `Fsum_tree` subclass; we could have easily created a more generic subclass by passing the function as a parameter to the constructor.

A subclass of Future should contain the following elements:

- Local storage for the parameters to the futurized function and its return value.
- A constructor or function-call operator for initialization. This member should accept the same parameters as does the function being futurized. The routine first saves the parameters in the instance variables and then calls `Future::init_future()` in order to insert the future into the work queue. (An optional integer argument can be used to specify *which* work queue.)
- An `evaluate()` member function. `Evaluate()` is a virtual member function that is called by a worker to compute the value of an unresolved `Future`. Thus, the redefined `evaluate` routine simply calls the futurized function with the instance variables

[5] Examples of the use of these features can be found in [8].

```
double psum_tree(NODE*);

class Fsum_tree : public Future {
    NODE *tree;
    double val;

  public:
    Fsum_tree(NODE *t) {
      tree = t;
      init_future();
    };
    // evaluate() is an "upcall"
    virtual void evaluate() {
      val = psum_tree(tree);
    };
    operator double() {
      resolve();
      return val;
    }
};

double psum_tree(NODE *tree) {
    if (!tree->left) {
      return(tree->value);
    } else {
      Fsum_tree right(tree->right);
      return (sum_tree(tree->left) + (double)right);
    }
}
```

Figure 5: Subclass of Future to parallelize `psum_tree`.

as parameters, and saves the return value (if any) in another instance variable.

- The appropriate type coercion operator(s). Each coercion operator should call `Future::resolve()`, which performs all necessary synchronization (including, if necessary, calling `evaluate()`). Once resolved, the future has been computed, and the type coercion operator returns the instance variable that is used to store the return value.

Thus, futurizing a C++ program is not as elegant as futurizing a Mul-T or Qlisp program, but it is by no means difficult.

One limitation of our implementation is that passing a `Future` to a function in which the corresponding formal parameter is not of type `Future` will cause the compiler to invoke a type coercion operator, which will force resolution of the future before the call occurs. Lisp-based languages do not have this problem because data values are dynamically typed. To get around this problem it is necessary to change the type of the formal parameter to `Future` (or the appropriate subclass). The function could still be called with a non-`Future` actual parameter because the `Future` class would provide an implicit type conversion from the non-`Future` to the `Future`.

An Efficient Implementation Scheme of Concurrent Object-Oriented Languages on Stock Multicomputers

Kenjiro Taura Satoshi Matsuoka
Akinori Yonezawa
Department of Information Science, The University of Tokyo*

Abstract

Several novel techniques for efficient implementation of concurrent object-oriented languages on general purpose, stock multicomputers are presented. These techniques have been developed in implementing our concurrent object-oriented language ABCL on a Fujitsu Laboratory's experimental multicomputer AP1000 consisting of 512 SPARC chips. The proposed intra-node scheduling mechanism reduces the cost of local message passing. The cost of intra-node asynchronous message passing is about 20 SPARC instructions in the best case, including locality checking, dynamic method lookup, and scheduling. The minimum latency of asynchronous inter-node message passing is about 9μs, or about 120 instructions, employing the self-dispatching mechanism independently proposed by Eicken et al. A large scale benchmark which involves 9,000,000 message passings shows 440 times speedup on the 512 nodes system compared to the sequential version of the same algorithm. We rely on simple hardware support for message passing and use no specialized architectural supports for object-oriented computing. Thus, we are able to enjoy the benefits of future progress in standard processor technology. Our result shows that concurrent object-oriented languages can be implemented efficiently on conventional multicomputers.

*Physical mail address: 7-3-1 Hongo, Bunkyo-ku, Tokyo 113, Japan. Phone 03-3812-2111 (overseas +81-3-3812-2111) ex. 4108. E-mail: {tau,matsu,yonezawa}@is.s.u-tokyo.ac.jp

4th ACM PPOPP,5/93/CA,USA

1 Introduction

Although a number of concurrent object-oriented programming languages (concurrent OOPL) have been proposed, relatively little attention has been paid to achieving high performance on *conventional* multicomputers such as CM-5, nCUBE/2, and AP1000[11].

Most work on high performance concurrent OOPLs has focused on combination of elaborate hardware and highly-tuned, specially tailored software [5, 14]. These software architectures (the compiler and the runtime system) exploit special features provided by the hardware in order to achieve the two key factors in high-performance concurrent OOPL implementation—efficient message passing between objects and efficient intra-node multithreading. The characteristics of the hardware features are: (1) Processors and the network are tightly connected—processors can send a packet to the network within a few machine cycles, and dispatching a task upon packet arrival takes only a few cycles as well. (2) The scheduling of threads is automatic and directly supported by hardware—the hardware manages the scheduling queue and the next runnable thread is scheduled automatically upon termination of the current thread. Some concurrent OOPLs on such fine-grain machines achieve impressive performance where the latency of message passing between objects on different nodes are 9μs[14], or about 200 machine cycles[5] for a request-reply cycle of method invocation.

The purpose of this paper is to demonstrate the techniques on conventional multicomputers that achieve comparable performance without the hardware facilities described above. Language implementation effort in this direction has been recently proposed; Culler et al. has proposed key features to efficiently manage fine-grain parallelism in a multicomputer setting in their work on TAM[4] and Active Message[13], using Id[8] as the primary target language. Although our work shares some characteristics with theirs, we propose several novel ideas which could be another essential step toward efficient parallel computing on conventional multicomputers.

To demonstrate this, we have developed a runtime environment for a concurrent OOPL called ABCL/onAP1000, which is based on the computation model ABCM[15]. The runtime environment features low-overhead intra-node scheduling and low-latency remote communication on conventional multicomputers which lack special hardware support such as message send instructions and hardware scheduling queues. The three key software technologies in our implementation of ABCL/onAP1000 are:

Integration of Stack-Based and Queue-Based Scheduling: Standard multiprocessing techniques on a single node employ a scheduling queue but suffers from the high overhead of software queue manipulation. Our scheduling mechanism avoids this overhead in many cases by employing efficient stack-based scheduling as much as possible.

Multiple Virtual Function Table: The *virtual function table* is a well-known technique for dynamic method dispatching in object-oriented languages. We propose techniques that extend its use in concurrent OOPLs with which several runtime checks in concurrent object execution can be avoided.

Hiding Latency of Remote Object Creation: The standard scheme for remote object creation requires inter-node communication, which causes unpredictable latency. Moreover, *split-phase allocation*, which works well on fine-grain machines, is not acceptable because of the high-overhead of context switching on conventional multicomputers. We present a technique which hides remote communication latency and avoids context switching in many cases.

The actual implementation of the language ABCL/onAP1000 was done on Fujitsu Laboratory's experimental multicomputer AP1000, which consists of 512 SPARC chips running at 25MHz, interconnected with a 25MB/s torus network. The preliminary measurements show the minimal cost of an asynchronous method invocation on a local object is 2.3μs, or about 20 instructions, including locality checking, method dispatching and scheduling. Also, the cost of an asynchronous message send between two objects on different nodes is 9μs in the best case. This is within a small factor of fine-grain machine performance[5, 14].

Our current prototype compiler generates C language source code. This decision was based on maintaining portability on various future machines.

2 Language Model

This section briefly describes our language, ABCL/onAP1000, which embodies characteristics common to most concurrent OOPL proposed so far[2]. A more comprehensive description of the language ABCL can be found in [15, 16].

2.1 Concurrent Objects and Message Passing

In our computation/programming model[15], computation is carried out by message transmissions among *concurrent objects*, which are units of concurrency and become active when they accept messages. More than one message transmission may take place in parallel and objects may become active simultaneously.

When an object *receives* a message, the message is placed in its *message queue*, and *accepted* for method invocation one-by-one (asynchronous buffered communication). Messages can contain *mail addresses* of concurrent objects as well as basic values such as numbers and booleans. When two messages are sent from the same sender to the same receiver, they arrive at the receiver in the same order as they were sent (*preservation of transmission order*). A sender can send a message to other concurrent objects only if it knows their mail addresses. Since the mail addresses of concurrent objects can be message arguments, the reference topology of concurrent objects is dynamic.

Each object has its own (autonomous) single thread of control, and its own encapsulated state variables (instance variables). The state of a concurrent object is also characterized by the *mode* of its execution; an object is in *dormant* mode if it has no messages to be processed, and it is in *active* mode if it is executing a method. Our model also facilitates *selective message reception* where an object waits for a certain set of messages within a method. Such objects are said to be in *waiting* mode.

2.2 Actions within A Method

A concurrent object can execute a sequence of the following five kinds of basic actions in its method:

1. *Message sends* to other concurrent objects.

   Messages could be *past type* (namely, "asynchronously send and no-wait", syntactically denoted by `[`*TargetObj* `<=` *Msg*`]`) or *now type* (namely, "asynchronously send and wait for a reply message", syntactically denoted by [*TargetObj* <== *Msg*]). The now-type is similar to procedure call, except that (1) the receiver of the request message may continue execution even after it has returned the reply message to the sender, and (2) the reply messages areo actually sent to another object, called *reply destination object* which resumes the original sender upon the reception of the reply message. The reply destination object may be passed to other objects, thus reply messages are not necessarily sent by the original receiver of the request message.

2. *Creation* of concurrent objects.
3. *Referencing and Updating* of the contents of its state variables.
4. *Waiting* for a specified set of messages (*Selective message reception*), including replies of now-type messages.
5. *Standard operations* (e.g., arithmetic operations) on values that are stored in its state variables and passed around by message transmissions.

2.3 Types and Objects

In this paper, we assume that types of variables and element types of containers (i.e., arrays and lists) are statically determined. Although a part of our proposed scheme is applicable regardless of the underlying type system, the overhead incurred by runtime tag handling in dynamic types may nullify our optimization. Objects are the only entities which could be referred to from remote nodes, while other data types, such as arrays and lists are private data of an object that are only referred to from the object.

2.4 Message Patterns

The syntax of a message is similar to that of Smalltalk, consisting of keywords and corresponding arguments. A message is distinguished from one another by its *pattern*, which is a combination of its keywords and its argument types. Unary messages (messages without arguments) are also supported. At compile time, a unique number is assigned to each message pattern.

2.5 Creation of Objects

Objects can be created dynamically on any node (processor). To provide the programmer with locality control, we provide two primitives, namely *local create* and *remote create*. In remote creation, the system determines where the object is created based on local information. The details are described in Section 5.2. We are currently developing a more sophisticated solution for issues on long-term locality management/load balancing.

3 Issues in Implementations of Concurrent OOPL

The major overhead in concurrent OOPL compared to sequential, single-node counterparts lies in: (1) overhead of intra-node communication/multiprocessing (e.g., scheduling queue manipulation) and (2) high cost of remote communication. Our proposed software architecture overcomes these problems.

A naive implementation of a message reception/method invocation for an object would require (1) allocation of an invocation frame, which holds local variables and message arguments of the method, (2) buffering a message into the frame, and (3) enqueueing the frame into the object message queue, and (4) enqueueing the object into the scheduling queue, if necessary (i.e., if the object is not already in the scheduling queue). The object enqueued in the scheduling queue will eventually get control. The above process is far more costly than the corresponding scheduling process for sequential OOPLs (i.e., method lookup + stack-based function call).

The remote communication overhead involves the start-up cost of message sends and the cost of dispatching appropriate tasks on the receiver node. This is complicated by the fact that the receiver node is not only required to service the messages between objects, but also must provide other services such as remote object creation, garbage collection, load monitoring, object migration, etc. On conventional multicomputers, these tasks are mostly done in software, thus consuming a significant amount of CPU time.

4 Intra-node Software Architecture of ABCL/onAP1000

As mentioned above, the naive method invocation schemes in concurrent OOPL are much more costly than that of sequential OOPLs. The source of inefficiency is heap-based (i.e., not stack-based) frame allocation/deallocation and queue manipulations (i.e., message queue and scheduling queue). In this naive scheme, frame allocation is done from the heap because scheduling of methods are not necessarily LIFO-based, that is, methods may be blocked in order to wait for messages and resumed upon the arrival of the message. The scheduling queue is also required for the same reason. In addition, since the processing of received messages may be postponed

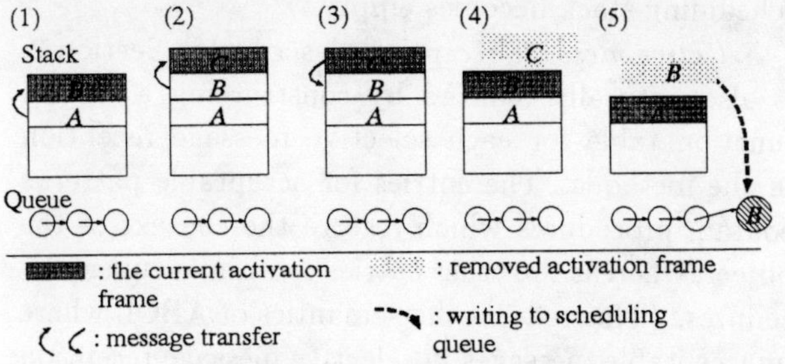

Figure 1: Intra-node scheduling strategy: (1) A sends a message to B. B starts execution immediately. (2) B sends a message to C. C starts execution immediately. (3) C sends the second message to B, and C continues execution because B is already active. (4) After C finished its execution, B executes the rest of the method. (5) When B finishes its method, B enqueues itself in the scheduling queue and will be scheduled later.

depending on the mode of the receiver object (e.g., messages to active objects cannot be processed immediately), each object must have its own message queue to which incoming messages are buffered, in addition to the global (node-wise) scheduling queue.

4.1 Intra-node Scheduling Strategy

Our key observation is that the full scheduling mechanism described above is not necessary in many cases. Instead, more efficient, stack-based scheduling similar to sequential language suffices. More specifically, in our scheduling strategy, if an object has no messages to be processed (i.e., *dormant*), its method is immediately invoked upon message reception without message buffering nor scheduling queue manipulation. In contrast, if it is already running (*active*), the message is buffered and the method is invoked later via a global scheduling queue.

To illustrate our scheduling strategy, consider three objects A, B and C, which execute the following sequence of actions on a single node (Figure 1). Assume that only A is initially active, the others are dormant, and each method is not blocked during its processing.

1. A sends a message to B.
2. B, in the method invoked by A, sends a message to C.
3. Then C, in the method invoked by B, sends a message to B.

In Step 1, B is invoked immediately because B is dormant, and the execution of A is temporarily suspended. Similarly, in Step 2, C starts its execution immediately, suspending the execution of B. On the other hand, in Step 3, since B is now active, the second message to B is buffered in its message queue and C continues execution. After C has finished its method, B resumes the execution of the rest of the method (Step 4 in Figure 1). At this point, there is a choice either to process the next message in the message queue of B, or resume A. We resume A in order to prevent B from monopolizing control; thus, B is enqueued into the global scheduling queue to be scheduled later (Step 5 in Figure 1). By this strategy, A would eventually get control even if B and C were to continue sending messages to each other.

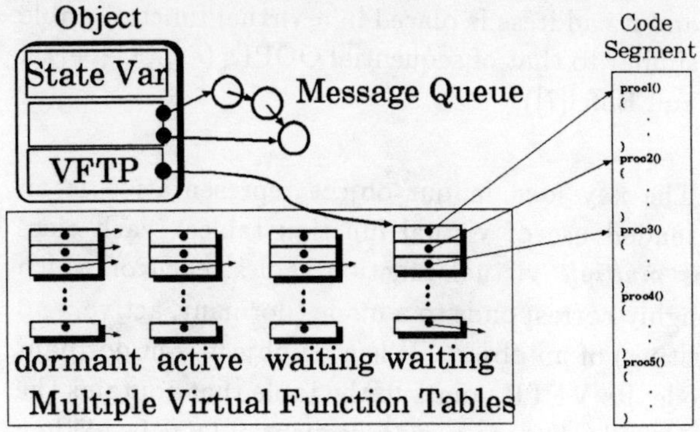

Figure 2: Components of an object.

4.2 Dynamic Method Dispatching via Multiple Virtual Tables

Although our scheduling strategy is now clear, the *mechanism* to implement it efficiently is not trivial. For example, it might seem that a runtime check is required on every intra-node message send in order to determine whether the receiver is dormant or not, making our scheme less attractive. Also, the scheduling mechanism must be *deadlock-free*, i.e., when the running object becomes *blocked* on the stack, other objects must be resumed. This and next sections describe an efficient realization of these strategies.

First, the representation of an object is an extension of that in sequential OOPLs. As in Figure 2, each object is composed of:

- A state variable box, which holds the state variables (i.e., instance variables) of the object. Each state variable is accessed with a fixed offset from the top of the object.
- A message queue, which is a list of received, unprocessed messages. Each item in the message queue is actually a heap-allocated frame which is allocated upon message reception. Each frame keeps its message arguments, local variables and other necessary fields for scheduling purpose.
- A *virtual function table pointer* (*VFTP*), which points to one of the *multiple virtual function tables*. A method of a class is compiled into a C function

and its address is placed in a virtual function table similar to that of sequential OOPLs (e.g., C++[12] and Eiffel[7]).

The key idea in our object representation is an extended use of virtual function tables: each class has *multiple* virtual function tables, each of which roughly corresponds to a mode (dormant, active, and waiting) of an object. When an object is in dormant mode, its VFTP points to the table that contains the method bodies, as is with sequential OOPLs. When the object becomes active, the VFTP is made to point to a virtual function table that holds tiny *queuing procedures* which simply allocates a frame, store the message into the frame and enqueues it to the message queue of the receiver object. Multiple virtual function tables liberate the sender object from the runtime checking of whether or not the receiver object is dormant, by incorporating it into the virtual function table look-up, which is already a necessary cost in OOPLs.

A message send begins with a runtime check to determine whether or not the receiver object is local by looking up the node ID of the object. (The locality check usually takes 3~4 SPARC instructions.) If the receiver object is local, we simply look-up the virtual function table with the statically-determined index number of the message pattern and call the indexed procedure with the message as arguments. As described above, if the object is in dormant mode, the procedure will be the method body itself, which is executed immediately. Otherwise, if the object is in active mode, the procedure will be a queuing procedure, which stores the message into a message box and returns execution to the sender. Each queuing procedure is customized according to the interface of the corresponding method (i.e., the number of the arguments and the types of each argument).

For now-type messages, the mail address of the reply destination object is passed as well. After the invoked procedure returned, the sender checks its reply destination object to see if the reply has arrived; if the reply has not arrived the object becomes blocked. (The details are described in Section 4.3.) Notice that return from a procedure does not imply the arrival of the reply as with sequential procedural languages; rather, the reply message is explicitly sent as normal message passing to the reply destination object.

Each object checks its message queue at the completion of a method, and if there are any pending messages, enqueues itself in the global scheduling queue. Objects in the scheduling queue are invoked when the scheduling stack becomes empty.[1]

Selective message reception, described in Section 2, is also naturally realized by constructing a virtual function table for each selective message reception in the methods. The entries for acceptable patterns contain procedures which restore the context of the object, whereas the other entries contain queuing procedures. (This reflects the semantics of ABCL where unacceptable messages in selective message reception are buffered into the message queue. Other semantics, e.g., discarding unacceptable messages, can also be facilitated easily.)

In addition, we utilize the VFTP for two other purposes. Firstly, an object initializes its state variables lazily when it receives a message for the first time. A naive implementation would require an additional flag indicating initialization, which would result in checking the flag on every message send. We avoid this by building a virtual function table which holds pointers to an initialization routine which calls the method body after the state variable initialization. Secondly, using the multiple virtual function tables solves a problem in fast remote creation of objects. The problem is that, a message to an object created on a remote node may arrive before the virtual function of the object is properly initialized. The details of the problem and its solution is described in Section 5.2.

4.3 Combining the Stack and Scheduling Queue

Upon invoking a method of a dormant object, a frame is allocated on the *stack* thereby achieving fast frame allocation/deallocation. When such an invocation is blocked in the middle of the thread for the first time, it allocates another frame lazily on the heap, and saves its context (i.e., local variables) to the frame which will be kept until termination of the method. On the other hand, upon reception of a message by an active object, a frame is allocated on heap and the message is immediately stored there.

The object that has its activation frame on the top of the stack is physically executing. When the running object becomes blocked as a result of a selective message reception or waits for a reply of a now-type message send, it pops off its own stack frame and saves its context (i.e., instruction pointer and local variables) into the heap-allocated frame, thereby resuming other objects. At the same time, it also

[1] Our scheduling mechanism also allows invocation of objects in the scheduling queue even if the stack is not empty, but we do not employ this for the purpose of fair scheduling between objects. (See Step 5 in Figure 1)

switches the VFTP to point to the virtual function table whose entries of awaited messages have the context restoration routine and others have the queueing procedures. (More precisely speaking, in the case of now-type messages, since the reply is sent to the reply destination object rather than to the sender object, all the entries of the VFTP of the sender are the queueing procedure; the reply destination object actually resumes the sender on the arrival of the reply message.) When one of the awaited messages later arrives, the context is restored and the object becomes active again. We stress that object is not blocked as long as it finds an awaited message when it first checks its message queue (or, the reply destination object for a now-type message). In particular, for intra-node now-type message passing, it is usually the case that the reply will have already arrived when the sender checks the reply destination object because we employ stack-based scheduling; in such cases, stack unwinding does not occur.

Let us examine an example case where stack unwinding occurs and how our scheme schedules runnable objects (Figure 3). Consider object S sends now type message m to *active* object R, whose current activation frame is buried in the lower part of the stack. When sending m, S invokes the queueing procedure of m because R is active. After the queuing procedure returns, S checks the reply destination object to see if a reply has already returned. Since there are naturally no replies, S saves its context into a heap-allocated frame and resumes the object which activated S (i.e., Object O in the Figure 3). When control reaches R again and R finishes its current method, it checks its message queue to find that there are some messages, thus enqueueing itself to the scheduling queue (Step 3 in Figure 3). Eventually R processes m and sends a reply message to S, resuming the saved context of S.

Although most part of our scheduling is done via the stack, we also employ a global (node-wise) scheduling queue as well. The purposes of the scheduling queue are twofold:

1. To invoke buffered messages in the FIFO scheduling—Messages that were once buffered in a message queue are scheduled through the scheduling queue, as we have seen in Section 4.1.

2. To preempt objects—Preemption occurs when an object falls into a long internal loop or a deep recursion. When preemption occurs, the object stores its context into a heap-allocated frame and enqueues itself into the scheduling queue.

Each item of the queue consists of a pointer to the

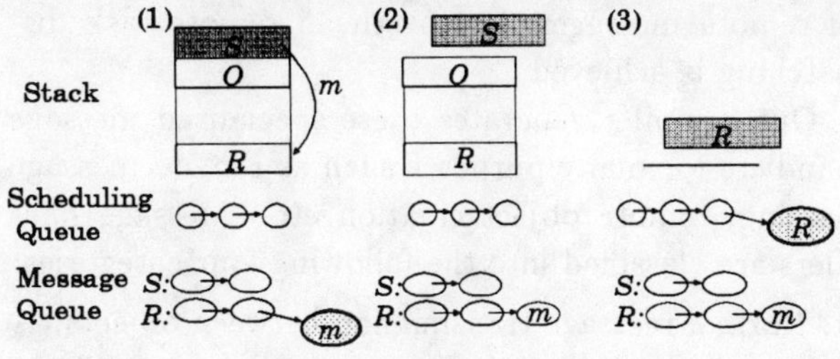

Figure 3: An example of stack unwinding. (1) S sends now type message m to R and m is enqueued. (2) S checks the reply destination object to find that no reply has arrived and saves its context into a heap-allocated frame. (3) When R gets control, it enqueues itself into the scheduling queue at the end of the method. m is eventually scheduled and the reply reaches S.

object which will be scheduled and a continuation address from which the object will restart execution. The system dequeues an item in the scheduling queue simply by transferring control to the continuation address contained in the item—the instructions starting from the continuation address perform the actual context restoration and activation of the scheduled object.

5 Inter-node Software Architecture of ABCL/onAP1000

We next describe the remote servicing aspects of our software architecture, such as message passing between objects on different nodes, and object creation on a remote node. Our software architecture assumes that the hardware (or message passing libraries) provides an interface to send and receive messages asynchronously. It is strongly desirable to be able to send/receive messages without OS kernel intervention. Supports for arbitrary length packets and preservation of message transmission order do simplify the implementation, although it is not a necessity. Message arrival may be notified by polling as in CM-5 or AP1000, or by interrupt as in nCUBE/2 or iPSC/2. Most multicomputers (including AP1000, our current target machine) support these facilities.

5.1 Efficient Remote Task Activation

As for underlying mechanisms of remote servicing aspects, we employed an "Active Message-like mechanism[13]",[2] which is a low overhead message dispatching mechanism for conventional multicomputers. The idea is that each kind of message attaches its own 'self-dispatching' message handler which is invoked immediately after the delivery of the message By giving a customized message handler for each kind

[2]We developed a technique similar to Active Message early 1992, and later found it in [13].

of remote messages, low overhead remote task dispatching is achieved.

Our compiler generates these specialized message handlers for many purposes such as remote message passing, remote object creation etc. Message handlers are classified into the following four categories:

1. Normal message transmission between objects.
2. Request for remote object creation.
3. Reply to remote memory allocation request.
4. Other services (load balancing, global garbage collection, etc.).

The handlers for Category 1 extract the pointer to the receiver object and arguments and schedule the receiver object in the manner described in Section 4.2. The compiler generates a specialized message handler for each message pattern (i.e., the number of arguments and the type of each message). Since the types of the arguments are statically determined, tags are no longer necessary and the arguments are processed efficiently by the specialized handler.

Categories 2 and 3 are used for remote object creation. The handlers for Category 2 create an object of a particular class at the address specified by the requester. The message handler returns the address of another memory chunk to the requester for its future use. The message handlers for Category 3 are provided as the handler address of this reply message. Our compiler generates a single (specialized) message handler of Category 2 for each class and one message handler of Category 3 for each chunk size. The details are described in the next section.

5.2 Remote Object Creation

In our software architecture a mail address of an object is uniformly represented as a pair ⟨ *processor number, a (real) pointer* ⟩. We employed this representation for maximum performance in local object access and to avoid the overhead of the export table management. One restriction is that in general it would prohibit the use of a simple copying/compacting garbage collector, as objects cannot be moved freely. We are now developing an algorithm whereby objects that are only referred to locally can be freely copied.

Under our representation scheme of mail addresses, object creation on a remote node requires a memory allocation on the target node in order to generate a remote mail address. Since the latency of remote communication is unpredictable, it is not acceptable to wait until a pointer to the allocated memory (chunk) is returned. *Split-phase allocation* is preferable on fine-grain machines where context switching to another thread effectively hide the latency[1]. On conventional multicomputers, however, split-phase allocation is undesirable because of high context-switching overhead. Rather, a scheme whereby the object can continue execution even in the presence of remote allocation request is preferable.

For this purpose, we employ a *prefetch scheme* where each node manages predelivered "stocks" of address of memory chunks on remote nodes, and the address for remote object allocation is obtained locally from the stock. Only when the stock is empty does context switching on remote object creation occur. The requested node later replies another chunk to replenish the stock. The stock is unlikely to become empty except when unusually frequent remote creations occur.

A typical sequence of remote object creation is as follows:

1. The requester node obtains a unique mail address locally from the stock.
2. A creation request message is sent to the node of the mail address.
3. The target node performs class-specific initialization (e.g., initialization of virtual function table) of the created object upon receipt of the creation message (message handler for Category 2).
4. The target node allocates a replacement chunk and returns its address to the requester node.
5. The requester replenishes the stock upon receipt of the address (message handler for Category 3).

An object on the requesting node can obtain the mail address of the created object in Step 1, rather than in Step 3, thereby effectively hiding the remote communication latency. Furthermore, this scheme avoids context switching (which, in contrast, is necessary for split-phase allocation) as long as some chunks remain in the stock.

There is one problem however: After the new mail address is locally obtained in Step 1, the request message sent in Step 2 must precede any messages to the object. Under our scheme, however, standard messages between objects could reach the uninitialized object when the obtained mail address is passed to other objects before the initialization message has reached the target node (Figure 4).

We again utilize the VFTP to solve this problem without adding any overhead to each message send. Each chunk is pre-initialized in the following way when its address is sent in Step 4: The message queue is empty and the VFTP is *temporarily* initialized to be the generic *fault function table*, whose entries are

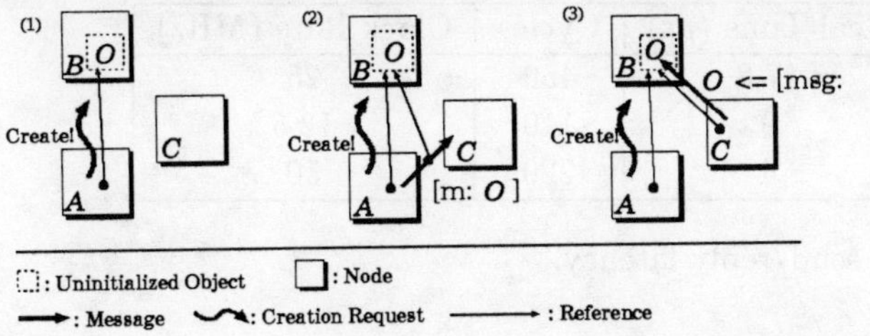

Figure 4: Initialization problem on remote object creation: (1) Sending creation request to B, an object on node A obtains the mail address of an uninitialized object O on node B from the stock. (2) The object on A sends a message which contains the mail address of O to some object on another node C. (3) It sends a message to O. This message may reach O before the actual initialization of O by the creation request.

	Time (μs)
Intra-node Message (to Dormant)	2.3
Intra-node Message (to Active)	9.6
Intra-node Creation	2.1
Latency of Inter-node Message	8.9

Table 1: Costs of basic operations.

entirely queuing procedures. This forces all messages to uninitialized objects to be enqueued. When the initialization message eventually arrives, the virtual function table is initialized to the proper one for the class of the object. In addition, the message queue of the object is checked for pending messages, and the first message is extracted and processed if it exists. This scheme works because the queuing procedures are generic for all objects, independent of their classes.

6 Preliminary Performance Measurement of ABCL/onAP1000

6.1 Efficiency of Basic Operations

Table 1 shows the cost of basic operations such as message passing or object creation. Our compiler generates C language code, which is in turn compiled with optimization level "-O4". Throughout all the measurements, Sun-OS 4.1.1 `cc` was used.

An intra-node past-type message send to a dormant object takes 2.3μs. This was measured by repeatedly invoking a null method with no arguments. Table 2 is the breakdown of this process. Further compile-time optimizations are possible under the following conditions: (1) Locality check can be eliminated for objects guaranteed to be local; for example, message passings which follow local object creation. (2) Switching of the VFTP is not necessary if the method does not send messages to other objects and is never blocked. (i.e., if the method is ensured to finish its execution without running other objects.) (3) Checking the message queue is not necessary if the object is not history sensitive. (4) Polling of remote message arrival is not always necessary, especially for small methods—we merely need to guarantee periodical polling of remote messages. Altogether, the overhead of an intra-node message to dormant objects varies from 8 (in this case, the overhead is truly comparable with virtual function call in C++) to 25 instructions.

	Instructions
Check Locality	3
Lookup and Call	5
Switch VFTP to Active Mode	3
Execution of Method Body	–
Check Message Queue	3
Switch VFTP to Dormant Mode	3
Polling of Remote Message	5
Adjusting Stack Pointer and Return	3
Total	25

Table 2: Breakdown of intra-node message to dormant object.

The cost of an intra-node message to an active mode object includes: (1) a frame allocation, (2) storing the message into the frame, (3) enqueueing the frame into the message queue of the object, (4) enqueueing the object to the global scheduling queue (if the object is not already in the scheduling queue), and (5) re-scheduling of the object from the scheduling queue. The total time is approximately 10μs, which is over 4 times (or even more if we adopt the above optimizations) that of the dormant case. Our scheduling mechanism specially optimizes dormant case by stack-based scheduling, thereby reducing the total intra-node scheduling overhead.

Minimum inter-node latency, 8.9μs, is obtained by repeatedly transmitting one word past-type messages between two objects. There are no objects other than these two objects in the system and both are dormant upon message reception. This shows that conventional multicomputers with appropriate software technologies have much higher inter-node message passing capability than previously believed. In comparison to fine-grain architecture (Table 3), send and reply latency is approximately 18μs, or 450 cycles, which is only about twice of [5] or about 4 times of [14] when normalized to the same clock speed. The instruction counts includes message setup (in the script of the sender), polling, extracting of the message (in the message handler), system message buffer management and script invocation. The sender node

	Instruction Counts	Real Time (μs)	Cycles	Clock Rate (MHz)
ABCL/onAP1000	160	17.8	450	25
ABCL/onEM4[14]	100	9	110	12.5
CST (on J-Machine)[5]	110	4	220	50

Table 3: Comparison of send/reply latency.

	$N = 8$	$N = 13$
# of Solutions	92	73,712
# of Objects Creation	2,056	4,636,210
# of Messages	4,104	9,349,765
Total Memory Used (KB)	130	549,463
Elapsed Time on SS1+	84 ms	461,955 ms

Table 4: The scale of the N-queen program ($N = 8, 13$).

takes about 20 instructions to setup and send a message which is a total of 4 words including routing information, the mail address of the receiver object and the message argument. The receiver node consumes a total of about 50 instructions for polling, extracting the message and management of the system message buffer. The script invocation cost is the same as intra-node message send to dormant objects (approximately 10 instructions). The remaining portion of the latency is due to hardware, which is roughly 1.5μs each way. By (1) reducing this hardware latency and (2) more appropriate interface to network, our speed further approaches that of implementations on fine-grain machines. Furthermore, such implementations on conventional multicomputers can directly benefit from advances in single-processor technology.

6.2 Benchmark Statistics

To evaluate the proposed techniques on real applications, we measured the performance of the N-queen exhaustive search algorithm varying N. The small program ($N = 8$) is the one which terminates within 100 milliseconds on single CPU SPARC station 1+, and the large program ($N = 13$) involves more than 4,500,000 object creations and $9,000,000$ message passings. Table 4 shows the scale of the algorithm where $N = 8$ and 13. Table 4 also shows the elapsed time of the sequential version of basically the same algorithm running on a single SPARC station 1+, which has the same CPU as the node processor of AP1000. The sequential version is written in C++ and compiled by g++ with optimize option.

Figure 5 shows the speedup of the N-queen program relative to the sequential version. Since the sequential version of the algorithm uses run-time stack for the depth first search, it requires no heap memory and there is no need for termination detection, while our parallel version uses heap extensively for parallel

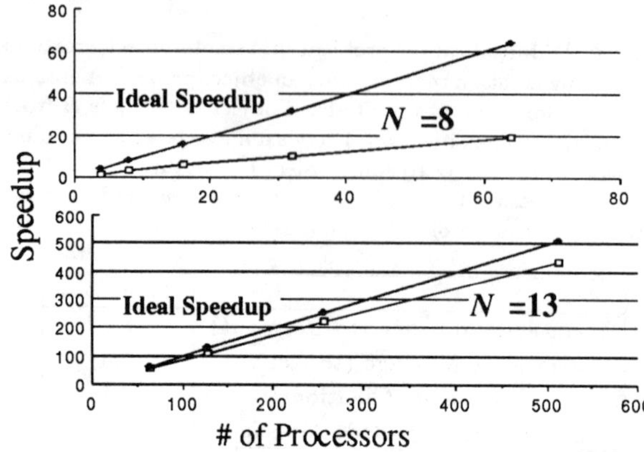

Figure 5: Speedup for N-queen problem ($N = 8, 13$).

search and acknowledgement message trace back the search tree for the termination detection. Nevertheless, approximately 20 times speedup is obtained for $N = 8$ on a 64 processors, and 440 times for $N = 13$ on 512 processors (approximately 85% utilization).

6.3 Effect of Stack-Based Scheduling

To demonstrate the effect of stack-based scheduling, we compare our performance to a more naive scheduling mechanism. The naive scheduling mechanism always buffers a message in the message queue of the receiver object and the object is scheduled through the scheduling queue.

Figure 6 shows the performance improvements in the N queen programs as N varies. In these programs, approximately 75% of local messages are sent to dormant mode objects. In general, we have observed approximately 30% speedup.

7 Related Work

Our work shares the goals of all attempts to make fine-grain computing feasible, not only for object-oriented concurrent languages but for other languages. Amongst them, our work is similar to Threaded Abstract Machine (TAM)[4] and Active Message[13] in aiming for high performance without elaborate hardware supports.

TAM is a multithreaded abstract machine whose instruction set, TL0, is intended to be mapped onto conventional instruction sets, so that TL0 can serve as an intermediate language on conventional multi-

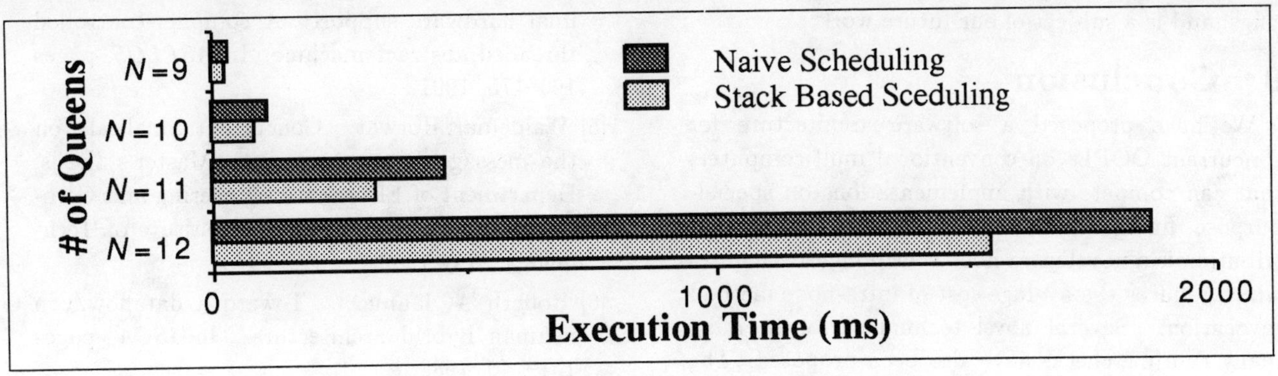

Figure 6: Effect of the stack scheduling.

computers for high-level parallel languages such as Id[8] and Multilisp[9]. The execution model of TAM is an extension of the hybrid dataflow model[6]: In addition to "threads" (instruction sequences which are exclusively executed), TAM recognizes a collection of logically related threads called the *code-block*. Under the TAM execution model, runnable threads within a code-block are ensured to be scheduled consecutively, thereby allowing inter-thread register allocation and inexpensive synchronization of threads. This unit of co-scheduling is called "quanta" in TAM.

8 Discussion

8.1 Stack-based Scheduling

Although TAM has shown an efficient dataflow synchronization and communication between threads *within* a code-block, its *code-block invocation* or *inter-code-block* communication (e.g., passing function arguments) mechanism has room for further improvement. That is, under the TAM execution mechanism, a code-block invocation (e.g., function call) always require frame allocation from heap, message buffering, and scheduling queue manipulation, while our implementation uses a stack as much as possible.

Although situations are different for our language and TAM, which is intended to support lenient[10] semantics where blocking in the middle of a function is more likely, we believe our stack-based scheduling mechanism is better in practical settings where small functions (or methods), which are not typically blocked, are extensively used.

The advantages of our stack-based scheduling are: (1) frames are cheaply allocated/deallocated as long as blocking does not occur, (2) messages are processed without buffering, (3) it is more likely that the result of a function (or method) has already arrived when the callee resumes the caller, because we run the callee (or the receiver object) first, and then resuming the caller (or sender object).

Of course, we do not claim that our stack-based scheduling is not unconditionally advantageous. It requires some registers to be saved before a function call, which is unnecessary under a TAM execution where a caller is never invoked until a callee is blocked. Nevertheless, the amount of registers to be saved will be typically small and the cost will be smaller than the cost of argument buffering and scheduling queue manipulation which is required in the TAM mechanism.

8.2 Method Inlining

Our implementation scheme relies on the fact that objects are always accessed through methods which are obtained from the virtual function table: The readers might point out that this would prohibit further optimization via inlining of method calls which is used extensively in sequential object-oriented language SELF[3] to achieve good performance. However, inlining is possible in the following way, as long as the class of a receiver object is known at compile time: let the class of the receiver be C, the virtual function table of class C for dormant mode be C_dormant_vft, and the method which should be invoked be C_method. The inlined code of the method call would be as follows:

```
if(receiver_node_id == my_cell_id){
    if(receiver_obj->vftp == C_dormant_vftp){
        inlined code of C\_method;
    } else {
        enqueue the message;
    }
} else {
    send the message to the receiver_node_id;
}.
```

This code still has additional checks for locality and the mode of the object. The full benefit of inlining is obtained by inferring such information and eliminating the checking code, but such inference is far more difficult than class inference in sequential OOPL settings, and is a subject of our future work.

9 Conclusion

We have proposed a software architecture for concurrent OOPLs on conventional multicomputers that can compete with implementations on special-purpose, fine-grain architectures. Our primary contribution is a novel intra-node scheduling mechanism which reduces the average cost of intra-node method invocation. Several novel techniques for avoiding many runtime checks have also been proposed. The preliminary measurements have shown that our performance compares favorably with the implementations on fine-grain machines. Restrictions of these mechanisms/techniques are small and they are widely applicable for various (even non-object-oriented) concurrent language implementations.

Acknowledgements

Our thought was improved through the discussion with Rishiyur S. Nikhil, who gave us many beneficial and thoughtful comments that go into details of our proposal. We thank to David E. Culler and Thorsten von Eicken for giving us many comments on our paper. The discussions with Bill Dally and Waldemar Horwat at our mutual visits were very fruitful. We would like to appreciate the offer of Fujitsu Laboratory in Kawasaki, Japan, which has provided us with the opportunity to use AP1000. Our special thanks go to Takeshi Horie for his helpful technical advices and access to the library sources of AP1000. We thank the members of the ABCL project group, especially Jeff MaAffer who substantially improved the presentation of our paper, and Masahiro Yasugi for daily technical discussion.

References

[1] Arvind and Robert A. Iannucci. Two fundamental issues in multiprocessing. In *4th International DFVLR Seminar on Foundations of Engineering Sciences*, volume 295 of *Lecture Notes in Computer Science*, pages 61–88, 1987.

[2] Henri E. Bal, Jennifer G. Steiner, and Andrew S. Tanenbaum. Programming languages for distributed computing systems. *ACM Computing Surveys*, 21(3):261–322, September 1989.

[3] Craig Chambers and David Ungar. Making pure object-oriented language practical. In *OOPSLA*, pages 1–15, 1991.

[4] David E. Culler, Anurag Sah, Klaus Erik Schauser, Thorsten von Eicken, and John Wawrzynek. Fine-grain parallelism with minimal hardware support: A compiler-controlled threaded abstract machine. In *ASPLOS*, pages 166–175, 1991.

[5] Waldemar Horwat. Concurrent Smalltalk on the message-driven processor. Master's thesis, Department of Electrical Engineering and Computer Science, Massachusetts Institute of Technology, May 1989.

[6] Roberb A. Iannucci. Toward a dataflow/von neuman hybrid architecture. In *ISCA*, pages 131–140, 1988.

[7] Bertrand Meyer. *Object-oriented Software Construction*. Prentice Hall, 1988.

[8] R. S. Nikhil. Id (version 88.0) reference manual. Technical Report 284, MIT Laboratry for Computer Science, March 1988.

[9] Jr. Robert H. Halstead. Multilisp: A language for concurrent symbolic computation. *acm Transactions on Programming Languages and Systems*, 7(4):501–538, April 1985.

[10] Klaus Erik Schauser, David E. Culler, and Thorsten von Eicken. Compiler-controlled multithreading for lenient parallel languages. In *Functional Programming Languages and Computer Architecture*, volume 523 of *Lecture Notes in Computer Science*, pages 50–72, 1991.

[11] Toshiyuki Shimizu, Takeshi Horie, and Hiroaki Ishihata. Low-latency message communication support for the ap1000. In *ISCA*, pages 288–297, 1992.

[12] Bjarne Stroustrup. *The C++ Programming Language, second edition*. Addison Wasley, 1991.

[13] Thorsten von Eicken, David E. Culler, Seth Copen Goldstein, and Klaus Erik Schauser. Active messages: a mechanism for integrated communication and computation. In *ISCA*, pages 256–266, 1992.

[14] Masahiro Yasugi, Satoshi Matsuoka, and Akinori Yonezawa. ABCL/onEM4: A new software/hardware architecture for object-oriented concurrent computing on an extended dataflow supercomputer. In *ICS*, pages 93–103, 1992.

[15] Akinori Yonezawa. *ABCL: An Object-Oriented Concurrent System — Theory, Language, Programming, Implementation and Application*. The MIT Press, 1990.

[16] Akinori Yonezawa, Jean-Pierre Briot, and Etsuya Shibayama. Object-oriented concurrent programming in ABCL/1. In *OOPSLA '86 Conference Proceedings*, pages 258–268, 1986.

The Shared Regions Approach to Software Cache Coherence on Multiprocessors

Harjinder S. Sandhu   Benjamin Gamsa   Songnian Zhou

Computer Systems Research Institute
University of Toronto

Abstract

The effective management of caches is critical to the performance of applications on shared-memory multiprocessors. In this paper, we discuss a technique for software cache coherence that is based upon the integration of a program-level abstraction for shared data with software cache management. The program-level abstraction, called *Shared Regions*, explicitly relates synchronization objects with the data they protect. Cache coherence algorithms are presented which use the information provided by shared region primitives, and ensure that shared regions are always cacheable by the processors accessing them. Measurements and experiments of the Shared Region approach on a shared-memory multiprocessor are shown. Comparisons with other software based coherence strategies, including a user-controlled strategy and an operating system-based strategy, show that this approach is able to deliver better performance, with relatively low corresponding overhead and only a small increase in the programming effort. Compared to a compiler-based coherence strategy, the Shared Regions approach still performs better than a compiler that can achieve 90% accuracy in allowing cacheing, as long as the regions are a few hundred bytes or larger, or they are re-used a few times in the cache.

1 Introduction

Shared-memory multiprocessors offer a simple and convenient model for programming parallel applications. For highly parallel architectures, the Non-Uniform Memory Access (NUMA) characteristics of these machines make memory access latency a central issue. Techniques for cache coherence attempt to exploit the advantages of low latency processor caches while minimizing cache management overhead. Weak consistency models attempt to tolerate memory access latency by integrating specific programming models with architectures that exploit buffering and pipelining using knowledge of synchronization events to relax the constraints on the ordering of memory operations. In this paper, we discuss a new approach to managing consistency on shared-memory multiprocessors that integrates an even weaker consistency model with software cache management.

Hardware cache coherence techniques that have been proposed include snoopy caches and directory schemes [LLG+90][CKA91]. A problem with hardware solutions is that they are either non-scalable or require complex and expensive hardware. Thus, software techniques that can guarantee consistency and achieve reasonable cache hit performance are desirable. On multiprocessors without hardware coherent caches, the task of enforcing consistency may be assumed by the user [PBG+85] [GKM+82] [MOR86], the compiler [CKM88] [CV90], or by the operating system [SUK92]. User-based approaches introduce significant complexity to the programming task, while compiler-based approaches require sophisticated static analysis which is difficult in explicitly parallel languages. Operating system-based approaches often perform poorly because they determine cacheability on a per-page basis.

Weak consistency models rely on the fact that synchronization points and memory accesses are related [AH90]. For instance, by assuming that the value of an element being written to by processor P_i will not be used by another processor until after the next synchronization point has been reached by P_i, P_i can avoid waiting for the completion of the write operation. Read operations initiated after a write operation has been started may overtake and complete before the write operation has completed. A weakly consistent system must be aware of synchronization points, and ensure consistency at those points. The Release Consistency [GLL+90] model is a weak consistency model that uses knowledge of two types of synchronization operations, *acquire* and *release*, to further relax the constraints on the ordering of memory operations.

Our approach, which we call the Shared Regions approach (SR), is an extension of the weak consistency concept in which synchronization objects are explicitly associated with the data they protect. The shared data in the application is

4th ACM PPOPP,5/93/CA,USA
© 1993 ACM 0-89791-589-5/93/0005/0229...$1.50

partitioned into shared regions of memory, and the application explicitly identifies the region it wishes to access. A processor that is accessing a shared region is guaranteed exclusive or read-shared access to that region. Because of this, shared regions are always *cacheable* by a processor accessing that region; the system has only to ensure consistency of a shared region at the shared region access control points in the application.

Unlike traditional weak consistency models, however, which relax the constraints on the ordering of memory operations and thereby improve performance, the primary motivation for the Shared Regions approach is to permit more effective management of caches and main memory. In this paper, we show that SR cache coherence can be implemented efficiently in software, with no special hardware support. NUMA memory management can also be enhanced by exploiting knowledge of shared regions, but this is discussed in a separate paper [SGZ92].

An overview of the rest of this paper is as follows: Section 2 discusses the program-level abstraction that relates synchronization objects with the data they protect. Section 3 presents algorithms for SR cache coherence. Section 4 presents some experiments from an implementation of SR cache coherence on a shared-memory multiprocessor using a few sample applications, and compares this strategy with some other software-based cache coherence strategies. Section 5 presents a comparative analysis of SR cache coherence and a compiler-based strategy. Section 6 summarizes the ideas presented in this paper.

2 Shared Regions

A Shared Region is a high-level programming abstraction for shared data. In much the same way as a user may specify the threads of execution in the application but leave the scheduling and management of those threads to the system, a user specifies the shared regions in the application and leaves the management of that data to the system. In this section, we discuss the specification and integration of shared regions into a high-level programming language such as C++.

A *shared region* is defined loosely as a set of memory locations that are accessed together (i.e., within the same task) and in the same mode (read or write) in a parallel application. A region may encompass an entire user-defined data object, it may encompass only some subsection of a data object, or it may comprise subsections of multiple data objects. For example, in a parallel matrix multiplication ($C = AB$) where each task computes a row of C using a row of A and the entire matrix B, each row of A and C may be defined as a separate shared region, while the entire matrix B may be defined as a single shared region.

Using the Shared Region abstraction, performance critical shared data is partitioned into shared regions, and accesses to those regions must be requested explicitly using shared region access primitives (called SR primitives). A *token* representing a shared region is explicitly bound to some data using a *BindRegion* call. The SR primitives *ReadAccess*, *ReadDone*, *WriteAccess*, and *WriteDone* are operations on shared regions. *ReadAccess* is a request for read-only access to the shared region, and *WriteAccess* is a request for exclusive write access to the shared region. A series of references to a region are preceded by a ReadAccess or WriteAccess call, and terminated by a ReadDone or WriteDone call.

The use of SR primitives for synchronization obviates the need for other synchronization mechanisms (such as semaphores or monitors) in many cases. However, this introduces a subtle shift in paradigm; whereas traditional synchronization constructs typically protect a critical section of code, the SR primitives protect a section of shared memory. Figure 1 shows an example of region specification and contrasts this with the use of semaphores. In this example, an array of regions r is defined, and each region is bound to a separate row of A (region $r[a]$ is bound to a section of memory encompassing RS bytes starting at address $\&A[a]$) much as a separate lock is associated implicitly with a row of A in the semaphore version.[1] A process requesting WriteAccess to a region must wait until all previous ReadAccess or WriteAccess requests to that region have completed. A process requesting WriteAccess to a region must wait until all previous ReadAccess requests to that region have completed.

Semaphore approach	Shared Regions approach

double A[N][N];
lock k[N];
 	
for (a=0; a<N; a++)
... initialize lock k[a]
 	
lock(k[i])
for (j=0; j<N; j++)
A[i][j] = ...
unlock(k[i])
	double A[N][N];
	Region r[N];
	
	for (a=0; a<N; a++)
	r[a].BindRegion(&A[a],RS)
	. . .
	r[i].WriteAccess()
	for (j=0; j<N; j++)
	A[i][j] = ...
	r[i].WriteDone()

Figure 1: C++ region specification example compared with semaphores.

In the case where Shared Region primitives replace other synchronization constructs, the programmer's task is not any more difficult than programming a non-Shared Region version of the same application, so the programming complexity of Shared Regions is minimal. Additionally, the cost of acquiring the shared region lock should not be considered an overhead of this technique. In other cases, however, the locking aspect of the region access primitives may be redundant, for example, when using ReadAccess where the region is already guaranteed not to be write-shared at that point in

[1] In this example, the *BindRegion* function specifies a contiguous region comprising one row of the matrix. Non-contiguous regions may be specified using a function which allows multiple contiguous regions to be referenced as a single region.

the application. In such cases, the ReadAccess call is still required for coherence purposes, but the locking overhead is avoided by using non-blocking versions of the SR primitives.

The advantage of the Shared Region approach is that the sharing characteristics of the application are exposed to the underlying system, thus permitting more efficient shared data management. The next section presents some algorithms for software cache coherence based upon the information provided by SR primitives. The utility of the Shared Region approach to software cache management will depend on: 1) the effectiveness of SR cache coherence, in terms of cache hit rates and application performance, 2) the overhead of managing the cache in software, and 3) the complexity of writing applications with Shared Region specifications. These issues are addressed using measurements and experiments in section 4.

3 SR cache coherence

In this section we discuss two algorithms for SR cache coherence. For an implementation of these algorithms, the following software cache control operations are required:

1. *cache-invalidate* (addr, size): invalidate *size* bytes starting at virtual address *addr*.
2. *cache-copyback* (addr, size): copy dirty bytes to memory for the specified address range.
3. *cache-flush* (addr, size): copyback any dirty bytes and also invalidate the address range.

For *write-through* caches, both the *cache-copyback* and the *cache-flush* operations become unnecessary, although for generality we assume that the cache is not write-through. We also assume that shared regions are aligned to cache line boundaries, since software cache control operations usually operate at cache line granularity.

Two algorithms for SR cache coherence are shown in Table 1. In the Cache-Flush algorithm, regions are invalidated from the cache at ReadDone time, and flushed at WriteDone time. Using the Cache-Validate algorithm, the region remains in the cache at ReadDone/WriteDone time, but it must be checked for validity at Access time. If the region has been modified since the last access by this processor, the region must be invalidated.

The Cache-Flush algorithm is the simplest SR cache management algorithm to implement, and behaves similarly to the user-based coherence approach described in earlier work [OA89, MOR86] and the compiler-based approach described by Cytron *et al* [CKM88]. However, the Cache-Flush algorithm may perform poorly for many applications because a region may be unnecessarily invalidated from the cache after every ReadDone or WriteDone operation. Invalidations from processor P_i are necessary only in those cases where P_j ($j \neq i$) modifies region R before P_i accesses it again. In all other cases, this algorithm incurs unnecessarily the overhead both of invalidating the region from the cache, as well as that of reloading the region on a subsequent access.

Access Primitive	SR Cache Management Algorithm: Cache-Flush	SR Cache Management Algorithm: Cache-Validate
ReadAccess and WriteAccess	-	if status[P] == HI cache-inval(R) status[P] = HV
ReadDone	cache-inval(R)	-
WriteDone	cache-flush(R)	cache-copyback(R) foreach Cache ≠ P & status[Cache] == HV status[Cache] = HI

Table 1: SR cache coherence algorithms: region R, processor P.

The Cache-Validate algorithm performs only necessary cache invalidations, and is thus preferrable to the Cache-Flush algorithm, but it introduces additional overhead in checking the status of a region prior to accessing it. To implement this algorithm, we associate with each region a state vector which contains information about the current state of all caches in the system with respect to that region. The cache states are: a) this cache does *Not Have* a copy of the region (state NH), b) this cache *Has* a *Valid* copy (state HV), and c) this cache *Has* an *Invalid* copy (state HI). For either ReadAccess or WriteAccess calls, the region's cache state vector is checked. If the current state of R for cache C_i is HI, then R has been modified by another processor since the last Done operation by processor P_i, and it must be invalidated from C_i before P_i may continue. At the time of a WriteDone operation on R by P_i, the state of those caches (except C_i) for which the current state is HV is set to HI to indicate that the region has been modified.

The state vector is left uncached in order to ensure that it remains consistent. A separate lock for the state vector should not be necessary as long as operations on individual state vector entries can be performed atomically, since, in the Cache-Validate algorithm, the state vector is accessed by a processor only after it has first acquired access to the region. A processor with WriteAccess to a region is guaranteed that no other processor is currently accessing the state vector, and it is free to modify the vector. A processor performing a ReadAccess will only access and potentially modify its own entry in the vector, so it will not interfere with other processors performing a ReadAccess, and it is ensured that another processor cannot be performing a WriteAccess and potentially modifying its entry. The performance issues related to managing the state vector are addressed in the next section.

4 Experiments

On a multiprocessor without hardware support for cache coherence, there are a few alternatives for cache management: 1) leave shared data uncached, 2) manage shared data within the operating system, as in Hurricane [SUK92], 3) allow the user to explicitly manage the cache from the application, as in the RP3 [PBG+85], the NYU Ultracomputer [GKM+82], and the ELXSI [MOR86], 4) use compiler-based techniques, as suggested in [CKM88] [CV90], and 5) use Shared Region-based techniques, as discussed in this paper. In this section, we examine the costs involved in using region-based techniques, and compare the performance of SR cache coherence with the first three alternatives. Section 5 presents an analysis comparing SR coherence with a compiler-based technique for cache management.

Experiments with SR coherence were done on a hierarchical shared-memory multiprocessor called Hector [VSLW91] using some sample applications. Hector is designed to accommodate up to 256 16 MHz MC88100 CPU's with 16 KB data and 16 KB instruction caches, and 4 MB local memory per processor. The interconnection consists of buses at the lowest level connected by a hierarchy of bit-parallel rings. Our experiments were done on a 16-processor configuration of 4 processors per bus and 4 buses on one ring.

Hector has no hardware cache coherence. By default, Hector's operating system, HURRICANE, maintains cache coherence on a per-page basis (where each page is 4 KB). According to the coherence protocol, cacheing of a page is disabled whenever writes to the page are detected by the hardware and the page is shared by multiple processors. In the SR implementation, the standard HURRICANE cache coherence mechanisms are disabled for a specific memory pool. Shared data that is defined as Shared Regions is allocated in a this memory pool, and coherence of this pool is controlled through region access control operations, using the Cache-Validate cache coherence algorithm by default. Typically, only shared data that is critical to performance is allocated in the region memory pool. Shared data that is not performance critical is managed using the existing HURRICANE cache management protocol, and accesses to that data do not need to be encapsulated in ReadAccess and WriteAccess calls.

4.1 Application description

Three applications were used in these experiments. We first describe each application, and then characterize the use and overhead of shared regions in each application. The applications are:

- LU-Decomposition (LU): Row-oriented LU decomposes a dense $N \times N$ matrix A into a lower triangular matrix L and an upper triangular matrix U. The sequential algorithm goes through $N-1$ phases; at phase i: 1) row i becomes the pivot row and is reduced, and 2) all rows j ($j > i$) are reduced using the pivot row. This continues until all rows have become the pivot once. LU-decomposition is performed in parallel by assigning the rows of A to the P processors in a round-robin fashion. Each row is defined as a separate shared region. In our experiments, the matrix size for LU is 512×512.

- Mean Value Analysis (MVA): MVA calculates average customer response times and queue lengths for a 2-class closed queueing network [RL80] by successively calculates the values for a system with n_1 and n_2 customers in each of the two classes, using the values for systems of populations $(n_1 - 1, n_2)$ and $(n_1, n_2 - 1)$. A task solving a system of a particular size requires the queue length vectors from its two parent tasks in order to proceed, and each queue length vector is defined as a shared region. Figure 2 shows a skeleton of the code for the task (n_1, n_2), together with the six lines of region access control code. In the experiments, there are 200 classes and 400 centers.

```
mva_task(n1, n2)
{
    ... allocate my queue length vector
    regions[n1, n2].WriteAccess();

    regions[n1, n2-1].ReadAccess();
    ... use left parent's vector to update mine
    regions[n1, n2-1].ReadDone();

    regions[n1-1, n2].ReadAccess();
    ... use right parent's vector to update mine
    regions[n1-1, n2].ReadDone();

    regions[n1, n2].WriteDone();
}
```

Figure 2: A single task in parallel MVA.

- Matrix Multiplication (MM): MM calculates the product of two $N \times N$ matrices A and B and places the result in matrix C. This is done in parallel by creating N threads and assigning to each thread one row of A and C each, and dividing the threads evenly among processors. The entire matrix B is read-shared by all threads. In the Shared Regions version, each row of A and C is defined as a separate region, while all of B is defined as a single shared region. Thus, each thread T_i, upon beginning execution, does a ReadAccess on row A_i, a ReadAccess for B, and a WriteAccess on C_i. A matrix size of 460x460 is used in the experiments.

4.2 Regions overhead in applications

Now we examine the use of shared regions in each application and their overheads. Figure 3 shows the number of region constructs (Access and Done pairs) in each application code and the number of calls to region primitives during program execution. The number of region constructs in the application code is one measure of the complexity of using the region paradigm in each application. In LU, region constructs replace synchronization constructs that are required in a non-SR version of this program, so the only additional effort on the part of the programmer is that of initially binding the regions to the data they protect. For each of these applications, there is a natural decomposition of data into shared regions, so the task of initially defining the regions is trivial.

	LU	MVA	MM
Synch constructs replaced with region constructs	2	0	0
New region constructs	0	3	3
WriteAccess/WriteDone calls	512	80,000	920
ReadAccess/ReadDone calls	8,190	160,000	1840

Figure 3: Application characteristics.

For the MVA and MM applications, no existing synchronization constructs are replaced, and three new region Access/Done pairs are added. From a synchronization point of view, the locking of the region is unnecessary, so the non-locking versions of the primitives are used in the MVA version to avoid the locking overhead. In the MM program, the region overhead was low enough (as shown later) that this overhead did not matter.

Even though both MVA and MM required new constructs in the region version, the programming effort required is insignificant, since there are only six lines of new code for shared region access primitives, and their use is intuitive in these applications (as an example, see Figure 2). However, the number of calls made to region primitives during execution is substantial. This is especially true in the case of MVA, which heavily taxes the region primitives.

Figure 4 shows breakdowns of the program execution times on 16 processors. For LU, only 2.9% of the time is spent executing region code. In MM, the region code execution time, at 0.2%, is completely insignificant. In the case of MVA, region code occupies a significant 11% of the execution time. This is to be expected considering the very large number of times region access primitives are called during execution for MVA. Because of the pair-wise sharing in MVA, however, this overhead should not increase significantly with system size.

Next, we examine the region access calls in more detail. A microsecond timer was used to measure separate time components of each call (Figure 5). For both the ReadAccess and WriteAccess functions, the time components are: 1) the time spent spinning to acquire the region, 2) the time to actually acquire the lock after spinning [2], 3) for the Cache-Validate

	LU	MVA	MM
user code	8.94 (97.1%)	7.65 (88.9%)	18.38 (99.8%)
region code	0.27 (2.9%)	0.96 (11.1%)	0.042 (0.2%)
total	9.21	8.61	18.42

Figure 4: Application runtime measurements (in seconds), 16 processors.

algorithm, the time required to invalidate the region if it is dirty, and 4) the region management overhead, which includes the time spent managing the region status vector. For the ReadDone and WriteDone operations, the time components are: 1) the time required to invalidate or copyback the region from the cache, and 2) the overhead, which includes the time required to update the region vector and the time to release the lock in the locking version of the SR primitives. Figure 5 shows the average time for each component for all calls to the region primitives, and the time spent as a percentage of the total program runtime.

Cost factor	LU	MVA	MM
ReadAccess/WriteAccess			
spin-wait	413 (2.6%)	-	0
lock acquire	7 (0.05%)	-	20 (0.01%)
cache-inval	0	8 (1.5%)	-
overhead	9 (0.05%)	9 (1.5%)	3 (0.001%)
ReadDone			
cache-inval	-	-	614 (0.17%)
overhead	5 (0.05%)	3 (0.08%)	15 (0.004%)
WriteDone			
cache-copyback	288 (0.07%)	202 (7.0%)	101 (0.01%)
overhead	9 (0.002%)	2 (0.07%)	5 (0.007%)

Figure 5: Application region primitives overhead measurements (in microseconds).

In the case of LU, most of the time is spent either spin-waiting to acquire the lock (2.6% of program execution time, or 90% of the time spent executing region code). This cannot be considered SR overhead since these locks replaced synchronization constructs that are necessary in LU. Copying back the region from the cache also occupies a significant amount of time for each call (288 μs). The actual region overhead is insignificant.

In MVA, the non-locking versions of the SR primitives are used so no time is required waiting or acquiring the region lock. As in LU, the average time spent flushing the cache is high compared to the other factors. The region overhead itself is relatively low.

In MM, most of the time in region code is spent invalidating B after every ReadDone. This average time is quite large

[2] In the non-locking versions of the SR primitives, lock spinning and acquisition time is zero.

since B itself is very large (1692800 bytes), and even though any particular element of B is unlikely to remain in the cache, simply executing a null invalidate (that is, an invalidate of an element that is not in the cache) requires a significant amount of time.

In summary, several observations can be made on the measurements in this section. First, the complexity of using Shared Regions is low for these applications. Second, the overhead of the SR primitives is generally low. Most of the time spent executing region code is spent either waiting to acquire the region, or invalidating or copying back the region to memory. It can be argued that neither of these factors can be considered region overhead, because lock acquisition can be turned off if it is not necessary to the algorithm, and the copyback and invalidation will likely be necessary regardless of which software cache management strategy is used.

4.3 Application performance

In this subsection, we present speedups for each of the applications, and compare the SR versions with 1) a version where Hurricane page-based cache management is used on an implementation of the application with little architecture specific code (the OSpage version), and 2) a version that was hand-tuned to take into account the specific architectural characteristics of the experimental platform with Hurricane's page-based cache management running underneath (the Handtuned version). The alternative of leaving shared data uncached was also initially considered, but for each application, the performance on 16-processors is worse than the 1-processor case, so this alternative will not be discussed further. The algorithm for user-controlled caches described in [OA89, MOR86], in which the user explicitly flushes data before leaving a critical section, is similar to the SR Cache-Flush algorithm, so we consider the performance of the Cache-Flush algorithm to be representative of this class of techniques.[3]

In the OSpage and Handtuned versions, the central concerns with respect to cacheing are the false sharing of data on fixed-sized pages and reenabling cacheing for a page after a write to the page has caused cacheing to be disabled. Thus, much of the hand-tuning for the Handtuned version focuses on addressing these concerns. The programming effort involved is considerable, requiring days of performance debugging in an application such as LU. In the SR version of the algorithm, we take a version that has no architecture specific code and insert SR primitives. For both LU and MM, there is no difference in the performance of the Cache-Flush and Cache-Validate algorithms, because of the cache reuse patterns and the small fraction of time spent executing region code. The difference in these two algorithms is shown only in the case of MVA.

[3] Unlike user-controlled caches, however, the task of coherence using the SR Cache-Flush algorithm is automated and the details hidden from the user, leading to a simpler programming interface.

Figure 6 shows the results for LU-decomposition using matrix size 512×512. Speedups are calculated relative to the best sequential version of the algorithm not using Shared Regions, and speedup curves are annotated with response times for the 16-processor cases. In the SR version, the rows are always cacheable by the accessing processor, and the corresponding region management overhead is low (as shown in the previous subsection). The Handtuned version is limited by the fact that data still must be managed at page granularity, and thus, it still performs slightly worse than the SR version which has close to linear speedup.

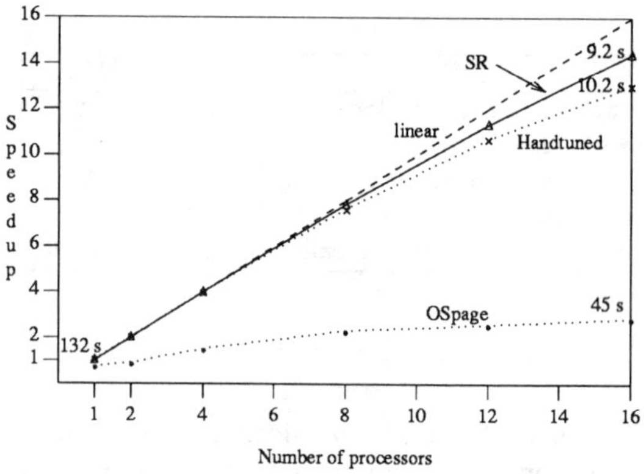

Figure 6: LU-decomposition on 512×512 matrix.

Results for MVA are shown in Figure 7. Here, a queue length vector is 1600 bytes long. Since each occupies only about 1/3 of a page, multiple vectors are dynamically allocated onto the same page. This makes the vectors uncacheable except in the SR version. Each task reads the queue length vector of each of its parents only once, and has only a 50% chance of being able to reuse its parents' cached data. Even with this low amount of cache reuse, and the significant fraction of time spent executing region code (11% from Figure 4), the speedup curve for the SR Cache-Validate version is straight and close to linear for up to 16 processors. The SR Cache-Flush algorithm does not perform as well, because it unnecessarily invalidates the region at every Done operation.

Figure 8 shows the results of matrix multiply on 460×460 matrices. In the Handtuned version, each processor is assigned a group of contiguous rows, but its perimeter rows of C fall on pages shared with other processors, causing these to become uncacheable. However, these perimeter rows account for only a small fraction of the total number of accesses, so, although the SR version allows full-cacheing of all rows and thus performance better than the Handtuned version, the difference is small. The substantial difference between the SR speedup and the linear curve is due to the lack of memory locality; a version of MM with B pre-replicated at each memory unit achieves linear speedup.

A number of other applications that are not discussed here were written using Shared Regions. These include Fast Fourier Transform, Mergesort, Hough Transforms, and

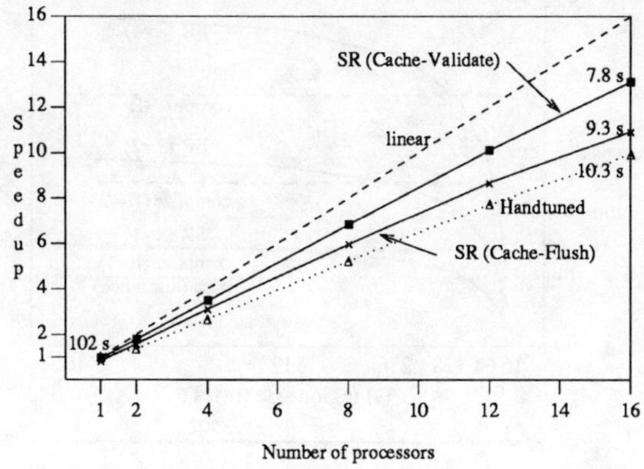

Figure 7: MVA for $C = 200, K = 400$

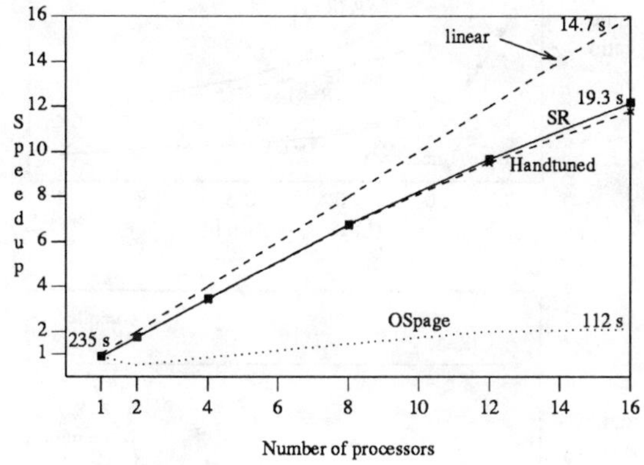

Figure 8: Matrix multiplication: 460x460 matrix.

Traveling Salesman. For the applications with regular data structures, using the Shared Regions approach is simple. For problems without regular data structures, such as the Traveling Salesman and Mergesort, using Shared Regions is not as straightforward. However, all of the applications perform well with Shared Regions compared with some of the other alternatives for cache coherence discussed here.

A number of conclusions can be drawn from the performance results in this section. Leaving shared data uncached is not a viable alternative to cache coherence. Having the operating system enforce cache coherence at fixed page-granularity requires the user to expend considerable effort tuning the application to deal with architecture specific problems. Even a hand-tuned version may not perform as well as a SR version if data is still managed at fixed page granularity. In comparison to the Cache-Flush algorithm (and hence the user-controlled cache management techniques that behave similarly), the Cache-Validate algorithm performs significantly better in the case of MVA, and approximately the same for LU and MM. In all cases, because data is always cacheable in SR, and the corresponding region overhead is relatively low, the applications are able to achieve good performance using the Cache-Validate algorithm.

5 Comparison to compiler based technique

In this section we compare the performance of the SR Cache-Validate strategy with the expected behavior of a compiler-based strategy. Although several algorithms for compiler-based cache management have been suggested, in [CKM88] and in the Cedar work [CV90], compiler techniques are limited by the fact that static analysis techniques are unable to accurately predict the runtime behavior of a program. In our comparison, the behavior of the compiler scheme is based upon the expectation that future advances in compiler technology will make these more feasible, using compiler error rate to parameterize the accuracy of the compiler. Adve *et al*[AAHV91] compare compiler-based techniques with hardware coherence techniques using a similar notion of compiler accuracy, but they are more comprehensive in classifying the types of errors the compiler may make. In our model, we will consider, for simplicity, only those errors in which data that could have been cached is accessed as uncacheable.

Contrasted with compiler techniques, SR manages the cache entirely at runtime. The advantage of this is that while a compiler technique will make conservative errors, in SR shared regions are always cacheable. The disadvantage is that there is some overhead for managing shared regions at runtime, in particular, that of managing the region state vector. We use a simple model to highlight the tradeoffs between static and runtime management of shared data.

The model has four high-level parameters: 1) region size S, in words, 2) region reuse R – the number of times a region is accessed for every Access/Done operation, 3) write probability W – the fraction of Access operations that are WriteAccess operations, and 4) compiler error rate E – the percentage of conservative errors made by the compiler. Default values for these parameters are also shown in Figure 9. The write probability (0.5) is intentionally pessimistic in order to strain both software coherence strategies.

Low level parameters used in this model, also shown in Figure 9, are based upon measurements in HECTOR and assume that all data is on non-local memory being accessed over the bus. For simplicity, we ignore both NUMAness and contention, and assume infinite size caches. Additionally, we assume that for a particular Access/Done session (referred to as a *region access*), the entire region is referenced or modified.

Within the model, processors randomly access a region, choosing to do a WriteAccess with probability W. For the base case, in which the region is uncacheable, the region access time is SRC_M. In the SR case, each region access costs C_O, plus $\frac{S}{4}C_L$ if the region is in the NH state at this processor, $SC_I + \frac{S}{4}C_L$ if the region is in the HI state, or SC_A if it is in the HV state. Since subsequent reuse of the region takes place in the cache, $SC_I(R-1)$ is also added. If the operation is a WriteAccess, cost $\frac{S}{4}C_B$ is also added to account for copying the region back to memory.

High Level Parameters		
parameter		default
region size	S	256 bytes
region reuse	R	4
write prob	W	0.5
compiler error	E	0.1

Low Level Parameters		
cost factor		Cost C
region overhead	C_O	200 cycles per Access/Done
cache-inval	C_I	1 cycle per cache-line
cache-copyback	C_B	70 cycles per line
cache access	C_A	1 cycle per word
memory word access	C_M	20 cycles
memory line access	C_L	30 cycles per line

Figure 9: Model parameters. A line is 4 words

In the compiler case, the compiler makes a conservative error with probability E and accesses the region as uncached, inducing cost SRC_M as in the uncached case, plus $\frac{S}{4}C_I$ if the region is already in the cache. Otherwise, the region is accessed as cacheable, with cost $\frac{S}{4}C_L + SC_A(R-1)$ if the region is not currently in the cache, or SC_AR if the region is currently in the cache. If the region is written to (probability W), cost $\frac{S}{4}C_B$ is also added to account for copying the region back to memory.

The ***region access time ratio*** is the average region access time of the base case divided by the average region access time of the other two techniques. A higher region access time ratio indicates an improvement in performance. Figure 10 shows a number of experiments using the region access time ratio as a performance metric.

Figure 10(a) shows a comparison of SR coherence with the compiler strategy for various region sizes and reuse factors. For a reuse factor of 1, SR coherence performs better than the compiler with 90% efficiency only when the region is larger than about 512 bytes. However, as the reuse factor increases, SR coherence performs comparatively better. For a reuse factor of 4, SR coherence performs better than the compiler technique when the region size is larger than about 100 bytes.

Figure 10(b) shows the effect of varying the write probability, with the default region size at 256 bytes. When the write probability is very low, SR coherence performs significantly better than the compiler with 90% efficiency when the reuse factor is 4. However, as the write probability approaches 1, both techniques perform similarly. The higher write probability induces more flush operations and decreases the benefits of the cache, so both techniques degrade for higher write probabilities.

Figure 10(c) shows the effect of varying the compiler efficiency from 0 to 1, with the region size again at 256 bytes and the write probability at 0.5. When the reuse factor is 1, the compiler requires 70% efficiency to perform better than

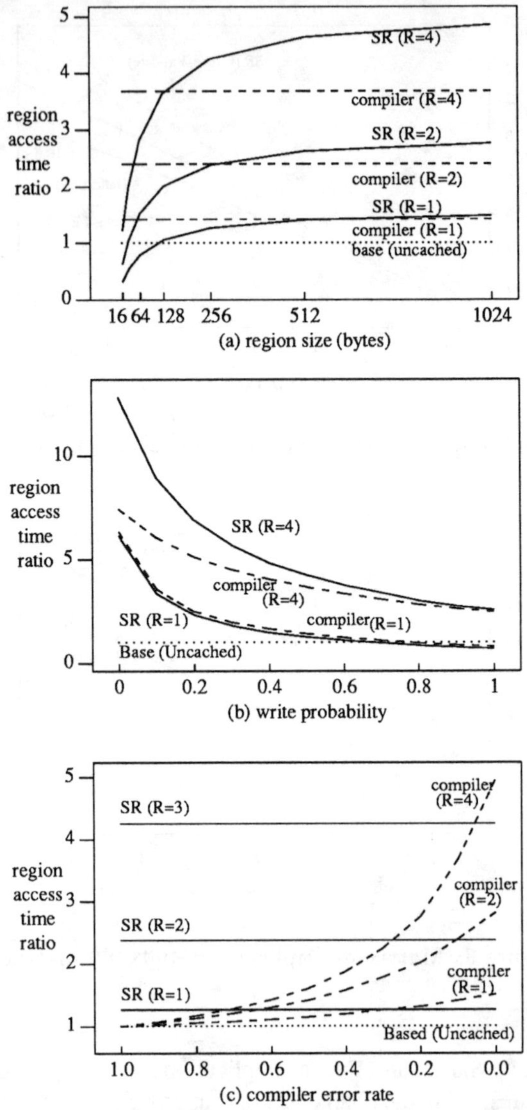

Figure 10: Comparison of SR Cache-Validate with compiler-based strategy

SR coherence. When the reuse factor is 4, the compiler requires about 95% efficiency in order to perform better than SR coherence.

In summary, the analysis in this section shows that good performance with the SR Cache-Validate requires that regions be sufficiently large or that they have a high reuse factor. In such cases, compiler techniques will require a high degree of accuracy in order to be competitive. In the applications discussed in the previous section, regions were both large and the reuse factor was high, thereby contributing to good performance.

6 Related Work

Methods for annotating programs to elicit greater information about program behavior has been proposed in a number of different contexts. Jade [LR91] proposes *with* and *withonly* constructs that expose sharing characteristics to the systems, but unlike our approach, the motivations for these constructs in Jade is to permit the compiler to detect concurrency. The tokens used in the Jade constructs are not explicitly related to the data they encapsulate. In the approach proposed in [HLRW92], called Cooperative Shared Memory (CSM), users may optionally annotate their programs with explicit *check-in* and *check-out* of shared data, which serve as hints to the underlying system. CSM has the advantage over the Shared Region approach that the annotations are only advisory and thus need not be put in. However, because these annotations are only advisory, the CSM hardware still needs to implement a limited directory strategy to manage coherence. The advantage of the Shared Regions approach is that no hardware support is required, and a wide variety of coherence strategies can be implemented without being constrained to hardware determined fixed block sizes.

The approach proposed in [FL92], called Versioned Distributed Object Management (VDOM), bears a closer resemblance to our work. VDOM's notion of *fragmented objects* appears to be closely related to our notion of Shared Regions, and the primitives used to access fragmented objects, AcquireRead/AcquireWrite, appear identical to our ReadAccess/WriteAccess primitives. In both approaches, coherence is managed at the granularity of shared regions or fragmented objects, but the differing environments that they have been applied to lead to entirely different solutions and problems. For instance, in the VDOM case, the loosely coupled distributed environment means that higher overhead in accessing the fragmented objects can be tolerated; in the tightly-coupled shared-memory environment we have assumed, the overhead of the ReadAccess/WriteAccess calls themselves become a fundamental issue, along with managing coherence at that granularity.

7 Conclusions

In this paper, we introduced a technique for software cache coherence based on the integration of an abstraction for shared data, called *Shared Regions (SR)*, with software cache management. Algorithms for cache coherence which exploit knowledge of shared regions were discussed. These algorithms can be implemented easily and efficiently in software, without any special hardware support.

An implementation of the Shared Region approach was done on a shared-memory multiprocessor, and experiments with a few sample applications show favorable results. Measurements of the overheads of software region management for these applications show that most of the time spent in region code is spent performing operations such as cache-invalidation and cache-copyback, which would be required using any cache management strategy; the actual overhead particular to shared regions is relatively low. Comparisons with other software coherence strategies such as user-controlled caches, and operating system based-coherence, show that the Shared Regions approach is able to deliver better performance with little programming complexity. Comparisons with a compiler-based cache management strategy show that the Shared Region approach performs well except when the region is very small or is only used in the cache once or twice. In most other cases, a compiler strategy would have to make fewer than 5% errors in order to be competitive.

Work is currently in progress to compare, using a simulation model, the Shared Regions approach to hardware directory strategies such as the full-map scheme used in DASH [LLG+90], and the LimitLESS scheme proposed in [CKA91], as well as strategies that require special hardware architectures or hardware support, such as VMP [CGB89] which relies on a hierarchical cache organization. Additionally, although the 16-processors experiments in this paper give some indication of the scalability of the Shared Regions approach, work is also in progress to analyze, via simulation, its behavior on much larger systems.

Acknowledgements

We are indebted to the HECTOR and HURRICANE groups for making the implementation and experiments in this paper possible, most notably: Michael Stumm, Ron Unrau, Orran Krieger, Ron White, and Tim Brecht. Additional thanks to the reviewers for their useful comments. Ben Gamsa was supported by a National Science and Research Council Scholarship and Bell-Northern Research Graduate Scholarship. Harjinder Sandhu was supported by an IBM Graduate Fellowship.

References

[AAHV91] S. Adve, V. Adve, M. Hill, and M. Vernon. Comparison of hardware and software cache coherence schemes. In *18th Intl. Symp. on Computer Architecture*. ACM, May 1991.

[AH90] S. Adve and M. Hill. Weak ordering - a new definition. In *17th Intl. Symp. on Computer Architecture*. ACM, May 1990.

[CGB89] D. Cheriton, H. Goosen, and P. Boyle. Multilevel shared cacheing techniques for scalability in VMP-MC. In *16th Intl. Symp. on Computer Architecture*. ACM, May 1989.

[CKA91] D. Chaiken, J. Kubiatowicz, and A. Agarwal. LimitLESS directories: A scalable cache coherence scheme. In *4th Intl. Conf. on Architectural Support for Programming Languages and Operating Systems*. ACM, April 1991.

[CKM88] R. Cytron, S. Karlovsky, and K. McAuliffe. Automatic management of programmable caches.

In *1988 Intl. Conf. on Parallel Processing*, 1988.

[CV90] H. Cheong and A. Veidenbaum. Compiler-directed cache management in multiprocessors. *IEEE Computer*, 1990.

[FL92] M. Feeley and H. Levy. Distributed shared memory with versioned objects. In *Conf. on Object-Oriented Programming Systems, Languages, and Applications*. ACM, October 1992.

[GKM+82] A. Gottlieb, C. Kruskal, K. McAullife, L. Rudolph, and M. Snir. The NYU Ultracomputer – designing an MIMD shared memoory parallel computer. In *9th Intl. Symp. on Computer Architecture*. ACM, 1982.

[GLL+90] K. Gharacharloo, D. Lenoski, J. Laudon, P. Gibbons, A. Gupta, and J. Hennessy. Memory consistency and event ordering in scalable shared-memory multiprocessors. In *17th Intl. Symp. on Computer Architecture*. ACM, May 1990.

[HLRW92] M. Hill, J. Larus, K. Reinhardt, and D. Wood. Cooperative shared memory: Software and hardware for scalable multiprocessors. In *5th Intl. Conf. on Architectural Support for Programming Languages and Operating Systems*. ACM, October 1992.

[LLG+90] D. Lenowski, J. Laudon, K. Gharachorloo, A. Gupta, and John Hennessy. The directory-based cache coherence protocol for the DASH multiprocessor. In *17th Intl. Symp. on Computer Architecture*. ACM, 1990.

[LR91] M. Lam and M. Rinard. Coarse-grain parallel programming in Jade. In *3rd Symp. on Principles and Practices of Parallel Programming*. ACM, April 1991.

[MOR86] S. McGrogan, R. Olson, and N. Roda. Parallelizing large existing programs - methodology and experience. In *1986 Spring COMPCON*, 1986.

[OA89] S. Owicki and A. Agarwal. Evaluating the performance of software cache coherence. In *3rd Intl. Conf. on Architectural Support for Programming Languages and Operating Systems*. ACM, 1989.

[PBG+85] G. Pfister, W. Brantley, D. George, S. Harvey, W. Kleinfelder, K. McAliffe, E. Melton, V. Norton, and J. Weiss. The IBM research processor prototype (RP3); introduction and architecture. In *1985 Intl. Conf. on Parallel Processing*, 1985.

[RL80] M. Reiser and S. Lavenberg. Mean value analysis of closed multichain queueing networks. *JACM*, April 1980.

[SGZ92] H.S. Sandhu, B. Gamsa, and S. Zhou. Region-oriented memory management in shared-memory multiprocessors. Technical Report 269, University of Toronto, April 1992.

[SUK92] M. Stumm, R. Unrau, and O. Krieger. Clustering micro-kernels for scalability. In *Microkernels and Other Kernel Architectures Workshop*. USENIX, April 1992.

[VSLW91] Z.G. Vranesic, M. Stumm, D.M. Lewis, and R. White. Hector - a hierarchically structured shared-memory multiprocessor. *Computer*, January 1991.

Computation Migration: Enhancing Locality for Distributed-Memory Parallel Systems

Wilson C. Hsieh, Paul Wang, William E. Weihl

Abstract

We describe *computation migration*, a new technique that is based on compile-time program transformations, for accessing remote data in a distributed-memory parallel system. In contrast with RPC-style access, where the access is performed remotely, and with data migration, where the data is moved so that it is local, computation migration moves part of the current thread to the processor where the data resides. The access is performed at the remote processor, and the migrated thread portion continues to run on that same processor; this makes subsequent accesses in the thread portion local.

We describe an implementation of computation migration that consists of two parts: an implementation that migrates single activation frames, and a high-level language annotation that allows a programmer to express when migration is desired. We performed experiments using two applications; these experiments demonstrate that computation migration is a valuable alternative to RPC and data migration.

1 Introduction

One of the most important factors for efficient program execution on a distributed-memory parallel system is the locality of data accesses. If there are many non-local memory accesses in a parallel program, it is unlikely that the program will exhibit good speedup. There are two important factors in ensuring locality of accesses: the placement of data, and how remote accesses are handled. We deal with the second issue — where and how remote accesses should occur — and propose a new mechanism for remote access called *computation migration*. For some applications, computation migration can significantly reduce the communication cost associated with accessing remote data compared to other existing techniques. The approach we describe in this paper allows the programmer to write programs in a shared-memory style; the compiler (perhaps with guidance from the programmer) then decides how to map the program onto a particular machine, and uses computation migration and other techniques to optimize communication.

Several mechanisms for accessing remote data are widely used. RPC, or remote procedure call (e.g., [BN84, CAL+89, JLHB88, SB90]), is used in both distributed and parallel systems for executing procedure calls on remote data. Remote procedure calls resemble local procedure calls; compiler-generated stubs hide the underlying complexity of executing a procedure remotely. Another mechanism for remote access is data migration or data-shipping (e.g., [CKA91, JLHB88, LLG+90, Li88]). Using data migration (an example of which is cache-coherent shared memory), the remote data is moved (or copied) so that it is local to the access. Yet another mechanism for remote access is thread migration (e.g., [PM83, SN90, TLC85]), which can be viewed as the converse of data migration. Using thread migration, a thread that makes a remote access is moved to the processor where the data resides, and it continues execution where the data is located.

Computation migration can be viewed as partial thread migration.[1] Migrating entire threads can be useful for load balancing, but is usually not an effective technique for handling accesses to remote data because the amount of state to be moved is large. However, if we generalize thread migration to allow only *part* of the thread to be moved (for example, the part corresponding to one or more activation frames at the top of the stack), the amount of state that must be moved may be relatively small, and it may be more effective to move this state than to use RPC or data migration to perform a remote access.

We do not propose that computation migration should always be used instead of RPC, data migration, or thread migration. Indeed, which approach is best depends on the characteristics of the application and of the architecture on which the application is being executed. We believe that programmers (or compilers) should be able to choose the option that is best for a specific application on a specific architecture. The evidence we present in this paper shows that computation migration can provide performance advantages over other techniques, and thus programmers should be able to choose it instead of RPC or data migration as the method used to perform a remote data access. In addition, we explain how we can use compiler transformations to generate programs that use computation migration; such structures do not have to be programmed explicitly.

We have designed and implemented a prototype of computation migration as part of the Prelude parallel programming language [WBC+91], which we have implemented on the Proteus simulator [BDCW91]. This implementation has two parts: the low-level implementation of computation migration, and high-level annotations in Prelude that allow a programmer to choose when to use computation migration.

We believe that supporting portability and tunability requires providing a comprehensive suite of mechanisms

---

Authors' address: MIT Laboratory for Computer Science, 545 Technology Square, Cambridge, MA 02139. Email: wchsieh@lcs.mit.edu. The first two authors were supported by NSF Graduate Fellowships. This research was also supported in part by the NSF under Grant CCR-8716884, by DARPA under Contract N00014-89-J-1988, by an equipment grant from DEC, and by grants from AT&T and IBM.

4th ACM PPOPP,5/93/CA,USA
© 1993 ACM 0-89791-589-5/93/0005/0239...$1.50

[1] By "thread", we mean threads in the sense of lightweight threads packages [CD88], as opposed to threads in TAM, which are much lighter-weight [SCvE91].

for performing remote accesses, including RPC, data migration, and computation migration. Our current prototype was designed for evaluating the effectiveness of computation migration relative to RPC and to data migration. It supports RPC, data migration, and migration of single activation frames; we are working on extending it to support migration of multiple and partial activations. We believe that this additional flexibility is necessary to allow a programmer to tune and port programs without being forced to restructure them by hand.

Section 2 explains in more detail how computation migration can reduce the cost of communication relative to other techniques, and presents a simple model of how computation migration saves messages. Section 3 describes an implementation of computation migration, and Section 4 describes experiments that we performed with our prototype. Section 5 discusses some related work. Finally, Section 6 summarizes our results and discusses directions for future work.

2 Motivation

We begin by discussing RPC, data migration, thread migration, and computation migration in more detail. We then compare RPC, data migration, and computation migration, and describe how computation migration saves messages over RPC and data migration.

2.1 RPC-style Access

The most common mechanism for implementing remote access in a message-passing system is remote procedure call, which has been used in both distributed and parallel systems [BN84]. RPCs resemble local procedure calls; the underlying message-passing is hidden by compiler-generated stubs. When an RPC occurs, a local call is made to a client stub, which marshals the arguments and sends a message to the processor where the data resides. At the remote processor, a server stub unmarshals the arguments and calls the procedure. When the remote procedure returns to the server stub, the server stub marshals any result values into a message and returns the message to the client stub; the client stub returns the results to the RPC caller.

A problem with RPC-style access is that each call requires two messages, one for the call and one for the reply; this can be expensive, as there is substantial overhead involved in marshaling values into and out of messages. The major problem with using RPC for a series of accesses to remote data, however, is that there is no locality of access; each access is remote.

One advantage of RPC is that it does not add "extra" load on a server; when a remote call finishes and returns, the thread that initiated the call does not consume any more resources on the server (until it makes another call). Another advantage of RPC is that it can work well in the case of write-shared data (shared data that is frequently written to), especially when compared to data migration.

2.2 Data Migration

Data migration involves moving remote data to the processor where a request is made. One example is hardware caching in shared-memory multiprocessors such as Alewife [CKA91] and DASH [LLG+90]; such systems provide automatic data replication as well as data migration. The Munin system [BCZ90] allows the programmer to choose among several different coherence protocols for shared data. The Emerald system [JLHB88] migrates entire objects without replicating them.

Data migration can perform poorly when the size of the data is large. In addition, data migration in the form of cache-coherent shared memory performs poorly for write-shared data because of the communication involved in maintaining consistency: when there are many writes to a replicated datum, it is expensive to ensure global consistency. Write-shared data appears to occur moderately frequently, resulting in data that migrates from one cache to another with relatively few copies existing at any one time [GW92]. Some researchers have tried to optimize their cache-coherence algorithms for migratory data [SBS92] to reduce the communication required to maintain consistency. Even so, RPC and computation migration will require fewer messages than data migration for write-shared data, and hence may result in better overall performance, particularly if message-passing is efficient (as in [vECGS92, HJ92]). (The performance results in Section 4 show that shared memory consumes significantly more network bandwidth than RPC or computation migration.)

One important advantage of data migration is that it can improve the locality of accesses: after the first access by a thread to some data, successive accesses will be local. In addition, cache-coherent shared memory increases concurrency for read-shared data (shared data that is rarely written) by replicating it in different caches that can be accessed concurrently.

2.3 Thread Migration

Thread migration can be used to improve load balance as well as locality, but its major problem is that the grain of migration is too coarse. Migrating an entire thread can be expensive, since there may be a large amount of state to move; it also may be unnecessary, since we often need to migrate only a small amount of state in a thread to improve locality substantially. In addition, migrating every thread that accesses a datum to the datum's processor could put too much load on that processor.

2.4 Computation Migration

Our proposed mechanism, computation migration, gives us the benefits of both thread migration and RPC. If we move part of a thread's stack to the remote data, we can receive the benefit of increased locality of accesses; for example, if the executing thread makes a series of accesses to the same data, there is a great deal to be gained by moving those accesses to the data. At the same time, we gain the benefit of RPC; we can vary the granularity of the computation to be performed at the remote processor. This allows us to avoid the problem of overloading the resources at a single processor, since we move only the amount of state necessary to improve locality.

The disadvantage of computation migration is that the cost of using it depends on the amount of computation state that must be moved. If the amount of state is large (such as a substantial portion of a thread) computation migration will be fairly expensive. In addition, when the amount of data that is accessed is small and rarely written, data migration (especially when done in hardware) should outperform computation migration.

Computation migration can also be viewed as the dual of data migration; instead of moving data to the computation, we move computation to the data. In the case where the data are not all on the same processor, some data migration may need to occur. In some cases it may be better to migrate the computation as well as some of

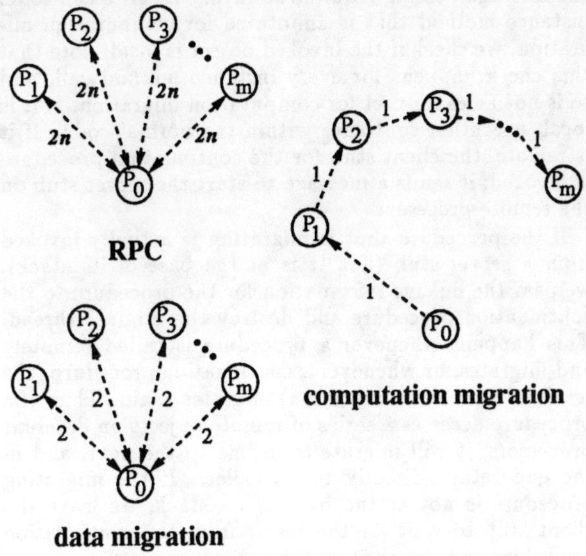

Figure 1: Message patterns under different mechanisms

the data; the pure data migration solution of always migrating all of the data to the computation may not always be the best.

Some applications require very little locality management: the computation of Fast Fourier Transform, in fact, requires data to be migrated exactly once during the entire computation; all accesses are local. However, we expect that for most applications (and dynamic time-shared systems), it will not be possible to layout the data once so as to achieve good locality.

Load balance is an issue that can conflict with locality management in parallel systems. For some regular numerical problems, it is sometimes possible to layout the data initially so as to provide both good locality and load balance under an "owner-computes" rule; languages such as Fortran D [HKK+91] and Vienna Fortran [ZBC+92] use such a rule. However, most applications (and certainly multiprogrammed systems) cannot be dealt with so simply. Markatos and LeBlanc have shown that for NUMA shared-memory multiprocessors, locality management can have a much larger impact on performance than load balancing [ML91]; even though computation migration can also be viewed as a mechanism to achieve load balance (since it is a form of thread migration), for most applications the locality aspects of computation migration are probably more important.

2.5 Comparison

In this section we compare the communication cost of computation migration to that of RPC and data migration by examining a scenario where a single thread makes a series of remote accesses to data on other processors. We measure cost in terms of the number of messages each mechanism requires; for the moment, we ignore other issues such as contention and message sizes.

Figure 1 illustrates the different message-passing patterns using RPC, data migration, and computation migration, where one thread on Processor P_0 makes n consecutive accesses to each of m data items on processors 1 through m, respectively. Relative to RPC, both computation migration and data migration can reduce the number of messages by making repeated accesses to the same data local.

Computation migration also saves messages by "short-circuiting" return messages. For each datum accessed, only one message needs to be sent; using data migration and RPC, at least two messages need to be sent per datum. (RPC sends two per access to each datum.) In addition, no communication is needed to maintain coherence of copies of data, which is necessary with cache-coherent shared memory when the data is written.

Reducing the total number of messages improves performance (as long as the messages do not get much larger) for two reasons. First, it can reduce the demands on network bandwidth. More important, it removes the various costs of extra message handling from the execution of the thread: marshaling and unmarshaling values, allocating packets, moving through the network, and dispatching to the code to execute.

It is important to remember that our model only counts the number of messages; there are other factors that can affect the relative costs of the three mechanisms. First of all, we do not take the size of data into account; if we must send a large amount of data, we will need to use multiple messages. More important, we do not take contention of any sort into account. Data contention, for example, will strongly affect whether data migration or computation migration is more efficient: if the data is write-shared between many threads, computation migration will almost always perform better than data migration; otherwise, data migration should perform better. Contention is likely to be a very important factor in determining the best mechanism to use, but we do not yet have a good model of its effects.

Our model also does not take into account techniques for hiding latency, such as prefetching and multithreading. Prefetching will lower the relative cost of performing data migration, since the delays involved with data migration can be overlapped with computation. We also do not model the effects of increased concurrency that results from replication in the case of cache-coherent shared memory.

3 Implementation

We have so far discussed computation migration abstractly, in terms of migrating portions of stacks; we now describe an implementation of computation migration that allows the programmer to migrate a single activation record on the top of the stack. There are two parts to our implementation: how migration is expressed by the programmer, and the low-level mechanics of migration. First we describe how the programmer can express the migration of an activation using a simple annotation, and we argue why such an annotation is much more desirable than coding computation migration explicitly into the structure of a program. Then we describe two mechanisms for migration: the first is the one we have implemented, and the second is a potentially more efficient one that is not possible on our prototype.

3.1 Annotations

Prelude [WBC+91] is an object-based language that provides procedures and instance methods, where instance methods always execute at the object on which they are invoked. Instance method calls are the remote accesses in our language, and we permit procedures (single activations) to migrate to objects on which they invoke instance methods. We do not permit instance method activations to migrate, as we currently require all instance method calls to run at the site of the invoked object.

We provide a simple program annotation that allows the programmer to migrate a procedure. The annotation indicates an instance method call within the procedure where computation migration should occur. Migration is conditional on the location of the computation: if the computation is already local to the datum accessed, it does not migrate.

There are several important characteristics of our approach. First, it is very simple to experiment with computation migration: changing where migration occurs simply involves moving the annotation, and the programmer can easily switch between using computation migration, RPC, and data migration. Second, the annotation affects only the performance of a program, not its semantics. Finally, computation migration imposes no additional cost on local accesses: if the data item being accessed is local, the cost of the access is not affected by the use of an annotation indicating that computation migration should occur.

Some languages permit a programmer to code a structure explicitly that mimics the effect of computation migration. For example, Actor-based languages [Man87] encourage a "continuation-passing" style for programs, in which each actor does a small amount of computation and then calls another actor to perform the rest of the computation. In effect, the computation migrates from actor to actor. By carefully designing the message-passing structure of the program, a programmer can optimize the communication cost.

For several reasons, we think it is an extremely bad idea to code computation migration explicitly in programs. The most important reason is that such programs are very difficult to tune and port. Performance decisions in such a program are closely intertwined with the description of the algorithm; changing the communication pattern may require substantial changes to the program, and may result in inadvertent errors being introduced into the computation. It is far better to separate the description of the computation from the decisions of how it is to be mapped onto a particular machine, and to let the compiler handle the details of the message-passing for computation migration.

In addition, our experience with both parallel and distributed systems indicates that programming in terms of explicit message-passing can lead to programs that are much more complex than ones written in terms of shared memory. Such an explicit programming style is also undesirable from a software engineering perspective, since it requires the modification of the interfaces of data objects to include additional procedures that represent the migrated computations.

3.2 Our Implementation

We implemented computation migration in the Prelude compiler and runtime system and ran experiments on the PROTEUS simulator [BDCW91]. Our current Prelude compiler generates C code, which does not give us the flexibility to code the implementation we describe in Section 3.3.

Our implementation generates a special "continuation" procedure to handle computation migration. The continuation procedure's body is the continuation of the migrating procedure at the point of migration; its arguments are the live variables at that point. Client and server stubs are generated for the special procedure to handle the message-passing required to invoke it. At a call to an instance method that is annotated for computation migration, we check if the invoked object is local; note that this check happens for every instance method call, and so is not an extra cost for computation migration. If it is local, execution continues within the normal code. If it is remote, the client stub for the continuation procedure is invoked; it sends a message to start the server stub on the remote processor.

If the procedure that is migrating is actually invoked from a server stub (i.e., it is at the base of its stack), we pass the linkage information for the procedure to the continuation procedure and destroy the original thread. This happens whenever a procedure is called remotely and migrates, or whenever a continuation procedure (the result of a previous migration) migrates again. Thus, if a procedure accesses a series of remote objects on different processors, it will migrate from one to the next, and in the end return directly to its caller. If the migrating procedure is not at the base of its stack, we leave the client stub to wait for the result from the continuation procedure and return it to the procedure's caller.

3.3 Alternate Implementation

The implementation we describe above suffers from several problems. First, it leads to a large expansion in the size of our generated code: for each occurrence of computation migration, we generate a continuation procedure and its two stubs. Second, it is somewhat inefficient, since the live variables at the point of migration need to be passed as arguments to the continuation client stub, and then marshaled into a message.

If we had control of the actual code generation for Prelude, we could avoid generating the extra continuation procedure. Instead, at the point of migration the live variables (which reside in the registers and on the stack) would be marshaled into a message, which would be sent to the destination processor. At the destination processor, an alternate entry point to the migrating procedure would be called, which would unmarshal the values (back into an identical activation record and into the registers), and would then jump back into the original procedure's code. The only tricky point would be if the migrating procedure was originally expected to return values on the stack; we must ensure that the code on the destination processor returns to a stub that returns a message to the original processor.

4 Experiments

We have performed experiments with two different applications, both of which are a form of distributed data structure traversal: a counting network and a distributed B-tree. We used the PROTEUS simulator [BDCW91] to run our experiments; we simulated a RISC machine similar to the Alewife machine, but without its multithreading capability [ACD+91]. In addition, our target machine, unlike Alewife, provides both private memory and shared memory; it uses the same cache coherence protocol that Alewife does [CKA91], and each processor has a 64K shared-memory cache with a line size of 16 bytes. For each application, we compared using RPC, cache-coherent shared memory, and computation migration for data accesses. We would like to compare our results to object migration, such as the mechanism in Emerald [JLHB88], but our group has not finished implementing object migration in Prelude yet.

It is important to remember that we are actually comparing a software implementation of RPC and computation migration to a hardware implementation of data migration, namely Alewife-style cache-coherent shared memory. Cache-coherent shared memory benefits from hardware support in three ways: it provides cheap message-passing, since data migration messages are implemented directly in hardware; it provides a global address space, without which a global object name space must be built in software; and it provides automatic replication.

We performed several experiments to estimate the effects of providing hardware support for RPC and computation migration. First, we estimated the effects of having hardware support for message-passing, as described by Henry and Joerg [HJ92]. In particular, we assumed that the network interface is mapped into ten additional registers in the register file, so that marshaling and unmarshaling would be cheaper; we did not take advantage of other modifications that Henry and Joerg describe. We also estimated the effects of having hardware support for global object identifier translation, as in the J-Machine [DCC+87].

The last benefit of cache-coherent shared memory, replication, is the biggest difference in performance between shared memory and computation migration, both of which outperformed RPC in our experiments. The results of our experiments show that computation migration with hardware support performs as well as cache-coherent shared memory in the counting network, and slightly worse on the B-tree. In our B-tree experiments, we implemented a software replication method for the root of the tree [WW90] to estimate the benefits of replication for computation migration; our results show that replication is the primary reason why shared memory performs better, and that it can also be used to improve performance when computation migration is used.

4.1 Counting Network

Our first application is a counting network [AHS91, HLN92]. A counting network is a distributed data structure that supports "shared counting"; multiple threads request values from a given range of values. For example, when a set of threads executes the iterations of a parallel loop, each iteration should be executed by exactly one thread. The simplest solution is to use a single counter protected by a lock to store the iteration count; a thread acquires the lock and updates the counter when it needs a loop index. This solution scales poorly due to contention; a counting network is a distributed data structure that trades latency under low-contention conditions for much higher scalability of throughput.

A counting network is built out of balancers; a balancer is a two-by-two switch that alternately routes requests between its two outputs. We performed our experiments on an eight-by-eight counting network, which is essentially a six-stage pipeline; each stage has four balancers in parallel. We laid out the counting network on twenty-four processors (one balancer per processor). We will not go into further detail on how counting networks function; please see the references for details.

We ran with eight, sixteen, thirty-two, forty-eight, and sixty-four threads making requests; each of the requesting threads was placed on a separate processor. We used two different think times, zero and ten thousand cycles.

Figure 2 shows the results for the counting network under high contention (zero think time) and lower contention (ten thousand cycle think time). Under high contention, computation migration with hardware support can perform better than shared memory. Every access to a balancer modifies it, so the balancers are essentially write-shared. Therefore, the performance benefit of replication due to shared memory is negligible: in our experiments we measured a twelve percent hit rate on data objects in shared memory.

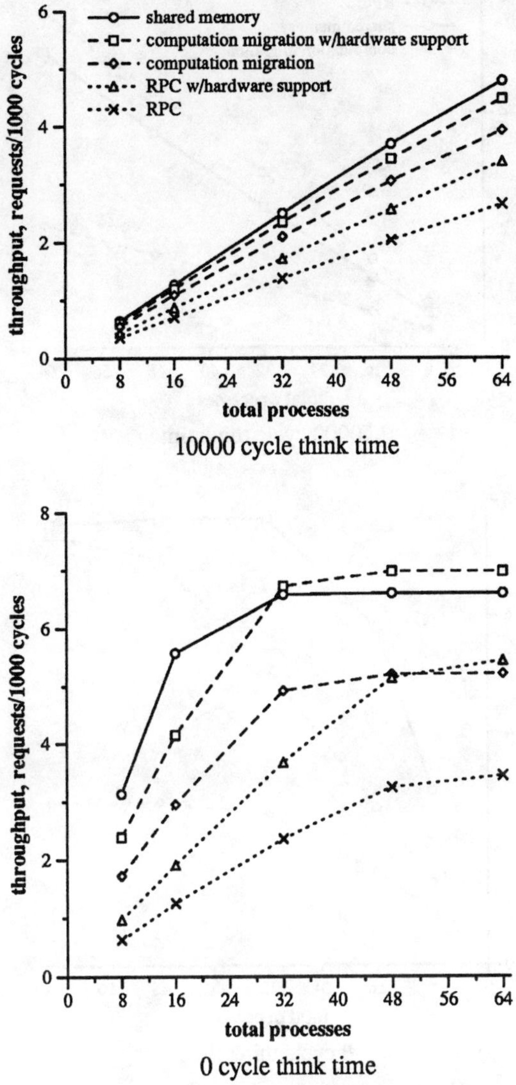

Figure 2: Throughput results

In fact, the automatic replication provided by shared memory consumes a great deal of bandwidth; even though shared memory often has the best overall performance in terms of request throughput, it puts a very high demand on the network. Figure 3 illustrates the bandwidth consumed by each mechanism. Computation migration requires less bandwidth than both RPC and shared memory. Shared memory requires the most bandwidth under high-contention conditions, due to the amount of coherence activity; at low contention, shared memory requires less bandwidth than RPC, but computation migration still requires less than half of the bandwidth of both RPC and shared memory.

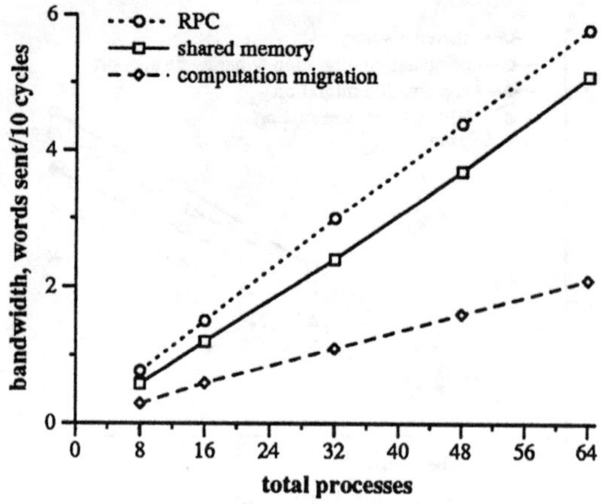

10000 cycle think time

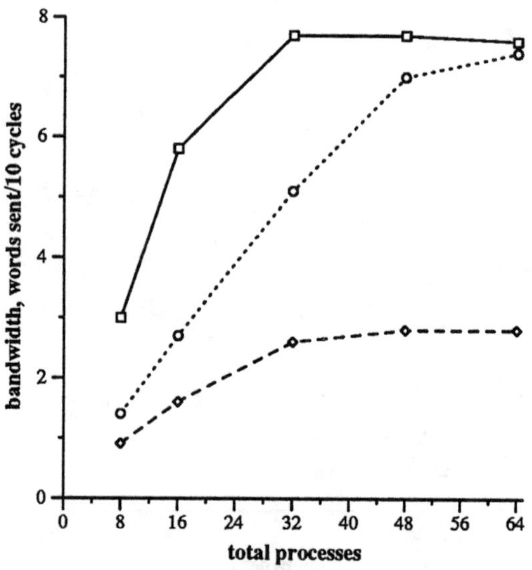

0 cycle think time

Figure 3: Bandwidth requirements

Under lower contention, we see that computation migration does not perform as well as shared memory. As we describe more precisely in Section 4.3, much of this is due to inefficiencies in our runtime system; if we were to tune the runtime, computation migration would probably perform as well as or better than shared memory.

4.2 B-tree

Our second application is a distributed B-tree. A B-tree [BM72] is a data structure designed to represent *dictionaries*; i.e., dynamic sets that support the operations *insert*, *delete*, and *lookup*. The basic structure and implementation of a B-tree is similar to that of a balanced binary tree. However, unlike a binary tree, the allowed maximum number of children for each B-tree node is not constrained to two; it can be much larger. Comer [Com79] presents a full discussion of the B-tree and its common variants.

Bayer and McCreight's original B-tree [BM72] was designed to support sequential applications. Since then, researchers have proposed many different algorithms to

Scheme	*Throughput (ops/1000 cycles)*
SM	1.837
RPC	0.3828
RPC w/HW	0.5133
RPC w/repl.	0.6060
RPC w/repl. & HW	0.7830
CP	0.8018
CP w/hardware	0.9570
CP w/repl.	1.155
CP w/repl. & HW	1.341

Table 1: Throughput results: 0 cycle think time

Scheme	*Bandwidth (words/10 cycles)*
SM	75
RPC	7.3
RPC w/HW	9.9
RPC w/repl.	7.0
RPC w/repl. & HW	9.3
CP	3.5
CP w/hardware	4.3
CP w/repl.	3.8
CP w/repl. & HW	3.9

Table 2: Bandwidth results: 0 cycle think time

support concurrent operations on the B-tree (e.g., [BS77, LY81, MR85, Sag86, LS86, CBDW91, Wan91, JC92]) and have conducted many studies examining their performance (e.g., [LS86, JS90, Wan91, Cos93]). Some algorithms [Wan91, CBDW91, JC92] are designed to run on a distributed-memory multiprocessor, where the B-tree nodes are laid out across several processors.

Two primary factors limit performance in distributed B-trees: *data* and *resource contention*. Data contention occurs when concurrent accesses to the same B-tree node must be synchronized. The most critical example of data contention is the *root bottleneck*, where an update to the tree's root node causes all incoming B-tree operations to block. Even if no synchronization among concurrent accesses is necessary, performance can still be degraded by resource contention. For example, since every B-tree operation accesses the root node, we would expect the memory module that contains it to be heavily utilized. If the rate of incoming operations exceeds the rate at which requests are serviced, then a bottleneck still exists.

Our distributed B-tree implementation is a simplified version of one of the algorithms proposed by Wang [Wan91] (it does not support the *delete* operation). In our experiments, we first constructed a B-tree with ten thousand keys and with the maximum number of children or keys in each node constrained to at most one hundred. The nodes of the tree were laid out randomly across forty-eight processors. We then created sixteen threads on separate processors that initiated requests into the B-tree; we ran experiments with two different think times, zero and ten thousand cycles.

Tables 1 and 2 present the results of the experiments using zero cycle think time (SM, CM, HW, and repl. represent shared memory, computation migration, hard-

Scheme	*Throughput (ops/1000 cycles)*
SM	1.071
CP w/repl.	0.9816
CP w/repl. & HW	1.053

Table 3: Throughput results: 10000 cycle think time

ware support, and software replication for the root of the B-tree, respectively). In all of the experiments, computation migration has higher throughput than RPC, but lower throughput than shared memory. In fact, even with hardware support for RPC and computation migration, the throughput of shared memory is over three times that of RPC and almost twice that of computation migration. As explained in Section 4.3, much of the relatively poor performance of computation migration and RPC can be attributed to the inefficiencies in the runtime system.

In addition, automatic replication contributes significantly to shared memory's throughput advantage. As stated above, one of the limiting factors to B-tree performance is the root bottleneck; it is the limiting factor for RPC and computation migration throughput. Computation migration, for instance, moves an activation for every request to the processor containing the root. The activations arrive at a rate greater than the rate at which the processor completes each activation. Shared memory, however, provides local copies of B-tree nodes to alleviate resource contention. In fact, the amount of work required to maintain cache coherence can be seen in Table 2; shared memory imposes a substantial load on the network. Furthermore, the cache hit rate was less than seven percent; we can conclude that shared memory benefited from its caches only because of its replication and not because of any locality.

We would expect computation migration's performance to improve considerably when software replication is provided for the root; as shown in Table 1, this is the case. However, the throughput of computation migration is still not as high as shared memory's. This is because we are still experiencing resource contention; instead of facing a root bottleneck, we experience bottlenecks at the level below the root — the root node has only three children. By changing the parameters of the experiments to alleviate this new source of resource contention, we get more favorable results.

In a separate experiment where the B-tree nodes are constrained to have at most only ten children or keys (but all other parameters are identical), the resulting throughput for continuation passing with root replication was 2.076 operations/1000 cycles vs. 2.427 operations/1000 cycles for shared memory. While shared memory still performs better, computation migration's throughput is better because the bottleneck below the root has been alleviated. The reason for this is twofold. First, the roots of the trees in these experiments have four (instead of three) children. Second, activations accessing smaller nodes require less time to service; this lowers the workload on the frequently accessed processors. From these experiments, we can conclude that the main reason for shared memory's performance advantage is the automatic replication due to hardware caches. This correlates with conclusions made by other studies examining B-tree performance and caching [Wan91, Cos93].

Scheme	*Bandwidth (words/10 cycles)*
SM	16
CP w/repl.	2.5
CP w/repl. & HW	2.7

Table 4: Bandwidth results: 10000 cycle think time

Category	*Cycles*	*Percent*
Total time	651	100%
User code	150	23%
Network transit	17	3%
Message overhead total	484	74%
Receiver total	341	52%
Copy packet (32 bytes)	76	10%
Thread creation	66	10%
Procedure linkage	66	10%
Unmarshaling	51	8%
Object ID translation	36	6%
Scheduler	36	6%
Forwarding check	23	4%
Allocate packet	16	2%
Sender total	143	22%
Procedure linkage	44	7%
Allocate packet	35	5%
Message send	23	4%
Marshaling	22	3%

Table 5: Approximate costs for migration in counting network

With the above information in mind, we should expect that the throughput of computation migration and shared memory to be much closer for a B-tree experiment where contention for the root is much lighter (thus reducing the advantage provided by caches for shared memory). Tables 3 and 4 show performance for experiments conducted with a ten thousand cycle think time; for brevity, RPC measurements have been omitted. With hardware support, computation migration and shared memory have almost identical throughput. Again, shared memory uses more bandwidth because it must maintain cache coherence.

4.3 Cost Breakdown

We measured the costs in RISC cycles for computation migration in Prelude; Table 5 shows an fairly accurate breakdown of the time to migrate one activation from one processor to another in the counting network application. As in most message-passing systems, the software overhead for sending a message dominates the execution time.

The table explains how our estimate of hardware support for message-passing improved our results by about twenty percent. When we assumed the presence of network interface registers, we assumed that we could reduce the copying overhead to approximately twelve cycles, removing about eight percent of the overhead. The registers also remove the need to allocate packets (since messages are composed in registers), and marshaling and unmarshaling costs are reduced by about half; this led to a removal of approximately another six percent of overhead. Finally, the assumption of hardware for global object identifier translation removed another six percent.

There are several obvious places where we could reduce the costs in Prelude. First, we spend ten percent of our time copying thirty bytes of data at the receiver, which is clearly inefficient. Eight percent of the time (fifty-one cycles) is spent unmarshaling data and translating global object identifiers on the receiving side; twenty-six of those cycles (eighteen for the translation and eight for linkage) are wasted because our implementation actually performs an unnecessary global object identifier translation during a computation migration.

We spend approximately another ten percent of our time creating a thread to handle the request and in copying the arguments for the thread (which were already copied once before). Currently, Prelude creates a new thread for most remote calls. If we were to move to an Active Messages-style implementation [vECGS92], we could avoid this overhead most of the time; for some of the short methods (such as remote record access) we already use such an approach, and it has proven to be quite effective.

As shown in the table, we also spend seventeen percent of the time in procedure linkage. If we were to rewrite portions of our runtime in assembly (or inline more of the procedures), we could eliminate almost all of this overhead. In addition, there is some additional overhead (which we did specifically measure) on the sending side due to our use of general-purpose stubs for all remote calls; we could increase performance by using special-purpose stubs for computation migration.

4.4 Summary

Our experiments show that computation migration and cache-coherent shared memory both outperform RPC. We should note, however, that we have optimized short methods in Prelude so that threads are not created for them; many of the extra calls performed using RPC call these faster short methods. If we were to perform similar optimizations for computation migration calls (as discussed in Section 4.3, computation migration would perform even better.

The factor that has the largest effect on computation migration is replication. In a counting network replication is not an issue, since all of the balancers are write-shared. Our experiments show that computation migration with hardware support for message-passing performs as well as cache-coherent shared memory at higher contention levels.

In a B-tree replication does become an issue. Even though cache hit ratios are still low in the B-tree, the lack of replication limits the overall throughput available using computation migration; we run into the problem that several activations all migrate to the same processor, thus causing resource contention. Shared memory, on the other hand, lets non-conflicting accesses run in parallel. When we add software replication to the B-tree, thus reducing resource contention, computation migration with hardware support exhibits the same performance as shared memory.

In terms of bandwidth consumption, computation migration puts a far smaller load on the network than shared memory. This would seem to indicate that as we push down message-passing costs, computation migration should perform better relative to shared memory. In fact, if we examine words transmitted per high-level operation (counting network or B-tree), computation migration still places a far smaller demand on the network. Finally, we showed that our current implementation of message-passing in Prelude is rather inefficient; given that we could remove quite a few wasted cycles from the fast path for message-passing, our results are pessimistic for both computation migration and RPC.

5 Related Work

Rogers, Hendren, and Reppy [RRH92] have developed mechanisms for migrating single activations that are similar to ours: on any access to remote data, they always migrate the top activation. The idea of migrating activations is similar to our work, but their approach is more restrictive than ours. Migrating an activation is often, but not always, the best approach. We let the user choose the appropriate mechanism; this flexibility can be vital for achieving good performance. In addition, fixing the granularity of migration to a single activation forces programmers to organize their programs so that procedures correspond to migration units; this will make it very difficult to tune or port programs. Our current prototype migrates only single activations, but an essential aspect of our overall approach is to provide the flexibility to migrate both larger and smaller units of computation.

Draves, *et al.* [DBRD91] suggest using a continuation-based structure to improve the performance of operating system services; they use continuations to reduce the amount of context-switching. They program continuations explicitly; the compilation techniques we use in this paper could probably be used to construct the continuations automatically, thus greatly reducing the programming effort involved in their approach.

Fowler and Kontothanassis [FK92] suggest using a similar "continuation-passing" structure to reduce context-switching costs in parallel programs. They also suggest using "object-affinity scheduling" to improve locality in parallel computations, where threads are scheduled based on information about what data they will reference in the near future. However, although they say that this information can be provided by the programmer or the compiler, they give no clear description of an implementation.

6 Conclusions

Ensuring high locality of data access is crucial to the performance of parallel systems. The choice of method for non-local accesses is critical: some methods of remote access can be far more expensive than others. We have described a new mechanism for remote access, computation migration, that for some applications can outperform traditional methods of access such as RPC and data migration.

Using a prototype we ran several experiments that demonstrate how computation migration outperforms RPC in applications that involve the traversal of distributed data structures, and how it can perform as well as cache-coherent shared memory. Computation migration also places a far smaller demand on the network than either shared memory or RPC. In non-shared memory systems, it would certainly be more efficient to use computation migration than data migration for the applications we have studied.

Our experiments showed that computation migration with hardware support performs as well as cache-coherent shared memory when replication is unnecessary. However, when replication is necessary, computation migration alone does not perform nearly as well as shared memory; this merely says that it is important to use replication with computation migration, just as when one uses data migration.

We intend to experiment with computation migration and replication more thoroughly to see if software replication and computation migration can perform as well as (or better than) shared memory. In addition, given the overheads of our message-passing implementation, we could certainly improve performance with further tuning. A rewrite of our runtime in an Active-Messages-style could lead to far better performance; the addition of hardware support, such as a register-based network interface, would also benefit computation migration.

We allow programmers to use computation migration with a simple program annotation; they do not need to code migration explicitly into the structure of their programs. Our program annotation affects only performance, not semantics, so the programmer can easily change the annotation to tune performance without affecting the correctness of a program; this should make tuning and porting parallel programs that use a migratory structure much easier.

Our current prototype allows the programmer to express single-activation migration. We are designing annotations to allow a programmer to express migration of multiple and partial activations. We believe this is essential for providing flexible control over the message-passing behavior of a program. We are also developing compiler analysis techniques for automatically choosing among the remote access mechanisms.

7 Acknowledgments

We would especially like to thank Anthony Joseph for helping us debug everything. Thanks to Anthony and Carl Waldspurger for helping us build Prelude; Eric Brewer for his help with PROTEUS; and Anthony, Carl, Eric, Ulana Legedza, Brad Spiers, Shail Aditya, Bradley Kuszmaul, Steve Keckler, John Keen, Sanjay Ghemawat, Donald Yeung, and the anonymous referees for giving us feedback on drafts of this paper.

References

[ACD+91] A. Agarwal, D. Chaiken, G. D'Souza, K. Johnson, D. Kranz, J. Kubiatowicz, K. Kurihara, B.H. Lim, G. Maa, D. Nussbaum, M. Parkin, and D. Yeung. "The MIT Alewife Machine: A Large-Scale Distributed-Memory Multiprocessor". In *Proceedings of Workshop on Scalable Shared Memory Multiprocessors*. Kluwer Academic Publishers, 1991. Extended version is MIT/LCS/TM-454.

[AHS91] J. Aspnes, M. Herlihy, and N. Shavit. "Counting Networks and Multiprocessor Coordination". In *Proceedings of the 23rd Annual Symposium on the Theory of Computing*, May 1991.

[BCZ90] J.K. Bennett, J.B. Carter, and W. Zwaenepoel. "Munin: Distributed Shared Memory Based on Type-Specific Memory Coherence". In *Proceedings of the 2nd PPoPP*, March 1990.

[BDCW91] E.A. Brewer, C.N. Dellarocas, A. Colbrook, and W.E. Weihl. "Proteus: A High-Performance Parallel Architecture Simulator". Technical Report MIT/LCS/TR-516, MIT LCS, September 1991. Shorter version appears in 1992 SIGMETRICS.

[BM72] R. Bayer and E.M. McCreight. "Organization and Maintenance of Large Ordered Indexes". *Acta Informatica*, 1(3):173–189, 1972.

[BN84] A.D. Birrell and B.J. Nelson. "Implementing Remote Procedure Calls". *ACM Transactions on Computer Systems*, 2(1):39–59, February 1984.

[BS77] R. Bayer and M. Schkolnick. "Concurrency of Operations on B-trees". *Acta Informatica*, 9:1–22, 1977.

[CAL+89] J.S. Chase, F.G. Amador, E.D. Lazowska, H.M. Levy, and R.J. Littlefield. "The Amber System: Parallel Programming on a Network of Multiprocessors". In *Proceedings of the 12th SOSP*, pages 147–158, December 1989.

[CBDW91] A. Colbrook, E. Brewer, C. Dellorocas, and W. E. Weihl. "Algorithms for Search Trees on Message-Passing Architectures". In *Proceedings of 1991 ICPP*, pages III138–III141, 1991.

[CD88] E.C. Cooper and R.P. Draves. "C Threads". Technical Report CMU-CS-88-154, CMU Computer Science Dept. June 1988.

[CKA91] D. Chaiken, J. Kubiatowicz, and A. Agarwal. "LimitLESS Directories: A Scalable Cache Coherence Scheme". In *Proceedings of the 4th ASPLOS*, pages 224–234, April 1991.

[Com79] D. Comer. "The Ubiquitous B-Tree". *ACM Computing Surveys*, 11(2):121–128, June 1979.

[Cos93] P.R. Cosway. "Replication Control in Distributed B-Trees". Master's thesis, MIT, 1993. To appear in May.

[DBRD91] R.P. Draves, B.N. Bershad, R.F. Rashid, and R.W. Dean. "Using Continuations to Implement Thread Management and Communication in Operating Systems". In *Proceedings of the 13th SOSP*, pages 122–136, October 1991.

[DCC+87] W.J. Dally, L. Chao, A. Chien, S. Hassoun, W. Horwat, J. Kaplan, P. Song, B. Totty, and S. Wills. "Architecture of a Message-Driven Processor". In *Proceedings of the 14th ISCA*, pages 189–196, June 1987.

[FK92] R.J. Fowler and L.I. Kontothanassis. "Improving Processor and Cache Locality in Fine-Grain Parallel Computations using Object-Affinity Scheduling and Continuation Passing (Revised)". Technical Report 411, Univ. of Rochester Computer Science Dept. June 1992.

[GW92] A. Gupta and W.D. Weber. "Cache Invalidation Patterns in Shared-Memory Multiprocessors". *IEEE Transactions on Computers*, 41(7):794–810, July 1992.

[HJ92] D.S. Henry and C.F. Joerg. "A Tightly-Coupled Processor-Network Interface". In *Proceedings of the 5th ASPLOS*, pages 111–122, October 1992.

[HKK+91] S. Hiranandani, K. Kennedy, C. Koelbel, U. Kremer, and C. Tseng. "An Overview of the Fortran D Programming System". In *Proceedings of the 4th Workshop on Languages and Compilers for Parallel Computing*, August 1991.

[HLN92] M. Herlihy, B.H. Lim, and N.Shavit. "Low Contention Load Balancing on Large-Scale Multiprocessors". In *Proceedings of the 4th SPAA*, June 1992.

[JC92] T. Johnson and A. Colbrook. "A Distributed Data-Balanced Dictionary Based on the B-Link Tree". In *Proceedings of the 6th IPPS*, pages 319–324, 1992.

[JLHB88] E. Jul, H. Levy, N. Hutchison, and A. Black. "Fine-Grained Mobility in the Emerald System". *ACM Transactions on Computer Systems*, 6(1):109–133, February 1988.

[JS90] T. Johnson and D. Shasha. "A Framework for the Performance Analysis of Concurrent B-tree Algorithms". In *Proceedings of the 9th ACM Symposium on Principles of Database Systems*, April 1990.

[Li88] K. Li. "IVY: A Shared Virtual Memory System for Parallel Computing". In *Proceedings of the 1988 ICPP*, volume II, pages 94–101, 1988.

[LLG+90] D. Lenoski, J. Laudon, K. Gharachorloo, A. Gupta, and J. Hennessy. "The Directory-Based Cache Coherence Protocol for the DASH Multiprocessor". In *Proceedings of the 17th ISCA*, pages 148–158, May 1990.

[LS86] V. Lanin and D. Shasha. "A Symmetric Concurrent B-Tree Algorithm". In *1986 Proceedings Fall Joint Computer Conference*, pages 380–386, November 1986.

[LY81] P.L. Lehman and S.B. Yao. "Efficient Locking for Concurrent Operations on B-Trees". *ACM Transactions on Database Systems*, 6(4):650–670, December 1981.

[Man87] C.R. Manning. "ACORE: The Design of a Core Actor Language and its Compiler". Master's thesis, MIT, August 1987.

[ML91] E.P. Markatos and T.J. LeBlanc. "Load Balancing vs. Locality Management in Shared-Memory Multiprocessors". Technical Report 399, Univ. of Rochester Computer Science Dept. October 1991.

[MR85] Y. Mond and Y. Raz. "Concurrency Control in B+ Trees Using Preparatory Operations". In *Proceedings of the 11th International Conference on Very Large Data Bases*, pages 331–334, August 1985.

[PM83] M.L. Powell and B.P. Miller. "Process Migration in DEMOS/MP". In *Proceedings of the 9th SOSP*, pages 110–119, 1983.

[RRH92] A. Rogers, J.H. Reppy, and L.J. Hendren. "Supporting SPMD Execution for Dynamic Data Structures", 1992.

[Sag86] Y. Sagiv. "Concurrent Operations on B-Trees with Overtaking". *Journal of Computer and System Sciences*, 33(2):275–296, October 1986.

[SB90] M.D. Schroeder and M. Burrows. "Performance of Firefly RPC". *ACM Transactions on Computer Systems*, 8(1):1–17, February 1990.

[SBS92] P. Stenström, M. Brorsson, and L. Sandberg. "An Adaptive Cache Coherence Protocol Optimized for Migratory Sharing", November 1992. Unpublished manuscript.

[SCvE91] K.E. Schauser, D.E. Culler, and T. von Eicken. "Compiled-Controlled Multithreading for Lenient Parallel Languages". In *Proceedings of 1991 FPCA*. Springer Verlag, August 1991.

[SN90] M.S. Squillante and R.D. Nelson. "Analysis of Task Migration in Shared-Memory Multiprocessor Scheduling". Technical Report 90-07-05, Univ. of Washington Dept. of Computer Science, September 1990.

[TLC85] M.M. Theimer, K.A. Lantz, and D.R. Cheriton. "Preemptable Remote Execution Facilities for the V-System". In *Proceedings of the 10th SOSP*, pages 2–12, December 1985.

[vECGS92] T. von Eicken, D.E. Culler, S.C. Goldstein, and K.E. Schauser. "Active Messages: a Mechanism for Integrated Communcation and Computation". In *Proceedings of the 19th ISCA*, pages 256–266, May 1992.

[Wan91] P. Wang. "An In-Depth Analysis of Concurrent B-Tree Algorithms". Master's thesis, MIT, January 1991. Available as MIT/LCS/TR-496.

[WBC+91] W. Weihl, E. Brewer, A. Colbrook, C. Dellarocas, W. Hsieh, A. Joseph, C. Waldspurger, and P. Wang. "PRELUDE: A System for Portable Parallel Software". Technical Report MIT/LCS/TR-519, MIT LCS, October 1991. Shorter version appears in *Proceedings of PARLE '92*.

[WW90] W.E. Weihl and P. Wang. "Multi-Version Memory: Software Cache Management for Concurrent B-Trees (extended abstract)". In *Proceedings of the 2nd IEEE Symposium on Parallel and Distributed Processing*, pages 650–655, December 1990.

[ZBC+92] H. Zima, P. Brezany, B. Chapman, P. Mehrotra, and A. Schwald. "Vienna Fortran — a Language Specification". Technical Report ICASE Interim Report 21, ICASE Nasa Langley Research Center, March 1992.

Data Locality and Load Balancing in COOL

Rohit Chandra, Anoop Gupta, John L. Hennessy
Center for Integrated Systems
Stanford University, Stanford CA 94305
Email: {chandra, gupta, hennessy}@cs.stanford.edu

Abstract

Large-scale shared memory multiprocessors typically support a multilevel memory hierarchy consisting of per-processor caches, a local portion of shared memory, and remote shared memory. On such machines, the performance of parallel programs is often limited by the high latency of remote memory references. In this paper we explore how knowledge of the underlying memory hierarchy can be used to schedule computation and distribute data structures, and thereby improve data locality. Our study is done in the context of COOL, a concurrent object-oriented language developed at Stanford. We develop abstractions for the programmer to supply optional information about the data reference patterns of the program. This information is used by the runtime system to distribute tasks and objects so that the tasks execute close (in the memory hierarchy) to the objects they reference.

We demonstrate the effectiveness of these techniques by applying them to several applications chosen from the SPLASH parallel benchmark suite. Our experience suggests that improving data locality can be simple through a combination of programmer abstractions and smart runtime scheduling.

1 Introduction

With rapid improvements in processor speeds, the memory system is increasingly the limiting factor in the performance of computer systems. The latency of memory accesses can be especially high in large-scale shared memory multiprocessors that have deep memory hierarchies. For example, in the Stanford DASH [9], while the local cache access takes only a single clock cycle, a miss serviced by the local portion of shared memory takes about thirty clock cycles, and a remote miss takes over a hundred clock cycles. Improving data locality in parallel programs can reduce the time spent by a processor waiting for data, and is critical for achieving good performance.

Data locality in parallel programs can be improved by scheduling computation and distributing data structures with an awareness of the underlying memory hierarchy, so that tasks execute close to the objects they reference. Determining an appropriate distribution of tasks and objects, however, requires knowledge about the program that is often beyond the scope of the compiler, but that may be readily known to the programmer. In this paper we focus on the support provided for such programmer intervention in COOL [3], a parallel programming language designed to express task-level parallelism. In addition to support for expressing parallelism, COOL provides abstractions for the programmer to supply hints about the data objects referenced by parallel tasks. These hints are used by the runtime system to appropriately schedule tasks and migrate data, and thereby exploit locality in the memory hierarchy; they do not affect the semantics of the program. This approach provides a clear separation of functionality: the programmer can focus on exploiting parallelism and supplying hints about the object reference patterns, leaving the details of task creation and management to the implementation.

Since our approach depends on programmer participation, it is important that the abstractions be intuitive and easy to use. At the same time the abstractions should be powerful enough to exploit locality at each level in the memory hierarchy, without compromising performance. We address these goals through the following key elements of our design. First, the abstractions are integrated with the task and object structure of the underlying COOL program so that the hints are easily supplied. Second, the abstractions are structured as a hierarchy of optional hints so that simple optimizations are easily obtained as defaults while more complex ones require incremental amounts of programmer effort. Finally, the abstractions are designed to enable experimentation with different optimizations, and address locality at each level in the memory hierarchy.

We demonstrate that our approach is both effective and easy to use, by applying it to several applications chosen from the SPLASH [15] parallel benchmark suite. We show how information about the program can be easily supplied by the programmer, usually with just a few lines of optional code, and how it is used by the runtime system for scheduling optimizations that improve both cache and memory locality. Performance improvements with these hints range from 60-135%, and are especially high in programs where locality of data references is critical. The primary conclusion of this work, therefore, is that a combination of simple programmer hints and smart runtime strategies is a highly effective approach for improving data locality and load balance.

The rest of this paper is organized as follows. Section 2 presents a brief overview of COOL. Section 3 reviews the basic techniques for improving data locality. Section 4 describes our approach, the abstractions that we provide, and the runtime scheduling mechanisms. Section 5 describes the implementation of the runtime scheduler. Section 6 applies these techniques to various programs, and presents performance results. We present related work in Section 7, and conclude in Section 8.

4th ACM PPOPP,5/93/CA,USA
© 1993 ACM 0-89791-589-5/93/0005/0249...$1.50

2 COOL Language Overview

COOL is a parallel programming language designed for applications using task-level parallelism on shared memory multiprocessors. It is an extension of C++, chosen because of its support for the definition of abstract data types and its widespread use. Our approach emphasizes the integration of concurrency and synchronization with data abstraction. Programs structured around objects have the advantage that they are modular. In addition, the object structure of COOL programs makes it easier to address load balancing and data locality issues. First, the objects referenced by tasks are more easily identified. Second, programs in COOL dynamically create light-weight tasks, providing the opportunity to schedule a task (when it is created) close to the objects it references with very low overhead.

In COOL, parallelism is expressed by identifying a function to be *parallel*; such functions execute asynchronously when invoked. Parallel functions communicate through program data in the shared address space and synchronize through monitors and condition variables [6]. Operations on shared objects may be declared *mutex*, signifying that they must acquire exclusive access to the object before executing. Event synchronization is expressed through operations on condition variables that allow a thread to wait for an event, or to signal a waiting thread when the appropriate event occurs. Finally, for convenience, we also provide a construct called *waitfor* to express fork-join style synchronization at the task level. The keyword waitfor can be attached to a scope in the program; upon reaching the end of that scope, the executing thread blocks until all tasks created within the scope of the waitfor have completed. We will see examples of COOL programs later in the paper, and a detailed description of COOL can be found in [3].

3 Exploiting Memory Hierarchy

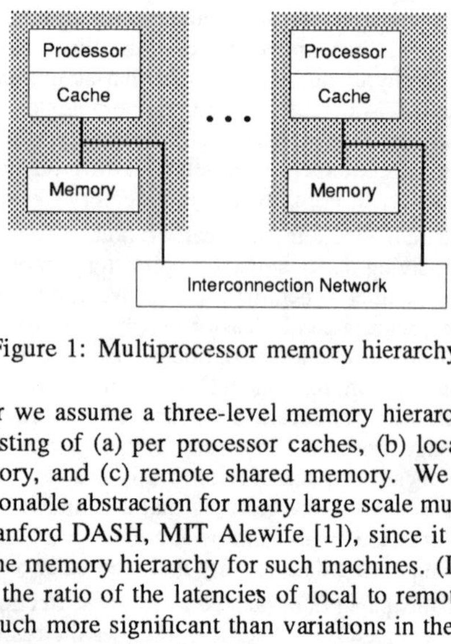

Figure 1: Multiprocessor memory hierarchy.

In this paper we assume a three-level memory hierarchy (see Figure 1) consisting of (a) per processor caches, (b) local portion of shared memory, and (c) remote shared memory. We believe that this is a reasonable abstraction for many large scale multiprocessors (e.g. the Stanford DASH, MIT Alewife [1]), since it captures the essence of the memory hierarchy for such machines. (In these multiprocessors the ratio of the latencies of local to remote references is usually much more significant than variations in the latencies to different remote processing elments).

For such architectures, the primary mechanisms to improve data locality in a parallel application are *task scheduling* and *object distribution*. The latency of references to an object can be reduced by scheduling computation and distributing objects so that a task executes on a processor that is close (in the memory hierarchy) to the objects referenced by the task. However, scheduling tasks to improve cache and memory locality often conflicts with the simultaneous goal of scheduling to achieve good load balance. Therefore, it is important to weigh the tradeoff between locality and load balance when determining a task schedule.

Given a specific task decomposition for an application, we can exploit *cache locality* (i.e. reuse in the cache) by scheduling tasks that reference the same objects on the same processor. Cache locality can be further enhanced by scheduling these tasks *back to back* to reduce possible cache interference caused by the intervening execution of other unrelated tasks. When cache locality alone is insufficient, we can exploit *memory locality* by identifying the primary object(s) referenced by a task and executing the task on the processor that contains the object(s) in its local memory. Thus, references to the object that miss in the cache will be serviced in local rather than remote memory, resulting in lower latency. However, ensuring a good load balance while exploiting memory locality requires both task scheduling and an appropriate distribution of objects across the local memories of processors. Finally, the impact of long-latency memory references can be further reduced by dynamically migrating the object, or by *prefetching* the object closer to the processor.

4 Language Abstractions and Runtime Support

Determining an efficient task and object distribution requires knowledge about the program that is often beyond the scope of a compiler, but may be known to the programmer. In COOL, therefore, we provide abstractions for the programmer to supply hints about the data reference pattern of the program. The COOL implementation has runtime mechanisms that use these hints to exploit locality at different levels in the underlying memory hierarchy. The abstractions are designed to be easy to use, and enable the programmer to supply hints naturally in terms of the objects referenced by a task. In addition, the hints are optional since they only affect the performance of the program.

We provide a *hierarchy* of control, ranging from smart defaults to simple hints to very specific hints. Smart default scheduling policies provide the basic optimizations without any programmer effort. When programmer participation becomes necessary, we have abstractions for providing simple hints about object usage. These hints are sufficient for most programs. For programs that require more complex optimizations, we have abstractions that provide greater control over task scheduling and data placement. These latter abstractions require a greater degree of understanding of the application and the memory hierarchy, but are within the same framework (as the simple abstractions) and still relatively easy to use.

For simplicity, we currently leave the burden of distributing and migrating objects across processors' memories to the programmer, and simply provide constructs to allow this to be expressed in the language. Ongoing compiler [7, 16] and operating systems [2, 8] research has enjoyed some success in automatically distributing objects, and could reduce this burden on the programmer.

4.1 The Abstractions

In COOL, information about the program is provided by identifying the objects that are important for locality for a task. Along with a parallel function, the programmer can specify a block of code that contains *affinity hints* (see Figure 2). This block of code is executed when the parallel function is invoked and a corresponding task is created. The affinity hints themselves are simply evaluated by the runtime system to determine their effect on the scheduling of the task; they do not affect the semantics of the program. We present the hierarchy of the affinity abstractions in this section.

Defaults: Parallel functions in COOL have a natural association

```
class column_c {
  ...
public:
  ...
  // Parallel function to reduce a column by a matrix.
  // Invocations of this function result in the
  // creation of a task to execute the function.
  parallel mutex void Reduce (column_c* src)
    // Code specifying affinity hints. The runtime executes
    // this code when the function is invoked, to determine
    // how to schedule the corresponding task.
    [
      // By default the task has affinity for the column
      // being reduced ("this").
      affinity (this);
      // To instead express affinity for the column "src"
      // being used to reduce the column.
      affinity (src);
    ];
} *column;

main () {
  int i, j;
  ...
  for (i=0; i<N; i++) {
    for (j=0; j<i; j++) {
      // Invocations of the parallel function.
      // The corresponding tasks are scheduled
      // based on the specified affinity hints (or default).
      column[i].Reduce (column+j);
    }
  }
}
```

Figure 2: Illustrating the affinity hints.

with the object that they are invoked on. So by default, tasks created by the invocations of a parallel function are scheduled on the processor that contains the corresponding object in its local memory.[1] The task is therefore likely to reference the object in local rather than remote memory. In addition, if there are several tasks that operate on that object, then only the first task will need to fetch the object from memory; the rest are likely to find the object in the cache. The runtime system executes such tasks *back to back* on that processor to reduce the cache interference caused by the execution of unrelated intervening tasks. This further improves cache locality.

Simple Affinity: When a parallel function would benefit from locality on an object other than the base object, the programmer can override the default by explicitly identifying that object through an *affinity* specification for the function. When affinity for an object is explicitly identified, the runtime system schedules the task in a manner similar to the default described above, except that the scheduling is based on the specified object rather than the default object. As a result, the object is likely to be referenced in the cache, and references to the object that miss in the cache are serviced in local rather then remote memory.

Task and Object Affinity: We have shown how to exploit both cache and memory locality by simply specifying the objects referenced by the parallel function. It is often useful to *simultaneously* exploit memory locality on one object and cache locality on a different object.

We illustrate this using Gaussian elimination on a matrix. In our algorithm, each column of the matrix is updated by the columns to

[1]Tasks created by invocations of parallel C style functions (as opposed to C++ member functions) are scheduled on the server that created them.

```
class column_c {
  ...
public:
  ...
  // update "this" column by the given source column
  parallel mutex void update (column_c* src)
    [
      // Object affinity for "this" exploits
      // memory locality on the destination column.
      affinity (this, OBJECT);
      // Task affinity for "src" exploits
      // cache locality on the source column.
      affinity (src, TASK);
    ];
};
```

Figure 3: COOL code illustrating TASK and OBJECT affinity in Gaussian elimination.

its left to zero out the entries above the diagonal element. Once the column has received all such updates (i.e. all entries above the diagonal element are zero), it is used to update other columns to its right in the matrix. A task in this algorithm is an invocation of the parallel function *update* (see Figure 3), which updates a destination column by a given source column. A desirable execution schedule and object distribution for this column-oriented algorithm are as follows (see Rothberg [13]). The algorithm exploits memory locality on the destination column by executing the task where the destination column is allocated (the number of columns per processor is so large that they are not expected to fit in the cache). Distributing the columns across processors in a round-robin fashion results in good load distribution. In addition, the algorithm exploits cache locality on the source column since each processor executes multiple updates that involve the same source column. However, it is important that each processor execute the tasks involving the same source column back to back; this avoids the execution of other tasks that might flush the source column from the cache.

The above example clearly shows that we wish to exploit cache locality on the source column and memory locality on the destination column. We therefore allow the keywords *OBJECT* and *TASK* to be specified with an affinity statement. The *TASK* affinity statement identifies tasks that reference a common object as a *task-affinity* set; these tasks are executed back to back to increase cache reuse. The *OBJECT* affinity statement identifies the object for memory locality; the task is collocated with the object. As shown in Figure 3, we can simultaneously exploit cache locality through task affinity on the source column, as well as memory locality through object affinity on the destination column. This exactly captures the way the algorithm was hand-coded using ANL macros [11] to run on the Stanford DASH multiprocessor; the same scheduling is very simply expressed in COOL.

Processor Affinity: Finally, for load balancing reasons it often becomes necessary to *directly* schedule a task on a particular processor (in practice the corresponding server process), rather than indirectly through the objects it references. We therefore provide *processor affinity* through the *PROCESSOR* keyword that can be specified for an affinity declaration. An integer argument is supplied instead of an object address, and its value (modulo the number of server processes) is used as the server number on which the task is scheduled.

Object Distribution: In addition to affinity hints for a task, we also allow the programmer to distribute objects across memory modules, both when they are allocated, as well as by dynamically migrating them to another processor's local memory. Since tasks with object affinity are executed where the object is allocated, distribut-

Table 1: Summary of affinity specifications and data distribution constructs.

Affinity Construct	*Description*	*Effect*
`affinity` (*obj-addr*)	Simple affinity	Collocate with object, schedule back-to-back
`affinity` (*obj-addr*, `OBJECT`)	Object affinity	Collocate with object
`affinity` (*obj-addr*, `TASK`)	Task affinity	Schedule tasks in task-affinity set back to back
`affinity` (*num*, `PROCESSOR`)	Processor Affinity	Schedule on specified processor
`x = new (P)` *type*	Allocate the object from the memory of processor P	
`migrate` (*obj-addr*, `P`)	Migrate the object to the memory of processor P	
`migrate` (*obj-addr*, `P, size`)	Migrate an array of 'size' objects to the memory of processor P	
`home` (*obj-addr*)	Return the processor P that contains the object in its local memory	

ing objects across memory modules can improve the load balance of the program.

By default, memory is allocated from the local memory of the requesting processor. To allocate memory from within the local memory of a particular processor, a processor number can be supplied as an additional argument to the `new` operator. For dynamic object distribution we provide a `migrate` function that takes a pointer to an object and a processor number, and migrates the object to the local memory of the specified processor (modulo the number of server processes). An optional third argument that specifies the number of objects to be migrated is useful to migrate an array of objects.[2] Finally, the `home` function returns the number of the processor that contains the given object allocated in its local memory.

The various affinity hints are summarized in Table 1. If affinity is specified for multiple objects then we currently schedule the task based on the first object. There are obvious better heuristics that would determine the relative importance of objects based on their size and schedule the task on the processor that has the *most* objects in its local memory, while prefetching the remaining objects. We plan to study such tradeoffs in the future.

4.2 The Runtime Scheduler

The runtime scheduler uses the affinity hints to schedule tasks as described above. To maintain good load balance an idle processor steals tasks from other processors. We are also experimenting with other optimizations that the runtime system may perform based on the hints about object usage. For instance, tasks in a task-affinity set should preferably be executed on the same processor, but the *particular* processor can be chosen based on load balancing considerations. In addition, tasks scheduled with task-affinity can be stolen as a *set* by an idle processor to improve load balance and still benefit from cache locality. In contrast, tasks scheduled with object-affinity should preferably not be stolen; moving such tasks away from the memory containing the objects they reference may result in an increase in effective memory latency arising from remote memory references to the objects.

5 Implementation

In this section we give a brief overview of the runtime system and the task queue structure used to support the task scheduling optimizations.

When a COOL program begins execution several server processes are created, usually one per available processor. Ideally a server process runs on the same processor throughout its lifetime. It continually fetches a task from the task queue and executes it (without preemption) until the task completes or blocks awaiting some synchronization event. There are two kinds of task queues per server — a *NewQ* for newly created tasks, and a *ReadyQ* for tasks that had blocked on some synchronization event and are now ready to run again. If a newly created task is fetched, then the server allocates a stack for the task and starts executing the parallel function associated with the task. If a ready task is fetched (one that had blocked on some event, but is now ready to execute), the task resumes execution where it had left off.

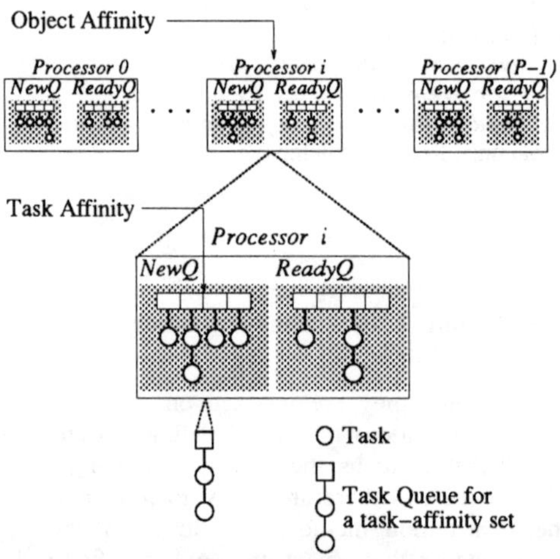

Figure 4: Task queue structure to support task and object affinity.

Object affinity requires that tasks be executed on the processor that contains the object allocated in its local memory, while task affinity requires that tasks be executed back to back on a processor. To support task scheduling for object affinity there is a task queue for each server process, and a task with object affinity is collocated with the object (see Figure 4). To support task-affinity sets, each processor must distinguish tasks belonging to different sets. Therefore each server actually has an *array* of queues, with each element of the array corresponding to a task affinity set.

Given the above task queue structure, when a task is created with affinity specified for some object, we schedule it on the processor that has the object allocated in its local memory.[3] In addition, within the array of queues for that processor, the task is enqueued on the queue determined by hashing the object's virtual address onto an element of the array. The hash function is a simple modulo operation of the object address with the size of the array.

If both task and object affinity are specified for a task, then the task is scheduled on the processor determined by the object affinity hint, i.e. on the processor that contains the specified object in

[2]The operating system on DASH supports data allocation at the page level only, therefore the migrate call on these machines is implemented through the migration of entire pages spanned by the object, rather than the object alone.

[3]An operating system call is available on DASH which, given a virtual address, returns the number of the processor that contains the physical page corresponding to that address. To avoid the cost of the system call, the runtime can maintain the location of an object in a special variable within the object.

its local memory. However, within that processor, it is scheduled on a queue based on the object specified in the task-affinity hint, thereby identifying tasks in that task affinity set. This allows us to simultaneously exploit both cache and memory locality on different objects, as illustrated by the example in Section 4.1. Tasks in the same task-affinity set therefore get mapped onto the same queue, and can be serviced back to back. Collisions of different task-affinity sets on the same queue can be minimized by choosing a suitably large array size.

This task queue structure is implemented efficiently. Determining where to schedule a task simply requires two modulo operations. Within the task queue structure of each processor, the non-empty queues in the array are linked together to form a doubly-linked list and provide fast enqueue and dequeue operations.

6 Case Studies

In this section we apply our approach to several scientific and engineering applications chosen from the SPLASH parallel benchmark suite. For each application we describe both the structure of the program and how the concurrency is expressed in COOL. We analyze the locality and load balancing issues in the application, and identify the potentially useful optimizations. We then show how the affinity hints are used to supply information about the program, and how they are effective in triggering different optimizations. We contrast the programmer effort required in our approach with that in a program written using the ANL macros, that do not provide any support for locality optimizations. Finally, we measure and analyze the performance impact of supplying these hints.

Through this analysis we hope to illustrate the following benefits of our approach. First, the hints are powerful enough to address locality at each level in the memory hierarchy. Second, the hints are flexible in that they enable the programmer to easily experiment with different optimizations. Finally, the underlying task and object structure of the program provides a natural framework in which the affinity hints are easily supplied.

We present results from five SPLASH applications. The first application (Ocean) has a simple structure, and simple affinity between tasks and objects is sufficient to improve both cache and memory performance. The next application (LocusRoute) illustrates the benefits of scheduling related tasks on the same processor to enhance reuse in the cache. The third application (Panel Cholesky) is more complex, and requires careful placement of objects and tasks to improve both cache and memory locality. For the final two applications, Barnes-Hut and Block Cholesky, we only present a summary of the results due to space limitations.

We present performance results running on a prototype of the Stanford DASH multiprocessor, consisting of thirty-two 33 MHz R3000 processors. The processors are organized into (eight) clusters, with each cluster containing four processors and some physical memory (28 MB each). Each processor has a 64 KB first level cache and a 256 KB second-level cache. References that are satisfied in the first-level cache take a single processor cycle, while hits in the second-level cache take about 14 cycles. Memory references to data in the local cluster memory take nearly 30 cycles, while references to the remote memory of another cluster take about 100-150 cycles. We measure the time spent in the parallel portion of the code, and plot its speedup with respect to the time taken by a serial version of the code running on one processor. We also use the hardware performance monitor on DASH [10], that enables us to monitor the bus and network activity in a non-intrusive manner.

```
class region_c {
    ... data declarations ...
public:
    parallel void laplace (region_c*);
    ...
};

class grid_c {
    ...
public:
    // Grid composed of regions.
    region_c* region;
    void laplace (grid_c* p) {
        int i;
        waitfor {
            for (i=0; i<N; i++)
                // Process all the regions in parallel.
                region[i].laplace (&(p->region[i]));
        } // 'waitfor' the operations to complete for all regions.
    }

    // Distribute the regions across processors.
    void distribute () {
        int i;
        for (i=0; i<N; i++)
            migrate (region+i, i);
    }
} A, B;

main () {
    A.distribute ();
    B.distribute ();
    ...
    A.laplace (B);
}
```

Figure 5: Concurrency and affinity in the Ocean code.

6.1 Ocean

Ocean is a program to study the influence of eddy and boundary currents on large-scale ocean currents. It simulates flows in a cuboidal basin over a series of time steps, solving a set of spatial partial differential equations within each step. In this case study we illustrate how a simple object distribution together with the default affinity works well in improving data locality.

The main data structures are twenty-five double precision floating point grids. Each grid is a two-dimensional array, representing the value of a state variable at different locations in the ocean basin. The computation involves very regular intra-grid (e.g. nearest neighbor) and inter-grid (e.g. adding corresponding elements of two grids) operations. To exploit concurrency, for both intra-grid and inter-grid operations we partition each grid into regions, and process different regions of the grid concurrently. This results in a uniform amount of work for each region, as well as minimal communication between processes working on different regions.

Figure 5 shows abstracted segments of the Ocean program expressed in COOL. The primary objects are *regions* and *grids*, with a grid composed of several regions. We chose to partition a grid into a single *array* of regions, although rectangular block decompositions are also possible. Concurrency within a grid operation is exploited by invoking a parallel function on each region within the grid. Synchronization for the completion of a grid operation is easily expressed by invoking the operations on the regions within a waitfor.

As part of initialization, the COOL programmer explicitly dis-

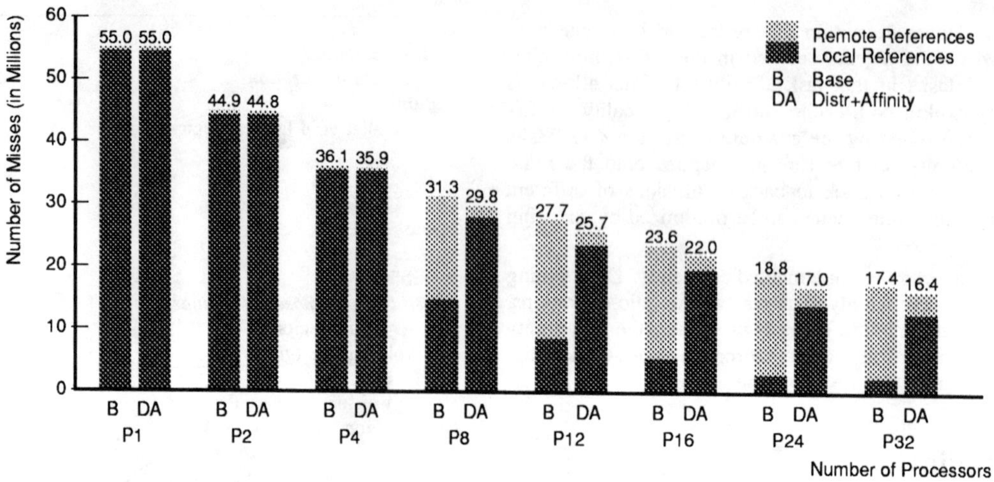

Figure 7: Cache miss statistics for Ocean, before and after affinity optimizations.

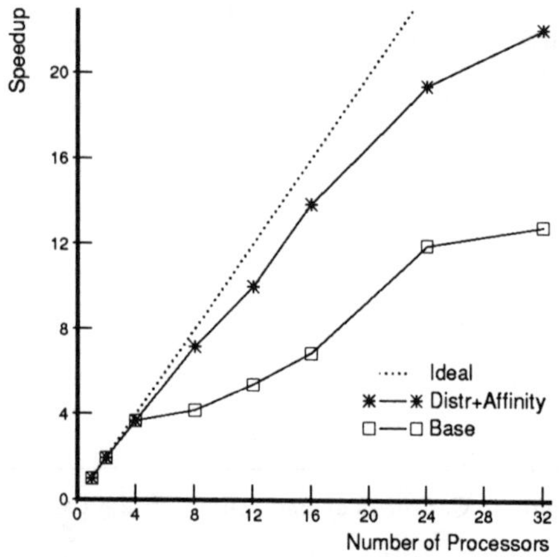

Figure 6: Performance improvement with affinity hints for Ocean.

tributes the regions of the grids across the memories of the processors so that corresponding regions of different grids are allocated within the same local memory (see the function *distribute*).[4] This is all that the programmer has to do; the runtime automatically schedules tasks for locality on the region objects, based on their default affinity. As a result both intra-grid and inter-grid tasks find the data they reference in local memory.

Figure 6 shows the performance results for the Ocean code on a square grid of 194x194 points (the input problem is kept fixed throughout).[5] Performance improves dramatically (75-100%) with the hints described above, compared to the base version in which tasks are scheduled on a single task queue. The statistics gathered with the hardware performance monitor on the 32-processor DASH are shown in the bar charts in Figure 7. The figure plots the total number of cache misses before (B) and after optimization (DA) during the execution of the parallel portion of the program, for different number of processors. Each bar corresponds to the total number of caches misses, and is partitioned into two regions. The dark region represents the cache misses that were serviced in local memory while the light region corresponds to misses that were to data in remote memory. As shown in the figure most misses are to remote memory before optimization, but with the optimizations nearly all (80-90%) of the cache misses are satisfied in local memory. Thus the primary performance gains are due to the objects being referenced in local rather than in remote memory.

Even though the problem is statically decomposable, this example demonstrates the ease with which the program was optimized. The COOL program is decomposed into tasks and objects, and the default affinity successfully improves both cache and memory locality. Explicit distribution of objects is required of the programmer, but is easily expressed through the migrate statement. Finally, experience with this example suggests an automatic object distribution strategy in which the objects associated with a parallel function are distributed in a round-robin manner across the local memories of processors. This appears to be a reasonable default, and would be sufficient for programs with a regular structure. For more complex programs the programmer could always override this default with explicit object distribution.

6.2 LocusRoute

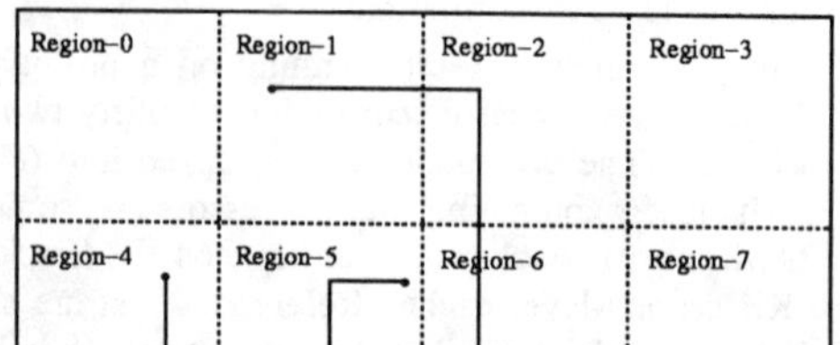

A, B, C: Wires within the CostArray

Figure 8: The CostArray composed of regions.

LocusRoute is a parallel algorithm for standard cell placement and routing in integrated circuits. Given a circuit consisting of modules and connections, and a placement of the circuit modules, the program does *routing* to determine the paths of the connecting wires. The objective is to find a route that minimizes the area of the circuit.

[4]Actually, although we impose a region and grid structure in the program, for simplicity the underlying grid elements are still maintained as a two dimensional array. Regions are distributed by migrating the corresponding elements of the two dimensional array. Thus object distribution can also be easily incorporated into existing codes without requiring a major restructuring of the data structures, and illustrates the flexibility of the basic mechanism.

[5]An ANL version of this code on DASH is still under development, hence we cannot compare the performance of the COOL program with the ANL version. However, we expect their performance to be similar.

```
// Function to determine the CostArray region that the
// wire lies in, based on the mid-point of the wire.
int Region (Wire*);

class Wire {
   ...
public:
   // Parallel function to route a wire.
   parallel void Route ()
      [ affinity (Region (this), PROCESSOR); ];
};

main () {
   ...
   for (i=0; i<NumIter; i++) {
      waitfor {
         for (all wires 'W' do) W->Route ();
         // Route the wires in parallel.
      } // Wait for all wires to be routed.
   }
}
```

Figure 9: Specifying affinity hints in LocusRoute.

The two main data structures are *Wires* and the *CostArray*. A wire object contains the list of pin locations to be joined, where a pin location corresponds to a routing cell in the circuit. The CostArray keeps track of the number of wires running through each routing cell, and contains two values: the number of wires that pass horizontally and vertically through the routing cell. These values are updated as wires are routed. The cost of a route is given by the sum of the CostArray values for all the routing cells that it traverses.

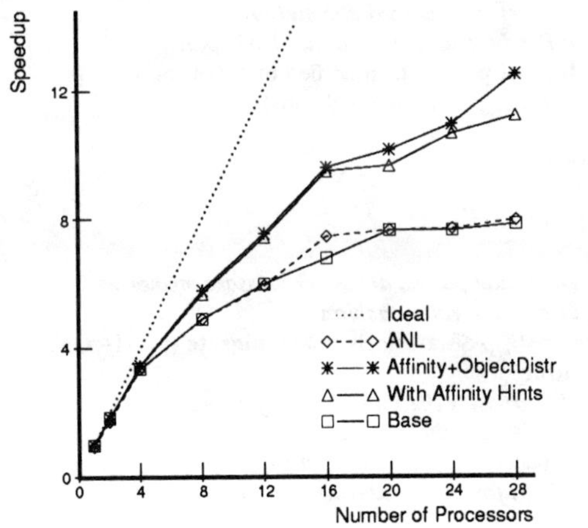

Figure 10: Performance improvements in LocusRoute with affinity hints.

The program iteratively converges to a route for each wire. Within each iteration, for every wire, LocusRoute rips out the previous route of the wire and tries to find a better route by reading the CostArray and examining the cost of alternate routes. If it finds a better route then it updates the CostArray with the new route. After all wires have been routed in an iteration, this process is repeated in the next iteration. However, different wires can be routed concurrently within an iteration. The COOL program to express this concurrency is shown in Figure 9, and consists of the parallel function `Route` on a Wire. This function reads the wire object and the portion of the CostArray spanned by the geographical end-points of the wire, tries to find a better route, and updates the CostArray with the new route. Synchronization for the completion of an iteration is expressed by wrapping a waitfor around an iteration.

The algorithm spends nearly all of its time in evaluating the cost of different routes for a wire, so locality on the CostArray is important. We can express this by viewing the CostArray as partitioned into geographical *regions* (see Figure 8), and identifying wires that lie within the same region of the CostArray as a task-affinity set. Executing these tasks back to back on a processor will hopefully reuse that region of the CostArray in the cache. To simultaneously distribute the load across processors as well, we actually exploit this locality using processor affinity: each region of the CostArray is (conceptually) assigned to a processor, and tasks within that region are directly scheduled on the corresponding processor. Besides reusing the same region in the cache, each region is likely to be referenced by only one processor, thereby reducing the invalidations of the CostArray in caches of other processors. Finally, depending on the degree of reuse, physically distributing the regions of the CostArray across the memories of different processors may further improve performance, since the misses to the CostArray will be to local rather than remote memory.

The code to express these hints is shown in Figure 9. The function `Region(CurrentWire)` computes the midpoint of the wire and returns the region number that the midpoint lies within, which is then used as the server number in the processor-affinity hint. Partitioning the CostArray into a few large regions (say one per processor) will have better locality but perhaps poorer load balance, while larger numbers of smaller regions will have better load balance at the expense of data locality. These tradeoffs can be easily explored in the COOL program by varying the Region function.

Since we had only small input circuits available to us, we demonstrate our technique using a synthetically constructed input consisting of a dense network of wires within regions of the circuit (we believe our results apply to larger realistic circuits as well). The performance results in Figure 10 show (a) the *Base* version of the program in which the wire tasks are scheduled across processors in a round-robin fashion without regard for locality, (b) the *Affinity* version in which processor affinity hint is supplied so that wires in a geographical region are likely to be routed by the associated processor, and (c) the *Affinity+ObjectDistr* version in which the regions of the CostArray are physically distributed across processors' memories as well. Overall speedups are small due to the high degree of communication of shared data. However, with the affinity hints most of the wire tasks (over 80%) in a region are routed on the corresponding processor, resulting in significant performance improvements. As shown by the cache miss statistics in Figure 11, affinity scheduling nearly halves the number of cache misses. Distributing the CostArray improves performance further, although the gains are smaller. The number of cache misses remain unchanged but more of them are serviced in local rather than remote memory.

In contrast to the COOL program that simply requires affinity hints, the ANL version requires the programmer to explicitly maintain task queues per processor, and manage task creation and scheduling based on the geographic locality described above. The COOL program outperforms the ANL code due to some additional optimizations for dynamic memory allocation. To factor out the effect of these optimizations, we present self-relative speedup for the ANL code in Figure 10. Even so, the COOL program exhibits better speedup, especially for larger number of processors.

While the actual affinity hints supplied are simple, it is important to realize that the hints are based on insights about the semantics of the application, that would be impossible for a compiler to deduce. For instance, a compiler simply cannot infer that wire objects have end-points that correspond to a region in the CostArray and have affinity for that region. Programmer intervention is therefore necessary for such programs.

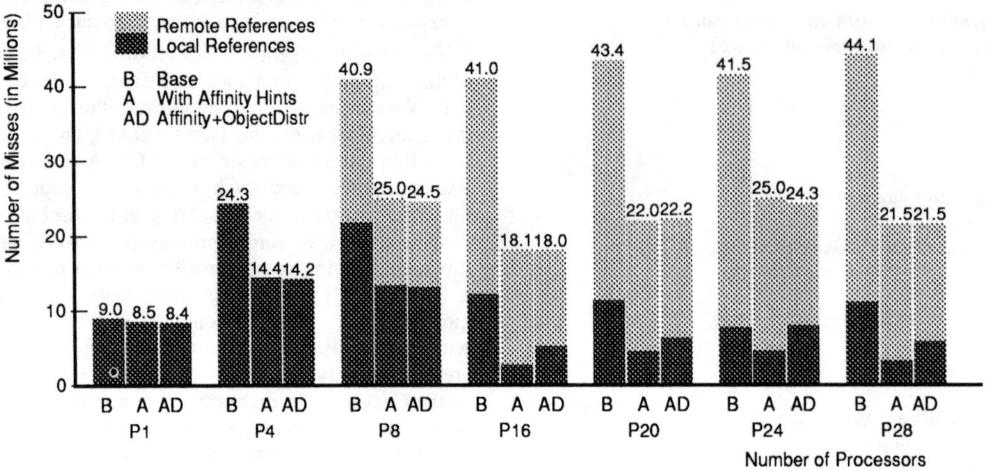

Figure 11: Cache miss statistics for LocusRoute, and the affect of the affinity optimizations.

6.3 Panel Cholesky

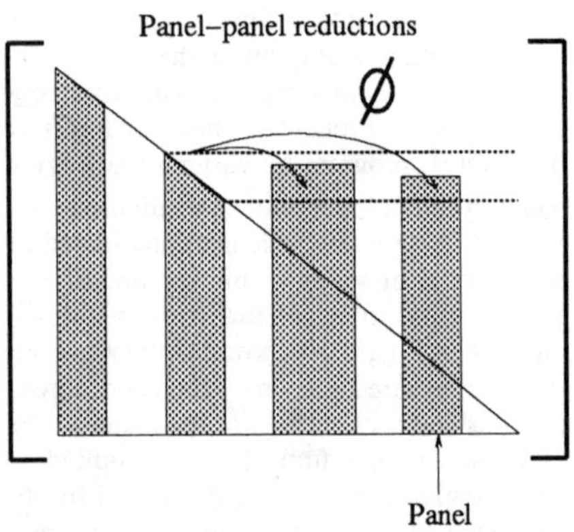

Figure 12: Panel reduction structure in Cholesky.

This program performs parallel Cholesky factorization of a sparse positive definite matrix [13]. That is, given a sparse matrix A, the program finds a lower-triangular matrix L, such that $A = LL^T$. The primary operation in a column-oriented sparse Cholesky factorization is the addition of a multiple of one column of A into another column to its right in order to cancel a non-zero in the upper triangle. This operation is typically referred to as a column modification. Rothberg and Gupta [13] have suggested a matrix representation in which columns with identical non-zero structure are organized into *panels*, as shown in Figure 12. Operations are performed between panels — each panel has updates peformed to it by relevant panels to its left, and once *all* the updates to a panel have been performed, the panel becomes 'ready', and can be used to update other panels to its right.

The COOL code expressing this computation is shown in Figure 13. The *main* procedure initially starts the computation by calling *CompletePanel* on the panels that are initially ready and do not require any modifications. This function performs some internal modifications, and then calls the parallel function *UpdatePanel* to update those panels to its right that are modified by this panel. Besides being a parallel function, UpdatePanel is also a mutex function since it requires exclusive access to the panel being updated. This ensures that multiple updates to a particular panel are serialized. Once all the modifications to a panel have been performed, the panel becomes ready, and CompletePanel is called on it.

```
class panel_c {
  ...
public:
  parallel mutex void UpdatePanel (panel* src)
    [ affinity (src, TASK); affinity (this, OBJECT);] {
    ... Update this panel by the given src panel ...
    if (all updates to this panel have been performed)
      // This panel is now ready.
      CompletePanel ();
  }

  parallel void CompletePanel () {
    ... Perform internal completion ...
    // Produce updates that need this panel.
    for (all panels 'p' modified by this panel)
      panel[p].UpdatePanel (this);
  }
} *panel;

main () {
  ...
  // Distribute panels across processors memories,
  // in a round robin fashion.
  for (p=0; p<MaxPanels; p++) migrate (panel+p, p);
  waitfor {
    // Start with the initially ready panels.
    for (all panels 'p' that are initially ready)
      panel[p].CompletePanel ();
  } // Wait for all updates to complete.
}
```

Figure 13: Expressing concurrency and affinity in Panel Cholesky.

Most of the work is done in UpdatePanel, which reads the source panel and modifies the destination panel. By default, tasks corresponding to UpdatePanel have affinity for the panel that they are invoked on (the destination panel), and are automatically scheduled to exploit both cache reuse and memory locality on the destination panel. In addition, by distributing the panels across processors' memories we can both distribute the associated work and distribute the memory bandwidth requirements.

This scheme should perform well. Since the destination panel is being modified, it is preferable that modifications to a panel be performed on the processor that contains the destination panel in its local memory; otherwise the destination panel will continually be

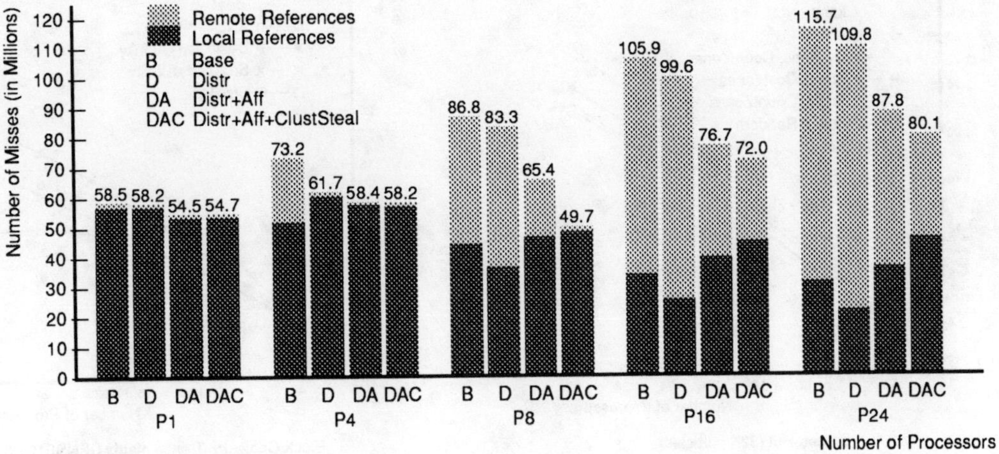

Figure 15: Cache miss statistics for Panel Cholesky, and the affect of the affinity optimizations.

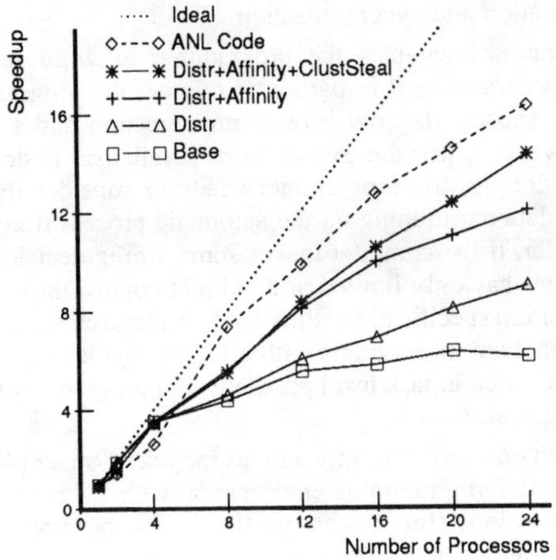

Figure 14: Performance improvement with affinity hints for Panel Cholesky (matrix BCSSTK33).

invalidated in different processors' caches. We can simultaneously exploit *cache reuse* on each source panel by identifying tasks with the same source panel as a task-affinity set. Each processor usually has multiple panels assigned to it that need to be modified by any given source panel. Executing these updates back to back on the processor will reuse the source panel in the cache.

These scheduling optimizations are easily obtained with the affinity hints shown in Figure 13. The panels are distributed across processors' memories in a round robin fashion. The default affinity for the base object automatically collocates tasks with the destination panel, while a task affinity hint supplied with UpdatePanel exploits reuse on the source panel.

The performance results are shown in Figure 14.[6] The *Base* version is executed with no optimizations. *Distr* includes round-robin distribution of panels across processors, but the tasks are scheduled randomly across processors. The improvement in performance is due to a better distribution of the memory bandwidth requirements. Performance further improves with scheduling tasks with affinity for the source and destination panels as described above, as shown by the plot *Distr+Aff*.

[6] We present results on upto 24 processors due to limitations in the amount of physical memory on the machine.

We now discuss an experiment we did with cluster-based scheduling. This experiment demonstrates the benefits of exploiting specific architectural features in improving data locality; the necessary optimizations, however, may require additional programmer abstractions and/or runtime support. Recall that although tasks are collocated with the destination panel on a particular processor, all processors within that cluster (in DASH) share the local memory containing the destination panel. We therefore ran the program with an idle processor allowed to steal tasks only from other processors within the same cluster; the stolen tasks would therefore continue to reference the destination panel in local rather than remote memory. This effect is controlled through a runtime flag that can be dynamically manipulated by the programmer. As shown by the plot *Distr+Aff+ClusterStealing*, stealing only within a cluster further improves performance.

Although in our experiments cluster scheduling was explicitly manipulated by the programmer, perhaps this effect can be automated within the runtime system. For instance, a runtime scheduler could always try to steal tasks from processors within the same cluster before trying to steal tasks from remote processors. Or, the scheduler may decide to steal tasks from remote processors based on the relative latencies of local and remote memory references. However, more experience is required before good defaults or automatic strategies can be developed; this example simply demonstrates the usefulness of such mechanisms.

As shown in the figure, the performance of the final COOL code is less than 10% slower than a hand-coded version of the code written using the ANL macros. Figure 15 displays the effect of the optimizations on the cache miss behavior of the program. Simply distributing the panels improves performance due to better utilization of the available memory bandwidth without affecting the cache performance. However, affinity scheduling and cluster scheduling significantly reduce the number of cache misses; in addition, since the tasks are collocated with the panel, more of the misses are serviced in local rather than remote memory.

6.4 Summary of other Applications

We have obtained similar good results with other SPLASH applications. Here we briefly summarize our experience with two applications, Barnes-Hut and Block Cholesky [14] (see Figure 16). Barnes-Hut is an N-body application, while the Block Cholesky program performs Cholesky factorization by representing the matrix as a set of *blocks* (instead of panels as studied in Section 6.3). Both

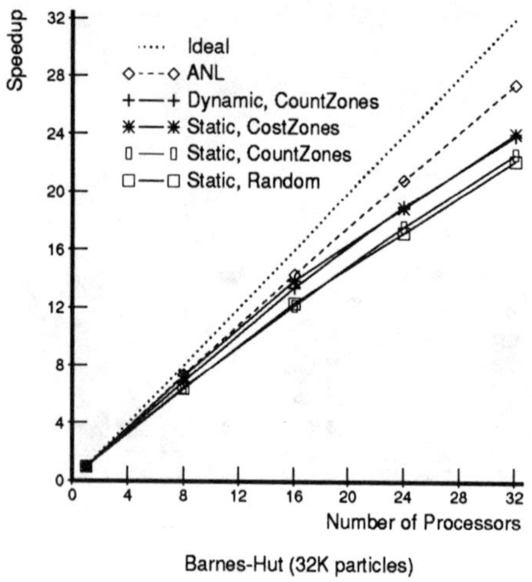

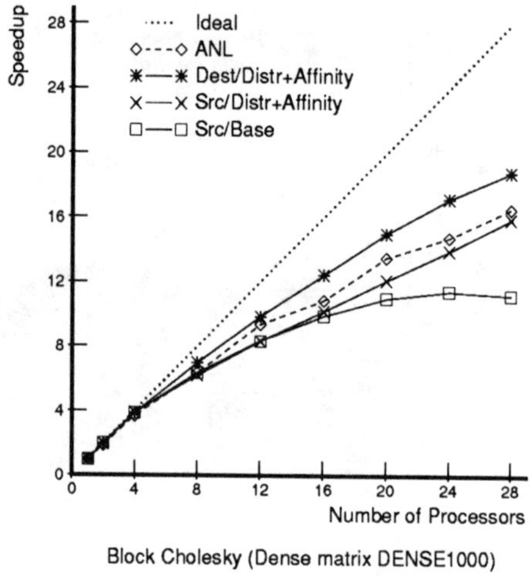

Figure 16: Performance improvement with affinity hints for Barnes-Hut and Block Cholesky.

these applications illustrate how the abstractions in COOL allow the programmer to easily explore several alternatives that tradeoff between locality and load balance. By simply changing the affinity hints the programmer could try different optimizations for locality, and depend on the runtime to dynamically correct any load imbalance. The COOL version of Barnes-Hut performs close to the hand-coded ANL version, while Block Cholesky in COOL gets even higher performance than the ANL program due to better load balancing.

7 Related Work

In this section we begin with a brief outline of automatic techniques to address data locality in programs. We then describe other approaches based on explicit programmer support, and contrast them with COOL.

Automatic Techniques: Compiler based approaches [7, 16] primarily address loop-level parallelism in regular numerical algorithms, and include optimizations such as loop transformations to improve reuse in the cache, and array alignment and distribution for better memory locality. However, these approaches focus on affine array accesses within a loop nest, while our target is a much broader class of programs with complex data reference patterns.

Operating system techniques [2, 8] address data locality in NUMA machines through smart page placement policies such as allocating private data in the local memory of a processor, allocating modified data in common global memory if any, and replicating those pages that are referenced but not modified (replicating pages in softwares requires that the system keep the multiple copies of a page consistent). Although such schemes don't require programmer intervention, their primary drawback is the limited amount of information available based on which pages must be distributed. In addition, these schemes are based only on page distribution to improve memory locality, and do not consider techniques such as task scheduling that can improve cache locality.

Explicit Programmer Hints: Along with other researchers, both Fortran-D [5], and Rogers and Pingali [12] have taken a data-centric view towards writing parallel programs in machines with distributed physical memory. The programmer writes a serial shared memory program and specifies a data distribution across processors; explicit constructs for predefined regular patterns as well as for irregular distributions are provided. The parallelism is automatically inferred by the compiler based on an *owner-computes* strategy. The compiler generates code for each processing node along with the necessary communication and synchronization.

This approach enables the programmer to write serial shared memory programs, and in particular relieves the programmer from having to specify the low level communication and synchronization. However, since the extraction of parallelism is driven by the data partitioning, the programmer needs to consider the effect of specified data partitioning on the automatic process decomposition. In particular, if the compiler makes some wrong decisions then the programmer has only limited and indirect control through the data decomposition specification. Finally, their research focuses on loop-level parallelism in programs with a highly regular structure, while we are interested in task level parallelism in programs with irregular and complex structures.

Research done concurrently with us includes Fowler [4], who provide a parallel programming environment with light-weight threads and continuations (for synchronization). The programmer can influence the scheduling of threads through object-affinity scheduling: objects derived from a base class `uses_OAS` have a field that stores a processor number, with methods for reading and writing this field. Tasks on an object derived from `uses_OAS` are scheduled on the processor specified by the field. By default, tasks are scheduled on a global queue, and acquire affinity for the processor that steals them once they get stolen. In addition, tasks or groups of tasks may also be scheduled on the local queue of a processor.

Their work is done in the context of SGI multiprocessor workstations, that have per processor caches but a single global shared memory. Therefore they focus on optimizations for cache reuse, such as scheduling tasks on the same object on the same processor, and scheduling tasks in a *template group* (i.e. tasks related through common synchronization) together on a processor. However, they do not consider the *temporal* aspect of cache reuse. Each processor has a single task queue that is simply serviced in FIFO order. In contrast, temporal reuse is explicitly addressed in COOL by identifying related tasks through task affinity for back to back execution on a processor. In addition, COOL provides support for exploiting memory locality on NUMA machines.

8 Concluding Remarks

The high latency of memory references in multiprocessors significantly hinders the efficient execution of parallel programs. In this paper we have shown how scheduling computation and distributing objects, with an understanding of the underlying memory hierarchy, can improve data locality. We develop an abstraction of the memory hierarchy of a shared-memory multiprocessor, that captures the essential components of the memory system. To exploit locality in this abstract memory hierarchy, we develop support in COOL for the programmer to supply hints about the program, and scheduling mechanisms in the runtime system that use these hints to distribute tasks and objects appropriately. Through several realistic examples we have shown how the hints can be naturally supplied within the task and object structure of the COOL program. The hierarchy of abstractions provides an increasing degree of control, while the flexibility of the abstractions makes it easy to experiment with different scheduling optimizations. The hints are highly effective, with performance improvements as high as 135%.

An important question that arises from this work concerns the feasibility of automating these techniques in a compiler. Are programmer supplied locality hints necessary in the long-term, or are they only a stop-gap measure that will be made obsolete with improvements in compiler technology? Our experience with the applications indicates the former. For instance, in the LocusRoute application, the locality hints are based on the semantic understanding of 'wires' (e.g. their 2-D spatial nature and that they are short), the 'cost array', and the relationship between the two. We do not believe that a compiler could automatically infer such semantics. At the same time, however, experience with programs such as Panel Cholesky and Ocean suggests that smart default strategies for object distribution and task scheduling can significantly reduce the burden on the programmer.

Our ongoing research focuses on experimenting and evaluating different runtime heuristics, supporting affinity for multiple objects, runtime support and abstractions for prefetching, and algorithms for automatic object distribution.

Acknowledgements: The Barnes-Hut code was developed by J. P. Singh and programmed in COOL by Avneesh Agrawal. Sparse Cholesky (panel and block) codes were developed by Edward Rothberg, and programmed in COOL by Maneesh Agrawal. This research has been supported by the Defense Advanced Research Projects Agency under DARPA contract #N00039-91-C-0138. Anoop Gupta is also supported by an NSF Presidential Young Investigator Award.

References

[1] A. Agarwal, B.-H. Lim, D. Kranz, and J. Kubiatowicz. April: A processor architecture for multiprocessing. In *Proceedings of the 17th International Symposium on Computer Architecture*, pages 104–114, May 1990.

[2] W. J. Bolosky, M. L. Scott, R. P. Fitzgerald, R. J. Fowler, and A. L. Cox. NUMA policies and their relation to memory architecture. In *ASPLOS*, pages 212–221, April 1991.

[3] R. Chandra, A. Gupta, and J. L. Hennessy. Integrating concurrency and data abstraction in the COOL programming language. Technical Report CSL-TR-92-511, Computer Systems Lab, Stanford University, February 1992.

[4] R. J. Fowler and L. I. Kontothanassis. Improving processor and cache locality in fine-grain parallel computations using object-affinity scheduling and continuation passing. Technical Report 411, Computer Science Department, University of Rochester, June 1992.

[5] S. Hiranandani, K. Kennedy, C. Koelbel, U. Kremer, and C.-W. Tseng. An overview of the Fortran D programming system. In U. Bannerjee, D. Gelernter, A. Nicolau, and D. Padua, editors, *Languages and Compilers for Parallel Computing*, pages 18–34. Springer-Verlag, August 1991. Lecture Notes in Computer Science No. 589.

[6] C. A. R. Hoare. Monitors: An operating system structuring concept. *Communications of the ACM*, 17(10):549–557, October 1974.

[7] K. Knobe, J. D. Lukas, and G. L. Steele. Data optimization: Allocation of arrays to reduce communication on SIMD machines. *Journal of Parallel and Distributed Computing*, 8:102–118, 1990.

[8] R. P. LaRowe Jr., C. S. Ellis, and L. S. Kaplan. The robustness of NUMA memory managament. In *Symposium on Operating System Principles*, pages 137–151, October 1991.

[9] D. Lenoski, J. Laudon, K. Gharachorloo, W.-D. Weber, A. Gupta, J. Hennessy, M. Horowitz, and M. Lam. The Stanford Dash multiprocessor. *IEEE Computer*, 25(3):63–79, March 1992.

[10] D. Lenoski, J. Laudon, T. Joe, D. Nakahira, L. Stevens, A. Gupta, and J. L. Hennessy. The DASH prototype: Implementation and performance. In *Proceedings of the 19th International Symposium on Computer Architecture*, pages 92–103, May 1992.

[11] E. Lusk, R. Overbeek, et al. *Portable Programs for Parallel Processors*. Holt, Rinehard and Winston, Inc., New York NY, 1987.

[12] A. Rogers and K. Pingali. Compiling for locality. In *International Conference on Parallel Processing*, pages 142–146, August 1990.

[13] E. Rothberg and A. Gupta. Techniques for improving the performance of sparse matrix factorization on multiprocessor workstations. In *Supercomputing '90*, pages 232–243, November 1990.

[14] E. Rothberg and A. Gupta. An efficient block-oriented approach to parallel sparse cholesky factorization. Technical Report CSL-TR-92-533, Computer Systems Lab, Stanford University, July 1992.

[15] J. P. Singh, W.-D. Weber, and A. Gupta. SPLASH: Stanford parallel applications for shared memory. *Computer Architecture News*, 20(1):5–44, 1992.

[16] M. E. Wolf and M. S. Lam. A data locality optimizing algorithm. In *Proceedings of the ACM SIGPLAN Conference on Programming Language Design and Implementation*, pages 30–44, June 1991.

~ Notes ~

~ *Notes* ~

~ Notes ~